Mastering™
Windows® XP Home Edition

Guy Hart-Davis

SYBEX®   San Francisco   Paris   Düsseldorf   Soest   London

Associate Publisher: Richard Staron

Acquisitions and Developmental Editor: Ellen Dendy

Editor: Ronn Jost

Production Editor: Shannon Murphy

Technical Editor: Mark Kovach

Electronic Publishing Specialist: Maureen Forys, Happenstance Type-O-Rama

Graphic Illustrator: Tony Jonick

Proofreaders: Emily Hsuan, Dave Nash, Laurie O'Connell, Yariv Rabinovitch, and Nancy Riddiough

Indexer: John S. Lewis

CD Coordinator: Christine Harris

CD Technician: Kevin Ly

Book Designer: Maureen Forys, Happenstance Type-O-Rama

Cover Designer: Design Site

Cover Illustrator: Tania Kac

Library of Congress Card Number: 2001091740

ISBN: 0-7821-2980-3

Manufactured in the United States of America

10 9 8 7 6 5 4

Software License Agreement: Terms and Conditions

The media and/or any online materials accompanying this book that are available now or in the future contain programs and/or text files (the "Software") to be used in connection with the book. SYBEX hereby grants to you a license to use the Software, subject to the terms that follow. Your purchase, acceptance, or use of the Software will constitute your acceptance of such terms.

The Software compilation is the property of SYBEX unless otherwise indicated and is protected by copyright to SYBEX or other copyright owner(s) as indicated in the media files (the "Owner(s)"). You are hereby granted a single-user license to use the Software for your personal, noncommercial use only. You may not reproduce, sell, distribute, publish, circulate, or commercially exploit the Software, or any portion thereof, without the written consent of SYBEX and the specific copyright owner(s) of any component software included on this media.

In the event that the Software or components include specific license requirements or end-user agreements, statements of condition, disclaimers, limitations or warranties ("End-User License"), those End-User Licenses supersede the terms and conditions herein as to that particular Software component. Your purchase, acceptance, or use of the Software will constitute your acceptance of such End-User Licenses.

By purchase, use or acceptance of the Software you further agree to comply with all export laws and regulations of the United States as such laws and regulations may exist from time to time.

SOFTWARE SUPPORT

Components of the supplemental Software and any offers associated with them may be supported by the specific Owner(s) of that material, but they are not supported by SYBEX. Information regarding any available support may be obtained from the Owner(s) using the information provided in the appropriate read.me files or listed elsewhere on the media.

Should the manufacturer(s) or other Owner(s) cease to offer support or decline to honor any offer, SYBEX bears no responsibility. This notice concerning support for the Software is provided for your information only. SYBEX is not the agent or principal of the Owner(s), and SYBEX is in no way responsible for providing any support for the Software, nor is it liable or responsible for any support provided, or not provided, by the Owner(s).

WARRANTY

SYBEX warrants the enclosed media to be free of physical defects for a period of ninety (90) days after purchase. The Software is not available from SYBEX in any other form or media than that enclosed herein or posted to www.sybex.com. If you discover a defect in the media during this warranty period, you may obtain a replacement of identical format at no charge by sending the defective media, postage prepaid, with proof of purchase to:

SYBEX Inc.
Customer Service Department
e-mail: info@sybex.com
WEB: HTTP://WWW.SYBEX.COM

After the 90-day period, you can obtain replacement media of identical format by sending us the defective disk, proof of purchase, and a check or money order for $10, payable to SYBEX.

DISCLAIMER

SYBEX makes no warranty or representation, either expressed or implied, with respect to the Software or its contents, quality, performance, merchantability, or fitness for a particular purpose. In no event will SYBEX, its distributors, or dealers be liable to you or any other party for direct, indirect, special, incidental, consequential, or other damages arising out of the use of or inability to use the Software or its contents even if advised of the possibility of such damage. In the event that the Software includes an online update feature, SYBEX further disclaims any obligation to provide this feature for any specific duration other than the initial posting.

The exclusion of implied warranties is not permitted by some states. Therefore, the above exclusion may not apply to you. This warranty provides you with specific legal rights; there may be other rights that you may have that vary from state to state. The pricing of the book with the Software by SYBEX reflects the allocation of risk and limitations on liability contained in this agreement of Terms and Conditions.

SHAREWARE DISTRIBUTION

This Software may contain various programs that are distributed as shareware. Copyright laws apply to both shareware and ordinary commercial software, and the copyright Owner(s) retains all rights. If you try a shareware program and continue using it, you are expected to register it. Individual programs differ on details of trial periods, registration, and payment. Please observe the requirements stated in appropriate files.

COPY PROTECTION

The Software in whole or in part may or may not be copy-protected or encrypted. However, in all cases, reselling or redistributing these files without authorization is expressly forbidden except as specifically provided for by the Owner(s) therein.

This book is dedicated to Rhonda.

Acknowledgments

MY THANKS GO TO THE following people for their help with this book:

- ◆ Gary Masters for thinking of me for this book
- ◆ Ellen Dendy for developing the book
- ◆ Ronn Jost for editing the book with patience and a light touch
- ◆ Mark Kovach for reviewing the manuscript for technical accuracy
- ◆ Shannon Murphy and Teresa Trego for coordinating the production of the book
- ◆ Maureen Forys for typesetting the book
- ◆ Emily Hsuan, Dave Nash, Laurie O'Connell, Yariv Rabinovitch, and Nancy Riddiough for proofreading the book
- ◆ John S. Lewis for creating the index
- ◆ Dan Mummert and Kevin Ly for helping put together the CD

Contents at a Glance

Contents

Introduction

WINDOWS XP HOME EDITION is a huge operating system—huge both in terms of its number of lines of programming code and the number of features it offers. Windows XP is also huge in that it's a huge improvement on its predecessors: Windows 95, Windows 98, and Windows Me. Not only does it offer features that can simplify your computing life, but it's extremely stable: It crashes seldom, and then only under extreme provocation.

Microsoft has worked hard to make Windows XP easier to use than the earlier versions of Windows. But there's still a huge amount you need to know about Windows XP in order to use it most effectively.

This book gives you that information.

Who Is This Book For?

This book is for beginning, intermediate, and advanced users who want to get the most out of Windows XP with the minimum effort.

Beginning, intermediate, *and* advanced—that's a wide brief. Because any book that covered absolutely everything to do with Windows in detail would be several thousand pages long, and this book isn't that long, it assumes that you want to get things done with Windows rather than know everything about Windows. Instead of presenting arcane trivia or every single way of doing something, the book presents useful information and the easiest and most effective ways of getting something done. (There *is* some arcane information in the book, but it's there because you may find it useful or interesting.) This book also presents the background that you need to know in order to make important decisions about how you configure and use Windows. But it doesn't hold your hand every step of the way.

NOTE   *In order to present the information you need within its limited number of pages, this book assumes that you have basic knowledge of Windows already. If you're new to Windows, see the Appendix, "Windows Basics," and the first few sections of the* Essential Skills *section for a quick orientation on the Windows Desktop and graphical user interface.*

What Does This Book Cover?

Glad you asked. Here's an overview of what the book covers:

The full-color *Essential Skills* section gives you a visual guide to some of the most important procedures you'll need to take with Windows. These procedures are also explained in full in the main text of the book, so you may want to flip between the visual treatment and the detailed text treatment of a topic.

Chapter 1, "Introducing Windows XP Home Edition," discusses what Windows XP is, what's new in it, whether you should upgrade to Windows XP from your current version of Windows, and whether (if you decide to upgrade) you should go to Windows XP Professional rather than Windows XP Home.

Chapter 2, "Installing Windows XP," discusses how to install Windows XP in each of the three ways you're likely to want to install it: as an upgrade to Windows 98 or Windows Me, as a dual-booting new installation alongside your current version of Windows, or as a clean installation on a computer with no other operating system installed. The chapter starts by discussing how to establish whether your computer is up to running Windows XP, and finishes by showing you how to install Windows XP automatically.

Chapter 3, "Getting Started with Windows," discusses how to log on and log off, how to switch from one user session to another, and how to exit Windows. It also discusses how you can find out who else is logged on to the computer when you're working at it and how you can get an idea of which programs the other users are running.

Chapter 4, "Customizing Your Desktop," discusses how to get your Desktop into shape so that you can work comfortably, effectively, and enjoyably. These changes range from those you should make immediately (such as choosing the best display resolution, configuring the keyboard and mouse, and setting any accessibility options you need) to changes you may want to make before too long (such as choosing a screen saver, changing your Desktop background, customizing the Start menu, and creating custom toolbars).

Chapter 5, "Installing, Removing, and Running Programs," discusses how to install, configure, remove, and run programs—and how to shut them down when they fail to respond to conventional stimuli.

Chapter 6, "Managing Your Files and Folders," discusses how to manage files and folders—everything from what files and folders actually are to what you can do with them and the tools that Windows provides for manipulating them.

Chapter 7, "Making the Most of the Bundled Programs," discusses the bundled programs that come with Windows: WordPad, Notepad, Character Map, Paint, Calculator, Windows Picture and Fax Viewer, and Command Prompt. These programs are deliberately limited—Microsoft would like you to buy extra programs—but they're useful for a variety of tasks. This chapter points out the most important features of the bundled programs, including features that most users miss.

Chapter 8, "Finding Help to Solve Your Windows Problems," discusses how to find the help you need to use Windows XP most effectively—both the new Help and Support Center and other resources that you may need to turn to for difficult problems.

Chapter 9, "Managing Users and Accounts," discusses how to manage users and accounts to give each user their own Desktop and folders and to maintain security. The chapter covers what user accounts are, what they're for, and why you should use them; the three different types of user account in Windows XP Home; and how to create, delete, and modify user accounts.

Chapter 10, "Sharing, Permissions, and File Types," shows you how to use Windows XP's sharing security features to share folders you want to share and keep private those you don't want to share. It also discusses the complex but essential topic of file extensions, file types, and file associations, which allow you to control what happens when you double-click different types of files in Explorer.

Chapter 11, "Managing Your Disks and Drives," discusses how to manage your disks and drives, showing you how to take actions such as formatting a disk, converting a disk's file system to NTFS, using compression to free up disk space, using quotas to allot disk space to users, and creating and deleting partitions.

Chapter 12, "Working with the Registry," discusses the Registry, the configuration database that contains most of Windows' settings, and how you can use the Registry Editor to examine it and change it. The chapter starts by detailing the step you *must* take before you make any changes to the Registry and concludes by showing you how to change the Registry so that you can crash your computer with two keystrokes—for testing purposes only, of course.

Chapter 13, "Installing, Configuring, and Managing Printers and Fonts," shows you how to install printers, configure them, and manage print jobs, including printing offline and printing to a file when necessary. This chapter also covers how to install, remove, and use fonts.

Chapter 14, "Managing Hardware, Drivers, and Power," discusses how to install hardware on your computer and how to install, update, and roll back device drivers, the software that makes hardware function. It also covers how to configure power management on your computer and install an uninterruptible power supply.

Chapter 15, "Using Windows on a Portable Computer," outlines the considerations for using Windows on a portable computer. Many of these considerations (such as the basics of power management) apply to desktop computers as well and so are covered in other chapters, but this chapter discusses using portable-specific power-management features, using PC Cards, using hardware profiles, and using different locations for dial-up networking.

Chapter 16, "Troubleshooting, Optimizing, and Dual-Booting Windows," shows you how to use the tools that Windows provides for dealing with hangs, crashes, and error messages. It also discusses some steps you may want to take to optimize Windows in the hope of keeping it running smoothly and as swiftly as your hardware permits. And it shows you how to set up a dual-boot arrangement so that you can use both Windows XP and another operating system on your computer.

Chapter 17, "Connecting to the Internet," covers how to connect to the Internet with Windows XP and how to secure your Internet connection. You'll learn about the different types of Internet connection and the benefits they offer; what dial-up networking is, how it works, and how to configure it; and how to work with digital certificates to verify the authenticity of a document or transaction.

Chapter 18, "Surfing the Web with Internet Explorer," discusses how to browse the Web with Internet Explorer and how to configure Internet Explorer to deliver the performance and security you should be demanding. Among many other things, this chapter covers how to control your browsing history and use the Content Advisor to screen out objectionable content. At the end of the chapter, you'll find the briefest of introductions to MSN Explorer, Microsoft's Internet service.

Chapter 19, "Using Address Book," shows you how to make the most of the Address Book program that comes built into Windows. Address Book is an unassuming program, but it's capable enough to be useful for home (and some home-office) contact management.

Chapter 20, "E-mail with Outlook Express," shows you how to use Outlook Express, the powerful e-mail and newsreader program built into Windows and Internet Explorer, for e-mail. The chapter covers setting up e-mail accounts; configuring Outlook Express' many options; creating, sending, reading, and replying to messages; filtering your messages; and working with both multiple e-mail accounts and multiple identities. This is a long chapter, but the topic is almost guaranteed to be of interest to you.

Chapter 21, "Reading News with Outlook Express," is a much shorter chapter. It shows you how to use Outlook Express's newsreader features to read messages posted to Internet newsgroups and to post messages yourself. It also covers configuring Outlook Express to access your news server.

Chapter 22, "Instant Messaging with Windows Messenger," shows you how to get started with Microsoft's entry into the IM arena: Windows Messenger. At this writing, Windows Messenger still can't exchange messages with AOL Instant Messenger, but apart from this severe drawback, it offers a full set of features, including voice calls, video calls, and file transfer. This chapter shows you how to use these features and more.

Chapter 23, "Faxing and Telephony," discusses how to send faxes and make telephone calls in Windows by using Fax Services and their various helper applications (for faxing) and Phone Dialer and HyperTerminal (for telephony).

Chapter 24, "Remote Desktop Connection and Remote Assistance," covers two of the remote-connection technologies built into Windows. Remote Desktop Connection lets you take control of a computer running Windows XP Professional and work on it as if you were sitting in front of it. (For example, you might access your work PC from home.) Remote Assistance lets you request assistance securely across the Internet to solve computer problems—or supply such assistance to someone else.

Chapter 25, "Sharing and Conferencing with NetMeeting," shows you how to make the most of NetMeeting, the collaboration, file-sharing, and videoconferencing package built into Windows. You'll also learn how to use NetMeeting's Remote Desktop Sharing feature to take control of your computer from a remote location, which is useful for computers that use Windows XP Home rather than Windows XP Professional (for which Remote Desktop Connection is a better bet).

Chapter 26, "Publishing Information to the Web," discusses the considerations to keep in mind when publishing information to the Web: the legalities of what you can publish, the options of where to publish it, and the most satisfactory methods for getting it there.

Chapter 27, "Windows Media Player," covers Windows Media Player, the powerful multimedia player incorporated in Windows XP. You'll learn how to configure Windows Media Player for optimum performance, copy CDs to your hard drive, tune into Internet radio, play DVDs, and deal with digital rights management. The chapter also shows you how to use Volume Control to control audio output and input, and how to use Sound Recorder to record sounds and convert audio files from one format to another.

Chapter 28, "Working with Pictures and Videos," shows you how to use image- and video-manipulation tools that Windows provides. Coverage includes installing scanners and digital cameras; scanning documents; retrieving images from a digital camera; and making your own movies with Windows Movie Maker.

Chapter 29, "Burning CDs," walks you through Windows XP's features for burning both audio CDs and data CDs. This chapter also discusses how to choose recordable CD media and how to choose a CD rewriter drive.

Chapter 30, "Playing Games on Windows XP," starts with a brief introduction to the single-player and multiplayer games included with Windows XP. It then discusses the hardware you need for serious gaming, how to add and configure games controllers, and how to get the best performance on games.

Chapter 31, "Understanding Windows Networking," discusses what a network is, why you might want to implement one in your home or home office, and what hardware you'll need to get in order to implement a network. It covers what you need to know about network architectures, network topologies, and network equipment in order to choose a network that's right for your situation.

Chapter 32, "Building a Home or Home-Office Network," discusses how to build an effective network for your home or your home office. It starts with the simplest type of network—a direct connection between two computers—before moving on to cover setting up wired and wireless networks by using the Home Networking Wizard.

Chapter 33, "Sharing Resources on Your Network," shows you how to go beyond what the Home Networking Wizard does and configure your network manually if necessary. You'll learn how to share your Internet connection with other computers, share folders, and share printers.

The Appendix, "Windows Basics," provides a quick introduction to the Windows Desktop and the main elements of the graphical user interface.

The CD contains a fully searchable electronic edition of the book together with a wide variety of software that you can use to extend XP's capabilities and make XP easier to use. See the inside back cover for details of the CD's contents.

Terminology and Conventions Used in This Book

To keep its waistline under control, this book uses a number of conventions to represent information concisely and accurately:

♦ The menu arrow, ➤, indicates selecting a choice from a menu or submenu. For example, "choose Edit ➤ Preferences" means that you should pull down the Edit menu and select the Preferences item from it.

♦ + signs indicate key combinations. For example, "press Ctrl+P" means that you should hold down the Ctrl key and press the P key. Likewise, "Ctrl+click" and "Shift+click" indicate that you should hold down the key involved and then click.

♦ *Italics* mostly indicate new terms being introduced, but sometimes they simply indicate emphasis.

♦ **Boldface** indicates text that you may need to type letter for letter.

♦ URLs: The book leaves off the http:// from each URL for brevity (and to prevent bad line breaks). For example, the URL http://www.sybex.com appears in the book as www.sybex.com. So you'll need to add the http:// to each URL you use, or have Internet Explorer add it for you.

Mastering™
Windows XP Home Edition

Essential Skills

The Essential Skills for Windows XP Home Edition

Welcome to the *Windows XP Home Edition Essential Skills* section! This visual section teaches you 56 of the most important Windows XP Home Edition skills through a series of easy-to-follow screens with step-by-step instructions. These numbered steps show you exactly what you'll see on your screen at every step along the way as you learn, hands-on, the skills that will enable you to take control of your computer quickly and effectively. In a matter of minutes, you'll learn how to perform important tasks ranging from logging on to Windows, to sharing folders on the network and changing hardware drivers. Each screen highlights elements you'll need to click.

These step-by-step directions are so easy to follow that you may want to simply sit at your computer and walk through all the procedures at once to get up and running with Windows XP quickly. Or you may prefer to flip to the *Essential Skills* section each time you need to perform a key task. You'll find references in the main text of the book to indicate when a step-by-step process is covered in the *Essential Skills* section, so that you can easily move from the detailed discussion of a topic to the graphical coverage of the steps involved.

None of the procedures covered in this section involve long textual explanations, background information, or troubleshooting. Those discussions occur in later sections of the book, when you have the background to understand them. In this section, you'll learn the important tasks that empower you to use Windows XP most efficiently. So sit yourself down at your PC with this section and master the most important Windows XP Home Edition skills hands-on!

Skills you'll learn in this section include:

- Logging on, logging off, switching user, and shutting down Windows
- Using and customizing the Start menu and Taskbar
- Setting up and using a dial-up Internet connection
- Copying, moving, renaming, and searching for files and folders
- Browsing the Web with Internet Explorer
- Copying files to a recordable CD or floppy disk
- Enjoying music and Internet radio with Windows Media Player
- Using views and navigating in Explorer
- Sharing folders with other users of the computer or network
- Installing and removing programs and hardware drivers
- Using Windows Update to keep Windows up to date
- Using System Restore to recover from installing bad software
- Defragmenting and cleaning up your hard disk
- Installing and sharing a printer

LOGGING ON TO WINDOWS

To begin using Windows XP, log on under your user account.

Windows is designed to be used by multiple users—for example, the members of a family. The Windows setup routine encourages you to create a user account for each user, so that each person can keep their programs and files separate and protect them if necessary.

By default, Windows displays the Welcome screen. If someone has turned off the Welcome screen, Windows displays the Log On to Windows dialog box instead.

1. Click your username on the Welcome screen.

If you don't have an account on this computer, and the Guest account is available, log on as the Guest user.

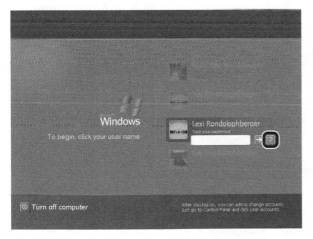

2. If you need to enter a password to log on, Windows displays the Type Your Password text box.

To see your password hint (if you have one), click the Password Hint button.

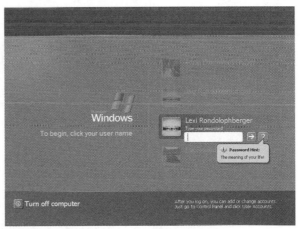

3. Windows displays the password hint.

Type the password and press Enter.

Windows logs you on and displays the Desktop.

LOGGING OFF FROM WINDOWS

The counterpart to logging on is (as you'd expect) logging off. When you've finished working in Windows, you can log off to end your user session.

When you log off, Windows closes any programs and files you've left open. If the files contain unsaved changes, Windows prompts you to save them. It's a good idea to close programs and files manually before logging off because it's easier to see which application you're working with than when Windows prompts you during logoff.

1. Click the Start button.

Click the Log Off button.

2. Windows displays the Log Off Windows screen.

Click the Log Off button.

3. If an open file contains unsaved information, Windows prompts you to save it. Choose Yes or No.

Windows then displays the Welcome screen, from which you (or other users) can log on.

SWITCHING FROM ONE USER TO ANOTHER

Instead of logging off and closing all the programs and files you were using, you can *switch user* and leave the programs running and the files open.

Switching user has several advantages over logging off. The main advantage is that when you log back on, you can resume your work from where you left off without needing to reopen programs and files. Another advantage is that you can leave tasks running. For example, you could switch user and leave a large download happening in the background.

Switching user also has disadvantages. Other users can't see which files you're using, so they may try to use the same files. They may even shut down the computer, which loses you any work you haven't saved. Also, leaving user sessions running in the background uses memory and processor power. This can slow down the computer for the active user.

1. Click the Start button.

Click the Log Off button.

2. Windows displays the Log Off Windows screen.

Click the Switch User button.

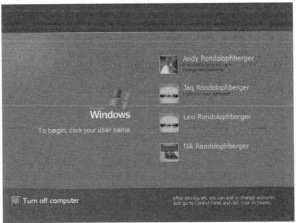

3. Windows displays the Welcome screen, from which other users can log on or you can resume your Windows session by clicking your username.

Your session remains active, and the programs and files you were using remain open.

SHUTTING DOWN WINDOWS

When you've finished using your computer for the day, week, or month, shut down Windows and power down your computer.

Before shutting down Windows, close any open programs and files and make sure that no other users have left sessions running. (See the section "Seeing Which Programs the Other Users Are Running" in Chapter 3.) If you shut down Windows while other users are still using it, they will lose any unsaved work in the programs they were using.

1. Click the Start button. Windows displays the Start menu.

Click the Turn Off Computer button. Windows displays the Turn Off Computer screen.

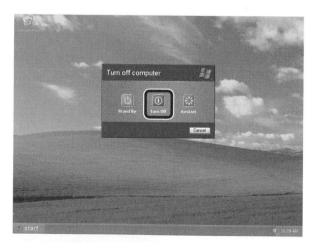

2. Click the Turn Off button.

Windows closes itself and turns off your computer.

Expert Advice

♦ You can also display the Turn Off Computer screen by pressing the power button on many computers.

♦ Windows automatically powers off most computers. If you have an older computer, you may need to power it off manually.

♦ If you're not sure whether other users are still logged on to the computer, use Task Manager to find out. (See Chapter 3.)

♦ From the Turn Off Computer screen, you can restart your computer by clicking the Restart button.

♦ If your computer supports hibernation, you can put it into hibernation by clicking the Hibernate button. If your computer supports standby, you can put it into standby by clicking the Stand By button.

USING THE START MENU

The Start menu and its submenus provide quick access to programs, settings, files, and help.

The Start menu's basic shape remains more or less the same, but its content changes. The current user's name appears at the top of the Start menu. One section of the Start menu automatically changes to display programs you've used recently. You can fix programs manually to this section of the Start menu so that they're always available. You can also perform some customization on the other parts of the Start menu.

When you install a program, its setup routine usually adds an entry for the program to the Start menu's All Programs submenu.

1. Click the Start button.

Windows displays the Start menu.

2. Click one of the items on the Start menu to open it.

The marked area of the left panel contains recently used programs.

The other items on the menu remain there unless you customize the menu.

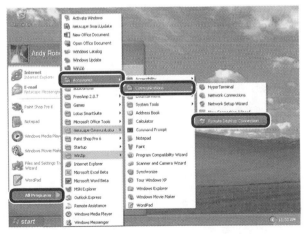

3. If the program or item doesn't appear on the first part of the Start menu, click the All Programs button.

Choose an item to open it, or open a submenu (indicated by an arrow) to access further items.

Highlights indicate new items.

USING THE TASKBAR TO ACCESS A WINDOW

The Taskbar lets you quickly access and manage the windows you have open.

The Taskbar displays a button for each open window or group of windows. The window you're working in is called the *active* window. The Taskbar button for the active window or group is visually highlighted in some way. For example, in the Windows XP theme, the button for the active window or group appears in a darker blue. In the Classic theme, the button appears lighter and pushed-in.

1. Click the Taskbar button once to display the window. Click the button again to minimize the window to its Taskbar button.

2. When the first row of the Taskbar is full, Windows groups the buttons for similar windows.

Click the group button to display a menu of the window buttons it contains.

3. When the buttons for open windows and groups won't fit on one row, the Taskbar displays scroll buttons for accessing subsequent rows.

Click the scroll buttons to scroll up or down a row of buttons.

RESIZING, MOVING, AND CLOSING A WINDOW

Each program displays one or more windows—rectangular (or nearly rectangular) areas containing information. Many programs use several windows. For example, Word for Windows uses a separate window for each document you create or open.

To display the programs you need to work with, you can resize and move windows about the screen. Most windows can appear in three states:

◆ Maximized: The window is expanded to fill the Desktop (apart from the Taskbar area).

◆ Minimized: The window is reduced to its Taskbar button, leaving the Desktop free for other windows.

◆ Normal: The window is not maximized or minimized, but is some size in between.

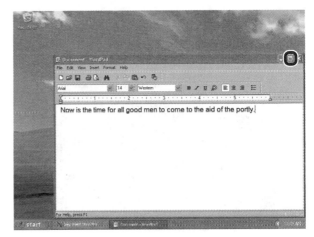

1. Open one or more program windows. To maximize a window, click the Maximize button.

Windows maximizes the window and replaces its Maximize button with the Restore Down button.

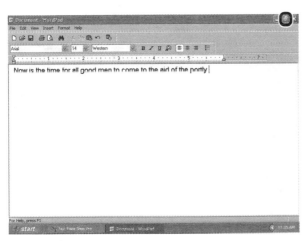

2. To restore a maximized window to the normal state, click the Restore Down button.

Windows restores the window to its previous size and replaces its Restore Down button with the Maximize button.

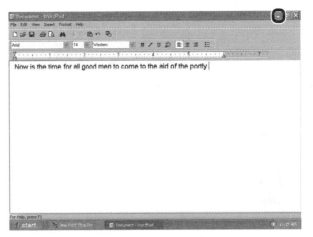

3. To minimize a window, click the Minimize button.

Windows reduces the window to its button on the Taskbar.

RESIZING, MOVING, AND CLOSING A WINDOW (continued)

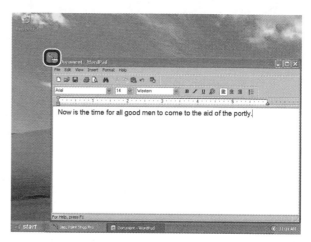

4. To restore a minimized window, click its Taskbar button.

Windows restores the window to its previous state—maximized or normal.

5. To resize a window, move the mouse pointer over an edge or corner of the window so that the pointer changes into a double-headed arrow.

Click and drag the window edge or corner to the size you want.

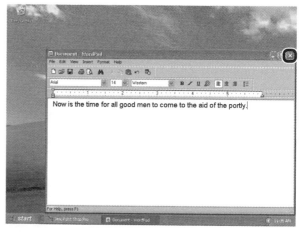

6. To move a window, click the title bar and drag the window to its new location.

7. To close a window, click its Close button.

Windows closes the window.

If the window contains unsaved information, the program may prompt you to save it.

ARRANGING WINDOWS BY USING THE TASKBAR

Windows provides the following automated commands for arranging windows easily:

◆ Cascade Windows: Displays the nonminimized windows overlapping each other so that you can see the title bar of each

◆ Undo Cascade: Restores the windows to the positions they were in before cascading

◆ Tile Windows Horizontally: Implements a horizontal tiling scheme for all nonminimized windows

◆ Tile Windows Vertically: Implements a vertical tiling scheme for all nonminimized windows

◆ Undo Tile: Restores the windows to the positions they were in before tiling

◆ Show the Desktop: Displays the Desktop by minimizing all nonminimized windows.

◆ Show Open Windows: Restores the windows to the positions they were in before minimization via the Show the Desktop command

1. Right-click the notification area or open space in the Taskbar. Windows displays the context menu.

Choose the appropriate command for the action you want to take.

2. Issuing a Show the Desktop command minimizes all windows.

To restore the windows to their previous positions, issue the Show Open Windows command.

3. Issuing a Tile Windows Horizontally command tiles the windows in a horizontal pattern.

To restore the windows to their previous positions, issue the Undo Tile command.

ARRANGING WINDOWS BY USING THE TASKBAR (continued)

4. Issuing a Tile Windows Vertically command tiles the windows in a vertical pattern.

To restore the windows to their previous positions, issue the Undo Tile command.

5. Issuing a Cascade Windows command arranges the windows in an overlapping pattern with their title bars visible.

To restore the windows to their previous positions, issue the Undo Cascade command.

6. To maximize a window, right-click its Taskbar button and choose Maximize from the context menu.

7. To close a window, right-click its Taskbar button and choose Close from the context menu.

UNLOCKING, RESIZING, AND MOVING THE TASKBAR

By default, the Taskbar is locked so that it cannot be resized or moved, and so that you cannot display any Desktop toolbars.

By unlocking the Taskbar, you can resize it, move it to another edge of the screen, and display and use the Desktop toolbars.

1. To unlock the Taskbar, right-click the notification area. Windows displays the context menu.

Choose the Lock the Taskbar item. Windows unlocks the Taskbar and removes the check mark from the context menu item.

2. To resize the Taskbar, move the mouse pointer over its border so that the pointer becomes a double-headed arrow.

Drag the border to enlarge or reduce the Taskbar.

3. To move the Taskbar to another edge of the screen, click open space in it and drag it to the edge you want. Windows moves the Taskbar.

To lock the Taskbar at its new size or position, right-click the notification area and choose Lock the Taskbar.

DISPLAYING AND USING DESKTOP TOOLBARS

To give you quick access to programs and features, Windows provides four Desktop toolbars: the Quick Launch toolbar, the Desktop toolbar, the Address toolbar, and the Links toolbar.

You can display any or all of these toolbars. Most people find the Quick Launch toolbar and the Desktop toolbar more useful than the Address toolbar or the Links toolbar.

When you've displayed a Desktop toolbar, you can resize or reposition it by dragging the dotted handle at its left or upper end. You need to unlock the Taskbar before you can move one of the Desktop toolbars.

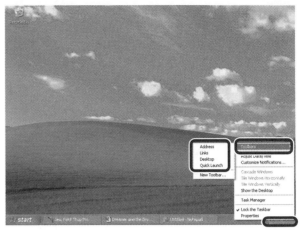

1. Right-click the notification area. Windows displays the context menu.

Select the Toolbars item. Windows displays the submenu.

Select the toolbar. Windows displays the toolbar.

2. The Quick Launch toolbar contains shortcuts for launching Internet Explorer, showing the Desktop, and launching Windows Media Player (from left to right).

3. The Desktop toolbar contains shortcuts to the items on your Desktop, to key items on the Start menu, and to Internet Explorer.

This toolbar is usually most useful with just its title and >> button displayed.

DISPLAYING AND USING DESKTOP TOOLBARS *(continued)*

4. The Address toolbar contains an address box and a Go button. Enter an URL or a network location and click the Go button to open an Internet Explorer window to that site or folder.

5. The Links toolbar displays your links from Internet Explorer. (You can customize these links in Internet Explorer.)

Click a link to display it in Internet Explorer.

6. To customize the Quick Launch toolbar, unlock the Taskbar, right-click the Quick Launch toolbar's handle and choose Open Folder from the context menu. Windows displays the Quick Launch folder.

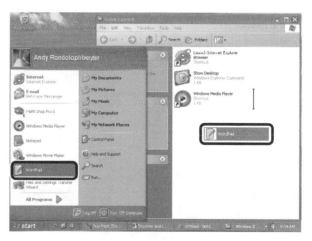

7. To add a shortcut to the Quick Launch toolbar, right-drag an item to the folder and drop it there.

Windows displays the context menu.

Choose Create Shortcuts Here. Windows creates a shortcut for the item.

CUSTOMIZING THE START MENU

You can customize the Start menu so that it contains the items you need. Because the Start menu is such a vital part of Windows XP, you can save time and make computing easier by customizing it. Besides, each user with a separate user account can customize the Start menu without affecting other users.

The easiest way to customize the Start menu is to "pin" an item to it, nailing that item in place permanently—or until you choose to "unpin" it. You can also easily remove an item from the Start menu's recently used–programs area. With a little more effort, you can customize the Start menu extensively.

1. Click the Start button. Windows displays the Start menu.

To remove an item from the recently used–programs area, right-click it and choose Remove from This List from the context menu.

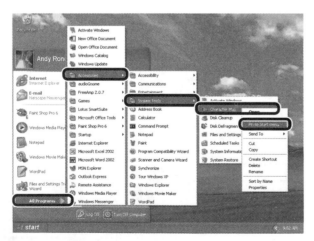

2. To pin an item to the Start menu, right-click it and choose Pin to Start Menu from the context menu.

Some items are not available for pinning to the Start menu.

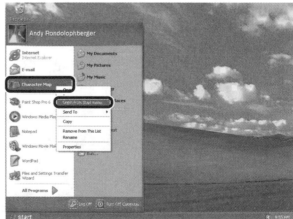

3. To remove a pinned item, unpin it by right-clicking it and choosing Unpin from Start Menu from the context menu.

CUSTOMIZING THE START MENU *(continued)*

4. To perform further customizations, right-click the Start button or open space on the Start menu and choose Properties from the context menu.

Windows displays the Start Menu page of the Taskbar and Start Menu Properties dialog box.

5. Click the upper Customize button.

Windows displays the General page of the Customize Start Menu dialog box.

6. Choose an icon size for programs.

Specify the number of programs to show on the Start menu (or click the Clear List button to clear the list).

7. To remove the Internet item or E-mail item from the Start menu, clear its check box.

To change the program for the item, use the drop-down list.

Click the Advanced tab. Windows displays the Advanced page of the Customize Start Menu dialog box.

CUSTOMIZING THE START MENU *(continued)*

8. Choose whether to open submenus when you hover the mouse over them (rather than clicking them) and whether to display a highlight for newly installed programs.

9. Choose which items to display on the Start menu and which features to enable (for example, dragging and dropping).

For some items, you can choose between displaying the item as a link (the default), as a menu, or not displaying it at all.

10. Select the List My Most Recently Opened Documents check box if you want the Start menu to include a menu of recently used documents (as in previous versions of Windows).

Click the OK button. Windows closes the Customize Start Menu dialog box.

11. Click the OK button. Windows closes the Taskbar and Start Menu Properties dialog box and applies your changes.

CUSTOMIZING THE NOTIFICATION AREA

The notification area (also known as the System Tray) appears at the right end of the Taskbar. The notification area contains items that it's useful to have displayed all the time (such as the clock, which is displayed by default), together with information and alerts (which are displayed at appropriate times).

By default, Windows XP Home collapses the notification area so that only the icons you've used most recently are displayed. To display the other icons in the notification area, click the < button at the left end of the notification area.

1. Right-click the notification area and choose Customize Notifications from the context menu.

Windows displays the Taskbar and Start Menu Properties dialog box and, in front of it, the Customize Notifications dialog box.

2. Use the Behavior drop-down list to specify when to display an item. Choose Hide when Inactive, Always Hide, or Always Show as appropriate.

Click the Restore Defaults button if you want to apply default settings to the notification area.

Click the OK button. Windows closes the Customize Notifications dialog box.

3. Select or clear the Show the Clock check box.

If you don't want Windows to hide inactive icons, clear the Hide Inactive Icons check box.

Click the OK button. Windows closes the Taskbar and Start Menu Properties dialog box.

NAVIGATING IN EXPLORER

Windows Explorer is a program for viewing and manipulating the contents of the drives and folders on your computer.

You can use Explorer for a wide variety of tasks including creating, deleting, and renaming files and folders; copying and moving files and folders; and finding files and folders you've lost.

1. Click the Start button. Windows displays the Start menu.

Choose one of the five circled links from it. If your computer isn't connected to a network, you won't have a My Network Places link.

2. The My Documents link displays the \My Documents\ folder, in which Windows automatically places files you create other than graphics, music, or video files. This folder contains the \My Pictures\ folder, the \My Music\ folder, and the \My Videos\ folder.

3. The My Pictures link displays the \My Pictures\ folder, in which Windows automatically places picture files you create and download. This folder contains features and links for manipulating pictures.

NAVIGATING IN EXPLORER *(continued)*

4. The My Music link displays the `\My Music\` folder, in which Windows automatically places music files you create and download. This folder contains features and links for working with music files.

5. The My Computer link displays a list of document folders and drives on the computer.

6. To perform a task on a file or folder, select it and use the File and Folder Tasks list.

7. To navigate to other frequently used places and folders, use the Other Places list.

To open a folder or file, double-click it.

USING VIEWS IN EXPLORER

Explorer provides five different views for looking at the contents of most files and folders, together with a specialized view for folders containing graphics. The different views are designed to make it easy to work with different types of folder contents.

   Some custom folders also have other views. You can apply these views from the View menu.

1. Display the View menu, then choose one of the views from it.

2. Thumbnails view displays a large icon for each file or folder. For graphics files, Thumbnails view displays a miniature version of each graphic.

3. Tiles view displays a medium-sized icon for each file or folder. It's good for viewing folders that contain relatively few files or folders.

USING VIEWS IN EXPLORER *(continued)*

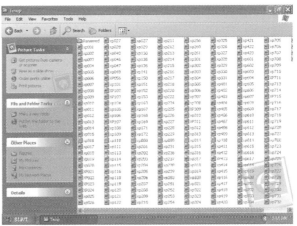

4. Icons view displays a small-ish icon for each file or folder. It's good for viewing folders that contain a moderate number of files or folders.

5. List view displays a list of folders and files, showing only the filename or folder name and a small icon for each. It's good for viewing folders that contain a large number of files or folders.

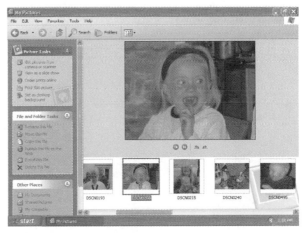

6. Details view displays a list of files and folders, including the filename or folder name, a small icon, the file size, the file type, and the date on which it was modified. You can sort by any of the columns displayed.

7. The \My Pictures\ folder and the \Shared Pictures\ folder also have a Filmstrip view designed for scrolling through a folder of images.

SELECTING AND DESELECTING FILES

In order to manipulate files and folders in Explorer, you need to select them first.

The easiest selection techniques use the mouse and the keyboard together. (You can also select files by using only the keyboard.) These selection techniques work the same on the Desktop, in most common dialog boxes in Windows applications, and in some Windows applications.

1. To select a file or folder, click it. The Details pane displays information about the file or folder.

To deselect a selected file or folder, click in empty space in the window.

2. To select a group of adjacent files, click the first file, then hold down Shift and click the last file in the group.

3. To select a group of nonadjacent files, select the first file, hold down Ctrl, and click each of the other files.

To deselect a file in a selected group, hold down Ctrl and click the file.

CREATING A FOLDER

Windows lets you create an almost unlimited number of folders in which to store your files. By using separate folders, you can group your files by category such as subject, type, or date, keeping the files organized and making it easy to find the ones you need.

You can create folders on your Desktop as well by using the technique shown here.

1. Open an Explorer window to the folder in which you want to create the new folder. For example, choose Start ➤ My Documents if you want to create the new folder in the \My Documents\ folder.

2. Click the Make a New Folder link.

   Windows creates a new folder named New Folder or a similar name (New Folder 1, New Folder 2, and so on) and displays an edit box around the name.

3. Type the name for the folder and press Enter. Windows renames the folder.

RENAMING A FILE OR FOLDER

Often, you'll need to rename a file or folder, to make its name shorter, longer, more explicit, or simply different from the names of other files or folders in the same folder. Including the drive and folder path to it, a filename can be up to 255 characters long, so you can get verbose if necessary.

Filenames can't contain the following characters: forward slashes (/), backslashes (\), colons (:), asterisks (*), question marks (?), double quotation marks ("), less-than (<) and greater-than (>) signs, or pipe characters (|).

To rename a file or folder, open an Explorer window to the appropriate folder. If the file or folder is on the Desktop, you can work directly on the Desktop using the same technique.

1. Select the file or folder you want to rename.

Click the Rename This File link or the Rename This Folder Link.

Windows displays an edit box around the name.

2. Type the name you want, and then press Enter.

Windows applies the new name to the file or folder.

Expert Advice

◆ Instead of clicking the Rename This File link or the Rename This Folder link, you can display an edit box around the filename or folder name by clicking it again a moment or two after selecting it.

◆ This two-click technique works on the Desktop and in common dialog boxes as well as in Explorer windows.

◆ If you can't get the hang of clicking twice slowly enough, select the file or folder and press F2, or right-click it and choose Rename from the context menu.

COPYING OR MOVING A FILE OR FOLDER

Often, you'll need to copy files or folders—for example, so that you can store copies in a safe location, or so that you can share the files or folders with someone else.

Similarly, you'll frequently need to move files or folders from their current location to a different location. For example, you might need to move a folder of files from your \My Documents\ folder to the \Shared Documents\ folder so that other users can work with it.

Windows provides several ways to copy or move a file or folder. This page shows you the easiest and most consistent way of performing each operation.

1. Select the file or folder.

To copy it, click the Copy This File link or the Copy This Folder link. Proceed to step 2.

To move it, click the Move This File link or the Move This Folder link. Proceed to step 3.

2. Navigate to the folder in which you want Windows to place the copy of the file or folder.

Click the Copy button. Windows closes the Copy Items dialog box and copies the file or folder.

3. Navigate to the folder to which you want Windows to move the file or folder.

Click the Move button. Windows closes the Move Items dialog box and moves the file or folder.

COPYING OR MOVING BY USING COPY, CUT, AND PASTE

You can also copy a file or folder by using the Copy and Paste commands, and move a file or folder by using the Cut and Paste commands.

The Copy, Cut, and Paste commands are most useful for copying and moving files and folders when you have two Explorer windows open, one showing the source folder and the other the destination folder. You can then quickly copy or move files or folders from the source folder to the destination folder. But you can also use the Copy, Cut, and Paste commands in a single window if you find them easy or convenient.

1. Open two Explorer windows and arrange them so that you can see both.

In one Explorer window, navigate to the source folder.

In the other Explorer window, navigate to the destination folder.

2. In the source folder, right-click the file or folder you want to copy or move.

From the context menu, choose Copy (to copy the item) or Cut (to move it).

3. Right-click in open space in the destination folder.

From the context menu, choose Paste.

Windows pastes the copy of the file or folder, or the file or folder itself, into the destination folder.

COPYING FILES TO A FLOPPY DISK OR REMOVABLE DISK

Because you'll often need to copy files to a floppy disk or another removable disk (such as a Zip drive), Windows provides a convenient way of doing so.

You can also use a similar technique for creating a shortcut located on the Desktop that refers to an item in the current folder.

1. Open an Explorer window to the folder that contains the file or folder you want to copy.

2. Right-click the file or folder. Windows displays the context menu.

Choose Send To. Windows displays the submenu.

Select the item for the floppy disk or removable disk. Windows copies the file or folder.

3. You can also create a shortcut on the Desktop to the file or folder by using a similar technique.

Right-click the file or folder and choose Send To ➤ Desktop (Create Shortcut).

Windows creates a shortcut on the Desktop.

COPYING FILES OR FOLDERS TO A RECORDABLE CD

If you have a recordable CD drive (CD-R) or a rewritable CD drive (CD-RW), you can copy files or folders to a recordable CD.

Because recordable CDs are capacious, inexpensive, durable, and (at least in theory) relatively long lasting, they're good for backup and archiving. Even if the CDs turn out not to last, they're good for transferring files from point A to point B in the short term, because most computers have CD drives.

Windows also provides features for recording an audio CD that you can play on most CD players—audio CD players as well as computer CD drives.

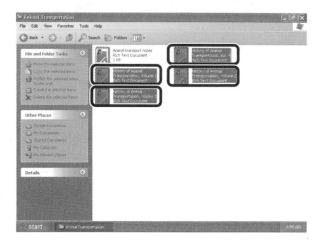

1. Load a blank CD in your recordable CD drive.

Open an Explorer window to the appropriate folder.

Select the files or folders you want to copy to the CD.

2. Right-click one of the selected files or folders and choose Send To ➢ CD Drive.

Windows copies the files or folders to a queue for writing to the CD drive and displays a notification-area icon and pop-up.

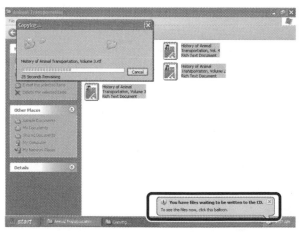

3. Add further files or folders to the CD list as necessary.

Click the notification-area pop-up to open an Explorer window showing the CD drive. (If the pop-up disappears, choose Start ➢ My Computer, then double-click the CD drive.)

COPYING FILES OR FOLDERS TO A RECORDABLE CD *(continued)*

4. Click the Write These Files to CD link. Windows starts the CD Writing Wizard.

5. Change or improve the name for the CD. (The Wizard suggests the current date for the CD's name.)

Click the Next button. The Wizard starts writing the files to the CD.

6. When the Wizard has finished writing the CD, it ejects the CD and displays the Completing the CD Writing Wizard page.

7. If you want to create another CD containing the same files, select the Yes, Write These Files to Another CD check box.

Click the Finish button. The Wizard closes or restarts, as appropriate.

DELETING A FILE OR FOLDER

When you no longer need a file, you can delete it to remove it from your disk. By default, deleting a file on your hard disk sends the file to the Recycle Bin, from which you can retrieve it if necessary. Deleting a file on a removable disk, a floppy disk, or a network drive gets rid of the file immediately.

Don't try to delete any Windows files. Doing so can prevent Windows from running. Usually, though, Windows simply reinstalls the files when it discovers they're missing, so deleting them achieves nothing.

Similarly, it's best not to delete any program files manually. Instead, use Windows' Remove Programs feature to remove the program, as discussed on page 66.

1. Select a file that you're sure you don't need.

Click the Delete This File link.

Windows displays the Confirm File Delete dialog box.

2. Click the Yes button.

Depending on where the file is stored, Windows moves the file to the Recycle Bin or deletes it.

3. To delete a folder, select it and click the Delete This Folder link.

Windows displays the Confirm Folder Delete dialog box, asking if you want to remove the folder and all its contents.

Click the Yes button.

RECOVERING A DELETED FILE OR FOLDER FROM THE RECYCLE BIN

If you move a file or folder to the Recycle Bin and subsequently wish you hadn't, you may be able to recover the file or folder.

Files or folders stay in the Recycle Bin until the Recycle Bin gets full or you empty it manually. When the Recycle Bin gets full, Windows discards the oldest files or folders to make space for new files or folders you delete.

Once Windows has deleted a file or folder from the Recycle Bin, you may be able to recover it using a specialized undelete utility, but there's no guarantee that this will work. So when you delete a file or folder by mistake, it's best to recover it immediately. When you recover a file or folder, Windows removes it from the Recycle Bin and restores it to the folder that previously contained it.

1. Double-click the Recycle Bin icon on the Desktop.

Windows opens an Explorer window showing the contents of the Recycle Bin.

2. Select the file or folder.

Click the Restore This Item link.

To restore all the files and folders in the Recycle Bin, click the Restore All Items link without selecting a file or folder.

3. To get rid of the files and folders in the Recycle Bin, click the Empty the Recycle Bin link.

Windows displays the Confirm Multiple File Delete dialog box.

Click the Yes button.

SEARCHING FOR FILES

If you create a lot of files, you'll probably forget before too long where one or more files are located.

Windows provides a feature called Search Companion for searching for files. You can search by all or part of a file's name, by its approximate size, by the date it was created, or even by a word or phrase contained in the body of the file.

Search Companion offers different features for searching for specific types of files such as document files or files containing pictures, music, or video. This example shows how to search for all file types, because this gives the most flexible search.

1. Choose Start ➢ Search.

Windows displays a Search Results window.

2. Click the All Files and Folders link.

Search Companion displays a panel of search options.

3. To search by filename, enter a distinctive part of the filename in the All or Part of the Filename text box.

SEARCHING FOR FILES *(continued)*

4. To search by contents, or to narrow a search by other criteria, you can enter a distinctive word or phrase in the A Word or Phrase in the File text box.

5. Specify the drives or folders to search.

6. To specify a range of dates when the file was modified, click the When Was It Modified? heading.

Use the options for specifying a time period.

7. To search only for files of a specified size, click the What Size Is It? heading.

Use the options for specifying an approximate size.

SEARCHING FOR FILES *(continued)*

8. To specify advanced options, such as searching hidden files or folders or tape backup, click the More Advanced Options heading.

By default, Search Companion searches system folders and subfolders.

9. Click the Search button. Search Companion performs the search and returns a list containing any matches it finds.

10. If Search Companion didn't find the right match, use the No, Refine This Search And… links to search again.

Otherwise, click the Yes, Finished Searching link to close Search Companion.

11. Select a file to display its details.

Double-click a file to open it.

Select a file and click the Open the Folder That Contains This Item link to open the folder.

CREATING A SHORTCUT ON YOUR DESKTOP

If you need quick access to a program or file, place a shortcut to it on your Desktop or in another convenient place. The shortcut acts as a pointer, making it easy to access the program or file. You can create any number of shortcuts to any given program or file.

You can create a shortcut in several different ways. This section shows two of the easiest ways to create a shortcut.

1. Right-click open space on the Desktop. Windows displays the context menu.

Choose New ➢ Shortcut.

Windows starts the Create Shortcut Wizard.

2. Click the Browse button.

Windows displays the Browse for Folder dialog box.

3. Navigate to the program or file and select it.

Click the OK button. Windows closes the Browse for Folder dialog box and enters the path and filename in the Create Shortcut Wizard.

CREATING A SHORTCUT ON YOUR DESKTOP *(continued)*

4. Click the Next button.

The Wizard displays the Select a Title for The Program page and suggests the file or program's name as the name for the shortcut.

5. Change the name if necessary.

Click the Finish button.

The Wizard creates the shortcut, names it, and places it on your Desktop.

6. You can also create a shortcut from an Explorer window.

Select the file. Then choose File ➢ Send To ➢ Desktop (Create Shortcut).

Windows creates a shortcut on the Desktop.

7. Change the name of the shortcut if necessary (See page 26 for details of how to rename a file).

Windows names shortcuts created this way *Shortcut to* and the filename.

CHANGING THE SCREEN RESOLUTION

If you want to display more or less information on the screen at once, change the screen resolution. Higher resolutions let you see more on-screen at the same time, but everything displayed is smaller; lower resolutions display less information, but everything is correspondingly larger.

1. Right-click the Desktop and choose Properties from the context menu.

Windows displays the Display Properties dialog box.

2. Click the Settings tab. Windows displays the Settings page.

3. Drag the slider in the Screen Resolution group box left to decrease the resolution or right to increase the resolution.

Click the Apply button. Windows displays the Monitor Settings dialog box.

CHANGING THE SCREEN RESOLUTION *(continued)*

4. If the screen looks okay, click the Yes button. If the screen looks bad, click the No button. If the screen isn't legible, wait 15 seconds.

5. Click the OK button. Windows closes the Display Properties dialog box.

6. Windows displays your Desktop at the new size. If you increased the resolution, you see more on-screen, but everything appears smaller. If you decreased it, you see less, but everything appears larger.

Expert Advice

♦ If you've previously used the resolution you're applying, Windows doesn't display the Monitor Settings dialog box.

♦ If your display becomes garbled or faded when you apply a higher screen resolution, wait 15 seconds, and Windows restores your previous video settings automatically.

♦ Once you've found a resolution you like, adjust your monitor so that the picture reaches all the way to each edge of the screen.

♦ In Windows XP, each user has to use the same screen resolution. When one user changes the screen resolution, Windows changes it for all other users as well.

♦ Most cathode-ray tube (CRT) displays can display several different resolutions. Most LCD screens can display only one resolution with acceptable clarity.

SETTING THE MY PICTURES SLIDESHOW SCREEN SAVER

The My Pictures Slideshow screen saver lets you have Windows automatically display a slideshow of the pictures in a specified folder when you're not using the computer.

Before setting up My Pictures Slideshow, group the pictures you want to use for the slideshow in a convenient folder. The default setting is to use the \My Pictures\ folder, but you might want to copy or move the pictures to a subfolder of the \My Pictures\ folder or use a shared folder rather than using all the pictures in the \My Pictures\ folder.

1. Right-click the Desktop and choose Properties. Windows displays the Display Properties dialog box.

   Click the Screen Saver tab. Windows displays the Screen Saver page.

2. Click the down-arrow button on the Screen Saver drop-down list.

   Select the My Pictures Slideshow item.

3. Click the Settings button. Windows displays the My Pictures Screen Saver Options dialog box.

SETTING THE MY PICTURES SLIDESHOW SCREEN SAVER *(continued)*

4. Drag the sliders to specify how often the pictures should change and how much of the screen they should take up.

Click the Browse button. Windows displays the Browse for Folder dialog box.

5. Navigate to and select the folder that contains the pictures you want to use for the slideshow.

Click the OK button. Windows closes the Browse for Folder dialog box.

6. Choose other options. It's best to clear the Use Transition Effects between Pictures check box, as the transition effects are visually distracting.

Click the OK button. Windows closes the My Pictures Screen Saver Options dialog box.

7. Enter the delay before the screen saver starts.

Clear the On Resume, Display Welcome Screen check box if you want Windows to display the Desktop after you cancel the screen saver.

Click the OK button.

SETTING UP A DIAL-UP INTERNET CONNECTION

In order to connect to the Internet via a dial-up connection, you need to give Windows the details of the connection: what technology to use, which number to call, and so on.

You can choose whether to set up the connection as the computer's default connection, whether to store the username and password or require each user to provide them, and whether to make a stored username and password available to all users.

Before starting to set up a dial-up Internet connection, make sure that your modem is connected to the computer, that it's connected to a working phone line, and that it's powered on (if it has its own power controls).

1. Choose Start ➢ Control Panel.

Click the Network and Internet Connections link.

Windows displays the Network and Internet Connections screen.

2. Click the Network Connections link.

Windows displays the Network Connections screen.

3. Click the Create a New Connection link.

Windows starts the New Connection Wizard.

SETTING UP A DIAL-UP INTERNET CONNECTION *(continued)*

4. Click the Next button.

5. Make sure the Connect to the Internet option button is selected.

Click the Next button.

6. Select the Set Up My Connection Manually option button.

Click the Next button.

7. Select the Connect Using a Dial-up Modem option button.

Click the Next button.

SETTING UP A DIAL-UP INTERNET CONNECTION *(continued)*

8. Enter the name you want to use for the connection. (This name doesn't have to be the ISP's name, but that may be clearest.)

Click the Next button.

9. Enter the phone number for your ISP, including the area code and long-distance code if appropriate.

Click the Next button.

10. Enter the username and password.

Select or clear the first two check boxes as appropriate.

Leave the Turn On Internet Connection Firewall for This Connection check box selected.

Click the Next button.

11. Select the Add a Shortcut to This Connection to My Desktop check box if appropriate.

Click the Finish button. The Wizard creates the connection, closes itself, and displays the Connect dialog box for the connection. Connect as described on next page.

USING A DIAL-UP INTERNET CONNECTION

When you set up a dial-up Internet connection (as described on the previous three pages), Windows stores the details of the connection so that you can reconnect to it quickly.

If you didn't store the username and password in the Internet connection, you'll need to enter them each time you use the connection. Storing this information can compromise your security, but it makes establishing the connection significantly quicker.

1. Choose Start ➤ Connect To.

Select the Internet connection from the Connect To submenu.

Windows displays the Connect dialog box for the connection.

2. Enter the username and password if necessary.

Select the Save This User Name and Password for the Following Users check box if appropriate. If you do, select the Me Only option button or the Anyone Who Uses This Computer option button.

3. Click the Dial button. Windows dials the connection.

USING A DIAL-UP INTERNET CONNECTION *(continued)*

4. If Windows is able to establish the connection, it displays a notification-area icon for the connection and a notification-area pop-up showing the connection speed.

5. To view brief information on the status of the connection, hover the mouse pointer over the notification-area icon.

Windows displays a pop-up of statistics.

6. To view detailed information about the status of the connection, click the notification-area icon.

Windows displays the Status dialog box for the connection.

Click the Close button to dismiss the Status dialog box.

7. To disconnect the connection, right-click the notification-area icon and choose Disconnect from the context menu.

BROWSING THE WEB

Windows XP includes Internet Explorer, a powerful program for browsing the Web. Internet Explorer can display many different types of Web content, including text, forms, graphics, and various kinds of animations.

Once you're connected to the Internet, you can access any available Web page by entering its address. A Web address is called a Uniform Resource Locator, or URL. Many Web pages contain hyperlinks (jumps) to other URLs. You can access these URLs by clicking the hyperlinks.

1. Choose Start ➢ Internet. Windows starts Internet Explorer, which displays your home page.

If you're not connected to the Internet, Windows prompts you to connect.

2. To open a Web page, click in the Address bar.

Internet Explorer highlights the current contents of the Address bar.

3. Type the URL for the Web site you want to display. You can omit the `http://` that appears at the beginning of many URLs. Internet Explorer adds this automatically.

BROWSING THE WEB *(continued)*

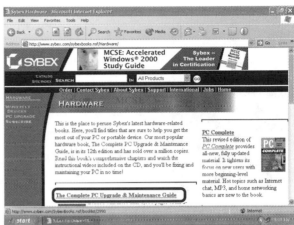

4. Press the Enter key or click the Go button.

Internet Explorer displays the Web page.

5. To follow a hyperlink, click it.

Most hyperlinks appear underlined, in a different color, or both.

The mouse pointer changes to a different shape when it's over a hyperlink. The status bar shows the linked URL.

6. To move back to the last Web page you visited, click the Back button.

To move forward again after moving back, click the Forward button.

7. To move back or forward several pages, click the arrow button on the Back button or the Forward button and choose the page from the list.

BROWSING THE WEB *(continued)*

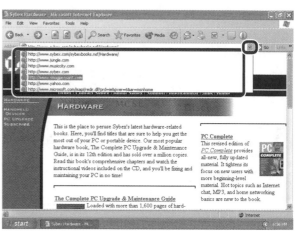

8. To stop a page being displayed (for example, if it's taking too long), click the Stop button.

9. To return to an URL you've visited recently, click the arrow button on the Address bar and select the URL from the list.

10. To refresh the current Web page with the latest information, click the Refresh button or press the F5 key.

11. To exit Internet Explorer, choose File ➢ Close or click the Close button.

CHANGING YOUR HOME PAGE

Your home page is the page that Internet Explorer automatically opens when you start it. You can also display your home page at any time by clicking the Home button on the toolbar or pressing Alt+Home.

Internet Explorer uses MSN as its default home page. You'll probably want to change this to a site of your choosing, so that you see information that interests you when you start Internet Explorer. You can use any valid URL for your home page. Alternatively, you can use a local file or folder as your home page. For example, you can create an HTML file that contains links to the sites you're most interested in, and use that file as your home page to give you quick access to those sites.

1. Navigate to the Web page, local file, or folder that you want to use as your home page.

    Choose Tools ➢ Internet Options.

    Internet Explorer displays the General page of the Internet Options dialog box.

2. Click the Use Current button.

    Click the OK button. Internet Explorer closes the Internet Options dialog box.

3. To access your home page, click the Home button.

SEARCHING THE WEB

With more pages being added every microsecond, the Web can seem an unnavigable maelstrom of information. But by using searching, you can usually produce some order out of the chaos—or at least find some pages containing the information you need.

Like Explorer, Internet Explorer uses Search Companion to present its search capabilities. For Internet Explorer, Search Companion uses a natural-language interface that lets you phrase your query as a full sentence if you prefer rather than boiling it down to the essential words.

1. Click the Search button. Internet Explorer displays Search Companion.

2. Enter your query in the What Are You Looking For? text box.

Press the Enter key or click the Search button. Internet Explorer performs the search and displays search results.

3. Click a result to display its page.

Alternatively, follow one of the search links in Search Companion.

Click the Search button again to hide Search Companion.

CREATING AND ACCESSING FAVORITES

Internet Explorer's favorites feature lets you keep a list of Web pages (or local files or folders) that you want to be able to access quickly. You can divide your favorites into folders to keep them organized, and you can export your list of favorites for backup or for use on another computer.

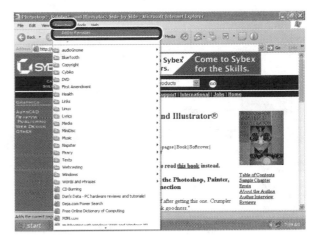

1. Open the Web page, file, or folder for which you want to create a favorite.

Choose Favorites ➢ Add to Favorites. Internet Explorer displays the Add Favorite dialog box.

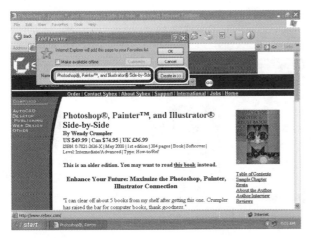

2. Check the name for the favorite. Change it if you want.

Click the Create In button. Internet Explorer expands the Add Favorite dialog box.

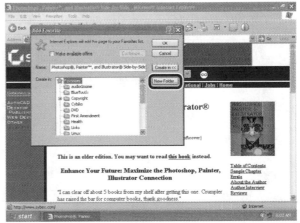

3. Select the existing folder in which to store the favorite.

To create a new folder, click the New Folder button. Internet Explorer displays the Create New Folder dialog box.

CREATING AND ACCESSING FAVORITES *(continued)*

4. Enter the name for the folder.

Click the OK button. Internet Explorer closes the dialog box, creates the folder, and selects it in the Add Favorite dialog box.

5. Click the OK button. Internet Explorer closes the dialog box and creates the favorite.

6. To access a favorite, select it from the Favorites menu.

7. To browse and access favorites, use the Favorites Explorer bar.

Click the Favorites button on the toolbar. Internet Explorer displays the Favorites Explorer bar.

LISTENING TO AN AUDIO CD

Windows Media Player is a capable multimedia player that you can use for listening to music and for watching video files. You can also watch DVDs with Windows Media Player if you add a DVD decoder to Windows.

If your computer has a CD drive, you can use it to listen to an audio CD or to copy the audio from a CD to your hard drive as Windows Media Audio (WMA) files.

If your computer has a sound card, connect the speakers or headphones to the output jack. If your computer doesn't have a sound card, connect the speakers or headphones to the output jack on your CD drive.

If Autoplay is disabled on your computer, the CD won't start playing automatically. Instead, start Windows Media Player manually by choosing Start ➤ All Programs ➤ Windows Media Player.

1. Load the CD in your CD drive. Windows Media Player opens automatically, starts playing the CD, and displays a visualization on the Now Playing page.

Use the visualization buttons to change the visualization.

2. Use the play controls to control the play.

Drag the Volume slider to control the volume.

Click the Mute/Sound button to mute and unmute the sound.

3. To jump to a track, double-click it in the playlist.

BUILDING A MEDIA LIBRARY

To make it easy for you to play and access audio and video files, Windows Media Player keeps a Media Library of all the audio and video files on your computer and network drives.

The first time you use Windows Media Player, follow this procedure for searching your computer for audio and video files. You can also use the procedure subsequently to add more media files, though you may not need to: When you copy music from CD, or when you purchase and download music, Windows Media Player automatically adds the copied or downloaded tracks to the Media Library.

1. Choose Tools ➢ Search for Media Files. Windows Media Player displays the Search for Media Files dialog box.

2. If necessary, specify the drive or drives. (You can accept the default setting, Local Drives.)

If you specify a drive, you can specify a starting folder in the Look In drop-down list by using the Browse button and Browse for Folder dialog box.

3. Click the Advanced button. Windows Media Player expands the Search for Media Files dialog box.

BUILDING A MEDIA LIBRARY *(continued)*

4. Choose further options as appropriate. You can specify minimum sizes for audio and video files, choose to add smaller files if you play them, or include media files in system folders.

Click the Search button.

5. Windows Media Player starts searching and displays another Search for Media Files dialog box showing its progress. The Cancel button changes to a Close button when the search is finished.

6. Click the Close button in each Search for Media Files dialog box. Windows Media Player adds details of the files to your Media Library.

7. To play a file, double-click it on the Media Library page.

COPYING A CD TO YOUR HARD DRIVE

Windows Media Player lets you "copy" an audio CD to your hard disk by extracting the audio data from the CD and encoding it to a compressed format called Windows Media Audio (WMA).

By storing tracks from your CDs as music files on your hard disk, you can create a jukebox-like selection of tracks that you can play back in Windows Media Player or another audio player (for example, Winamp or MusicMatch Jukebox). You can also use WMA files with some portable audio players.

The first time you copy a CD, choose quality settings as described here. After that, change quality settings only when necessary.

1. Load the CD.

If Windows Media Player doesn't start automatically, choose Start ➢ All Programs ➢ Windows Media Player.

2. Click the Copy from CD tab. Windows Media Player displays information for the CD.

If Windows Media Player doesn't display CD information, start your Internet connection and click the Get Names button.

3. Choose Tools ➢ Options. Windows Media Player displays the Options dialog box.

COPYING A CD TO YOUR HARD DRIVE *(continued)*

4. Click the Copy Music tab. Windows Media Player displays the Copy Music page of the Options dialog box.

5. Drag the slider to select the encoding quality.

Clear the Protect Content check box if you will need to transfer the tracks to another computer or device.

Click the OK button.

6. Select the tracks to copy by selecting and clearing the check boxes. Clicking the top-most check box selects or clears all the check boxes.

Click the Copy Music button.

7. Windows Media Player copies the tracks. It creates a folder with the CD's name inside a folder with the artist's name and names each track with the track number and name shown on the Copy from CD page.

USING SKIN MODE

Windows Media Player supports skins—custom graphical looks that you can apply to change its look and shape. Windows Media Player comes with a number of skins built in. You can download further skins from the WindowsMedia.com site by clicking the More Skins button on the Skin Chooser page. You can even make your own skins for Windows Media Player and post them on WindowsMedia.com.

By default, Windows Media Player appears in its Full mode, which takes up a large chunk of an average-sized Desktop. When you're listening to audio with Windows Media Player, you can use its Skin mode instead to save space on-screen—and to apply slick, colorful, or attractive skins.

1. Click the Skin Chooser tab. Windows displays the Skin Chooser page.

2. Select a skin whose look appeals to you.

Click the Apply Skin button. Windows Media Player applies the skin and switches to Skin mode.

3. Most skins provide play controls, volume controls, and visualization controls.

USING SKIN MODE *(continued)*

4. You can issue some commands by clicking the anchor window and choosing from the menu displayed.

5. Click the Return to Full Mode button—wherever it may be on the skin—to display Windows Media Player in Full mode again.

6. Alternatively, right-click the skin and choose Switch to Full Mode from the context menu.

7. To return to Skin mode with the same skin, click the Switch to Skin Mode button.

LISTENING TO INTERNET RADIO

Windows Media Player provides good features for tuning into Internet radio—radio broadcast across the Web via streaming audio servers such as SHOUTcast, icecast, or RealAudio.

Some Internet radio stations are commercial stations, but most are amateur stations broadcasting only on the Internet. You can search for radio stations by a variety of information, including format, band, location, callsign, keywords in their description, or language.

1. Click the Radio Tuner tab. Windows displays the Radio Tuner page.

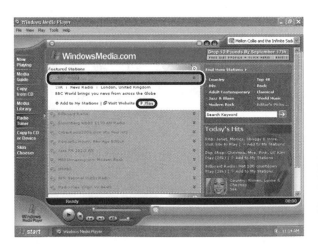

2. To listen to one of the featured stations, click its heading, then click the Play link.

Windows Media Player opens the station, buffers it (which takes a few seconds), and starts to play it. It also opens an Internet Explorer window to the station's Web site.

3. Use the Pause button, Stop button, Mute/Sound button, and Volume control to control the playback of the radio station.

LISTENING TO INTERNET RADIO *(continued)*

4. You can browse for a radio station by following the category links under the Find More Stations heading.

To search for a station, click the Find More Stations link.

5. From this screen, you can search by keyword or zip code.

Click the Use Advanced Search button.

6. Specify the criteria you want: Genre, Language, Country, State (in the U.S. only), Speed, Band (AM, FM, or the Net), or Keyword, Call Sign, or Frequency.

Click the Search button.

7. To listen to a station you've found, click its heading to expand the listing, then click the Play link.

INSTALLING A PROGRAM

Windows comes with a modest selection of mostly limited programs (such as Notepad, WordPad, and Paint, all discussed in Chapter 7), but you'll probably want to add various programs to supplement them.

If you got the program on a physical medium, such as a floppy disk, a CD-ROM, a DVD, or a removable disk, load the disk in the appropriate drive. If you downloaded the file, you need only know where you saved it.

Before installing a program, it's a good idea to close all open programs. This isn't always necessary, but it's possible for the files you're installing to conflict with files that are being used by open programs.

1. Choose Start ➤ Control Panel. Windows displays Control Panel.

2. Click the Add or Remove Programs link. Windows displays the Add or Remove Programs window.

3. Click the Add New Programs button. Windows displays the Add New Programs page.

INSTALLING A PROGRAM *(continued)*

4. Click the CD or Floppy button. Windows displays the Install Program from Floppy Disk or CD-ROM page.

5. If the program is on a CD or a floppy, and you haven't inserted the disk already, do so now.

Click the Next button. Windows searches your floppy drives and CD drives for a setup file and displays the Run Installation Program dialog box.

6. If Windows found a setup file, it lists it in the Open text box. Make sure this is the right file. If not, or if Windows didn't find the file, click the Browse button and use the Browse dialog box to locate the setup file.

Click the Finish button. Windows starts the setup routine for the program.

7. Follow the prompts, supplying decisions and information as necessary.

REMOVING A PROGRAM

If you cease to find a program useful, or if you replace it with a better program, you can remove the program to reclaim the space it occupied on disk.

To remove a program, always use the procedure shown on this page. If you try to remove a program by deleting its files, you'll usually be able to remove only part of it, so it'll still take up some space on the disk. Worse, Windows won't know that you've disabled the program, which may cause problems.

Before you remove a program, make sure that no other user still needs it. Make doubly sure that no other user is currently using it.

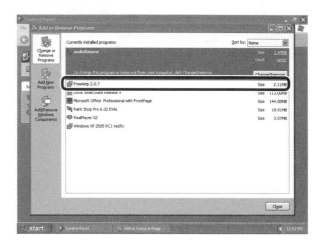

1. Take steps 1 and 2 of the previous item to display the Change or Remove Programs page of the Add or Remove Programs window.

Select the program. The window displays information about the program and buttons for changing it or removing it.

2. Click the Remove button or the Change/ Remove button. Windows starts the uninstall routine for the program.

Most uninstall routines display some kind of confirmation dialog box.

3. Choose the confirmation button in any confirmation message box.

You may also need to choose uninstall options and confirm the removal of some files.

KEEPING WINDOWS UP-TO-DATE WITH WINDOWS UPDATE

Windows Update keeps your copy of Windows up-to-date and secure by downloading and installing the latest updates, additions, and security patches that Microsoft releases. In order to use Windows Update, your computer needs to be connected to the Internet.

By default, Windows Update runs itself periodically, downloads update files you might want to install, and prompts you to install them. If you prefer, you can run Windows Update manually as described in this section. You can also run Windows Update from Help and Support Center.

Because Windows Update is implemented via the Microsoft Web site, the interface may have changed from the screens shown here.

1. Choose Start ➢ All Programs ➢ Windows Update. Windows opens an Internet Explorer window to the Windows Update Web site.

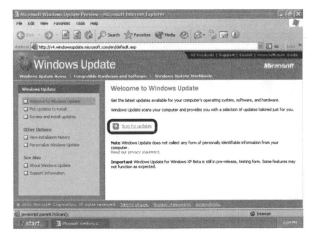

2. Click the Scan for Updates link. Windows scans the available updates and presents a list.

If you see a Security Warning dialog box asking you to install controls signed by Microsoft Corporation, choose the Yes button.

3. Click the Review and Install Updates link. Windows displays information on the updates.

If there are no critical updates, you can choose other updates in the Pick Updates to Install area.

KEEPING WINDOWS UP-TO-DATE *(continued)*

4. Click the Remove button to remove any update you don't want to install.

Click the Install Now button. Windows may display a license agreement.

5. Click the Accept button if the license is acceptable.

6. Wait while Windows downloads and installs the updates. When it has finished, it may display the Installation Complete screen or may require you to shut down your computer (as shown here).

7. Click the OK button to restart your computer. Windows restarts your computer and finishes installing the update.

CONFIGURING AUTOPLAY

Windows includes an Autoplay feature that's set by default to spring into action when you insert a removable storage item such as a CD, a DVD, a removable disk (for example, a Zip disk), or a CompactFlash card or SmartMedia card.

Autoplay is designed to take different actions for different types of content: audio files (for example, MP3 files), picture files (for example, digital photos), video files, and mixed content. By configuring Autoplay, you can make Windows take the actions you want for a given type of content.

1. Choose Start ➢ My Computer. Windows opens an Explorer window showing your drives.

2. Right-click the removable drive and choose Properties from the context menu. Windows displays the Properties dialog box for the drive—in this example, a CD drive.

3. Click the Autoplay tab. Windows displays the Autoplay page.

CONFIGURING AUTOPLAY *(continued)*

4. In the drop-down list, select the type of content you want to set Autoplay for.

The Actions group box displays actions for that type of content.

5. To have Windows perform an action, select the Select an Action to Perform option button, then select the action in the list box.

6. To have Windows prompt you for an action each time, select the Prompt Me Each Time to Choose an Action option button.

7. Set Autoplay options for other content types.

Click the OK button. Windows closes the Properties dialog box and applies your settings.

INSTALLING A PRINTER

In order to print documents on a printer, you need to install the printer on your computer. Installing the printer lets Windows know that the printer is there, what type of printer it is, and which driver (software) to use for it.

You can install a printer locally (as described in this section) or connect to a shared printer on another computer to which your computer is networked (as described in "Connecting to a Shared Printer" on page 76).

Windows may detect a local printer when you connect it to your computer. If so, it installs the driver if it can; otherwise, it prompts you to start the installation process. If Windows does not detect your printer, you can install it manually as described here.

1. Choose Start ➢ Control Panel. Windows displays Control Panel.

2. Click the Printers and Other Hardware link. Windows displays the Printers and Other Hardware screen.

3. Click the Add a Printer link. Windows starts the Add Printer Wizard, which displays its first page.

INSTALLING A PRINTER *(continued)*

4. Click the Next button. The Wizard displays the Local or Network Printer page.

5. Make sure the Local Printer Attached to This Computer option button is selected.

Make sure the Automatically Detect and Install My Plug and Play Printer check box is selected.

Click the Next button. If the Wizard finds the printer, go to step 12.

6. Click the Next button. The Wizard displays the Select a Printer Port page.

7. Select the port in the Use the Following Port drop-down list.

Click the Next button. The Wizard displays the Install Printer Software page.

INSTALLING A PRINTER *(continued)*

8. Select the manufacturer and printer model.

Click the Next button. The Wizard displays the Name Your Printer page.

9. Change the name for the printer if you want to. If your computer has another printer installed, the Wizard offers to make this the default printer. Choose the Yes or the No option button.

Click the Next button. The Wizard displays the Printer Sharing page.

10. If you want to share the printer with other computers, select the Share Name option button and enter the name in the text box.

Click the Next button. The Wizard displays the Print Test Page page.

11. Select the Yes option button or the No option button as appropriate.

Click the Next button. The Wizard displays the Completing the Add Printer Wizard page, which summarizes the choices you made.

INSTALLING A PRINTER (continued)

12. Click the Finish button. The Wizard installs the files for the printer.

If you chose to print a test page, the Wizard prints the page and displays a dialog box checking that it printed okay.

13. Click the OK button to close the dialog box. (If the page didn't print correctly, click the Troubleshoot button and follow the Printing Troubleshooter.)

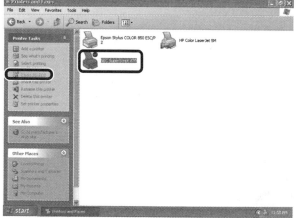

14. The default printer is designated by a black circle containing a white check mark.

To set a different default printer, right-click the printer and choose Set As Default Printer from the context menu.

15. To pause printing on a printer, select it and click the Pause Printing link in the Printer Tasks list.

To resume printing, click the resulting Resume Printing link in the Printer Tasks list.

SHARING A PRINTER

Windows XP lets you share a printer with other users so that they can use it as if it were attached to their computer.

If you didn't set up your printer for sharing while installing it by using the Add Printer Wizard (as described on pages 71–74), you can set it up for sharing as described in this section.

1. Display the Printers and Other Hardware screen as described in steps 1 and 2 on page 71.

Click the View Installed Printers or Fax Printers link. Windows displays the Printers and Faxes screen.

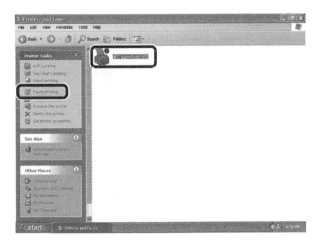

2. Select the printer you want to share.

Click the Share This Printer item in the Printer Tasks list. Windows displays the Sharing page of the Properties dialog box for the printer.

3. Select the Share This Printer option button.

Check—and if necessary, change—the name Windows suggests for the shared printer.

Click the OK button. Windows shares the printer and closes the Properties dialog box.

CONNECTING TO A SHARED PRINTER

Instead of installing a local printer, you can connect to a printer shared by a computer to which your computer is networked. Such a printer is called a *network printer*. Provided that the computer to which the network printer is attached is running, you can print to the network printer as you would to a local printer.

1. Display the Local or Network Printer page of the Add Printer Wizard by following steps 1 to 4 on pages 71–72.

Select the A Network Printer, or a Printer Attached to Another Computer option button. Click the Next button.

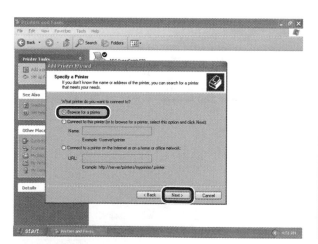

2. Make sure the Browse for a Printer option button is selected.

Click the Next button. The Wizard displays the Browse for Printer page.

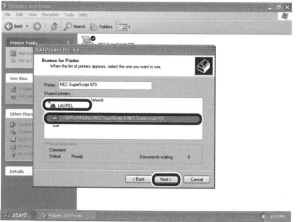

3. Expand the appropriate workgroup and computer, then select the shared printer.

Follow through the remaining steps of the Wizard for specifying whether this is the default printer and finishing the Wizard (see pages 73–74).

DEFRAGMENTING YOUR HARD DISK

To keep your hard disk in good shape, and to improve disk performance, defragment it regularly by using Disk Defragmenter. How frequently you need to run Disk Defragmenter depends on how actively you use your computer and how often you create, modify, or delete files. Try running Disk Defragmenter once a week and see if it recommends defragmenting your disks. If not, decrease the frequency with which you run Disk Defragmenter.

Defragmenting a volume (a drive) can take several hours, and it's best not to use the computer during defragmentation. Set Disk Defragmenter running when you don't need to use the computer for a few hours—for example, at night.

Before defragmenting a disk, close all open programs and make sure no one else is logged on to the computer.

1. Choose Start ➢ All Programs ➢ Accessories ➢ System Tools ➢ Disk Defragmenter. Windows starts Disk Defragmenter.

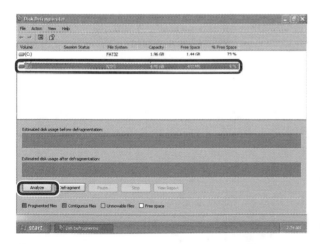

2. Select the volume you want to defragment. Click the Analyze button. Disk Defragmenter analyzes the volume and displays a summary.

3. If the volume needs defragmentation, click the View Report button. Disk Defragmenter displays the Analysis Report dialog box.

If the volume doesn't need defragmentation, click the Close button and go to step 7.

DEFRAGMENTING YOUR HARD DISK *(continued)*

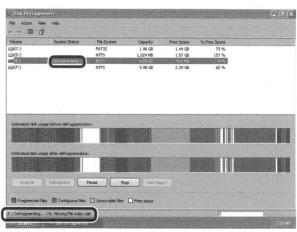

4. If you want, click the Print button to print the analysis report, or click the Save As button to save it.

Click the Defragment button to start defragmentation.

5. Disk Defragmenter displays its status and its progress.

You can pause defragmentation by clicking the Pause button or stop it by clicking the Stop button.

6. When defragmentation is complete, Disk Defragmenter displays another Disk Defragmenter dialog box telling you so.

Click the View Report button to display the defragmentation report on the volume's status, or click the Close button to close the dialog box.

7. Defragment other volumes as necessary.

Choose File ➢ Exit. Disk Defragmenter closes.

You can now resume computing as normal.

RUNNING DISK CLEANUP

Windows' Disk Cleanup feature lets you keep your hard disk in order by removing temporary files, emptying the Recycle Bin, and compressing old files. By getting rid of old files, you can reclaim disk space.

It's a good idea to run Disk Cleanup once every few weeks. If you find it hard to remember to run Disk Cleanup, you can schedule it to run automatically at a convenient time, as described in the next section.

See "Cleaning Up Your Disks with Disk Cleanup" in Chapter 11 for a discussion of the pros and cons of removing the various types of files that Disk Cleanup rounds up for deletion.

1. Choose Start ➤ All Programs ➤ Accessories ➤ System Tools ➤ Disk Cleanup. Windows starts Disk Cleanup, which displays the Select Drive dialog box.

2. Select the drive to clean up.

Click the OK button. Disk Cleanup scans the drive and displays the Disk Cleanup dialog box.

3. Select the items you want to delete.

Click the OK button. Windows removes the items and closes the Disk Cleanup dialog box.

SCHEDULING A TASK TO RUN AUTOMATICALLY

You can schedule tasks to run automatically at times and frequencies that suit you. Scheduling tasks can be useful for tasks that are best run automatically, when no one is using the computer, at an antisocial hour, or on a regular schedule that makes them hard to remember. You can also schedule tasks that you need to run only once at some point in the future—either at a specific point in time or when a particular event occurs, such as a user's logging on.

1. Choose Start ➤ All Programs ➤ Accessories ➤ System Tools ➤ Scheduled Tasks.

Windows displays the Scheduled Tasks folder.

2. Double-click the Add Scheduled Task icon. Windows starts the Scheduled Task Wizard.

3. Click the Next button. The Wizard displays the next page.

SCHEDULING A TASK TO RUN AUTOMATICALLY *(continued)*

4. Select the program in the list.

If the program isn't in the list, click the Browse button and use the Select Program to Schedule dialog box to select the program.

Click the Next button.

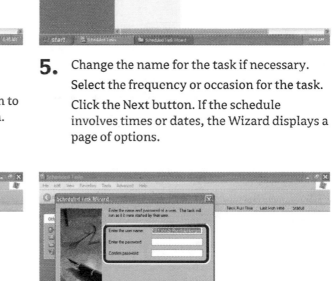

5. Change the name for the task if necessary.

Select the frequency or occasion for the task.

Click the Next button. If the schedule involves times or dates, the Wizard displays a page of options.

6. Choose schedule options as appropriate.

Click the Next button. The Wizard displays the name and password page.

7. Specify the username and password under which to run the task. The Wizard suggests your username.

Click the Next button. The Wizard displays its final page.

SCHEDULING A TASK TO RUN AUTOMATICALLY *(continued)*

8. Select the Open Advanced Properties for This Task when I Click Finish check box.

Click the Finish button. The Wizard adds the task to your schedule and displays the Properties dialog box for the task.

9. You can turn the task on or off by selecting or clearing the Enabled check box.

Click the Schedule tab. Windows displays the Schedule page.

10. Choose further settings on the Schedule page as necessary.

Click the Settings tab. Windows displays the Settings page.

11. Choose further settings on the Settings page as necessary.

Click the OK button. Windows closes the Properties dialog box and applies your changes.

SETTING SYSTEM RESTORE POINTS

The System Restore feature lets you roll back your computer's software state following a change of software that doesn't turn out satisfactorily. For example, you might update a device driver but find that the new driver didn't work correctly. Or you might install a program that doesn't work as it should   and which won't uninstall correctly.

System Restore lets you return your computer to a system restore point created in the past. Windows automatically creates system restore points both periodically and when you use Windows Update, and you can create them manually whenever you want—for example, before installing or updating software or changing configuration settings. With typical settings, Windows retains two to three weeks' worth of restore points, giving you good flexibility in recovering from software and hardware mishaps.

1. Choose Start ≻ All Programs ≻ Accessories ≻ System Tools ≻ System Restore. Windows starts System Restore.

2. Click the System Restore Settings link. System Restore displays the System Restore page of the System Properties dialog box.

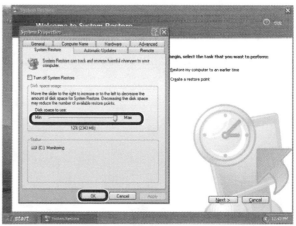

3. If necessary, use the Disk Space to Use slider to adjust the amount of space System Restore uses. (If your system has multiple drives, click the Settings button and use the Settings dialog box.)

Click the OK button.

SETTING SYSTEM RESTORE POINTS *(continued)*

4. Select the Create a Restore Point option button.

Click the Next button. System Restore displays the Create a Restore Point screen.

5. Enter the name for the restore point.

Click the Create button. System Restore creates the restore point and displays the Restore Point Created screen.

6. Click the Close button. System Restore closes.

Expert Advice

◆ You can turn off System Restore by selecting the Turn Off System Restore check box (or the Turn Off System Restore on All Drives check box, if you have multiple drives) on the System Restore page of the System Properties dialog box, but doing so isn't a good idea: Although Windows XP is reliable and stable, badly written software or drivers can still prevent it from running. But you may be able to save disk space by reducing the amount of space System Restore can take up. System Restore needs at least 200MB of space.

◆ If you have multiple hard drives, you can save disk space by turning off System Restore for data-only drives. Keep System Restore turned on for the drive that contains your Windows files and your program files.

RESTORING YOUR SYSTEM

When a software installation or a driver upgrade doesn't work as planned, you can use System Restore to return Windows to one of the restore points that you or Windows created.

Because System Restore changes the software configuration of your computer, it's best to use it only when your software goes seriously wrong. If you experience a problem that you can solve by changing a driver or rolling back a driver to the previously installed driver, it's better to solve the problem that way than by using System Restore. (Pages 92–95 discuss how to change a driver, and page 96 illustrates how to roll back a driver.)

1. Choose Start ➢ All Programs ➢ Accessories ➢ System Tools ➢ System Restore. Windows starts System Restore.

2. Make sure the Restore My Computer to an Earlier Time option button is selected.

Click the Next button. System Restore displays the Select a Restore Point screen.

3. Use the calendar to select the date to which you want to restore the computer. Bold dates indicate restore points.

Select a restore point in the list for the date.

Click the Next button. System Restore displays the Confirm Restore Point Selection screen.

RESTORING YOUR SYSTEM *(continued)*

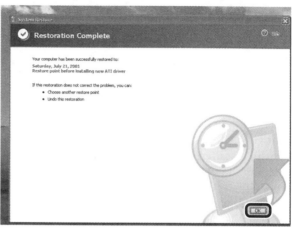

4. Close any other open programs.

Click the Next button. System Restore restores your system to the restore point you chose, then restarts Windows and displays the Restoration Complete page after you log on.

5. Click the OK button. System Restore closes.

Check your system to see if it's running properly.

6. If the restoration didn't produce the effect you wanted, run System Restore again. You can either choose a restore point further in the past or undo your last restoration.

Expert Advice

◆ System Restore stores several weeks' worth of restore points, depending on how much space you've allocated to it.

◆ Restoring your system affects only your system files—it doesn't affect your data files. So any data files that you've created since the restore point to which you're restoring Windows will still be there after the restoration.

◆ Conversely, this also means that you can't use System Restore to rescue a data file that you've deleted or damaged. For example, if you delete the contents of an Excel workbook and then save it, you can't recover an earlier version of the file by using System Restore.

SHARING FILES OR FOLDERS WITH OTHER USERS OF THE COMPUTER

To share a file or folder with other users of your computer, copy or move it to the \Shared Documents\ folder or one of its subfolders. Windows provides the \Shared Documents\ folder for shared documents, the \Shared Music\ folder for shared music files, the \Shared Pictures\ folder for shared pictures, and the \Shared Videos\ folder (when you start working with video) for shared video files.

If you copy the file or folder (as described here), you can keep the original to yourself. If you move the file or folder, anyone can change the original.

1. Open an Explorer window to the folder that contains the file or folder.

2. Select the file or folder.

Click the Copy This File link or the Copy This Folder link. Windows displays the Copy Items dialog box.

3. Select the Shared Documents icon.

Click the Copy button.

Windows copies the file or folder to the \Shared Documents\ folder.

KEEPING A FOLDER PRIVATE

Even if you don't share a folder under your \My Documents\ folder, other Computer Administrator users of your computer can access it. To prevent them from doing so, you need to mark the folder as private.

If you don't have a password on your user account, you need to set one. (Otherwise, other users can log on as you and see your folders.)

1. Right-click the folder and choose Sharing and Security from the context menu.
Windows displays the Sharing page of the Properties dialog box.

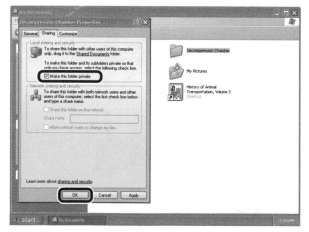

2. Select the Make This Folder Private check box.
Click the OK button. Windows closes the Properties dialog box and makes the folder private.

Expert Advice

◆ If you don't have a password on your user account, Windows displays the Sharing dialog box warning you that because you don't have a password, anyone can log in as you and then access the folder you've made private.

◆ Click the Yes button in the Sharing dialog box. Windows displays the Create a Password for Your Account screen of User Accounts.

◆ Enter the password in the top two text boxes.

◆ If you want, enter a cryptic word or phrase for a password hint.

◆ Click the Create Password button. Windows applies the password to your account. The folder is then securely private.

SHARING A FOLDER ON THE NETWORK

Instead of sharing a folder only with other users of
your computer, you can share it with them and
with other users of computers networked to yours.

1. Select the folder.

Click the Share This Folder link.
Windows displays the Sharing page of the
Properties dialog box for the folder.

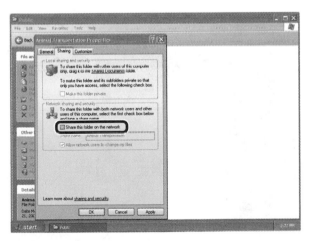

2. Select the Share This Folder on the Network
check box. Windows enables the other sharing options.

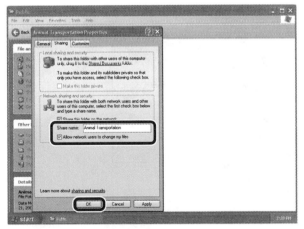

3. Adjust the share name if you want to.

Select or clear the Allow Network Users to
Change My Files check box as appropriate.

Click the OK button. Windows shares the
folder.

CONNECTING A NETWORK DRIVE

If your computer is connected to a network, you can connect to any drive that a computer on the network has shared. You can then work with the files and folders on that network drive as if it were a drive on your computer.

1. From an Explorer window, choose Tools ➢ Map Network Drive. Windows displays the Map Network Drive dialog box.

2. Specify the drive letter to use for the network drive. Windows starts with the letter Z, the last letter used.

Click the Browse button. Windows displays the Browse for Folder dialog box.

3. Expand the Microsoft Windows Network item. Expand the appropriate workgroup item.

CONNECTING A NETWORK DRIVE *(continued)*

4. Expand the item for the computer that contains the shared folder.

Select the shared folder.

Click the OK button. Windows closes the Browse for Folder dialog box and enters the folder path and name in the Folder text box.

5. To automatically connect this network drive each time you log on, select the Reconnect at Logon check box.

To specify a different username for connecting to the network drive, click the Connect Using a Different User Name link.

6. Enter your username. If necessary, preface it with the computer name and a backslash.

Enter your password.

Click the OK button. Windows closes the Connect As dialog box.

7. Click the Finish button. Windows closes the Map Network Drive dialog box and maps the drive.

CHANGING A DRIVER

You can often improve a device's performance by updating its driver, the software that enables Windows to communicate with it. Most hardware manufacturers release updated drivers periodically for their hardware to remove bugs and add new features. Once you've downloaded the driver, you can install it as described in this section.

If a new driver doesn't work satisfactorily, you can roll the driver back (as described in the next section) or use the System Restore feature to restore your system's state to before you installed the driver.

1. Choose Start ➢ Control Panel. Windows displays Control Panel.

(Alternatively, press Winkey+Break and go directly to step 4.)

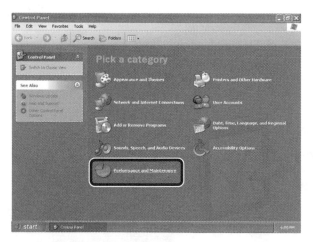

2. Click the Performance and Maintenance link. Windows displays the Performance and Maintenance screen.

3. Click the System link. Windows displays the System Properties dialog box.

CHANGING A DRIVER *(continued)*

4. Click the Hardware tab. Windows displays the Hardware page.

5. Click the Device Manager button. Windows displays Device Manager.

6. Select the device for which you want to change the driver.

Click the Update Driver button. Windows starts the Hardware Update Wizard.

7. Select the Install from a List or Specific Location option button.

Click the Next button. The Wizard displays the Please Choose Your Search and Installation Options page.

CHANGING A DRIVER *(continued)*

8. Select the Don't Search. I Will Choose the Driver to Install option button.

Click the Next button.

If the Wizard displays the Hardware Type page first, leave the Show All Devices item selected and click the Next button.

9. Click the Have Disk button. The Wizard displays the Install from Disk dialog box.

10. Click the Browse button. The Wizard displays the Locate File dialog box.

11. Navigate to and select the file containing the driver information.

Click the Open button. The Wizard closes the Locate File dialog box and enters the driver name in the Install from Disk dialog box.

CHANGING A DRIVER *(continued)*

12. Click the OK button. The Wizard closes the Install from Disk dialog box and enters the driver name on the Select the Device Driver You Want to Install for This Hardware page.

13. Click the Next button. The Wizard installs the software and displays the final page of the Wizard.

14. Click the Finish button. The Wizard closes.

15. Click the Close button to close Device Manager.

Click the Close button to close the System Properties dialog box.

Click the Close button to close the Performance and Maintenance window.

ROLLING BACK A DRIVER

In case a driver upgrade doesn't work correctly, Windows stores information about the previous driver used for the hardware in question so that you can easily restore that driver. Windows calls this process *rolling back* the new driver to the previous driver.

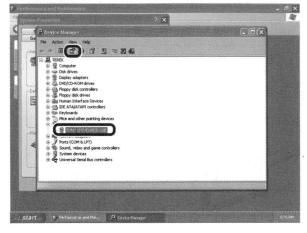

1. Follow steps 1 to 5 of the previous section to display Device Manager.

Select the device whose driver you want to roll back.

Click the Properties button. Windows displays the Properties dialog box for the driver.

2. Click the Driver tab. Windows displays the Driver page of the dialog box.

Click the Roll Back Driver button. Windows displays a confirmation dialog box.

3. Click the Yes button. Windows restores the previous driver.

Click the OK button. Windows closes the Properties dialog box.

Close Device Manager, the Performance and Maintenance window, and the System Properties dialog box.

Part I

Up and Running with Windows XP Home Edition

Chapter 1

Introducing Windows XP Home Edition

THIS CHAPTER DISCUSSES WHAT Windows XP Home Edition is, what it does, and who it's for. It covers in some detail the features and improvements in Windows XP Home, so that you'll know what the operating system offers, and mentions which chapter of the book covers which feature.

The chapter then discusses whether you should upgrade from your current version of Windows. As you might imagine, the answer depends on which version of Windows you're currently running, what you're trying to do with it, and what degrees of success and satisfaction you're experiencing. But for most people who have adequate hardware, Windows XP offers significant improvements over all previous versions of Windows.

At the end of the chapter, you'll find a discussion of the main ways in which Windows XP Professional differs from Windows XP Home, because you may want to consider Professional rather than Home if you need any of the additional features that Professional offers.

If you're already up to speed on all of Windows XP's features, skip straight ahead to the next chapter and get started on installing XP.

This chapter covers the following topics:

◆ What is Windows XP Home Edition?

◆ What's new in Windows XP Home Edition?

◆ Should you upgrade to Windows XP Home Edition?

◆ Should you upgrade to Windows XP Professional Edition instead?

What Is Windows XP Home Edition?

In a nutshell, Windows XP Home Edition is the latest version of Windows aimed at the consumer market. Windows XP Home comprises a feature set designed for home users, while its more powerful (and more expensive) sibling Windows XP Professional offers features designed for professional and corporate users.

If you've used Windows before, or if you're currently using Windows, you may wonder what the big deal is. The good news is that Windows XP *is* a big deal, especially if you've had less than satisfactory experiences with Windows in the past. Windows XP isn't the be-all and end-all of operating systems, but it's a great improvement on its predecessors.

As you probably know, through the second half of the 1990s and up until 2001, Microsoft offered two main categories of Windows versions for personal computers: the Windows 95 family and the Windows NT family. In the Windows 95 family were Windows 95 itself, naturally enough; Windows 98; Windows 98 Second Edition, which (despite its unassuming name) was a major upgrade to Windows 98; and Windows Millennium Edition, also known as Windows Me. In the Windows NT family were Windows NT versions 3.1, 3.5, 3.51, and 4, each of which came in a Workstation version and a Server version, and then Windows 2000, which came in a Professional version and several Server versions.

The Windows 95 family, widely referred to as Windows 9*x* in a brave attempt to simplify Microsoft's inconsistent naming, offered impressive compatibility with older hardware (*legacy hardware*, as it's sometimes politely termed) and software (*legacy software*), including full (or full-ish) DOS capabilities for running games and character-based programs. These versions of Windows kept their hardware demands to a reasonable minimum. They were aimed at the consumer market. When things went wrong (which happened regrettably often), they became unstable. And they crashed. Frequently.

Many of those people—both professionals and home users—who couldn't stand or afford to lose their work because of Windows 9*x*'s frequent crashes migrated to Windows NT instead. (Others tried OS/2 while it lasted, then returned disconsolately to Windows. Others went to Linux, and mostly stayed with it.) NT, which stands for New Technology, had a completely different underpinning of code than Windows 9*x*. NT was designed for stability, and as a result, it crashed much less frequently than Windows 9*x*. Unfortunately, though, NT wasn't nearly as compatible as Windows 9*x* with legacy hardware and software. Most games and much audio and video software wouldn't run on NT, and it was picky about the hardware on which it would run. (Actually, this wasn't unfortunate at all—it was deliberate on Microsoft's part, and probably wise. But the result was far from great for many users.)

So for the last half-dozen years, users have essentially had to decide between stability and compatibility. This led to a lot of unhappy users, some of whom couldn't run the software they wanted, and others who kept losing work or at least having to reboot their computers more than they should have had to.

The Windows 9*x* line culminated in Windows Me, which tacked some stability and restoration features onto the Windows 9*x* code base. NT culminated in Windows 2000 Professional, which featured increased compatibility with programs over NT (which wasn't saying all that much), a smooth user interface, and usability enhancements.

Windows 2000 Professional was arguably the most stable operating system that Microsoft had produced until Windows XP came along. (Some old-timers reckoned Windows NT 3.51 was more stable.) But Windows 2000 Professional's stability came at a price: It had no interest in running any games or other demanding software that wouldn't conform to its stringent requirements. And while it was compatible with quite an impressive range of legacy hardware, many items still wouldn't work. Even up-to-date hardware could be problematic, especially if it connected via USB.

Since the late 1990s, Microsoft had been promising to deliver a consumer version of Windows that melded the stability of NT and the compatibility of Windows 9x. In Windows XP Home Edition, that version of Windows is finally here.

What's New in Windows XP Home Edition?

This section outlines the most striking and appealing new features in Windows XP, starting with installation and upgrading, moving through the user interface and visible features, and ending up with the features hidden under the hood.

Some of these new features fall into convenient categories, and this section presents them in categories. Others don't; this section presents these features individually.

Easier Installation and Updating

Windows XP includes several features designed to make it easier to install and keep up to date. These include Dynamic Update and Windows Update; the Files and Settings Transfer Wizard; more Wizards for a variety of tasks; a wider selection of device drivers; simplified installation for multifunction devices; and effective uninstall back to Windows 98 and Windows Me.

DYNAMIC UPDATE AND WINDOWS UPDATE

If you're installing Windows XP, one of the first new features that you'll notice is Dynamic Update, which runs during setup and offers to download the latest patches, packages, and fixes so that they can be installed during the setup process.

Dynamic Update may prove to be a great feature. It goes hand in hand with its terrible twin, Windows Update, which runs periodically after setup and offers to download the latest patches, packages, and fixes and install them so that your copy of Windows is as up to date, secure, and compatible as possible. (You can also run Windows Update manually whenever you want to.)

Chapter 2 discusses Dynamic Update and Windows Update.

FILES AND SETTINGS TRANSFER WIZARD

Making its debut in Windows XP is the Files and Settings Transfer Wizard, a feature that Windows users have been demanding for a good 10 years. The Files and Settings Transfer Wizard provides a way of transferring designated files and settings from one computer to another, or from one installation of Windows to another on the same computer. You'll still need to reinstall all your programs on the new computer or new installation of Windows, but you can transfer your data and a good amount of information about your work environment easily.

If you're migrating from an old computer to a new computer, or if you're installing Windows XP as a dual-boot with an existing version of Windows, you can use the Files and Settings Transfer Wizard to clone your existing Desktop and files and transfer them to the new computer or new version of Windows.

Chapter 2 discusses how to use the Files and Settings Transfer Wizard.

MORE WIZARDS TO MAKE TASKS EASIER

Windows XP includes a slew of Wizards designed to walk you through complicated processes (and some that aren't so complicated). Perhaps most welcome are the improvements to the Network Setup Wizard (discussed in Chapter 32), which provides effective configuration of simple networks and Internet connection sharing, and the two Hardware Wizards, the Add Hardware Wizard and the Found New Hardware Wizard (discussed in various chapters, but primarily in Chapter 14).

On the less useful front, Windows XP also includes Wizards such as the Desktop Cleanup Wizard, which pops out periodically like the neighborhood dog and tries to persuade you to let it herd the stray icons on your Desktop into a folder where they'll be available but less obtrusive. If you refuse, it wags its tail and goes away for a while.

MORE DEVICE DRIVERS

Windows XP comes complete with drivers for a large number of devices, including scanners, digital still cameras, digital video cameras, printers, and so on. So there's a better chance than with another version of Windows (say Windows Me or Windows 2000) that when you plug in a new device, Windows XP will be able to load a driver for it and get it working without any fuss.

You'll probably want to take this improvement with a grain of salt. It's great when Windows XP installs a new device without any effort on your part. But to enjoy the latest features and the best performance from a new device, you may well need to install the driver that comes with the device or (better) download the latest version from the manufacturer's Web site rather than wait for updated drivers to filter through Windows Update.

Like hardware, drivers pop up in various places throughout the book, but most of the action is in Chapter 14.

SIMPLIFIED INSTALLATION FOR MULTIFUNCTION DEVICES

Apart from having more drivers (as described in the previous section), Windows XP makes it easier to install multifunction devices—for example, a multifunction printer/scanner/fax device (the kind that people sometimes call *hydra* machines), a PC Card that combines a network interface card with a modem, or a sound board with extra features.

Previous versions of Windows tended to recognize the component pieces of multifunction devices separately in sequence. If you installed a hydra, Windows would recognize the printer and demand the installation software for it. Once that was done, Windows would recognize the fax and demand the software for *that*. After that, it would recognize the scanner and suggest you might want to install yet more software. Windows XP improves on this social ineptitude by recognizing multifunction devices as such the first time you introduce it to them, and so it demands the installation software only once.

EFFECTIVE UNINSTALL BACK TO WINDOWS 98 AND WINDOWS ME

Windows XP Home provides an effective uninstall feature for rolling back the Windows XP installation to your previous installation of Windows 98 or Windows Me. You can't uninstall Windows XP Home and revert to an operating system other than these two. (Windows XP Professional supports upgrading from and uninstalling back to a different set of previous versions of Windows, as you'll see later in this chapter.)

Effective Multiuser Capabilities

Windows XP provides far better multiuser capabilities than Windows 9x. You'll notice this at once when you start Windows XP, because by default the Welcome screen that's displayed when Windows starts lists each user who has an account on the computer.

While Windows 9x let anybody log on to the computer by creating a new account, Windows XP requires an existing account in order to log on. By default, no account has a password in Windows XP Home, though, so in effect anybody can log on using one of the existing accounts until you require passwords—and you ought to require passwords immediately to protect your data.

Windows 9x let you create a profile for each separate user, so that each user could have their own Desktop, Start menu, and set of programs; but it didn't offer any features for preventing one user from seeing another user's files. By contrast, Windows XP takes the approach of NT and Windows 2000, which keep each user's files separate, letting you set Windows up so that no user can see another user's files unless they have been shared deliberately.

Windows XP goes further than NT and Windows 2000, though, in that it lets multiple users be logged on at the same time, each with programs running. Only one user can be actually *using* the computer, or *active* in Windows XP parlance, at any one time, but the other user sessions continue running in the background (*disconnected,* in Windows XP parlance). When you've finished with the computer for the time being, you can log off Windows, just as you did in previous versions of Windows. Logging off closes all the programs you were using and frees up the memory they took up. But if you stop using the computer only temporarily, you may prefer to *switch user,* which leaves your programs running but lets someone else use the computer in the interim. Further encouraging you to switch user, Windows' default screen saver setting is to display the Welcome screen after 10 minutes of inactivity, performing the equivalent of a Switch User command as it disconnects the user but leaves their session running hidden in the background.

As you might imagine, having multiple user sessions running like this can cause some problems. For example, what happens when one user has a shared file open for editing in their (disconnected) session, and along comes another user, logs on, opens the same file, and starts editing it? And what happens if a disconnected session has the Internet connection open, preventing the currently active user from using the phone line?

Turn to Chapter 5 to find out the answer to the first question, and Chapter 33 to learn the answer to the second question.

Enhanced User Interface

Windows XP has a completely revamped user interface with a large number of visual enhancements and improved functionality. Some of the visual enhancements improve usability, while others are mere eye candy. But the overall effect is mostly easy to use and mostly looks good—and if you don't like the look, you can restore the "classic" Windows look with minimal effort.

The following sections discuss the main changes to the user interface.

REDESIGNED START MENU

Windows XP sports a redesigned Start menu that's supposedly easier and quicker to use. Whether you find it so depends on your experience with the Start menu found in Windows 9x and Windows 2000. But don't worry if you like the "classic" Start menu—you can restore it easily enough with a few clicks of the mouse, as discussed in Chapter 4.

The Start menu appears as a panel containing two columns (shown in Figure 1.1). The right-hand column remains the same unless you customize it. The left-hand column starts off with items Microsoft thinks you ought to know about immediately after installation. It then automatically reconfigures itself to show your most used programs. You can pin an item to the Start menu to prevent it from moving and keep it available.

FIGURE 1.1

The redesigned Start menu contains a static column of choices on the right and a variable column of choices on the left.

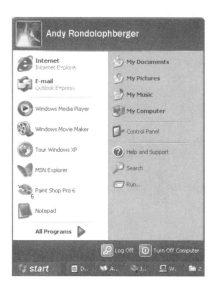

As you can see in the figure, the current user's name appears in a bar across the top of the Start menu, and the Log Off button and Turn Off Computer button appear at the bottom of the menu.

REDESIGNED EXPLORER

Explorer windows use a pair of technologies called WebView and ListView to present context-sensitive lists of tasks you may want to perform or other locations you may want to access. If that sounds a bit vague, that's because WebView and ListView mean that what you see in an Explorer window changes depending on the item that's displayed.

For example, when you select a file (as in Figure 1.2), you see a list of File and Folder Tasks (including links for Rename This File, Move This File, and Delete This File), a list of Other Places (other folders you may want to access from this folder), and a list of Details (which contains information about the file selected and is off the screen in the figure). When you select a folder, Explorer displays a list of File and Folder Tasks (including links for Rename This Folder, Copy This Folder, and Publish This Folder to the Web). When you select your My Network Places folder, you get a Network Tasks list (including links for View Network Connections and Set Up a Home or Small Office Network). When you select the Recycle Bin…. Okay, you get the idea.

Context menus (right-click menus) in Explorer are also improved, with more context-sensitive commands added where appropriate. But most of the action takes place in the Tasks list for the selected item. That's because some 80 percent of users apparently weren't using the context menus successfully—an impressive and frightening statistic thrown up by Microsoft's research on Windows users.

FIGURE 1.2

Explorer windows use the new Web-View and ListView technologies to present lists of tasks associated with the selected item.

REDESIGNED CONTROL PANEL

Windows XP also has a redesigned Control Panel (shown in Figure 1.3) that uses WebView and ListView technology to present Control Panel as categories of items and actions you can take with them. (If you regard Control Panel as an oddly behaved Explorer window, it should come as no surprise after reading the previous section that Control Panel uses WebView and ListView.)

New users will likely find the Category view of Control Panel easy to use. Users comfortable with the regular manifestation of Control Panel in Windows 9x, Windows NT 4, and Windows 2000 will probably prefer to use the Classic view.

FIGURE 1.3

Control Panel also uses WebView and ListView by default, dividing its bevy of icons into categories. You can use the Classic view to see all the icons at once.

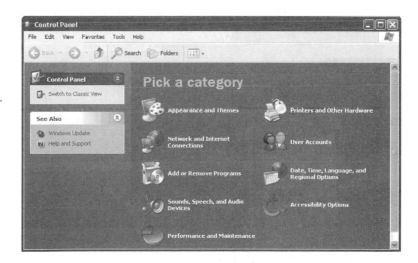

EYE CANDY

To complement its highly graphical interface, Windows XP includes a dangerous amount of eye candy. Most people will like at least some of it. Some people will love it all. And no doubt some people will claim to detest every pixel of it.

The prime example of eye candy is the My Pictures Slideshow screen saver, which lets you set up an automated (or mouse-controlled) slideshow of designated pictures instead of a regular screen saver. This feature seems destined to be widely popular.

Less assured of a rapturous welcome are the staggering amounts of adornment in the interface, such as shadows under the mouse pointer and under menus; the color gradient in the title bar of windows; and the effect of sliding icons, controls, and Taskbar buttons. This overbearing emphasis on graphics places heavy demands on your graphics card and processor, and if your computer's hardware tends to the lukewarm rather than the hot, you may find that the eye candy exacts an unacceptable performance penalty. Microsoft has had the sense to let you set performance options to balance the demands of appearance against your need for performance, so you can turn off the least necessary effects and speed up your computer. (Chapter 11 discusses how to set performance options.)

Taskbar Changes and Enhancements

Windows XP includes a number of tweaks to the Taskbar. These seem designed for beginners, so if you're an experienced Windows user, you may find some good and others bad. Fortunately, you can change the Taskbar's behavior back to how it was in previous versions of Windows. You'll find the details in Chapter 4.

TASKBAR LOCKING

By default, the Taskbar is locked in Windows XP Home so that you cannot resize it or move it. Presumably this is intended to help prevent users from dragging their Taskbar to an inaccessible line at the edge of the screen, but it will annoy experienced users who want to be able to resize and move their Taskbar freely. (You can unlock it easily enough.)

TASKBAR SCROLLING

If you read the previous paragraph, you probably started raising objections: If the Taskbar is a fixed size, the buttons for the running programs must become tiny and useless as soon as you've got 10 or more programs running.

Two other changes come into play here, of which the first is Taskbar scrolling. When the Taskbar is locked, Windows keeps the buttons bigger than a minimum size. To accommodate the buttons, Windows increases the depth of the Taskbar, but displays only its top row. On the displayed portion of the Taskbar, Windows puts scroll buttons so that you can scroll the Taskbar up and down one row of buttons at a time.

TASKBAR BUTTON GROUPING

The second change that makes Taskbar locking reasonable is Taskbar button grouping.

By default, Windows XP groups related Taskbar buttons once you've opened enough windows to more or less fill the Taskbar. Whereas other versions of Windows displayed one Taskbar button for each program window, Windows XP groups them onto a pop-up menu from a single Taskbar button.

For example, if you open nine Internet Explorer windows in Windows 98, Windows displays nine Internet Explorer buttons on the Taskbar. Having all these buttons can make it easy to find the window you want, but the buttons take up a lot of space (or each button on the Taskbar gets shrunk to a tiny size to fit them all in).

In Windows XP, if the program has multiple open windows, the Taskbar button displays the number of windows, the title of the current active window or last active window, and a drop-down arrow. To access one of the other open windows, click the Taskbar button. Windows displays a list of the windows by title (shown in Figure 1.4). Select the window you want, and Windows displays it.

FIGURE 1.4

Unlike previous versions of Windows, Windows XP can group related Taskbar buttons onto a single button.

Notification Area

By default, Windows XP Home collapses the notification area (also known as the System Tray) so that only the icons you've used most recently are displayed. To display the other icons in the notification area, click the < button at the left end of the notification area.

Better Audio and Video Features

Windows XP includes a slew of new features and improvements for audio and video. These include a new version of Windows Media Player; better features for grabbing and handling images from digital input devices such as scanners and cameras; and Windows Movie Maker, a modest video-editing program.

Windows Media Player Version 8

Front and center among the improved audio and video features of Windows XP is Windows Media Player version 8, which combines a video and DVD player, a CD player, an Internet radio tuner, and a jukebox for playing and organizing digital-audio files such as Windows Media Audio (WMA) files and MP3 files. Windows Media Player 8 comes with a number of visually interesting *skins* (graphical looks) that you can apply at will. You can even create your own skins if you have the time and talent to invest.

All in all, Windows Media Player 8 is a huge improvement over the 98-pound weakling version of Windows Media Player shipped with all previous versions of Windows except Windows Me. (Me included Windows Media Player 7, which offered many of the features of version 8.) Windows Media Player can even burn audio CDs at the full speed of your CD-R or CD-RW drive.

Windows Media Player is a strong program, but two missing features will disappoint many users:

♦ Windows Media Player has no codec (coder/decoder) for playing back DVDs. If you want to watch DVDs, you'll have to add a codec of your own—and almost certainly pay for the privilege.

♦ Windows Media Player can encode audio to the universally popular MP3 format—but only if you add a third-party encoder. You'll probably have to pay for this too.

Chapter 27 discusses Windows Media Player.

MY MUSIC FOLDER AND MY PICTURES FOLDER

Like several of its predecessors, Windows XP uses custom folders for music (the My Music folder) and pictures (the My Pictures folder). Again like its predecessors, it tries none too subtly to persuade you to save your music in these folders. But Windows XP goes further, in that it makes these folders much more useful than they were in earlier versions of Windows.

As you'd expect, the My Music folder and the My Pictures folder use WebView and ListView to present customized lists of actions you can take with music files and picture files. Some of these actions tend to the commercial—for example, the Order Prints Online link in the Picture Tasks list, and the Shop for Music Online link in the Music Tasks list. But others are solidly useful—for example, the Play All link in the Music Tasks list, which lets you play all the music in a folder without spelunking into it, or the View As a Slide Show link in the Picture Tasks list, which lets you set a whole folder of pictures running as a slideshow with a single click.

Not surprisingly, the My Music folder works hand in hand (or is it glove?) with Windows Media Player. Windows Media Player is definitely happy for you to keep your music in the My Music folder, though it will let you keep your music elsewhere as well. Better yet, Windows Media Player's features for cataloging music tracks are flexible enough to keep track of music files even when you move them from one folder to another.

The My Pictures folder works closely with Windows Image Acquisition, Windows Picture and Fax Viewer, and Paint (all three of which are discussed in the next section). The folder includes a slideshow applet and a filmstrip view, and it can publish your pictures to the Web.

BETTER IMAGE ACQUISITION AND HANDLING

Windows XP provides strong features for capturing images from scanners, still cameras, and video cameras. It also provides better throughput for video streams, though unless you have a duplicate computer running an older version of Windows to use as a benchmark, you could be forgiven for failing to go into raptures over the improvement. Less cynically, the improvement in throughput is unquestionably a good thing, and on decent hardware, Windows XP delivers adequate to impressive video performance; but the chances of your confusing your PC with your Dreamcast remain poor.

One of the central tools for image acquisition and handling is the Scanner and Camera Wizard. This Wizard has a variety of duties, including transferring image files from still cameras and digital media (for example, CompactFlash cards and SmartMedia cards) to the computer. Most of its capabilities stay on the useful side of the esoteric. For example, you can scan multiple pages into a single image file, an ability that can come in handy in both home and business settings.

Windows XP provides some basic tools for handling still images. As mentioned in the previous section, the My Pictures folder acts as a default repository for images and provides some basic image-handling abilities, such as rotating an image. Windows Picture and Fax Viewer feature lets you examine an image (and annotate a fax). And Paint, the basic image-manipulation and drawing package that's been included with Windows since Windows 3.x, has been beefed up as well. Paint can now open—and save—JPEG, GIF, TIFF, and PNG images as well as Windows bitmap (BMP) files, making it about five times as useful as before.

WINDOWS MOVIE MAKER

Windows XP includes Windows Movie Maker, a basic package for capturing video, editing video and audio, and creating video files in the Windows Media format. You won't find yourself making the next *Timecode* or *Traffic* with Windows Movie Maker, but it's good enough for home-video editing. You can also create video slideshows with still images for those family occasions on rainy weekends or holidays.

Chapter 28 discusses how to get started with Windows Movie Maker.

CD Burning

Windows XP comes with built-in CD-burning capabilities. You can burn CDs from an Explorer window with minimal effort. You can also burn CDs directly from Windows Media Player, which lets you easily create audio CDs that you can play in regular CD players.

Chapter 29 discusses how to burn CDs.

Compressed Folders

Windows XP has built-in support for compressed folders in both the ubiquitous ZIP format and the Microsoft Cabinet (CAB) format. You can create ZIP folders containing one or more files or folders. Better still, you can view the contents of a ZIP or CAB folder seamlessly in Explorer as if it were a regular folder.

Chapter 6 discusses how to work with compressed folders.

Improved Features for Sending Attachments

Windows XP includes improved features for sending files and folders as attachments to e-mail messages. Instead of blindly attaching the files and folders identified by the user, Windows offers to optimize the file size and display size of the pictures so that they transfer faster and fit onto the recipient's screen when they arrive. If the recipient is using Windows XP, they get to choose whether to open the file or files at the original size or at the optimized size.

Because this feature can actually change the files sent, it seems suspect. But if it reduces the number of multimegabyte digital pictures landing on your ISP's mail server, you may well find it a positive feature—even if you choose never to use it yourself.

Chapter 20 discusses how to use Outlook Express for e-mail, including attachments.

Search Companion

Windows XP includes Search Companion, an enhanced search feature for finding information both on your PC and in the wider world. You can use Search Companion to search for files, for computers or people online, or for information in Help and Support Center. Search Companion brokers the search requests that you enter and farms them out to the appropriate search mechanisms.

You can choose between having Search Companion appear in a straightforward and unexceptionable window and having it manifest itself using one of various animated characters reminiscent of the Microsoft Office Assistant.

Chapter 6 discusses how to use Search Companion.

Easy Publishing to the Web

Windows XP makes it easier to publish files or folders to a Web site by using a Web-hosting service. Windows XP includes a feature called Web Digital Authoring and Versioning (WebDAV for short) that lets you save information to the Web from any program rather than having to use the regular Web-publishing protocols.

Chapter 26 discusses how to publish information to the Web.

A Sane Implementation of Autoplay

If you've used Windows 9x, NT 4, or 2000, you'll know all about the Autoplay feature and how it used to drive people crazy. You remember Autoplay—the moment you insert a CD, it starts playing the music from it or installing any software it contains. By default, Autoplay was enabled, so you had to switch it off (or override it by holding down the Shift key while closing the CD tray) to prevent this from occurring.

Windows XP includes a new version of Autoplay that's improved in several ways. First, you can customize it. Second, you can configure it to take different actions depending on what the CD (or other medium) contains. For example, you might want Windows to play your audio CDs automatically when you insert them (okay, you don't—but you *might*), or you might want Windows to display a slideshow automatically when you insert a CD containing nothing but pictures.

What's that about *other medium*? That's the third thing: In Windows XP, Autoplay works for CDs, DVDs, assorted flash cards (including CompactFlash, Memory Stick, and SmartMedia), PC Cards, Zip and other removable disk drives, and FireWire hot-plug external drives.

Chapter 6 discusses how to configure Autoplay.

More Games

Windows XP includes more games than previous versions of Windows. Some of these are single-player games (for example, Spider Solitaire). Others are multiplayer games that you can play across the Internet via MSN's Zone.com Web site.

Chapter 30 discusses the games that Windows XP includes and how to configure Windows XP for playing more demanding games.

Remote Desktop Connection

Windows XP Home includes Remote Desktop Connection, a technology that lets you use your computer to access a remote computer (for example, your computer at the office) that's running

Windows XP Professional. Once you've connected to the remote computer, you can control it as if you were sitting at it.

Chapter 24 discusses how to use Remote Desktop Connection.

A More Useful Winkey

A what? *Winkey*, pronounced "win-key" rather than as the diminutive of *wink*, is the Windows key on the keyboard—the key with the Windows logo. Most keyboards have one or two Winkeys, usually located next to the Alt key or keys.

Windows XP includes more functionality for the Winkey. You can still press the Winkey to open or close the Start menu, but you can also use it in a number of key combinations. For example, pressing Winkey+M issues a Minimize All command (showing the Desktop), and pressing Winkey+Shift+M issues an Undo Minimize All command.

For the full list of Winkey combinations, see the section "Using the Winkey" in Chapter 3. You'll also find Winkey combinations throughout the book when you may want to take a Winkey action.

Improvements for Portable Computers

Windows XP includes several improvements for portable computers.

First, Windows XP supports processor power control, which lets the computer make use of features in chips such as Intel's SpeedStep, in which the processor runs at full speed when the computer is plugged into the main power supply (or told that it's plugged in) but at a lower speed to save power when it's running on battery power (or told that it is).

Throttling back the processor like this reduces the computer's power usage a bit, improving battery life, but in most portables, the screen consumes far more power than the processor. Windows XP also targets the screen, providing a couple of features designed to reduce power use when the computer is running on battery power. First, Windows XP turns off the display when the user closes the computer's lid, on the basis that the user probably isn't looking at the display. Second, it runs the screen at a dimmer brightness when the computer is running off the battery. The cynical among you will point out that the better-designed portables implement both these functions already in hardware. Still, it shouldn't do any harm to have Windows help out for the manufacturers who design their machines a little less carefully. Anyway, Chapter 15 discusses these features.

Windows XP also includes some other less obvious visual enhancements, such as support for ClearType, a Microsoft text-display technology that improves the look of fonts on LCD screens that have digital interfaces. While these screens aren't strictly confined to portables, that's where the bulk of the market is.

Faxing

Windows XP Home contains a built-in fax client that's more than adequate for most home needs and many home-office needs. You can send faxes from any program that supports printing, and you can specify whether to print out incoming faxes automatically or store them in a folder. You can even configure different fax/modems to take different roles. For example, if you use faxes extensively, you might want to keep separate incoming and outgoing fax lines. You'll need a modem for each of the phone lines involved, but that's about as difficult as it gets.

Chapter 23 discusses faxing and telephony.

More Help

Windows XP delivers more help—and more different types of help—than any other version of Windows.

If you've searched fruitlessly for information in the past, you'll be aware that Windows' Help files have never exactly delivered the ultimate in user satisfaction. Digging information out of help often felt so difficult that if you knew Windows well enough to find help on the right topic, you could probably solve the problem without help's assistance.

Windows XP takes a new approach to help. There are Help files on your hard drive still, but they're integrated into a program called Help and Support Center. Help and Support Center not only works with the Help files but also with the Microsoft Knowledge Base (a database of support queries) and other online sources of information. For example, if you run a query within Help and Support Center to find information on hardware, it might return some information from local files, some information from the Microsoft Web site, and some information from hardware manufacturers' Web sites, all packaged into one window so that you can access the information conveniently.

Help and Support Center also provides a gateway to other areas of support, including Microsoft Assisted Support and Microsoft Communities, and to programs that you can use to get help from other users (such as Remote Assistance) and troubleshoot your computer (such as System Configuration Utility and System Restore).

The following sections discuss some of the Help and Support Center features. Chapter 8 discusses how to use Help and Support Center.

MICROSOFT ASSISTED SUPPORT

Windows XP's Microsoft Assisted Support feature lets you automatically collect information on a problem you're having and submit it to Microsoft electronically. A Microsoft technician then sends a solution, which appears as a pop-up in your System Tray. You can read the response in the Help and Support Center window and apply the wisdom it contains to fix the problem.

Microsoft Assisted Support is designed to bypass the problems inherent with tech support via phone call, namely that it's difficult for the user to tell the help technician what's wrong with their computer; it's even harder for the technician to get a good idea of what's going wrong without knowing a fair bit of technical information about the computer; and waiting on hold for tech support is nobody's idea of fun, especially if you're paying for a long-distance call as well as for the support.

WINDOWS NEWSGROUPS

Instead of contacting a Microsoft technician via Microsoft Assisted Support, you can try to get support from the Windows Newsgroups, which are Microsoft-hosted newsgroups dedicated to Windows. Your mileage *will* vary in the Windows Newsgroups depending on whether helpful users answer your query soon and whether the stars have decided to shine on your horoscope for the day.

REMOTE ASSISTANCE

Remote Assistance is an ingenious feature by which you can get assistance from a friend or other knowledgeable person remotely by computer.

Here's the brief version of how Remote Assistance works. You send out an invitation file via e-mail, via Windows Messenger instant messaging, or via a file saved to the network (for example, in a business environment) or floppy disk. Your helper receives the invitation and responds to it. Remote Assistance sets up a secure connection between their computer and yours, using a password to verify their identity. Your helper can then view your screen remotely and chat with you (via text chat and voice). If you trust your helper, you can even let them control your computer so that they can take actions directly.

Chapter 24 discusses how to use Remote Assistance.

HELP QUERIES: ERRORS, EVENTS, AND COMPATIBILITY

You can use Help queries to search for information on error messages, event messages, and compatibility. Help and Support Center's integrated approach lets you search seamlessly across multiple Web sites (for example, the Microsoft Knowledge Base and the hardware manufacturer's Web site) to find the information you need.

TOOLS CENTER

Help and Support Center includes a Tools Center that gives you quick access to information about your computer (My Computer Information and Advanced System Information) and its configuration (System Configuration Utility); network diagnostic tools (Network Diagnostics); the System Restore feature; and more. In addition to the tools that Microsoft makes available in the Tools Center, OEMs (original equipment manufacturers) can add tools of their own, so you may also find custom tools provided by your computer manufacturer.

Many of the tools accessible through the Tools Center are also accessible in other ways through the Windows interface. For example, Windows XP includes an improved version of Disk Defragmenter, which you can use to keep your hard disk from becoming fragmented (fragmentation decreases performance). You can run Disk Defragmenter from Tools Center, but you can also run it from the System Tools submenu of the Start menu (Start ➤ All Programs ➤ Accessories ➤ System Tools ➤ Disk Defragmenter). Similarly, you can run Windows Update from inside Help and Support Center. This can be convenient, but it offers no great advantage over running Windows Update from the Start menu.

FIXING A PROBLEM TOOL

Help and Support Center includes an area called Fixing a Problem that contains a number of troubleshooters for walking you through the steps of diagnosing and curing various common problems. Fixing a Problem isn't a panacea, but it's a good place to start, and it can save you a call to a guru or even a trip to your local computer shop.

DEVICE DRIVER REFERRAL SITE

Help and Support Center contains a system for referring searches for drivers that don't come with Windows or with the hardware device. When you plug in a new hardware device, and Windows finds that it doesn't have a driver for it and you can't supply a driver, Windows invites you to send information about the hardware to Microsoft. Once you've sent the information, you can take a variety of actions depending on what information is available. For example, you might be able to view a list of compatible devices (if any), search for information on compatible devices or Knowledge Base articles about the hardware, or find a link to the vendor's Web site.

OTHER HELP IMPROVEMENTS

Help and Support Center includes assorted other help improvements that can save you time. For example, you can print out a whole chapter of help information at once instead of having to slog through it screen by screen. And you can open multiple Help and Support Center windows at the same time. This makes it easier to pursue different avenues of exploration for the information you need. When you find useful information, you can create a favorite for it so that you can access it quickly again when you need it.

Network Connectivity

Windows XP provides various improvements in network connectivity, from creating a home or home-office network to joining a computer to two separate networks. There are also great improvements in Internet connectivity, discussed in the next section.

NETWORK SETUP WIZARD

The Network Setup Wizard simplifies the process of creating a network; sharing printers, Internet connections, and other resources; and configuring protocols and security.

Chapter 32 discusses how to use the Network Setup Wizard to set up a network.

ALL-USER REMOTE ACCESS SERVICE

The All-User Remote Access Service lets you create a credential for all users of the computer so that they can share a connection. For example, you can make your high-speed Internet connection available to all the users of the computer without divulging the account password to them. The name is a bit intimidating and the acronym is nonsensical, but the process is easy.

Chapter 17 discusses how to do this.

ALTERNATIVE TCP/IP CONFIGURATION

Windows XP provides an alternative TCP/IP configuration that allows you to connect to a network that has a DHCP server and to a network that doesn't without changing your TCP/IP settings. For example, you might use a laptop at work (where the network has a DHCP server) and at home (where your network doesn't).

This feature is (jargon alert) transparent to the user—in other words, you won't usually notice it. Nevertheless, Chapter 33 discusses it briefly.

NETWORK BRIDGING

Windows XP's network-bridging capability lets you use a computer with two or more network adapters to join two separate networks. You're perhaps unlikely to have two (or more) networks at home or in a small office—unless you have a wired network to which you've added a wireless component to provide roaming capabilities for some of the computers.

Internet Connectivity and Web Browsing

Windows XP provides a number of enhanced features for Internet connectivity and Web browsing, from Internet connnection sharing and firewalling to a new version of Internet Explorer.

INTERNET CONNECTION SHARING AND INTERNET CONNECTION FIREWALL

Like Windows 98 Second Edition, Windows Me, and Windows 2000, Windows XP includes an Internet Connection Sharing (ICS) feature that lets you share an Internet connection on one computer with one or more networked computers. Windows XP's version of Internet Connection Sharing has some tweaks, such as that you can disconnect the shared Internet connection from another PC if necessary—for example, if you need to use the phone line that the connection is using. Windows XP includes a Quality of Service Packet Scheduler that works to optimize the utilization of a shared Internet connection.

Internet Connection Sharing is a great convenience, particularly if you have a high-speed connection such as a DSL or a cable modem—but it lays your network open to assault from the Internet. Windows XP goes one better than its predecessors by including a firewall (called Internet Connection Firewall) to protect the Internet connection (whether shared or not).

Chapter 17 discusses Internet Connection Firewall, and Chapter 33 discusses Internet Connection Sharing.

NEW VERSION OF INTERNET EXPLORER

Windows XP includes Internet Explorer 6, the latest version of Internet Explorer. Even if you feel you've already had it up to here with new versions of Internet Explorer, stifle your impatience, because Internet Explorer 6 offers a number of welcome innovations, including the following:

- You can save images, music, and videos more easily to your computer.

- The new Media bar lets you listen to streaming audio directly in Internet Explorer and (perhaps a less welcome feature) access WindowsMedia.com easily.

- Internet Explorer provides better handling of cookies and digital certificates for securing information transfer and authenticating content.

- Internet Explorer can automatically resize an image you've displayed directly. If you've ever used Internet Explorer to open a digital photo, and found it displayed bigger than your screen so that you could see only part of it, you may appreciate this feature. (But you'd be better off opening the photo in Paint in the first place.)

- Internet Explorer 6 has more integrated functionality for handling different file types. This won't strike you over the head; you'll simply find that more file types open without your being prodded to download and install extra components. For example, Internet Explorer 6 has built-in support for Macromedia Flash and Shockwave animations, and support for Cascading Style Sheet (CSS) Level 1. The net result is that more animations will play without your needing to add software, and documents formatted with CSS1 style sheets will be displayed as their authors intended. (They may still look horrible, but at least you'll know that they're meant to look that way.)

Chapter 18 discusses how to configure and use Internet Explorer.

MSN EXPLORER

Windows XP includes MSN Explorer, an Internet client dedicated to MSN. If you don't have an ISP, you may want to use MSN Explorer to connect to the Internet.

Chapter 17 provides a brief introduction to MSN Explorer.

.NET PASSPORT INTEGRATION

In order to implement many of its Internet services, Windows XP relies heavily on Microsoft's .NET Passport feature. For example, you need to get a .NET Passport in order to use Windows Messenger for instant messaging, to use Hotmail (Microsoft's Web-based e-mail service), to create Web pages on MSN, or to visit a Web site that requires a Passport sign-in (for instance, to download certain files from the Microsoft Web site).

.NET Passport (or, more simply, just *Passport*) is an electronic identifier that's associated with your user account on your PC. (If you use the same Passport with multiple PCs, it can be associated with multiple user accounts.) You can sign up for a Passport by using an existing e-mail account. If you don't have an e-mail account, Microsoft encourages you to base your Passport on a Hotmail account or an MSN account.

Passport enables many cool features—but it also locks you into using Microsoft technologies when you may not want to use them. Worse, it can (or *could*) give Microsoft a way to track some of your actions online. Microsoft protests that it is committed to your online privacy, and does give you the choice of opting out of some of the tracking features, but you don't need to be paranoid to find Passport's possibilities frightening.

You can use Passport Wallet features to (in Microsoft's words) "simplify your online shopping experience"—in other words, spend money faster online and with less effort. You get to decide whether this is a good idea. (Hint: Evaluate Passport Wallet carefully. Don't rush into anything.)

What's Hiding under the Hood

The features mentioned so far catch the eye—some even on a cursory scan of the Windows XP Desktop and interface.

Less glamorous, but more important in the long run, are the enhancements hiding under Windows XP's hood. This section discusses the major enhancements that you probably *won't* see.

PROTECTED MEMORY MANAGEMENT

Windows XP improves on Windows 9x (Windows 95, 98, and Me) by offering fully protected memory management. Windows 9x didn't protect the areas of memory used by the operating system. This meant that if a program tried to store information in memory already used by another program or by the operating system, the program could crash not only itself but also the operating system. If you've used any version of Windows 9x for any length of time, you're probably familiar with these crashes. Typically, you see a succession of instances of the Blue Screen of Death with assorted error messages, and eventually have to perform a warm reboot (Ctrl+Alt+Delete) or a hard reboot (by powering the computer down and back up again). In the meantime, you lose any unsaved work in the programs you're using.

With protected memory management, Windows XP can handle memory errors with more aplomb. When a program tries to access memory that doesn't belong to it, Windows XP can close the program without affecting any other running program. You still lose any unsaved work in the guilty program, but all your other programs continue running.

While Windows XP is dealing with the misbehaving program, you can move the program's window so that it doesn't obstruct your view of any other programs you have open.

SYSTEM FILE PROTECTION

Windows XP offers a feature called System File Protection that protects your system files from ill-advised actions on your part.

Windows XP tries to persuade you not to view the contents of folders that you probably shouldn't be messing with, by refusing to show them to you until you demand it show them. You can then delete system files if you want (except for any file that's actively in use, which is locked automatically). But the next time that Windows boots, or if it catches the damage you've done before you reboot it, it replaces the files you deleted without notifying you.

This is about all you need to know about System File Protection, so the book doesn't discuss it further.

SYSTEM RESTORE

Windows XP offers a System Restore feature similar to but more effective than the System Restore feature in Windows Me. System Restore automatically creates restore points both periodically and each time you make a change to the system—for example, by installing a program or a driver. You can also create system restore points manually. When one of your changes leads to an unwelcome result, such as your computer failing to work as well as it did before, you can use System Restore to roll back the change to an earlier point at which the system was working properly.

Chapter 16 discusses how to use System Restore.

DEVICE DRIVER ROLLBACK

Device drivers have long been the bane of Windows—okay, *one* of the banes of Windows. By installing the wrong driver, or a buggy driver, you could render your computer useless until you reinstalled Windows (or turned in frustration to another operating system).

Windows XP tracks the drivers you install and lets you roll back the installation of the driver—in other words, you can revert to the driver you were using before.

Better yet, Windows XP stores details of the previous driver in what's called the Last Known Good Configuration—the configuration used the last time the computer seemed to be running okay. This means that if installing a new driver prevents your computer from booting as normal, you can use the Last Known Good Configuration to restore the previous driver.

Chapter 14 discusses how to roll back a device driver, and Chapter 12 discusses how to use the Last Known Good Configuration.

NTFS

Where Windows 9*x* versions used the FAT (File Allocation Table) and VFAT (Virtual File Allocation Table) file systems, Windows XP prefers NTFS, the NT file system. NTFS provides security features (including file-level security) and stability that FAT and VFAT do not.

Chapter 2 discusses how to install (or upgrade to) NTFS.

COMPATIBILITY WITH WINDOWS 9x PROGRAMS

Windows XP aims to be able to run all programs that would run on Windows 9x, Windows NT, and Windows 2000. As you'll know if you've struggled to run a Windows 9x program on NT or Windows 2000, this is quite a challenge. NT-based operating systems (including Windows XP) handle memory and hardware access in a different way than Windows 9x operating systems. These differences mean that programs designed for Windows 9x often won't run satisfactorily on NT and Windows 2000.

Being able to run these legacy programs is a big feature of Windows XP—but because Microsoft has implemented this feature very successfully, it remains hidden most of the time. Usually, you can simply install a legacy program and run it without complications. Behind the scenes, Windows XP may be running the program in its Compatibility mode or applying one of its new AppFixes to the program (to prevent it from detecting the wrong operating system and from causing problems such as referencing memory once it's been freed up), but you often won't know about it. You may need to specifically run some programs in Compatibility mode, and you may see Windows Update automatically downloading new information for AppFixes to keep your copy of Windows up to date, but most of the time, your old programs will simply work—which of course is the way it should be.

Chapter 5 discusses how to use Compatibility mode when necessary.

Should You Upgrade to Windows XP Home Edition?

Whether you should upgrade to Windows XP Home Edition depends on your needs, how well your current version of Windows is fulfilling them, and whether your hardware is up to the test. The decision is wholly yours (of course), but the following sections offer some suggestions, depending on where you're coming from.

Windows 9x

If you're using one of the versions of Windows 9x—Windows 95, Windows 98, Windows 98 Second Edition, or Windows Me—the main attractions of Windows XP Home are much greater stability, the enhanced user interface, and the extra features that Windows XP includes.

Exactly which extra features Windows XP includes depends—obviously enough—on which version of Windows 9x you have. Not surprisingly, later versions of Windows 9x offer more features than earlier versions. For example, the Internet Connection Sharing feature debuted in Windows 98 Second Edition, so ICS might be a reason to upgrade to Windows XP if you have Windows 95 or Windows 98 (first edition), but not if you have Windows 98 Second Edition or Windows Me. (The Internet Connection Firewall feature, however, is new, and is a strong attraction unless you're already using an effective hardware or software firewall.) Likewise, Windows Me includes Windows Media Player 7, a version that greatly improved on the earlier, anemic versions of Windows Media Player but isn't as capable as Windows Media Player 8, the version included in Windows XP. From Windows Me, the new version of Windows Media Player provides only a modest incitement to upgrade, whereas from earlier versions of Windows 9x, it provides much more encouragement—assuming you're interested in multimedia, that is.

Whichever version of Windows 9x you're using, you'll need to make sure that your hardware is up to scratch for Windows XP. Very generally speaking, if your computer is capable of running

Windows 98 or Windows Me at a decent clip, it should be able to run Windows XP without much trouble (though you might need to add memory).

You'll find details of Windows XP's hardware requirements in Chapter 2.

Windows 3.1

If you're still using Windows 3.1 and DOS as your main operating system, Windows XP Home Edition represents a considerable upgrade. There are two major considerations in taking this step:

◆ Unless you've installed Windows 3.1 on a modern system (as you might have done for backward compatibility with ancient programs), you'll almost certainly need to get a new PC to run Windows XP. You *could* upgrade an older system, but it'd be a real grandfather's ax of an upgrade: hard drive, processor, RAM, graphics card.... (Don't you remember the anecdote? There's this guy in the bar (or wherever) who says "I have my grandfather's ax. My father replaced the handle, and I gave it a new blade. But it still cuts great!" Your upgraded Windows 3.1 computer would be like that ax.)

◆ If you will need to continue running DOS programs and 16-bit Windows programs (rather than upgrading to 32-bit programs that provide similar functionality), check to make sure that these programs are compatible with Windows XP before upgrading. As mentioned earlier, Windows XP runs older 32-bit Windows programs quite impressively, but it has problems with some 16-bit programs.

Windows 2000 Professional

If you're currently using Windows 2000 Professional and are happy with it, stick with it for the time being. The "natural" upgrade path from Windows 2000 Professional is to Windows XP Professional Edition, but make this upgrade only after carefully evaluating the benefits that Windows XP Professional will provide. If Windows 2000 Professional is currently fulfilling all your computing needs, stick with it.

Should You Upgrade to Windows XP Professional Edition Instead?

So you've decided that Windows XP offers features that you must have—but should you get Windows XP Home Edition or Windows XP Professional Edition? This section discusses the biggest differences between the two. This isn't an exhaustive breakdown of all the differences—just the ones that will probably affect your decision the most.

Intended Usage

As its name suggests (and is designed to suggest), Windows XP Professional is geared toward use in a professional setting—for example, in an office or in a corporate setting. That doesn't mean you can't use it at home if you want, just that it has features designed for use in office and corporate settings. For example, it's designed to connect to Windows 2000 servers running Active Directory domains, and it has features for being managed remotely by administrators. Professional also has features for using a portable computer as a complement to a desktop computer (rather than instead of a desktop computer) and lets you easily synchronize files between two computers.

By contrast, Windows XP Home is designed for home use. It features more relaxed security settings than Windows XP Professional, comes set up for sharing files and folders easily among users of the same computer, and has no interest in being managed remotely by administrators or anyone else.

Cost

As you'd expect, Windows XP Professional is more expensive than Windows XP Home, though if you need the extra features it offers, it's affordable enough. But you'll certainly want to avoid first buying Windows XP Home and then upgrading to Windows XP Professional.

Hardware Requirements

Windows XP Professional runs adequately on the same hardware as Windows XP Home. While Professional doesn't actually *need* better hardware than Home, it probably *appreciates* better hardware more than Home does, because its extra features (detailed after the next section) can use some extra memory and processing power.

Upgrade Paths to Windows XP

You can upgrade to Windows XP Professional from Windows 98, Windows 98 Second Edition, Windows Me, Windows NT 4 Workstation, and Windows 2000 Professional. You can upgrade to Windows XP Home from only Windows 98, Windows 98 Second Edition, and Windows Me.

Windows XP Professional Features

Professional is essentially a superset of Home: It has all the features that Home has, plus extra features. You can also look at this the other way around, and say that Home is a subset of Professional. In some ways, this might be truer, as Home can be regarded as Professional with a number of features—some very attractive, some less so—taken out.

The following list details the features that Professional has that Home does not have, in descending order of excitement.

Personal Web Server and Internet Information Services   Windows XP Professional includes Personal Web Server and Internet Information Services, which let you run a modest-scale Web server on XP.

Fax sharing   As mentioned earlier in the chapter, Windows XP Home has strong fax features for the individual user. Windows XP Professional goes one better by letting you share a fax/modem with other computers: Your computer can provide fax services to other computers to which it is networked, or your computer can send a fax via a fax/modem on another computer. These features can save a great deal of time and effort, not to mention phone lines.

Backup and Automated System Recovery (ASR)   Windows XP Professional includes a Backup utility and an Automated System Recovery feature that can be activated from boot-up to restore a damaged system. Windows XP Home doesn't have these features—though, as mentioned earlier in this chapter, Windows XP Home does have the System Restore feature for rolling back the installation of bad drivers and programs.

Offline files   Offline files let you cache (store) copies of files located on network drives on your local drive so that you can work with them when your computer is no longer connected to the network. Windows XP Professional can encrypt the Offline Files database to help keep the information in the files secure. Windows XP Home offers neither offline files nor encryption.

Multiprocessor support   Windows XP Professional Edition offers multiprocessor support, while Home doesn't. You probably won't care about this omission in Home unless you're one of the (very) few people who have a multiprocessor computer at home, but in a way it's rather sad, because the multiprocessor code is all written and available—Microsoft just decided to take this functionality out of Home, presumably to provide another point of differentiation with Professional. So if you do have a multiprocessor machine, and you want to use both processors, you need Professional rather than Home. (You might also consider Linux, which will love the extra processor and will cost you less.)

Remote Desktop   Windows XP Professional offers Remote Desktop technology, while Home doesn't. Remote Desktop is a little confusing because of the terminology. The Remote Desktop component lets you make a computer available for remote control. Professional has this capability; Home doesn't. The Remote Desktop *Connection* component lets you use a computer to access a remote computer that's running Remote Desktop. Both Professional and Home have Remote Desktop Connection. So you can use a computer running Home to access a computer running Professional, but not the other way around. If you need to be able to connect to your computer remotely via Remote Desktop Connection, you need Professional rather than Home. (Alternatively, you can use NetMeeting's remote features to control a Home computer, or one of the many third-party remote-control packages.)

Ability to upgrade from more versions of Windows   You can upgrade to Windows XP Professional from Windows 98, Windows 98 Second Edition, Windows NT 4 Workstation, and Windows 2000 Professional.

Security features   Windows XP Professional includes a number of security features that Windows XP Home lacks. For example, Windows XP Professional lets you control access at the level of individual files as well as folders, while with Windows XP Home, you can control access only at the folder level. Windows XP Professional supports the Encrypting File System (EFS) for encrypting files on the local disk; Windows XP Home does not support EFS.

Networking features   Windows XP Professional has many networking features that Windows XP Home does not. These include the Simple Network Management Protocol (SNMP), the Client Service for NetWare, Simple TCP/IP Services, and the Multiple Roaming feature. If you need to connect to a NetWare server, or if you need to use roaming profiles, you'll need Windows XP Professional rather than Windows XP Home.

Management features   Windows XP Professional has extensive management features that allow remote administration. Windows XP Home can't log on to an Active Directory domain, so it doesn't have management features associated with domains and remote administration. For example, Windows XP Home doesn't support Group Policy or Microsoft's IntelliMirror feature. Similarly, Windows XP Professional can wake up a laptop via a CardBus LAN card, while Windows XP Home cannot.

One other thing—there will be a 64-bit version of Windows XP Professional for the Intel Itanium processor. By contrast, Windows XP Home runs only on 32-bit Pentiums and their equivalents.

Up Next

This chapter has discussed what you need to know about Windows XP Home Edition in order to decide whether to upgrade to it, stay with your current version of Windows, or buy Windows XP Professional Edition instead.

The next chapter discusses how to install Windows XP Home Edition, both as an upgrade and as a clean installation from scratch.

Chapter 2

Installing Windows XP

THIS CHAPTER DISCUSSES HOW to install Windows XP Home Edition in each of the three ways in which you may want to install it: as an upgrade to Windows 98 or Windows Me; as a new installation on a computer that already has installed an operating system that you want to keep; and as a clean installation on a computer that doesn't have an operating system installed (or a computer whose operating system you want to wipe). Each of these installation paths starts in a distinct way, and the chapter covers these separately. Toward the end of the installation, all three installation paths join each other for the last few steps, so the chapter covers these steps only once.

At the end of the chapter, you'll find a discussion of how to perform an unattended installation, which can be useful if you need to install the same operating system multiple times.

This chapter covers the following topics:

- ◆ Making sure your computer can run Windows XP Home
- ◆ Choosing a method of installing Windows XP
- ◆ Preparing for installation
- ◆ Upgrading Windows 98 or Windows Me to Windows XP
- ◆ Performing a new installation of Windows XP
- ◆ Performing a clean installation of Windows XP
- ◆ Using the Files and Settings Transfer Wizard to transfer files and settings
- ◆ Uninstalling Windows XP and reverting to Windows 98 or Windows Me
- ◆ Removing your old version of Windows
- ◆ Keeping Windows updated
- ◆ Performing an unattended installation

The Order of Business

Here's the order of business for installing Windows XP successfully:

◆ First, make sure that your computer will be able to run Windows XP Home. Start by comparing your system specifications with the minimum requirements, and see if you need to upgrade any components.

◆ Then—assuming your computer has an operating system loaded already—load the Windows XP CD in your computer and run the Windows Upgrade Advisor.

◆ If you want to perform a new installation or a clean installation of Windows XP rather than an upgrade, but you want your new installation or clean installation to pick up your current settings and some of your files, run the Files and Settings Transfer Wizard to save the settings from your current version of Windows.

◆ Then perform the upgrade, new installation, or clean installation.

◆ If you ran the Files and Settings Transfer Wizard, run it again to apply your settings to Windows XP and to make your files available.

Will Your Computer Be Able to Run Windows XP Home Edition?

First, make sure that your computer will be able to run Windows XP Home Edition. The following sections discuss the main requirements.

Processor

Windows XP requires a minimum of a Pentium 166 processor. But realistically, it's barely worth using Windows XP with a processor slower than a Pentium II 266, a Celeron 300, or a K6 300, because performance is unacceptably slow. A 600MHz or faster processor delivers good performance.

If you don't know what processor your computer has, watch the information that comes up as it boots. This will give you at least the processor speed, though it may give an incorrect classification of the chip. For example, some systems classify Celeron chips as Pentium III chips. (Midrange Celeron chips *are* in fact cut-down Pentium III chips, but your system should really know the difference.)

RAM

Windows XP requires a minimum of 64MB of RAM to install and run. This too is an absolute minimum and delivers poor performance unless your processor is extremely fast (in which case the lack of RAM cannibalizes processor performance). 128MB of RAM gives good performance for one concurrent user session. For multiple concurrent user sessions, get 256MB or more RAM. (At this writing, 256MB RAM modules are selling for prices as low as $45, so upgrading your RAM is relatively painless.)

If you don't know how much RAM your computer has, watch the count of RAM when you boot. If the number is in kilobytes, divide by 1024 to get the number in megabytes. Alternatively, right-click the icon for your computer on the Windows Desktop and choose Properties from the context menu. Windows displays the System Properties dialog box with the General page foremost. At the bottom of the page is a readout of the amount of RAM in the computer.

EXPERT KNOWLEDGE: GET PLENTY OF RAM

Huh, you may be thinking: *that's* "expert knowledge"? Everyone knows that you need plenty of RAM to run Windows. That's true—up to a point. But most people still have too little RAM in their computers.

Windows XP will run—well, more like stagger along—on 64MB RAM. If the computer has a fast processor, and if you don't use any large programs or large files, performance may be tolerable. But the hard disk will be kept busy as Windows continually uses virtual memory to store the information that won't fit in the RAM.

If you're buying a new computer, you'll be much better off saving a little money on the processor and putting it into RAM. Unless you're running the latest 3-D games or performing terrain mapping or other advanced imaging, you'll notice little benefit from having a few hundred extra megahertz on your processor. But another 128MB (better, another 256MB) of RAM will make a huge difference over 64MB on a system with just about any processor.

Windows XP runs adequately on an antiquated processor such as a Pentium II 266 provided the computer has enough RAM—128MB for a single user session running a "normal" number of programs, 192MB for a single user session running a heavy number of programs, and 256MB or more for multiple user sessions running concurrently.

Given this, it's sad to see that many companies that should really know better—including IBM, Dell, and Compaq—are plugging computers with gigahertz-plus processors and 64MB RAM. They'll happily sell you as much extra memory as you specify, of course—but the implication is that a computer with 64MB RAM is adequately configured to run Windows, which it isn't.

Free Disk Space

Windows XP requires approximately 600MB of free disk space to install, plus space for your paging file (by default, 1.5× the amount of RAM in your computer) and for your hibernation file (the same size as the amount of RAM) if your computer supports hibernation. On top of that, you'll need space for any programs you want to install and any files you want to create.

In practice, it's a good idea to have at least 1GB of free space on the drive on which you install Windows XP, plus space for your programs and files. To see how much space is free on a drive, right-click the drive in an Explorer window and choose Properties from the context menu. The General page of the resulting Properties dialog box for the drive shows how much free space it has.

SVGA-Capable Video Adapter and Monitor

Your video adapter and monitor need to be capable of SVGA resolution (800×600 pixels) with 256 or more colors for you to enjoy Windows XP in all its glory. Beyond that, just about any PCI or AGP video adapter should work (drivers permitting, of course), as should any CRT or LCD monitor.

CD Drive or DVD Drive

You need a CD drive or DVD drive, or access to one or the other, to install Windows XP. If the drive is on another computer, you can install across a network or copy the files to your local drive and run them from there.

Checking System Compatibility

To check whether Windows XP thinks your computer will be able to run it, run the Windows Upgrade Advisor program by following these steps:

1. Insert the Windows XP CD. If your computer doesn't automatically start running the CD, open an Explorer window, navigate to the CD, and double-click the SETUP.EXE program.

2. On the opening screen, click the Check System Compatibility link. Setup offers the choices Check My System Automatically and Visit the Compatibility Web Site.

3. Click the Check My System Automatically link.

4. If an Internet connection is available, Setup runs Dynamic Update to download any new files that may help with the installation. It then runs the Windows Upgrade Advisor program and displays the Upgrade Report page of the Microsoft Windows Upgrade Advisor. Figure 2.1 shows an example of an upgrade report.

FIGURE 2.1

Use the Microsoft Windows Upgrade Advisor to check whether your computer will be able to run Windows XP.

5. If your computer seems to be fit for Windows XP, the report tells you that the check found no incompatibilities or problems. Any problems are listed in the list box in summary form. Click the Full Details button to view the details (broken up into categories such as Blocking Issues, Warnings, and Helpful Information) and advice on what to do about the problems. (Click the resulting Summary button to return to the summary view.) Click the Save As button to save the information to file, or click the Print button to print a copy of it.

6. Click the Finish button. Windows closes the Microsoft Windows Upgrade Advisor.

Follow the Upgrade Advisor's advice to get your computer ready for upgrading to Windows XP. In particular, you need to take care of any blocking issues that the Advisor has identified. An example of a blocking issue is not having enough disk space to install Windows XP. You might need to remove some existing files, or reconfigure your partitions (for example, by using a tool such as Partition-Magic), in order to resolve such an issue.

Choosing a Method of Installing Windows XP

Once you've decided to install Windows XP, your next decision is how to install Windows XP on your computer. You can install Windows XP in three different ways:

Upgrade If you have Windows 98 or Windows Me, you can perform an upgrade, essentially overwriting the previous version of Windows with Windows XP. (It's not entirely overwritten, because you can restore it if you so choose.) Upgrading like this transfers all your files, settings, and programs to Windows XP, so (in theory) you can pick up your work or play straight away in Windows XP where you left off in Windows 9x.

New installation You can install Windows XP alongside your current version of Windows. Windows XP creates a dual-boot setup (or modifies an existing dual-boot setup to create a multi-boot setup) so that you can run either operating system. Installing like this lets you compare Windows XP with your previous version of Windows. You can use the Files and Settings Transfer Wizard to copy your files and settings from your previous version of Windows to Windows XP. You'll need to install all the programs you want to use on Windows XP.

Clean installation You can install Windows XP from scratch on your computer, setting it up as the only operating system but not upgrading from your current operating system. Again, you can use the Files and Settings Transfer Wizard to copy your files and settings from your previous version of Windows to Windows XP. You'll need to install all the programs you want to use on Windows XP.

Which type of installation to perform can be a tricky decision. The longer you've been running Windows on this computer since installing it, the stronger the arguments are for both an upgrade and a clean installation:

♦ By now, you've probably installed all the programs you need and got them working together. By upgrading, you can transition your whole work environment to Windows XP, so that your Desktop, Start menu, and folder structure retain their current settings and your programs all work as before.

♦ Then again, you probably have programs that you no longer use, or programs that no longer work. By performing a clean install, you can strip your system down to only the software you need. It'll take longer, but the result may be better. Similarly, your data folders could probably do with some cleaning out and archiving.

If you need to install a new hard drive as your main hard drive, you'll need to perform a clean install. (The exception is if you use a hard drive cloning or migration package such as DriveImage or Ghost. These packages are often used for upgrading the hard drives in laptops, where the lack of expansion room forces you to replace the current hard drive rather than add a drive, but some of them work for desktops as well.)

Preparing for Installation

Once you've established that your computer should be able to run Windows XP, prepare for installation by taking those of the following steps as are applicable to the type of installation you're planning (upgrade, new installation, or clean installation).

Back Up All Your Data Files

For safety, back up all your data files shortly before installation using your usual backup medium.

Write Down Internet Connection Information

If you're planning a new installation or clean installation rather than an upgrade, and you use a dial-up Internet connection, write down the information you need to create the connection: your ISP account username, your password, your ISP's phone number, and your ISP's primary DNS server and secondary DNS server.

Plug In and Switch On All Hardware

Make sure that all the hardware you intend to use with the computer is attached to it and powered on. For example, if you'll use a printer and scanner with the computer, make sure these devices are attached to the computer and powered on, so that Setup can detect them if it's smart enough.

Use the Files and Settings Transfer Wizard to Transfer Settings

Windows XP includes a Wizard for transferring files and settings from one computer or operating system to another. You don't need to use this Wizard, which is called the Files and Settings Transfer Wizard, if you're upgrading Windows 98 or Windows Me to Windows XP, because Windows automatically transfers all your settings when you perform an upgrade. But the Wizard can save you a great deal of time when you want to transfer files and settings either to a new computer that's running Windows XP or to a new installation of Windows XP on the same computer on which you've kept your previous installation of Windows as a dual-boot. For example, if you choose to test Windows XP on a new partition before committing yourself to it, you can use the Files and Settings Transfer Wizard to transfer your work environment to the new partition so that you can use your regular settings and files.

Before you use the Files and Settings Transfer Wizard, make sure you've connected any network drive you want to use, or that you have a removable disk or recordable CD ready. To transfer files and settings, you'll need plenty of storage. You can save settings files to a floppy drive, but most data files will be too big.

To use the Files and Settings Transfer Wizard, follow these steps:

1. Insert the Windows XP CD. If your computer doesn't automatically start running the CD, open an Explorer window, navigate to the CD, and double-click the SETUP.EXE program. Windows displays the Welcome to Microsoft Windows XP screen.

2. Click the Perform Additional Tasks link.

3. On the next screen, click the Transfer Files and Settings link. Setup starts the Files and Settings Transfer Wizard.

4. Click the Next button. If this computer is running Windows XP, the Wizard displays the Which Computer Is This? screen. If it does, select the Old Computer option button and click the Next button. (If this computer isn't running Windows XP, the Wizard knows it's the old computer.) The Wizard then displays the Select a Transfer Method page (shown in Figure 2.2).

FIGURE 2.2

On the Select a Transfer Method page of the Files and Settings Transfer Wizard, specify how you want to transfer files and settings from the old computer to the new computer.

5. Select the Direct Cable option button, the Home or Small Office Network option button (if it's available), the Floppy Drive or Other Removable Media option button (select the drive in the drop-down list), or the Other option button as appropriate. The Other option button lets you use the Browse button and the resulting Browse for Folder dialog box or the Folder or Drive text box to specify a removable drive or a network drive.

6. Click the Next button. The Wizard displays the What Do You Want to Transfer? page (shown in Figure 2.3).

FIGURE 2.3

On the What Do You Want to Transfer? page of the Files and Settings Transfer Wizard, specify which settings and files you want to transfer to the new computer (or to Windows XP).

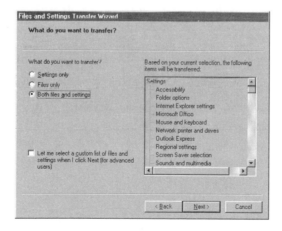

7. In the What Do You Want to Transfer? list, select the Settings Only option button, the Files Only option button, or the Both Files and Settings option button as appropriate. The list box on the right side of the dialog box lists the types of settings and files that will be affected.

8. If you want to customize the list of settings, files, or both, select the Let Me Select a Custom List of Files and Settings when I Click Next check box. Customizing the list of files lets you specify particular folders for transfer. By default, the Wizard transfers the `\Desktop\` folder, the `\Fonts\` folder, the `\My Documents\` folder, and the `\Shared Desktop\` folder.

9. Click the Next button. If you selected the Customize check box, the Wizard displays the Select Custom Files and Settings page (shown in Figure 2.4).

FIGURE 2.4

On the Select Custom Files and Settings page of the Files and Settings Transfer Wizard, choose the files and settings to transfer.

10. Select the files and settings to transfer:

- To add a setting, click the Add Setting button. The Wizard displays the Add a Setting dialog box. Select the setting or settings in the list box and click the OK button. The Wizard closes the Add a Setting dialog box and adds the setting or settings to the list.

- To add a folder, click the Add Folder button. The Wizard displays the Browse for Folder dialog box. Select the folder and click the OK button. The Wizard closes the Browse for Folder dialog box and adds the folder to the list.

- To add a file, click the Add File button. The Wizard displays the Add a File dialog box (a common Open dialog box in disguise). Select the file and click the Open button. The Wizard closes the Add a File dialog box and adds the file to the list.

- To add a file type, click the Add File Type button. The Wizard displays the Add a File Type dialog box (shown in Figure 2.5). Select the file type in the Registered File Types list box; if it's not listed there, enter its extension in the Other text box. Then click the OK button. The Wizard closes the Add a File Type dialog box and adds the file type to the list.

- To remove a setting, folder, file, or file type, select it in the list box and click the Remove button.

11. Click the Next button. The Wizard may display the Install Programs on Your New Computer page, suggesting some programs that you may want to install on your new computer (or new installation of Windows) before transferring settings. If so, note these suggestions.

FIGURE 2.5

Use the Add a File Type dialog box to add a file type to the list of file types to transfer.

12. The Wizard then displays the Collection in Progress page (shown in Figure 2.6) while it collects your files and settings. It then displays the Completing the Collection Phase page.

FIGURE 2.6

The Wizard collects the files.

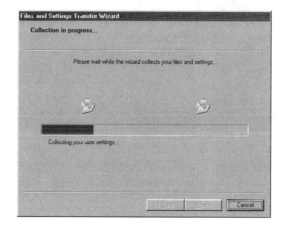

13. Click the Finish button. The Wizard closes itself.

For details of how to apply your saved files and settings to your new installation of Windows, see "Applying Your Files and Settings" later in this chapter.

Stop Any Anti-Virus Software or Disk Utilities

Stop any anti-virus software or disk utilities before running the Windows installation, because the installation process needs direct access to your hardware.

Upgrading Windows 98 or Windows Me to Windows XP

This section discusses the procedure for upgrading your current installation of Windows 9x to Windows XP. When you upgrade, the installation procedure copies the settings from your current version of Windows 9x and applies them to the installation of Windows XP. If the installation doesn't work correctly, or if you find Windows XP doesn't suit you, you can uninstall it and revert to your previous installation of Windows 9x.

To perform an upgrade, take the following steps:

1. Insert the CD in a CD drive or DVD drive. If Autoplay is enabled on your computer, Windows displays the introductory screen (shown in Figure 2.7). If not, open an Explorer window and double-click the CD. This should trigger the Autoplay action. If it doesn't, double-click the SETUP.EXE file on the CD to run it.

FIGURE 2.7

To start the upgrade, select the Install Windows XP link.

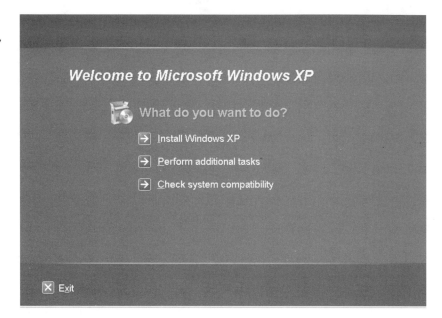

2. Click the Install Windows XP link. Setup displays the Welcome to Windows Setup page (shown in Figure 2.8).

3. In the Installation Type drop-down list, choose the Upgrade item.

FIGURE 2.8

On the Welcome to Windows Setup page, choose the Upgrade item in the Installation Type drop-down list.

4. Click the Next button. Setup displays the License Agreement page. Read it.

5. If you agree to the license, select the I Accept This Agreement option button and click the Next button. (If you don't agree to the license, Setup exits.) Setup displays the Your Product Key page.

6. Enter your product key and click the Next button. Setup displays the Upgrade Report page (shown in Figure 2.9).

FIGURE 2.9

On the Upgrade Report page of Setup, choose the type of upgrade report you want for this computer.

7. Choose the type of upgrade report you want by selecting the Show Me Hardware Issues and a Limited Set of Software Issues option button, the Show Me the Full Report option button, or the Do Not Show Me the Report option button.

8. Click the Next button. Setup displays the Get Updated Setup Files page (shown in Figure 2.10), which lets you choose whether to use Dynamic Update to download any new Setup files that Microsoft may have released since your copy of Windows XP was pressed.

9. To download any available files, leave the Yes, Download the Updated Setup Files option button selected, as it is by default. To skip Dynamic Update, select the No, Skip This Step and Continue Installing Windows option button.

FIGURE 2.10

On the Get Updated Setup Files page of Setup, choose whether to let Dynamic Update download the latest Setup files.

NOTE *You can download any updated files by using Windows Update after you finish installing Windows XP. The only advantage to Dynamic Update comes if the new files are needed for any of the hardware on your computer during installation.*

10. Click the Next button. If you chose to use Dynamic Update, Setup contacts the Microsoft Web site and downloads any relevant files. Setup then starts analyzing your computer for possible problems in upgrading to Windows XP.

   ◆ If you don't have enough space to install Windows XP, you'll see a Windows XP Setup dialog box such as that shown in Figure 2.11 warning you of the problem. Click the Quit Setup button, retire disconsolately from the fray, and return when you've made more space available.

FIGURE 2.11

Setup warns you if you don't have enough space available to install Windows XP.

11. If you have any incompatible hardware or software, Setup displays the Upgrade Report page (of which Figure 2.12 shows a sample). You can click the Full Report button to view the details of the hardware and software, click the Save As button to save the information to file, or click the Print button to print a copy of it. If you don't take up one of these options, Setup displays the Windows XP Setup dialog box, which warns you that some devices on your computer may not work with Windows XP and offers you a View Report button, a Continue button, and a Quit Setup button. Click the Continue button if you want to continue.

FIGURE 2.12

The Upgrade Report page of Setup summarizes any potential hardware and software upgrade problems you may face.

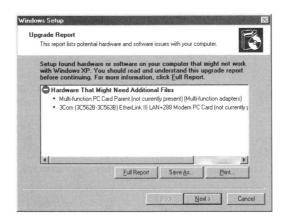

12. Click the Next button. Setup continues running the setup routine, reboots your computer, and takes the installation all the way to the Welcome to Microsoft Windows screen. Skip ahead to "The Installation Paths Converge" later in the chapter.

Performing a New Installation of Windows XP

To perform a new installation of Windows XP (without upgrading your current version of Windows), follow these steps:

1. Insert the CD in a CD drive or DVD drive. If Autoplay is enabled on your computer, Windows displays the introductory screen (shown in Figure 2.13). If not, open an Explorer window and double-click the CD. This should trigger the Autoplay action. If it doesn't, double-click the SETUP.EXE file on the CD to run it.

FIGURE 2.13

To start the upgrade, select the Install Windows XP link.

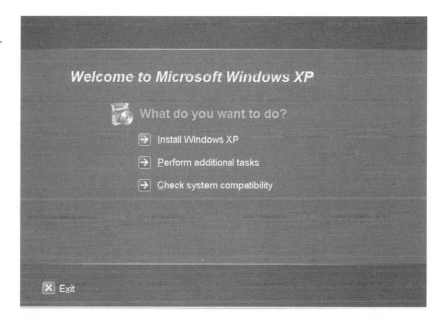

2. Click the Install Windows XP link. Setup displays the Welcome to Windows Setup page (shown in Figure 2.14).

FIGURE 2.14

On the Welcome to Windows Setup page, choose the New Installation item in the Installation Type drop-down list.

3. In the Installation Type drop-down list, choose the New Installation item.

4. Click the Next button. Setup displays the License Agreement page. Read it.

5. If you agree to the license, select the I Accept This Agreement option button and click the Next button. (If you don't agree to the license, Setup exits.) Setup displays the Your Product Key page.

6. Enter your product key and click the Next button. Setup displays the Setup Options page (shown in Figure 2.15). From this page, you can choose language options, installation options, and accessibility options.

FIGURE 2.15

When you perform a new installation, Setup displays the Setup Options page, on which you can choose advanced options and accessibility options.

7. To change the language used, select the language in the Select the Primary Language and Region You Want to Use drop-down list. If you want to install support for East Asian languages, select the Install Support for East Asian Languages check box.

8. To set the advanced options, which let you control the installation folder and specify that you want to select the installation partition, click the Advanced Options button on the Setup Options page. Setup displays the Advanced Options dialog box (shown in Figure 2.16), which offers the following options:

◆ The Copy Installation Files from This Folder text box lists the path from which you ran the Setup program (or it ran itself). Usually, you won't need to change this path, but you can if necessary.

FIGURE 2.16

In the Advanced Options dialog box, you can specify the installation folder and tell Setup that you want to choose the installation partition.

◆ The To This Folder on My Hard Drive text box shows the location to which Setup is planning to install Windows XP: your current Windows folder. If you don't want Windows XP to overwrite your current version of Windows, choose a different folder. For example, you may want to create a dual-boot setup so that you can compare Windows XP to your current version of Windows without yet removing the latter from your computer.

◆ The Copy All Installation Files from the Setup CD check box enables you to force Setup to copy all its files to the hard drive rather than leaving them on the CD. Use this option when installing Windows XP from a CD that will not be available after Setup reboots the computer. For example, when installing Windows XP on a laptop computer using an external CD drive (such as a parallel-port drive, a USB drive, or a PC Card–connected drive), you'll probably need to copy all setup files to the hard drive because the CD drive will not be available from the reboot until Setup is complete. You may also need to use this option if your CD drive will not read the Windows XP CD reliably during the setup routine after the reboot. (This shouldn't happen, but it does. After the reboot, Setup uses a different CD driver that apparently disagrees with some CD drives.) By default, this check box is cleared unless you're installing from a network drive, in which case it's not available (as in Figure 2.16).

◆ The I Want to Choose the Install Drive Letter and Partition during Setup check box lets you tell Setup to display the partitioning screen so that you can specify the partition on which to install Windows XP. If you're performing a new installation of Windows XP, you don't need to select this check box, because Setup automatically displays the partitioning screen so that you can specify where to install Windows XP.

9. Click the OK button. Setup closes the Advanced Options dialog box.

10. During Setup, Windows XP offers two accessibility options, Magnifier and Narrator. (Beyond these, Windows XP includes a large number of accessibility options, which we'll examine in detail in "Choosing Accessibility Options" in Chapter 4.) Magnifier is designed for people with limited but viable vision and displays an enlarged version of the selected portion of the screen. Narrator is designed for the blind and those with more limited vision. It reads the contents of the screen aloud. To use these options, click the Accessibility Options button on the Setup Options page. Setup displays the Accessibility Options dialog box (shown in Figure 2.17). Select the Use Microsoft Magnifier during Setup check box or the Use Microsoft Narrator during Setup check box as appropriate. Then click the OK button. Setup closes the Accessibility Options dialog box and applies your choices.

FIGURE 2.17

Setup offers Magnifier and Narrator accessibility options for those with limited vision and the blind.

11. Once you've finished choosing special options, click the Next button on the Setup Options page. Setup displays the Get Updated Setup Files page (shown in Figure 2.18), which lets you choose whether to use Dynamic Update to download any new Setup files that Microsoft may have released since your copy of Windows XP was pressed.

FIGURE 2.18

On the Get Updated Setup Files page of Setup, choose whether to let Dynamic Update download the latest Setup files.

12. To download any available files, leave the Yes, Download the Updated Setup Files option button selected, as it is by default. To skip Dynamic Update, select the No, Skip This Step and Continue Installing Windows option button.

13. Click the Next button. If you chose to use Dynamic Update, Setup contacts the Microsoft Web site and downloads any relevant files. Setup then continues running the setup routine, reboots your computer, and displays the partitioning screen. Go to the "Choosing a Hard Disk Partition" section in the "Performing a Clean Installation of Windows XP" section, a little later in this chapter.

EXPERT KNOWLEDGE: WHY IS THE FOLDER CALLED *I386*?

If you're looking at the Advanced Options dialog box, the Copy Installation Files from This Folder text box is probably listing a path that ends in \i386\. What's this all about?

i386 stands for Intel 386. The 386, as you'll remember if you've been computing for a while, was Intel's hottest processor at the end of the 1980s. But it's also the descriptor for the entire family of chips that has continued through the 486 chips and Pentium chips (renamed from 586, which wasn't trademarkable) to the Pentium IV chips of today.

But why is i386 there? Why's the folder not called something intuitive like *Files*? It's because NT was originally written to be processor independent so that it could run on various types of processor without major rebuilding.

The early version of NT ran on Intel chips, Alpha chips, MIPS chips, and PowerPC chips. The installation CD came with a separate folder for each of these. Over the years (or, more correctly, over the versions of NT), Microsoft gradually dropped support for processors other than the Intel 386 family. But the \i386\ folder survives as a hangover of the old days.

Performing a Clean Installation of Windows XP

To perform a clean installation of Windows XP, put the Windows XP CD in your CD-ROM drive or DVD drive and boot from it. (You may have to change the boot settings in your computer's BIOS to boot from the CD.) Setup automatically launches itself.

First, Setup displays the Welcome to Setup screen. From here, press the Enter key to start the installation. (Press the F3 key if you've reached this stage by mistake and need to quit.) Setup displays the partitioning screen.

Choosing a Hard Disk Partition

The partitioning screen lets you create and delete partitions as well as specify the installation partition. The screen lists the current partitions on the disk, their label, their type (for example, *NTFS* for an NTFS partition, *FAT32* for a FAT partition, and *Raw* for a new, unformatted partition), their size, and the amount of space free on each. Any unpartitioned space is listed as such. Any space you've deliberately left unpartitioned will of course be free, but there will often be a few megabytes of unpartitioned space left over after you've tried to allocate all the space on the disk.

To choose an existing partition for the installation, use ↓ and ↑ to move the highlight to it. Then press the Enter key.

To create a new partition, select some unpartitioned space and press the C key. Setup displays a details screen. Specify the size of the partition in megabytes and press the Enter key.

If you want to install Windows XP and use up the full amount of unpartitioned space, you don't need to explicitly create a partition first. Just select the Unpartitioned Space item and press the Enter key to start the installation.

To delete an existing partition, select it in the list and press the D key. Setup displays a screen confirming the action. Press the L key. If the partition is a system partition, Setup displays a more extensive warning. And if the partition is the partition on which Setup has installed its temporary files for carrying out the installation of Windows, Setup refuses to delete the partition.

Once you've chosen a partition, Setup proceeds. If the partition is a new partition, Setup offers you the choice of formatting it with NTFS or with FAT. For each, there's the option of a quick format. A full format includes a scan of the disk for bad sectors; a quick format skips this scan. Unless you're in a tearing hurry and have checked the disk recently for bad sectors, go with the full format.

NOTE   *If you choose to install Windows XP on a partition that already contains another operating system, Setup displays a page warning you that this may cause problems. Press the C key if you're prepared to continue. Press the Esc key to return to the partitioning screen and select another partition.*

Converting the Partition to NTFS

If you're installing Windows XP on an existing partition that uses FAT, Setup offers you the option of converting the installation partition to NTFS. Think seriously about doing so, because NTFS is one of the major improvements in Windows XP Home Edition over Windows Me and other Windows 9x versions.

NTFS offers two compelling advantages over FAT. First, NTFS has security features (including auditing) that FAT does not. And second, NTFS keeps a log of activities so that it can restore the disk to order after a hardware or power failure; FAT simply loses your data instead.

WARNING   *Don't convert the partition to NTFS if you're creating a dual-boot configuration with a version of Windows 9x, because Windows 9x cannot read NTFS partitions.*

Next, you see the license agreement. Read it and press the F8 key if you agree and want to proceed. Press the Esc key to cancel installation.

Choosing Regional and Language Options

After this, Setup entertains itself for a few minutes as it performs part of the installation. Next, you see the Regional and Language Options page. From here, you can change the computer's standards and formats setting so that it displays numbers, currencies, and dates in the appropriate formats for the country or user. You can also change the default keyboard layout.

To change the standards and formats setting, click the Customize button. Setup displays the Regional and Language Options dialog box with the Region Options page foremost, as shown in Figure 2.19. In the Standards and Formats group box, select the language and locale you want to use. The text boxes in the Samples area show samples of a number, a currency, a time, a short date, and a long date for that language and locale. (You can change these by clicking the Customize button and working in the Customize Regional Options dialog box.) In the Location drop-down list, select your geographical location so that Windows knows which part of the world you're in when its services try to present you with local information. Click the OK button. Setup closes the Regional and Language Options dialog box.

FIGURE 2.19

On the Region Options page of the Regional and Language Options dialog box, specify the standards and formats setting to use and tell Windows your location.

To change the keyboard layout, click the Details button. Setup displays the Text Services and Input Languages dialog box (shown in Figure 2.20). Select the language in the Default Input Language drop-down list. To add an input language, click the Add button and use the resulting Add Input Language dialog box to specify the input language and keyboard layout. For example, if you use the Dvorak layout for your keyboard, set it as the default keyboard layout. Then click the OK button. Setup closes the Text Services and Input Languages dialog box.

Click the Next button to continue the setup process.

FIGURE 2.20

Use the Text Services and Input Languages dialog box to change your default input language.

Entering Your Name and Organization

Next, Setup displays the Personalize Your Software page, which demands your name and your organization's name. Enter these with due care and consideration, as they get deeply buried within the Windows Registry. (Chapter 12 discusses how to change them if you get them wrong.) You must enter some text in the Name text box, but you can leave the Organization text box empty if you want.

Click the Next button to proceed.

Entering Your Product Key

Next, for a clean installation (but not for a new installation), Setup displays the Your Product Key page. Enter the 25-character product key (it should be on a yellow sticker on the back of the folder or CD box your Windows CD came in) and click the Next button to proceed.

TIP   If there's any risk of your misplacing your product key, write it on the Windows CD using a permanent pen.

Entering the Computer Name

Next, Setup displays the What's Your Computer's Name? page. By default, Setup suggests a complex and unmemorizable name that starts with the first part of the organization name you entered on the Personalize Your Software page. Change this name to something descriptive that you'll be able to remember and associate easily with this computer. The name can be up to 63 characters long, but you'd do well to keep it shorter than this to make it manageable. Names of more than 15 characters will be visible to other computers only via TCP/IP; via other network protocols, they won't be visible.

Click the Next button once again.

Entering the Modem Dialing Information

Next, if the computer has a modem that Setup was able to detect, Setup displays the Modem Dialing Information page. Specify your country or region (for example, United States of America), your area code (which is compulsory), any number you dial to get an outside line, and whether the phone system uses tone dialing or pulse dialing. Then click the Next button to proceed.

Checking the Date and Time

Next, Setup displays the Date and Time Settings page. Check the date, time, and time zone, and select or clear the Automatically Adjust Clock for Daylight Saving Changes check box as appropriate. Then click the Next button.

Specifying Networking Settings

Next, Setup installs some networking components and attempts to detect any network cards installed in your computer. Setup then displays the Networking Settings page, which offers you the choice of Typical Settings or Custom Settings.

The Typical Settings option installs the Client for Microsoft Networks, the QoS Packet Scheduler, File and Print Sharing for Microsoft Networks, and TCP/IP with automatic addressing. You can install other services after Setup completes (or remove these services), of course, but usually you'll be better off choosing the Custom Settings option and specifying suitable settings as described in the rest of this section.

If you select the Custom Settings option button and click the Next button, Setup displays the Networking Components page.

You can adjust the default settings by adding other services, uninstalling the default services, or choosing not to apply the selected services to this network adapter. When you remove a service, you make it unavailable to any of the network or dial-up adapters on your computer. So if you need to install a service but not use it for your primary network connection, let Setup install it, but clear its check box on the Networking Components page.

UNINSTALLING A SERVICE

To uninstall one of the services, select it and click the Uninstall button. Setup displays a confirmation message box warning you that uninstalling the component removes it from all network connections. Click the Yes button if you want to remove the service.

ADDING A SERVICE

To add other services to the default services, follow these steps:

1. Click the Install button. Setup displays the Select Network Component Type dialog box.

2. Select the type of component you want to add—Client, Service, or Protocol—and click the Add button. Setup displays the Select Network Client dialog box, the Select Network Service dialog box, or the Select Network Protocol dialog box, as appropriate.

3. Select the client, service, or protocol in the list box. To add an unlisted client, service, or protocol that you have on disk, click the Have Disk button and use the resulting Install from Disk dialog box to identify the file.

4. Click the OK button. Setup installs the client, service, or protocol and closes the Select Network Component Type dialog box.

CONFIGURING TCP/IP

Some of the network components have parameters you can configure. Of these, the key component is TCP/IP, the Internet protocol suite. If you don't run Internet Connection Sharing (ICS) on this computer, connect to the Internet through a computer running ICS, or connect to a DHCP server, you'll probably want to configure TCP/IP manually.

To configure your TCP/IP settings for the primary network card, follow these steps:

1. Select the Internet Protocol (TCP/IP) item in the list box on the Networking Components page.

2. Click the Properties button. Setup displays the Internet Protocol (TCP/IP) Properties dialog box.

3. On the General page, select the Use the Following IP Address option button.

4. Enter the IP address in the IP Address text box (for example, 192.168.0.11).

5. Enter the subnet mask in the Subnet Mask text box (for example, 255.255.255.0). Setup automatically enters a suggested subnet mask appropriate to the IP address you enter, but you may need to change it.

6. Enter the IP address of the default gateway in the Default Gateway text box.

7. Select the Use the Following DNS Server Addresses option button.

8. Enter the IP address of your primary DNS server in the Preferred DNS Server text box.

9. Enter the IP address of your secondary DNS server (if you have one) in the Alternate DNS Server text box.

10. Click the OK button. Setup closes the Internet Protocol (TCP/IP) Properties dialog box and applies your settings.

NOTE   *If necessary, you can also set advanced TCP/IP settings by clicking the Advanced button on the General page of the Internet Protocol (TCP/IP) Properties dialog box and working in the resulting Advanced TCP/IP Settings dialog box.*

Click the Next button to proceed with the installation. You've now chosen all the custom options.

CHANGING DISPLAY SETTINGS

If Setup detects that your screen has a recommended resolution (for example, if it is an LCD panel), or if it detects that you were using the 640X480 screen resolution, Setup displays the Display Settings dialog box, which announces that Windows will automatically adjust your screen resolution to improve the appearance of visual elements. Click the OK button. Windows adjusts the resolution and displays a Monitor Settings dialog box asking if you want to keep the change. Click the OK button if you do. If not, click the Cancel button or (if the screen isn't legible after the change) wait 30 seconds, after which Windows restores the previous screen resolution.

The Installation Paths Converge

The installation paths converge at the Welcome to Microsoft Windows screen, at which Setup starts playing active elevator music while an animated help logo struts its stuff. Click the Next button to move along.

Setting Up Your Internet Connection

Setup then tries to get you connected to the Internet. It tests any detected network adapter to see if it can find an Internet connection. If it detects an Internet connection, Setup displays the Will This Computer Connect to the Internet Directly, or through a Network? screen. Select the Yes, This Computer Will Connect through a Local Area Network or Home Network option button or the No, This Computer Will Connect Directly to the Internet option button as appropriate. (To skip the step of connecting to the Internet, click the Skip button.) Click the Next button. Setup displays the Ready to Activate Windows? screen.

If Setup doesn't detect an Internet connection, it displays the How Will This Computer Connect to the Internet? screen, which offers three options: the Telephone Modem option button, the Digital Subscriber Line (DSL) or Cable Modem option button, or the Local Area Network (LAN) option button.

Select the appropriate option button. If you don't want to configure an Internet connection at the moment—for example, you don't have your ISP or network information—click the Skip button.

The following sections describe what happens when you select each of these options.

TELEPHONE MODEM

If your computer connects with a telephone modem, select the Telephone Modem option button, then click the Next button. Setup displays the Ready to Activate Windows? screen.

After the step of activating Windows (or your turning down the invitation to do so), Setup displays the Do You Want to Set Up Internet Access Now? screen, which asks if you want to set up your computer to connect to the Internet. Select the Yes, Help Me Connect to the Internet option button or the No, Not at This Time option button as appropriate.

If you choose the Yes option button, Setup displays the Let's Get on the Internet screen. This offers three choices: The Get Online with MSN option button, the Use My Existing Internet Account with Another Service Provider (ISP) option button, and the Create a New Internet Account after I Finish Setting Up Windows option button. Select the appropriate option button and click the Next button to proceed.

If you choose the Get Online with MSN option button, Setup walks you through the process of signing you up for a new account on MSN (the Microsoft Network) or letting Windows know the details of your current MSN account.

If you choose to use your existing Internet account, Windows displays the Do You Want Help Finding an Internet Service Provider? screen. If you want assistance setting up your account, select the Yes, I Need Help Finding Information about My Account option button. When you click the Next button, Setup dials a toll-free number to the Microsoft Referral Service to walk you through the steps of identifying your ISP. If you know the details of your account, select the No, I Have My

User Name, Password, and My ISP's Name and Phone Number Handy option button. When you click the Next button, Windows displays the Set Up Your Internet Account screen.

Enter your username, password, and ISP phone number. By default, Windows selects the Obtain IP Automatically (DHCP) check box and the Obtain DNS Automatically (DHCP) check box. If you need to specify a static IP address rather than have the IP address be assigned automatically, clear the Obtain IP Automatically (DHCP) check box and enter the IP address in the Static Internet Protocol (IP) Address text box. Similarly, if your ISP does not supply DNS information automatically, clear the Obtain DNS Automatically check box and enter the IP addresses of the primary and secondary DNS servers in the Preferred DNS text box and the Alternate DNS text box.

When you click the Next button, Setup displays a Congratulations screen telling you that you can connect to the Internet using your phone line. Bear in mind that this isn't necessarily true—you've entered the information, but Windows hasn't checked that it works.

If you choose to create a new account, Setup walks you through the process of selecting an ISP from Microsoft's list and entering the connection information for it.

DIGITAL SUBSCRIBER LINE (DSL) OR CABLE MODEM

If your computer connects with a DSL or cable modem, select the Digital Subscriber Line (DSL) or Cable Modem option button, then click the Next button. Setup displays the Do You Use a Username and Password to Connect to the Internet? screen. Select the Yes, I Use a Username and Password to Connect option button or the No, This Computer Is Always Connected to the Internet option button as appropriate. Click the Next button. Setup displays the Ready to Activate Windows? screen.

LOCAL AREA NETWORK (LAN)

If your computer connects through a local area network (LAN), select the Local Area Network (LAN) option button, then click the Next button. Setup displays the Setting Up a High Speed Connection screen.

If your network is set up to automatically supply an IP address and Domain Name System (DNS) information, this screen is easy: Select the Obtain IP Automatically check box and the Obtain DNS Automatically check box, and you're all set. If your network isn't set up to deliver the goods, leave these check boxes cleared and enter your static IP address, your subnet mask, and your default gateway in the left stack of text boxes; your primary DNS server's IP address in the Preferred DNS text box; and your secondary DNS server's IP address (if you have one) in the Alternate DNS text box.

Click the Next button to proceed. Setup displays the Ready to Activate Windows? screen.

Activating Windows

Next, Setup displays the Ready to Activate Windows? screen, prompting you to activate Windows. Select the Yes, Activate Windows over the Internet Now option button or the No, Remind Me Every Few Days option button as appropriate.

Activation is a one-time procedure that you need to perform within 30 days of installing Windows. If you don't activate Windows, it stops working. The activation procedure is intended to reduce software piracy. A side effect is to increase the annoyance to legitimate software users.

In theory, setup is a convenient time for activating Windows, because you get the activation out of the way once and for all. But it's much best to wait until you're sure that all your hardware works before activating Windows. This needn't take long, and it's much better than needing to get your activation revoked because you need to install Windows on another computer instead. If you don't activate Windows at setup, it reminds you every few days until you activate it or your grace period ends.

Activation is a little creepy, even though it doesn't involve supplying any personal information. Windows creates what it calls "a unique hardware configuration that represents the configuration of the PC at the time of activation." At this writing, it's hard to tell how many problems upgrading your PC will cause if you need to reinstall Windows.

The Windows Product Activation Privacy Statement reassures you that "Windows can detect and tolerate minor changes to your PC configuration" and that only a complete overhaul will need reactivation. But you have to wonder: If you upgrade, say, the BIOS, the processor, and the network card, how will Microsoft be able to tell that it's the same computer? Doubtless there will be plenty of horror stories about activation going wrong—and pirates will offer hacks and cracks for circumventing activation.

Registering Windows

During activation, you're heavily encouraged to register your copy of Windows XP with Microsoft.

If you've already registered on Microsoft's Web site, your Windows registration information gets merged into your current information. If you haven't registered, Microsoft creates a new profile for you with a personal information number (PIN) and adds the PIN to your hard drive in a cookie file. When you then visit the Microsoft Web site, it prompts you to create a Registration ID (not usually acronymed to RID). You can keep a profile with personal information—and you can opt out of the communications that Microsoft and the other companies it "occasionally" allows to offer its customers information will bombard you with.

Creating User Accounts

When you've finished with activation and registration, or when you've skipped both, Setup displays the Who Will Use This Computer? screen, which provides an easy way of setting up accounts for one to five users. This screen contains five text boxes. The first is named Your Name; the rest are numbered 2nd User through 5th User.

NOTE   *When you're upgrading from Windows 9x, Setup creates an account for the username under which you upgraded if you yourself forget to do so.*

Enter the names of the users in the text boxes. Each name can be up to 20 characters long, and each must be unique. Names cannot use the characters " * + , / : ; < = > ? [ ] \ or |, and no name can consist of all spaces, all periods, or a combination of the two.

Click the Next button. Setup displays the Thank You! screen telling you you're ready to start using Windows.

Click the Finish button. Setup completes a few odds and ends, and then displays the Welcome screen for you to log in. Turn ahead to the next chapter for coverage of this and other basic Windows procedures.

Applying Your Files and Settings

To apply the files and settings you saved by using the Files and Settings Transfer Wizard to your new installation of Windows, take the following steps:

1. Choose Start ➤ All Programs ➤ Accessories ➤ System Tools ➤ Files and Settings Transfer Wizard. Windows starts the Files and Settings Transfer Wizard, which displays the Welcome to the Files and Settings Transfer Wizard page.

2. Click the Next button. The Wizard displays the Which Computer Is This? page.

3. Select the New Computer option button.

4. Click the Next button. The Wizard displays the Do You Have a Windows XP CD? page, which offers to create a Wizard disk that you can use to collect the information from your old computer.

5. Select the I Don't Need the Wizard Disk. I Have Already Collected My Files and Settings from My Old Computer option button.

6. Click the Next button. The Wizard displays the Where Are the Files and Settings? page (shown in Figure 2.21).

FIGURE 2.21

On the Where Are the Files and Settings? page of the Files and Settings Transfer Wizard, tell the Wizard where you saved the files and settings.

7. Select the Direct Cable option button, the Floppy Drive or Other Removable Media option button, or the Other option button as appropriate.

   ◆ If you select the Floppy Drive or Other Removable Media option button, select the drive in the drop-down list.

   ◆ If you select the Other option button, use the text box and (if necessary) the Browse button and the resulting Browse for Folder dialog box to specify the location of the files and settings.

8. Click the Next button. The Wizard displays the Transfer in Progress page (shown in Figure 2.22) as it transfers the files and settings.

FIGURE 2.22

The Files and Settings Transfer Wizard transfers the files and settings.

9. If the Wizard displays a dialog box telling you that you need to log off for the settings to take effect and inviting you to log off now, choose the Yes button. The Wizard logs you off and finishes applying the settings.

10. Log back in, and your files and settings are available.

Uninstalling Windows XP and Reverting to Windows Me or 98

If you upgraded from Windows Me or Windows 98 to Windows XP, you can uninstall Windows XP and revert to your previous version of Windows if necessary. To do so, take the following steps:

1. Choose Start ➤ Control Panel. Windows displays Control Panel.

2. Click the Add or Remove Programs link. Windows displays the Add or Remove Programs window with the Add or Remove Programs page foremost.

3. Select the Windows XP Uninstall item. Windows displays its details, including a Change/Remove button.

4. Click the Change/Remove button. Windows displays the Uninstall Windows XP dialog box (shown in Figure 2.23).

FIGURE 2.23

In the Uninstall Windows XP dialog box, choose whether to uninstall Windows XP or to remove the backup of your old version of Windows.

5. Select the Uninstall Windows XP option button.

6. Click the Continue button. Windows displays a confirmation dialog box checking that you're absolutely sure.

7. Click the Yes button. Windows closes, runs the uninstall procedure, and automatically restarts your computer with your previous version of Windows.

Removing Your Old Version of Windows

If you decide to stick with Windows XP after upgrading to it, you can reclaim the space taken up by the backup of your old version of Windows. To do so, follow the first four steps in the previous section but select the Remove the Backup of My Previous Operating System option button in the Uninstall Windows XP dialog box. Click the Continue button and confirm your choice, and Windows deletes the backup of your previous operating system.

Keeping Windows Updated

Windows XP includes a feature called Windows Update that's designed to keep Windows up-to-date by automatically downloading Windows updates, such as patches and fixes for security holes, and offering to install them. If you need to run old programs that have compatibility problems, Windows Update may be of particular interest, because it also includes new fixes for programs to run on Windows XP.

There are several things you should know about Windows Update before you find it springing into action: how it works, how to configure it, and what to do when an update presents itself.

When Windows Update Runs

By default, Windows Update runs automatically, but only when an Administrator user is logged in. (Microsoft assumes that you don't want Limited users—let alone guests—to install or refuse updates.) If multiple Administrator users are logged on to the computer at the same time, Windows Update runs for only one of them.

You can also run Windows Update manually by choosing Start ➤ All Programs ➤ Windows Update. (If you prefer to run Windows Update manually, you may also want to turn off automatic updating. Read on.)

Windows Update's default setting is to automatically download updates when they're available (and an Administrator user is logged on) and then invite the Administrator to install them. You can change this default behavior, as described in the next section.

Here's what happens:

◆ Windows Update decides it's time to run (or an Administrator runs it manually).

◆ Windows Update goes online and checks which updates are available, then compares the list to those that have already been applied to the computer and those that have been offered to the computer but refused by an Administrator.

◆ If update files are available, Windows Update downloads them in the background, using bandwidth-throttling technology to make sure it doesn't prevent you from using your Internet connection by grabbing all bandwidth when you need it. (*Bandwidth-throttling* means that Windows Update throttles back the amount of bandwidth the download is taking up, not that it throttles your bandwidth.) If you're not using your Internet connection, Windows Update downloads the update files as fast as possible.

◆ Once the update files are downloaded, Windows Update notifies you (assuming you're an Administrator) that they're available and invites you to install them.

Configuring Windows Update

To configure Windows Update, follow these steps:

1. Press Winkey+Break. Windows displays the System Properties dialog box. (Alternatively, click the Start button to display the Start menu, then right-click the My Computer item and choose Properties from the context menu.)

2. Click the Automatic Updates tab. Windows displays the Automatic Updates page (shown in Figure 2.24).

FIGURE 2.24

You can configure Windows Update on the Automatic Updates page of the System Properties dialog box.

3. In the Notification Settings group box, choose one of the three option buttons:

Download the Updates Automatically and Notify Me when They Are Ready to Be Installed option button The default, this setting is convenient if you want to use automatic updating and you have a fast Internet connection.

Notify Me before Downloading Any Updates and Notify Me Again before Installing Them on My Computer option button Use this setting if you want to use automatic updating but want to be aware of when Windows Update is downloading updates. You might want to know this because your Internet connection isn't fast enough to support your surfing (or downloading MP3s) at the same time as Windows is trying to squeeze a large update through it, or because you don't like unexplained activity across your Internet connection.

Turn Off Automatic Updating. I Want to Update My Computer Manually option button Select this option button if you prefer to control not only when Windows Update downloads and installs updates but when it checks for them—or if you don't want to use Windows Update at all.

4. If you have previously declined updates that Windows has offered you, you can click the Restore Declined Updates button in the Previous Updates group box to make them available again. (Until you've declined an update, the Restore Hidden Items button is unavailable.)

5. Click the OK button. Windows closes the System Properties dialog box.

Running Windows Update Manually

If you don't want to wait for Windows Update to run automatically on schedule, or if you don't like to have your computer calling Microsoft secretly in the wee hours of dark and stormy nights, you can run Windows Update manually. You can do so either from the Start menu (Start ➢ All Programs ➢ Windows Update) or from the Help and Support Center window. See pages 67–68 of the *Essential Skills* section for a visual guide to running Windows Update.

EXPERT KNOWLEDGE: AUTOMATING THE INSTALLATION OF WINDOWS XP

The installation procedure described in this chapter is effective and relatively straightforward once you know what the options mean. But it still takes between 45 and 90 minutes to complete, depending on the speed of your computer, and requires you to be there at odd moments to answer prompts, so it's a bit of a waste of time.

Still, you need to run the installation procedure only once on any computer. Or do you? Some people find that they need to install Windows multiple times on the same computer. Every installation of Windows gradually accumulates unneeded programs, files, and settings. These can cause Windows to slow down or even become unstable. Windows 98 was so notorious for this that the joke went that its name specified the number of days that you could reasonably run it before expecting enough trouble to set in that would require a reinstall to fix.

Windows XP improves your chances of not needing to reinstall by providing tools such as System Restore (discussed in Chapter 16), device driver rollback (discussed in Chapter 14), and Disk Cleanup and Disk Defragmenter (both discussed in Chapter 11) to keep your system in working order. But even these can't fix every problem. If you need a fresh start, or if you maintain a test computer, you may want to blow away all the old files and settings and virtual dust-bunnies by performing a new installation.

To help you do so, Windows XP includes a tool for performing an unattended installation. (You can, of course, use these tools to set up Windows XP the first and only time, but most people don't find it worth their while to do so.)

Continued on next page

EXPERT KNOWLEDGE: AUTOMATING THE INSTALLATION OF WINDOWS XP *(continued)*

If you had to guess at how the procedure works, you'd probably figure that it'd consist of creating a file ahead of time that gives Windows the information for which it normally prompts you during setup, and then feeding that file to the Setup procedure. That's just how it works. The file is called an *answer file* for obvious enough reasons. There's a Wizard to help you create the answer file, but then you may want to edit it a bit by hand.

To perform an unattended installation, take the following steps:

1. Extract the tools from the \Support\Tools\Deploy.cab folder on the CD to a convenient location. If you already have Windows XP installed on one of your computers, you can extract these files by using Explorer. If you have an earlier version of Windows, use a Zip program (for example, WinZip) from Windows or the EXTRACT command from a command prompt instead. (See the Expert Knowledge sidebar "Extracting a Compressed File from a Cabinet File" in Chapter 16 for information on using the EXTRACT command.)

2. Open an Explorer window to the folder to which you extracted the files.

3. Double-click the SETUPMGR.EXE program. Windows starts the Windows XP Setup Manager Wizard, which displays its first page.

4. Click the Next button. The Wizard displays the New or Existing Answer File page.

5. Leave the Create a New Answer File option button selected (as it is by default) unless you already have an answer file that you want to tweak. In that case, select the Modify an Existing Answer File option button and enter the path and filename in the text box, either by typing or by clicking the Browse button and using the resulting Open dialog box.

6. Click the Next button. The Wizard displays the Product to Install page (shown below).

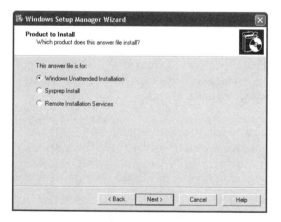

7. Make sure the Windows Unattended Installation option button is selected.

8. Click the Next button. The Wizard displays the Platform page (shown next).

Continued on next page

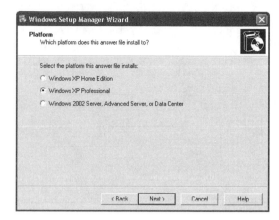

9. Select the Windows XP Home Edition option button.

10. Click the Next button. The Wizard displays the User Interaction Level page (shown below).

11. Select the Fully Automated option button.

12. Click the Next button. The Wizard displays the Distribution Folder page, which lets you specify that the Wizard create a distribution folder on your computer or on a networked drive containing the Windows source files.

◆ Creating a distribution folder lets you not only install without the CD but also add extra files (such as device drivers) to the custom installation. If you like unattended installation so much that you'd like to buy the company that made it—that is, if you want to run unattended installations frequently and you have a convenient drive or folder—you'll probably want to try this option. For the moment, we'll stick with installing from the CD.

13. Select the No, This Answer File Will Be Used to Install from a CD option button.

Continued on next page

14. Click the Next button. The Wizard displays the License Agreement page.

15. Select the I Accept the Terms of the License Agreement check box and click the Next button. The Wizard displays the Windows Setup Manager window (shown below).

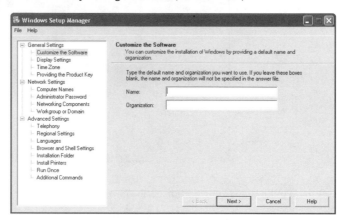

16. Select each page in turn and specify those settings applicable to your installation. Browsing through the pages feels like a sort of Redmond Roulette, because you must fill in any required fields (such as the Name text box on the Customize the Software page) before leaving any given page. If you don't, the Wizard halts you in your tracks with a peremptory message box pointing out your omission. So it's best to deal with the pages in order. You can move from page to page by clicking items in the list box or by clicking the Next button.

Customize the Software page   Enter your name in the Name text box (compulsory). If appropriate, enter the organization in the Organization text box.

Display Settings page   You can use the Colors drop-down list, the Screen Area drop-down list, and the Refresh Frequency drop-down list to specify the colors, screen area, and refresh rate to use instead of accepting the Windows defaults. For custom settings, click the Custom button and specify them in the Custom Display Settings dialog box.

Time Zone page   Select the time zone in the Time Zone drop-down list.

Providing the Product Key page   Enter the product key on this page. (This is compulsory for creating a fully automated answer file.)

Computer Names page   Enter the computer name in the Computer Name text box (compulsory).

Administrator Password page   Enter the password for the Administrator account in the Password text box and the Confirm Password text box. Select the Encrypt Administrator Password in Answer File check box if you want to do just that. To have Windows log the Administrator on automatically, you can select the When the Computer Starts, Automatically Log On As Administrator check box and specify the number of times in the Number of Times to Auto Logon text box. (Autologon can be useful for the first boot, but beyond that, it's a severe security threat.)

Continued on next page

Networking Components page   Select the Typical Settings option button or the Customize Settings option button as appropriate. If you select the latter, customize the settings as discussed in "Specifying Networking Settings" earlier in the chapter.

Workgroup or Domain page   Leave the Workgroup option button selected and enter the name of the workgroup in the Workgroup text box.

17. Click the Next button. Windows displays the Windows Setup Manager dialog box shown below telling you that it has created an answer file and inviting you to specify the location for it.

18. Enter the appropriate location and change the filename from its default UNATTEND.TXT to WINNT.SIF. Click the OK button. Windows XP Setup Manager creates the file and saves it under that name.

19. Choose File ➢ Exit. Windows XP Setup Manager closes itself.

Now you've created the basic file. It's ready to go—but before you run it, you probably want to take a look at the contents. (You might also want to add extra parameters. Consult the Setup Manager Help file for possibilities.) Right-click the file in an Explorer window, choose Open With from the context menu, select Notepad in the Open With dialog box, and click the OK button. Windows opens the file in Notepad. Depending on the options you chose, it should look something like this:

```
;SetupMgrTag
[Data]
    AutoPartition=1
    MsDosInitiated="0"
    UnattendedInstall="Yes"

[Unattended]
    UnattendMode=FullUnattended
    OemSkipEula=Yes
    OemPreinstall=No
    TargetPath=\WINDOWS

[GuiUnattended]
    AdminPassword=*
    EncryptedAdminPassword=NO
```

Continued on next page

EXPERT KNOWLEDGE: AUTOMATING THE INSTALLATION OF WINDOWS XP *(continued)*

```
        OEMSkipRegional=1
        TimeZone=85
        OemSkipWelcome=1

    [UserData]
        ProductID=NNNNN-NNNNN-NNNNN-NNNNN-NNNNN
        FullName="Andy Rondolophberger"
        OrgName="Rondolophberger Pharmaceuticals"
        ComputerName=Verwirrung

    [Display]
        BitsPerPel=32
        Xresolution=800
        YResolution=600
        Vrefresh=85

    [Identification]
        JoinWorkgroup=LAUREL

    [Networking]
        InstallDefaultComponents=Yes
```

If you've chosen other options—for example, customizing networking or choosing language settings—you'll see further lines covering them. You can also add other lines as necessary to take other actions, such as specifying that the installation repartition the hard drive or convert the file system to NTFS. You'll find details of the possibilities in the Help files contained in DEPLOY.CAB.

If you make any changes, save the file. Then close it and copy it to a floppy disk. Then boot the computer from the Windows XP CD and put the floppy disk in the floppy drive. Windows installs automatically using the settings you specified.

Up Next

This chapter has discussed how to install Windows, either as a clean install or as an upgrade to your current version of Windows 9x. You've also learned how to use the Windows Update feature to keep your copy of Windows updated, compatible, and secure, and how to create an answer file to perform an unattended installation.

The next chapter discusses how to get started with Windows XP: logging on and off, switching users, finding out who's logged on, and shutting down Windows.

Chapter 3

Getting Started with Windows

THIS CHAPTER DISCUSSES HOW to get started with Windows. It covers how to log on and log off; how to switch from one user session to another; and how to exit Windows. It also discusses how you can find out who else is logged on to the computer when you're working at it; how you can get an idea of which programs the other users are running; and how you can log off another user (or all other users) in order to reclaim the resources they're using.

Logging on and off and switching user are straightforward as they should be, because you'll probably perform each action several times each day you use the computer. But behind these mundane actions lie some important concepts of multiuser computing that you need to understand in order to use Windows most effectively. So even at this basic level of getting to grips with Windows, we need to lift the hood and glance at what it's hiding beneath it. To do so, we'll use Task Manager, a handy administration tool built into Windows.

This chapter covers the following topics:

◆ Logging on and logging off

◆ Switching from one user to another

◆ Seeing who else is logged on to the computer

◆ Logging another user off

◆ Sending a message to another user

◆ Using the Winkey

◆ Shutting down Windows

NOTE   *Before we start, here's something you need to know. Windows XP Home supports three types of users: Computer Administrator users, Limited users, and the Guest user. By default, all named users are set up as Computer Administrator users, which gives them full authority to configure and customize the computer. Limited users, which you create manually, can perform only minimal configuration and customization. The Guest user, an account that's created automatically by Windows, can perform no configuration or customization. This chapter assumes you're logging on as a Computer Administrator user, because that's most likely to be the case. Chapter 9 discusses how to create and manage user accounts.*

Logging On and Logging Off

Logging on and off in Windows XP work differently than in previous versions of Windows. Logging on and off could hardly be easier, but it's important to understand what happens when you log on and off, and how logging on and off differ from switching user.

In earlier versions of Windows, only one user at a time could be logged on to a computer running Windows. For a second user to log on, the first user needed to log off. Logging off involved closing all the open programs and files: Either the user could close the programs and files manually before logging off, or Windows would close them automatically when the user issued the Log Off command (and confirmed that they wanted to log off).

EXPERT KNOWLEDGE: FAST USER SWITCHING, PERFORMANCE, AND FILE INTEGRITY

Having multiple users logged on to Windows at the same time affects performance because each user who's logged on takes up some of the computer's memory. Having a user logged on itself takes up relatively little memory, but each program that the user has running, and each file that they have open, adds to the amount being used.

Windows XP needs a minimum of 64MB of RAM to run at an acceptable speed. For each light user, reckon another 32MB of RAM; for each moderate user, 64MB; and for each heavy user, 128MB. If you have 256MB of RAM, you should be able to have two or three users logged on and running several programs each without running short of memory.

Having multiple users logged on at once can also affect file integrity. For example, what happens when two users try to change the same file at the same time? The short answer is: It depends.

Some programs are smart enough to realize that someone else has a copy of the file open. For example, if you try to open in Word 2002 the same document that another user has open, Word displays the File in Use dialog box (shown below) to warn you that the document is locked for editing and to offer you ways to work with the document (open a read-only copy; create a local copy and merge your changes later; or receive notification when the original copy is available).

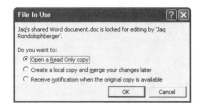

Other programs aren't smart enough to spot the problem. For example, WordPad (Windows XP's built-in word processing program) lets you open a document that another user has open, change it, and save the changes. The other user can then save *their* changes to the same file, which can end up with some of the changes you've made and some that the other user has made. And this is assuming that only two users are editing the document at the same time. For all WordPad knows, half the people in Delaware could be editing the document at the same time and wiping out each other's changes.

If your computer has a modest amount of RAM—say, 64MB, 96MB, or 128MB—or if you're having problems with users opening files at the same time, turn off the Fast User Switching feature as discussed in the section "Turning Off Fast User Switching" in Chapter 9. When you turn off Fast User Switching, only one user can be logged on to the computer at any given time, and that user must log off before another user can log on. This reduces the amount of memory needed and avoids most problems with shared files.

Once all the programs and files were closed, and all network and Internet connections were closed as well, Windows displayed the Log On to Windows dialog box or the Enter Network Password dialog box, depending on whether the computer was attached to a network. Another user could then log on to Windows, run programs, open files, establish network and Internet connections, and so on.

In Windows XP, multiple users can be logged on at the same time, though of course only one user can actually be using the computer. Each of those users who is logged on can have programs running and files open. Windows XP lets you switch quickly between users without closing the programs and files.

Only one user can be *active*—actually using the computer—at any time. (Given that most computers have only one keyboard, mouse, and monitor, this may seem too obvious to mention—but things are very different in Unix and Linux, in which multiple users can be actively using the same computer at the same time, some locally and some remotely.) A user who is logged on but not active is said to be *disconnected*.

This means that, for example, Jane and Jack can keep their programs open while Ross is using the computer. When Jane logs back on (in the process disconnecting Ross, who perhaps stepped away for a cup of coffee), Windows resumes her session from where she left it off, displaying the programs she had running and the files she had open. Windows reestablishes any of Jane's persistent network connections, including any Internet connection that's set to connect automatically.

Being able to leave multiple users up and running is great—up to a point. But it has serious implications for performance and file integrity. The following sections discuss these considerations briefly.

Logging On

To start using Windows, log on from the Welcome screen. Figure 3.1 shows an example of the Welcome screen, which displays a list of the users who have accounts set up on the computer. (See page 3 of the *Essential Skills* section for a visual guide to logging on.) Any programs a user has running appear listed under the username, together with the number of e-mail messages waiting for them. If a user is logged on but has no programs running, the Welcome screen displays *Logged on* beneath their name.

FIGURE 3.1

The Welcome screen lists the users with accounts on this computer, any tasks the user has running, and any unread e-mail messages they have.

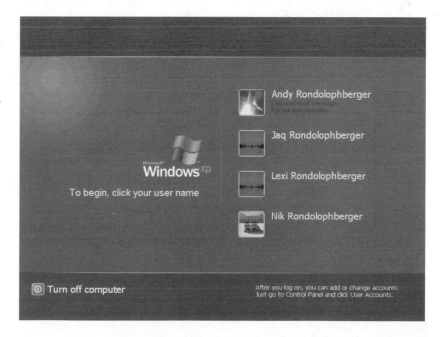

By default, user accounts in Windows XP Home are set up without passwords, so you log on by clicking the username under which you want to log on. (If an administrator has set up Windows to require passwords, you'll need to enter the password for the account as well.)

When it accepts your logon, Windows displays your Desktop with its current settings. (The section "Using the Desktop and Start Menu" a little later in this chapter discusses the basics of the Desktop and Start menu. The next chapter discusses how to customize the Desktop.)

The first time you log on, Windows creates your folders and sets up program shortcuts for you—so the logon process takes a minute or two. Subsequent logons are much quicker.

Logging Off

The counterpart to logging on is (unsurprisingly) logging off. When you log off, Windows closes all the programs and files you've been using. If the files contain unsaved changes, Windows prompts you to save them.

To log off, display the Start menu by clicking the Start button, and click the Log Off button. Windows displays the Log Off Windows dialog box (shown in Figure 3.2). Click the Log Off button to log off. See page 4 of the *Essential Skills* section for visual coverage of logging off.

FIGURE 3.2

The Log Off Windows dialog box lets you log off, cancel the command, or switch to another user.

NOTE   If you leave your computer unattended for a while, the screen saver usually kicks in—unless you have something open than prevents the screen from starting (or you've disabled the screen saver). For example, a dialog box open on-screen usually prevents the screen saver from starting. The default setting is for the screen saver to start after 10 minutes and to display the Welcome screen. The screen saver gives you some protection against prying eyes (particularly if you're using passwords for logging on), but it also makes it harder to see who's doing what on the computer. Chapter 4 discusses how to choose screen saver settings.

Using the Desktop and Start Menu

Once you've logged on successfully, Windows displays the Desktop. Figure 3.3 shows what the Desktop looks like the first time you start Windows and start a couple of programs. Because you can customize the Desktop extensively (as discussed in the next chapter), your Desktop might not look anything like the Desktop shown in the figure: The wallpaper might be different; the Taskbar could be located at a different side of the screen; or various toolbars might be displayed. About the one unchanging thing about the Desktop is the Start menu button—but even this might not be displayed if someone has chosen to hide the Taskbar (of which the Start button is part).

FIGURE 3.3

The components
of the Windows
Desktop

Icon · Program Windows · Desktop Background

Start Button · Taskbar Buttons · Taskbar · Notification Area

We'll examine the Desktop in more detail in the forthcoming chapters, but these are the basic actions for navigating it:

- ♦ The Desktop contains one or more shortcuts to items. Usually, there's an icon for the Recycle Bin, if nothing else. Double-click an icon to run the program associated with it.

- ♦ The Start menu provides access to the full range of programs and features currently installed on Windows. Click the Start button to display the Start menu. Choose one of the items that appears on it, or click the All Programs button to display a cascading menu containing further items. See page 7 of the *Essential Skills* section for a visual guide to using the Start menu.

- ♦ The Taskbar gives you quick access to each program that's currently running. The Taskbar displays a button for each active program window. To display that window in front of all other windows, click its button. To minimize the program, click its Taskbar button again. See page 8 of the *Essential Skills* section for coverage of how to use the Taskbar to access a window, and pages 11–12 for coverage of how to use the Taskbar to arrange windows.

- ♦ The notification area contains items that it's useful to have displayed all the time (such as the clock, which is displayed by default), together with information and alerts (which are displayed at appropriate times).

- ♦ The Desktop background is a graphic that you can change at will.

Switching to Another User

As you saw in Figure 3.2, the Log Off Windows dialog box also contains a button called Switch User. When you click the Switch User button, Windows keeps your programs running (instead of closing them, as it does when you log out) and displays the Welcome screen so that you can log on as another user or (more likely) another user can log on as themselves. See page 5 of the *Essential Skills* section for visual coverage of this procedure.

EXPERT KNOWLEDGE: USING THE CONNECT COMMAND TO SWITCH USER QUICKLY

Switching user as described above is easy but takes a few clicks. There's a quicker way of switching—by using Task Manager as follows:

1. Right-click open space in the Taskbar and choose Task Manager from the context menu. Windows opens Task Manager.

2. Click the Users tab. Windows displays the Users page (shown in Figure 3.4, later in the chapter).

3. Right-click the user as whom you want to connect and choose Connect from the context menu. If the user's account has a password, Windows displays the Connect Password Required dialog box. When you enter the password correctly (or if the account has no password), Windows disconnects your session and connects you as the user you selected.

Locking the Computer

To leave your current session running but display the Welcome screen quickly, press Winkey+L. (If you're not using the Welcome screen, Windows displays the Log On to Windows dialog box instead.)

Microsoft calls this action *locking* the computer, though the term is neither accurate nor helpful with Windows XP Home's default settings. The computer isn't locked in any useful sense unless all user accounts are protected with effective passwords.

However, if you turn off the Welcome screen and Fast User Switching (as discussed in Chapter 9), Windows manages a semblance of locking. When the current user disconnects their session, Windows displays a blank background topped by the Unlock Computer dialog box, which tells the user that the computer is in use, that it has been locked, and that only the current user or an administrator can unlock it. If you've applied passwords, this is true; if you haven't, anyone can click the OK button in the Unlock Computer dialog box to unlock the computer and log on as the current user.

Checking Which User Is Currently Active

If you're in any doubt as to which user is currently active, display the Start menu (by clicking the Start button or pressing the Winkey) and check the username displayed at the top.

Seeing Who Else Is Logged On to the Computer

As you saw a page or two ago, the Welcome screen displays details of each user logged on to the computer and the number of programs they're running. But if you don't want to display the

Welcome screen (and disconnect your session by doing so), you can find out which other users are logged in by using Task Manager as follows:

1. Right-click the Taskbar and choose Task Manager from the context menu. Windows displays Task Manager.

2. Click the Users tab. Windows displays the Users page (shown in Figure 3.4), which lists the users and their status.

FIGURE 3.4

The Users page of Task Manager shows you which other users are logged on to the computer. You can send them messages, switch to their sessions, or log them off forcibly.

NOTE   *Limited users and the Guest user can't see which other users are logged on or which processes they're running. As a result, Limited users and the Guest user can't switch directly to another user's session by using Task Manager, though they can disconnect their own session or log themselves off by using Task Manager.*

Seeing Which Programs the Other Users Are Running

It's not easy to see exactly which programs the other users of the computer are running unless you know the names of the executable files for the programs, but you can get an idea by using the Processes page of Task Manager. This page also shows you how much memory each program is using, which helps you establish whether—or why—your computer is running short of memory.

Follow these steps to start Task Manager and display its Processes page:

1. Right-click the Taskbar and choose Task Manager from the context menu. Windows displays Task Manager.

2. Click the Processes tab. Windows displays the Processes page, which lists the processes you're running.

3. Select the Show Processes from All Users check box. (This check box is cleared by default.) Task Manager adds to the list all the processes that the other users are running as well. Figure 3.5

shows an example of the Processes page. You can sort the list of processes by any column by clicking the column heading. In the figure, the processes are sorted by the User Name column so that it's easy to see which process belongs to which user.

FIGURE 3.5

Use the Processes page of Task Manager to see which programs the other users are running.

As you can see in the figure, three of the Rondolophbergers are running programs, and between them they're using quite a chunk of memory: The Commit Charge counter in the lower-right corner of the Processes page shows that 172,932K (about 169MB) out of 633,656K (about 619MB) of memory has been used up. In the list, you can see some of the principal offenders: copies of WIN-WORD.EXE (Word for Windows) that Andy and Jaq are running (24,624K and 18,148K, respectively), several instances of EXPLORER.EXE, and some programs with unpronounceable names such as DEVLDR32.EXE and WPABALN.EXE.

Some of the other names are readily identifiable. For example, WMPLAYER.EXE is the executable for Windows Media Player, as you'd expect, and TASKMGR.EXE is the executable for Task Manager itself. You don't need to memorize the mapping of each executable filename to its program, but if you look at Task Manager now and then, you'll learn to scan the list of processes and see which is running. This will help you decide whether you should go ahead and log another user off Windows (as described in the next section) or whether doing so will trash their work and ruin their life.

While you're looking at Task Manager, there are a couple of other things you might as well know.

First, you can also see in the figure that it's not just the Rondolophbergers who are using memory like there were no tomorrow—Windows also has a number of processes open on its own account. The LOCAL SERVICE account is running SVCHOST.EXE (service host), as is the NETWORK SERVICE account. The SYSTEM account is running a dozen or more processes, of which you can see only the top few in the figure. Of these, the first, the System Idle Process, is consuming 91 percent of the processor cycles. (This is actually good news. When the System Idle Process is taking up most of the processor cycles like this, the computer is idling along—goofing off until the user does something that presses it into action.)

EXPERT KNOWLEDGE: WHICH NAME CORRESPONDS TO WHICH PROGRAM?

To find out which program corresponds to each executable file, display the Applications page of Task Manager. Right-click a program and choose Go to Process from the context menu. Task Manager displays the Processes page and selects the process for that program.

That's easy enough—but there are many more processes running than programs. Try closing all the programs listed on the Applications page of Task Manager, and you'll see that there's still a goodly list of processes left. Try stopping any obvious services that you can temporarily dispense with, and see if an associated process disappears. For instance, try closing your Internet connection or stopping your PC Cards. Did either of those actions lose you a process? Then you have an idea of what that process does.

If you're desperate to find out which function or service an executable runs, try searching for the executable. (Chapter 6 describes how to search for a file, and pages 34–36 of the *Essential Skills* section illustrate searching.) The folder that contains the executable may give you a clue as to the program, or there may be a comment on the executable that reveals its purpose. Then again, the executable may prove to be one of the mysterious system files stored in the \Windows\ folder or the \Windows\System32\ folder. If the latter is the case, figure it's something unknowable and leave it alone.

Second, you may have noticed that the numbers in the Mem Usage column don't add up to anything like the 172,932K listed as being committed (even though you can't see the whole column). That's because that committed figure is both physical memory (RAM) used and virtual memory (hard disk space being used to simulate more RAM). If you want to see how much virtual memory each process is taking up, follow these steps:

1. Choose View ➤ Select Columns. Task Manager displays the Select Columns dialog box (shown in Figure 3.6).

FIGURE 3.6

Use the Select Columns dialog box to add further columns of information to Task Manager's Processes page.

2. Select the Virtual Memory Size check box.

   ◆ Also select the check boxes for any other information you want to see in Task Manager. Many of the items here are somewhat arcane, but you might want to look at CPU Time or Peak Memory Usage.

3. Click the OK button. Task Manager closes the Select Columns dialog box and adds the columns you chose to the Processes page.

Figure 3.7 shows the Processes page of Task Manager with the Virtual Memory Size column added and the processes sorted by that column. Notice that the two copies of Word have very heavy memory usage indeed (when you add the Mem Usage column and the VM Size column). SVCHOST.EXE also shows itself as a heavyweight, using a little over 11MB of virtual memory in addition to its 10MB of RAM.

FIGURE 3.7

If you want to see virtual memory usage, add the Virtual Memory Size (VM Size) column to the Processes page in Task Manager.

Logging Another User Off

If necessary, any Computer Administrator user can log another user off the computer.

Logging someone else off isn't usually a great idea, because while you can use Task Manager to see which processes they're running (as described in the previous section), you can't see whether they have any unsaved work in them. If you don't use passwords to log on to Windows, it's much better to log on as the other user and close the programs and documents manually. Then log off (as the other user) and log back on as yourself. If you do use passwords, you'll need to know the other user's password to log on as them, which kinda defeats the point of having passwords in the first place.

That said, you may need to log another user off if they are running enough programs to affect the computer's performance or if they have open a single-user program or a document that you need to use. If you do so, you may want to send them a message as described in the next section so that they know what's happened.

To log another user off:

1. Right-click the Taskbar and choose Task Manager from the context menu to display Task Manager.

2. Click the Users tab. Windows displays the Users page (shown in Figure 3.8).

FIGURE 3.8

From the Users page of Windows Task Manager, you can log another user off the computer.

3. Select the user and click the Logoff button. (Alternatively, right-click the user and choose Log Off from the context menu.) Windows displays the Windows Task Manager dialog box (shown in Figure 3.9) asking if you want to log the selected user off.

4. Click the Yes button. The other user's session is toast—as is any unsaved work they had open.

FIGURE 3.9

You can log another user off the computer—but be aware that doing so will cost them any unsaved work.

Sending a Message to Another User

You can send a message to another user logged in to this computer. Because the other user can't be using the computer at the same time as you, this feature is no use for real-time communication—it's not exactly instant messaging—but it can be useful for making sure a family member or a colleague gets a message the next time they use the computer. (For example, you might ask them not to shut down the computer because you're still using it.) It's also useful for notifying another user that you've had to terminate a program that they were using.

To send a message to another user:

1. Right-click the Taskbar and choose Task Manager from the context menu to display Windows Task Manager.

2. Click the Users tab to display the Users page.

3. Right-click the user and choose Send Message from the context menu. Windows displays the Send Message dialog box (shown in Figure 3.10).

FIGURE 3.10

Use the Send Message dialog box to send a message to another user logged on to this computer.

4. Enter the message title in the Message Title text box and the message in the Message text box.

◆ To start a new line, press Ctrl+Enter. (Pressing the Enter key on its own registers a click on the OK button, sending the message.)

◆ To type a tab, press Ctrl+Tab. (Pressing the Tab key on its own moves the focus to the next control.)

5. Click the OK button to send the message.

The next time the user logs on to Windows, they receive the message as a screen pop. Figure 3.11 shows an example.

FIGURE 3.11

When you send a message, the user receives a screen pop like this when they start using the computer.

Using the Winkey

As mentioned in Chapter 1, Windows XP provides a number of keyboard combinations for the Winkey, the key (or keys) with the Windows logo on the keyboard. If you're comfortable leaving your hands on the keyboard, these combinations are doubly convenient, because not only can you avoid reaching for the mouse but you can also display with a single keystroke a number of windows and dialog boxes that lie several commands deep in the Windows interface.

Table 3.1 lists the Winkey combinations.

TABLE 3.1: WINKEY COMBINATIONS

WINKEY COMBINATION	WHAT IT DOES
Winkey	Toggles the display of the Start menu
Winkey+Break	Displays the System Properties dialog box
Winkey+Tab	Moves the focus to the next button in the Taskbar
Winkey+Shift+Tab	Moves the focus to the previous button in the Taskbar
Winkey+B	Moves the focus to the System Tray
Winkey+D	Displays the Desktop
Winkey+E	Opens an Explorer window showing My Computer
Winkey+F	Opens a Search Results window and activates Search Companion
Winkey+Ctrl+F	Opens a Search Results window, activates Search Companion, and starts a Search for Computer
Winkey+F1	Opens a Help and Support Center window
Winkey+M	Issues a Minimize All Windows command
Winkey+Shift+M	Issues an Undo Minimize All command
Winkey+R	Displays the Run dialog box
Winkey+U	Displays Utility Manager
Winkey+L	Locks the computer

Shutting Down Windows

You can shut down Windows in several ways:

- ◆ By clicking the Turn Off Computer button at the bottom of the default Start menu or by choosing Start ➤ Turn Off Computer from the classic Start menu. See page 6 of the *Essential Skills* section for visual coverage of this method.

- ◆ By clicking the Turn Off Computer button on the Welcome screen, then clicking the Turn Off button on the Turn Off Computer screen (shown in Figure 3.12).

FIGURE 3.12

To turn off the computer, click the Turn Off button on the Turn Off Computer screen.

◆ By choosing Shut Down ➤ Turn Off from Windows Task Manager.

◆ By pressing Alt+F4 with the Desktop active and then clicking the Turn Off button on the Turn Off Computer screen.

From the Turn Off Computer screen, you can also click the Stand By button to make your computer hibernate or the Restart button to restart the computer and Windows. If your computer doesn't support hibernation, the Hibernate button doesn't appear on the Turn Off Computer screen.

TROUBLESHOOTING: POWERING DOWN YOUR COMPUTER WHEN WINDOWS HAS CRASHED

If Windows won't shut down because it has crashed, you'll need to shut it down the hard way. To do so, press the power button on the computer. On ACPI-compliant computers, you may need to hold the power button down for four seconds or more to shut the system down—short presses of the power button may have no effect.

On some computers, a short press of the power button may make Windows display the Turn Off Computer screen so that you can specify whether to hibernate, turn off the computer, or restart it. Under normal circumstances, catching the power signal like this is pretty smart, helping to dissuade users from powering down the computer without exiting Windows first. But if Windows has crashed, you won't be able to do anything from the Turn Off Computer screen.

Up Next

This chapter has discussed how to get started with Windows XP. You now know how to log on and log off, switch from one user to another, "lock" the computer, and (if necessary) log another user off by force. More importantly, you understand the implications of having two or more users logged on to the computer and using programs at the same time, and you know how to see which users are logged on and get a rough idea of which programs each is using.

The next chapter discusses how to customize your Desktop so that you can work comfortably, efficiently, and quickly.

Chapter 4

Customizing Your Desktop

THIS CHAPTER DISCUSSES HOW to get your Desktop into shape so that you can work comfortably, effectively, and enjoyably. Some of these changes are so important to working (or playing) ergonomically in Windows that you should perform them right away. These include choosing the best display resolution, configuring the keyboard and mouse, and setting accessibility options (if you need them).

This chapter covers these topics first. After that, it discusses changes that you don't *need* to implement right away, but that you may well want to make before too long. These changes include choosing a screen saver, changing your Desktop background, customizing the Start menu, creating custom toolbars, and so on.

This chapter covers the following topics:

- Configuring your display and monitor for best viewing
- Configuring the keyboard and mouse
- Choosing accessibility options
- Choosing a screen saver
- Applying themes and backgrounds
- Using Desktop Web pages
- Changing the appearance of the Desktop
- Choosing system sounds
- Configuring the Start menu and Taskbar
- Using the Desktop toolbars

NOTE   *Some of the topics covered in this chapter are considered "advanced" by some users and many other books. But in order to use Windows most effectively, you should know about them right away—so this book presents them now. If you find you don't need them at the moment, skip over them for the time being.*

Choosing the Best Display Resolution

First, set the best display resolution for you and your computer. If you're squinting at the screen, or if it's flickering at you, or if the display slops over the edges of the monitor, you won't be productive or happy.

Choosing the best display resolution involves three things: your eyesight, your monitor, and your graphics card. The first is up to you and your optometrist. The second and third are discussed below.

Your Monitor

As you'll know from being bombarded with computer ads, there are two widely used types of computer monitors: cathode-ray tube (CRT) monitors, which tend to be bulky and heavy but affordable, and liquid crystal display (LCD) panels, which tend to be thin and light in form but heavy on the wallet.

Most CRTs are capable of multiple resolutions. For example, most modern 15-inch monitors can handle 640×480 resolution, 800×600 resolution, and 1024×768 resolution. Most 17-inch monitors can handle these and 1280×1024 resolution as well. Most 19-inch monitors can also manage 1600×1200 resolution, and larger monitors (such as 20-inch, 21-inch, 22-inch, and 24-inch) can handle resolutions up to 2048×1536—with the right graphics card, of course.

Most LCD panels and some other monitors are designed to deliver optimal quality at only one resolution and only one refresh rate. Some LCD panels will display lesser resolutions as well as their optimum resolution, but the result is jagged and awkward to look at. A few LCD panels—usually on laptops—can display a *higher* resolution than their normal resolution. This can be useful for special effects, but it means that you can't see all of the screen at once, so you have to scroll to see the southern and eastern regions.

Table 4.1 lists all the resolutions you're likely to see on modern monitors, together with some unusual ones.

TABLE 4.1: STANDARD AND NONSTANDARD SCREEN RESOLUTIONS

RESOLUTION (PIXELS)	NAME	ABBREVIATION	COMMENTS
640×480	Video Graphics Array	VGA	Standard resolution
800×600	Super VGA	SVGA	Standard resolution
1024×480	—	—	Super-wide resolution (laptop LCDs)
1024×768	Extended Graphics Array	XGA	Standard resolution
1152×864	—	—	Standard resolution
1280×1024	—	—	Standard resolution
1400×1050	Ultra XGA	UXGA	Used almost exclusively on Dell laptops
1600×1024	—	—	Super-wide resolution (desktop LCDs)
1600×1200	—	—	Standard resolution
1792×1344	—	—	Standard resolution
1800×1440	—	—	Standard resolution
2048×1536	—	—	Standard resolution

Most CRTs support a variety of refresh rates, while most LCD panels support only one or two. (The *refresh rate* is the frequency with which the graphics card redraws the picture on the monitor. More details in a few pages' time.)

Your Graphics Card

The graphics card in your computer sends information to the monitor. The resolutions and refresh rates that the graphics card supports depend on the amount of video memory it contains.

Choosing Video Settings

To choose video settings, you use the Settings page of the Display Properties dialog box (shown in Figure 4.1): Right-click the Desktop and choose Properties from the context menu. Windows displays the Display Properties dialog box. Then click the Settings tab. Windows displays the Settings page.

FIGURE 4.1

On the Settings page of the Display Properties dialog box, you can specify the screen resolution and the number of colors Windows uses.

NOTE   *Windows XP supports multiple monitors—you can use up to 10 monitors on a single computer so that you can see a larger amount of information at once. See Chapter 14 for coverage of this feature.*

CHANGING THE SCREEN RESOLUTION

See pages 39–40 of the *Essential Skills* section for a visual guide to changing the screen resolution.

To change the amount of information displayed on the screen, you change the *screen resolution*. The screen resolution affects the number of pixels Windows displays on the screen. The more pixels displayed, the more you can see—but the smaller everything on-screen appears. (*Pixel* is short for *picture element* and means one of the elements that make up the display you see on your screen.)

For example, say you're working in a word processing document. At 640×480 resolution, you might see about 500 words of average length in the document window (with some of the screen taken up by the Taskbar, the program's menu bars and toolbars, and so on). At 800×600 resolution, you might see 850 words—not twice as much, but more than one-and-a-half times as much. At

1024×768 resolution, you might see about 1600 words—almost twice as much again. (This example is a little unfair in that the menu bar, toolbars, and the Taskbar take up correspondingly more space at the lower resolution, but it does illustrate roughly what you may see in practice.) Likewise, if you were working with a large spreadsheet, you'd be able to see much more of it on-screen at once by using a higher resolution.

As you can imagine, the higher resolutions let you see more on-screen at the same time, but everything displayed is smaller. In the example with the word processing document, you might need to zoom the display so that you could read the words comfortably at the higher resolution.

WARNING *For some unknown reason, all users of the computer must use the same Desktop resolution. The Welcome screen also uses this resolution. If some of your users see like hawks and others like field mice, try to find a compromise resolution that won't make anyone suffer unduly. Any user can change the resolution, but in doing so, they change it for all other users as well.*

To change the screen resolution, drag the slider in the Screen Resolution group box on the Settings page of the Display Properties dialog box to the left or right. The readout under the slider shows the next available resolution, and the graphic at the top of the dialog box shows an approximation of how your Desktop and a window will look at that resolution.

NOTE *Which resolutions are available depends on your graphics card and your monitor—and whether Windows has identified them correctly. (If it hasn't, see the sections "Changing the Video Driver" and "Changing the Monitor Type" in Chapter 14.)*

To apply the screen resolution you chose, click the Apply button. If you haven't used this resolution before, Windows displays the Monitor Settings dialog box (shown in Figure 4.2). If you can see the Monitor Settings dialog box, all is probably well. Click the Yes button to apply the screen resolution. (If you have used this resolution before, Windows applies it without displaying the Monitor Settings dialog box.)

FIGURE 4.2

If you can see this Monitor Settings dialog box clearly, the screen resolution probably works.

If your display becomes garbled or faded, or if you don't like what you see, either click the No button in the Monitor Settings dialog box or wait the 15 seconds until Windows restores your previous video settings.

CHANGING THE NUMBER OF COLORS

You can also change the number of colors that Windows uses for the display. Some LCD displays are limited in the number of colors they can display, maxing out at 65,536 colors (High Color), but most CRTs can display the full range of colors—16 million or 24 million, depending on your graphics card.

As you'd expect, the more colors Windows uses, the more lifelike, vibrant, and generally appealing the display looks. But the more colors used, the more video memory is needed on the graphics card, and the slower performance tends to be.

For performance' sake, it's not a good idea to ratchet the colors up as far as they can go if you're spending most of your time working with documents, spreadsheets, and e-mail, which all look more or less as good in 256 colors as they do at True Color. Even if you are working with files that need True Color—for example, if you're retouching digital photographs—you'll get better performance at 24-bit True Color than at 32-bit True Color, though in theory 32-bit True Color offers a better representation of every color.

By default, the Windows XP installation routine sets your system to use the highest color quality that your monitor and graphics card support at a reasonable refresh rate. (If you upgrade your installation of Windows, or if you use the Files and Settings Transfer Wizard to transfer your old settings, you should end up with the same color quality as you were using before.) If your graphics performance isn't satisfactory, use the Color Quality drop-down list on the Settings page of the Display Properties dialog box to specify a lower color quality. That should improve graphics performance.

Color settings tend to use confusing terms: either number of colors (from 16 colors up to 16 million or more), number of color bits (16-bit color, 24-bit color), or terms describing the number of colors used (High Color, True Color). Table 4.2 shows you what the terms mean.

TABLE 4.2: NUMBER OF COLORS, COLOR BITS, AND DESCRIPTIVE TERMS

NUMBER OF COLORS	COLOR BITS	DESCRIPTIVE TERM
16	4-bit	—
256	8-bit	—
65,536	16-bit	High Color
16,777,216	24-bit	True Color (24-bit)
4,294,967,296	32-bit	True Color (32-bit)

EXPERT KNOWLEDGE: HOW MUCH VIDEO MEMORY DO YOU NEED?

The number of colors and resolution your graphics card can display depends on the amount of memory it contains. Basically, the more memory the graphics card has, the higher the resolution and the higher the number of colors it should be able to display—up to a point.

This is true only up to a point because there's a limit to the number of colors used in conventional computing (4 billion colors, 32-bit color) and to the resolution that off-the-shelf monitors support (2048×1536 resolution is about the maximum widely used resolution).

In theory, calculating how much video memory you need is straightforward. To get the amount of video memory, you multiply the number of color bits per pixel by the number of pixels on the screen, then divide the result by 8 to get the number of bytes. For example, say you want 24-bit color at 800×600 resolution.

Continued on next page

EXPERT KNOWLEDGE: HOW MUCH VIDEO MEMORY DO YOU NEED? *(continued)*

Okay: 800×600 means 480,000 pixels on the screen. Multiplying 480,000×24 gives 11,520,000 bits. Divide that by 8 and you get 1,440,000 bytes, or a little under 1.4MB of video memory. Given that normal amounts of video memory for current video cards are 4MB, 8MB, 16MB, 32MB, and 64MB, and that older cards have 256KB, 512KB, 1MB, and 2MB sizes as well, you'd need a 2MB video card or better to display 24-bit color at 800×600 resolution.

Table 4.3 (which appears after this sidebar) shows the effective amount of memory required to display the color depths at the most widely used resolutions. In this table, the amounts of memory are rounded up to the nearest standard amount of video memory. For example, 1280×1024 resolution at 256 colors requires around 1.25MB of memory—but the nearest larger standard video size is 2MB, so the table lists that.

That calculation seems easy enough, doesn't it? But it's no longer that simple. Here's the problem: In 2001, entry-level video cards come with 8MB or 16MB of video memory. Serious video cards come with 32MB or 64MB. Gear-head video cards have 128MB.

Some of those 8MB cards can manage 1600×1200 resolution, just as the table says they should be able to—but many of them can't. Similarly, to get those really high resolutions—1800×1440 and 2048×1536—you typically need a graphics card with 64MB RAM, not one with the 16MB that the calculation gives you.

What's going on here?

Basically, only some of the RAM on the high-end graphics card is dedicated to creating the bitmap that's shunted off to be displayed on your monitor. The rest of the RAM is trying to display multiple images more quickly (for example, when you're watching a video or playing Quake) and smooth out unevenness in the transfer of information from one component to another. The results of these endeavors are mostly good, but it means that in order to find out how much memory you need on a graphics card to support a certain resolution and color depth, you need to consult the box (or preferably, the specifications) for each graphics card you're considering rather than just performing the above calculation.

More positively, if you use only a modest resolution (say, 1024×768) on your monitor, or if you have a graphics card with 32MB of RAM or more, you seldom need to worry about video memory, because you've probably got enough already.

TABLE 4.3: VIDEO MEMORY REQUIRED TO DISPLAY COLORS AND RESOLUTIONS

COLORS	BITS	640×480	800×600	1024×768	1152×864	1280×1024	1600×1200	1800×1440	2048×1536
16	4	256KB	256KB	512KB	512KB	1MB	1MB	2MB	2MB
256	8	512KB	512KB	1MB	1MB	2MB	2MB	4MB	4MB
65,536	16	1MB	1MB	2MB	2MB	4MB	4MB	8MB	8MB
16,777,216	24	1MB	2MB	4MB	4MB	4MB	8MB	8MB	16MB
4,294,967,296	32	2MB	2MB	4MB	4MB	8MB	8MB	16MB	16MB

CHANGING THE REFRESH RATE

If your screen flickers noticeably, try adjusting the *refresh rate*—the number of times per second that the video card sends a full screen of information to the monitor. The refresh rate is measured in hertz (Hz)—cycles per second, not the car-rental agency.

NOTE   *Technically, this is the vertical refresh rate, as opposed to the horizontal refresh rate. Just about the only time you need to worry about the horizontal refresh rate of your monitor is when you're setting an X Windows configuration in Linux. So most of the time people just say "refresh rate" without specifying the dimension involved.*

Flicker is produced by the video card redrawing the image on the monitor slowly enough for you to be able to notice. As a result, your eyes have to work a bit harder to decode what they're seeing, which tends to lead to eye strain and headaches, particularly if you don't take those ergonomically recommended breaks from staring at the screen.

Flicker shows more on large monitors than small monitors. This is not just because there's more of the screen to look at, but also because most people notice flicker more out of the corner of their eye than straight on, and you see more of a larger screen in your peripheral vision.

Some people are much more sensitive to flicker than others. At 60Hz—60 cycles per second—most people find flicker very noticeable on cathode-ray tube (CRT) monitors. At 70Hz, many people don't see it. By 75Hz, things look good to most people. At 85Hz, few people can detect flicker. Above that, you're entering the hypochondriac zone—though if your hardware supports a very high refresh rate, there's no reason why you shouldn't use it.

LCD screens flicker far less than CRTs, so they don't need such high refresh rates. Many LCD screens are designed for optimal performance at a refresh rate of 60Hz, and produce a beautifully stable picture at this rate, which would produce very pronounced flicker on a CRT. Other LCDs support refresh rates of 72Hz or 75Hz. Most LCDs don't support refresh rates faster than 75Hz.

Which refresh rates are available to you depends on your graphics card and your monitor. As you'd imagine, both the card and the monitor need to support a refresh rate for you to be able to use it.

To set the refresh rate, take the following steps:

1. Click the Advanced button on the Settings page of the Display Properties dialog box. Windows displays the Monitor and Graphics Card dialog box.

2. Click the Monitor tab. Windows displays the Monitor page (shown in Figure 4.3).

3. In the Screen Refresh Rate drop-down list, choose one of the settings. If you've configured Windows correctly for your hardware, you should be safe choosing the fastest refresh rate listed.

4. Click the Apply button. If you haven't used this refresh rate before, Windows displays a Monitor Settings dialog box asking you whether you want to keep the settings. (If you have used this refresh rate, Windows simply applies the settings.)

5. If you click the Yes button, Windows keeps the settings. If you click the No button, or if you wait 15 seconds, Windows reapplies your previous settings.

FIGURE 4.3

Set the refresh rate
on the Monitor page
of the Monitor and
Graphics Card dia-
log box.

As you can see in Figure 4.3, the Monitor Settings group box on the Monitor page also contains
the Hide Modes That This Monitor Cannot Display check box, which is selected by default. You *can*
clear this check box to force Windows to list in the Screen Refresh Rate drop-down list refresh rates
that Windows thinks your monitor doesn't support, and you *can* apply these refresh rates—but doing
so is usually a really bad idea, because you can permanently damage a monitor by setting a refresh
rate higher than it supports. The only reason to try this is if you are unable (for whatever reason) to
get Windows to recognize your monitor correctly and you need to trick Windows into applying a
refresh rate that you know from the monitor's documentation is supported.

NOTE   *If your screen settings still aren't satisfactory, you may need to take further steps, such as changing hardware
acceleration, changing the video driver, or changing Windows' misperception of which monitor you're using. Turn to Chapter 14 for details on how to take these (and other) actions.*

Adjusting Your Monitor if Necessary

Once you've settled on a display resolution, color depth, and frequency, adjust your monitor to maximize the image area so that you're seeing the whole image as large as possible. (It's amazing how many
people leave an inchwide band of unused space at each edge of the monitor and then complain that
they have to peer closely at the image.)

Monitor controls vary, but almost all monitors let you adjust the height, width, and vertical and
horizontal positions of the image. Open a program and maximize its window so that you can clearly
see where the edges of the screen are. Then use the monitor controls to make your Windows Desktop at your chosen resolution fill the display area of your monitor.

Configuring the Keyboard and Mouse

Your next order of business should be to configure the keyboard and mouse (or other pointing device;
for simplicity, this section uses the word *mouse*). Both these input devices are vital to getting information into and out of your computer, and each can be a source of great discomfort if you let it.

TIP   If configuring the keyboard and mouse don't give you the control you need, try the accessibility options. "Choosing Accessibility Options," later in this chapter, discusses these options.

Configuring the Keyboard

Windows offers three keyboard configuration options:

♦ The *repeat delay* (the length of time that Windows waits before repeating a key when you hold it down)

♦ The *repeat rate* (the speed with which a key repeats its character once the repeat delay is over)

♦ The rate at which the cursor blinks

To configure your keyboard, follow these steps:

1. Choose Start ➤ Control Panel. Windows displays Control Panel.

2. Click the Printers and Other Hardware link. Windows displays the Printers and Other Hardware screen.

3. Click the Keyboard link. Windows displays the Keyboard Properties dialog box.

4. On the Speed page (shown in Figure 4.4) of the Keyboard Properties dialog box, choose settings by adjusting the Repeat Delay slider, the Repeat Rate slider, and the Cursor Blink Rate slider. Use the Click Here and Hold Down a Key to Test Repeat Rate text box for testing your repeat rate.

FIGURE 4.4

You can adjust the repeat rate, repeat delay, and the cursor blink rate of your keyboard on the Speed page of the Keyboard Properties dialog box.

5. Click the OK button. Windows closes the Keyboard Properties dialog box.

NOTE   The Hardware page of the Keyboard Properties dialog box lets you see which type of keyboard Windows thinks you're using. From here, you can access the Properties dialog box for this type of keyboard, so that you can change the driver that it's using.

Configuring the Mouse

To configure your mouse, follow these steps:

1. Choose Start ➤ Control Panel. Windows displays Control Panel.

2. Click the Printers and Other Hardware link. Windows displays the Printers and Other Hardware screen.

3. Click the Mouse link. Windows displays the Mouse Properties dialog box.

NOTE   *The Mouse Properties dialog box in these figures has the standard controls. If your mouse has custom software, you may see other pages of options in the Mouse Properties dialog box.*

4. The Buttons page (shown in Figure 4.5) offers these options:

Switch Primary and Secondary Buttons check box   Select this check box if you want to swap the functions of the primary and secondary mouse buttons. This setting is most useful for changing a mouse from right-hand configuration to left-hand configuration.

Double-Click Speed slider   Drag this slider toward its Fast end or its Slow end to set the double-click speed of your mouse. Double-click in the Test Area box to see if Windows is registering your double-clicks properly. When the area registers a double-click, the folder opens; when it registers another, the folder closes.

Turn on ClickLock check box   Select this check box to turn on the ClickLock feature, which lets you drag without holding down the mouse button all the time. (You click the mouse button again to release the locked item after dragging it.) ClickLock can be useful if you get the hang of it, but it can be an annoyance if you find yourself setting the lock unintentionally when clicking. If you turn ClickLock on, click the Settings button and use the resulting Settings for ClickLock dialog box to tune the lock setting.

FIGURE 4.5

Choose button options on the Buttons page of the Mouse Properties dialog box.

5. If you want to use different pointers for your mouse, click the Pointers tab. Windows displays the Pointers page (shown in Figure 4.6). This page offers a variety of mouse pointer schemes, some of them fun (for example, the Dinosaur scheme) and others more useful (such as the various large, extra large, and inverted schemes, which can make the mouse pointers much easier to see).

- ◆ In the Scheme drop-down list, select the scheme you want to use.

- ◆ To customize the scheme, select a pointer in the Customize list box. Then click the Browse button, use the resulting Browse dialog box to specify the pointer you want to use instead, and click the Open button. (Windows displays the `\Windows\Cursors\` folder in the Browse dialog box, but you can navigate to other folders as necessary.) You can also click the Use Default button to use the standard Windows pointer in place of the selected pointer.

- ◆ To turn off pointer shadows, clear the Enable Pointer Shadow check box. (It's selected by default.)

- ◆ To save your customized scheme, click the Save As button, enter the name for the scheme in the Save Scheme dialog box, and click the OK button. Custom pointer schemes are stored in the Registry (in the `HKEY_CURRENT_USER` key) and are not available to other users.

FIGURE 4.6

Choose a pointer scheme—or create a custom pointer scheme—on the Pointers page of the Mouse Properties dialog box.

6. Click the Pointer Options tab to display the Pointer Options page (shown in Figure 4.7). This page offers the following options:

Motion group box Drag the slider toward its Slow end or its Fast end to adjust the speed at which the pointer moves. By default, the Enhance Pointer Precision check box is selected. This feature makes the mouse pointer decelerate more quickly on-screen as you stop moving the mouse. If you want to try more gradual deceleration, clear this check box.

NOTE   *Unlike in most dialog boxes, Windows applies the settings on the Pointer Options page of the Mouse Properties dialog box immediately, so you can see them in action without needing to click the Apply button.*

Automatically Move Pointer to the Default Button in a Dialog Box check box   Select this check box if you want Windows to automatically position the mouse pointer over the default button in each dialog box you display. This automatic movement can save you time, but it can also be confusing, because once a dialog box is displayed, the mouse pointer is no longer where you left it.

Display Pointer Trails check box and slider   Select this check box if you want the mouse pointer to display a contrasting trail of phantom pointers when you move it. This option is most useful for dual-scan LCD screens, on which it can be hard to discern the mouse pointer. If you turn this feature on, adjust the slider to give you the length of pointer trails that suits you.

Hide Pointer while Typing check box   Select this check box if you want Windows to hide the mouse pointer when you're typing. (In some programs, Windows hides the pointer when you're typing even if this check box isn't selected.)

Show Location of Pointer when I Press the Ctrl Key check box   Select this check box if you want to be able to make Windows identify the mouse key by zooming in a circle on it when you press the Ctrl key. This feature is useful for LCD screens on which the mouse pointer tends to disappear.

FIGURE 4.7

On the Pointer Options page of the Mouse Properties dialog box, you can change the speed and the behavior of the mouse pointer.

EXPERT KNOWLEDGE: CHOOSING ADVANCED SETTINGS FOR YOUR MOUSE

Windows offers several advanced settings for configuring your mouse. To access these settings, take the following steps:

1. Display the Mouse Properties dialog box as discussed in the previous section.

2. Click the Hardware tab. Windows displays the Hardware page.

3. Click the Properties button. Windows displays the *Mouse Type* Mouse Properties dialog box. For example, the illustration below shows the Mouse Properties dialog box for a PS/2 Compatible mouse.

4. Click the Advanced Settings tab. Windows displays the Advanced Settings page (shown in the illustration).

5. Choose advanced settings for the mouse:

   Sample Rate text box The value in this text box specifies how often Windows checks the position of the mouse. To increase mouse sensitivity, increase this value; to decrease sensitivity, decrease the value.

   Wheel Detection drop-down list This drop-down list controls whether Windows checks your mouse for a mouse wheel (or similar rotating button for scrolling). Select the Detection Disabled item if you don't want to use a mouse wheel. Select the Assume Wheel Is Present item if you don't want Windows to check whether the mouse has a wheel. Select the Look for Wheel item if you want Windows to determine whether the mouse has a wheel. If selecting the Look for Wheel item disables a mouse that has a wheel, Microsoft suggests selecting the Assume Wheel Is Present item instead.

   Input Buffer Length text box The value in this text box specifies the number of packets of information to store in the input buffer for your mouse's location. Increase this number if your mouse is behaving erratically.

   Fast Initialization check box This check box controls whether Windows uses fast initialization for the mouse. *Fast initialization* reduces Windows' start-up time, but it can make the mouse behave erratically—for example, the mouse pointer may move itself, or the mouse may register clicks you haven't generated. If your mouse does this, clear this check box.

6. Click the OK button. Windows closes the Mouse Properties dialog box and returns you to the Hardware page of the Mouse Properties dialog box.

Choosing Accessibility Options

For users with disabilities, Windows offers a good selection of accessibility options.

The easiest way to get started with the accessibility options is to run the Accessibility Wizard (Start ➤ All Programs ➤ Accessories ➤ Accessibility ➤ Accessibility Wizard). The Accessibility Wizard walks you through the process of configuring most of these options by asking questions about which accessibility areas you need help with and choosing options accordingly.

To adjust these options, you can run the Accessibility Wizard again. Alternatively, you can use the Accessibility Options dialog box, as discussed in the next section. To display the Accessibility Options dialog box, choose Start ➤ Control Panel, click the Accessibility Options link to access the Accessibility Options screen, and then click the Accessibility Options link (yes, another one).

Keyboard Accessibility Options

This section discusses the options that Windows provides to make the keyboard more accessible: keyboard accessibility options, On-Screen Keyboard, and the option of attaching a SerialKey device.

STICKYKEYS, FILTERKEYS, TOGGLEKEYS, AND EXTRA KEYBOARD HELP

Windows offers the following keyboard accessibility options on the Keyboard page of the Accessibility Options dialog box (shown in Figure 4.8):

StickyKeys This feature lets you enter keyboard combinations involving the Shift, Ctrl, or Alt keys one key at a time rather than needing to hold down the modifier key while you press subsequent keys.

FilterKeys This feature lets you tell Windows to ignore either repeated keystrokes (such as those caused by holding down a key for longer than a single keypress) or quick keystrokes (such as those caused by accidentally blipping a key while trying to press another key).

ToggleKeys This feature makes Windows sound a tone when you press the Caps Lock key, the Num Lock key, or the Scroll Lock key.

Show Extra Keyboard Help in Programs check box This feature makes programs show any extra help they contain about using the keyboard.

FIGURE 4.8

The Keyboard page of the Accessibility Options dialog box offers StickyKeys, FilterKeys, Toggle-Keys, and extra keyboard help.

ON-SCREEN KEYBOARD

On-Screen Keyboard displays a keyboard in a window on-screen so that you can enter keyboard commands with a mouse or other pointing device. To start On-Screen Keyboard, choose Start ➤ All Programs ➤ Accessories ➤ Accessibility ➤ On-Screen Keyboard.

Key (no pun intended) options for On-Screen Keyboard include:

◆ To make the keyboard click when you press a key, choose Settings ➤ Use Click Sound. (The click sound makes it easier to notice when you've misclicked or clicked twice.)

◆ To make the keyboard enter a key when you hover the pointer over it (so that you don't need to click), choose Settings ➤ Typing Mode. In the resulting Typing Mode dialog box, select the Hover to Select option button and specify the reaction time in the Minimum Time to Hover text box. Click the OK button.

◆ To display a standard keyboard rather than an enhanced keyboard, or to use a block layout rather than the regular offset layout, or to use a 102-key or 106-key keyboard instead of a 101-key keyboard, choose the appropriate command from the Keyboard menu.

ATTACHING A SERIALKEY DEVICE

If you can't (or won't) use a standard keyboard, you can attach a SerialKey device or other augmentative communication device to your computer instead. To use the SerialKey device, select the Use Serial Keys check box on the General page of the Accessibility Options dialog box. Then click the Settings button. Windows displays the Settings for SerialKeys dialog box. Specify the serial port and baud rate to use, then click the OK button.

Mouse Accessibility Options

Apart from the control over the mouse that the Mouse Properties dialog box offers, Windows provides a feature called MouseKeys that lets you control the mouse pointer by using your keyboard's numeric keys.

To use MouseKeys, select the Use MouseKeys check box on the Mouse page of the Accessibility Options dialog box. Then click the Settings button and choose appropriate settings in the Settings for MouseKeys dialog box. You can change the top speed and acceleration of the mouse pointer, and specify whether to use the Ctrl key to speed up the pointer's movement and the Shift key to slow it down. Click the OK button to make Windows close the Settings for MouseKeys dialog box, and then click the Apply button in the Accessibility Options dialog box.

Display Accessibility Options

In addition to the assorted color schemes and font sizes that you can set in the Display Properties dialog box, Windows provides a Magnifier feature and a High Contrast display option for improving display accessibility. You can also change the blink rate and the width of the cursor so that it's easier to see.

MAGNIFIER

Magnifier displays a magnified version of the section of the screen around the mouse pointer, the keyboard focus, or the section of text you're editing. This section appears in a panel at the top of the screen. You can resize this panel so that it takes up as much as half of the screen.

Start Magnifier by choosing Start ➢ All Programs ➢ Accessories ➢ Accessibility ➢ Magnifier, then choose settings in the Magnifier Settings window. You can set a magnification level from 1 (normal size) to 9; specify which items to track (the mouse cursor, the keyboard focus, and text editing); choose to invert the colors displayed for the magnified panel; choose to start Magnifier minimized; and choose whether to show Magnifier. Minimize the Magnifier Settings window to get it out of your way.

To stop using Magnifier, click the Exit button in the Magnifier Settings window.

TIP   If Magnifier doesn't give you the flexibility you need, check the list of magnification utilities for Windows at www.microsoft.com/enable.

HIGH CONTRAST

The High Contrast display option makes Windows use fonts and colors that are designed to be easy to read (as opposed to, say, looking good). To use this option, select the Use High Contrast check box on the Display page of the Accessibility Options dialog box (shown in Figure 4.9). Then click the Settings button to display the Settings for High Contrast dialog box and select the shortcut to use for toggling high contrast on and off and the color scheme to use.

FIGURE 4.9

On the Display page of the Accessibility Options dialog box, you can apply a high-contrast color scheme to Windows and change the blink rate and width of the cursor to make it more visible.

CHANGING THE BLINK RATE AND CURSOR WIDTH

If you find the normal Windows cursor hard to see, use the Width slider in the Cursor Options group box on the Display page of the Accessibility Options dialog box to adjust the cursor's width and the Blink Rate slider to change its blink rate.

Sound Accessibility Options

Windows offers sound accessibility options that fall into two categories: visual warnings for cues normally indicated by sound, for those with hearing impairments; and reading on-screen text aloud, for those with vision impairments.

VISUAL WARNINGS: SOUNDSENTRY AND SHOWSOUNDS

The SoundSentry option displays visual warnings to indicate when Windows makes a sound. To use SoundSentry, select the Use SoundSentry check box on the Sound page of the Accessibility Options dialog box. Click the Settings button to display the Settings for SoundSentry dialog box. Choose the visual warning you want: flashing the active caption bar, flashing the active window, or flashing the Desktop.

The ShowSounds option causes programs to display captions when they make sounds or convey information via spoken words. To use ShowSounds, select the Use ShowSounds check box on the Sound page of the Accessibility Options dialog box.

READING ALOUD: NARRATOR

The Narrator program can read aloud a variety of things from the screen: menu commands, dialog box controls, and characters you type. The voice is synthesized, and its phrasing and cadence make it hard to understand. It's usable in a pinch, but for sustained use you may want to check www.microsoft.com/enable for more powerful alternatives.

Start Narrator by choosing Start ➤ All Programs ➤ Accessories ➤ Accessibility ➤ Narrator. In the Narrator window, select the check boxes for the items you want Narrator to read. Three of the options—Read Typed Characters, Move Mouse Pointer to the Active Item, and Start Narrator Minimized—are self-explanatory. The Announce Events on Screen check box controls whether Narrator announces the program window you're working in and any dialog box on-screen and the controls it contains (or the control you're working with).

To adjust the voice used and the pitch, speed, and volume, click the Voice button and use the options in the Voice Settings dialog box.

To stop using Narrator, select the Exit button in the Narrator window and choose the Yes button in the Exit Narrator dialog box that tries to stop you.

Setting General Accessibility Options

The General page of the Accessibility Options dialog box contains additional controls for specifying accessibility options:

Automatic Reset group box   To turn off accessibility features automatically after a time, select the Use the Turn Off Accessibility Features after Idle for *NN* Minutes check box and specify the period of time in the text box.

Notification group box   Leave the Give Warning Message when Turning a Feature Off check box and the Make a Sound when Turning a Feature On or Off check box selected (as they are by default) if you want Windows to warn you when turning a feature off or on.

SerialKey Devices group box   Use these controls (as discussed earlier in this chapter) to set up SerialKey devices.

Administrative Options group box   Select the Apply All Settings to Logon Desktop check box if you want to use the accessibility settings set in the Accessibility Options dialog box each time the current user logs in. Select the Apply All Settings to Defaults for New Users check box if you want to apply these settings to each new user created on this computer. (Normally, it's best to apply the accessibility settings only when a user specifically needs them.)

Using Utility Manager to Start Magnifier, Narrator, and On-Screen Keyboard Automatically

To specify when Windows runs Magnifier, Narrator, and On-Screen Keyboard, use Utility Manager (shown in Figure 4.10). Press Winkey+U to start Utility Manager. In the list box, select the entry for Magnifier, Narrator, or On-Screen Keyboard. Then select the Start Automatically when I Log In check box, the Start Automatically when I Lock My Desktop check box (if it's available), and/or the Start Automatically when Utility Manager Starts check box as appropriate. (You can also start and stop the selected utility by using the Start button and Stop button.)

FIGURE 4.10

Use Utility Manager to specify when to run Magnifier, Narrator, and On-Screen Keyboard.

The changes discussed so far in this chapter—display and monitor settings; keyboard and mouse settings; and accessibility settings—are the most vital changes to make. The next changes are less crucial, but can make Windows easier to look at and easier to use.

Choosing a Screen Saver

A *screen saver* is a program that blanks out your monitor or displays a moving pattern over it when you haven't used the keyboard or mouse for a specified period of time. Windows comes with a variety of screen savers built in. You can also buy commercial screen savers or download them for free from philanthropists, egomaniacs, and advertisers.

Screen savers used to be important in the 1970s and 1980s, because they would save your screen—literally. In those days, text-based displays would burn into the phosphors of the monitor, creating a ghost image that then overlaid whatever else was being displayed. These days, most monitors aren't susceptible to phosphor burn-in, and in any case, graphical displays pose fewer problems with burn-in than text-based displays.

Nowadays, there are only two reasons to use a screen saver:

◆ First, to hide your work (or play) from prying eyes when you've left your computer idle for more than a certain length of time. When you use a screen saver to hide your work, apply a password to the screen saver so that only you can turn off the screen saver.

◆ Second, to have your monitor display something pretty or intriguing to amuse you when you're not actively using the computer. Most screen savers, true to their phosphor-protecting heritage, display moving patterns that can be entertaining to look at, but some display trivia, quizzes, or educational flashcards. Windows XP includes a screen saver called My Pictures Slideshow that displays the pictures in a designated folder one by one. This screen saver seems destined to become a living-room favorite, as it lets you turn the unused computer into a slide show.

EXPERT KNOWLEDGE: AVOID SCREEN SAVERS IF POSSIBLE

Screen savers are notorious for causing trouble, some through malice and some through incompetence.

On the malice front: Free, downloadable screen savers are a favorite tool of the writers of viruses and malware. When they create a screen saver of something diverting (say, a dog relieving itself on the steps of a government office) or an attractive female celebrity (say, Cox Arquette, Kournikova, or Klum), the writer can be almost certain of achieving widespread distribution. They can then use the screen saver as a Trojan horse to get a virus onto the downloader's system, and the virus is free to execute at a time of the writer's choosing.

On the incompetence front: Because they kick in and interrupt normal operations on the computer, screen savers can cause software conflicts and crashes. You can—actually, make that *should be able to*—assume that the screen savers that Microsoft supplies with Windows are robust and safe, but *any* screen saver might destabilize your system.

To avoid security threats, never download a third-party screen saver, however attractive it may seem.

To apply a screen saver, follow these steps:

1. Right-click the Desktop and choose Properties from the context menu. Windows displays the Display Properties dialog box.

2. Click the Screen Saver tab. Windows displays the Screen Saver page (shown in Figure 4.11).

FIGURE 4.11

Use the Screen Saver page of the Display Properties dialog box to configure a screen saver.

3. In the Screen Saver drop-down list, select the screen saver to use.

   ◆ To see how a screen saver looks full screen, click the Preview button. Windows displays the screen saver in all its glory. Move the mouse or press any key on the keyboard to stop the preview.

4. To choose settings for the screen saver, click the Settings button and work in the resulting Settings dialog box.

◆ Which settings are available depends on the type of screen saver you chose. Some screen savers have no settings; others have a dozen or more.

◆ Figure 4.12 shows the My Pictures Screen Saver Options dialog box, which offers a variety of settings for customizing the slide show, including the following: how frequently the pictures should change, how much of the screen the pictures should occupy, which pictures to use, and whether to use transition effects between pictures. (Tip: Turn off the transition effects unless you're a fan of overdone PowerPoint presentations.) See pages 41–42 of the *Essential Skills* section for a visual guide to setting up the My Pictures screen saver.

◆ Use the Preview button again after choosing settings to see if the settings you chose meet your liking.

FIGURE 4.12

Use the Options dialog box, Settings dialog box, or Setup dialog box for the screen saver to configure it. For example, in the My Pictures Screen Saver Options dialog box, you can specify settings including the size of the pictures, how frequently Windows should change the picture, and whether to use transition effects.

5. In the Wait text box, enter the number of minutes of inactivity that you want before the screen saver kicks in.

6. If your computer is using the Welcome screen, and you want Windows to display the Welcome screen when a user reactivates the computer after the screen saver has been running, select the On Resume, Display Welcome Screen check box. If you're not using the Welcome screen, Windows offers a different option: To protect the screen saver with your logon password, select the On Resume, Password Protect check box.

7. Click the Apply button. Windows applies your screen saver preferences.

NOTE *From the Screen Saver page of the Display Properties dialog box, you can click the Power button in the Monitor Power group box to display the Power Options Properties dialog box. Power management is an involved topic and is discussed in Chapter 14.*

Applying a Theme

A *theme* is a coordinated look for various different aspects of the Windows screen: the Desktop background, colors, font styles and sizes, window sizes, sound events, mouse pointers, icons, and even the screen saver. By applying a different theme, you can change the way Windows looks.

To apply a theme, take the following steps:

1. Right-click the Desktop and choose Properties from the context menu. Windows displays the Display Properties dialog box with the Themes page (shown in Figure 4.13) foremost.

FIGURE 4.13

Use the Themes page of the Display Properties dialog box to apply themes to Windows.

2. In the Theme drop-down list, select the theme to apply. Watch the Sample box to see how the different themes look.

   ◆ To select a theme that doesn't appear in the Theme drop-down list, select the Browse item. Windows displays the Open Theme dialog box. Navigate to and select the file containing the theme, then click the Open button.

3. Click the Apply button. Windows applies the theme.

TIP   To create a custom theme, select a theme to start with, and modify it to suit your taste. Then use the Save As button on the Themes page of the Display Properties dialog box, and the resulting Save As dialog box, to save the theme in your My Documents folder. Windows then makes the theme available in the Theme drop-down list, from which you can apply it as you would any other theme.

Changing the Background

You can change the background pattern or image on your Desktop by using the Desktop page of the Display Properties dialog box (shown in Figure 4.14). If you like the default background, there's no obligation to change it—though there is a good reason to do so.

FIGURE 4.14

On the Desktop page of the Display Properties dialog box, you can select a background picture or color for your Desktop.

Generally speaking, your computer's graphics performance suffers when you load up a complex picture as a background for your Desktop (though if your graphics card has plenty of memory to spare, you may not notice the hit). The Bliss graphic that's the default background for the Windows XP Home theme is large (about 1.4MB), whereas most of the other pictures are much smaller. For example, the Vortec Space graphic is only about 60K—so if your graphics card seems to be overcome with Bliss as the background, try applying a different background and see if performance improves.

If you do want to change the background pattern or image, select the item in the Background list. To use an image that's not listed, click the Browse button and use the resulting Browse dialog box to navigate to and select the file.

NOTE   By default, Windows lists any BMP, JPG, and GIF files in the Windows folder (whatever this folder is called), the \Web\ *folder in the Windows folder, and the* \Wallpaper\ *folder in the* \Web\ *folder.*

If the image you choose is smaller than the screen, you can select one of the choices in the Position drop-down list—Center, Tile, or Stretch—to specify whether to center it, tile it across the screen, or stretch it to fill the screen. If you choose the Center option, or if you choose to have no background image (by selecting the None item), you can change the color by selecting the color you want in the Color drop-down list.

If the image you want to use is a picture from a high-resolution digital camera, it may be *bigger* than the screen. In this case, the Tile option isn't much use. The Center option centers the center of the picture on the screen, so you'll see only part of it. And the Stretch option shrinks the picture to fit the screen.

If the image doesn't have the same proportions as the screen, the Stretch command distorts the image. If you want to have a full-screen picture without distortion, open the image in a graphics program (for example, Paint), crop it to the right proportions, and save the cropped version under a different name for use on your Desktop.

Changing Desktop Items and Desktop Web Pages

As you know, Windows displays some items on your Desktop by default, such as the Recycle Bin. You can't get rid of these by conventional means such as deleting them. But you can remove them and, if you wish, add other items by using the Desktop Items dialog box. You can also add live content to your Desktop by using Desktop Web pages.

Changing the Items Displayed on Your Desktop

To change the items displayed on the Desktop, click the Customize Desktop button on the Desktop page of the Display Properties dialog box. Windows displays the Desktop Items dialog box (shown in Figure 4.15) with the General page foremost.

FIGURE 4.15

Use the Desktop Items dialog box to specify which items appear on your Desktop.

In the Desktop Icons group box, specify which items to display by selecting and clearing the My Documents check box, the My Computer check box, the My Network Places check box, and the Internet Explorer check box.

To change the icon displayed for one of the first three of these items, or for the Recycle Bin in its empty or full state, select the item in the Change Desktop Icon list box and click the Change Icon button. Windows displays the Change Icon dialog box. In the Select an Icon from the List Below list box, choose the icon you want to use, and click the OK button to apply it. You can reapply the default icon for an item by selecting the item and clicking the Restore Default button in the Desktop Items dialog box.

TIP   If you don't see an icon you like in the Change Icon dialog box, click the Browse button and use the resulting Change Icon dialog box (a common Open dialog box in disguise) to select a file that contains icons. The file SHELL32.DLL *in the* \Windows\System32\ *folder contains a wide variety of icons, and the file* MORICONS.DLL *(in the same folder) contains a selection of older icons, some of which have amusement value. You can also find a wide variety of icons on the Web, or create your own icons with icon-editor programs.*

Adding Web Content via Desktop Web Pages

If you want, you can add Web content to your Desktop. Doing so can make your Desktop more lively and interesting, which can be handy if you spend long periods staring at the Desktop or if you want to keep a stock ticker going. On the other hand, Web content tends to be a time-sink. And if you spend most of your time working in a maximized program window, you'll miss the action on your Desktop.

To use Desktop Web pages:

1. Display the Desktop Items dialog box by clicking the Customize Desktop button on the Desktop page of the Display Properties dialog box.

TIP *Once you've started using Desktop Web pages, you can also display the Desktop Items dialog box by clicking the Active Desktop menu button and choosing Customize My Desktop from the menu.*

2. Click the Web tab. Windows displays the Web page (shown in Figure 4.16).

FIGURE 4.16

Use the Web page of the Desktop Items dialog box to arrange Desktop content.

3. By default, Windows lists your current home page in the Web Pages list box. To use this page, select its check box. (Windows doesn't apply the Web page to your screen until you close the Desktop Items dialog box *and* click the Apply button in the Display Properties dialog box, so don't worry that nothing happens at this point.)

4. To add a page, click the New button. Windows displays the New Desktop Item dialog box (shown in Figure 4.17).

5. In the Location text box, type in the URL for the Web page. Alternatively, if you have the location stored in a favorite, or if you want to add an HTML page that you have stored as a file, click the Browse button. Windows displays the Browse dialog box, which is an Open dialog box in disguise, listing your favorites. Navigate to and select the file, and then click the Open button.

6. Click the OK button. Windows closes the New Desktop Item dialog box.

FIGURE 4.17

Use the New Desktop Item dialog box to add a Web page to your Desktop.

NOTE *At this point, if you have already set this item up as an offline favorite (as discussed in Chapter 18), Windows displays the Active Desktop Item dialog box, telling you that you already have a subscription for this Active Desktop item, warning you that the subscription settings for the item will be lost if you continue, and asking if you still want to add this Active Desktop item. As you'll see in a moment, Desktop Web pages offer fewer customization settings than offline favorites: You don't get to specify the depth of additional pages to download (because downloading additional pages would be pointless), nor do you get to choose not to download certain items.*

7. Windows displays the Add Item to Active Desktop dialog box (shown in Figure 4.18).

FIGURE 4.18

In the Add Item to Active Desktop dialog box, click the Customize button if you need to enter a password for the Web site you're adding to the Desktop.

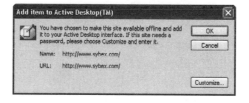

8. If you want to add the Web page just as it is to your Active Desktop, click the OK button and skip ahead to step 16. But if you want to create an update schedule for the Web page, or if you need to enter a password and username to access it, click the Customize button. Windows starts the Offline Favorite Wizard.

9. The first time you run the Wizard, you'll see an introductory page. Select the In the Future, Do Not Show This Introduction Screen check box and click the Next button. Windows displays the synchronization page of the Offline Favorite Wizard (shown in Figure 4.19).

10. Specify how you want to synchronize this favorite. You can choose among the Only when I Choose Synchronize from the Tools Menu option button, the I Would Like to Create a New Schedule option button (which lets you create a custom synchronization schedule for the favorite), and the Using This Existing Schedule option button (which lets you use an existing schedule from the drop-down list). (The Using This Existing Schedule option button becomes available once you've created a schedule.)

FIGURE 4.19

On this page of the Offline Favorite Wizard, specify whether you want to use an existing synchronization schedule, create a new schedule, or synchronize the Web page manually.

11. Click the Next button. If you chose to create a custom synchronization schedule for the favorite, Windows displays the Offline Favorite Wizard page shown in Figure 4.20.

FIGURE 4.20

If you chose to create a custom synchronization schedule for the favorite, specify the details on this page of the Offline Favorites Wizard.

12. Specify the schedule:

 ◆ Enter the interval (in days) and the time for the update at the top of the dialog box.

 ◆ Enter a name for the schedule in the Name text box. (The name is displayed when you go to apply an existing schedule to a new offline favorite you create, so make it descriptive, memorable, or both.)

 ◆ If you want your computer to connect to the network or Internet automatically if it is not connected when the time for the synchronization arrives, select the If My Computer Is Not Connected when This Scheduled Synchronization Begins, Automatically Connect for Me check box.

13. Click the Next button. Windows displays the password page of the Offline Favorite Wizard (shown in Figure 4.21).

FIGURE 4.21

On the final page of the Offline Favorite Wizard, enter your username and password if the site requires you to log on.

14. If the site requires a username and password, select the Yes, My User Name and Password Are: option button and specify your username and password (twice).

15. Click the Finish button to finish scheduling the update. Windows closes the Offline Favorite Wizard and returns you to the Add Item to Active Desktop dialog box.

16. Click the OK button. Windows closes the Add Item to Active Desktop dialog box and displays the Synchronizing dialog box while it synchronizes the Web page.

17. Add further items to the Web Pages list if you want.

18. Make sure the check box for each Desktop Web page that you want to use is selected.

19. When you're finished specifying Desktop Web pages, click the OK button. Windows closes the Desktop Items dialog box.

20. Click the OK button in the Display Properties dialog box. Windows closes the dialog box and applies your Web content to the Desktop.

Windows initially displays the first Desktop Web page across most of the Desktop (except for the part taken up by icons), with other Desktop Web pages appearing as small windows. Move the mouse pointer over the top of a window to display its title bar. You can then click the left control icon (a Maximize button) on the title bar to maximize the Web page across your whole Desktop (so that the icons appear on top of it) or click the right icon (a Restore button) to spread the Web page across the portion of your Desktop that doesn't have icons on it.

You can also resize a Desktop Web page by clicking the down-arrow button at the left end of the title bar and choosing Cover Desktop, Split Desktop with Icons, or Reset to Original Size from the drop-down menu.

NOTE *You can also add a new Desktop item by clicking the Visit Gallery button. Windows opens a browser window showing what's available in the Microsoft Desktop Gallery. At this writing, the Desktop Gallery offers an assortment of items including a weather map and a satellite tracker.*

Managing Your Desktop Web Pages

To manage your Desktop Web pages, you can take the following actions:

◆ To switch between Active Desktop Web pages, use the Web Pages text box on the Web page of the Desktop Items dialog box.

◆ To remove a Desktop Web page from being available, select it in the Web Pages list box and click the Remove button. Windows displays a confirmation message box. Click the Yes button.

◆ To hide your Desktop icons, right-click open space on the Desktop and choose Arrange Icons By ➤ Show Desktop Icons from the context menu. Windows removes the check mark from the Show Desktop Items item. To display the icons again, repeat the command.

◆ To lock the items on your Desktop so that they cannot be moved or rearranged, right-click open space on the Desktop and choose Arrange Icons By ➤ Lock Web Items on Desktop from the context menu. Windows places a check mark next to the Lock Desktop Items item to indicate the locking. To unlock locked items, right-click and choose Active Desktop ➤ Lock Web Items on Desktop again. Windows removes the check mark from the Lock Desktop Items item.

Changing the Appearance of Windows Items

You can customize the appearance of your Desktop by working on the Appearance page of the Display Properties dialog box (shown in Figure 4.22) and in the Advanced Appearance dialog box.

FIGURE 4.22

The Appearance page of the Display Properties dialog box

NOTE *In previous versions of Windows, the customization features of the Appearance page of the Display Properties dialog box and the Advanced Appearance dialog box all appeared on the Appearance page of the Display Properties dialog box. This was handy for power users but confusing for beginners. Windows XP separates the customization features, making it simpler to see what you're doing. But if you're used to customizing Windows from the Appearance page of the Display Properties dialog box, you may find Windows XP's approach frustrating.*

The Appearance page of the Display Properties dialog box offers three adjustments:

Windows and Buttons drop-down list   This drop-down list offers two choices of looks for windows and buttons: Windows XP Style or Windows Classic Style. You can choose advanced customizations only for Windows Classic Style.

Color Scheme drop-down list   This drop-down list provides a selection of color schemes. For the Windows XP style, you can apply only a few color schemes. For the Windows Classic style, you can choose from a wide variety of schemes that range from Windows Classic and Windows Standard through assorted color schemes and some high-contrast schemes.

Font Size drop-down list   This drop-down list gives you three choices of font size for Windows fonts: Normal, Large, and Extra Large.

If these three options don't give the effect you want, click the Advanced button. Windows displays the Advanced Appearance dialog box (shown in Figure 4.23), in which you can change the color of just about any part of the screen.

FIGURE 4.23

Use the Advanced Appearance dialog box to customize the look of Windows.

To change the color of an item, select the item in the Item drop-down list, either by selecting it from the list or by clicking its representation in the demo box at the top of the dialog box. Then select attributes in the Size, Color 1, and Color 2 controls as appropriate for the object. If the Font drop-down list is available, you can also specify a font, font size, color, and style for the item.

When you've finished making Windows look attractive (or peculiar), click the OK button. Windows closes the Advanced Appearance dialog box. Click the Apply button in the Display Properties dialog box to apply your choices.

Choosing Desktop Effects

Windows uses a number of visual effects to try to make your Desktop look appealing. Some people find these effects distracting and prefer to turn them off.

To work with effects, click the Effects button on the Appearance page. Windows displays the Effects dialog box (shown in Figure 4.24).

FIGURE 4.24

In the Effects dialog box, you can specify the effects that Windows uses for your Desktop.

Use the Following Transition Effect for Menus and Tooltips check box and drop-down list
When this check box is selected, Windows uses the effect specified in the drop-down list—Fade Effect or Scroll Effect—for the display of menus and tooltips. Clear this check box if you don't like the effect.

Use the Following Method to Smooth Edges of Screen Fonts check box and drop-down list
Select this check box if you want to have Windows smooth the edges of screen fonts so that they look less jagged and are easier to read. (Smoothing is usually a good idea.) Then choose one of the options from the drop-down list: Standard or ClearType. ClearType is a Microsoft font-rendering technology that uses subpixel rendering to smooth the edges of fonts, making them easier to read. (Briefly: Instead of turning on a whole pixel, or turning it off, ClearType can turn on *part* of a pixel to achieve a more graduated, less blocky effect.) ClearType is most effective on LCD screens, though it also has some effect on cathode-ray tube screens as well. If you're used to reading on-screen, ClearType may make you rub your eyes at first, as its effect is to blur the edges of the letters.

Use Large Icons check box   Select this check box if you want Windows to display icons at a larger size than usual. This option is useful for high screen resolutions, which can make it hard to distinguish one icon from another.

Show Shadows under Menus check box   Leave this check box selected (as it is by default) to have Windows display shadows at the bottom and right-hand edge of menus to give a 3-D effect. Clear this check box if you prefer your menus plain.

Show Window Contents while Dragging check box   Leave this check box selected (as it is by default) to have Windows display the contents of a window when you're moving it or resizing it. If your video card struggles to display the window's contents, try clearing this check box. Windows then displays only the window's frame when you move or resize it, then displays the contents when you've finished the maneuver.

Hide Underlined Letters for Keyboard Navigation until I Press the Alt Key check box   When this check box is selected (as it is by default), Windows doesn't display the underscores under the access keys in menus and dialog boxes until you press the Alt key. (An *access key* is the key you press to access a menu or control. For example, most programs use *F* as the access key for the File menu.) If you use the keyboard rather than the mouse to select options, clear this check box. You'll then be able to see access keys without needing to press the Alt key.

Choosing System Sounds

If you've got speakers or headphones attached to your computer, you'll have noticed by now that by default Windows plays sounds when certain system events occur. For example, when you log on to Windows, it plays a sub–Brian Eno tinkle, and when you take an action Windows has been programmed to consider unwise, it plays a peremptory little chord at you. (If you don't have speakers or headphones attached to your computer, congratulations—you're saving yourself a good amount of grief.)

Fortunately for your sanity, you can change these sounds. For example, if you decide that you can't abide having a program close without Windows declaring "It's just a flesh wound," you could assign a file containing that sound to the Close Program event. You can even create sound schemes so that you can keep multiple sets of system sounds and switch from one set to another as the fancy takes you. To protect other users of the computer from your sonic frenzies, sound schemes are stored in the Registry (in the HKEY_CURRENT_USER subtree, if you're interested; Chapter 12 discusses what the Registry is and how to work with it) and are available only to the user who created them.

To assign system sounds, follow these steps:

1. Choose Start ➤ Control Panel. Windows displays Control Panel.

2. Click the Sounds, Speech, and Audio Devices link. Windows displays the Sounds, Speech, and Audio Devices page.

3. Click the Change the Sound Scheme link. Windows displays the Sounds and Audio Devices Properties dialog box with the Sounds page (shown in Figure 4.25) foremost.

FIGURE 4.25

Use the Sounds and Audio Devices Properties dialog box to configure the sounds assigned to various Windows events.

4. To apply an existing sound scheme, select it in the Sound Scheme drop-down list. (To apply peace and quiet, select the No Sounds scheme.)

   ◆ If you were using a custom sound scheme before, but you haven't saved it, Windows displays the Save Scheme dialog box prompting you to save it. Choose the Yes button or the No button as appropriate.

5. To customize the current sound scheme:

   ◆ Select an event in the Program Events list box.

   ◆ In the Sounds drop-down list, select the sound you want to assign to the event. To find out how a sound sounds, click the Play button with the sound selected.

   ◆ The Sounds list box lists all the WAV files in the `\Windows\Media\` folder. To make your own WAV files available in the Sounds list box, copy or move them to this folder beforehand. Alternatively, use the Browse button to locate individual files you want to assign to events.

   ◆ To save the customized scheme, click the Save As button. Windows displays the Save Scheme As dialog box. Enter the name for the scheme and click the OK button. Once you've saved a scheme, it's available from the Sound Scheme drop-down list. If you tire of it, you can delete it by clicking the Delete button.

6. Click the Apply button to apply your sound settings.

7. Click the OK button. Windows closes the Sounds and Audio Devices Properties dialog box.

Arranging Icons on Your Desktop

By default, Windows starts you off with just the Recycle Bin on the Desktop. (Your computer's manufacturer may have added other icons to the Desktop.) As you saw earlier in the chapter, you can add icons for My Documents, My Computer, My Network Places, and Internet Explorer by selecting the check boxes on the General page of the Desktop Items dialog box. You can save files to the Desktop and create shortcuts there as you need them (more on this later in the chapter). And many programs place one or more shortcuts on the Desktop when you install them.

One way or another, your Desktop normally gathers icons like an ungroomed dog gathers fleas. To keep things in order, you can arrange the icons on your Desktop by dragging them to wherever you want them to appear or by using one of the commands on the Arrange Icons By submenu of the context menu for the Desktop:

   ◆ The Name command, Size command, Type command, and Modified command arrange the icons by that attribute. You can choose only one of these commands at a time. Windows displays a dot next to the currently selected item on the menu when the Auto Arrange command is active.

   ◆ The Auto Arrange command controls whether Windows automatically arranges the icons into neat columns and rows, starting with a column beginning at the upper-left corner of the screen. You can toggle this command on and off. When it's on, the menu displays a check mark next to it.

◆ The Align to Grid command controls whether Windows aligns icons on an invisible grid or lets you place them wherever you want them. You can toggle this command on and off by selecting it; again, it displays a check mark when it's on. This command is notionally independent of the Auto Arrange command, but in practice the Auto Arrange command essentially overrules it: When you let Windows arrange your icons, it parks them according to the grid whether the Align to Grid command is on or off.

◆ The Show in Groups command lets you arrange icons in groups. This command is much more useful in Explorer windows than on the average Desktop.

◆ To remove the icons from your Desktop, right-click the Desktop and choose Arrange Icons By ➤ Show Desktop Icons to remove the check mark from the Show Desktop Icons item. To restore the icons, repeat the command.

Desktop Cleanup Wizard

If you leave any of the icons on your Desktop unused for 60 days, the Desktop Cleanup Wizard pops up a prompt in the System Tray urging you to let it help you clean up your Desktop. If you accept this invitation, the Wizard displays a list of shortcuts you've never used, or haven't used for a long time, suggesting that you move them to a folder called Unused Desktop Shortcuts, which the Wizard creates on your Desktop the first time it runs. Choose which (if any) icons you want to move there, and the Wizard will do the rest. You can then access the shortcuts from the folder if you need to—or drag them back to your Desktop so that you can use them directly.

You can run the Desktop Cleanup Wizard manually at any time by clicking the Clean Desktop Now button on the General page of the Desktop Items dialog box. To prevent the Desktop Cleanup Wizard from running, clear the Run Desktop Cleanup Wizard Every 60 Days check box, also on the General page of the Desktop Items dialog box.

Configuring the Taskbar

Both the Taskbar and the Start menu have changed considerably in Windows XP from the way they were in its predecessors, and you may want to restore some of their old behavior. This section discusses how to configure the Taskbar to meet your needs. The section after this discusses how to configure the Start menu.

Resizing and Repositioning the Taskbar

By default, the Taskbar appears at the bottom of the Desktop and is locked so that you cannot expand, shrink, or reposition it. To unlock the Taskbar, right-click open space on it (for example, the partial button at the Taskbar's right end) or in the notification area and select the Lock the Taskbar item from the context menu. Windows removes the check mark from the Lock the Taskbar item. (To lock the Taskbar again, repeat this command.)

NOTE *You can also unlock the Taskbar by clearing the Lock the Taskbar check box on the Taskbar page of the Taskbar and Start Menu Properties dialog box, but this technique is handy only if you have this dialog box displayed already.*

Once you've unlocked the Taskbar, you can resize it or reposition it:

◆ To reposition the Taskbar, click open space in it and drag it toward (or to) one of the edges of the screen so that the Taskbar snaps to it. See page 13 of the *Essential Skills* section for visual coverage of unlocking, resizing, and repositioning the Taskbar.

◆ To resize the Taskbar, drag its inside edge to expand or shrink the Taskbar. The inside edge is the edge nearest to the center of the screen. For example, in the Taskbar's default position at the bottom of the screen, the top edge is the inside edge.

When the Taskbar is positioned at the top or bottom of the screen, it grows and shrinks in increments of its original depth rather than gradually, so you can drag it to one-button depth, two-button depth, and so on. When the Taskbar is positioned at the side of the screen, it grows and shrinks gradually, so you can get exactly the width you want.

TIP   Unless you have a lot of windows open, placing the Taskbar at the side of the screen tends to waste space, because the buttons have a standard depth, leaving the lower half of the Taskbar unused. If you do have a lot of windows open, placing the Taskbar at the side of the screen lets you read the button titles quickly in a column—and you can drag the column width to display more or less of each title as you need.

Using the Taskbar to Navigate between Programs

In Windows XP, the Taskbar looks more decorative than its utilitarian old version in previous versions of Windows, but its function remains the same: to let you see which programs are open; navigate quickly to a program; and maximize, minimize, restore, or close programs easily.

The Taskbar displays a button for each open program window. Note that this said *program window* rather than just *program*: If a program displays multiple separate program windows, the Taskbar shows one button for each window. If the program uses only one program window (including if the program has several document windows open within a program window), the Taskbar shows only one button for it. For example, if you have Excel 2002 or Word 2002 set to display multiple program windows (by selecting the Windows in Taskbar check box on the View page of the Options dialog box in each of the programs), Windows displays a Taskbar button for each program window. If you have these programs set to display only one program window, the Taskbar displays only one button for the program.

When the Taskbar has taken up all the available space with buttons, and making the buttons any smaller to display more buttons would make them impractically small, it uses two techniques to present the buttons when you take an action that would add another button to the Taskbar:

◆ First, it groups any related buttons into a single button for the category. For example, if you have five Word documents open, it groups their five buttons into a single group button that contains a menu of the buttons. While the individual buttons bear the names of the document windows, the group button bears the program name and the number of windows the program has open—in this case, 5 Microsoft Word. Similarly, the Taskbar will display an Explorer button named 4 Windows Explorer containing a Control Panel button, a Network Connections button, a My Computer button, and a Recycle Bin button.

◆ Second, if you take actions that require disparate Taskbar buttons that can't be grouped, Windows starts a second row of Taskbar buttons and displays scroll buttons at the right end of the Taskbar. Click the scroll buttons to scroll up and down the rows of Taskbar buttons to access the buttons you need.

To display a program, click its button on the Taskbar. (See page 8 of the *Essential Skills* section for visual coverage of using the Taskbar to access a window.) If the button is grouped into a group button, click the group button to display the menu of buttons, then choose the button from the menu. Figure 4.26 shows an example of working with a group button.

To resize, move, or close a program window, right-click its Taskbar button and choose Restore, Move, Size, Minimize, Maximize, or Close from the context menu.

FIGURE 4.26

When a program's windows are grouped into a group button, you activate a program window by clicking the group button and choosing the button from the menu displayed.

To arrange all the program windows, right-click open space in the Taskbar or in the notification area and choose the appropriate command from the context menu. This offers the Cascade Windows command, the Tile Windows Horizontally command, the Tile Windows Vertically command, and the Show the Desktop command. When you've issued a Show the Desktop command, the context menu also contains the Show Open Windows command and the Undo Minimize All command.

TIP   Two quick tips: First, right-click a group button to manipulate all its windows at once. The context menu offers Cascade, Tile Horizontally, Tile Vertically, Minimize Group, and Close Group commands. Second, to work with multiple windows at once, hold down the Ctrl key and select the Taskbar button for each window. Then right-click one of the windows and choose the action from the context menu.

Configuring the Taskbar's Behavior

To configure the Taskbar, right-click open space in it (in other words, don't click a button) or in the notification area and choose Properties from the context menu. Windows displays the Taskbar page of the Taskbar and Start Menu Properties dialog box (shown in Figure 4.27).

The Taskbar Appearance group box offers these five options:

Lock the Taskbar check box   Select this check box (which is selected by default) to prevent the Taskbar from being moved to another edge of the screen or resized. Clear the check box if you want to move or resize it.

FIGURE 4.27

Use the Taskbar page of the Taskbar and Start Menu Properties dialog box to configure the Taskbar to your liking.

Auto-Hide the Taskbar check box   Select this check box (which is cleared by default) to make the Taskbar hide itself until you move the pointer over its edge of the screen. This option is useful for maximizing the amount of the screen available to you, especially when you've increased the size of the Taskbar to accommodate more programs.

Keep the Taskbar on Top of Other Windows check box   Select this check box (which is selected by default) to have the Taskbar appear on top of any window. Instead of using the Auto Hide feature to hide the Taskbar, you can clear this check box so that the Taskbar remains on-screen. You can then display another window on top of the Taskbar if you want.

Group Similar Taskbar Buttons check box   Select this check box (which is selected by default) to have Windows display only one button per program on the Taskbar. (See the previous section for further explanation and an example.) Individual buttons can make it easy to find the window you want, but the buttons take up a lot of space (or each button on the Taskbar gets shrunk to a tiny size to fit them all in).

Show Quick Launch check box   Select this check box to display the Quick Launch toolbar on the Taskbar. See "Using the Desktop Toolbars" later in this chapter for a discussion of the Quick Launch toolbar.

The Notification Area group box offers two options:

Show the Clock check box   Select this check box to have the notification area show the clock (as it does by default). Clear the check box to get rid of the clock and reclaim the space it takes up.

Hide Inactive Icons check box   Select this check box (which is selected by default) to have Windows automatically remove from the notification area any items that you haven't used recently. Windows hides the items and displays a Show Hidden Icons button that you can use to display them. This option can be useful for keeping your notification area uncluttered. If you find it unsettling to have icons disappear, clear this check box. You can also customize Windows' treatment of notification-area icons by clicking the Customize button and working in the Customize Notifications dialog box (shown in Figure 4.28). Select the item in the Current Items list or the Past Items list (which doesn't appear in the figure), then choose Hide when Inactive, Always Hide, or Always Show from the context menu. (If you mess up, click the Restore Defaults button to restore Windows' default behavior with the notification area.)

FIGURE 4.28

If you choose to have Windows clean up the notification area, use the Customize Notifications dialog box to specify that some icons always appear.

Customizing the Start Menu

As you'll notice from your first session with Windows XP, Microsoft has given the Start menu not only a new look but also new behavior. By default, the Start menu appears as a wide panel (shown in Figure 4.29) that automatically adjusts its contents to show your most recently used and most used programs.

FIGURE 4.29

The new-look Start menu appears as a two-column panel with the current user's name at the top.

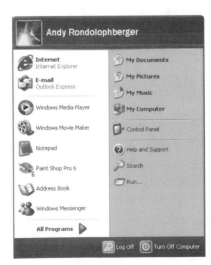

TIP   If you prefer the "classic" Start menu used in Windows 9x, Windows NT 4, and Windows 2000, you can easily restore it: Select the Classic Start Menu option button on the Start Menu page of the Taskbar and Start Menu Properties dialog box, then click the Apply button. This book assumes that you're using the XP-style Start menu, so if you choose the classic Start menu, you'll need to choose Start menu commands a little differently. The section after next discusses how to customize the classic Start menu, but after that, all coverage uses the XP Start menu.

Whether you use the XP Start menu or the classic Start menu, you can customize it to make your computing a little easier. The following sections discuss how to do so.

See pages 16–18 of the *Essential Skills* section for a visual guide to customizing the Start menu.

Customizing the XP Start Menu

Because the XP Start menu automatically configures itself, it offers fewer customization options than the classic Start menu (which is discussed in the next section).

To customize the XP Start menu:

1. Display the Start menu, then right-click it and choose Properties from the context menu. Windows displays the Start Menu page of the Taskbar and Start Menu Properties dialog box.

2. Click the upper Customize button to display the Customize Start Menu dialog box.

3. Choose options on the General page (shown in Figure 4.30):

FIGURE 4.30

On the General page of the Customize Start Menu dialog box, you can specify how many programs the Start menu should show.

Select an Icon Size for Programs group box   Choose the Large Icons option button or the Small Icons option button as suits you.

Programs group box   Use the Number of Programs on Start Menu drop-down list to specify the number of programs the Start menu should display. You can set any number from 0 to 30. To wipe the current list of programs, click the Clear List button.

Show on Start Menu group box   To display an Internet item on the Start menu, leave the Internet check box selected (as it is by default); to remove this item, clear it. If you leave the check box selected, you can use the drop-down list to select the program used for browsing the

Internet. The default is Internet Explorer. Similarly, to display an E-mail item on the Start menu, leave the E-mail check box selected, and specify the program in the drop-down list. The default is Outlook Express.

4. Click the Advanced tab. Windows displays the Advanced page (shown in Figure 4.31).

5. Choose options in the Start Menu Settings group box:

   Open Submenus when I Pause on Them with My Mouse check box   Leave this check box selected (as it is by default) if you want the Start menu to display its submenus when you hover the mouse pointer over them for more than a few milliseconds. Clear this check box if you prefer to have the submenus appear only when you click them.

FIGURE 4.31

On the Advanced page of the Customize Start Menu dialog box, you can specify which items to show on the menu and whether to include the recently used documents list.

Highlight Newly Installed Programs check box   Leave this check box selected (as it is by default) if you want Windows to display a yellow highlight on the Start menu and its submenus to show you the path to newly installed programs. Windows removes the highlighting once you've used the program. This highlighting can be useful, but because Windows applies it to each new shortcut the freshly installed program has created, the highlighted path persists until you've used each shortcut—which may be awhile for shortcuts to uninstall features, Help files, and documentation. If you don't like the highlighting, clear this check box.

6. The Start Menu Items list box presents a number of items that can appear on the Start menu. Those with an icon and three option buttons (the Display As a Link option button, the Display As a Menu option button, and the Don't Display This Item option button) let you specify whether they appear as a link or as a submenu. For example, you can have Control Panel appear as a link (which opens a Control Panel window), as a menu (which lets you access its categories directly), or never. Those items with a check box let you specify simply whether the item appears (for example, select the Printers and Faxes check box to have the Start menu display a Printers and Faxes entry) or whether a feature is implemented (for example, select the Scroll Programs check box if you want Windows to display the All Programs menu as a

scrolling item or as multiple pages should it be too long to fit on the screen). Select the check boxes and the option buttons as appropriate.

7. In the Recent Documents group box, select the List My Most Recently Opened Documents check box if you want the Start menu to display a menu for recently used documents. Displaying this item lets you access your recent documents quickly, but it also lets anyone logged on to the computer as you see which documents you've been working with. Click the Clear List button to clear the list of recent documents.

8. Click the OK button. Windows closes the Customize Start Menu dialog box.

9. Click the OK button. Windows closes the Taskbar and Start Menu Properties dialog box.

TIP   *To prevent Windows from moving an item on the Start menu, pin it in place. Right-click the item in the Start menu and choose Pin to Start Menu from the context menu. To unpin an item you've pinned, right-click it in the Start menu and choose Unpin from Start Menu from the context menu.*

Customizing the Classic Start Menu

You can customize the classic Start menu so that it contains exactly the items you want. To do so, you add items to the menu, remove existing items, and sort the menu if necessary.

Begin by choosing Start ➤ Settings ➤ Taskbar and Start Menu to display the Taskbar and Start Menu Properties dialog box. Select the Classic Start Menu option button if it isn't already selected (if you're using the classic Start menu, it should be selected already). Then click the lower Customize button. Windows displays the Customize Classic Start Menu dialog box (shown in Figure 4.32).

FIGURE 4.32

The Customize Classic Start Menu dialog box lets you customize the classic Start menu extensively to put the items you need most right at hand.

You can add items to the Start menu and remove items from it as follows:

◆   To add an item to the Start menu, click the Add button and follow the steps in the Create Shortcut Wizard that Windows displays.

- To remove an item from the Start menu, click the Remove button. Windows displays the Remove Shortcuts/Folders dialog box (shown in Figure 4.33). Select the item you want to remove, and then click the Remove button.

- To add and remove items freely, click the Advanced button. Windows opens an Explorer window showing the Start menu. You can then create and delete shortcuts as you see fit by using standard Explorer techniques.

TIP *Your Start menu folder is stored in the* \Documents and Settings*Username*\Start Menu\ *folder. You can navigate to it by using Explorer and manipulate it without bothering the Customize Classic Start Menu dialog box.*

FIGURE 4.33

Use the Remove Shortcuts/Folders dialog box to remove items from the Start menu.

- To sort the Start menu alphabetically, click the Sort button.

- To clear the details of recently used documents, programs, and Web sites, click the Clear button.

In the Advanced Start Menu Options list box, choose settings for the following options:

Display Administrative Tools check box   Select this check box to have Windows display the Administrative Tools menu on the Programs menu. You can also access these tools through the Administrative Tools page of the Control Panel, but using the menu is quicker for frequent access. This check box is cleared by default.

Display Favorites check box   Select this check box to have Windows display the Favorites menu on the Start menu. This menu lets you quickly access your favorites, but it can become unwieldy if you have a large number of favorites. This check box is cleared by default.

Display Run check box   Leave this check box selected (as it is by default) to have the Start menu include the Run item, which you can use for running a program. Clear this check box to remove the Run item. You might want to do this to help discourage users from running programs not on the Start menu.

Enable Dragging and Dropping check box   Leave this check box selected (as it is by default) if you want to be able to use drag-and-drop to move or copy items from one location on the Start menu to another location. Clear this check box to disable drag-and-drop.

Expand Control Panel check box   Select this check box if you want Windows to display a menu of Control Panel items instead of opening a Control Panel window when you select Start ➤ Settings ➤ Control Panel. This menu gives you faster access to the Control Panel items than does opening a Control Panel window. This check box is cleared by default.

Expand My Documents check box   Select this check box if you want Windows to display a menu listing the items in the My Documents folder instead of displaying a window when you choose Start ➤ Documents. This menu gives you quick access, but it can be hard to navigate if you accumulate many documents and folders in the My Documents folder. This check box is cleared by default.

Expand My Pictures check box   Select this check box if you want Windows to display a menu listing the items in the My Pictures folder when you choose Start ➤ My Documents ➤ My Pictures.

Expand Network Connections check box   Select this check box if you want Windows to display a menu of network connections instead of displaying a window when you choose Start ➤ Settings ➤ Network Connections. This check box is cleared by default.

Expand Printers check box   Select this check box if you want Windows to display a menu of printers instead of displaying a window when you choose Start ➤ Settings ➤ Printers and Faxes. This check box is cleared by default.

Scroll Programs check box   Select this check box if you want Windows to display the Programs menu as a scrolling menu when it is too tall to fit on the screen. With this check box cleared, Windows displays the Programs menu as two or more columns. This check box is cleared by default.

Show Small Icons in Start Menu check box   Select this check box to have Windows display small icons instead of large icons in the Start menu. Small icons let you pack more items on the Start menu but make it harder to read. This check box is cleared by default.

Use Personalized Menus check box   Leave this check box selected (as it is by default) to have Windows automatically tailor the Start menu to what it thinks are your needs. For example, if you don't use a program for a long time, Windows removes its item from the Start menu on the assumption that you don't need it. When Windows has removed items like this, it displays a button at the foot of the menu with a double arrow pointing downward to indicate that more items are available. Click this button to display the items that have been removed.

When you've finished customizing the classic Start menu, click the OK button. Windows closes the Customize Classic Start Menu dialog box and applies your choices.

Using the Desktop Toolbars

Windows offers four built-in toolbars that you can display on the Desktop. As you'll see in a moment, you can also create custom toolbars of your own to give you quick access to folders and Web pages of your choice.

The four toolbars are as follows:

Address toolbar   This toolbar works in the same way as the Address bar in Internet Explorer. Enter a URL and click the Go button (or press the Enter key) to open a Web page in Internet Explorer. Enter a drive letter or folder name to open it in an Explorer window. Enter a filename and path to open the file in the program associated with its file type.

Desktop toolbar   This toolbar displays an icon for each item on your Desktop and menus for key folders (for example, the My Computer folder and the My Network Places folder). By displaying this toolbar, you can save yourself having to display the Desktop to access a program, a folder, or a file. Many people find this toolbar most useful reduced to a button. You can then click the toolbar's expansion arrow to get a menu of the items on your Desktop.

Links toolbar   This toolbar is the Links toolbar from Internet Explorer. You can use it to provide quick access to Web sites you want to be able to access frequently.

Quick Launch toolbar   This toolbar provides quick access to programs and documents you designate. The Quick Launch toolbar initially contains four icons and appears to the right of the Start button (when the Taskbar is at the bottom of the screen): Launch Internet Explorer Browser, Launch Outlook Express, MSN Explorer, and Show Desktop (which brings the Desktop to the foreground, in front of all open windows). You can add other icons to suit your needs, as discussed in the section after next.

Displaying and Hiding the Desktop Toolbars

To display or hide a toolbar, right-click the notification area, choose Toolbars from the context menu, and select the toolbar from the submenu. (See pages 14–15 of the *Essential Skills* section for visual coverage of displaying and using Desktop toolbars.)

Figure 4.34 shows the Quick Launch toolbar, the Desktop toolbar (with its menu displayed), and the Address toolbar. As you can see, cramming several toolbars onto a single-line Taskbar like this makes them impractically small. (The Address toolbar in particular is more or less useless at this size.)

FIGURE 4.34

You can display one or more Desktop toolbars to give you quick access to your programs, your Desktop, and Web pages.

Customizing the Quick Launch Toolbar

As you've seen, the new-style Start menu tries to put your most-used programs at your fingertips (or at your mouse pointer) by juggling the Start menu items and letting you pin items to the Start menu. But you may find it even easier to put the programs and documents you use most often on the Quick

Launch toolbar and not have to worry about pinning them (or having Windows "disappear" them to make room for another program).

There are two easy ways to add a shortcut to the Quick Launch toolbar:

♦ Drag the target file from an Explorer window (or from the Desktop) to the Quick Launch toolbar. Windows creates a shortcut to the file (document or program) there.

NOTE   *Shortcuts on the Quick Launch toolbar don't show the usual shortcut arrow, though if you look at the Quick Launch folder, you'll see that the shortcut arrows are there.*

♦ Right-click open space in the Quick Launch toolbar and choose Open Folder from the context menu. Windows displays the Quick Launch folder. (If you want to open this folder the hard way, you'll find it in your `\Documents and Settings\`*Username*`\Application Data\ Microsoft\Internet Explorer\Quick Launch\` folder.) Create shortcuts by right-dragging any file or folder to this folder and choosing Create Shortcut Here from the context menu.

Once you have the shortcuts you need on the Quick Launch toolbar, drag their icons into the order in which you need them, left to right. This way, if only part of the Quick Launch toolbar is displayed on-screen, you'll be able to access your most-needed icons without needing to display the hidden portion of the toolbar.

Creating and Using Custom Toolbars

In addition to using the four ready-made toolbars, you can create custom toolbars to display the contents of any folder or any Web site that your computer can access. Using custom toolbars can be a great way of giving yourself access to the documents you use frequently. Custom toolbars aren't much use for Web pages—you can't see much of the page on the toolbar. This seems to be a feature that Microsoft implemented because it could rather than because it would benefit users.

To create a custom toolbar, take the following steps:

1. Right-click the Taskbar and choose Toolbars ➢ New Toolbar from the context menu. Windows displays the New Toolbar dialog box (shown in Figure 4.35).

FIGURE 4.35

Use the New Toolbar dialog box to create a new toolbar for the Desktop.

2. Navigate to and select the folder in the list box, or type a URL in the Folder text box (if you want to try creating a useless toolbar of a Web page).

3. Click the OK button. Windows creates a toolbar for the folder or Web page.

Managing Your Desktop Toolbars

If you have the Taskbar locked (as it is by default), you can't resize or move the toolbars you display. But if you unlock the Taskbar, you can resize and move them pretty much to your heart's content by dragging their sizing handles (the dotted area at the left end or upper end of the toolbar). You can drag a toolbar to a large size on the Taskbar, to a free-floating panel on the Desktop, or to a docked position at one of the edges of the screen.

Docking a toolbar like this may seem useless at first, because the toolbar takes up screen real estate that you probably have better uses for. But if you right-click the toolbar once and select the Always on Top attribute, then right-click again and select the Auto Hide attribute, you'll end up with a toolbar that disappears until you move the mouse pointer over its edge of the screen. Using such a toolbar can be a handy way to keep documents quickly accessible.

You can turn off the display of a toolbar's text by right-clicking the toolbar and clicking the Show Text item on the context menu to remove its check mark, or turn off the display of a toolbar's title by right-clicking the toolbar and clicking the Show Title item on the context menu to remove its check mark.

Up Next

This chapter has discussed how to configure your Desktop to suit your working needs. By now, you should have chosen display settings, customized the Windows Desktop, configured the Start menu and Taskbar, and applied any accessibility options you need in order to use your computer effectively.

The next chapter discusses how to install, remove, and run programs.

Chapter 5

Installing, Removing, and Running Programs

HOWEVER WONDERFUL THE FEATURES built into Windows XP—and some of them *are* pretty wonderful; some less so; see the rest of the book for details—they're not the be-all and end-all of computing. The programs bundled with Windows XP (most of which are discussed in Chapter 7) let you perform a few basic tasks, from creating simple documents to playing music and video to creating simple video movies of your own. But sooner or later, you're going to want to install a third-party program and run it so that you can carry on with your business and your life.

On the assumption that this is probably going to happen sooner rather than later, this chapter discusses how to install, configure, remove, and run programs—and how to shut them down when they fail to respond to conventional stimuli.

The chapter uses various programs as examples, ranging from the latest (and supposedly greatest) programs specially designed for Windows XP to Windows 9x programs to DOS programs that are still only just starting to suspect that graphical environments exist. The odds are overwhelmingly against these programs being the ones you want to use with your copy of Windows XP, but these programs provide examples of many of the issues you'll encounter with installing, running, and removing programs.

This chapter covers the following topics:

- ◆ Understanding compatibility issues
- ◆ Understanding multiuser considerations
- ◆ Who can install and remove programs
- ◆ Installing and removing programs
- ◆ Running programs in Compatibility mode
- ◆ Installing and removing DOS-based programs
- ◆ Running programs
- ◆ Making programs run at start-up
- ◆ Killing a program that's not responding

NOTE If you performed an in-place upgrade of your previous version of Windows to Windows XP, the installation processes should have configured all your programs for use already, so you shouldn't need to reinstall them. However, if you have old programs that you find don't run properly on Windows XP, you may need to run them in Compatibility mode. If so, turn to the section "Running Programs in Compatibility Mode," later in this chapter.

Good News on Compatibility

If you've used any of the versions of Windows NT, or if you've used Windows 2000, you'll know that program compatibility has been a major issue for the NT code base. In order to make NT stable and crash-proof, the designers made heavy sacrifices in compatibility. Many Windows 9x programs flat out wouldn't run on NT. Games and other programs that tried to access hardware directly were particularly problematic: Windows 9x lets a program access hardware directly, whereas NT's Hardware Abstraction Layer (HAL) forces all hardware requests to be brokered by the operating system.

In Windows 2000 Professional, Microsoft greatly increased the number of programs that would run on the NT code base—but some Windows 9x programs still wouldn't run, and many DOS-based games wouldn't run either. Direct hardware access was still a problem, because the HAL was still there. Briefly, if the program could run in protected mode, letting the HAL handle the communications with the hardware, it would usually run, though it might've run a bit more slowly than on other versions of Windows (or on DOS). If the program insisted on trying to communicate with the hardware directly, HAL gave it grief. (Fill in your own *2001* pun here: "I'm sorry, DOOM, I'm afraid I can't do that," and so on.)

On this front, Windows XP brings very welcome good news: XP is able to run most 32-bit Windows programs without problems. It can also run many 16-bit Windows programs. And it can run a number of DOS programs. Most of this happens transparently: You install the program by running its setup routine or installation routine as usual; you run the program as usual; and that's that. Behind the scenes, Windows XP provides more flexibility in providing the program with the type of environment it needs. On the surface, all is serene.

That's for many programs—perhaps most programs. But some programs don't run properly like this. For some, you need to explicitly use Windows XP's Compatibility mode to fool the program into thinking that it's running on the version of Windows that it expects. Windows XP then mimics the environment of that version of Windows for that program, sustaining the illusion that things are to the program's liking. For example, if a program expects Windows 95 and won't run without it, Compatibility mode tells the program that it's running on Windows 95 and tries to prevent it from finding out the truth. Usually the program then runs fine, though you may notice some loss of performance as Windows XP mollycoddles the program.

NOTE If you're familiar with the Mac, you might be wondering how Windows XP's Compatibility mode compares with Mac OS X and its Classic technology for running programs that won't run on OS X. Basically, there are similarities between Compatibility mode and Classic, but Compatibility mode is both less gruesome conceptually and far lighter on the memory. Classic essentially loads a hefty chunk of System 9.1 (on top of OS X, which isn't exactly svelte itself) and uses it to run the program, whereas Windows XP essentially dupes the program into a false sense of security by giving it the cues it expects. This duping requires a bit more memory and system resources, but nothing like the overhead that the Mac needs to run a program in Classic mode. But then Windows XP is less of a drastic change from its predecessors than OS X, which is essentially mutated Unix with a new graphical interface.

EXPERT KNOWLEDGE: 16-BIT PROGRAMS AND 32-BIT PROGRAMS

Okay, time out. What *is* a 16-bit program, and what's a 32-bit program? Where does the number of bits come from, and what does it mean?

A layperson's answer to the first question might be that 16-bit programs are programs designed to run on 16-bit versions of Windows (for example, Windows 3.1) and 32-bit programs are programs designed to run on 32-bit versions of Windows (Windows 9*x*, Windows NT, Windows 2000, and Windows XP).

Actually, it's not quite that simple. To get a fraction more technical, 16-bit programs are written to the Win16 application programming interface (API), and 32-bit programs are written to the Win32 API. The APIs are sets of rules that tell programmers how they can access the functionality that an operating system exposes to them and how a program should behave so that it gets along with the operating system and other programs running on it.

Normally, 32-bit programs *are* written for 32-bit operating systems, and 16-bit programs *are* (or, you might hope, *were*) written for 16-bit operating systems (which have largely gone the way of the dodo). But by using the Win32s extensions—a 32-bit operating system extension that sat on top of the 16-bit Windows 3.1 operating environment (which in turn sat on top of the 16-bit DOS operating system)—you could run a 32-bit program on Windows 3.1. So some 32-bit programs were written for a 16-bit operating system. And because 32-bit operating systems can normally run 16-bit programs, many 16-bit programs are used to this day, running more or less happily in virtual machines on 32-bit operating systems. The 32-bit operating system may have to perform a process called *thunking*, essentially gearing down to run a 16-bit program. Thunking typically involves some overhead and a slight loss of performance. But if the 16-bit program ran at an acceptable speed on Windows 3.1 with, say, a 486 processor, it should run at a decent speed on even a modest Celeron or Duron processor, even with any thunking needed.

Just as 32 valves are better than 16 (for making a satisfactory engine growl if not for reaching the speed limit ahead of that pickup in the next lane at the traffic signal), 32 bits are better than 16. The advantage of 32 bits is that you can move more information at once—*much* more information. 32 bits can represent a range of more than 4 billion integer values (4,294,967,296, to be precise), whereas 16 bits can represent only 65,536 integer values. 64 bits can represent correspondingly more than 32 bits, and 64-bit PC operating systems are on their way. In fact, the other versions of Windows XP (Professional and Server) will have 64-bit versions for the forthcoming 64-bit Itanium processor from Intel.

That still hasn't answered the second question: Where does the number of bits come from, and what does it mean? The bit-ness of a program essentially comes from the *word size* of the computer it's running on. The word size is the biggest number that the computer can handle in one operation. 286 systems, those fire-breathing speed-demons of the mid-1980s, used a 16-bit word size, enabling them to handle much more data at once than the (exhaust-breathing) 8-bit systems that preceded them. 386 systems upped the ante to a 32-bit word size, at which it has stayed for several generations of chips: Even Pentium IV and Athlon systems use 32-bit words. The Itanium processor will have a 64-bit word size, enabling it to handle impressively large chunks of data in a single operation.

When you're installing programs on Windows XP, you seldom need to worry about how many bits they're going to use, because Windows XP handles any necessary transitions between 32-bit and 16-bit code seamlessly. You *do* sometimes have to worry about *where* you install older programs so that all users of the computer can use them—but more on this a little later in the chapter.

Once you've set up Compatibility mode for a program, it runs in Compatibility mode each time, so you shouldn't need to tweak it any further unless some of its features misbehave.

Compatibility mode is very impressive, and it's great when it works. But some ancient programs (particularly DOS programs) may never work, even with Compatibility mode. In these cases, your choices of course of action are approximately a) give up on the program, b) dual-boot your system with the version of Windows with which the program was last known to work, or c) use emulation software such as VMWare to run on top of Windows XP a session of the version of Windows with which the program works.

NOTE   *One major category of program that this chapter* doesn't *talk about is games, which are a subject all to themselves. Games are cordoned off in Chapter 30.*

Programs You Shouldn't Even *Try* to Run on Windows XP

No matter how impressive Windows XP's compatibility with programs designed for earlier versions of Windows (or for DOS), there are some types of programs you should never try to run on Windows XP. These include the following:

Operating systems   Obviously, you can't install DOS, an earlier version of Windows, or another operating system or operating environment on top of Windows XP—at least, not without using some kind of PC-emulation software (such as VMWare).

Old anti-virus programs   Anti-virus programs designed for previous versions of Windows don't know how to deal with Windows XP. You may be able to update the program. More likely, you'll need to get a whole new version.

Old troubleshooting and cleanup utilities   Most troubleshooting and cleanup utilities designed for earlier versions of Windows will give XP nothing but grief. So will disk utilities (for example, Norton Utilities) designed for earlier versions. As with the anti-virus programs, these utilities don't know how Windows XP works—in fact, most of them assume that Windows works in a completely different way. So despite Windows XP's ability to restore your system after bad software goes on the rampage, it's a mistake to let old troubleshooting and cleanup utilities loose on your system in the first place. Where you still need the added functionality to supplement Windows XP's capabilities, invest in a new utility specifically designed for Windows XP.

Some potential offenders are smart enough to figure out the problem and quit on their own. Figure 5.1 shows the Incorrect Operating System dialog box that an old version of Network Associates' VirusScan displays if you try to install it on Windows XP without using Compatibility mode.

FIGURE 5.1

This old version of VirusScan is smart enough to refuse to be installed on Windows XP.

Multiuser Considerations

As you saw earlier in the book, Windows XP offers strong multiuser capabilities. From the start, Windows XP encourages you to set up your computer for multiple different users to use, allowing each their own custom settings. Moreover, multiple users can be logged on to the computer at the same time (though only one user can be active); other users can be running programs in the background (as it were) while the current user is working away unaware of them.

Windows XP's multiuser capabilities raise some issues for programs and files, as discussed in the next section.

Who Can Install Programs?

First, you'll remember that Windows XP Home supports three types of users: Computer Administrator users, Limited users, and the Guest user. Only Computer Administrator users can install and remove programs. Limited users and the Guest user cannot install or remove programs.

If a Limited user or the Guest user tries to install a program, Windows displays the Install Program As Other User dialog box (shown in Figure 5.2), telling them that they'll probably need administrator rights to do so. The user can specify a valid Computer Administrator username in the User Name text box and the appropriate password in the Password text box in order to proceed with administrative privileges.

FIGURE 5.2

To install or uninstall a program, you need to have Computer Administrator rights. If you don't, Windows stops you in your tracks with a warning such as this one.

If the user tries to continue with the installation without supplying Computer Administrator credentials, they usually run into an error message and abrupt termination of the setup routine. Figure 5.3 shows a couple of examples from Microsoft Office under different circumstances.

FIGURE 5.3

The Microsoft Office installation grinds to a halt if the user doesn't supply Computer Administrator credentials.

Figure 5.4 shows an example from a program that would prefer to remain nameless.

FIGURE 5.4

Perhaps the ultimate tight-lipped error message. Again, this signified that the installation had crashed because of a lack of permissions.

Who Is the Program Available To?

In some operating systems, you can install a program for some users but not for others. By contrast, Windows XP Home by default makes any program you install available to all users of the computer—provided that the program's setup routine does things in the right way. For example, if you install Office XP, the setup routine automatically creates shortcuts for all users to use the programs, so the next time any user logs on, they'll have a swath of new programs that they can use from the Start menu.

Office XP of course knows all about Windows XP, because they're both Microsoft products and they're roughly the same vintage. Eudora Pro 4.2, on the other hand, is a couple of years old at this writing and hasn't heard of Windows XP. But it installs fine, and is available to all users after installation, because its setup routine was (presumably) constructed along Microsoft's guidelines.

If the program's setup routine is deficient, you may need to install the program to an explicitly shared location or create shortcuts for it manually. For example, if you install Lotus SmartSuite Millennium Edition on Windows XP by using its setup routine, the user who installs SmartSuite gets the full set of shortcuts for it (plus a slew of shortcuts clogging the notification area, plus the indescribably wretched SmartCenter program-launcher and general menace). Other users get none of these—except for shortcuts to Net-It Now! Starter Edition, little-known Web-publishing companion software that was included with SmartSuite. This isn't useful, helpful, or even amusing.

TIP Windows expects all programs to be installed into the `\Program Files\` folder. Putting them there seems to help make them available for all users, though it's not a guarantee of success. Putting them in another folder is usually not a good idea, though if you need to make small programs easily accessible to all users, you might be tempted to put them in the `\Documents and Settings\All Users\` folder.

What Happens when Multiple Users Open the Same File at the Same Time?

As discussed in Chapter 3, problems arise with some programs when different users have the same file open. In Chapter 3, you saw how multiple users can open the same WordPad file at the same time, and each can save their changes into (or through) the other's changes. The result is pretty horrible.

Of course, some files are *designed* to be accessed by multiple users at the same time. For example, most database files are designed so that they can routinely be accessed by dozens, hundreds, or even thousands of users at the same time. The program prevents any *record* from being accessed by more than one user at a time. Some database programs prevent users from accessing records adjacent to any record being accessed by another user, to avoid the problems that can occur when records are added to or deleted from the database, either of which actions changes the numbering of records. But as long as each user is (virtually) cordoned off from all other users in the recordset, all is well. Similarly, Excel lets you explicitly share workbooks with other users.

At the risk of generalizing absurdly, more complex (or perhaps more smartly designed) programs use some form of locking mechanism so that they can tell when another user has a file open. This locking mechanism can consist of flags on the file in question, but often it's implemented as a separate file that's created when the file is opened and is deleted when the file is safely closed. You can see this easily enough with Word, which creates a locking file in the same folder as the document you've opened (or just saved, in the case of a new document) *and* sets a flag on the document. The locking file replaces the first two characters of the file's name with the characters ~$, so that a document named PENGUINS.DOC would generate a locking file named ~$ENGUINS.DOC. (Before you ask what happens with two-character filenames—if the file's name is six characters or fewer, Word *adds* the ~$ to the beginning of the filename. Seven characters, it replaces the first character. Eight characters, it replaces the first two.) If you open the locking file in a text editor (such as Notepad), you'll see that it contains the name of the current user (several times over, with variations in the spacing), some extended characters, and a variety of spaces.

NOTE *Word's locking files are hidden, so you won't see them in Explorer or in common dialog boxes unless you've selected the Show Hidden Files and Folders option button in the Advanced Settings list box on the View page of the Folder Options dialog box (Tools ➤ Folder Options) in Explorer.*

When you go to open a file, Word takes a quick look through the folder that contains the file to see if there's a locking file for it. If there is, it displays the File in Use dialog box to let you know about the problem and offer you options for proceeding. When you close the file that was open, Word deletes the locking file. But if you delete the locking file while the file is open, Word still knows that the file is open, because the flag is still set on the file, locking file or no.

As you might imagine, any program that doesn't use a locking mechanism so that it can tell when its files are open is going to have problems with multiple users accessing the same file. Very generally speaking, the less complex the program, the less likely it is to check that a file is open, and the more likely you are to have a problem with multiple users opening a file at the same time.

This problem also arises with files that can be opened with two or more different programs that are available on the computer. For example, if you use WordPad to open a Word document, it opens the document without any locking. You can then open the same document in Word while it's still open in WordPad. Word then locks the document, and you won't be able to save changes to the original file from WordPad.

What Happens when Multiple Users Run the Same Program at the Same Time?

By and large, having two or more users open the same document file at the same time (in the same program or in different programs) is more of a problem than having two or more users run the same program at the same time.

The brief answer to this question is as follows:

♦ Some programs are designed to be used by multiple users at once, so they don't cause problems.

◆ Some programs are too dumb to notice that they're being used by multiple users at once, so each session is happy enough. Some of these programs are designed to run multiple instances for any given user anyway, so they're in good shape to run multiple instances for multiple users.

◆ Some programs notice there's a problem with multiple sessions and deal with it gracefully.

◆ Some programs notice there's a problem and sulk conspicuously.

With most programs, the problem comes not with the executable files and libraries (DLLs) but with the settings files. Windows XP handles the executables and libraries, running each in a separate memory space and segregating each user's programs from all other users' programs. But if a program is designed to use a central settings file rather than to implement a separate settings file for each user, the settings file can cause problems. If the program locks the settings file when the first user runs the program, the settings file won't be available when the second user runs the program. The same goes if the settings information is stored in a central location in the Registry.

Perhaps the easiest way around this is to use a separate settings file for each user, or to keep separate Registry entries. As you'd imagine, that's what the Microsoft Office programs do. For example, if you're familiar with Word, you probably know that it stores a lot of information in the global template, which is saved in the file NORMAL.DOT. The global template is always loaded when you're running Word, so Word maintains a separate global template for each user. This way, it avoids problems when users in separate sessions of the same installation of Word change their settings at the same time.

Problems also arise when separate instances of a program try to use the same hardware resources on the computer at the same time—for example, the COM ports, the audio output, or the microphone input—or the same set of data files.

How a program handles a problem gracefully depends on what the program does and what the problem is. In a program that can manage only one instance running on the computer at the same time, when you start a new instance in another user session, you'll typically see a warning dialog box that lets you choose to either cancel running the new instance of the program or forcibly terminate the other user's session of the program.

As you'd expect, some programs are smarter than others. In particular, it shouldn't come as a shattering surprise to learn that current Microsoft programs are much more aware of Windows XP's multiuser functionality than earlier Microsoft programs or programs from other software companies.

For example, Windows Media Player lets you switch user while you're still playing music or video, or copying a CD. The music (or video) continues to run even while the Welcome screen is displayed. If you then log back on as the same user, Windows Media Player simply keeps going without interruption. Only when you log on as another user does Windows Media Player stop playing the music or video (or copying the CD). And—perhaps more important—it exits the instance that was playing or copying for the other user, freeing up the sound and video circuitry together with whatever system resources it was using. (Before you ask—Windows Media Player quits when you switch to another user even if it wasn't playing.)

TIP   *If you're experiencing problems with programs that can't run multiple instances successfully at the same time, or with shared documents being opened by multiple users at once, turn off Fast User Switching as discussed in Chapter 10. All these problems should disappear in a quick puff of logic.*

Installing a Program

After all that buildup, you're probably raring to install a program. You can do this in a couple of ways. The more formal way is to use the Add/Remove Programs window. The less formal way is to run the setup program manually.

Whichever method you choose, if the program you want to install is on a CD, DVD, or other removable medium, load it into the appropriate drive on your computer. If the program is on a network drive, establish a connection to that drive.

If you have Autoplay enabled, the setup routine may start automatically when you insert the CD or other medium in its drive. Cancel out of the setup routine if you want to use the Add/Remove Programs window for the installation. Alternatively, use the manual installation method described in the section after next.

NOTE *The section "Customizing and Turning Off Autoplay " in Chapter 6 discusses how to customize and turn off Autoplay.*

Installing a Program Using the Add/Remove Programs Window

The Add/Remove Programs window provides the more formal way of installing a program. This way has no particular advantages over the next method except that, because Windows explicitly manages the process, it should have no excuse for professing ignorance of the program after you've installed it.

1. Choose Start ➤ Control Panel. Windows displays Control Panel.

2. Click the Add or Remove Programs link. Windows displays the Add or Remove Programs window.

3. Click the Add New Programs button in the left-hand column of the window. Windows displays the Add New Programs page of the window (shown in Figure 5.5).

FIGURE 5.5

The formal way to install a new program is to use the Add New Programs page of the Add or Remove Programs window.

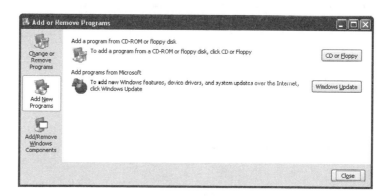

4. Click the CD or Floppy button, even if the program you want to install is on a removable disk, on a network drive, or on your hard drive. Windows displays the Install Program from Floppy Disk or CD-ROM page of the Add Programs Wizard.

5. If the program is on a CD or a floppy, and you haven't inserted the disk already, do so now.

6. Click the Next button. Windows searches your floppy drives and CD drives for a SETUP.EXE file and displays the Run Installation Program dialog box (shown in Figure 5.6). If Windows found a SETUP.EXE file, it lists it in the Open text box and invites you to make sure it's the correct file; if it didn't (as in the figure), it suggests you browse to find the file manually.

FIGURE 5.6

If Windows doesn't find a setup file in your floppy drive or CD drive, the Run Installation Program dialog box lets you choose the file manually.

7. If Windows didn't find a SETUP.EXE file, or if it found the wrong one (which can happen easily enough if you have multiple CD drives and install software frequently), click the Browse button. Windows displays the Browse dialog box. Navigate to the folder that contains the setup file, select it, and click the Open button. Windows closes the Browse dialog box and enters the program's path and filename in the Open text box.

TIP If the setup program has a name other than SETUP.EXE, NNSETUP.EXE, INSTALL.EXE, or another widely used name or name variation for setup programs, Windows may not list it in the Browse dialog box. Select the Programs entry in the Files of Type drop-down list in the Browse dialog box to make Windows list all executable files in the folder. If the setup program isn't an executable file (unlikely but possible), select the All Files entry in the Files of Type drop-down list.

8. Click the Finish button. Windows closes the Run Installation Program dialog box and starts the program's setup routine.

What happens next depends on the whims of the setup routine's programmers or (more commonly) on which of the two commonly used Windows installers they used—InstallShield or WISE. Suffice it to say that the usual steps for installing a program include agreeing to its license agreement, choosing which of the program's components to install, selecting a Start menu folder (often still called a Program Group, in an embarrassing hangover from Windows 3.*x* days), and twiddling your thumbs (or taking a break). For some programs, you'll have to reboot as well.

At the end of the setup routine, you usually get a message box telling you that setup completed successfully. When you dismiss this message box, Windows returns you to the Add or Remove Programs window, from which you can add further programs or simply click the Close button.

NOTE You might be tempted to use the Change or Remove Programs page of the Add or Remove Programs window to see how much space the program you just installed is taking up—but don't bother, because the Change or Remove Programs page doesn't list the new program until you close the Add or Remove Programs window and reopen it.

You may see some amusing messages when installing old programs. Figure 5.7 shows an example: a Windows 95 Detected dialog box from the setup routine for PhotoWorks 2.01. PhotoWorks identifies Windows XP as Windows 95, tells you that Windows 95 is still in beta, and warns you that PhotoWorks may not work properly because of that. (After this gaffe, PhotoWorks figured out that Windows XP didn't need Win32s, the 32-bit subsystem for Windows 3.1*x*; installed itself correctly; and then ran without problems.)

FIGURE 5.7

The PhotoWorks 2.01 setup routine identifies Windows XP as Windows 95— and warns you that it's still in beta.

If Windows knows about a problem with an application you're installing, it displays a dialog box warning you of the problem. Figure 5.8 shows an example in which Windows has detected an issue with Lotus Approach 9.*x*. (If you're using Autoplay, Windows performs such a check before even starting the setup routine for the software.) Click the Continue button, the Cancel button, or the Details button as appropriate.

FIGURE 5.8

Windows alerts you to any known issues with software that you're about to install.

Installing a Program by Running Its Setup Routine Manually

If you don't like jumping through hoops unnecessarily, you may want to forsake using the Add or Remove Programs window for installing programs, because you can add a program just as easily by running its setup routine manually.

To run a setup routine manually, double-click its file in an Explorer window or on the Desktop. Alternatively, use the Run dialog box as follows:

1. Choose Start ➤ Run or press Winkey+R. Windows displays the Run dialog box (shown in Figure 5.9).

FIGURE 5.9

You can also run a setup routine directly from an Explorer window or from the Run dialog box.

2. In the Open text box, enter the path and filename of the setup program. Either type in the path and filename or browse to it. (Click the Browse button. Windows displays the Browse dialog box. Navigate to and select the file, then click the Open button.)

3. Click the OK button. Windows closes the Run dialog box and starts running the setup program.

Removing a Program

Removing a program is usually even easier than installing a program, because you don't usually have to have the setup medium (CD, floppy, or whatever) and you have to make even fewer decisions. Follow these steps to remove a program:

1. Choose Start ➤ Control Panel. Windows displays Control Panel.

2. Click the Add or Remove Programs link. Windows displays the Add or Remove Programs window.

3. If the Change or Remove Programs page of the window isn't displayed, click its tab. Windows displays the page.

4. In the Currently Installed Programs list box, select the entry for the program you want to remove. The Add or Remove Programs window displays information about the program—its size (the approximate amount of space it's taking up on disk), a rough description of how often you've used it over the last 30 days (Frequently, Occasionally, or Rarely), and the date you used it last—together with a Change/Remove button. Figure 5.10 shows these details.

    ◆ If you have a lot of programs installed, use the Sort By drop-down list to sort the programs. You can sort by Name, Size, Frequency of Use, and Date Last Used. Obviously enough, the Name category is useful for finding programs by name. The Size category is good for determining which programs are hogging disk space when you need to free some up in a hurry. And the Frequency of Use category and Date Last Used category are useful for rooting out the programs you installed on a whim and have used hardly at all.

FIGURE 5.10

Use the Change or Remove Programs page of the Add or Remove Programs dialog box to uninstall a 32-bit program.

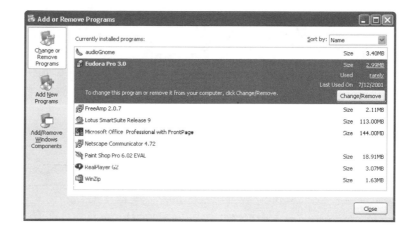

5. Click the Change/Remove button. Windows checks to see if other users are using the computer (because they might be using the program that you're about to remove). If any other user is logged on, Windows displays the Warning dialog box shown in Figure 5.11.

   ◆ At this point, you can click the Switch User button to display the Welcome screen, then log on as each user from there and log them off. But usually you'll find it easier to use the Users page of Task Manager to either switch to the other users or simply log them off.

   ◆ When you're ready, click the Continue button if the Warning dialog box is still displayed. (If it's not, click the Change/Remove button in the Add or Remove Programs dialog box instead.)

FIGURE 5.11

Before letting you uninstall a program, Windows warns you if other users are logged on to the computer.

6. Once you've cleared the Warning hurdle, Windows invokes the uninstall routine for the program. The next steps vary depending on the program (or on its programmers or the tool they chose), but in most cases, you either specify which parts of the program to uninstall (if the program contains discrete components) or simply confirm that you want to get rid of the program:

   ◆ Figure 5.12 shows the Confirm File Deletion dialog box that Windows displays when you issue the Change/Remove command for Eudora Pro.

FIGURE 5.12

Windows invokes the program's uninstall routine. In this case, Eudora Pro offers no partial uninstall and so treats the uninstall as a deletion.

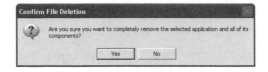

◆ Figure 5.13 shows the Select Lotus SmartSuite Applications dialog box, which lets you specify which SmartSuite programs to uninstall or uninstall the lot.

FIGURE 5.13

Windows invokes the program's uninstall routine, which lets you specify which components to uninstall (as in the case with Lotus Smart-Suite here) or confirm the uninstallation.

7. Choose uninstall options and click the appropriate button. You'll then typically see something like Figure 5.14, in which unInstallShield (InstallShield's evil twin) is removing Eudora Pro.

FIGURE 5.14

Here's an example of what you see when uninstalling a program. Here, unInstallShield is removing Eudora Pro.

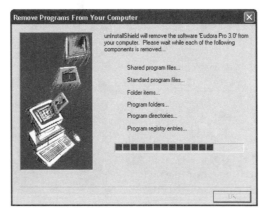

8. If the uninstall routine tells you that it was unable to remove some parts of the program that you've asked to uninstall completely, it usually lets you know which parts are left. For example, unInstallShield provides a Details button that you can click to display a dialog box such as that shown in Figure 5.15. In this case, it's easy enough to delete these folders manually by using Explorer.

FIGURE 5.15

If unInstallShield can't remove all the components of a program, it provides details in the Details dialog box.

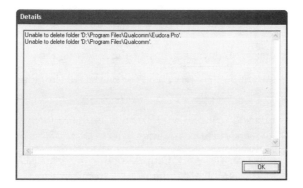

TROUBLESHOOTING: UNINSTALLING 16-BIT WINDOWS PROGRAMS AND DOS PROGRAMS

Windows' Add or Remove Programs feature tracks all 32-bit programs installed on the computer, and it's able to track many 16-bit programs as well. But some 16-bit Windows programs and most DOS programs don't show up in the Add or Remove Programs dialog box, so you can't remove them that way.

The preferred way of removing a program that doesn't show up in the Add or Remove Programs window is to run its uninstall routine manually. Some Windows programs add a shortcut to their uninstall routine to the program folder (or, in Windows XP, to the Start menu submenu) that contains their other shortcuts. If there's no shortcut, you'll need to dig through the folder that contains the program to see if it has one. The file might be an EXE file, but it might also be a BAT (batch) file.

If the program doesn't have an uninstall routine, you'll need to remove it manually. (If you've only just installed the program, you *could* use the System Restore feature to return your system to its state before you installed the program—but usually you'll have made other changes to your computer since installing the program. Chapter 16 discusses how to use System Restore.) This usually means deleting the folder (or folders) that contains the program and removing any references to it that you can find.

There are two problems with removing a program manually like this. First, you don't necessarily know where the program has put all its files. This is usually more of a problem with Windows programs, which (following Microsoft's own recommendations) often put shared files into the \Windows\ folder or one of its subfolders, than with DOS programs (which probably don't know that the \Windows\ folder exists, and certainly don't care about it even if they do know). So if you simply delete the folder or folders the program created, it may leave detritus in other folders. (This is why uninstall routines exist, of course.)

The second problem is that the program may also have added commands to configuration files of their era (such as AUTOEXEC.BAT or WIN.INI) that will cause errors when you've deleted its files. You'll need to discover these additions manually (usually when you get an error message) and delete them or comment them out manually. Because Windows XP uses these configuration files only for compatibility, these errors are likely to cause you annoyance rather than grief—unlike in the old days, when a command for a missing program could make Windows 3.1 refuse to load.

Running Programs

In Windows, you can start a program in any of several ways. If you've used a previous version of Windows, you'll probably be familiar with these ways. They break down into two categories: starting a program directly by opening it, and starting a program indirectly by opening a file whose file type is associated with the program. (Chapter 6 discusses file types and how you can associate them with programs.)

You can start a program directly in any of the following ways:

- Click its shortcut on the Start menu (or on the All Programs submenu, or on one of its submenus).

- Double-click a shortcut on the Desktop or in an Explorer window. (Chapter 6 discusses how to create shortcuts wherever you want.)

- Click a shortcut on the Quick Launch toolbar or another Desktop toolbar. (Chapter 4 discusses the Desktop toolbars and how to customize them.)

- Choose Start ➢ Run. Windows displays the Run dialog box. Enter the name of the program in the Open text box, either by typing or by browsing for it. (Click the Browse button. Windows displays the Browse dialog box. Navigate to and select the file, then click the Open button.) Then click the OK button.

NOTE   *Using the Run dialog box seems a clumsy way of running a program, but it's useful for running Windows utilities for which Windows doesn't provide a Start menu entry (for example, the Registry Editor, discussed in Chapter 12) and for running programs for which you don't want to create a shortcut but whose path and filename you can type (or otherwise enter) without undue effort.*

- Double-click the icon or listing for the program in an Explorer window (or on the Desktop). You can also use the Search feature (discussed in Chapter 6) to locate the program you want to run.

Almost all setup routines create shortcuts to their programs automatically. Usually, the setup routine puts a shortcut on the Start menu or in a subfolder of the Start menu. Some setup routines place a shortcut directly on the Desktop; some consult you first; others don't. Some setup routines offer to also put a shortcut in the notification area; other setup routines do so without consulting you; while others yet are civilized enough to respect Microsoft's guidelines for notification-area use—that the notification area should be used for warnings and information rather than loaded with shortcuts for every program in sight.

Running Programs in Compatibility Mode

If a program won't run normally on Windows XP, try running it in Compatibility mode. As mentioned earlier in the chapter, Compatibility mode lets you tell Windows XP to emulate Windows 95, Windows 98, Windows NT 4, or Windows 2000 so that a program thinks it's running on the operating system it knows and likes.

TIP   *Often, you'll need to run the program's setup routine in Compatibility mode to get the program to install in the first place. Then run the program itself in Compatibility mode as well.*

Windows XP comes with the Microsoft AppCompat database of compatibility problems known about programs. AppCompat is automatically updated by the Windows Update, which gives you another incentive to accept Windows Update's offers to download every update available—at least until your computer's hardware and all your software are working as perfectly as you could wish.

NOTE   You can set Compatibility mode only on files on local drives. You can't set Compatibility mode on a program located on a network drive. But you can create a shortcut on a local drive to a program located elsewhere, and then specify Compatibility mode for the shortcut.

Windows provides two ways of setting up a program to run in Compatibility mode. The first way is formal and cumbersome, but it lets you test whether the Compatibility mode you choose works for the program. The second way is much quicker, but you run the risk of getting a program comprehensively hung if Compatibility mode doesn't work.

Let's take it from the top.

The Formal Way of Setting Compatibility Mode

Here's the formal way to run a program in Compatibility mode:

1. Choose Start ➤ All Programs ➤ Accessories ➤ Program Compatibility Wizard.
   Windows displays a Help and Support Center window and starts the Program Compatibility Wizard in it.

2. Read the information and cautions on the Welcome to the Program Compatibility Wizard screen and click the Next button. Windows displays the How Do You Want to Locate the Program That You Would Like to Run with Compatibility Settings? screen (shown in Figure 5.16).

FIGURE 5.16

On the How Do You Want to Locate the Program That You Would Like to Run with Compatibility Settings? screen in Help and Support Center, choose how to select the program you want to run in Compatibility mode.

3. Use one of the following three ways to locate the program:

   ◆ To set Compatibility mode for a program that's already installed, select the I Want to Choose from a List of Programs option button and click the Next button. The Wizard scans your hard drive and displays a list of programs (Figure 5.17 shows an example). Select the program and click the Next button.

FIGURE 5.17

Select a program from the list that the Program Compatibility Wizard assembles.

◆ To set Compatibility mode for a program you're installing from CD, insert the CD, select the I Want to Use the Program in the CD-ROM Drive option button, and click the Next button.

◆ To set Compatibility mode for a program that isn't installed and whose installation medium isn't on CD, or if you're just feeling ornery, select the I Want to Locate the Program Manually option button and click the Next button. The Wizard displays the Which Program Do You Want to Run with Compatibility Settings? screen (shown in Figure 5.18). Enter the path in the text box, either by typing or by clicking the Browse button and using the resulting Please Select Application dialog box (a common Open dialog box) to select the program. Click the Next button.

FIGURE 5.18

If necessary, or if you prefer, you can identify the program manually on the Which Program Do You Want to Run with Compatibility Settings? screen of the Program Compatibility Wizard.

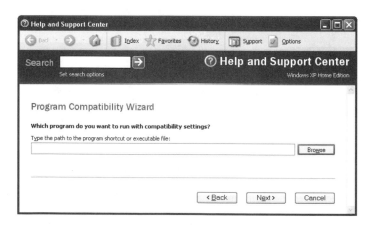

4. The Wizard displays the Select a Compatibility Mode for the Program screen (shown in Figure 5.19).

FIGURE 5.19

On the Select a Compatibility Mode for the Program screen of the Program Compatibility Wizard, select the Compatibility mode you want to use.

5. Select the option button for the operating system you think the program needs: Windows 95, Windows NT 4.0 (Service Pack 5), Windows 98/Windows Me, or Windows 2000.

6. Click the Next button. The Wizard displays the Select Display Settings for the Program screen (shown in Figure 5.20).

FIGURE 5.20

On the Select Display Settings for the Program screen of the Program Compatibility Wizard, you can apply limitations to the display settings used for the program.

7. If you know the program needs display limitations, select the 256 Colors check box, the 640×480 Screen Resolution check box, or the Disable Visual Themes check box.

◆ For most programs, you don't need to select any of these display limitations.

8. Click the Next button. The Wizard displays the Test Your Compatibility Settings screen (shown in Figure 5.21).

FIGURE 5.21

On the Test Your Compatibility Settings screen of the Program Compatibility Wizard, check through the settings you've chosen, then click the Next button to test them.

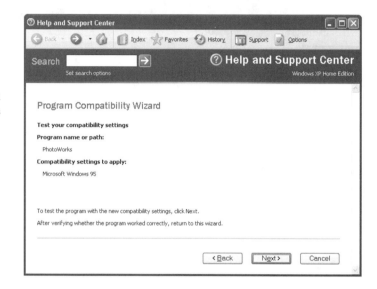

9. Check the settings you've chosen, then click the Next button. The Wizard launches the program with the compatibility settings you specified and displays the Did the Program Work Correctly? screen (shown in Figure 5.22).

FIGURE 5.22

On the Did the Program Work Correctly? screen, tell the Program Compatibility Wizard whether the program launched correctly with the computer settings.

10. Choose the appropriate option button:

◆ If the program ran okay, select the Yes, Set This Program to Always Use These Compatibility Settings option button. The Wizard displays the Program Compatibility Data screen (shown in Figure 5.23), on which you can choose whether to send Microsoft information on the program, the settings you chose, and whether they solved the problem.

FIGURE 5.23

On the Program Compatibility Data screen of the Program Compatibility Wizard, you can choose whether to send Microsoft information on a program that you couldn't get to work.

◆ If the program didn't run correctly, but you want to try other settings, select the No, Try Different Compatibility Settings option button. Click the Next button. The Wizard returns to the Select a Compatibility Mode for the Program screen. Return to step 5 and try again.

◆ When no compatibility settings seem to work, select the No, I Am Finished Trying Compatibility Settings option button. Click the Next button. The Wizard displays the Program Compatibility Data screen (discussed above). In this case, you have more incentive for sending Microsoft information, as it may help them fix the problem with this program in the future.

11. Choose the Yes button or the No button as appropriate.

12. Click the Next button. If you chose the Yes button, the Wizard sends the compatibility data. Either way, it displays the Completing the Program Compatibility Wizard page.

13. Click the Finish button. The Wizard closes itself.

Remember that old version of VirusScan from earlier in the chapter that didn't want to install on Windows XP? It was happy to install in Compatibility mode for Windows 95—but parts of it wouldn't run on Windows XP (see Figure 5.24).

FIGURE 5.24

VirusScan decided it really didn't like Windows XP after all.

The Quick Way of Setting Compatibility Mode

The quick way of setting Compatibility mode is as follows:

1. Right-click the shortcut for the program and select Properties from the context menu. Windows displays the Properties dialog box for the shortcut.

2. Click the Compatibility tab. Windows displays the Compatibility page. Figure 5.25 shows an example of this page.

FIGURE 5.25

You can also choose Compatibility mode settings on the Compatibility page of the Properties dialog box for the shortcut.

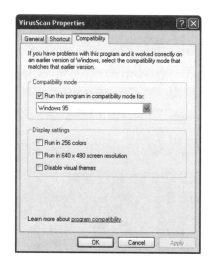

3. Select the Run This Program in Compatibility Mode For check box if it's not already selected.

4. In the drop-down list, select the mode you want to use.

5. In the Display Settings group box, select the Run in 256 Colors check box, the Run in 640×480 Screen Resolution check box, or the Disable Visual Themes check box as necessary. (Again, for most programs, you won't need to set these options.)

6. Click the OK button. Windows applies your choice and closes the Properties dialog box.

Even with Compatibility Mode, Some Programs Don't Work

Some programs plain don't work even when you use Compatibility mode. For example, Lotus Smart-Suite 96 won't install on Windows XP, no matter whether you try to run it from the CD or copy its files to a local drive and use Compatibility mode. When you run the SmartSuite 96 installation routine on Windows XP, you get to specify the program folder and the type of installation (typical, minimal, custom). Then the installation crashes with the Output message box shown in Figure 5.26. This message box mentions an overflow (trying to put more information in a memory register than will fit), but beyond that, it tells you next to nothing useful.

FIGURE 5.26

Lotus SmartSuite 96's installation routine crashes with an Output CNTR+318: Overflow message box.

After this message box, the program terminates. If you're feeling determined, and you lather, rinse, and repeat, exactly the same thing happens over.

NOTE *Microsoft may have fixed this problem with SmartSuite 96 by the time you read this book. But given that Lotus used to be a major competitor of Microsoft's in the programs field, and that IBM (which owns Lotus) used to make OS/2, and that this version of SmartSuite is a good five years out of date, they may not have gotten around to bothering.*

Making Programs Run at Start-up

If you want a program to start every time you log on to Windows, place a shortcut to it in your Startup folder. Starting programs automatically like this can save you a few seconds each time you start Windows if you always need to use the same programs.

Your Startup folder is the `\Documents and Settings\`*Username*`\Start Menu\Programs\Startup\` folder. Navigating to this folder usually takes nearly as long as placing in it the shortcuts you want. (See the next chapter for instructions on creating shortcuts.)

TIP *To make a program start automatically each time any user of your computer logs on to Windows, place a shortcut to the program in the Startup folder for All Users. As you'd guess, this folder is the* `\Documents and Settings\` `All Users\Start Menu\Programs\Startup\` *folder.*

To prevent a program from running at start-up, obviously enough, you remove its shortcut from the Startup folder.

Specifying the Size at Which a Program Runs

By default, most programs start in a "normal" window—one that's not maximized and not minimized. If you'd like the program to start up maximized or minimized, right-click its shortcut and choose Properties from the context menu. In the Properties dialog box that Windows displays, choose Maximized or Minimized in the Run drop-down list on the Shortcut page, and click the OK button.

You can do this for any shortcut to a program or to a file—so if you want, you can have shortcuts open different-sized windows for files of the same file type.

EXPERT KNOWLEDGE: RUNNING A PROGRAM AS ANOTHER USER

Sometimes you may need to run a program under a user account other than the user as which you're currently logged on to Windows. For example, your current user account might not have permission to access the file or folder you want to manipulate with the program, but you have access to another account that does have permission for that file or folder.

To run a program as another user, create a shortcut to it and set the advanced property called Run with Different Credentials, as described in the section "Setting Advanced Properties for a Shortcut" in the next chapter. When you open that shortcut, Windows displays the Run As dialog box, in which you can specify the user account under which you want to run the program.

Killing a Program That's Not Responding

Programs run pretty well on Windows XP—but not all programs run well all the time. Sooner or later, a program will hang or crash on you.

When this happens, first, make sure the program doesn't have an open dialog box that you can't see. When you're working with multiple programs, you can easily get an open dialog box stuck behind another open window. If the dialog box is *application modal*, it prevents you from doing anything else in the program until you dismiss it. (Dialog boxes can also be *system modal*, in which case they prevent you from doing anything else on your computer until you deal with them.)

Minimize all other open windows (right-click the Taskbar and choose Show the Desktop from the context menu), and see if the dialog box appears. If not, you'll probably have the program that's not responding still displayed on your screen, probably with only some parts of the window correctly drawn. For example, typically the areas of the program that were covered by other programs or windows will not be redrawn (or not redrawn correctly).

Next, try using Alt+Tab to switch to the program and bring out from behind it any dialog box that's hiding. Chances are that this won't work either, but it's worth a try. If the dialog box appears, deal with it as usual, and the program should come back to life.

If that didn't work, try using Task Manager to switch to the program:

1. Right-click the Taskbar and choose Task Manager from the context menu. Windows displays Task Manager.

2. If the Applications page isn't displayed, click the Applications tab. Windows displays the Applications page (shown in Figure 5.27), which lists each running program and its status. The status can be either Running (all is well with the program, as far as Windows is concerned) or Not Responding (Windows believes that the program is not responding to conventional stimuli).

3. Select the program that's not responding.

4. Click the Switch To button. Task Manager attempts to switch to the program, and minimizes itself in the process.

FIGURE 5.27

The Applications page of Task Manager lists all running programs and their status: Running or Not Responding.

If that didn't work either, it's probably time to kill the program. Take the following steps:

1. Restore Task Manager by clicking its button on the Taskbar.

2. Decide whether the program has hung or crashed. (See the nearby sidebar "*Not Responding Status Isn't Always Terminal*" for advice on determining whether the program is still viable.)

3. Select the task in the Task list.

4. Click the End Task button. Windows displays the End Program dialog box (shown in Figure 5.28).

FIGURE 5.28

To terminate the program, click the End Now button in the End Program dialog box.

5. Click the End Now button. Windows terminates the program and frees up the memory it contained.

If killing the program like this doesn't work, you have several options. Here they are, in descending order of preference:

◆ Close all other programs that are responding. Then log off Windows. Doing this should shut down any programs you're running.

◆ If you can't close the program and can't log off Windows, but Task Manager is still working (apart from not being able to kill the program), use Task Manager to switch to another user, then log off the user session that contains the crashed program.

◆ At this point, you're pretty much out of options. Reach for the Reset button on your computer.

EXPERT KNOWLEDGE: *NOT RESPONDING* **STATUS ISN'T ALWAYS TERMINAL**

When you see a program listed as having Not Responding status on the Applications page of Task Manager, you may be tempted to kill it off right away. But you'd do better to stay your hand for a minute or two. Why? Because Not Responding status doesn't necessarily mean that a program has hung or crashed:

◆ First, Not Responding may mean nothing more than that a program is responding more slowly than Windows expects; if you give it a few seconds, or perhaps a few minutes, it may start responding normally again. If your computer seems unresponsive overall, back off and give it a few minutes to sort itself out.

◆ Second (and often related to the first point), Not Responding may mean that Windows is struggling to allocate enough memory to the program; this often causes the program to run slowly. Task Manager is a little harsh in this respect—it's Windows' fault that the program isn't responding, but Task Manager points the finger at the program.

◆ Third, VBA-enabled programs (for example, Microsoft Word and Microsoft PowerPoint) are often listed as Not Responding when they're running a VBA routine or macro. In this case, Not Responding means only that VBA temporarily has control over the program. When VBA releases control of the program— in other words, when the routine ends—Task Manager lists the program as Running again. (If the program shouldn't be running a macro, try pressing Ctrl+Break to stop it.)

Up Next

This chapter has discussed how to install programs, how to run them—using Compatibility mode if necessary—and how to remove them when you tire of them. It's also touched on the types of programs you shouldn't even try to install on Windows XP, and it's shown you how to use Task Manager to kill a program that's crashed.

The next chapter discusses how to manage files in Explorer.

Chapter 6

Managing Your Files and Folders

THIS CHAPTER DISCUSSES HOW to manage files and folders. It starts off by touching briefly on what files and folders *are* (if you've used a computer before, you probably know this already) before getting into what you can do with them and the tools that Windows provides.

Tools? It's more like *tool*, actually, because most of your file management takes place in Explorer. As you'll see, you can use Explorer to search for files and folders; to manipulate them; to view them in different ways; and to dispose of them. You can also use Explorer to compress and uncompress files and folders, either to save space or to make archive files that are easy to handle.

At the end of the chapter, after all the other excitement, you'll find a section on how to configure Autoplay's behavior and how to customize folders in Explorer.

This chapter covers the following topics:

- ◆ The basics of files and folders
- ◆ Understanding what Explorer is
- ◆ Investigating the Windows XP folder structure
- ◆ Navigating in Explorer
- ◆ Copying, moving, and deleting files and folders
- ◆ Finding files and folders
- ◆ Creating and using shortcuts
- ◆ Configuring Autoplay
- ◆ Customizing Explorer

The Basics of Files and Folders

If you've used computers much in the past, you'll be familiar with the concept of a *file*—a named object containing information that's stored on a disk. The disk in question can be a local hard drive; a networked drive (including a Web server); a CD, DVD, or other removable drive; a tape drive; or even a humble floppy drive. Whichever type of drive the file's on, it's stored in a number of clusters on some form of disk. You don't have to worry about the number of clusters a file occupies. In fact, you need worry about the fact that each file occupies various clusters only when your drive needs defragmenting (which you'll find discussed in Chapter 11) or when you need to either wipe out all trace of a file that you've deleted or restore a file that you've deleted (a topic discussed later in this chapter).

Anyway, each file has a name so that you and the computer can distinguish it. In Windows XP, each filename can be up to 255 characters long. Filenames can include letters, numbers, and some punctuation, such as commas (,), periods (.), semicolons (;), single quotation marks (' '), or apostrophes ('). Filenames cannot contain forward slashes (/), backslashes (\ ), colons (:), asterisks (*), question marks (?), double quotation marks ("), less-than (<) and greater-than (>) signs, or pipe characters (|), because Windows either uses those characters literally or assigns special meanings to them. For example, a colon is used to denote a drive (for instance, C: refers to the C drive), and an asterisk is a wildcard character that represents one or more characters in searches and commands.

The 255 characters include the path to the file. The *path* (also sometimes called the *directory path*) gives the sequence of drive and folders that describes the location of the file and folders. For example, if a file is in the \My Documents\ folder in the \Nik\ folder of the \Documents and Settings\ folder on the C: drive, the path to that file is C:\Documents and Settings\Nik\My Documents\. That path is 43 characters long, including the backslashes and the spaces, so any file stored in that folder can have a filename of up to 212 characters (255 minus the 43 characters in the path).

A *folder* is a file that can contain other files. (You don't *have* to put any files in a folder, but an empty folder is little use to man or beast.) By using folders, you can organize your files into logical categories (or whimsical categories, if you prefer). Folder names can be up to 255 characters long, but you'll need to keep them shorter than this if you want to use long filenames within the folders. The possible length of a folder name also includes the path to the folder and the length of any filenames that the folder already contains. (If you rename a folder so that the path and filename of a file it contains add up to more than 255 characters, you can no longer access the file.)

When working in a graphical environment such as Windows, you don't normally need to type paths to files the way you often had to in DOS and similar text-based operating systems. Instead, you use graphical representations of folders and files to navigate to the folders and files you need, and then manipulate them in graphical windows. Some of this you do with Explorer (discussed in the next section), and some via dialog boxes in the individual programs.

Using Explorer

This section discusses Explorer, starting off with the trickiest thing about it—understanding what it is.

What *Is* Explorer?

If you've used Explorer before, you may think this a dumb question—but Explorer is actually a very complex program. You can use it almost effortlessly in several simple ways. But to understand why it behaves as it does when you take certain actions with it, you need to understand what it is and does. That means wrapping your mind around a few slithery concepts.

Ready?

First, Explorer is the shell for Windows. Briefly, in computing terms a *shell* is a logical layer that provides an interface between the user and the computer. In this case, it's a graphical interface—a *very* graphical interface. The Desktop, with its icons and pretty background picture, is run by Explorer, as are the Taskbar, the notification area, and so on. (If you doubt this, see the next sidebar.) Explorer essentially gives you a way to interact with Windows without talking code.

Second, Explorer is a utility for managing files and folders—all kinds of files and folders, including the files and folders that make up the Start menu, those that make up Control Panel, and so forth. File management is how most people view Explorer's role, because Explorer windows are the most obvious manifestation of Explorer. We'll investigate Explorer's file-management capabilities in some detail in this chapter.

Third, Explorer is intimately related to Internet Explorer, the Web browser that's built into Windows. If you look at them together, you see that Explorer (in its second role) and Internet Explorer are basically the same program with somewhat different manifestations and different roles. On the one hand, many of the commands—menu commands, toolbars, keyboard shortcuts—are the same. On the other hand, the Options dialog boxes are substantially different, as are the toolbars. On that first hand, you can use them to do many of the same things (for example, to display the contents of a folder). On that other hand, they're clearly designed to be used in different ways. Most of the time, anyway.

Back to that first hand again, the programs act in much the same way. In fact, Explorer can even switch itself to Internet Explorer when you're using it. This can be freaky until you learn to expect the unexpected. If you enter a URL in the Address bar in Explorer and click the Go button, Explorer opens the Web site and transmutes itself into Internet Explorer. By contrast, if you enter a local drive letter or path in the Address bar in Internet Explorer, it doesn't entirely change into Explorer. Instead, it just stays as Internet Explorer and displays the contents of the drive or the folder—but with all the Explorer features. For example, if you pull down the Tools menu, you'll see a Folder Options item (the Explorer menu item) rather than an Internet Options item.

But you've got better things to do than worry about how Windows Explorer and Internet Explorer might really be two heads of the same Cerberus-Explorer whose third head is the Desktop shell. If you use Windows Explorer for interacting with files and folders on local and network drives, and Internet Explorer for interacting with anything that might consider itself a Web site, you'll get on fine.

Besides, Explorer *isn't* Cerberus—at least, in that hewing off one of the heads doesn't affect the body. When you run Internet Explorer, it shows up as a separate process on the Processes page of Task Manager—a process named IEXPLORE.EXE. If you point Explorer at a Web site so that it turns into Internet Explorer, its Taskbar button takes on an Internet Explorer icon, but the process associated with it is EXPLORER.EXE, not IEXPLORE.EXE. If you terminate Explorer (as described in that next sidebar), Internet Explorer isn't affected. Likewise, if you terminate Internet Explorer, Explorer shouldn't be affected.

To try to keep things clear, the rest of this book uses *Explorer* to refer to Explorer windows (including those for My Computer, Network Connections, Control Panel, and so on), *Internet Explorer* to refer to any Explorer window that calls itself Internet Explorer, and descriptive terms such as *the Desktop, the Taskbar,* and *the notification area* to refer to the named components of the shell.

EXPERT KNOWLEDGE: PROVING THAT EXPLORER RUNS THE DESKTOP AND TASKBAR

If you doubt that Explorer really runs the Desktop, the Taskbar, and so on, you might want to try this little experiment. It's not exactly *recommended*, because it gives Windows a vigorous elbow in the solar plexus. But because Windows is quite stable and resilient, winding it a little doesn't usually do any damage.

Take these steps:

1. Close all the programs you're running.

2. Right-click open space on the Taskbar and choose Task Manager from the context menu. Windows displays Task Manager.

3. Click the Processes tab. Windows displays the Processes page.

4. Select the process named EXPLORER.EXE.

5. Click the End Process button. Task Manager displays a Task Manager Warning dialog box warning that terminating the process could lose you data or cause your system to be unstable.

6. Click the Yes button. Task Manager terminates Explorer. The Taskbar and notification area disappear, together with the Start button and all your Desktop icons. Task Manager keeps on chugging along happily enough.

7. Try right-clicking the Desktop. You won't get even a hint of a context menu.

8. Back in Task Manager, click the Applications tab. Windows displays the Applications page.

9. Click the New Task button. Windows displays the Create New Task dialog box.

10. Enter **explorer** in the Open text box.

11. Click the OK button. Windows closes the Create New Task dialog box and runs Explorer. Back come your icons, the Start button, the Taskbar, and the notification area, together with all their functionality.

You don't *have* to try this little experiment at home—but if you just tried it, wasn't it instructive? (Or at least entertaining?) Now, it might be a good idea to restart Windows in case it's feeling a little peculiar.

Starting Explorer

You can start Explorer in a variety of ways. The easiest way to start Explorer is to click the Start button so that Windows displays the Start menu, and then choose one of the shortcuts associated with Explorer: My Documents, My Pictures, My Music, My Computer, or (if you have it) My Network Places. Each of these opens an Explorer window to the specified folder in Open mode, one of the two modes that Explorer supports.

To open one of these folders in Explore mode (the other mode), click the Start button to display the Start menu, right-click the item for the folder, and choose Explore from the context menu.

You can also run Explorer by choosing Start ➢ All Programs ➢ Accessories ➢ Windows Explorer. Doing so opens a My Computer window in Explore mode.

EXPLORING MY COMPUTER

If you choose Start ➢ My Computer, Windows displays an Explorer window showing the contents of the My Computer folder in Open mode, as in the example shown in Figure 6.1.

FIGURE 6.1

The My Computer folder open in an Explorer window

There's a whole bunch of stuff to look at here, even (or especially) if you've used Windows before.

The first thing to notice is how different this looks from Explorer windows in earlier versions of Windows. The window has a title bar as usual, of course, and a menu bar and a toolbar. There's no Address bar, as there was by default in My Computer windows in earlier versions of Windows, but you can display it easily enough by choosing View ➢ Toolbars ➢ Address Bar. (And when you do, you may notice that the toolbar and the Address bar together look suspiciously like those in Internet Explorer....)

The main action is on the left side of the screen, where Explorer is displaying three collapsible panes courtesy of the new WebView and ListView features:

Tasks pane This pane provides a list of tasks that you might want to perform on the folder or, when you select an object that's displayed, on that object. (More on this in a moment.) For the My Computer folder, the Tasks pane is named System Tasks.

Other Places pane This pane provides a short list of other folders that you might want to access from the current folder. This list of folders changes to suit the current folder. The list usually includes the parent folder of the current folder (the *parent* of an object is the folder that contains it) and a carefully selected variety of widely used folders such as the Desktop folder, the My Computer folder, the My Documents folder, the Shared Documents folder, and (if your computer is connected to a network) the My Network Places folder. Each of the folders is presented as a link in the list, so you can access the folder by clicking it.

Details pane   This pane displays information about the selected folder or file. For example, when a file is selected, the pane displays the filename, the file type (such as WordPad Document), and the date that the file was modified.

Each pane collapses down to its title bar to save space and make room for its fellow panes. To collapse a pane, or expand it again, click its title bar. If you're feeling the need for precision, you can click the double-arrow button at the right end of the title bar, but the effect is the same as clicking the title bar, so it's not worth making the extra effort.

As you can see in the figure, the main part of the window presents several lists:

Files Stored on This Computer   This list shows the shared folders available to the current user. For a Limited user or the Guest user, this is typically a short list, containing only the \Shared Documents\ folder, which is shared among all users of the computer. Computer Administrator users can see other users' shared folders as well, as in the figure.

Hard Disk Drives   This list shows all the hard drives on the computer.

Devices with Removable Storage   This list shows all the devices with removable storage, such as floppy drives, CD drives, DVD drives, Zip drives, CompactFlash disk reader, and so on.

Network Drives   This list shows all the network drives (if any) to which the computer is attached for the current user.

Below the Network Drives list appears a Scanners and Cameras list if you have one or more scanners or cameras.

The lists of items in the Tasks pane and the Other Places pane are links, so you click them once to take the action on the selected file or folder or to access the other place. The items displayed on the right side of the screen are objects. An *object* is a general descriptor for a distinct entity on a computer—a file, a folder, a computer, and so on. Basically (no pun intended), everything that you see in Explorer is an object. A file is an object; a folder is an object; a computer you can see across the network is an object. Even the links displayed in the Tasks list and the Other Places list are objects.

Each object has *properties*—attributes—that you can view and, in some cases, set. For example, most objects have a name property that contains the name of the object. Many also have a read-only property that can be turned on and off and that determines whether a user can change the object (if the property is off) or not (if the property is on). Most objects also have *methods*—actions associated with the object. For example, many objects have a click method that determines what takes place when you click the object. Link objects execute when you click them, whereas objects such as files and folders become selected when you click them and execute when you double-click them.

WebView and ListView make the display more graphical, and provide quick access to a number of tasks and quick navigation to folders connected to the current folder. In essence, WebView and ListView try to simplify navigating from folder to folder and taking frequently used actions. In particular, they target navigating via the folder tree and taking actions via the context menu. As mentioned earlier in the book, usability tests suggested that 80 percent of Windows users weren't using the context menu effectively.

If you're new to Windows, or if you've never gotten the hang of navigating via the folder tree (*where* was that folder again?) or using the context menus, WebView and ListView may prove welcome. But if you're used to using the folder tree and the context menus, you probably won't find WebView and ListView much of an improvement. You may even find them detrimental, because they make it harder to navigate

Windows in your time-tested ways. If so, you can turn them off easily enough, as discussed in the section after next. Context menus, which have been enhanced for many folders in Windows XP, almost always contain more commands than the Tasks list, and they're easier to access with the mouse than the Tasks list.

EXPLORE MODE

Okay, so that was My Computer in Open mode. Now open it in Explore mode to see the difference. Click the Start button to display the Start menu, then right-click the My Computer item and choose Explore from the context menu. You get a window like that shown in Figure 6.2.

FIGURE 6.2

Viewed in Explore mode, the My Computer window displays the Folders Explorer bar on the left side for quick navigation.

As you can see, in Explore mode, Explorer displays a pane called Folders at the left side of the window pane. The formal name for this pane is the Folders Explorer bar. Clicking the Folders button on the toolbar or choosing View ➤ Explorer Bar ➤ Folders from a My Computer window displayed in Open mode gives you the same effect as opening the window afresh in Explore mode.

Explore mode makes moving up and down the directory tree easy, so Explorer hides the WebView and ListView panes in Explore mode. This also makes more room on the right side of the screen for the files or folders you're presumably interested in. If you find Explore mode useful, you'll probably want to make it the default action for Explorer (as discussed in the next sidebar).

TURNING OFF WEBVIEW AND LISTVIEW

If you're used to blazing up and down a directory tree with a few well-placed clicks of the mouse, you may well find WebView and ListView irritating or worse. You can turn them off easily enough. Follow these steps:

1. From an Explorer window, choose Tools ➤ Folder Options. Explorer displays the Folder Options dialog box with the General page foremost.

2. In the Tasks group box, select the Use Windows Classic Folders option button.

3. Click the OK button. Explorer closes the Folder Options dialog box and applies the change, removing WebView and ListView from all Explorer windows displayed.

To turn WebView and ListView back on, display the Folder Options dialog box again, select the Show Common Tasks in Folders option button in the Tasks group box, and click the OK button. This book assumes you're using WebView and ListView.

EXPERT KNOWLEDGE: SETTING EXPLORER TO USE EXPLORE MODE BY DEFAULT

If you've used a previous version of Windows and you're used to navigating via a tree of folders, you may find Explore mode so much easier and more useful than Open mode that you want to use it all the time. To make Explorer use Explore mode rather than Open mode by default, follow these steps:

1. From an Explorer window (in either Open mode or Explore mode), choose Tools ➤ Folder Options. Windows displays the Folder Options dialog box.

2. Click the File Types tab. Windows displays the File Types page.

3. Select the (NONE) Folder item. The *(NONE)* bit is in the Extensions list; the *Folder* bit is in the File Types list.

4. Click the Advanced button. Windows displays the Edit File Type dialog box for the Folder file type. (You'll find a discussion of file types toward the end of this chapter.)

5. In the Actions list box, make sure the Explore action is selected. (Windows usually selects it automatically.)

6. Click the Set Default button. Windows applies Explore as the default action for folders.

7. Click the OK button. Windows closes the Edit File Type dialog box, returning you to the Folder Options dialog box.

8. Click the Close button. Windows closes the Folder Options dialog box.

From now on, Windows opens folders using Explore mode. To switch back to Open as the default action, repeat the above steps but choose the Open action in step 5.

Investigating Windows XP's Folder Structure

This section discusses the folder structure that Windows XP creates on your hard drive. You don't *need* to understand the folder structure in order to use Windows XP effectively, because the WebView and ListView features provide an easy way to navigate among the folders that Windows wants you to use. But if you want to administer the computer and make the best use of Windows' management features, or if you just want to know a bit more about what's going on behind the curtain, it's a great help to understand the folder structure.

Windows XP Home has firm ideas about where it wants you to keep the files you install, create, and use. By and large, you'll get along best if you stick to these guidelines, but they can sure feel restrictive. (If you've used earlier versions of Windows, they'll probably seem familiar.) Windows also has firm ideas about what you should look at and what you shouldn't. If you use WebView and ListView, Windows attempts to shield you from seeing system folders and program folders. In fact, it tries to discourage you from looking in any folder except those that contain your documents and those that contain settings it expects you to change, such as the Control Panel folder and the Network Connections folder.

NOTE   *The folder structure discussed in this section is the one you get when you install a fresh copy of Windows on your computer without monkeying around with any settings. If anyone has customized your computer, things might look a bit different.*

Windows places all these folders on the same drive Windows itself is on.

From the My Computer window (Start ➢ My Computer), double click the hard disk drive that contains Windows. (If you have only one hard disk drive, you shouldn't have a problem. If you have multiple drives, you may need to work out which contains Windows.) You'll see something like Figure 6.3, which tells you that "This folder contains files that keep your system working properly. You should not modify its contents."

FIGURE 6.3

By default, Windows tries to shield you from the details of the system folders and program folders on your computer.

Click the Show the Contents of This Drive link in the System Tasks task list. Windows displays the folders it was hiding. You should see something like Figure 6.4.

FIGURE 6.4

Click the Show the Contents of This Drive link to make Windows display the folders.

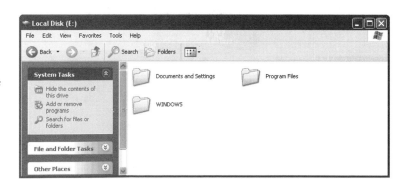

But that's not all the folders. By default, Windows hides what it calls *protected operating system files*—translation, any files or folders it would prefer you not to see or mess with. It also hides hidden files and folders—files and folders marked with the hidden attribute. (For example, you'll remember from the previous chapter that Word uses hidden locking files to prevent the same file from being accessed by more than one person at the same time.)

To display hidden files and protected operating system files, follow these steps:

1. Choose Tools ➢ Folder Options. Windows displays the Folder Options dialog box.

2. Click the View tab. Windows displays the View page.

3. In the Advanced Settings list box, select the Show Hidden Files and Folders option button. (By default, the Do Not Show Hidden Files and Folders option button is selected.)

4. A little further down the Advanced Settings list box, clear the Hide Protected Operating System Files check box. Windows displays the Warning dialog box shown in Figure 6.5 when you clear this check box.

FIGURE 6.5

Windows displays this Warning dialog box when you choose to display the protected operating system files.

5. Click the Yes button. Windows closes the Warning dialog box and returns you to the Folder Options dialog box.

6. Click the OK button. Windows closes the Folder Options dialog box and applies the changes. You should now see a list of folders similar to that in Figure 6.6.

FIGURE 6.6

Here's the folder structure that Windows creates.

The folder structure contains the `\Windows\` folder, the `\Program Files\` folder, and the `\Documents and Settings\` folder. The following sections discuss these folders. There's also the `\Recycler\` folder, which controls the Recycle Bin, and the `\System Volume Information\` folder, which Windows keeps locked against user intrusion to protect its contents.

THE *WINDOWS*\ FOLDER

The \Windows\ folder contains most of the files needed to keep Windows running. (As you'll see in a moment, there are a couple of others.) If you open this folder, you'll see a plethora of subfolders and files. (You know how people use the word *plethora* when they really just mean *more than a handful?* Well, this really is a plethora.)

Windows is right that it's not a good idea for you to mess with these files: There's very little you can do to them that will benefit you or your PC, and a fair amount you can do to them that will harm your PC. (That said, Windows XP is able to restore many system files after they've accidentally been deleted.)

THE *PROGRAM FILES*\ FOLDER

The \Program Files\ folder is designed to hold (almost) all the files for all the programs on the computer. The setup routines for most programs know that they're supposed to install the programs in the \Program Files\ folder, and do so unless you explicitly specify a different location.

Because Microsoft a) created Windows and b) is an 800-pound gorilla, however, it can put its program files wherever it wants to. For example, you'll find the program files for Notepad (a limited text-editor program included with Windows XP) in the \Windows\ folder rather than in the \Program Files\ folder.

You'll need to mess with the contents of the \Program Files\ folder only seldom—for example, when something goes wrong with an uninstall routine, or when you're trying to perform a special tweak on a program. But if you have even an averagely curious disposition, you'll probably want to spelunk through this folder to see what it contains.

THE *DOCUMENTS* AND *SETTINGS*\ FOLDER

The \Documents and Settings\ folder contains the documents and settings for each user for whom you create an account on the computer and who has logged on at least once, together with a \My Documents\ folder for the Guest user (also, once they've logged on). This is the place where Microsoft would like you to hang out—though Microsoft would prefer you to access it via the My Documents shortcut, which automatically lands the user in his or her own directory.

If you've been following along, go ahead and double-click the icon for the \Documents and Settings\ folder. You'll see something like the window shown in Figure 6.7.

FIGURE 6.7

The contents of the \Documents and Settings\ folder

The number of folders you see in your \Documents and Settings\ folder depends on the number of user accounts you set up on the computer. In the figure, the Rondolophbergers have four user accounts, so there's a folder for each of them: the \Andy Rondolophberger\ folder, the \Jaq Rondolophberger\ folder, the \Lexi Rondolophberger\ folder, and the \Nik Rondolophberger\ folder. Then there's an \All Users\ folder, which contains documents and settings that are available to all users. There's the \Default User\ folder, which contains settings that are applied to all new users created (until the user comes along and customizes them). There's the \Guest\ folder, which contains documents and settings for the Guest user. And then there's a \LocalService\ folder and a \NetworkService\ folder. We'll get to these folders in a minute or two.

Each user's folder contains the same folder structure—until the user changes it, anyway. Figure 6.8 shows an example.

FIGURE 6.8

Each user's folder contains this folder structure (until someone changes it).

Table 6.1 provides a quick breakdown of the folder structure. We'll examine the \My Documents\ folder in a minute or two. The other folders we'll examine as needed later in the book.

TABLE 6.1: FOLDERS IN EACH USER'S FOLDER STRUCTURE

FOLDER NAME	CONTENTS
\Application Data\	Your settings for programs, including your Address Book data and program templates
\Cookies\	Your cookie files (information used to allow Web sites to provide user-specific services)
\Desktop\	Your Desktop shortcuts (apart from the standard Desktop shortcuts that Windows provides, such as My Computer and the Recycle Bin)
\Favorites\	Your Explorer favorites and Internet Explorer favorites

TABLE 6.1: FOLDERS IN EACH USER'S FOLDER STRUCTURE *(continued)*

FOLDER NAME	CONTENTS
\Local Settings\	Your Internet Explorer history, temporary files, temporary Internet files, and Desktop settings
\My Documents\	Your documents
\My Recent Documents\	Shortcuts to files and folders you've used recently
\NetHood\	Information about mappings to any network drives that your computer connects to
\PrintHood\	The mappings for any network printers that your computer is set up to use
\SendTo\	The shortcuts, files, and folders that make up your Send To menu
\Start Menu\	Your shortcuts for the Start menu
\Templates\	Templates for programs you install
\Windows\	Your Windows settings

THE *MY DOCUMENTS*\ FOLDER

The \My Documents\ folder is where Microsoft would like you to keep all your data files except those that you explicitly want to share with other people. The main advantages to using the \My Documents\ folder (which you can rename to whatever you want) are first that you have a central point of administration that you can protect or back up easily, and second that all the programs know where to look for files.

As you might imagine, which user is active governs which folder is connected to the My Documents link on the Start menu. For example, when Andy Rondolophberger is logged on and active, choosing Start ➢ My Documents causes Explorer to display the \Documents and Settings\Andy Rondolophberger\My Documents\ folder rather than any of the \My Documents\ folders in the other users' folders.

Each user's \My Documents\ folder contains a \My Music\ folder and a \My Pictures\ folder. When you start using videos (for example, the first time you start Windows Movie Maker), Windows adds a \My Videos\ folder as well. You get no prizes for guessing what's intended to go in each of these folders. Windows XP–aware programs use these folders by default. For example, WordPad automatically uses the \My Documents\ folder. Windows Media Player has been schooled to save music you copy to folders within the \My Music\ folder, though you can teach it without difficulty to save music elsewhere if you prefer. And Paint uses the \My Pictures\ folder, as does Windows Picture and Fax Viewer.

PAGEFILE.SYS AND HIBERFIL.SYS

As mentioned a page or two ago, not *all* the files needed to keep Windows running reside in the \Windows\ folder. There are a couple of massive exceptions: the paging file and the hibernation file.

If you look at the root of the drive on which Windows is installed, you should see a large file named PAGEFILE or PAGEFILE.SYS. This is the *paging file*—a file in which Windows stores information temporarily to supplement the RAM (physical memory) in your computer. (Chapter 11 discusses what the paging file does and how you can optimize and move it.) Don't mess with this file via

Explorer. It's locked, because it's perpetually in use, so all you can do is stub your toes on it. You probably have better things to do with your time.

You may also see another large file, this one called HIBERFIL or HIBERFIL.SYS. This is the *hibernation file*—the file in which Windows stores the contents of RAM when you put the computer into Hibernation mode. It takes up as many megabytes of disk space as you have RAM. Don't mess with this file either. If you don't like sacrificing a chunk of disk space to it, turn off hibernation as discussed in Chapter 14.

You may also see a file called ERRORLOG or ERRORLOG.TXT. As its name suggests, this is a log of critical errors that have occurred on your computer. If you haven't had any critical errors, there won't be an error log file yet.

THE *LOCALSERVICE*\ FOLDER AND *NETWORKSERVICE*\ FOLDER

The \LocalService\ folder and the \NetworkService\ folder are created and maintained automatically by Windows XP in order to manage local services and network services. These folders are locked so that you cannot access them. You *can* circumvent the locking so that you can open the folders and make changes in them, but there's no point in doing so, because it will make Windows seriously unhappy and can do you no conceivable good.

RESTORING THE FOLDER OPTIONS

Now that we've finished our quick tour of the folder structure, you might want to hide the program folders, system folders, and hidden files again so that you see Windows as nature—that is, Microsoft—intended. To do so, follow these steps:

1. Choose Tools ➢ Folder Options. Windows displays the Folder Options dialog box.

2. Click the View tab. Windows displays the View page.

3. In the Advanced Settings list box, select the Do Not Show Hidden Files and Folders option button and the Hide Protected Operating System Files check box.

4. Click the OK button. Windows closes the Folder Options dialog box and applies the changes.

Using Views

Explorer supports a number of views to let you browse folders and files comfortably and be able to tell what you're looking at:

Thumbnails view   This view displays a largish icon for each file or folder. Thumbnails view is good for finding the graphics you need, because Explorer displays a miniature version of each graphic. For file types other than graphics, Explorer displays only the icon associated with the program.

Tiles view   This view displays a medium-sized icon for each file or folder. Explorer displays icons rather than miniatures for graphics files. Tiles view is good for sorting through folders that contain relatively few files or folders.

Icons view   This view displays a smallish icon for each file or folder. Again, Explorer displays icons rather than miniatures for graphics files. Icons view is good for sorting through folders that contain a moderate number of files or folders.

List view   This view displays a list of folders and files, showing only the filename or folder name and a small icon for each. List view is good for sorting through folders that contain a large number of files or folders.

Details   This view displays a list of files and folders, showing the filename or folder name, a small icon, the file size, the file type, and the date on which it was modified. (You can customize the details displayed for a folder. See the end of the chapter for, uh, details.) Details view is good for sorting files and folders by different types of information to quickly locate the file or folder you need.

You can apply a view in any of these ways:

♦ Pull down the View menu and choose Thumbnails, Tiles, Icons, List, or Details from it.

♦ Click the View button on the toolbar and choose Thumbnails, Tiles, Icons, List, or Details from the menu it displays.

♦ Right-click in an Explorer window, choose View from the context menu, and choose Thumbnails, Tiles, Icons, List, or Details from the submenu that appears.

See pages 22–23 of the *Essential Skills* section for a visual guide to using views.

Arranging Icons

Once you've applied a view, you can choose how to arrange the icons displayed in the view. Explorer lets you arrange icons in the following ways:

Name   This arrangement sorts the icons alphabetically by name.

Size   This arrangement sorts the icons by size.

Type   This arrangement sorts the icons by their file type. If the folder contains more than a few files, sorting by file type produces groups by file type, so it's a good way of finding all the documents of a particular type (for example, text file) that the folder contains.

Modified   This arrangement sorts the icons by the date the file they represent was last modified.

NOTE   In some special folders, Explorer offers other arrangements. For example, in the My Computer folder, it offers Total Size, Free Space, and Comments arrangements.

Once you've chosen the arrangement, you can turn on the Show in Groups option to arrange the icons into groups by the attribute on which they're currently sorted. For example, if you're using Details view, and you've sorted by the Modified column, turning on the Show in Groups option divides the icons into groups such as Today and Earlier This Month. If you've sorted Details view by the Type column, turning on the Show in Groups option creates groups based on the types of file—for example, File Folder, Text Document, and so on.

There are two further options that you can toggle on and off as suits you:

Auto Arrange   This option tells Explorer to arrange the icons into the specified order automatically. This option is good for keeping the icons in order.

Align to Grid   This option tells Explorer to snap the icons back to an invisible grid, thus tidying up the window.

To specify the sorting and arrangement, pull down the View menu, or right-click in open space in the Explorer window to display the context menu. Choose the Arrange Icons By item from the menu, and then select the command from the submenu.

TIP   In Details view, you can sort quickly by clicking the heading of the column by which you want to sort. The first click produces an ascending sort (alphabetical order; smallest numbers first). A second click produces a descending sort (reverse alphabetical order; largest numbers first).

Using the Standard Buttons Toolbar

The main Explorer toolbar, which is called the Standard Buttons toolbar, contains six graphical buttons for actions you may well need to take frequently:

Back button   Click this button to move back to the previous folder that was displayed. Click the down arrow at the right side of the button to display a drop-down list of the previous folders so that you can move back several steps at once.

Forward button   This is the counterpart to the Back button, and becomes available only when you've used the Back button. After you've moved back along the path of folders you've browsed through, you can use the Forward button to move forward through them again. As with the Back button, use the drop-down list to move forward several steps at once.

Up button   Click this button to browse to the parent folder of the current folder. (The parent, you'll remember, is the folder that contains the object in question.)

Search button   Click this button to display Search Companion, the tool for searching for files, folders, or computers. (The section "Finding a File or Folder," later in this chapter, discusses how to use Search Companion.)

Folders button   Click this button to toggle the display of the Folders Explorer bar.

Views button   Click this button to display a menu from which you can choose a view for the current window.

USING THE ADDRESS BAR AND THE LINKS BAR

Isn't *Standard Buttons toolbar* quite a mouthful for a plain old toolbar (especially one with only six buttons)? It sure is. But this toolbar needs a distinctive name because Explorer provides two other toolbars: the Address bar and the Links bar. To toggle the display of these toolbars, choose View ➢ Toolbars ➢ Address Bar or View ➢ Toolbars ➢ Links, or right-click the menu bar or a displayed toolbar and choose Address Bar or Links from the context menu.

The Address bar contains a drop-down list box that gives access to folders and files on local and network drives. Figure 6.9 shows an example. Alternatively, you can type in a path or a URL and click the Go button.

The Links toolbar provides links to Web sites. We'll discuss this toolbar more when we examine Internet Explorer in Chapter 18.

FIGURE 6.9

The Address bar provides quick access to the folders on your computer.

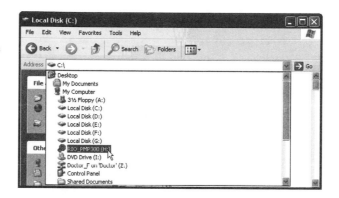

REARRANGING THE MENU BAR AND TOOLBARS

By default, the toolbars and menu bar are locked so that you can't move them. To unlock toolbars (and the menu bar, which is an honorary toolbar), right-click the menu bar or a displayed toolbar and choose Lock the Toolbars from the context menu, or choose View ➤ Toolbars ➤ Lock the Toolbars.

Once you've unlocked the toolbars, you can drag them and the menu bar to different sizes or arrangements by clicking and dragging the sizing handles (the rows of dots) at their left ends. For example, you can display the Address bar on the same row as the Standard Buttons toolbar to save space.

When the toolbars and menu bar are where you want them, you can lock them again (by repeating the process described two paragraphs above) if you want to prevent yourself from moving them by accident.

Navigating Explorer with the Keyboard

If you prefer the keyboard to the mouse, you can perform some basic navigation with menu commands and keyboard shortcuts. Table 6.2 lists these keyboard shortcuts and menu commands.

TABLE 6.2: KEYBOARD SHORTCUTS AND MENU COMMANDS FOR NAVIGATING EXPLORER

ACTION	KEYBOARD SHORTCUT	MENU COMMAND
Back	Alt+←	View ➤ Go To ➤ Back
Forward	Alt+→	View ➤ Go To ➤ Forward
Up One Level	Backspace	View ➤ Go To ➤ Up One Level
Home Page	Alt+Home	View ➤ Go To ➤ Home Page
My Computer	—	View ➤ Go To ➤ My Computer
Display Address bar drop-down list	F4	—
Refresh	F5	View ➤ Refresh

Navigating Using the Address Bar

You can also navigate from folder to folder by using the Address bar. To display the Address bar, choose View ➢ Toolbars ➢ Address Bar. By default, the Address bar appears below the toolbar.

Navigating by Using Type-Down Addressing

Instead of navigating with the mouse, you can navigate through folders by using the keyboard and type-down addressing. This technique works best for accessing a file or folder whose name and location you know, but you can also use it for browsing through folders or files if you find it fast and comfortable.

Type-down addressing sounds forbidding, but it's easy and intuitive—and a great saver of time and effort. To use type-down addressing, you put the focus in the appropriate area—for example, in an Explorer window or in the Address bar. You can then type down through the contents of the folder. As you type each letter, the program (in this case, Explorer; the technique works for all properly implemented Windows programs) selects the files or folders that match what you've typed, progressively narrowing down the possibilities until you reach the file or folder you want. At that point (or before), you can select it as usual.

That sounds a bit vague, doesn't it? Type-down addressing is much easier to do than to describe. Here's an example:

1. Choose Start ➢ My Computer. Windows displays an Explorer window showing the contents of the My Computer folder.

2. Click the Address bar to select the current entry (My Computer). Alternatively, press the F4 key and then the Esc key.

   ◆ If the Address bar isn't displayed, choose View ➢ Toolbars ➢ Address Bar to display it.

3. Type the letter of the hard drive on which Windows is installed, followed by a colon and a backslash. For example:

   `C:\`

4. Explorer displays a drop-down list of the matching folders and files.

5. Type **m**. Windows narrows down the selection to the files and folders that start with the letter *m*—typically, the `\My Music\` folder (unless you've created other folders).

6. Press the ↓ key to select the `\My Music\` folder.

7. You can then type down through the `\My Music\` folder to reach the folder or file you want.

Refreshing the Listing in a Folder

If you take an action in an Explorer window that causes the contents of the folder displayed to change, Explorer automatically refreshes the display. For example, if you create a new folder within the folder, Explorer updates the display to show the new folder along with the previous contents. If you delete a file from the folder, Explorer removes the file from the display.

But if the contents of the folder displayed in an Explorer window change because of an action *not* taken in the window, Explorer doesn't usually notice right away. Periodically, it will re-read the contents of the folder and update the display. But if you don't want to wait, you can refresh the display manually. To do so, press the F5 key, or choose View ➤ Refresh, or right-click empty space in the folder and choose Refresh from the context menu.

Creating a New Folder

To create a new folder, right-click open space in the folder in which you want to create the new folder and choose New ➤ Folder from the context menu. Alternatively, choose File ➤ New ➤ Folder. Windows creates a new folder, assigns it a default name based on New Folder (New Folder, New Folder (2), and so on), and displays an edit box around the name. Type the name for the folder and press the Enter key or click elsewhere in the window.

NOTE *You can create a new folder in any folder for which you have permission to make changes. If you're not able to create a folder, the folder you're working in probably belongs to someone else who has chosen not to give you permission to make changes in it.*

See page 25 of the *Essential Skills* section for a visual guide to creating a folder.

Copying a File or Folder

Windows supports a variety of ways to copy a file or folder. Because copying is an action you'll need to perform often, this section shows you most of the convenient ways to copy a file or folder. (Comprehensive as these ways may seem, there are a couple of unorthodox ways of copying a file or folder that this section *doesn't* show.) You may end up using only one or two of these ways, but you should try them all out and see which you find easiest in which circumstances.

Some of the ways of copying a file involve opening multiple Explorer windows (or having the Desktop visible). For others, you need have only one Explorer window open (or the Desktop).

This section says "a file or folder," but most of the techniques work just as well for multiple files or folders. As you'll see, one technique doesn't work so well.

See pages 27–28 of the *Essential Skills* section for a visual guide to copying and moving a file or folder.

Copying a File or Folder by Using Drag-and-Drop

To copy a file or folder to another folder on the same drive, take the following steps:

1. Open an Explorer window to the folder that contains the source file or folder.

2. Open another Explorer window to the destination folder.

3. Select the file or folder in the source folder.

4. Hold down the Ctrl key and drag the file or folder to the destination folder. Windows displays a plus (+) sign on the mouse pointer to indicate that the file or folder will be copied to the destination.

5. Release the mouse button and the Ctrl key. Windows copies the file or folder. While it does so, it displays the Copying dialog box (shown in Figure 6.10), which lists the file or folder being copied and an estimate of how long the whole Copy operation will take.

FIGURE 6.10

The Copying dialog box shows you the progress of the Copy operation.

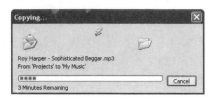

To copy a file or folder to another folder on another drive, use the technique described in the above list, but don't hold down the Ctrl key. When you drag a file to another drive, Windows automatically copies the file rather than moving it.

TIP   Because it's easy to get confused about which drive a folder is on, you may prefer to use the right-drag-and-drop technique described in the next section instead of the plain drag-and-drop technique.

Copying a File or Folder by Using Right-Drag-and-Drop

You can also copy a file or folder by using the right-drag-and-drop technique. Follow these steps:

1. Open an Explorer window to the folder that contains the source file or folder.

2. Open another Explorer window to the destination folder.

3. Right-click the file or folder in the source folder and right-drag it to the destination folder. Windows displays a context menu of options, as shown below.

4. Select the Copy Here item. Windows copies the file or folder.

The advantage of this technique over the plain drag-and-drop technique is that you can always choose whether to copy the file or move it.

Copying a File or Folder by Using Copy and Paste Commands

You can also copy a file or folder by using the Copy and Paste commands. Follow these steps:

1. Open an Explorer window to the source folder.

2. Select the file or folder.

3. Issue a Copy command by right-clicking and choosing Copy from the context menu or pressing Ctrl+C.

4. Navigate to the destination folder, either in the same Explorer window or in another Explorer window.

5. Select the destination folder.

6. Issue a Paste command by choosing Edit ➢ Paste, right-clicking and choosing Paste from the context menu, or pressing Ctrl+V. Windows pastes the copy of the file or folder into the destination folder.

Copying a File or Folder by Using the Copy to Folder Command

Another way of copying a file or folder is by using the Copy to Folder command as follows:

1. Select the file or folder you want to copy.

2. Click the Copy This File link or the Copy This Folder Link in the File and Folder Tasks list, or choose Edit ➤ Copy to Folder. Windows displays the Copy Items dialog box (shown in Figure 6.11).

FIGURE 6.11

You can also use the Copy to Folder command to copy a file or folder.

3. Navigate to the folder in which you want to create the copy of the file or folder.

   ◆ To create a new folder in the currently selected folder, click the Make New Folder button. Windows creates a folder named New Folder and displays an edit box around it. Type the name for the folder and press Enter. Windows renames the folder and leaves it selected.

4. Click the Copy button. Windows copies the file and closes the Copy Items dialog box.

Copying a File or Folder by Using the Send To Command

If you frequently need to copy files or folders to a particular location, using the Send To menu is usually the quickest and most convenient way to do so. For example, you might need to copy files or folders to another folder in order to burn backups of them to CD. You can customize the Send To menu (as described in the nearby sidebar) so that it offers the folder locations you need.

To copy a file or folder via the Send To menu, right-click the file or folder, choose Send To from the context menu, and select the location from the submenu. Figure 6.12 shows an example of using the Send To menu.

FIGURE 6.12

The Send To menu provides a fast and convenient way to copy files or folders into regularly used locations.

Expert Knowledge: Customizing the Send To Menu

To make the most of the Send To menu, customize it so that it contains the folders and programs you use most. Take the following steps:

1. Open an Explorer window to My Computer and navigate through the \Documents and Settings\ folder to the \SendTo\ folder. It's under \Documents and Settings*Username*\.

   ◆ In order to be able to customize the Send To menu, you must have told Windows to show hidden files and folders. (From Explorer, choose Tools ➢ Folder Options, display the View page, and select the Show Hidden Files and Folders option button. Click the OK button.)

2. Open another Explorer window and navigate to a folder or program that you want to add to the Send To menu.

3. Arrange the two Explorer windows so that you can see both of them. (For example, if these two windows are the only windows open and not minimized, right-click the Taskbar and choose Tile Windows Horizontally or Tile Windows Vertically from the context menu.)

4. Right-click the program or folder and right-drag it to the \SendTo\ folder. Windows displays a context menu.

5. Select the Create Shortcut(s) Here item from the context menu. Windows adds a shortcut to the SendTo folder.

Now, when you display the Send To menu, the folder or program appears on it.

To create a cascading menu off the Send To menu, create a folder in the \SendTo\ folder, then place in that folder shortcuts to programs.

Moving a File or Folder

Windows' drag-and-drop techniques for moving a file depend on whether the source folder (the folder the file is currently in) and the destination folder (the folder to which you want to move the file) are on the same drive or on different drives. You'll notice that the techniques for moving are closely related to the techniques for copying a file.

Moving a File or Folder to a Folder on the Same Drive

To move a file or folder to a folder on the same drive:

1. Arrange one or two Explorer windows so that you can see the source folder and the destination.

2. Drag the file or folder from the source folder to the destination folder, and drop it there. Windows moves the file or folder.

Moving a File or Folder to a Folder on a Different Drive

To move a file or folder to a folder on a different drive:

1. Arrange one or two Explorer windows so that you can see the source folder and the destination.

2. Select the file or folder.

3. Hold down the Shift key.

4. Drag the file or folder to the destination folder.

5. Release the Shift key and the mouse button. Windows moves the file.

NOTE   This technique doesn't work well for multiple files or folders, because holding down the Shift key and clicking the selected files or folders (in preparation for dragging them) changes the selection.

Moving a File or Folder by Using Right-Drag-and-Drop

You can also move a file or folder by using the right-drag-and-drop technique. Follow these steps:

1. Open an Explorer window to the folder that contains the source file or folder.

2. Open another Explorer window to the destination folder.

3. Right-click the file or folder in the source folder and right-drag it to the destination folder. Windows displays a context menu of options.

4. Select the Move Here item. Windows moves the file or folder.

TIP   As with copying a file or folder, the right-drag technique has the advantage of eliminating any ambiguity caused by the result of a drag-and-drop operation depending on whether the destination folder is on the same drive as the source folder.

Moving a File or Folder by Using the Move to Folder Command

Another way of moving a file or folder is by using the Move to Folder command as follows:

1. Select the file or folder you want to move.

2. Click the Move This File link or the Move This Folder link in the File and Folder Tasks list, or choose Edit ➢ Move to Folder. Windows displays the Move Items dialog box.

3. Navigate to the destination folder.

    ◆ To create a new folder in the currently selected folder, click the Make New Folder button. Windows creates a folder named `New Folder` and displays an edit box around it. Type the name for the folder and press Enter. Windows renames the folder and leaves it selected.

4. Click the Move button. Windows copies the file and closes the Move Items dialog box.

Moving a File or Folder by Using the Cut and Paste Commands

You can also move a file or folder by using Cut and Paste commands. Follow these steps:

1. Open an Explorer window to the source folder.

2. Select the file or folder.

3. Issue a Cut command by choosing Edit ➢ Cut, right-clicking and choosing Cut from the context menu, or pressing Ctrl+X.

4. Navigate to the destination folder, either in the same Explorer window or in another Explorer window.

5. Select the destination folder.

6. Issue a Paste command by choosing Edit ➤ Paste, right-clicking and choosing Paste from the context menu, or pressing Ctrl+V. Windows pastes the cut file or folder into the destination folder.

EXPERT KNOWLEDGE: UNABLE TO COPY OR MOVE A FILE OR FOLDER

If you find you can't copy or move a file or folder, especially one on a network drive, you probably don't have the necessary permission. Because moving a file involves deleting its original from the folder it's in, you need permission to change a folder in order to move a file from it. Likewise, you need permission to create a file in the destination folder.

Deleting a File or Folder

Deleting a file or folder is easy once you understand the two-stage process that Windows uses to help prevent you from deleting any files or folders unintentionally.

By default, Windows maintains a holding area called the Recycle Bin for files or folders that you've deleted. (If you're familiar with Mac OS, you'll find similarities between the Recycle Bin and the Trash.) By default, when you tell Windows to delete a file or folder that's stored on a local drive, it confirms that you're sure about the deletion and then moves the file or folder from its current folder to the Recycle Bin. When a file or folder is in the Recycle Bin, it hasn't been deleted yet, and you can retrieve it easily. Windows calls this *restoring* a file or folder—restoring it from the Recycle Bin to its previous folder.

Files or folders stay in the Recycle Bin until either you empty it or the Recycle Bin grows to occupy its full allocation of disk space, at which point Windows starts discarding the oldest files (or folders) in the Recycle Bin without consultation to make space for further files (or folders) you delete.

WARNING   *When you tell Windows to delete a file or folder on a network drive, it deletes it immediately without moving the file to the Recycle Bin. Unless you work strictly with files or folders on local drives, it's a bad idea to rely on the Recycle Bin to rescue from careless Delete operations.*

If you want, you can turn off the confirmation of deletion, and you can stop Windows from using the Recycle Bin. That way, when you delete a file or folder, it's deleted instantly without confirmation, and there's no easy way of restoring it. (You can sometimes restore deleted files or folders with third-party undelete utilities, but you should bank on doing so no more than you should bank on winning the lottery.)

See page 32 of the *Essential Skills* section for a visual guide to deleting a file or folder.

Moving a File or Folder to the Recycle Bin

All that said, moving a file or folder to the Recycle Bin is easy. Take any of the following actions:

- Select the file or folder and press the Delete key.

- Right-click the file or folder and choose Delete from the context menu.

- Select the file in an Explorer window and click the Delete This File link. For a folder, click the Delete This Folder link.

- Select the file or folder and drag it to the Recycle Bin on the Desktop.

Once you've issued a Delete command, Windows displays the Confirm File Delete dialog box (shown in Figure 6.13). Click the Yes button if you're sure you want to send the file to the Recycle Bin.

FIGURE 6.13

By default, Windows displays the Confirm File Delete dialog box to double-check that you want to move the file to the Recycle Bin when you issue a Delete command.

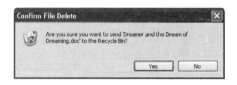

Deleting a folder works in almost exactly the same way as deleting a file, except that you need to worry about the contents of the folder as well as the folder itself. When you delete a folder, Windows displays the Confirm Folder Delete dialog box (shown in Figure 6.14) to make sure you've thought about what you're doing. Click the Yes button to proceed.

FIGURE 6.14

When you delete a folder, Windows displays the Confirm Folder Delete dialog box to make sure you realize you're deleting the folder's contents as well.

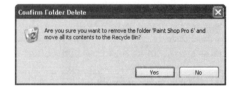

If you accidentally delete a file or folder in an Explorer window, you can recover it by choosing Edit ➢ Undo Delete or by pressing Ctrl+Z before taking any other actions in Explorer.

Deleting a File or Folder without Moving It to the Recycle Bin

To delete a file or folder without moving it to the Recycle Bin, hold down the Shift key as you issue the Delete command:

- Select the file or folder, hold down the Shift key, and press the Delete key.

- Right-click the file or folder, hold down the Shift key, and press the Delete key.

- Select the file or folder in an Explorer window, hold down the Shift key, and click the Delete This File link or the Delete This Folder link.

Windows displays the Confirm File Delete dialog box (shown in Figure 6.15) or the Confirm Folder Delete dialog box with different wording. Click the Yes button to delete the file.

FIGURE 6.15

Windows also double-checks when you choose to delete a file. Note the different wording in this dialog box from the dialog boxes in the two previous figures.

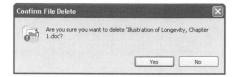

EXPERT KNOWLEDGE: FILE DELETION AND RESTORATION

Each file is stored in a number of clusters on your hard disk. The file system—NTFS or FAT—maintains an allocation table of which sectors each file is stored in. When a program goes to open a file, Windows gets from the file system the location of the clusters that contain the file and instructs the hard disk to retrieve the information. These clusters may be located pretty much anywhere on the disk partition that contains the drive. If they're located near each other, the hard disk can retrieve them faster, but if your drive is fragmented, they may be scattered all over the place. Either way, the file system puts them together so that Windows can present them as a single file in the correct order.

When you delete a file (when you perform a real Delete operation, that is—not when you put a file in the Recycle Bin), Windows tells the file system to get rid of the file. The file system does this by deleting the entry that tells it where the clusters containing the file are located. The clusters that the file is actually stored in remain intact but are marked as being available for storing data, so they may be overwritten by another Save operation at any point.

This method of deletion is why some undelete utilities can recover files that have been "deleted" by the operating system. Before the clusters containing the file have been overwritten, the information can be reassembled by synthesizing the entry in the allocation table. This may not work perfectly—often, the result is a bit rough—but it works surprisingly often. After the clusters containing the file have been overwritten, it's much harder to restore the file—though specialists can usually do it. If you followed the Monica Lewinsky affair, you'll probably remember that the NSA was able to restore the contents of Lewinsky's hard drive even though it had been formatted over several times.

If you want to be sure that nobody can easily restore the files you delete, get a shredder utility that overwrites the clusters in which the file's data is stored as soon as you delete the file. But if you want to be entirely sure that nobody will ever be able to read the data on your hard disk again, you'll probably need to destroy it. A sledgehammer, an oxy-acetylene lamp, or strong acid might be needed.

Recovering a File or Folder from the Recycle Bin

See page 33 of the *Essential Skills* section for a visual guide to recovering a deleted file or folder from the Recycle Bin.

To recover a file or folder from the Recycle Bin, open the Recycle Bin by double-clicking its icon on the Desktop. Right-click the file or folder in question and choose Restore from the context menu.

(Alternatively, select the file or folder and choose File ➤ Restore.) Windows restores the file or folder to its previous location.

If you've created another file with the same name in the folder the file to be restored previously occupied, Windows displays the Confirm File Replace dialog box to let you decide whether to over-write the newer file with the one you're restoring.

If you restore a folder from the Recycle Bin after you've created another folder with the same name in the folder into which it'll return, Windows displays the Confirm Folder Replace dialog box, which lets you specify whether to overwrite any files in the new folder that have the same names as those that you're restoring. Choose the Yes button, the Yes to All button, the No button, or the Cancel button as appropriate.

Emptying the Recycle Bin

Under normal usage, your Recycle Bin will gradually silt up with files and folders you delete. As mentioned earlier, Windows lets the Recycle Bin fill and then automatically deletes the oldest files or folders in it when it needs space for newer files or folders you delete, so you don't *need* to empty the Recycle Bin. But for security, it's a good idea to clear out old files you wouldn't want others to see. So every now and then, visit the Recycle Bin, look through it, recover anything you want to keep, and empty out the rest.

To empty the Recycle Bin, right-click the Recycle Bin icon on your Desktop and choose Empty Recycle Bin from the context menu. (If you've been reviewing the contents of the Recycle Bin and have the Recycle Bin window open, click the Empty the Recycle Bin link in the Recycle Bin Tasks list instead.) Windows displays the Confirm Multiple File Delete dialog box asking you to confirm the deletions. Click the Yes button to proceed.

Avoiding Using the Recycle Bin

If you want the files you delete to be removed immediately and stay deleted, you can tell Windows not to use the Recycle Bin at all. Right-click the Recycle Bin icon on your Desktop and choose Properties from the context menu. Windows displays the Recycle Bin Properties dialog box with the Global page (shown in Figure 6.16) foremost. The Recycle Bin Properties dialog box also contains a page for each hard drive on your computer.

Select the Do Not Move Files to the Recycle Bin. Remove Files Immediately when Deleted check box on the Global page. Click the OK button. Windows closes the Recycle Bin Properties dialog box.

Turning Off Confirmation of Deletion

If you're careful or sure in your actions, you may want to prevent Windows from double-checking that you know what you're doing each time you delete a file. Right-click the Recycle Bin icon on your Desktop and choose Properties from the context menu. Windows displays the Recycle Bin Properties dialog box with the Global page foremost. Clear the Display Delete Confirmation Dialog check box on the Global page. Click the OK button. Windows closes the Recycle Bin Properties dialog box. From now on, Windows will send files straight to the Recycle Bin without confirming the action.

FIGURE 6.16

If you don't want to use the Recycle Bin, you can tell Windows to remove files immediately when you delete them.

EXPERT KNOWLEDGE: RESIZING AND MOVING THE RECYCLE BIN

By default, the Recycle Bin is set to take up 10 percent of the space on each hard drive installed in your computer. Depending on the size of your drives and the number and nature of deleted files you want to keep hanging around, this may be far too much space. For example, if you have a couple of 80GB drives in your computer, you probably don't want to devote 16GB of precious space to deleted files.

To configure the maximum amount of space on your drive that the Recycle Bin can take up, right-click the Recycle Bin icon on the Desktop and choose Properties from the context menu. Windows displays the Recycle Bin Properties dialog box with the Global page foremost.

On the Global page, you can drag the Maximum Size of Recycle Bin (Percent of Each Drive) slider to change the percentage from 10 percent to a smaller number (or a higher number if you need a larger Recycle Bin). But to give yourself the most control on a computer with multiple drives, select the Configure Drives Independently option button, then use the Maximum Size of Recycle Bin (Percent of Drive) slider on the page for each drive to specify the percentage of that drive you want to set aside for the Recycle Bin.

On each page, you can also select the Do Not Move Files to the Recycle Bin. Remove Files Immediately when Deleted check box if you want to delete files on that drive rather than moving them to the Recycle Bin.

Renaming a File or Folder

To rename a file or folder, right-click it and choose Rename from the context menu. Alternatively, select the file or folder and then click its name. In an Explorer window, you can also select the file and either click the Rename This File link (or the Rename This Folder link) or choose File ➤ Rename.

Whichever of the above actions you take, Windows displays an edit box around the filename or folder name, as shown below. Type the new name into the edit box and press the Enter key or click in open space outside the filename.

EXPERT KNOWLEDGE: PERFORMING FILE OPERATIONS IN COMMON DIALOG BOXES

You can perform file operations such as Copy, Paste, Rename, and Delete in many common dialog boxes used by Windows programs. Just right-click the listing for a file to display a context menu of the actions you can take, as in the illustration below.

Doing this can save you time because you don't need to open an Explorer window. For example, say you're working in Word and need to save the active document under a name that another document in the same folder already has without overwriting that document. Instead of opening an Explorer window, you can click the listing for the original file twice (with a pause between the clicks) to display an edit box around it, and rename it there.

Viewing and Setting Properties for a File or Folder

As you'll remember from earlier in the chapter, files and folders are objects, and objects have properties.

To view the properties for a file or folder, right-click it and choose Properties from the context menu. (Alternatively, select it and choose File ➢ Properties.) Windows displays the Properties dialog box for the file or folder.

Figure 6.17 shows an example of the General page of the Properties dialog box for a file. As you can see, this page contains a lot of information about the file—its name, its file type, its location, its size, and the dates on which it was created, last modified, and last accessed. This page also shows the program that's set to open the target file—in this case, Notepad. (You can change the associated program by clicking the Change button. Chapter 10 discusses the implications of doing so.)

At the bottom of the page, the Attributes line shows the status of the read-only attribute (which governs whether users can modify the file or only view it) and the hidden attribute (which governs whether Windows displays the file when Explorer is set to hide hidden files). You can toggle these attributes on and off by selecting or clearing the Read-Only check box and the Hidden check box. You can set advanced attributes for the file or folder by clicking the Advanced button and working in the Advanced Attributes dialog box that Windows displays. (Chapter 10 discusses these options.)

The Summary page of the Properties dialog box contains information about the file or folder. This page has two views, Simple view (shown on the left in Figure 6.18) and Advanced view (shown on the right), which you can switch between by clicking the Simple button or the Advanced button. (These buttons replace each other as appropriate.) You can use this page to view existing information, modify it, or add information. Any field whose icon includes a pen in Advanced view is editable; the others are not. For example, in the figure, the Protected field and the Duration field are not editable, but the other fields are.

FIGURE 6.18

The Summary page
of the Properties
dialog box for a
file offers a Simple
view (left) and
an Advanced
view (right).

When you've finished examining or changing properties, click the OK button. Windows closes the Properties dialog box.

Finding a File or Folder

Unless you're incredibly well organized or have the world's most amazing memory (or you never create any files), you'll probably forget where a particular file or folder is located. Windows provides a powerful Search Companion feature that you can use to find files by their name, their size, the date they were created, or even by a word or phrase contained in the body of the file.

See pages 34–36 of the *Essential Skills* section for a visual guide to searching for files.

Displaying Search Companion

First, display Search Companion:

◆ If you have an Explorer window open, click the Search button on the toolbar. (Alternatively, chose View ➤ Explorer Bar ➤ Search or press Ctrl+E.)

◆ Choose Start ➤ Search from the simple Start menu. (From the classic Start menu, choose Start ➤ Search ➤ For Files or Folders.)

Figure 6.19 shows Search Companion in an Explorer window.

FIGURE 6.19

Use Search Companion to search for files or folders. Search Companion offers custom procedures for searching for pictures, music, or video files, and for searching for documents.

TIP   The following sections discuss the different types of search separately, but you can also combine several types of search to really pinpoint the file you need. For example, you can combine searching by filename with searching by a word or phrase in the file, searching for a particular file type, and specifying the time frame in which the file was modified.

Configuring Searching

By default, Windows displays an animated screen character to walk you through your searches. You can turn off this character by clicking the Turn Off Animated Character link that appears at the bottom of the Search Companion pane the first time you display Search Companion (as in Figure 6.19, above). The following examples illustrate searching without the animated screen character.

You can also choose several options for configuring searching at any time by clicking the Change Preferences link. Windows displays the How Do You Want to Use Search Companion? box. Click one of the following links to turn that option on or off:

With an Animated Screen Character/Without an Animated Screen Character link   Click this link to toggle between using an animated screen character and not using one. If you use a character, you can click the With a Different Character link to reach a screen on which you can select the character to use.

With Indexing Service (for Faster Local Searches)/Without Indexing Service link   Click this link to toggle Indexing Service on and off. (Turning on Indexing Service lets your computer spend some of its idle moments creating and updating an index of the files stored on it. Having an updated index speeds up searches.) Windows displays the Indexing Service screen. Select the Yes, Enable Indexing Service option button and click the OK button. To turn Indexing Service off, click the Without Indexing Service link, then click the No, Do Not Enable Indexing Service link on the Indexing Service screen and click the OK button.

Change Files and Folders Search Behavior link   Click this link to display a screen that lets you choose between the Standard search options (the default) and Advanced search options. Advanced search options provide less hand-holding and give you more freedom of action.

Change Internet Search Behavior link   Click this link to display a screen that lets you choose between searching with Search Companion and searching with Classic Internet Search. You can also select your default search engine.

Don't Show Balloon Tips/Show Balloon Tips link   Click these links (which replace each other as appropriate) to turn balloon tips off and on.

Turn AutoComplete Off/Turn AutoComplete On link   Click these links (which replace each other as appropriate) to turn the AutoComplete feature on and off. AutoComplete suggests the remaining text of items you're typing based on entries you've used before.

Searching for Pictures, Music, Video, or Documents

Search Companion provides custom features for searching for pictures, music, and video files, and for searching for documents (such as Word documents or Explorer workbooks):

◆ To search for pictures, music, or video files, click the Pictures, Music, or Video link in the What Do You Want to Search For? pane and follow the prompts.

◆ To search for document files, click the Documents (Word Processing, Spreadsheet, etc.) link and follow the prompts.

With each of these custom search features, you can also choose advanced options as described in the next sections, which describe the general procedures for searching.

Searching for All Files

To search for a file or folder by name, follow these steps:

1. In the What Do You Want to Search For? pane, click the All File Types link. Windows displays the Search Companion screen shown in Figure 6.20.

FIGURE 6.20

The Search Companion screen for general searching

2. In the All or Part of the File Name text box, enter the entire filename or part of the filename:

   ◆ Enter only as much of the name as you're sure of. Usually, it's better to get multiple results from a search using part of the name than to get no results from using search criteria that are too specific and not quite right.

   ◆ If you know the extension of the file, it's worth entering it. If you're not sure of the extension, omit it.

   ◆ You can use the wildcards * and ? to increase the scope of your search. The wildcard * represents any number of characters, while ? represents just one character. For example, searching for Letter* returns a list of all files whose names start with the word *Letter*, while searching for Letter? return a list of all files whose names include *Letter* plus only one other character (for example, *Letters* or *Letter2*).

   ◆ To search for files or folders whose name contains two or more specified words, enter the words separated by spaces. Windows searches for any filename that includes both words, irrespective of the order in which they appear.

   ◆ To search for files or folders whose name contains one or more specified words, enter the words separated by semicolons.

NOTE   If you don't include wildcards in your search, the Search Results pane returns a list of all the files whose file-names include the text you searched for. For example, if you search for Letter, *the Search Results pane lists all files whose names include* Letter, *not just those that start with* Letter.

3. If you can remember a distinctive word or phrase that the file contains, enter that word or phrase in the A Word or Phrase in the File text box.

   ◆ Make the search word or phrase as distinctive as possible to reduce the number of results returned. Windows treats the search word or phrase as a literal item; you can't use a semi-colon to indicate you want one word or another.

4. In the Look In drop-down list, specify the drives or folders to search.

   ◆ If you opened the Search pane from an Explorer window, the Look In text box suggests the current folder as the starting point for the search. Otherwise, the Look In text box suggests Local Hard Drives.

   ◆ The Look In drop-down list offers further choices, including all local drives (hard drives, CD or DVD drives, floppy drives, or removable drives), mapped network drives, the My Documents folder, and any shared documents folders on this computer.

   ◆ To specify a folder of your choice, click the Browse item on the Look In drop-down list and use the resulting Browse for Folder dialog box to identify the folder.

   ◆ To specify multiple folders, enter them in the Look In text box separated by semicolons. For example, you might search Local Hard Drives (C:; D:); Z:\Users to search both your local hard drives and a folder on a networked drive.

NOTE   If you search My Computer, Windows includes any floppy drives, removable drives, CD drives, or DVD drives that contain media.

5. By default, Windows searches all the subfolders of the folder or drive you specify. This is the best way of finding all matching files or folders, but if the locations you specified contain many subfolders and files, the search can take a long time. If you want to restrict the search to only the folder or folders you specified in step 4, expand the More Advanced Options area to display the advanced options. Then clear the Search Subfolders check box.

6. If you remember when the file was modified, expand the When Was It Modified? area by click-ing its heading and select the appropriate options. By default, the Don't Remember option but-ton is selected, excluding dates from the search criteria. You can select the Within the Last Week option button, the Past Month option button, the Within the Past Year option button, or the Specify Dates option button. If you choose the Specify Dates option button, use the drop-down list to select Modified Date, Created Date (the date on which the file was first saved), or Last Accessed Date as appropriate, then use the From drop-down list and the To drop-down list to designate the range of dates.

   ◆ To choose dates with the mouse, click the drop-down button and use the resulting panel to specify the date you want. You can change the month and year in the panel by clicking them and using the controls that appear.

◆ To specify dates with the keyboard, use the → key and the ← key to move between month, day, and year. Use the ↑ key and the ↓ key to increase or decrease the value for the selected item.

7. To restrict the search to files smaller than or larger than a given size, expand the What Size Is It? area by clicking its heading. Figure 6.21 shows this part of the list. By default, the Don't Remember option button is selected, excluding size from the search criteria. Select the Small (Less Than 100KB) option button, Medium (Less Than 1MB) option button, or Large (More Than 1MB) option button as appropriate. Or select the Specify Size option button, choose At Least or At Most in the drop-down list, and specify the size in the text box. For example, to find files over 5MB in size, you might specify At Least 5120KB (or, more realistically, At Least 5000KB).

FIGURE 6.21

You can use the What Size Is It? area of Search Companion to specify the approximate size of the file you're searching for.

8. To choose further options, expand the More Advanced Options area by clicking its heading. Figure 6.22 shows the options this area contains.

Search System Folders check box   Select this check box to force Windows to include the system folders in the search. Unless you mix your documents in with your system files (which you shouldn't do), you'll need to search your system folders only to find system files, readme files, and the like.

Search Hidden Files and Folders check box   Select this check box if you want the search to include files and folders marked with the hidden attribute.

Search Subfolders check box   Select this check box (which is selected by default) if you want the search to include the subfolders of the specified folder. This is usually a good idea.

Case Sensitive check box   Select this check box (which is cleared by default) to make your searches case sensitive. Case-sensitive searches tend to be most useful when searching for a word or phrase in a file, because you can use distinctive capitalization to search for a word in, say, a title or heading.

Search Tape Backup check box   Select this check box (which is cleared by default) to include an attached tape backup drive in your search. Searching a tape backup drive can be nearly as slow as watching grout dry, so don't select this check box until it's necessary.

FIGURE 6.22

You can also select options in the More Advanced Options area.

9. Click the Search button. Search Companion starts the search.

As the search progresses, Search Companion returns a list of matching files and folders in the Search Results window. When the search is finished, Search Companion displays a summary of the results, together with links for finishing searching, starting Indexing Service to make future searches faster (if Indexing Service is not currently running), refining the search, and starting a new search. Figure 6.23 shows an example of the Search Results window. You can sort and arrange these as you would any other files in an Explorer window. For example, to get an overview of the results, you might choose View ➢ Details and then click the Name column heading to sort them by name.

FIGURE 6.23

Search Companion displays the files it has found, together with options for refining the search and starting a new search.

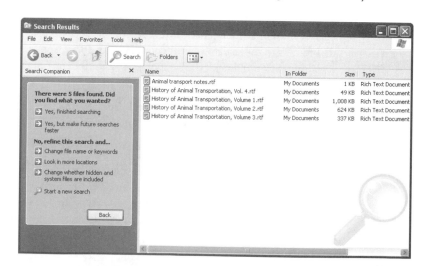

From the Search Results window, you can perform most actions that you can from any Explorer window: Select a file to display its information in the Details pane; double-click a file to open it; press the Delete key to move the selected file to the Recycle Bin; drag a file to another folder; and so on. To open the folder that contains a file you've found, select the file and click the Open Containing Folder link in the Search Results Tasks list. Alternatively, right-click the search result and choose Open Containing Folder from the context menu.

Working with Compressed Files

As you'll know if you've needed to transfer files or store them on limited-capacity media, file-compression programs can save you a lot of time or trouble. There are two widely used forms of compressed files: Zip files and cabinet files. Zip files have the ZIP extension. Cabinet files have the CAB extension and are mainly used by Microsoft for distributing files. Windows XP lets you create Zip folders but not cabinet files.

Windows XP reads compressed files in both formats seamlessly, displaying both Zip files and cabinet files as folders that you can open and browse in Explorer as you would any other folder. A Zip folder appears in Explorer as a closed folder icon with a zipper across it, and a cabinet folder appears as a filing cabinet with an open drawer busy consuming a document. Figure 6.24 shows these icons.

FIGURE 6.24

Zip files appear as folders zipped closed, while cabinet files appear as hungry filing cabinets.

 Blueprints 1.cab
77,026 KB

 Blueprints1.zip
77,422 KB

You can create compressed folders in the Zip format from one or more files or folders as follows:

- To create a compressed folder with the same name as the file or folder it contains, right-click the file or folder and choose Send To ➤ Compressed (Zipped) Folder from the context menu.

- To create a new compressed folder, choose File ➤ New ➤ Compressed (Zipped) Folder in an Explorer window, or right-click and choose New ➤ Compressed (Zipped) Folder from the context menu. Windows creates a new compressed folder named `New Compressed (zipped) Folder` (or `New Compressed (zipped) Folder.ZIP`, if you've displayed extensions) and selects the name so that you can enter a new name. Type the new name and press the Enter key (or click elsewhere in the window) to apply it.

Once you've created a compressed folder, you can add files to it by dragging them to the folder and dropping them in or on it.

Creating and Organizing Shortcuts

This section discusses how to create and organize shortcuts to save time and effort.

What Is a Shortcut?

A *shortcut* is a pointer to a file or folder. (If you're used to the Mac, a shortcut is like an alias.) By placing shortcuts in convenient places, you can give yourself quick access to files and folders stored in remote locations. For example, you could create a shortcut on your Desktop to a WordPerfect document stored in the nethermost subfolder of a network drive. By double-clicking the shortcut from the comfort of your Desktop, you could open the document without browsing through the drives and folders to reach it.

You can create as many shortcuts as you want for any file or folder. You can even create a shortcut to a shortcut if you feel the need. Each shortcut is typically less than 1KB in size, so unless you create a few million of them, you don't need to worry about the amount of disk space they take up.

Shortcuts have been around for many versions of Windows, but Microsoft has been improving them along the way. In the old days, if you renamed or moved the target file or folder to which a shortcut referred, Windows would be unable to find the target file when you double-clicked the shortcut. Nowadays, Windows can almost always find the target file unless you move it to somewhere truly inaccessible.

You can tell a shortcut icon on the Desktop or in an Explorer window by the small white box containing an upward-curling black arrow in its lower-left corner. Figure 6.25 shows a text file (on the left) and a renamed shortcut to it. When you let Windows name a shortcut, it creates a name consisting of *Shortcut to* and the filename, but you can change the name to anything you want by using standard Windows renaming techniques. (Renaming is discussed earlier in this chapter.)

FIGURE 6.25

A shortcut icon (on the right) bears an upward-curling black arrow in its lower-left corner but can have the same name and icon as the file it leads to.

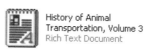

History of Animal
Transportation, Volume 3
Rich Text Document

History of Animal
Transportation, Volume 3
Shortcut

NOTE *Shortcuts that appear on the Start menu or on toolbars do not have this arrow.*

It's always safe to delete a shortcut, because deleting a shortcut never deletes the file that it's associated with. And as you saw in Chapter 4, you can customize a shortcut so that it launches the associated program in Compatibility mode or in a window of a specified size.

Creating a Shortcut

You can create a shortcut in several easy ways. The setup routines of most programs install shortcuts automatically for you, so you should already be equipped with shortcuts to your programs. Most of these shortcuts will be on the Start menu. Some programs place shortcuts on the Desktop or in the notification area, despite Microsoft's guidelines to programs designers telling them not to do this. Better-designed programs are courteous enough to consult you before placing shortcuts like this. Other programs go right ahead and please themselves.

See pages 37–38 of the *Essential Skills* section for a visual guide to creating a shortcut on the Desktop by using the Create Shortcut Wizard.

CREATING A SHORTCUT THE QUICK WAY

To create a shortcut the quick way, follow these steps:

1. Right-click the file on your Desktop or in an Explorer window and drag it (holding down that right mouse button) to where you want the shortcut to be.

2. Release the mouse button and choose Create Shortcuts Here from the context menu. Windows creates a shortcut named *Shortcut to* and the name of the file.

3. If you want to rename the shortcut, right-click it and choose Rename from the context menu. Enter the new name in the resulting edit box and press the Enter key.

CREATING A SHORTCUT ON THE DESKTOP OR IN AN EXPLORER WINDOW

To create a shortcut on the Desktop or in an Explorer window (the more formal way), follow these steps:

1. Right-click open space on the Desktop or in an Explorer window and choose New ➤ Shortcut from the context menu. (Alternatively, choose File ➤ New ➤ Shortcut.) Windows displays the Create Shortcut dialog box.

2. Enter the location of the file to which you want to create the shortcut. Either type it in, or click the Browse button, use the resulting Browse for Folder dialog box to navigate to and select the file, and click the OK button.

3. Click the Next button. Windows displays the Select a Title for the Program dialog box.

4. Enter the name that you want the shortcut to have. This can be just about anything, so make it descriptive and memorable.

5. Click the Finish button to create the shortcut.

Setting Properties for a Shortcut

To set properties for a shortcut, right-click it and choose Properties from the context menu. Windows displays the Properties dialog box. For a shortcut to a document, this dialog box contains two pages: a General page and a Shortcut page. For a shortcut to a program, this dialog box contains a Compatibility page as well.

The General page is just like the one you saw earlier in this chapter, while the Shortcut page (of which Figure 6.26 shows an example) contains a number of items of interest.

Target text box This contains the path and filename of the target file (or folder). To open an Explorer window showing the target in its folder, click the Find Target button.

Start In text box This text box contains the path to the target file. You may need to change this setting occasionally, but not regularly.

Shortcut Key text box To set a shortcut key to run the shortcut, click in this text box and press the letter you want to use. By default, Windows creates a shortcut using the Ctrl key and the Alt key, so if you press **P**, it creates the shortcut Ctrl+Alt+P. You can override this default by pressing Ctrl+Shift or Alt+Shift as you enter the letter.

Run drop-down list   As discussed in the section "Specifying the Size at Which a Program Runs" in Chapter 5, you can use this drop-down list to make the program run minimized, maximized, or in a "normal" window.

Comment text box   In this text box, you can enter a comment associated with the shortcut.

Change Icon button   To change the icon displayed for the shortcut, click this button and use the Change Icon dialog box to select an icon you like. As mentioned in Chapter 4, SHELL32.DLL and MORICONS.DLL (both in the \Windows\System32\ folder) contain a selection of icons.

FIGURE 6.26

The Shortcut page of the Properties dialog box for a shortcut

When you've finished tweaking the shortcut, click the OK button. Windows closes the Properties dialog box and applies your changes.

SETTING ADVANCED PROPERTIES FOR A SHORTCUT

You can set two advanced properties for shortcuts that lead to program files. To do so, click the Advanced button on the Shortcut page of the Properties dialog box for the shortcut. Windows displays the Advanced Properties dialog box (shown in Figure 6.27).

FIGURE 6.27

The Advanced Properties dialog box for a shortcut to a program lets you specify whether to run the program with different credentials (in other words, as a different user). If the program is 16 bit, you can also choose not to run it in separate memory space.

Run with Different Credentials check box   Select this check box to have Windows display the Run As dialog box when you execute the shortcut. This dialog box (shown in Figure 6.28) lets you specify a different user account under which to run the program. This is useful for accessing files of a file type associated with this program in a folder for which the current user account does not have sufficient permission.

FIGURE 6.28

When you've selected the Run with Different Credentials check box in the Advanced Properties dialog box for a program, Windows displays the Run As dialog box when you start the program from the shortcut. You can then choose whether to run the program under your current identity or as a different user.

Run in Separate Memory Space check box   You can change this setting only for 16-bit programs, which you can choose *not* to run in a separate memory space. (Windows always runs all 32-bit programs in separate memory spaces to prevent them from corrupting each other.) By default, Windows runs all 16-bit programs in separate memory spaces, but you may sometimes need to run two or more 16-bit programs in the same memory space so that they can communicate directly with each other (for example, via DDE).

Click the OK button. Windows closes the Advanced Properties dialog box and applies the settings you chose.

Customizing Explorer

This section discusses the main ways in which to customize Explorer. It starts off by covering that bane of Windows users, Autoplay. The bad news is that Autoplay is still in Windows, and it's still enabled by default. The good news is that not only can you disable Autoplay (as you could before), but you can now customize it so that it takes appropriate actions for different types of files.

After discussing Autoplay, this section shows you how to customize folders, how to customize the toolbar, and how to specify the columns Explorer displays in Details view.

Customizing and Turning Off Autoplay

By default, Windows is set to use its Autoplay feature, which tries to automatically run any CD that you insert in your CD drive. What *run* means depends on the contents of the CD and the action that the CD's developer has specified in the CD's AUTORUN.INF initialization file, a hidden file stored at the root of the CD's file system. If the initialization file doesn't contain specific instructions, or if there's no initialization file, Windows may pop up a dialog box offering you a choice of possible actions to take with the CD.

These are the usual actions for Autoplay:

◆ For a music CD, Autoplay activates the default player for files of the CD Audio Track type. Usually, this means that Windows Media Player (or whichever program has ousted Windows Media Player as the default player) starts playing the CD.

◆ For a software installation CD, Autoplay usually activates the setup routine. There's more good news here: Windows XP is much better than Windows 9x at detecting that you've installed software already, so it doesn't blindly rerun the setup routine when you insert the same CD again. (Windows XP isn't infallible on this score, but it does pretty well.)

◆ For a game CD, Autoplay usually starts playing the game.

◆ For a CD containing video files, Autoplay may start playing a file.

◆ For a DVD containing a video, Autoplay may start playing the video.

Autoplay also manifests itself in other ways, such as the Removable Disk dialog box, which lets you specify an action to take when you insert a disk that contains a specific type of file.

SUPPRESSING AUTOPLAY TEMPORARILY

To suppress Autoplay temporarily, hold down the Shift key as you close the CD drive after inserting a CD. Release the Shift key when Windows has loaded the CD (for example, when you see the CD's name and contents appear in an Explorer window).

CUSTOMIZING AUTOPLAY—AND TURNING IT OFF

You can customize Autoplay for six different types of content: music files, pictures, video files, mixed content, a music CD, and a DVD movie. *Mixed content* is a peculiar description, but in essence it means any CD that isn't exclusively pictures, exclusively music files, or exclusively video, and that isn't an audio CD or a DVD.

To customize Autoplay, or turn it off, follow these steps:

1. Choose Start ➢ My Computer. Windows opens an Explorer window showing your drives.

2. Right-click the CD drive or removable drive you want to affect and choose Properties from the context menu to display the Properties dialog box for the drive.

3. Click the AutoPlay tab. Windows displays the AutoPlay page. Figure 6.29 shows an example of the AutoPlay page for a DVD drive.

4. In the list box, select the type of files for which you want to specify an action: Music Files, Pictures, Video Files, Mixed Content, Audio CD, or (for a DVD drive) DVD Movie.

5. In the Actions group box, choose the Select an Action to Perform option button or the Prompt Me Each Time to Choose an Action option button. If you choose the Select an Action to Perform option button, choose an action from the list box:

   ◆ For Music Files, you can choose Play, Open Folder to View Files, or Take No Action.

FIGURE 6.29

Customize
Autoplay—or
turn it off—on the
AutoPlay page of
the drive's Properties
dialog box.

- For Pictures, you can choose Copy Pictures to a Folder on My Computer, View a Slideshow of the Images, Print the Pictures, Open Folder to View Files, or Take No Action.

- For Video Files, you can choose Play, Open Folder to View Files, or Take No Action.

- For Mixed Content, you can choose Open Folder to View Files or Take No Action.

- For Audio CD, you can choose Play Audio CD, Open Folder to View Files, or Take No Action.

- For DVD Movie, you can choose Play DVD Video, Open Folder to View Files, or Take No Action.

6. Click the OK button. Windows applies your choices and closes the Properties dialog box.

Customizing a Folder

You can customize a folder by designating a particular type of role for it, by applying a picture to it (for Thumbnails view), and by changing the icon displayed for it (for all views other than Thumbnails).

To customize a folder, take the following steps:

1. Right-click the folder and choose Properties from the context menu. Windows displays the Properties dialog box for the folder.

2. Click the Customize tab. Windows displays the Customize page (shown in Figure 6.30).

3. In the Use This Folder Type As a Template list box, you can select a template for the folder. Windows offers assorted templates for documents, pictures and photos, and music. These

templates contain suitable WebView and ListView settings for the folder. For example, the music templates offer links for playing music.

◆ If you'll be creating subfolders of this folder and putting the same type of content in them, select the Also Apply This Template to All Subfolders check box.

FIGURE 6.30

Use the Customize page of a folder's Properties dialog box to customize the folder.

4. To specify the picture that Windows displays on the folder in Thumbnails view, click the Choose Picture button. Windows displays the Browse dialog box. Navigate to the picture you want to use, select it, and click the Open button.

◆ To reapply the default picture to the folder, click the Restore Default button.

5. To specify the icon that Windows displays for the folder in all views other than Thumbnails view, click the Change Icon button. Windows displays the Change Icon dialog box. Select an icon and click the OK button.

6. Click the OK button. Windows closes the Properties dialog box and applies your choices to the folder.

Customizing the Toolbar

As mentioned earlier, Explorer's Standard Buttons toolbar has a half-dozen buttons by default. But you can customize it by adding and removing buttons so that it contains the actions you need.

To customize the toolbar, take the following steps:

1. Right-click the toolbar and choose Customize from the context menu, or choose View ➢ Toolbars ➢ Customize. Windows displays the Customize Toolbar dialog box (shown in Figure 6.31).

2. To add a button to the toolbar:

   ◆ In the Current Toolbar Buttons list box, select the button above which you want the new button to appear.

   ◆ Select the new button in the Available Toolbar Buttons list box.

   ◆ Click the Add button. Explorer adds the button to the toolbar.

FIGURE 6.31

Use the Customize Toolbar dialog box to customize the Explorer toolbar so that it contains the buttons you want.

3. To remove a button, select it in the Current Toolbar Buttons list box, then click the Remove button. Explorer removes the button from the Current Toolbar Buttons list box and adds it to the Available Toolbar Buttons list box.

4. To rearrange the order of the buttons in the Current Toolbar Buttons list box, select the button you want to move and use the Move Up button and Move Down button to move it to the position you want.

5. To change the text labels, choose one of the items in the Text Options drop-down list:

   ◆ Show Text Labels makes the text label appear beneath the graphic on each button.

   ◆ Selective Text on Right makes the text labels appear on some buttons (such as Search and Folders) to the right of the graphic. Other buttons display no text label. When a button has no text label, Internet Explorer displays a ScreenTip when you hover the mouse pointer over the button so that you can identify it easily.

   ◆ No Text Labels removes the text labels from the buttons. This option lets you fit more buttons on the toolbar.

6. In the Icon Options drop-down list, select Small Icons or Large Icons to suit your preference. For example, choose small icons and no text labels to really pack the toolbar.

7. Click the Close button to close the Customize Toolbar dialog box.

Choosing the Columns to Display in Details View

You can customize Details view to display the columns you want in any given folder. For example, you might want to add the artist, album, track name, and bitrate to a folder containing MP3 files. Similarly, you might want to display the title and subject for office documents so that you had another means of identifying them apart from their names.

To choose detail settings, follow these steps:

1. Choose View ➢ Choose Details. Windows displays the Choose Details dialog box (shown in Figure 6.32).

FIGURE 6.32

Use the Choose Details dialog box to specify the columns you want to see in Details view in a folder.

2. In the list box, select the check boxes for the columns you want Explorer to display. Clear the check boxes for any currently displayed columns that you want to hide.

   ◆ Which columns are available depends on the template applied to the folder.

3. Use the Move Up button and Move Down button to arrange the columns into the order in which you want them to appear from left to right.

4. To specify the width for a column, enter it in the Width of Selected Column (in Pixels) text box. (Usually it's easier to resize a column manually when you have information displayed and can see how much space it needs.)

5. Click the OK button. Windows closes the Choose Details dialog box. Explorer displays the columns you selected.

Up Next

This chapter has discussed what files and folders are, what Explorer is, and how to use Explorer to perform a wide variety of manipulations on files and folders. You've also seen how to apply some simple customizations to Explorer.

This chapter was uncomfortably long. The next chapter is much shorter and discusses how to make the most of the programs that come bundled with Windows XP.

Chapter 7

Making the Most of the Bundled Programs

THIS CHAPTER DISCUSSES THE bundled programs that come with Windows: WordPad, Notepad, Character Map, Paint, Calculator, Windows Picture and Fax Viewer, and Command Prompt.

These programs have relatively limited functionality; they're intended to take care of some basic tasks, but not to discourage you from buying fuller programs from either Microsoft or its competitors. Because they're limited, most of these programs are relatively small and easy to use. So as not to waste time belaboring the obvious, this chapter discusses only the most important features of the programs, leaving you to work out the easy stuff on your own.

This chapter covers the following topics:

- WordPad
- Notepad
- Character Map
- Paint
- Calculator
- Windows Picture and Fax Viewer
- Command Prompt

WordPad

WordPad is a lightweight word processing program. It provides rudimentary features including font formatting, bulleted lists, paragraph alignment, margin placement, and support for different sizes of paper. It also lets you insert objects such as graphics and parts of other documents, so at a pinch you can create attractive documents with it. WordPad's Print Preview feature (File ➤ Print Preview) lets you make sure your documents look okay before you commit them to paper. But WordPad has no advanced features; for example, it doesn't offer style formatting, tables, or macros. It also lacks a spelling checker or grammar checker, so you'll need to proof and check your documents visually.

Because of these limitations, if you have Microsoft Word, Corel WordPerfect, Star Office, or another full-fledged word processor, you'll probably have little use for WordPad. But if you don't have another word processor, and if you need to create only simple documents, you may find Word-Pad useful.

WordPad can open documents in Word format, Windows Write format, Rich-Text Format (RTF), and text formats. (Windows Write was WordPad's predecessor for Window 3.x versions.) If you have font-formatted documents created in another word processing program, Rich-Text Format may prove the best format for getting them into WordPad.

TIP   Because WordPad can open Word documents but doesn't support macros, you can safely use WordPad to view Word documents that may contain dangerous macros or customizations. WordPad doesn't render all Word's formatting faithfully, but you'll be able to see if the document is valuable or merely a vector for macro viruses. (You can also get a free viewer for Word documents that lets you examine their contents without worrying about macros and viruses. Visit the Microsoft Web site, `www.microsoft.com`.)

Each instance of WordPad can have only one document open at once, but you can run multiple instances of WordPad if you need to have two or more documents open at the same time. Each instance of WordPad typically takes up around 4MB of memory (RAM and virtual memory) plus the size of the document, so if you have 128MB RAM or more, you should be able to have several instances of WordPad open without degrading your computer's performance or impairing its ability to run larger programs at a good speed.

The most complex part of WordPad is the Options dialog box (View ➤ Options), which has six pages: Options, Text, Rich Text, Word, Write, and Embedded:

◆ The Options page (of the Options dialog box—WordPad gets a little recursive here) lets you choose measurement units: Inches, Centimeters, Points, or Picas. (Points and picas are typesetting measurements. A *point* is $1/72$ inch, and a *pica* is $1/6$ inch, so there are 12 points to the pica.) It also contains the Automatic Word Selection check box, which controls whether WordPad selects the whole of each second and subsequent word when you click and drag to select from one word to the next. If Automatic Word Selection is turned off, WordPad lets you select character by character. (If you've used Word, you're probably familiar with this behavior.)

◆ The Text, Rich Text, Word, Write, and Embedded pages contain options for the different document types that WordPad can handle. For each, you can choose word-wrap settings (No Wrap, Wrap to Window, or Wrap to Ruler) and whether you want to display the toolbar, the Format bar, the ruler, and the status bar.

Notepad

Notepad is a *text editor*, a program designed for working with text files. A *text file* is a file that contains only text (characters): It has no formatting and no graphical objects.

To make life tolerable in the Spartan environment of text files, Notepad lets you select a font for the display of text on-screen (choose Format ➤ Font). It has a word-wrap option (choose Format ➤ Word Wrap) so that lines of text don't reach past the border of the window to the horizon on your right. And you can insert the time and date in a Notepad file by choosing Edit ➤ Time/Date or pressing the F5 key.

TIP *Notepad automatically adds the TXT extension to files you save. To save a file under a different extension, enter the filename and extension in double quotation marks in the File Name text box in the Save As dialog box.*

Generally speaking, you shouldn't spend any more time using Notepad than you need to, because Notepad is a very limited program. But it's good for several tasks:

◆ Because Notepad is small and simple, you can keep it running without worrying about it slowing your computer down. Because Notepad takes up little memory, you can run multiple instances of Notepad without slowing your computer down appreciably. This can be useful for taking a variety of notes. Notepad lets you open only a single file at a time, but by opening multiple instances of Notepad, you can open as many files as you need.

◆ Notepad is good for editing configuration files for such Windows programs as still use them. But if you're editing any of the standard Windows configuration files that remain in Windows XP (for example, AUTOEXEC.BAT or WIN.INI), use the System Configuration Editor instead. The System Configuration Editor is essentially Notepad after a couple of doses of steroids and customizations for editing system files. (To run the System Configuration Editor, choose Start ➤ Run or press Winkey+R, enter **sysedit** in the Open text box in the Run dialog box, and click the OK button.)

◆ Apart from working with self-declared text files, Notepad is good for creating and editing other text-only files. For example, it's good for editing playlists for programs such as MP3 players. These are text files, though they use extensions such as M3U and PLS to give them file-type functionality. If you create such a file using Notepad, remember to use double quotation marks around the filename when saving it.

◆ You can use Notepad to open documents other than text files. (Select the All Files item in the Files of Type drop-down list in the Open dialog box.) For example, if Word for Windows crashes, you may end up with a corrupted file that Word itself cannot open. By opening up the file in Notepad, you may be able to save part of the text. You'll see a lot of nonalphanumeric characters that represent things like Word formatting (for example, styles), but you'll also find readable text. Figure 7.1 shows an example of this. If the document has been saved using Word's Fast Save feature, you'll even find deleted parts of the document still in the file—which can be intriguing or embarrassing, depending on whether you wrote the document.

FIGURE 7.1

You can use Notepad to recover text from a corrupted Word document—or to view deleted parts of a fast-saved Word document.

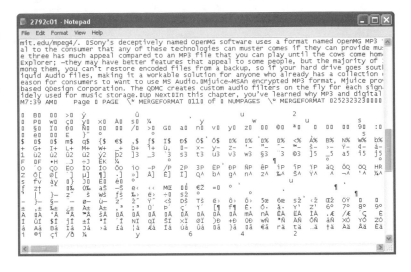

Character Map

Character Map is a small utility that lets you insert in your documents characters and symbols that don't appear on your keyboard. Figure 7.2 shows Character Map in its Standard view with the graphical symbols font Webdings displayed.

FIGURE 7.2

Character Map lets you select any character in any font installed on your computer.

Windows hides Character Map on the System Tools menu (Start ➤ All Programs ➤ Accessories ➤ System Tools ➤ Character Map). If you don't find it there but think it's installed on your computer, choose Start ➤ Run (or press Winkey+R) to display the Run dialog box, enter **charmap** in the Open text box, and click the Open button. Failing that, search for **charmap.exe** (it should be in your \Windows\System32\ folder) and run it from the Search Results window.

Inserting a Character

To insert a character with Character Map:

1. Select the font in the Font drop-down list.

2. Scroll the list box until the character is visible:

   ◆ To display a magnified view of a character, click it. Alternatively, use the arrow keys ($\rightarrow$, $\leftarrow$, $\uparrow$, and $\downarrow$) to select it, and then press the spacebar.

   ◆ Once you've displayed a magnified view, you can use the arrow keys to move the magnifier around the grid of characters.

   ◆ To remove the magnified view, click the magnified character or press the spacebar.

3. Select the character and click the Select button. Character Map copies it into the Characters to Copy text box.

4. Select other characters as necessary, then click the Copy button to copy the character or characters to the Clipboard.

5. Activate the program and paste the characters into it.

NOTE   Some text-based programs cannot accept graphical characters and convert them to the nearest character they support. For example, if you paste a Wingdings telephone character into Notepad, Notepad converts it to a mutated parenthesis. If you paste the same telephone character into WordPad, WordPad displays it correctly. Similarly, many e-mail programs strip incoming messages down to text, so it's a waste of time to send the users of such programs messages that contain unusual characters.

Inserting a Character in Advanced View

Character Map's Standard view is fine for inserting many weird and wonderful characters in your documents. But if you want to work with a particular character set, you need to use Advanced view. (Character sets are discussed in the nearby sidebar.) Select the Advanced View check box to display Character Map in Advanced view (shown in Figure 7.3).

As you can see in the figure, Character Map in Advanced view has several extra controls:

Character Set drop-down list   Use this drop-down list to select the character set you want to work with. The default selection is Unicode.

Group By drop-down list   When necessary, choose a grouping for the character set. Depending on the character sets installed on your computer, you'll see options such as All, Ideographs by Radicals, Japanese Kanji by Hiragana, Japanese Kanji by Radical, Japanese Shift-JIS Subrange, and Unicode Subrange.

Go to Unicode text box   Use this text box to display the Unicode character associated with a character code. Type the code into this text box. When you type the fourth character of the code, Character Map displays the associated Unicode character.

Search For text box and Search button   Use this text box and button to search for a character by its description. For example, to find the inverted question mark character (¿), enter text such as **question inverted** or **inverted question** and click the Search button. Character Map displays all characters that match the criteria.

FIGURE 7.3

Select the Advanced View check box to work with a particular character set.

TIP   If you don't see the character sets you need, they may not be installed on your computer. To install a character set, open Control Panel and click the Date, Time, Language, and Regional Options link. Click the Add Support for Additional Languages link. Windows displays the Regional and Language Options dialog box. Click the Advanced tab to display the Advanced page, then specify the languages to add.

Here's an example of inserting a Japanese kanji using Advanced view:

1. In the Character Set drop-down list, select the Windows: Japanese item.

2. In the Group By drop-down list, select the grouping you want. In the example, this is Japanese Kanji by Hiragana. Character Map opens a window displaying the kanji.

3. In the Japanese Kanji by Hiragana window, select the hiragana (phonetic character) that represents the sound of the kanji character. The main Character Map window (shown in Figure 7.4 with the Japanese Kanji by Hiragana window) displays a scrolling list of kanji that can be pronounced with that sound.

4. Select and copy the character as usual, then paste it into the document.

If you need to enter a particular character frequently in your documents and don't want to have to access Character Map each time, select the character in Character Map and memorize the Alt code displayed in the status bar. (Only some characters have these Alt codes.) To enter the character at the insertion point in a document, make sure that Num Lock is on, then hold down the Alt key and type the code for the character.

FIGURE 7.4

Using Character Map's Advanced view to select Japanese kanji

EXPERT KNOWLEDGE: ASCII, UNICODE, AND CODE PAGES

Okay, time out: What's ASCII? (It sounds kinda familiar....) What's Unicode? And what are code pages?

Briefly, these are all ways of mapping the binary codes that computers use to store characters to a) the characters on whichever keyboard you happen to be using, and b) what you see on-screen.

ASCII (American Standard Code for Information Interchange) and Unicode are both standard character-encoding schemes for text-based data. In other words, if you have information that can be represented in characters (such as this paragraph, for example), you can encode it in ASCII or in Unicode so that a computer can store it.

In ASCII, each character is represented by one byte. There are two forms of ASCII: *Standard ASCII* uses a 7-bit binary number combination to represent each character, which gives enough combinations for 128 characters. *Extended ASCII*, which is also known as *high ASCII*, uses an 8-bit number combination for each character, which gives enough combinations for 256 characters.

Given that the English alphabet uses 26 uppercase letters, 26 lowercase letters, 10 numbers, some punctuation (comma, period, parentheses, and so on), and control characters, standard ASCII's capacity for 128 characters starts to look paltry. Extended ASCII doubles the ante and adds some foreign characters (for example, ¿), graphic symbols, and symbol characters to standard ASCII's set.

Extended ASCII works pretty well provided you're satisfied with 256 characters. But even 256 characters is a pathetic number if you want anything beyond the main European languages.

Enter Unicode. In Unicode, each character is represented by two bytes (16 bits), which gives 65,536 character combinations (256×256)—enough to cover most of the characters in the world's many languages. As of the year 2000, about 39,000 of those 65,536 combinations had been assigned, with Chinese alone accounting for about 21,000 of them. (Japanese, with its borrowed and mutated kanji, is another of the greedier languages for Unicode combinations.)

continued on next page

EXPERT KNOWLEDGE: ASCII, UNICODE, AND CODE PAGES *(continued)*

When do you have to worry about ASCII and Unicode? Windows XP is pretty savvy about Unicode, so usually you don't have to worry about whether you're using Unicode or ASCII, because Windows XP uses Unicode almost exclusively.

For programs that don't support Unicode, you can use code pages to enable the programs to communicate effectively with the user. Briefly, a *code page* is a table that maps a program's character codes (which are binary) to the keys on the keyboard, the characters on the display, or (preferably) both. Previous versions of Windows used code pages.

If you need to use a program that can't handle Unicode, assign a code page for it as follows:

1. Choose Start ➢ Control Panel. Windows displays Control Panel.

2. Click the Date, Time, Language, and Regional Options link. Windows displays the Date, Time, Language, and Regional Options screen.

3. Click the Regional and Language Options link. Windows displays the Regional and Language Options dialog box.

4. Click the Advanced tab. Windows displays the Advanced page.

5. In the drop-down list, choose the language in which to display the program.

6. In the Code Page Conversion Tables list box, make sure the check box for the language is selected. If it isn't, select the check box to install the code page conversion table. (You'll need to provide your Windows CD or be connected to a network source of Windows installation files.)

7. If you want to make the code page settings available to yourself and to all new user accounts that you or other Computer Administrator users set up on this computer, select the Apply All Settings to the Current User Account and to the Default User Profile check box.

8. Click the OK button. If you chose to install a code page conversion table, Windows prompts you for your CD or installation source.

EXPERT KNOWLEDGE: USING PRIVATE CHARACTER EDITOR TO CREATE YOUR OWN CHARACTERS

Windows XP includes a hidden applet called Private Character Editor that you can use for creating your own characters and logos. To run Private Character Editor, choose Start ➢ Run or press Winkey+R. Windows displays the Run dialog box. Enter **eudcedit** in the Open text box and click the OK button.

Paint

Paint (Start ➢ All Programs ➢ Accessories ➢ Paint) is a basic illustration program that's been included with almost all known desktop versions of Windows. XP's incarnation of Paint lets you create bitmap files (BMP, DIB), GIF files, JPEG files (JPG and JPEG), and TIFF files (TIF)— enough to make it useful for basic illustration needs, and significantly better than the versions of Paint in most versions of Windows 9x, which could work only with bitmaps.

If you're into creating drawings or paintings on the computer, you'll find that Paint's limitations present more challenges than its capabilities do. Paint's Image menu provides tools for flipping and rotating images, stretching and skewing images, changing their attributes (for example, changing a color file to black and white), and inverting colors—but that's about it. If you want to do serious illustration work, consider a heavy-duty illustration program such as Paint Shop Pro (of which you'll find an evaluation copy on the CD) or Adobe Photoshop.

If you're *not* into creating drawings or paintings on the computer, you'll probably find Paint quite useful for some basic graphical tasks such as the following:

Creating background images for your Desktop If you want to use a digital photo or a scan as a background image for your Desktop, you may need to rotate it from a portrait orientation to a landscape orientation or crop it down to size.

Capturing images directly from a Web camera You can capture images directly from a Web camera by using the File ➢ From Scanner or Camera command. Chapter 28 discusses how to work with pictures and video.

Cleaning up scanned images Images you scan can easily pick up dots from specks of dirt on the scanner or from damage to the picture. You can use Paint to edit pictures and remove small defects such as these.

Capturing screens If you're preparing documentation on how to use software, you may want to capture the screen, or a window. To capture the whole screen to the Clipboard, press the PrintScreen (PrtScn) key. To capture only the active window to the Clipboard, press Alt+PrintScreen. Then choose Edit ➢ Paste to paste the screen or window into Paint, where you can work with it as you would any other graphic.

Calculator

Calculator (Start ➢ All Programs ➢ Accessories ➢ Calculator) seems such a basic program that it barely deserves mention. But there are several things you should know about it:

♦ Calculator displays itself by default in its Standard view, but it also has a Scientific view that's useful if you need to work in hexadecimal, binary, or octal; calculate degrees or radians; or perform similar tasks. To switch Calculator to Scientific view, choose View ➢ Scientific. (To switch Calculator back to Standard view, choose View ➢ Standard.) Figure 7.5 shows Calculator in Scientific view calculating hex. For hex, octal, and binary, you can choose from four display sizes: Byte (8-bit representation), Word (16-bit representation), Dword (32-bit representation), and Qword (64-bit representation).

♦ When you switch Calculator from Standard view to Scientific view, or switch it back, it wipes the display. To take the current number from one view to the other view, use the MS button to store it, switch view, and then use the MR button to retrieve it. Binary, octal, or hex numbers get converted to decimal when you move them to Standard view by using this technique.

♦ You can operate Calculator entirely from the keyboard if you want to. Choose Help ➢ Help Topics to open the Help file, then investigate the "Using Keyboard Equivalents of Calculator Functions" topic.

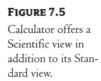

FIGURE 7.5

Calculator offers a Scientific view in addition to its Standard view.

- ◆ You can use key sequences as functions. For example, the sequence **:p** performs the equivalent of clicking the M+ key. Check the "Using Key Sequences as Functions" topic in the Help file for more information.

- ◆ If you're working with long numbers, you may want to choose View ➤ Digit Grouping to have Calculator group the digits into threes separated by commas. For example, with digit grouping, 4444444444 appears as 44,444,444,444, making it easier to read.

- ◆ Press Esc to clear Calculator.

Windows Picture and Fax Viewer

Windows Picture and Fax Viewer is a sort of stealth program. It's largely subsumed into Windows Explorer, for which it provides the preview functionality (in views such as Thumbnails view), the Filmstrip view in the My Pictures folder, and slideshow views. There's no shortcut for Windows Picture and Fax Viewer on the Start menu, and there's no convenient way to start it other than by opening one of the file types with which it's associated.

Even when Windows Picture and Fax Viewer is running, Windows refuses to acknowledge it as such. The window it runs in is titled Windows Picture and Fax Viewer, but the window is treated as an Explorer window for Taskbar-grouping purposes. This isn't particularly helpful, as it's counterintuitive and means that the Windows Picture and Fax Viewer windows tend to disappear in the welter of Explorer windows that characterizes the busy Desktop. But no doubt it's logical enough. And Task Manager shows you on its Applications page that Windows Picture and Fax Viewer is running, but its Processes page shows only Explorer.

However, when you double-click a picture file in your My Pictures folder (or right-click the file and choose Preview from the context menu), Windows Picture and Fax Viewer springs into action, opening its own window. Figure 7.6 shows an example.

Basic Manipulation of Images

Unlike (almost) all good Windows programs, Windows Picture and Fax Viewer spurns a menu bar in favor of a toolbar. The toolbar icons are marginally intuitive, and Windows Picture and Fax Viewer

FIGURE 7.6

Windows Picture and Fax Viewer is a stealth program that hides under Explorer's virtual skirts most of the time.

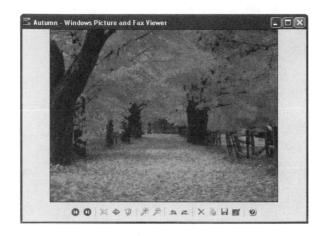

displays ScreenTips when you hover the mouse pointer over them—but Windows Picture and Fax Viewer displays a different set of buttons depending on which type of image you have opened. Figure 7.7 shows the basic set of buttons on the Windows Picture and Fax Viewer toolbar with labels.

FIGURE 7.7

Windows Picture and Fax Viewer uses a toolbar rather than a menu structure to give you access to its commands.

All these buttons are self-explanatory except for the Actual Size button, which displays the image at 100 percent of its actual size (in other words, not zoomed in or zoomed out at all).

To make Windows Picture and Fax Viewer usable from the keyboard despite its lack of menus, most of these buttons have keyboard equivalents. Table 7.1 lists these keyboard equivalents.

TABLE 7.1: KEYBOARD EQUIVALENTS FOR WINDOWS PICTURE AND FAX VIEWER TOOLBAR BUTTONS

BUTTON	KEYBOARD EQUIVALENT
Previous Image	Ctrl+Page Up
Next Image	Ctrl+Page Down
Best Fit	Ctrl+B

continued on next page

TABLE 7.1: KEYBOARD EQUIVALENTS FOR WINDOWS PICTURE AND FAX VIEWER TOOLBAR BUTTONS *(continued)*

Actual Size	Ctrl+A
Start Slide Show	F11
Zoom In	+ on numeric keypad
Zoom Out	– on numeric keypad
Slide Show	—
Rotate Clockwise	Ctrl+K
Rotate Counterclockwise	Ctrl+L
Delete	Delete
Print	Ctrl+P
Copy To	Ctrl+S
Close Program and Open Image for Editing	Ctrl+E
Help	F1

Annotating an Image

Viewing images quickly palls, even if you use the slideshow feature, unless of course the images are unusually stimulating. To counter accusations that it's a featherweight, Windows Picture and Fax Viewer also provides features for annotating TIFF images. You might say that this isn't a task you feel compelled to perform with anything approaching frequency, but these features can be especially useful for annotating incoming faxes before printing them out or shunting them along to your colleagues.

To annotate a TIFF, open it by double-clicking it in an Explorer window. The Windows Picture and Fax Viewer window opens, including the image annotation tools on the toolbar. Figure 7.8 shows the extra buttons with labels.

These annotation tools are mostly self-explanatory and easy to use. The one distinction that you need to know is that a text annotation is plain text with no background, while an attached note annotation is a colored rectangular background to which you can add text. A text annotation works well in open space on the document (for example, in one of the margins), while an attached note annotation is good for slapping over part of the document.

Once you've applied an annotation, you can click the Edit Info button with the annotation selected to display the Annotation Properties dialog box, in which you can change the font or color for the annotation.

Continuing its attempt to build a reputation as a maverick Windows program, Windows Picture and Fax Viewer provides some annotation functionality that's available only through the keyboard (as opposed to being available through both keyboard and mouse, as is the case with most functionality in most Windows programs):

◆ Select an annotation and press ← or → to move it 1 pixel to the left or right.

◆ Select an annotation and press ↑ or ↓ to move it 1 pixel up or down.

- Select an annotation and press Ctrl+← or Ctrl+→ to move it 10 pixels to the left or right.

- Select an annotation and press Ctrl+↑ or Ctrl+↓ to move it 10 pixels up or down.

When you've finished annotating an image, save it and close the Windows Picture and Fax Viewer window.

FIGURE 7.8

You can use the annotation tools on the Windows Picture and Fax Viewer tool bar to annotate TIFF files, such as faxes.

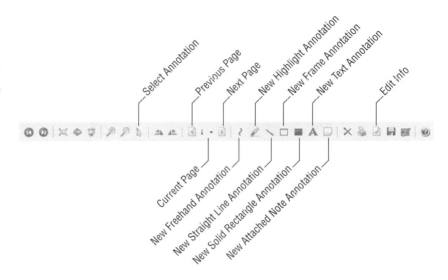

Command Prompt

Command Prompt (Start ➤ All Programs ➤ Accessories ➤ Command Prompt) gives you a DOS-like command prompt window that you can use to run character-mode programs or to issue commands. Command Prompt is especially useful for command-line utilities such as ping and tracert, which missed the line when the deity of the GUI was doling out interfaces. Figure 7.9 shows ping running in a Command Prompt window.

FIGURE 7.9

Running ping in a Command Prompt window

```
E:\>ping 192.168.0.1

Pinging 192.168.0.1 with 32 bytes of data:

Reply from 192.168.0.1: bytes=32 time=1ms TTL=128
Reply from 192.168.0.1: bytes=32 time<1ms TTL=128
Reply from 192.168.0.1: bytes=32 time<1ms TTL=128
Reply from 192.168.0.1: bytes=32 time<1ms TTL=128

Ping statistics for 192.168.0.1:
    Packets: Sent = 4, Received = 4, Lost = 0 (0% loss),
Approximate round trip times in milli-seconds:
    Minimum = 0ms, Maximum = 1ms, Average = 0ms

E:\>
```

For most purposes, there's no advantage in using Command Prompt to issue commands instead of using the Run dialog box (Start ➤ Run, or Winkey+R) except that in Command Prompt you can see the history of the commands you've issued in this session.

Command Prompt may look as simple as an unadorned DOS prompt—and you can use it as simply as that. But if you use Command Prompt extensively, you'd do well to use its editing capabilities and customize its behavior to suit your needs.

If you *really* want Command Prompt to look like a DOS prompt, try running it full screen instead of in a window. To toggle Command Prompt between a window and full screen, press Alt+Enter. There's also an option setting for this, as you'll see in a moment.

Recalling a Command You've Used

Often, you'll need to reuse a command you've used earlier in the current Command Prompt window, or you'll need to issue a similar command. Command Prompt stores the last few commands you've used (as you'll see in a moment, you can customize the number of commands it stores), so that you can recall them quickly.

To recall a command from the current session, press the ↑ key. The first press displays the previous command, the second the command before that, and so on. If you go too far back in the list, press the ↓ key to go back through the list toward the later commands.

Once you've reached the command you want to use, you can edit it or add to it, or simply press the Enter key to run it.

Selecting, Copying, and Pasting in Command Prompt

Selecting, copying, and pasting in Command Prompt windows are much clumsier than in graphical windows, but they work well enough once you know how to do them.

To use the mouse to select text in Command Prompt, you need to turn on QuickEdit mode. You can turn it on either temporarily (choose Edit ➤ Mark from the title-bar context menu or from the control menu) or permanently (select the QuickEdit Mode check box on the Options page of the Console Windows Properties dialog box or the Command Prompt Properties dialog box).

Once you've turned on QuickEdit, click to place an insertion point, or drag to select a block of text.

To copy, right-click after making a selection. (Alternatively, press Enter, or choose Edit ➤ Copy from the title-bar context menu or from the control menu.) Issuing a Copy command in any of these ways collapses the selection, so that it looks as though the Copy operation has failed, but in fact Windows has copied the selection to the Clipboard, from which you can paste it into another Windows program or back into the Command Prompt window.

You can also copy information from another Windows program and paste it into Command Prompt by placing the insertion point, then choosing Edit ➤ Paste from either the title-bar context menu or the control menu.

Customizing Command Prompt

By default, Command Prompt uses a white system font on a black background—to look as DOS-like as possible, perhaps—but there's no reason to keep it that way if you don't like that look. You can customize Command Prompt easily enough by using its Properties dialog box.

Actually, it's a little more complicated than that. You can customize the settings for the current Command Prompt window, or you can customize the default settings for the Console Window, which affects all Command Prompt windows you open. You can also choose to apply the settings you specify for the current Command Prompt window to the shortcut from which you started Command Prompt, which means that further Command Prompt windows you start from that shortcut will start with those properties. (This is different from changing the default settings for the Console Window—changing the shortcut affects only the Command Prompt windows you start from the shortcut.)

Let's take it from the top.

CUSTOMIZING THE CURRENT COMMAND PROMPT WINDOW

To customize the current Command Prompt window, right-click its title bar and choose Properties from the context menu. (Alternatively, open the control menu and choose Properties from it.) Command Prompt displays the Properties dialog box.

Options Page

The Options page of the Command Prompt Properties dialog box (shown in Figure 7.10) contains four group boxes of options:

Cursor Size group box   Choose the Small option button, the Medium option button, or the Large option button as appropriate.

Command History group box   In the Buffer Size text box, you can adjust the number of commands that Command Prompt stores in its buffer. (Storing more commands needs a little more memory, but if your computer can run Windows XP at a tolerable speed, it probably has plenty of memory to store a few extra commands.) In the Number of Buffers text box, you can adjust the number of processes allowed to have distinct history buffers. Select the Discard Old Duplicates check box if you want the buffered list to omit repeated commands. Omitting them reduces the list and can make it more manageable.

FIGURE 7.10

On the Options page of the Command Prompt Properties dialog box, specify cursor size, command history, display options, and editing options.

Display Options group box   If you want your Command Prompt sessions to be displayed full screen, select the Full Screen option button. Otherwise, leave the Window option button selected, as it is by default.

Edit Options group box   Select the QuickEdit Mode check box if you want to be able to use the mouse for cutting and pasting in Command Prompt. Leave the Insert Mode check box selected (as it is by default) if you like the standard way of inserting text at the cursor, moving along any characters to the right of the cursor instead of typing over them. If you prefer typeover, clear this check box.

Font Page

On the Font page of the Command Prompt Properties dialog box, select the font and font size you want to use for the Command Prompt window.

Layout Page

On the Layout page of the Command Prompt Properties dialog box (shown in Figure 7.11), specify how the Command Prompt window should look, where it should appear on the screen, and how many commands it should retain:

Screen Buffer Size group box   In the Width text box, specify the number of characters that you want each line in the buffer to contain. (Note that this is the buffer, not the window.) In the Height text box, specify the number of lines of data that you want to store.

FIGURE 7.11

On the Layout page of the Command Prompt Properties dialog box, specify how you want the Command Prompt window to appear.

Window Size group box   In the Width text box, specify the number of characters for the width of the window. Usually it's best to set this to the same value as the width of the screen buffer. (You can set it to a smaller value and have the window display scroll bars, but you can't set it to a larger value.) In the Height text box, specify the number of lines for the height of the window.

Window Position group box   By default, the Let System Position Window check box is selected, which lets Windows position the Command Prompt window as it sees fit. You can clear this check box and use the Left text box and the Top text box to specify the position of the left side and the top of the window.

Colors Page

On the Colors page of the Command Prompt Properties dialog box, you can choose colors for the screen text, the screen background, the pop-up text, and the pop-up background. Use the preview boxes to get an idea of the effect you're creating.

When you click the OK button in the Command Prompt Properties dialog box, Windows displays the Apply Properties to Shortcut dialog box asking whether you want to apply the properties you chose to the current window only or to modify the shortcut that you used to open this window. Select the Apply Properties to Current Window Only option button and click the OK button. Windows closes the Apply Properties to Shortcut dialog box and applies your choices.

CUSTOMIZING ALL COMMAND PROMPT WINDOWS STARTED FROM A PARTICULAR SHORTCUT

To change how future Command Prompt windows will be displayed, select the Modify Shortcut That Started This Window option button in the Apply Properties to Shortcut dialog box. Then click the OK button.

CUSTOMIZING THE CONSOLE WINDOW SETTINGS

To customize the Console Window settings, right-click the title bar of a Command Prompt window and choose Defaults from the context menu. (Alternatively, choose Defaults from the control menu.) Command Prompt displays the Console Windows Properties dialog box. Choose your customizations and click the OK button to apply them. Note that these customizations don't affect the current Command Prompt window, but they do affect Command Prompt windows that you start by using a shortcut that hasn't been customized or by issuing the **cmd** command.

Up Next

This chapter has discussed the more challenging features of the programs that come bundled with Windows XP. Between them, these programs provide the bare minimum of features for you to accomplish a number of tasks.

The next chapter discusses how to use Windows XP's help system to find the information you need when things go wrong or just won't work.

Chapter 8

Finding Help to Solve Your Windows Problems

THIS CHAPTER DISCUSSES HOW to find the help you need to use Windows XP most effectively. XP includes a greater amount of help than previous versions of Windows and presents that help in a new interface, the Help and Support Center program. This chapter describes how to use Help and Support Center and the various areas it offers. It also mentions other resources that you may need to turn to when you run into less tractable problems.

This chapter covers the following topics:

◆ Finding your way around Help and Support Center

◆ Searching for help

◆ Searching the Knowledge Base

◆ Browsing for help

◆ Using the support options

◆ Other help resources

Help and Support Center

Help and Support Center is the latest in Microsoft's efforts to provide help resources powerful enough to silence the ringing of the phones on its costly support lines. Windows XP's Help and Support Center builds on the improvements introduced in the Help and Support Center in Windows Me, which introduced a Web-style interface to replace the old-style Help-file interface in earlier versions of Windows, by integrating many more external resources. For example, you can now search the Microsoft Knowledge Base, an online database of questions and answers, directly from Help and Support Center instead of having to access it separately by using Internet Explorer. And many hardware manufacturers are now providing product-support information that's accessible through Help and Support Center.

Starting Help and Support Center

Choose Start ➤ Help and Support to open Help and Support Center at the Home page. You should see something like Figure 8.1, except that it will contain some updated information. (Your hardware manufacturer may also have customized Help and Support Center by adding content to it or by adapting its interface.)

FIGURE 8.1

The Home page in Help and Support Center provides links to the many different areas of Help and Support Center.

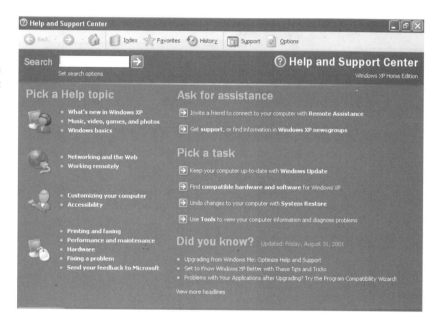

As you can see in Figure 8.1, the Help and Support Center window has a toolbar (at the top, starting with the Back button) for primary navigation rather than a menu bar. This toolbar is called the *navigation bar*. Below the navigation bar appears the Search bar.

TIP   *You can open multiple Help and Support Center windows at once, which can be a help when you're searching for different pieces of help information or navigating different routes in search of the same piece of information.*

Finding Your Way around Help and Support Center

Help and Support Center has access to a large amount of information in Help files that Windows installs on your hard drive, together with troubleshooters for stepping you through the process of finding solutions to common problems and links for running Windows programs (such as Remote Assistance and the System Configuration Utility) that may help you solve or eliminate problems. But Help and Support Center's strongest feature is that it also provides a gateway to information resources on the Web and Internet.

Because of the amount of information and resources that Help and Support Center offers, you may find that it takes you a while to get the hang of navigating around Help and Support Center. This section highlights the main ways of finding the information you need: searching, browsing, using the History feature, and using the Index.

SEARCHING FOR HELP

If you don't see an immediately appropriate link on the Help and Support Center Home page, the easiest way to find information on a particular topic is to search for it.

To search, enter the search term or terms in the Search text box and click the Search button. Help and Support Center displays the Search Results pane on the left side and adds a toolbar containing four buttons (Add to Favorites, Change View, Print, and Locate in Contents) under the right side of the Search bar.

The Search Results list box breaks up the results into three categories:

Suggested Topics   Suggested topics are keyword matches—one or more of your search terms match a keyword in each of these topics. These topics are further broken up into subcategories such as Pick a Task and Overviews, Articles, and Tutorials.

Full-Text Search Matches   Full-text matches are topics that contain one or more of your search terms in the body text of the help topic rather than in the keywords. Because the search term isn't one of the keywords for the help topic, the mention of the search term is likely to be peripheral rather than central to the topic. But you may still dig up nuggets of vital information from full-text matches.

Microsoft Knowledge Base   These results are from the Microsoft Knowledge Base (see the next sidebar). Use them to glean extra or extraneous information beyond that offered by the topics listed in the Suggested Topics and Full-Text Search Matches lists.

To display a category, click its heading. Then click a search result to display it in the right pane, as in the example in Figure 8.2. By default, Windows highlights the word or words you searched for, as in the figure. If there are one or two instances, this can be a help, but if there are many instances, this highlighting appears as more of a defacement than an enhancement. But you can get rid of it, as described after the sidebar.

FIGURE 8.2

Click a search result in the Search Results pane to display the page in the right pane.

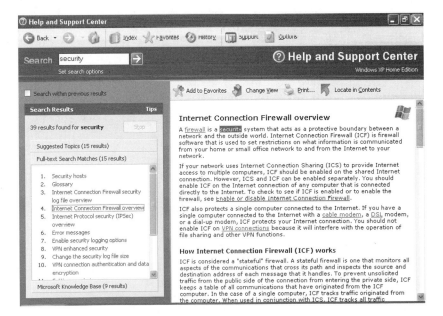

EXPERT KNOWLEDGE: MAKING THE MOST OF THE MICROSOFT KNOWLEDGE BASE

The Microsoft Knowledge Base is an online repository of knowledge and wisdom accumulated by Microsoft about its products. Given that the Knowledge Base is one of the main tools that Microsoft's support engineers use for troubleshooting customer problems with Windows, it's a great resource for searching for solutions to problems that Windows' local help resources don't know about.

The disadvantage to the Knowledge Base, and the reason perhaps why it's not more heavily emphasized in Microsoft's battery of help solutions, is the way it's arranged and the necessarily scattershot nature of its coverage. The Knowledge Base consists of a large number of answers that Microsoft's support engineers and other experts have written to questions that frustrated users and developers have submitted. The answers vary greatly in length, depending on the complexity of the problem and user level, ranging from beginner topics to super-advanced (developer-level) topics. Coverage is patchy, because the questions tend to be answered only when they're not covered in the Help files and other more accessible resources. This is why the Help and Support Center Search Results pane presents the Microsoft Knowledge Base list after the Suggested Topics list and the Full-Text Search Matches list: The Knowledge Base's offerings may be helpful, but they may equally well be completely irrelevant to your needs.

Each article is identified by an Article ID number, which consists of the letter Q followed by a six-digit number (for example, Q201950). Each article has a title that describes the problem it covers, information on which products and versions it covers, a summary that you can scan to get an idea of the contents, and the full text of the article. Beyond this, each article is tagged with keywords describing the main areas of its content. By searching for keywords, you can avoid passing references to words you might have included in the search, thus producing a more focused set of results.

For power use, you may get better results by searching the Knowledge Base directly by using Internet Explorer or another browser, because the Knowledge Base's Web interface offers extra options that Help and Support Center does not, such as searching for what's new in the last few days on a particular product and being able to display either titles and excerpts from hits found or just titles. To search the Knowledge Base directly, point your browser at search.support.microsoft.com/kb/c.asp.

If you know the number of a particular query, enter it in the Search text box. For example, if you read newsgroups on Microsoft-related subjects, you'll often see references to particular queries (or, more accurately, to the *answers* to particular queries) mentioned as the place to find a fix for a given problem.

NOTE   *You can also start searching for help from Search Companion by clicking the Information in Help and Support Center link. There's no advantage to starting searching this way unless you happen to have Search Companion displayed when you want help.*

SETTING SEARCH OPTIONS

Help and Support Center lets you specify how you want it to search. To set search options, take the following steps:

1. Click the Options button on the navigation bar. Help and Support Center displays the Options screen.

2. In the Options list in the left pane, click the Set Search Options link. Help and Support Center displays the Set Search Options screen (shown in Figure 8.3).

FIGURE 8.3

Choose search options on the Set Search Options screen in Help and Support Center.

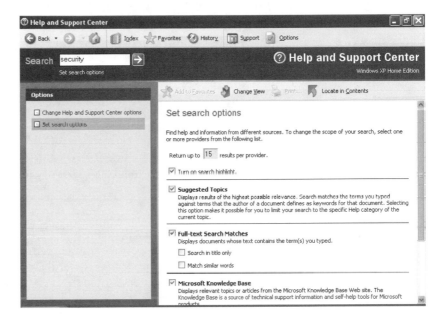

3. In the Return Up to *NN* Results per Provider text box, enter the number of search results you want Help and Support Center to get at once from each source of help. The default setting is 15, but you may want to increase this number if you find 15 doesn't give you the information you need. The disadvantage to returning more search results is that it takes longer to download those that come across your Internet connection.

4. Clear the Turn On Search Highlight check box if you don't want Help and Support Center to highlight your search terms in each result it displays.

5. If you don't want to use the Suggested Topics category, clear the Suggested Topics check box. (Usually, this category is well worth using, but in some circumstances you might want to set up Help and Support Center to search only the Knowledge Base.)

6. If you don't want to use full-text searching, clear the Full-Text Search Matches check box. If you do use full-text searching, you can refine it by selecting the Search in Title Only check box to limit full-text searches to the titles of documents instead of including their body text, or the Match Similar Words check box to have full-text searching include matches with words it thinks are similar to (instead of identical to) your search terms.

7. Clear the Microsoft Knowledge Base check box if you don't want to search the Knowledge Base. You might want to avoid searching the Knowledge Base if you find its suggestions too esoteric or if you're working offline. If you continue to search the Knowledge Base, you can set the following search options to target the results:

◆ In the Select a Product or Topic drop-down list, select the product or topic to search for.

◆ In the Search For drop-down list, choose the search method you want by selecting the All of the Words item, the Any of the Words item, the The Exact Phrase item, or the The Boolean Phrase item. (A *Boolean phrase* is one that uses terms such as AND, OR, or NOT—for example, "Internet NOT Explorer" to search for documents that contain *Internet* but do not contain *Explorer*.)

◆ Select the Search in Title Only check box if you want to limit searches to the titles of documents instead of including their body text.

SETTING HELP AND SUPPORT CENTER OPTIONS

While you're setting search options, your eye will probably be caught by the Change Help and Support Center Options link in the Options pane on the Options screen. These are the options you can set:

Show Favorites on the Navigation Bar check box   Leave this check box selected (as it is by default) to have Help and Support Center display the Favorites button on the toolbar. Clear this check box to remove the Favorites button.

Show History on the Navigation Bar check box   Leave this check box selected (as it is by default) to have Help and Support Center display the History button on the toolbar. Clear this check box to remove the History button.

Font Size Used for Help Content list   Select the Small option button, the Medium option button, or the Large option button to set a font size you find comfortable.

Options for Icons in the Navigation Bar list   Specify whether Help and Support Center should display text on the navigation bar buttons by selecting the Show All Text Labels option button, the Show Only Default Text Labels option button, or the Do Not Show Text Labels option button.

Browsing for Help

As you saw in Figure 8.1, Help and Support Center provides a list of a dozen or so *help topics* on the left side of its Home page. You can browse any of these help topics by clicking its link. Figure 8.4 shows an example of a help topic.

Click one of the links in the topic area to display the links or information available. Figure 8.5 shows an example of help subtopics.

Similarly, Help and Support Center provides a list of key support topics on the right side of its Home page. The Ask for Assistance list provides links to Remote Assistance, Support (from Microsoft), and Windows XP Newsgroups. The Pick a Task list includes links to tools such as

Windows Update and System Restore, the Tools area of Help and Support Center for help-specific tools, and Help and Support Center's features for finding XP-compatible hardware and software.

FIGURE 8.4

Follow the links in the Pick a Help Topic list to reach help topic areas.

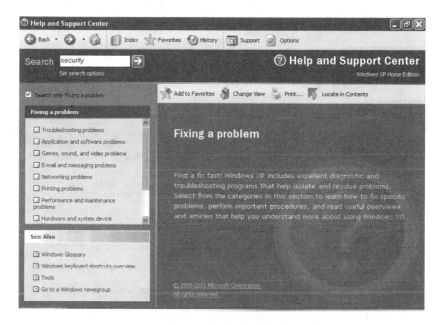

FIGURE 8.5

Drill down to find the information you need.

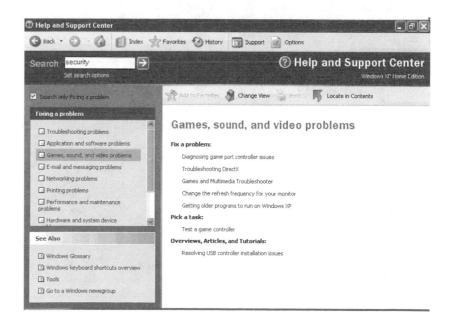

SUPPORT PAGE

The Support page (shown in Figure 8.6 with Remote Assistance information displayed) offers a variety of support tools, some of them items that actually provide support (such as Remote Assistance—accessed via the Ask a Friend to Help link—and Microsoft Online Support) and some that are just links to Windows utilities (such as My Computer Information and System Configuration Utility).

FIGURE 8.6

The Support area contains tools and links to Windows utilities.

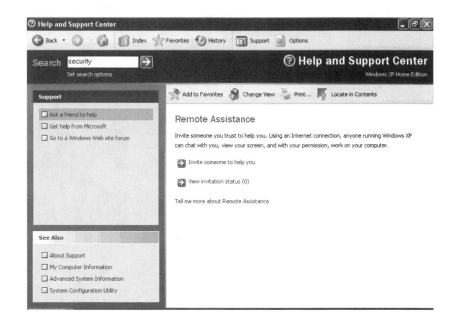

WINDOWS UPDATE PAGE

The Windows Update page provides an alternative method of accessing Windows Update. (As you saw in Chapter 2, you can also access Windows Update from the Start menu.)

COMPATIBLE HARDWARE AND SOFTWARE PAGE

The Compatible Hardware and Software page (shown in Figure 8.7) provides a mechanism for searching for information on whether particular products are compatible with Windows XP.

TOOLS PAGE

The Tools page (shown in Figure 8.8 with the Advanced System Information screen displayed) contains the Tools Center, which provides access to a number of tools for configuring and troubleshooting Windows. You'll notice that some of these tools have already popped up on other Help and Support Center pages you've seen so far. This illustrates the large number of redundant paths deliberately built into Help and Support Center to make it easier for you to find the information and tools you need to solve a problem.

FIGURE 8.7

Use the Compatible Hardware and Software page to search for compatibility information for a specific product.

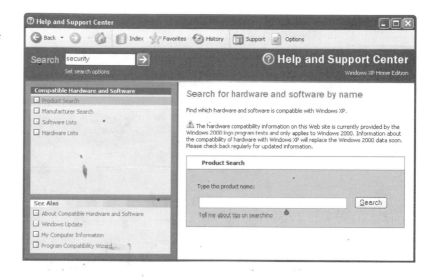

FIGURE 8.8

The Tools page provides links to a large handful of system tools.

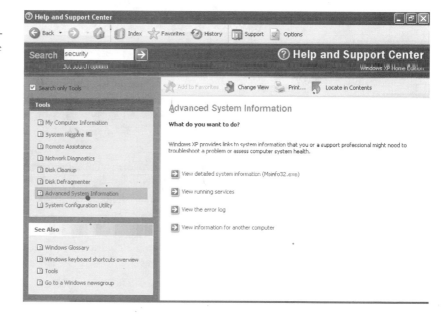

Creating and Using Favorites in Help

You can create favorites in Help and Support Center so that you can access pages of information quickly whenever you need to.

To add the current page to your favorites, click the Add to Favorites button. Help and Support Center adds the favorite to your Favorites list and displays a message box telling you that it is doing so.

To access a favorite, click the Favorites button on the toolbar. Help and Support Center displays the Favorites pane (shown in Figure 8.9). Select the favorite you want to display and click the Display button.

FIGURE 8.9

You can create favorites to give yourself quick access to topics in Help and Support Center.

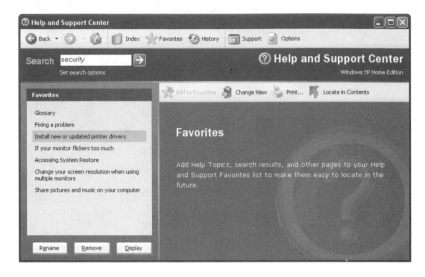

To rename a favorite, click it in the Favorites pane, then click the Rename button. Help and Support Center displays an edit box around the favorite's name. Type the new name and press the Enter key.

To delete a favorite, select it in the Favorites pane and click the Remove button.

Using Views

Designed to display a serious amount of information and options at the same time, the Help and Support Center window can threaten visual overload or simply swamp a small screen. To help you retain your sanity and your screen estate, the Help and Support Center window has a reduced view as well.

Click the Change View button to toggle between the full Help and Support Center window (including the left navigation pane, the Search bar, and the toolbar) and the reduced window, which contains only the content page and an abbreviated version of the toolbar. Figure 8.10 shows an example of the reduced window.

Navigating with Help History

You can navigate backward and forward in the chain of pages you've browsed by using the Back button and Forward button on the toolbar. If you want to see the history of where you've been, click the History button. Help and Support Center displays the History pane (shown in Figure 8.11). Click the topic you want to access.

FIGURE 8.10

Click the Change View button to reduce the Help and Support Center window to its smaller size when you've found the information to solve your problem and you need to see other windows on-screen.

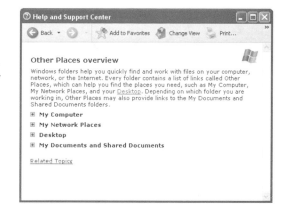

FIGURE 8.11

Use the History pane to return to topics you've visited recently.

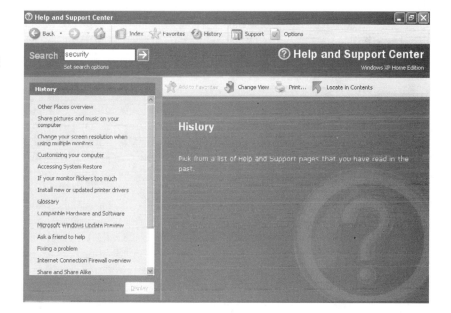

Printing Out Help Information

It goes without saying that you can print out help information if you want to have a hard copy of it handy. To print the current topic, click the Print button, and then click the Print button in the Print dialog box that Help and Support Center displays.

But it's worth pointing out that, instead of printing just an individual screen at a time, you can print a whole section of help by selecting the Print All Linked Documents check box on the Options page of the Print dialog box. You can also select the Print Table of Links check box if you want to print a table of linked pages.

Using the Support Options

This section briefly discusses the three items in the Support pane on the Support page in Help and Support Center. You can access the Support page by clicking the Support button on the navigation bar or the Support link on the Home page in Help and Support Center.

Remote Assistance (Ask a Friend to Help)

The most direct way in which you can get help is by using Windows XP's Remote Assistance feature to let someone else connect to your computer from a remote computer so that they can see what's happening and offer advice via text-based chat or via voice. If you trust your helper well enough, you can even let them take control of your computer so that they can take actions to fix the problem.

The section "Remote Assistance" in Chapter 24 discusses how to configure and use Remote Assistance.

Microsoft Online Support (Get Help from Microsoft)

Microsoft Online Support lets you automatically collect information on a problem you're having and submit it to Microsoft electronically. A Microsoft technician then sends a solution, which appears as a pop-up in your System Tray. You can read the response in the Help and Support Center window and apply the advice it contains to fix the problem.

Microsoft Online Support lets you avoid both long waits on hold and the difficulty of explaining complex problems and system configuration over the phone.

To use Microsoft Online Support, you need to have a Microsoft Passport or a Hotmail account. If you don't have one, Help and Support Center walks you through the process of getting one.

To connect to Microsoft Online Support, click the Get Help from Microsoft link in the Support pane and follow through the steps the Help and Support Center presents. For obvious reasons, your computer needs to have a working Internet connection to use this feature.

Windows Newsgroups (Go to a Windows Web Site Forum)

The Windows Newsgroups are an assortment of Windows-related online newsgroups that you can access through a Web-based front end. Though these newsgroups are run under the auspices of Microsoft, they suffer to some extent from the problems of noise and irrelevance that characterize public newsgroups. (See Chapter 21 for a discussion of newsgroups and how to use Outlook Express to access them.)

To access the Windows Newsgroups, take the following steps:

1. Display the Support page of Help and Support Center.

2. In the Support pane, click the Go to a Windows Web Site Forum link. Help and Support Center displays the Windows Newsgroups screen.

3. Click the Go to Windows Newsgroups link. Help and Support Center activates or launches Internet Explorer (or your default browser) and displays the Windows XP Newsgroups home page, which lists the newsgroups.

4. Click one of the newsgroup links. Internet Explorer activates or launches Outlook Express (or your default newsreader) and opens that newsgroup in it.

Using the Troubleshooters

Windows XP includes a number of troubleshooters for troubleshooting common problems with hardware and software configuration. Help and Support Center provides a central starting point for running these tools, though Windows also offers you the chance to run the appropriate troubleshooter when it detects that you've run into a configuration problem.

To run one of the troubleshooters, follow these steps:

1. From the Help and Support Center Home page, click the Fixing a Problem link. Help and Support Center displays the Fixing a Problem screen.

2. Click the Troubleshooting Problems link in the Fixing a Problem pane. Help and Support Center displays the Troubleshooting Problems screen.

3. Click the List of Troubleshooters link in the Overviews, Articles, and Tutorials list. Help and Support Center displays the List of Troubleshooters page.

4. Click the link for a troubleshooter to run it. Figure 8.12 shows the first screen of the Video Display Troubleshooter.

FIGURE 8.12

Windows XP includes troubleshooters that attempt to walk you through the steps of solving a problem.

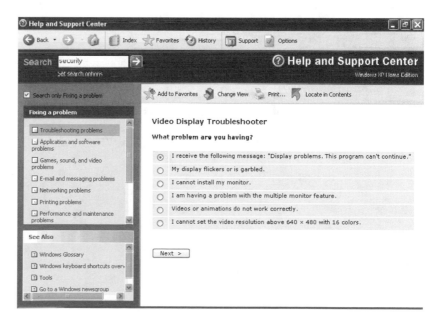

Finding Help on the Internet and Web

If you can't find the information you need through Help and Support Center, try the Internet and the Web.

Help on the Web

With earlier versions of Windows, the first port of call when looking for help on the Web was the Microsoft Web site, which offered all sorts of resources from the latest patches and drivers to the Knowledge Base. But now that Help and Support Center both seamlessly searches the Microsoft Web site and provides links to some hardware and software manufacturers' offerings, and Windows Update can automatically download and prompt you to install updates and patches to Windows, there's less reason to access the Microsoft Web site manually unless you need, say, the extra search capabilities that the Knowledge Base Web site offers.

To find information from hardware and software manufacturers not partnered closely enough with Microsoft to rate inclusion in Help and Support Center's repertoire, to download the latest drivers, or to find other sources of information, the Web can be either valuable or invaluable, depending on your luck and your persistence in searching.

Chapter 18 discusses how to surf the Web with Internet Explorer.

Help in Newsgroups

Another good source of information and help are the many computer-related public newsgroups (such as the `comp.sys` hierarchy) and the Microsoft public newsgroups (in the `microsoft.public` hierarchy).

Chapter 21 discusses how to use Outlook Express to read news.

Up Next

As you've seen in this chapter, Microsoft has done a nice job of integrating internal and external resources into Help and Support Center, bringing many separate sources of information together into a single, searchable front end. But you'll sometimes need to go beyond these offerings to find the solutions to your Windows problems. In particular, you may want to go to the newsgroups for unfiltered advice, and to third-party Web sites for the latest drivers, patches, and tips.

That's the end of the first part of the book. By now, you should be handling Windows XP with aplomb.

The next part of the book discusses how to administer and troubleshoot Windows.

Turn the page.

Part II

Administering and Troubleshooting Windows

In this section:

Chapter 9

Managing Users and Accounts

As you've read several times already in this book, Windows XP is designed to be a multiuser operating system. To help you keep your users divided if not conquered, Windows XP's setup routine encourages you heavily to create a separate user account for each user. If you do so, each user can keep their own preferences and settings, which helps keep the users from each other's throats. You can also assign users different types of user accounts to reflect the freedom and responsibility you want to give them or (perhaps more likely) the restrictions you want to impose on them in the name of harmony and democracy.

This chapter discusses how to manage users and accounts. First, it muses briefly on what user accounts are and what they're for. Then it details the three different types of user account that Windows XP Home supports, together with their limitations. After that, it tells you how to create, delete, and modify user accounts; how to require passwords for them; how to turn off the Welcome screen; and sundry other associated goodies.

This chapter covers the following topics:

◆ Understanding what user accounts are and what they're for

◆ The three different types of user accounts

◆ Creating and deleting user accounts

◆ Making Windows require passwords

◆ Using password reset disks to recover from lost passwords

◆ Applying a .NET Passport to an account

◆ Turning off the Welcome screen

◆ Turning off Fast User Switching

◆ Turning on the Guest account

NOTE   *If you're the only person who ever uses your computer, you hardly need to worry about user accounts. But if you share your computer with anybody else, you should use user accounts to the full, because they offer great benefits and require minimal setup and administration. Read on.*

What Are User Accounts and What Are They For?

A *user account* is a logical entity that lets you tailor the Windows environment to each regular user. By using user accounts, you can let each user set and maintain different preferences on the computer, so they can maintain a custom Desktop that provides the look they like and the shortcuts and information they need. Each user can also keep separate favorites and histories in Internet Explorer. (Chapter 18 discusses Internet Explorer's history and favorites features.) Each user can protect their user account with a password if they choose, and they can choose to share folders with other users via the network. (Chapter 10 discusses how to share folders with other users.)

By using accounts effectively and setting passwords, you can control access to your computer, and you can allow different privileges to different users. For example, you could prevent the less responsible members of the household from accessing critical files by storing them in secure folders. User accounts are particularly useful when your computer is networked (including always-on connections to the Internet).

Three Types of User Accounts

Windows XP Home supports three types of user accounts: Computer Administrator, Limited, and Guest. (Windows XP Professional supports a fourth type, Standard, as well as these three.) The following sections discuss what each account can do and which type of account is suitable for which type of user.

Computer Administrator Accounts

Computer Administrator accounts are intended for power users who administer the computer. A Computer Administrator account can perform just about any action on the computer, including installing programs and hardware on the computer and creating, modifying, and deleting user accounts. A Computer Administrator account can access all the files on the computer.

NOTE *A Computer Administrator account in Windows XP is roughly equivalent to the default type of account in Windows 9x.*

By default, during setup Windows XP creates each account as a Computer Administrator account, presumably to spare people from needing to make an awkward decision under (real or imagined) pressure of time. Having everyone be a Computer Administrator suits only groups of people with the most open computing arrangements imaginable. So if you created accounts during setup, you'll probably want to change some of them to Limited accounts.

Limited Accounts

As its name suggests, a Limited account is limited in what it can do—very limited. A Limited account user can change their own picture or password, or remove their password (so that they do not need to use a password to log on to Windows).

A Limited user can create, edit, and delete their own files (of course), but they can't read other files. A Limited account user cannot install or remove most programs (they can install *some* programs); cannot install any hardware; cannot create, modify, or delete user accounts; cannot see via Task Manager which other users are logged on to the computer, or log off another user who's locked the computer; and cannot make systemwide changes. Limited users may also have problems running programs designed for older versions of Windows—programs that assumed the user had free rein to use the computer.

If you want to prevent a household member from rampaging across the computer, making them a Limited user does the job quite nicely.

The Guest Account

The Guest account is a special account for use by guests—either literally guests of your household or company, or figuratively in the sense that the user will need to use the computer only briefly. For longer-term use, create a dedicated account for the user—probably a Limited account.

You can't require a password for the Guest account. That's to prevent one guest from locking out another guest. And you can have only one Guest account on an installation of Windows, so the account needs to be shared among guests. You can't create or delete the Guest account, but you can turn it off and on. (For instructions, see the section "Turning the Guest Account On and Off," later in this chapter.) By default, the Guest account is off until you turn it on.

The Guest account cannot access password-protected folders. It can change only supposedly harmless settings. For example, the Guest account can change screen resolution and color schemes, but the only user account option it can change is the picture displayed for Guest. (Given that the screen resolution applies to all users when you're using Fast User Switching, changing screen resolution can sorely vex other users.)

Creating a User Account

Windows XP encourages you to create user accounts at the end of the setup routine. But you can also create accounts at any time as needed.

NOTE   *If you're used to using Windows in a corporate setting that uses NT domains or Windows 2000 domains, you may be wondering how Windows XP Home behaves when you connect it to a network that uses a domain configuration rather than a workgroup configuration. The answer is that it doesn't: You can't connect Windows XP Home to a domain. For that, you have to use Windows XP Professional.*

To create a user account, log on as a Computer Administrator user and take the following steps:

1. Choose Start ➢ Control Panel. Windows displays Control Panel.

2. Click the User Accounts link. Windows displays the User Accounts screen (shown in Figure 9.1).

3. In the Pick a Task list, click the Create a New Account link. Windows displays the Name the New Account screen (shown in Figure 9.2).

4. Enter a name for the account:

   ◆ Usernames can be up to 20 characters long and are not case sensitive.

   ◆ Names can contain letters, numbers, and most symbols. They cannot contain any of these characters: *, ?, +, =, , (comma), : (colon), ; (semicolon), <, >, | (pipe character), " (double quotation marks), [,], /, or \.

   ◆ Names can start with letters, numbers, or symbols. Names can even consist of nothing but underscores.

FIGURE 9.1

From the User Accounts screen in Control Panel, you can create, delete, and modify user accounts.

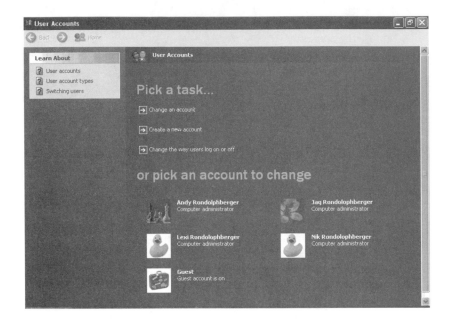

FIGURE 9.2

On the Name the New Account screen, enter the name for the new user account.

TIP It can be amusing to create idiosyncratic names, but consider using a naming convention if you're creating more than a few user accounts and want to keep things formal and organized.

5. Click the Next button. Windows displays the Pick an Account Type screen.

6. By default, Windows selects the Computer Administrator option button. Select the Limited option button if you want the account to be Limited instead.

7. Click the Create Account button. Windows creates the account and displays the User Accounts screen again, with the new user listed.

Deleting a User Account

If you lose a member of your company or excommunicate a member of your family, you may want to delete their user account from your computer. Deleting the user account is easy, but you need to decide whether to keep the user's Desktop configuration files and their My Documents folder.

To delete a user account, log on as a Computer Administrator user and take the following steps:

1. Choose Start ➤ Control Panel. Windows displays Control Panel.

2. Click the User Accounts link. Windows displays the User Accounts screen.

3. Click the user's icon. Windows displays the What Do You Want to Change about *Username*'s Account? screen (shown in Figure 9.3).

FIGURE 9.3

Use the What Do You Want to Change about *Username*'s Account? page of User Accounts to make changes to the account.

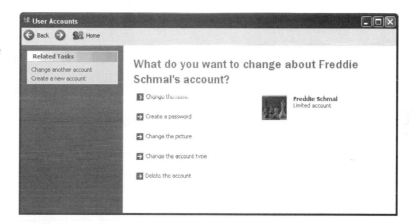

4. Click the Delete the Account link. Windows displays the Do You Want to Keep *Username*'s Files? screen (shown in Figure 9.4).

FIGURE 9.4

When you delete a user, you get to choose whether to keep the user's files.

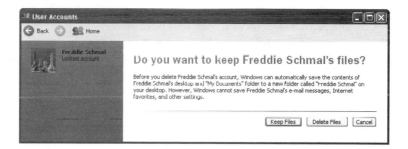

5. Click the Keep Files button or the Delete Files button as appropriate. Windows displays the Are You Sure You Want to Delete *Username*'s Account? page to make sure you've thought about what you're doing.

   ◆ If you chose to keep the files, Windows tells you that it will save the user's files to a folder on your Desktop. The folder will bear the soon-to-be-ex-user's name.

6. Click the Delete Account button if you're sure you want to proceed. Windows deletes the account and displays the User Accounts screen.

EXPERT KNOWLEDGE: DELETING YOUR OWN ACCOUNT

Sometimes—almost certainly not often—you'll need to delete your own account from a computer. You can't delete it directly from your own user session, because the account is active and (as it were) doesn't have a self-destruct button.

So (you've guessed it) you need to delete your account from another Computer Administrator account. If yours is the only Computer Administrator account on the computer, you'll need to create a new Computer Administrator account (either from scratch or by promoting a Limited account to Computer Administrator status) in order to delete your account.

Changing a User Account

If you set up a user account but don't quite get it right, don't worry—you can change it easily. You can change a user account from Limited to Computer Administrator or vice versa; change the account name; change the picture; or add a password to the account.

The actions you can take for a user's account are grouped on the What Do You Want to Change about *Username*'s Account? page (shown in Figure 9.3 above). To display this page, click the user's name on the User Accounts page.

You can then change the account by taking one or more of the actions detailed in the next sections.

Assigning a Picture to a User Account

Assigning a picture to a user account is likely to be one of the most popular account changes made in Windows XP. Even the Guest user can change their picture.

The picture for a user's account can be of the BMP, GIF, JPG, PNG, or TIF file type. Windows shrinks the picture down to the appropriate size, but you'll need to take care of any cropping or rotating first. (Windows Picture and Fax Viewer can handle the rotation. Paint can handle both rotation and cropping. See Chapter 7 for a brief discussion of these built-in programs.)

To change the picture for a user, follow these steps from the What Do You Want to Change about *Username*'s Account? page:

1. Click the Change the Picture link. Windows displays the Pick a New Picture for *Username*'s Account page (shown in Figure 9.5).

2. To use a built-in picture, select it in the list box. To use a picture of your own, click the Browse for More Pictures link. Windows displays an Open dialog box.

3. Navigate to the picture you want to use, select it, and click the Open button. Windows adds the picture to the list box.

4. Select the picture and click the Change Picture button.

Now disconnect your session so that you can see how the picture looks on the Welcome screen.

FIGURE 9.5

Any user can change the picture shown for them on the Welcome screen.

Requiring a Password for an Account

As you've seen, by default Windows XP Home Edition doesn't require a password for any user: Anyone for whom you've created an account can log on by clicking their username on the Welcome screen, and anyone else can log in as Guest once the Guest account is active. (Needless to say, guests can log in under any of the existing user accounts if they're not password protected.)

If you need to tighten your security, start by using passwords. Passwords are more or less mandatory in any serious business setting, and they can be a good idea in many family or dorm situations as well.

You can require passwords from some users but not from others if you want, but in practice this makes little sense, as anyone can log on to any account that doesn't have a password. If you leave a Computer Administrator account unprotected, any user who logs on to that account can make wholesale changes to Windows. So if you're going to implement passwords, you should implement them for every user (except the Guest user, who can't have one).

Unfortunately, Windows XP doesn't have an ideal arrangement for implementing passwords. Ideally, there'd be a setting that you (the Computer Administrator user) could set that would make each user apart from the Guest user create a password for their account the next time they used the computer. Each user would then create a password that only they would know, and the computer would be secure against unauthorized users logging on. Each user would be able to change their password whenever they wanted to (or, better, would be made to change the password frequently) and wouldn't be able to remove password protection from the account.

From a security and administration point of view, such an arrangement would be more or less ideal. And in fact this is a crude description of the security you get in Windows XP Professional when you use it in a Windows domain (rather than a workgroup). But in Windows XP Home? Dream on.

Given that Windows XP doesn't have this ideal security arrangement, there are two ways in which you can proceed.

- ◆ Encourage—no, make that *heavily encourage*—each user to create a password right this moment, change it at least halfway frequently, and never remove it. Stress the benefits of having a strong password that only the user knows.

◆ Create passwords for each user yourself from a Computer Administrator account. This method has two disadvantages. First, you know the passwords. Second, and much worse, *the user loses all the personal certificates they've stored, together with any passwords they've saved for network resources (such as folders and printers) and for Web sites.* Losing the user this information will make you deservedly unpopular, so the only sensible time to implement passwords in this manner is before the user has used their account.

To make Windows require passwords, take these steps from the What Do You Want to Change about *Username*'s Account? page:

1. Click the Create a Password link. Windows displays the Create a Password for *Username*'s Account screen (shown in Figure 9.6). If you're creating a password for your own account, you get the same text boxes but not the excitable warnings.

FIGURE 9.6

Use the Create a Password for *Username*'s Account screen to create a password and (if necessary) a password hint for the account.

2. Enter the password in the Type a New Password text box and the Type the New Password Again to Confirm text box. For security (is someone looking over your shoulder?), Windows displays each character as an asterisk (*). Make sure the two instances of the password match.

3. If you think it appropriate, enter a password hint in the Type a Word or Phrase to Use As a Password Hint text box. Anybody trying to log on to the computer can display the password hint, so you need to tailor it carefully to the person. The password hint must mean something to the user without meaning anything to anyone else. It's much easier to get this wrong than right—and in any case, for security, you shouldn't use password hints. (Every user should memorize their password. Period.)

4. Click the Create Password button. Windows applies the password to the account.

5. When you create a password for your own user account, and you're a Computer Administrator user, Windows displays the Do You Want to Make Your Files and Folders Private? screen (shown in Figure 9.7), which offers to make your files and folders private so that Limited users won't be able to see them. To accept this offer, click the Yes, Make Private button. To decline it, click the No button. (See Chapter 10 for information on sharing files and folders with other users and implementing security on your computer.)

FIGURE 9.7

Windows displays the Do You Want to Make Your Files and Folders Private? screen when you create a password for your own Computer Administrator account.

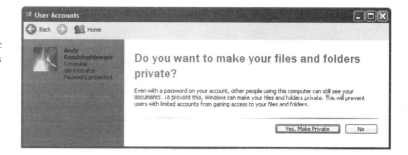

When you require passwords, Windows prompts the user for a password when they click their name on the Welcome screen. The user can click the Password Hint link to display the hint for the password.

When a user account is password protected, Windows displays *Password protected* under the account type on the User Accounts screens.

EXPERT KNOWLEDGE: HOW—AND WHY—TO CREATE SECURE PASSWORDS

If you use passwords—and you should, if you value your data—it's vital to make sure that they're effective. You wouldn't believe the number of people who don't understand why passwords are important and who see them as an irritant.

Actually, you *might* believe that. But would you believe that between 90 and 95 percent of *all* passwords are the same 100 words? This is what some security experts estimate based on the passwords they see in daily use. Crackers (malevolent hackers) try these popular passwords first when trying to guess a password because they work so often.

In order to create a secure password, it helps to understand how crackers go about breaking a password. The most common method is to use a *dictionary attack*. The attacker runs a script that tries to match each word in a specified dictionary with your password until it gets a hit. The dictionary can be in any language or a mixture of languages, and will usually contain all popular passwords in all major languages at its beginning. (The dictionary isn't so much a dictionary in the conventional sense as a list of words arranged in some kind of descending order of probability—most likely words first.)

Dictionary attacks are often effective. But if the would-be victim has created a tough password (by using the methods described below), the cracker may resort to *social engineering*—the art of extracting passwords from the unsuspecting by posing as someone in authority (for example, as a system administrator or a troubleshooter for your ISP). Again, security experts tend to be amazed by how freely many users give up their passwords over the phone.

Continued on next page

EXPERT KNOWLEDGE: HOW—AND WHY—TO CREATE SECURE PASSWORDS *(continued)*

To keep your password secure, *never* write it down (and if you must write it down, don't stick the paper containing it onto your computer or monitor) and *never* tell anyone else what it is. You are the only person who ever needs to know your password. No ISP and no system administrator should need to be given your password, over the phone or in person. ISP personnel and system administrators may need to reset your password or assign you a new password—for example, if you forget your password. In this case, *they'll* give *you* the new password. You then log in with it and create a new, secure password for yourself immediately. (At least, that's the theory.)

Follow these rules to create a secure password:

◆ Create a password of an appropriate length. Windows, many ISPs, and most services will let you create passwords of any length between 6 characters and 15 characters. Treat 6 characters as the absolute minimum. Aim for a password of at least 8 characters, and more like 12 if you're feeling insecure. Passwords of 5 characters or fewer are relatively easy to crack by brute force; passwords of 6 characters are much harder; and longer passwords are much harder yet. If you're allowed to create a password of any length, be sensible and limit the password to a length that you can remember and type without undue stumbling.

◆ Never use a real word in any language for a password. Real words can be broken easily by a dictionary attack.

◆ Instead, use symbols (@, $, %, ^, !, &, and so on) as substitute characters in a word or phrase, or reduce a phrase or sentence to its initial letters or key letters. Mix letters and numbers. Use uppercase and lowercase creatively (passwords are case sensitive). Alternatively, open a text editor, close your eyes, and type randomly for a few seconds, making sure to hold down the Shift key at intervals. Then pick a particularly cryptic part of the result to use as a password.

◆ Never use any example password that you see, no matter how compelling it may seem. For example, books on security provide example passwords. These may look wonderfully cryptic, but you should assume that they're all known to crackers and included in cracking dictionaries.

◆ Never use any option that offers to save a password for you. For example, Windows offers to store your dial-up passwords so that you can access your dial-up accounts more easily. These passwords not only let unauthorized users of your computer access your dial-up accounts effortlessly, but also can be cracked easily by commonly available programs.

◆ Use a different password for each account or program that requires one. That way, if one password is compromised, the others will still be secure. (Yes, of course it's difficult. If security were effortless, nobody in the world would have a problem with it.)

◆ Change your passwords frequently, even if you have no reason to suspect that they've been compromised.

◆ As soon as you suspect that a password may have been compromised, change it. Also change any associated passwords.

◆ Never repeat a password you've used in the past. Create an entirely new password each time you change a password.

◆ Memorize your passwords. Never write them down. If you write a password down, you've compromised it. If you must write a password down, keep it in the safest of places. If that place is virtual rather than physical, protect your password stash with another password—a good one.

◆ Never tell anybody any of your passwords—not even the ones you've stopped using. (They might be able to use these passwords to guess at your newer passwords.)

Continued on next page

EXPERT KNOWLEDGE: HOW—AND WHY—TO CREATE SECURE PASSWORDS *(continued)*

If you can follow the simple advice in this list, you'll be ahead of 99 percent of the computer-using population—and measurably (perhaps immeasurably) more secure than any of them.

That said, be warned that no password is totally secure. Any password can be broken by an attacker who has sufficient time, determination, and computer operations. But most crackers will not be prepared to spend more than a few minutes (or, at the most, hours) on any given password, and will swiftly move on to other pastures that promise to prove greener. So your goal is to keep your passwords secure against random attackers, not against the NSA. If the NSA is on your case, you'll have much worse things to worry about than whether your passwords are strong enough.

TIP   One problem that can occur with passwords is having the Caps Lock feature switched on, either when you're creating the password (Windows has no method for warning you of this) or when you're subsequently entering it. If you're sure of the letters and shifting of the password, but Windows won't accept it, double-check that Caps Lock isn't on (or, if you used Caps Lock for your password, make sure it isn't off). On keyboards with an embedded numeric keypad, such as those on most notebooks, you can give yourself a similar problem by having the Num Lock feature on while typing the password.

Removing Password Protection from an Account

Just as a Computer Administrator user can apply password protection to another user's account, so they can remove it. But the same problem applies to removal as to application: The user loses all the personal certificates they've stored, together with any passwords they've saved for network resources (such as folders and printers) and for Web sites. So if you need to remove password protection from an account, it's far better to have the users do it themselves.

To remove password protection from an account, click the Remove the Password link on the What Do You Want to Change about *Username*'s Account? screen. On the Are You Sure You Want to Remove *Username*'s Password? screen, click the Remove Password button.

Creating a New Password for a User

If a user forgets their password, they won't be able to log on to Windows. They'll need to get a Computer Administrator user to create a new password—a replacement password, as it were   for them. But again, as with applying and removing passwords, the user loses all the personal certificates they've stored, together with any passwords they've saved for network resources (such as folders and printers) and for Web sites.

To create a replacement password for another user, log on as a Computer Administrator user and click the Change the Password link on the What Do You Want to Change about *Username*'s Account? screen. Windows displays the Change *Username*'s Password screen, which works in the same way as the Create a Password for *Username*'s Account screen shown a page or two earlier: You type a password, confirm it, enter a password hint if appropriate, and click the Change Password button.

You're probably thinking that all this losing of the user's personal certificates and passwords should be avoidable, even if the user is unwise enough to forget their password. And it is avoidable. Read on.

Using Password Reset Disks to Recover from Lost Passwords

If a Limited user forgets their password, they need to get a Computer Administrator user to create a new password for them or remove the password from the account. That's easy enough—but if there's no Computer Administrator user around, it could prove a big waste of time. And the user loses any personal certificates and passwords they have stored.

If any Computer Administrator user forgets their password, they'll need to have another Computer Administrator user create a new password for them (because they won't be able to log on to their own account). That too is easy enough—provided that there's another Computer Administrator user, and that they're handy. Again, though, those personal certificates and passwords go overboard.

But if all available Computer Administrator users forget their passwords, you have a problem bigger than the personal certificates and passwords taking a permanent hike. If you don't prepare for this eventuality, and those Computer Administrator users forget their passwords, you'll need to reinstall Windows to get it working again.

To prepare for this eventuality, you need to create a password reset disk. Both Computer Administrator users and Limited users can—and should—do this. You can do this only for your own account.

CREATING YOUR PASSWORD RESET DISK

To create a password reset disk, follow these steps:

1. Click your account on the Pick an Account to Change screen. Windows displays the What Do You Want to Change About Your Account? screen.

2. Click the Prevent a Forgotten Password link in the Related Tasks list. Windows launches the Forgotten Password Wizard, which displays the Welcome to the Forgotten Password Wizard page.

3. Click the Next button. The Wizard displays the Create a Password Reset Disk page, which prompts you to insert a blank, formatted floppy into your A drive.

4. Insert a blank, formatted floppy disk in the drive.

   ◆ If you have multiple floppy drives, choose the option button for the one you put the floppy in.

   ◆ The floppy doesn't actually have to be blank. The Wizard creates only one file, USERKEY.PSW, which is typically only a couple of kilobytes large. So unless the floppy is completely full, the file will usually fit.

5. Click the Next button. The Wizard displays the Current User Account Password page (shown in Figure 9.8).

6. Enter your password in the Current User Account Password text box.

7. Click the Next button. The Wizard displays the Creating Password Reset Disk page asking you to wait while it creates the disk. When it has finished, it makes the Next button available.

8. Click the Next button. The Wizard displays the Completing the Forgotten Password Wizard screen.

FIGURE 9.8

On the Current User Account Password page of the Forgotten Password Wizard, enter your password.

9. Click the Finish button. The Wizard closes itself. Remove the disk, label it clearly (or confusingly, if you plan to store it in a shared place), and put it somewhere safe. You can't create another password reset disk without invalidating this disk, so don't try making multiple disks—only the last one will work.

This disk doesn't store your password as such. Instead, it stores encrypted information that enables you to create a new password.

USING YOUR PASSWORD RESET DISK

To use the password reset disk, take the following steps:

1. When you get stuck at the Welcome screen and can't remember your password, insert the disk.

2. Click the green arrow button without entering your password. Windows displays the Did You Forget Your Password? pop-up.

3. Click the Use Your Password Reset Disk link in the pop-up. Windows starts the Password Reset Wizard, which displays its Welcome screen.

4. Click the Next button. The Wizard displays the Insert the Password Reset Disk screen.

5. Insert the disk, specify the drive if necessary, and click the Next button. The Wizard displays the Reset the User Account Password page (shown in Figure 9.9).

6. Enter your new password twice, and enter a hint if you think it wise.

7. Click the Next button. The Wizard displays the Completing the Password Reset Wizard page.

8. Click the Finish button. The Wizard closes itself and returns you to the Welcome screen.

9. Log on using the new password. Remove the password reset disk and put it away somewhere safe. (You don't need to update it.)

FIGURE 9.9

On the Reset the User Account Password page of the Password Reset Wizard, enter a new password for yourself.

Applying a .NET Passport to an Account

As mentioned earlier in the book, many of Windows XP's communications features (such as Windows Messenger's text, audio, and video messaging capabilities) require you to use a Microsoft .NET Passport.

You can apply a Passport to your user account either indirectly—by signing up for a Passport or using a Passport while logged in to the account—or directly by taking the following steps from the What Do You Want to Change about Your Account? page. You'll need to be online at the time. Note that Microsoft tweaks its Hotmail and Passport sign-up procedures now and then, so you may use a different procedure from that described here.

1. Click the Set Up My Account to Use a .NET Passport link. Windows starts the .NET Passport Wizard, which displays its Add a .NET Passport to Your Windows XP User Account page.

2. Click the Next button. The Wizard displays the Do You Have an E-mail Account? page (shown in Figure 9.10).

3. Select the Yes option button or the No. Please Open a Free MSN.com E-mail Address for Me option button as appropriate.

FIGURE 9.10

On the Do You Have an E-mail Address? page of the .NET Passport Wizard, specify whether to use an existing e-mail account for your Passport or to get a new account with MSN.

4. Click the Next button.

   ◆ If you chose the Yes button, the Wizard displays the What Is Your E-mail Address? page (shown in Figure 9.11).

FIGURE 9.11

On the What Is Your E-mail Address? page of the .NET Passport Wizard, enter the e-mail address you want to associate with the passport.

   ◆ The Wizard displays a series of pages that walk you through the steps of creating an MSN e-mail account that also serves as your passport. You need to give your first name, last name, country or region, state, zip code, time zone, birth date, gender, and occupation. You then get to choose a sign-in name and password and set a secret question and answer for securing the account. By default, the .NET Passport Wizard sets you up to use MSN Explorer to access your e-mail. If you prefer to use another e-mail program, clear the Use MSN Explorer to Access My E-mail check box. You then get to choose whether Microsoft Passport shares your e-mail address, your name, and your other registration information with sites that use Passport. Passport then creates your .NET Passport and applies it to your computer. The Wizard ends.

5. Enter the e-mail address in the E-mail Address or Passport text box.

6. Click the Next button. The Wizard displays the Type Your .NET Password page (shown in Figure 9.12).

FIGURE 9.12

On the Type Your .NET Password page of the .NET Passport Wizard, enter the password for your Passport.

7. Enter your password.

8. By default, the Wizard selects the Save My Passport in My Windows XP User Account check box. Clear this check box if you want to apply your Passport manually to this account or another account.

9. Click the Next button. The Wizard checks the password against the Passport and displays the You're Done! screen.

10. Click the Finish button. The Wizard closes. You should now be able to access Passport-enabled sites and services from this account.

If necessary, you can change the .NET Passport associated with your user account by clicking the Change My .NET Passport link on the What Do You Want to Change about Your Account? page of User Accounts and clicking the Use a Different Passport button on the resulting What Do You Want to Change about Your .NET Passport? page.

Turning Off the Welcome Screen

If you don't like the Welcome screen, or if you don't want users logging on to the computer to be able to see the list of other users, you can make Windows display the Log On to Windows dialog box instead of the Welcome screen.

NOTE   *Turning off the Welcome screen also turns off Fast User Switching, which means that multiple users won't be able to be logged on to the computer at the same time.*

To turn off the Welcome screen, make sure you're the only user logged on, and then take the following steps:

1. Choose Start ➤ Control Panel. Windows displays Control Panel.

2. Click the User Accounts link. Windows displays the User Accounts screen.

3. In the Pick a Task list, click the Change the Way Users Log On or Off link. Windows displays the Select Logon and Logoff Options screen (shown in Figure 9.13).

FIGURE 9.13

On the Select Logon and Logoff Options screen, you can turn off the Welcome screen and Fast User Switching.

4. Clear the Use the Welcome Screen check box.

5. Click the Apply Options button.

Thereafter, Windows displays the Log On to Windows dialog box instead of the Welcome screen. This dialog box neither lists the user accounts on the computer nor offers password hints, so it's more secure than the Welcome screen. However, Windows displays the name of the last user in the Log On to Windows dialog box as a convenience in case the same user needs to log back in—so if this account isn't protected by a password, anyone can log on with no trouble at all.

Turning Off Fast User Switching

By default, Windows' Fast User Switching feature is turned on, allowing you to have multiple user sessions running at the same time (with only one of them active at a time, of course). Fast User Switching is convenient for multiuser situations such as a family computer, but if several users leave a number of programs running, the computer's performance can suffer, especially if the computer has a modest amount of RAM (128MB or less). There's also the risk that one user will try to shut down the computer while another user has unsaved work still open, which will almost always lose the unsaved work. And even if no one terminates anyone else's session, users can have problems trying to open the same files or run the same programs, as discussed in Chapter 5.

To turn off Fast User Switching, make sure you're the only user logged on to the computer. (Log off any other users. If you don't, Windows can't turn off Fast User Switching.) Then display the Select Logon and Logoff Options screen as discussed in the previous section, clear the Use Fast User Switching check box, and click the Apply Options button.

Turning the Guest Account On and Off

Next, ask yourself if you want to have the Guest account enabled on your computer. If you want your computer to be moderately secure, it's a good idea to leave the Guest account turned off until you need it.

In a family setting, the Guest account can be a good idea, particularly if nobody keeps secrets on the computer. In an office, dorm, or just about any other setting, the Guest account is a bad idea because it compromises the security of your computer. The Guest account is more limited in what it can do than Computer Administrator accounts and Limited accounts, but even so, it has the potential to cause trouble, either with local files or via a network or Internet connection.

The Guest account is disabled by default in Windows XP Home Edition. To turn it on, follow these steps:

1. Choose Start ➤ Control Panel. Windows displays Control Panel.

2. Click the User Accounts link. Windows displays the User Accounts screen.

3. Click the Guest link. Windows displays the Do You Want to Turn On the Guest Account? screen.

4. Click the Turn On the Guest Account link. Windows turns on the Guest account and displays the User Accounts screen again.

To disable the Guest account, click the Guest link on the User Accounts page. Windows displays the What Do You Want to Change about the Guest Account? page. Click the Turn Off the Guest Account link.

Up Next

This chapter has discussed what user accounts are, what they're for, and how to work with them to keep users separated from each other and give users scope to take only the actions they need to take. You know why passwords are vital for protecting your data, and you know how to create strong passwords. And you've seen how to turn on and off the Welcome screen, the Fast User Switching feature, and the Guest account.

If this has whetted your taste for administration, turn the page. The next chapter discusses how to share folders with other users, how to use the auditing and security options that Windows XP Home offers, and how to work with file types to make files behave the way you want them to.

Chapter 10

Sharing and File Types

THIS CHAPTER DISCUSSES SHARING and file types—two topics you really need to know about in order to make the most of Windows.

The chapter starts with a little background about Windows XP Home's approach to security and sharing. After that, it discusses how to share folders with other users of the computer, and how to prevent other users (including Computer Administrator users) from examining folders you want to keep private. It also shows you how to use the Shared Folders snap-in to see at a glance which folders you're sharing and which user has which file open.

Sharing folders is easy. But the topic covered at the end of the chapter—file extensions, file types, and file associations—is tough enough to annoy well-seasoned Windows veterans. If you've gotten confused about why different things happen when you double-click different types of files in Explorer; if you wish you could change the action that results for one file type or another; or if you want to see extensions for all your files—if any of these is the case, read this section.

This chapter might not sound like your idea of fun, but you should probably read it at some point—not necessarily right now, but perhaps when you start having problems with your house-mates accessing your secret files, or with extensions and file types misbehaving.

Part of the problem is that Windows XP Home simply tries to be too friendly, so its security model is wide open by default. Each user created during setup is automatically made a Computer Administrator user, which gives them access to every folder and file on the computer. If you want privacy, you have to tell Windows XP Home so, and tell it explicitly.

This chapter covers the following topics:

- ◆ The background to sharing
- ◆ Sharing folders
- ◆ Making a folder private
- ◆ Seeing which folders and files you're sharing
- ◆ Understanding what file types are
- ◆ Changing the action associated with a file type
- ◆ Creating a new file type

The Background to Sharing

Windows NT and Windows 2000, as you'll know if you've worked with them, have an impressive range of security and management features, including three different categories of permissions (share permissions, folder permissions, and special permissions) that allow pico-management of what any particular user or group of users can do with a given folder or file. For example, you could allow one user to open files in a particular folder but not change them. Or you could prevent another user from seeing those files in that folder, but allow them to navigate through that folder to a subfolder it contained (and allow them to work with one of the files in that subfolder).

Because Windows XP has the NT/2000 code base under its hood, it has most of these capabilities too: When you connect a computer running Windows XP Professional to a Windows 2000–server-based network, you can implement a set of permissions extensive enough to stun medium-sized mammals. But because Windows XP Home is designed for home use rather than for corporate or military use, and because you don't (or *shouldn't*) need to set permissions such as these in the typical home or home-office setting, Windows XP Home simplifies permissions and security a great deal. These are the basic parameters:

◆ Windows XP Home differentiates between local sharing and network sharing. Once you read those terms, you probably have a pretty good idea as to what they mean: *Local sharing* is the sharing of files and folders with other users of your computer. *Network sharing* is the sharing of files and folders with users of other computers to which your computer is networked.

◆ By default, most files and folders in Windows XP Home are shared locally. (More on this in a moment.) By default, no files are shared on the network.

◆ Windows XP Home provides a separate area of the file structure for each user: the \My Documents\ folder and its subfolders. Files and folders within the \My Documents\ folder and its subfolders are automatically protected from Limited users and the Guest user. By default, Computer Administrator users can see the contents of any user's \My Documents\ folder and its subfolders, but you can make the contents of your \My Documents\ folder and its subfolders private so that only you can see them.

◆ Windows XP Home provides folders that are automatically shared with all users of your computer (the \Shared Documents\ folder structure). You can't remove this sharing from these folders.

◆ For any folder apart from folders owned and protected by the operating system, you can choose to share the folder on the network. You can even share your \My Documents\ folder if you so choose.

◆ When you share a folder on the network, you can decide whether the users you're sharing it with can only read its contents or can read them and change them. If you let other users change your files, they can delete them as well.

◆ A subfolder inherits privacy from its parent folder (the folder that contains it). For example, say you have a folder named \My Secret Stuff\, located in your \My Documents\ folder, that you make private. If you create a folder named \Top Secret\ within the \My Secret Stuff\ folder, it automatically is made private too. You can't remove privacy from the subfolder of a private folder without removing it from the parent folder.

◆ By contrast, a subfolder *does not* inherit being shared on the network from its parent folder: You need to specify sharing explicitly for the subfolder of a shared parent folder.

◆ You can't set sharing on individual files, so to implement sharing on files, you need to put them in shared folders or private folders as appropriate.

As mentioned in Chapter 6, Windows XP Home would like you to keep all the documents that you don't want to share in the \My Documents\ folder and its subfolders (such as the \My Pictures\ folder, the \My Music\ folder, and the \My Videos\ folder) and all the documents that you do want to share in the \Shared Documents\ folder and its subfolders (such as the \Shared Music\ folder, the \Shared Pictures\ folder, and the \Shared Videos\ folder). Windows programs are trained to put documents you create using them in the \My Documents\ folder or the appropriate subfolder by default and to look for them there. In theory, this helps you, the user, because you don't lose files, and each program opens automatically in the right folder for the types of files you're likely to want to open in it. Other Windows programs and features also use these folders as appropriate. For example, the My Pictures Slideshow screen saver by default looks for pictures in the \My Pictures\ folder.

Sharing a Folder

Windows XP Home provides two easy ways of sharing a folder:

◆ Using the \Shared Documents\ folder to share the folder with all other users of the computer

◆ Using the "share on the network" technique to share the folder with all other users of the same computer and users of computers networked to this computer

The next two sections discuss these ways of sharing a folder.

Sharing a Folder with All Other Users of This Computer

Windows XP provides an easy way to share a folder with all the other users of the computer. To share a new folder, create it in the \Shared Documents\ folder. To share an existing folder, move it to the \Shared Documents\ folder. All other users of the computer can then access the contents of the folder and (by default) change them.

Sharing a Folder "on the Network" with All Other Users

The second way of sharing a folder is called "share on the network." The name is misleading—perhaps intentionally so. A folder shared in this way *is* shared on the network, so that users of other computers networked to this computer can access the folder's contents. But the folder is also shared with all other users of this computer.

Before we get into this topic, there are a couple of things you need to know:

◆ First, before you can share a folder on the network, you need to enable remote access to your computer by running the Network Setup Wizard. If you haven't done so, turn to Chapter 32 for coverage of the Network Setup Wizard. Alternatively, you can click the If You Understand the Security Risks but Want to Share Files without Running The Wizard, Click Here link that Windows displays in the Network Sharing and Security group box on the Sharing page of the Properties dialog box for a folder until you've run the Network Setup Wizard (or clicked this link). When you click this link, Windows displays the Enable File Sharing dialog box. Select the Just Enable File Sharing option button and click the OK button. Windows closes the Enable File Sharing dialog box and makes the Share This Folder on the Network check box available in the Network Sharing and Security group box.

◆ Second, Windows prevents you from using the share-on-the-network technique for folders in the \Program Files\ folder and the \Windows\ folder structure. These limitations are of course in your best interests, but you need to know about them upfront so that you don't trip over them.

To share a folder on the network, follow these steps:

1. Create the folder (if you haven't created it already) in a suitable location for sharing on the network. (That means you shouldn't put it in your \My Documents\ folder—it's best to keep that to yourself—and you can't put it in the \Program Files\ folder structure or the \Windows\ folder structure.) If the folder already exists, and is located in a less-than-prime location, move it to a suitable location.

2. Right-click the folder and choose Sharing and Security from the context menu. (Alternatively, select the folder and choose File ➤ Sharing and Security.) Windows displays the Sharing page of the Properties dialog box for the folder. Figure 10.1 shows an example of the Sharing page.

   ◆ If you're sharing a drive, the Sharing page of the Properties dialog box at first contains nothing but a note warning you that sharing the root of a drive isn't recommended (for security reasons) and a link that you can click to acknowledge that you understand the risk but want to share the root of the drive anyway. If you want to share the drive, click this link, and Windows displays the controls for the Sharing page.

FIGURE 10.1

Use the Sharing page of the Properties dialog box for a folder or drive to share the folder or drive "on the network."

3. Select the Share This Folder on the Network check box. Windows enables the Share Name text box and enters the folder's name in it. Windows also enables the Allow Network Users to Change My Files check box.

4. Change the name in the Share Name text box if you want. You'll often want to change this to something more descriptive. For example, you might want to change the name to indicate which computer the folder is located on.

   ◆ Remove any commas or semicolons from the share name. Windows doesn't allow them, though they're fine in the folder name (and so are entered in the share name automatically). Periods and exclamation points are okay. (If you don't remove these characters, Windows hits you with a Sharing dialog box telling you that the share name "contains invalid characters" when you close the Properties dialog box.)

   ◆ You'll need to reduce the share name to 12 characters or fewer if you want to be able to access it from computers running Windows 98, Windows Me, or Windows NT 4. If you don't shorten a long name, Windows hits you with another Sharing dialog box to this effect when you close the Properties dialog box.

5. If you don't want other users to be able to change your files, clear the Allow Network Users to Change My Files check box.

6. Click the OK button. Windows closes the Properties dialog box and shares the folder with the degree of permissions you specified.

Explorer displays a different icon for a shared folder—an open hand appears underneath the folder—to give you a quick graphical cue to which folders are shared and which aren't. Figure 10.2 shows an example.

FIGURE 10.2

Windows displays an icon with an open hand to indicate a shared folder.

Documents and Settings

Video Factory

Making a Folder Private

So far in this chapter, you've seen how to share a folder with all other users of this computer, with them and users of networked computers, and with users you specify.

But what if you want to share a folder with none of the above—in other words, if you flat-out don't want to share a folder? Simply not sharing it (using any of the methods described above) isn't good enough, because Computer Administrator users can see the contents of any folder that isn't specifically protected against them. You need to make it private.

To make a folder private, take the following steps:

1. Right-click the folder and choose Sharing and Security from the context menu. (Alternatively, select the folder and click the Share This Folder link in the File and Folder Tasks list.) Windows displays the Sharing page of the Properties dialog box.

2. Select the Make This Folder Private check box.

3. Click the OK button. Windows closes the Properties dialog box and applies privacy to the folder.

◆ If you don't have a password on your user account when you select the Make This Folder Private check box, Windows displays the Sharing dialog box shown in Figure 10.3, warning you that anyone can log in as you, and so access the folder, and inviting you to create a password. If you click the Yes button, Windows displays the Create a Password for Your Account screen of User Accounts so that you can create the password immediately.

FIGURE 10.3

When you make a folder private, Windows displays this Sharing dialog box to prompt you to password-protect your user account if it's not already protected.

When you make a folder private, other users can still see the folder is there (because they can list the contents of the parent folder), but they can't view its contents. When they try to open it, they get a message such as that shown in Figure 10.4 that the folder is inaccessible and access is denied.

FIGURE 10.4

When you've made a folder private, other users of the computer can't access it.

WARRNING   *When you move a folder that you've made private, it loses its private status unless the folder to which you move it is private as well. (By contrast, when you move a folder that isn't private to a folder that is private, Windows doesn't make the moved folder private.) So after moving a private folder, explicitly check its sharing status and reapply privacy if necessary.*

Seeing What Files and Folders You're Sharing

However tidy a structure of shared folders you set up, it's easy to lose track of what's being shared and where. You can of course open one or more Explorer windows and go spelunking through your drives looking for shared icons, but this gets old fast, and in any case, Explorer can't show you whether anyone is accessing your shared folders at any given point.

Windows XP's Computer Management tool provides a feature called Shared Folders for seeing which folders and files you're sharing.

To access Shared Folders, follow these steps:

1. Choose Start ➤ Control Panel. Windows displays Control Panel.

◆ Alternatively, click the Start button to display the Start menu, right-click the My Computer item, and choose Manage from the context menu. Windows opens the Computer Management window. Go to step 5.

2. Click the Performance and Maintenance link. Windows displays the Performance and Maintenance screen.

3. Click the Administrative Tools link. Windows displays the Administrative Tools screen.

4. Double-click the Computer Management icon. Windows opens the Computer Management window (shown in Figure 10.5).

FIGURE 10.5

Open a Computer Management window to access the Shared Folders feature to see which folders and files you're sharing.

5. Expand the System Tools object in the left pane if it's collapsed.

6. Expand the Shared Folders object under the System Tools object.

7. To examine and work with shared folders, select the Shares object. Computer Management displays the list of folders currently being shared and the number of client connections on each. Figure 10.6 shows an example.

8. To see which users are connected to the computer, select the Sessions object. Computer Management displays a list of the users, the computer from which they're connecting, the number of files they have open, and the length of time for which they've been connected. Figure 10.7 shows an example.

FIGURE 10.6

Select the Shares object under the Shared Folders object to see the folders currently shared.

FIGURE 10.7

Select the Sessions object under the Shared Folders object to see the current sessions connected to the computer.

9. To see which files are open, select the Open Files object. Computer Management displays a list of the files and the users accessing them. Figure 10.8 shows an example.

FIGURE 10.8

Select the Open Files object under the Shared Folders object to see the files that users currently have open.

10. When you've finished using Computer Management, choose File ➤ Exit. Windows closes the program.

Working with File Associations, File Extensions, and File Types

As you know, if you double-click a file with an EXE extension, Windows runs the file. If you double-click a file with a TXT extension, Windows opens the file in Notepad (or your default text editor; or in WordPad if the file is too big for Notepad to handle). If you double-click a file with an MP3 extension, Windows starts it playing in Windows Media Player (or your default audio player for MP3 files).

In each of these examples, the double-click triggers a different action keyed by the file type with which the file extension is associated. This section discusses file extensions, file types, and file associations; how they interact; and how you can customize them to suit your working needs.

What Are File Extensions?

The *extension* is that part of the filename that appears after the last period in the filename. For example, in a file named September 2001 Report.doc, the extension is doc. In a file named September 2001 Report. Edited by Rikki.doc, the extension is still doc, even though there's an earlier period in the filename. A filename doesn't have to have an extension, but almost all files do, because the extension identifies the file type associated with the file, and the file type contains information on the program and action to use for the file. (More on this in a minute.) If a file doesn't have an extension, Windows doesn't know what to do with it—unless the file is one of the file types designed to have no extension, such as a folder or a DVD. (By contrast, the Mac splits its files up into a resource fork and a data fork. The resource fork contains information about the file type, while the data fork contains the file's data.)

Most extensions are three characters (for example, EXE, DOC, or AVI), but some are four characters (for example, JPEG, MPEG, or HTML). Extensions can be up to 200 characters long, but this length is impractical and unnecessary for all but the most specialized purposes (though it sure lets you create plenty of different extensions). Despite the proliferation of programs and file types, many three-character extensions remain unused and available, though developers who need to create a new file type may prefer a distinctive four-character extension to an unmemorable three-character extension. Users—particularly those who grew up using DOS—tend to be familiar with three-character extensions, so four-character extensions seem strange or a bit wrong.

What Are File Types?

Ideally, each file extension is linked to a *file type*, a descriptive category with which actions can be associated. For example, the BMP extension is linked by default to the Bitmap Image file type. The default action associated with the Bitmap Image file type is Open. So when you double-click a file with the BMP extension, Windows opens the file in the default program (Paint). Other actions associated by default with the Bitmap Image file type are Edit, Print, and PrintTo.

Each extension can be linked to only one file type at a time. If an extension isn't linked to a file type, when you double-click the file, Windows displays the Open With dialog box so that you can tell it which program you want to use to open the file. A file that doesn't have a registered file type associated with it is listed as being of the file type "File." (You could argue for or against this really being the file type, just as you could argue about how you can't really call a poem or song "Untitled.")

Multiple extensions can be linked to a given file type. For example, by default the extensions MPA, MPE, MPEG, MPG, and MPV2 are linked to the Movie File (MPEG) file type. So when you double-click a file with any one of those five extensions, Windows performs the default action for the Movie File (MPEG) file type: Play.

Registering File Types and Associations

File types and associations are stored in the Windows Registry. You can dig at them there (by using the techniques described in Chapter 12), but it's seldom a good idea unless you know exactly what you're doing. Windows provides mostly adequate tools for viewing and changing file types and associations, so you don't need to visit the Registry unless you're trying to create very special effects. (*Mostly* adequate? Yes. More on this in a few pages' time. Hold your horses.)

When you install a program, the setup routine typically handles the registration of any file types associated with the program. The better setup routines check with you before registering the file types, because they may already be registered to other programs. But more aggressive programs monitor the file types associated with them and try to reclaim them each time you run the program. Audio players (particularly MP3 players) and video players tend to be the worst offenders on this front, but they're by no means the only ones. The better programs let you specify whether they should reclaim file types automatically and, if so, which file types.

Specifying the File Type of a File

Typically, you specify the file type of a file by adding the appropriate extension (or one of the appropriate extensions) to it. Most Windows programs use common dialog boxes for Save operations. These common dialog boxes include a Save As Type drop-down list that you use to specify the file type for the file. (By default, the program displays the most likely file type in the Save As dialog box.) If you don't explicitly specify the extension for the file, the program adds it. For example, if you save a workbook file in Excel, Excel suggests the Microsoft Excel Workbook file type in the Save As Type drop-down list. If you don't add an extension to the filename, Excel automatically adds the extension XLS, which is linked to the Microsoft Excel Workbook file type.

Finding Out Which File Type a File Is

Your first clue to which file type a file is should be the icon that Windows uses for the file. But if you have a less-than-perfect memory for icons, or if the icon is too small to be identifiable, there are other ways of finding out.

To find out which file type a file is, right-click it in an Explorer window or on the Desktop and choose Properties from the context menu. The General page of the Properties dialog box for the file displays its file type. Figure 10.9 shows an example.

Alternatively, switch the Explorer window to Details view and look at the Type column.

Displaying All File Extensions

Windows has an engrossing love/hate relationship with file extensions. It can't live without them, but it'd sure like to keep them out of sight in the laundry room. It's kinda like that episode of *Friends* where Monica and Chandler are pretending that they're not—don't you remember? Well, never mind.

As mentioned a page or two ago, Windows needs file extensions so that it knows the actions it can take with a particular file. But Microsoft seems to feel that extensions look ugly, so it makes Windows hide them for as long as possible. This improves the cosmetic look of long filenames and a few other things, but it also has some very undesirable consequences, as you'll see a little later in the chapter.

So by default, Windows hides file extensions for registered file types, relying on icons in their various forms (thumbnails, tiles, and icons) to identify the file type and, by (as it were) extension, the extension. In Details view, the Type column in Explorer windows and dialog boxes displays the file type. And because most every file type is registered either by Windows or by the program you install that creates that type of file, all file extensions remain hidden until you change the settings.

FIGURE 10.9

If you can't identify a file's file type by its icon, display the General page of the Properties dialog box.

If you're comfortable with and used to icons, this is more or less okay. But if not, you can display most file extensions by choosing Tools ➤ Folder Options from an Explorer window to display the Folder Options dialog box, clearing the Hide File Extensions for Known File Types check box on the View page, and clicking the OK button.

Instead of displaying most file extensions, you can display selected ones by selecting the Always Show Extension check box in the Edit File Type dialog box for the file type. See the next section for details.

Wait a minute—what was that about *most* file extensions? Well, Windows kinda figures that there are some file extensions that you really don't need to know about. These extensions include the following:

File Extension	File Type
URL	Internet shortcut or URL
JSE	JScript Encoded file
JS	JScript file
SHS	Scrap object
LNK	Shortcut
SHB	Shortcut to section of a document
JOB	Task Scheduler Task Object file
VBE	VBScript Encoded Script file
VBS	VBScript Script file
SCF	Explorer command file
WSF	Windows Script file

Even when you clear that Hide File Extensions for Known File Types check box and apply the change, Windows keeps these extensions hidden. This is partly for the cosmetic reasons mentioned earlier (which sort of stand up) but perhaps more because Microsoft thinks you shouldn't be messing with these files too much, which is (shall we say) misguided. And the overall effect can be disastrous.

As you can see in the list, the LNK file type is used for shortcuts. So if you make Windows display the extension for LNK files, you'll see a LNK extension popping up for shortcuts on your Desktop, for shortcuts on your Start menu, and for shortcuts in Explorer windows. The LNK extensions on the Desktop are entirely harmless, but the extensions on the Start menu *are* actually kinda ugly and make it a little more awkward to use. For one thing, the four extra characters—the period and LNK—make each of the cascading menus wider than it would otherwise be. And apart from the visual distraction, it's conceptually a little distracting to realize that many of the items on the Start menu are plain old shortcuts. It's not quite like pulling aside the Wizard's curtain, but it gives a feeling that the Start menu is held together by virtual string and sealing wax.

Similarly, the URL file type is for Internet shortcuts and URLs. So if you make Windows display the URL extension, it appears on all Internet shortcuts, including those on your Favorites menus. This too looks less than great, and you can see why Microsoft doesn't want these extensions displayed.

The problem with not displaying extensions is that some file types can be used to deliver viruses. All the scripting file types—VBE and VBS files, JSE and JS files, WSF files, even SCF files—can perform a wide variety of actions on your computer without consulting you.

Of course, no savvy user will run a script that arrives unsolicited: It could be just about anything, and the chances of it doing anything pleasant are slimmer than Calista Flockhart. But because Windows hides these extensions, a script file can easily masquerade as another file type. For example, say a malefactor creates a script file and names it `Latest Britney Clip.mp3.vbs`. Because the VBS extension is hidden, this file shows up as `Latest Britney Clip.mp3`. If the user double-clicks it, thinking that doing so will start the file playing in their default MP3 player (for example, Windows Media Player), they're in for an unpleasant surprise, because the script will execute instead. The icon will be wrong, but people often miss this, particularly in Details view in Explorer or when opening an attachment from e-mail. (As you know perfectly well, you should never open an attachment without virus-checking it—but people do all the time. Hence the big success of many macro viruses, including the Melissa virus of 1999 and the Anna Kournikova virus of 2001.)

Because of the dangers posed by hidden file extensions, it's best to display *all* file extensions so that you always know exactly what type of file you're double-clicking.

You can display the hidden file extensions by using the manual technique described in the section "Choosing Other Options in the Edit File Type Dialog Box" later in this chapter, but it takes a little while. Another way is to use a program called X-Setup, of which you'll find a copy on the companion CD. (Expand the Appearance item, then the Files&Folders item, and then the Files item. Then select the Show/Hide File Extensions item and work with the options it displays.)

Changing the File Type Linked to an Extension

As mentioned earlier, some programs grab file types without asking, either during their setup routines or each time you run them. Other programs ask for permission before grabbing. Either way, you'll sometimes need to change file types so that they're associated with the program you want rather than with the grabbiest program around.

To change the file type linked to an extension, follow these steps.

1. Right-click a file with the extension and choose Properties from the context menu. Windows displays the Properties dialog box for the file. Figure 10.10 shows an example. The General page displays information including the type of file (the Type of File item) and the program associated with it (the Opens With item).

FIGURE 10.10

You can change the file type linked to an extension from the Properties dialog box.

2. Click the Change button. Windows displays the Open With dialog box (shown in Figure 10.11).

FIGURE 10.11

Use this Open With dialog box to specify the program with which you want to open the file.

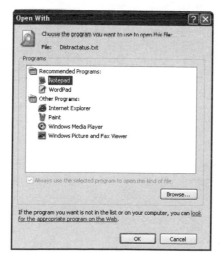

3. In the Programs list box, select the program with which to open the file:

   ◆ Windows breaks down the programs it offers into two categories: Recommended Programs and Other Programs.

   ◆ If neither category lists the program you want to use, click the Browse button. Windows displays a second Open With dialog box. This dialog box is an Open dialog box in disguise. Navigate to and select the program, then click the Open button. Windows closes the second Open With dialog box and returns you to the first Open With dialog box.

4. Click the OK button. Windows closes the first Open With dialog box and links the extension to the file type you selected.

5. Click the OK button. Windows closes the Properties dialog box for the file.

Restoring the File Type Linked to an Extension

When you customize the file type linked to an extension, Windows stores the previous file type for that extension so that you can easily change it back if necessary.

To restore a file association, choose Tools ➤ Folder Options from an Explorer window. Windows displays the Folder Options dialog box. Click the File Types tab. Windows displays the File Types page. In the Registered File Types list box, select the extension you customized. Click the Restore button (shown in Figure 10.12) to restore the file type previously linked to the extension. Click the Close button to close the Folder Options dialog box.

FIGURE 10.12

When you've customized the file type linked to an extension, the Folder Options dialog box provides a Restore button so that you can restore the previous file type easily if needed.

Changing the Program or Action Associated with a File Type

As you saw in the previous couple of sections, you can change the file type linked to an extension easily enough. Chances are, you'll need to do this only occasionally. Much more often, you'll need to change the program associated with a file type, because one program often grabs another program's file types.

NOTE   *One way to reassociate a program with all its default file types is to reinstall the program. But if you've customized the program, or if the installation process is complex or lengthy, you'll do better to edit the file associations manually as described in this section.*

To change the program or action associated with a file type, open the Edit File Type dialog box as described in the following list:

1. From an Explorer window, choose Tools ➤ Folder Options. Windows displays the Folder Options dialog box.

2. Click the File Types tab. Windows displays the File Types page (shown in Figure 10.13).

FIGURE 10.13

Use the File Types page of the Folder Options dialog box to edit file types and extensions.

3 In the Registered File Types list box, select the file type you want to change. By default, this list is sorted alphabetically by extension, but you can sort by file type by clicking the File Types column heading.

NOTE   *At this point, you can also change the file type linked to the extension. (Click the Change button. Windows displays the Open With dialog box. Select the program as described earlier in this section and click the OK button.) But usually it's easier to change the file type linked to the extension from the Properties dialog box of a file of that type, as described in the previous section.*

4. Click the Advanced button. Windows displays the Edit File Type dialog box (shown in Figure 10.14).

Then perform one or more of the changes described in the following sections.

FIGURE 10.14
Use the Edit File
Type dialog box to
change the behavior
or appearance of a
file type.

CHANGING THE NAME OF THE FILE TYPE

To change the name of the file type, enter the new name in the text box at the top of the Edit File
Type dialog box.

CHANGING THE ICON WINDOWS DISPLAYS FOR THE FILE TYPE

To change the icon that Windows displays for the file type, follow these steps:

1. Click the Change Icon button. Windows displays the Change Icon dialog box, showing the
   icons associated with the current program for the file type.

2. Either select an alternate icon or click the Browse button and use the resulting Change Icon
   dialog box (which is a renamed Open dialog box) to identify the icon or the program or
   library file containing it:

   ◆ Select Icon Files, Programs, Libraries, Icons, or All Files in the Files of Type drop-down
     list as appropriate.

   ◆ Click the Open button. Windows closes the second Change Icon dialog box and returns
     you to the first Change Icon dialog box.

TIP   *As mentioned in Chapter 4,* SHELL32.DLL *and* MORICONS.DLL *(both in the* \Windows\System32\ *folder)*
contain a selection of icons.

3. Select the icon if necessary.

4. Click the OK button. Windows closes the first Change Icon dialog box.

CHANGING THE ACTION ASSOCIATED WITH THE FILE TYPE

Next, you can change the action associated with the file type. For example, instead of having files of
the Movie File (MPEG) file type play when you double-click them, you might want to have them
open instead.

Some file types have only one action associated with them. Others have anywhere from two up to a half-dozen. You can create new actions, edit existing actions, remove existing actions, and set the default action to be executed when you double-click the file (or select it and press the Enter key).

The default action appears in boldface in the Actions list box.

Creating a New Action

To create a new action for the file type, follow these steps:

1. Click the New button. Windows displays the New Action dialog box (shown in Figure 10.15).

FIGURE 10.15

Use the New Action dialog box to specify the name and program for a new action.

2. In the Action text box, enter the name for the action. Put an ampersand (&) before the letter that you want to use as the access key for the action. Make sure this letter is different from all other access keys on the context menu for this file type.

3. In the Application Used to Perform Action text box, enter the path and name of the program you want to use. Either type in the path and name or use the Browse button and the resulting Open With dialog box to enter them. If you type in the path and name, enclose them in double quotation marks. (If you use the Open With dialog box, it supplies the double quotation marks for you.)

4. After the program's path and name, enter any switches or parameters the program needs to perform the action. (You'll usually need to consult the program's Help files to discover these.)

5. After the switches or parameters (if any), add the parameter "%1" if you need to pass the filename to the program.

6. If the program uses Dynamic Data Exchange (DDE), select the Use DDE check box and choose further options in the Use DDE group box and extra section of the dialog box that Windows displays. Most modern programs don't use DDE, which is an older way of exchanging information, but some older programs still use it.

7. Click the OK button. Windows closes the New Action dialog box and adds the new action to the Actions list in the Edit File Type dialog box.

Editing an Existing Action

To edit an existing action, select it in the Actions list box and click the Edit button. Windows displays the Editing Action for Type dialog box (shown in Figure 10.16), in which you can edit the action along the lines discussed in steps 2 through 6 in the previous section.

FIGURE 10.16

The Editing Action for Type dialog box is the New Action dialog box in disguise. Use it to edit an existing action for the file type.

Removing an Existing Action

To remove an existing action, select it and click the Remove button. Windows displays a File Types message box to confirm the removal. Click the Yes button if you're sure you want to proceed.

It's not a good idea to remove actions built into Windows programs because you may remove functionality that you subsequently need. However, feel free to remove any custom actions you've created.

Changing the Default Action for the File Type

To change the default action (the action that takes place when you double-click the file), select the action you want in the Actions list box and click the Set Default button.

CHOOSING OTHER OPTIONS IN THE EDIT FILE TYPE DIALOG BOX

The Edit File Type dialog box contains three other options that you may want to be aware of:

Confirm Open after Download check box   Select this check box if you want Windows to prompt you before opening a downloaded file of this type; clear it if you want Windows to open downloaded files without prompting. This check box is selected by default for most file types because of the dangers of opening downloaded files without virus-checking them. The check box is cleared by default for file types such as Windows Media Audio (WMA) files and Video Clip (AVI) files. Clear this check box only for file types that you're sure pose no security risk to your computer.

Always Show Extension check box   Select this check box if you want Windows to display extensions for this file type. (If you've set Windows to display all extensions already, this check box affects only the extra-hidden file types discussed earlier in the chapter.)

Browse in Same Window check box   Select this check box to make files of this type open in the existing window rather than in a new window. This check box is not available for many file types. Examples of file types for which this check box *is* available include Microsoft Word Document and Microsoft PowerPoint Presentation.

Opening a File with a Program Other than the Associated Program

Once you've got the correct file association in place, double-clicking a file opens it in the associated program. But sometimes you may want to open the file in a different program. For example, you might want to use WordPad instead of Word to open a DOC file or trusty old Notepad instead of your custom 350-BHP multifile text editor to open a TXT file.

To open a file with a program other than the associated program:

1. Right-click the file and choose Open With from the context menu. Windows displays the Open With dialog box.

   ◆ If Windows displays an Open With submenu, select the Choose Program item.

2. In the Choose the Program You Want to Use list box, select the program with which to open the file. Use the Browse button and second Open With dialog box if you need to select a program that doesn't appear in the Recommended Programs list or the Other Programs list.

3. If you want Windows to create an Open With submenu for this file type and place an item for this program and the default program for this file type on the submenu, select the Always Use This Program to Open These Files check box.

4. Click the OK button. Windows closes the Open With dialog box.

If you selected the Always Use This Program to Open These Files check box in step 3, Windows adds an Open With submenu to the context menu for the file type.

EXPERT KNOWLEDGE: CREATING AND REGISTERING A NEW FILE TYPE

If you want, you can create a file of an unregistered file type simply by specifying an extension that hasn't been used. For example, open Notepad, enter a space, and save the new document it automatically creates under the name "Adventures in an Orinda Landscape.888". You'll need to enter the filename and extension within double quotation marks, because otherwise Notepad automatically assigns the TXT extension, which is associated with the TXT File file type. Exit Notepad.

Now open an Explorer window to that folder, and you'll see the 888 extension displayed. Rather touchingly, Explorer decides that the file type for this file is "888 File"; you've created a new file type.

At this point, you can probably still contain your excitement: Creating the file hasn't done you much good. Nor has creating the file type. But now try the following:

1. Double-click the file in Explorer. Wait while Windows consults the Registry about the file type and comes up dry. Windows then displays the Windows Cannot Open This File dialog box, shown below.

Continued on next page

EXPERT KNOWLEDGE: CREATING AND REGISTERING A NEW FILE TYPE *(continued)*

2. Choose the Select the Program from a List option button. Windows displays the Open With dialog box shown below.

3. In the Type a Description That You Want to Use for This Kind of File text box, enter the name you want to assign to the file type. Make it as concise and descriptive as possible.

4. In the Programs list box, select the program you want to associate with the file type. If the program isn't listed, click the Browse button and use the resulting Open With dialog box to identify it.

5. Leave the Always Use the Selected Program to Open This Kind of File check box selected, as it is by default.

6. Click the OK button. Windows creates the file type, creates Registry entries for it, and opens the file in the specified program.

At the end of this maneuvering, when you double-click a file of your new file type, Windows invokes the program you specified, which performs the action you designated.

NOTE   To delete a new file type you've created, use the Remove button on the File Types page of the Folder Options dialog box.

Up Next

This chapter has discussed how to share folders and how to keep folders private, even from Computer Administrator users. It has also covered how to work with file types so that files of a given file type open with the program and the action you want.

The next chapter discusses how to manage your disk and drives.

Chapter 11

Managing Your Disks and Drives

THIS CHAPTER DISCUSSES HOW to manage your disks and drives, showing you how to understand and undertake the key actions you'll need to perform with them. These actions range from formatting a disk to converting a disk's file system to NTFS; from using compression to free up disk space on an NTFS disk to using quotas to prevent users from grabbing more than their fair share; and from defragmenting your disks to creating and deleting partitions.

This chapter covers the following topics:

- ◆ Formatting a disk
- ◆ Changing the computer's name, description, and workgroup
- ◆ Converting a disk to NTFS
- ◆ Using compression to free up space
- ◆ Using quotas to apportion disk space
- ◆ Defragmenting and cleaning up disks
- ◆ Creating and deleting partitions

Formatting a Disk

Be it hard, removable, or floppy, a disk needs to be formatted before it's usable. *Formatting* imposes a file system on the disk's physical sectors, arranging them into logical clusters that Windows can access and manipulate.

You use the same procedure for formatting hard, removable, and floppy disks. By contrast, recordable (CD-R) and rewritable (CD-RW) discs and writable DVDs need a different kind of formatting because they use different file systems.

To format a disk, follow these steps:

1. Open an Explorer window. (Usually, choosing Start ➢ My Computer gives you the best view for formatting disks.)

2. Right-click the disk and choose Format from the context menu. Windows displays the appropriate Format dialog box for the disk:

◆ For a local hard disk, Windows displays the Format Local Disk dialog box (shown in Figure 11.1).

FIGURE 11.1

In the Format Local Disk dialog box, specify the file system to use for the disk.

◆ For a floppy disk, Windows displays the Format $3\frac{1}{2}$ Floppy dialog box.

◆ For a removable disk, Windows displays a dialog box named after the drive's name. For example, for a Zip 100 drive, Windows displays a Format ZIP-100 dialog box.

3. If you're formatting a floppy disk, make sure that the Capacity drop-down list is showing approximately the right size for the disk. You shouldn't be able to change this setting for a hard disk, but you should check it in case Windows XP is having trouble reading the disk, which could indicate a physical problem with the disk.

NOTE   Good news: Windows XP fixes a problem with previous versions of Windows, in which a format operation would grind to a halt if an Explorer window was showing the contents of the disk you tried to format. This problem was especially annoying when you displayed the disk in Explore mode to check that it didn't contain anything worth keeping, and then issued a command from the Folders Explorer bar while the contents were still displayed in the right-hand pane.

4. In the File System drop-down list, choose the file system with which to format the disk: NTFS or FAT32 for a hard disk. You'll recall from Chapter 2 that NTFS offers advantages of security and stability over FAT32 and that the main reason for using FAT32 is if you need an operating system not based on NT—for example, Windows 9x—to be able to read the disk.

5. In the Allocation Unit Size drop-down list, you can specify the cluster size for the disk. By default, Windows selects the Default Allocation Size item. Typically the options for NTFS are 512 bytes, 1024 bytes, 2048 bytes, and 4096 bytes. You shouldn't need to specify the cluster size, but see the next sidebar if you're curious as to why not.

6. In the Volume Label text box, you can enter a name for the volume. FAT32 volume names can be up to 11 characters long, while NTFS volume names can be up to 32 characters long. There's no obligation to enter a volume label, but doing so makes the volume easier to identify. (This tends to be less important for a floppy disk than for a hard disk volume, especially if you label the outside of the floppy.)

7. In the Format Options group box, select the Quick Format check box if you want to skip scanning the disk for bad sectors. Skipping the scan speeds up the format significantly, because it means that all Windows has to do is remove the files from the disk. But it's almost always a good idea to perform the scan by running a standard format. The only exception is if you've very recently scanned the disk for bad sectors and it's come up clean.

8. If the Enable Compression check box is available, you can select it to enable compression on the drive. Compression is available only on NTFS drives. The section "Using Compression to Free Up Space," later in this chapter, discusses the pros and cons of compression.

9. Click the Start button. Windows displays a warning dialog box (shown in Figure 11.2) checking that you're sure you want to format the disk.

FIGURE 11.2

Because you're about to wipe the contents of the disk, Windows double-checks with this warning dialog box to make sure you know what you're doing.

10. If you *are* sure, click the OK button. Windows starts the formatting operation.

11. When Windows has finished formatting the disk, it displays a Formatting Local Disk dialog box (or a Formatting $3^1/_2$ Floppy dialog box, or a Formatting ZIP-100 dialog box, or whatever), such as that shown in Figure 11.3, to tell you that the format is complete.

FIGURE 11.3

Windows displays a dialog box such as this when it has finished formatting the disk.

12. Click the OK button. Windows closes the Formatting Local Disk dialog box and returns you to the Format Local Disk dialog box (or whichever variant of the Format dialog box was previously displayed).

13. Click the Close button. Windows closes the Format Local Disk dialog box.

You can now use the formatted disk to store files.

NOTE *The Create an MS-DOS Startup Disk check box lets you create a floppy disk that boots DOS. You can't do much from DOS to an XP computer, so you probably won't need to use this capability.*

EXPERT KNOWLEDGE: WHAT IS THE CLUSTER SIZE, AND SHOULD YOU SPECIFY IT?

The *cluster size* is the smallest amount of disk space that you can allocate for storing a file. As you'll remember from Chapter 6, Windows uses clusters as a logical overlay to let it get at the physical sectors on the disk in which the information is actually stored. Most files take up multiple clusters; the smaller the cluster size, obviously enough, the more clusters a file of any given size takes up.

In the days when both disks and files were smaller than they are today, cluster size used to be more of an issue than it is now. Operating systems that used the FAT16 file allocation table, such as DOS and Windows 95, essentially weren't able to create enough clusters to handle large disks efficiently: For a drive of 120MB, FAT16 uses a 2KB cluster size, which is fine; for a 512MB drive, 16KB, which is—let's say—lavish; and for a 3GB drive, 64KB, which is prodigal. Any space not used in the cluster is wasted, so if you stored a 1KB file on that 3GB drive under FAT16, you were wasting 63KB—far worse overheads, so to speak, than in the Mall of the Americas.

Unlike FAT16, FAT32 and NTFS *can* create enough clusters to handle even large disks, so cluster size shouldn't be an issue with Windows XP. As mentioned a moment ago, you can specify cluster sizes of 512 bytes (0.5KB), 1KB, 2KB, and 4KB: all good, small sizes. If you're creating files smaller than 4KB these days, you're doing well—and in any case, hard disks have grown so much that occasionally wasting a few KB seldom causes much pain anymore.

The best cluster size depends on the size of the disk in question. If you're familiar with the cluster size recommended for the size of disk you have, you *can* specify the cluster size you want to use. But because Windows is preloaded with information about cluster sizes, it's usually best to let Windows allocate the cluster size automatically. To do so, leave the Default Allocation Size entry (the default) selected in the Allocation Unit Size drop-down list.

Changing the Computer's Name, Description, and Workgroup

Each computer has a name and a description, and belongs to a workgroup:

◆ The *name* isn't the name for My Computer (which you can rename to anything you want without affecting anything more than the user interface): It's the name by which the computer appears on the network (if any) to which it's attached. The name is partly for your benefit, partly for the benefit of other users, partly for that of Windows, and partly for that of other computers on the network: It enables you, other users, Windows, and the other computers to identify your computer.

◆ The *description* is entirely for your and other users' benefit: It's a text field that lets you describe the computer identified by the name. Windows doesn't assign a description by default, so the computer doesn't have a description until you enter one.

◆ The *workgroup* is a logical collection of computers intended to work together. By default, the Windows XP Home setup routine adds your computer to a workgroup named MSHOME. As you'll see in Chapter 32, it's a good idea to change the workgroup name, especially if you have a cable modem.

You can change the computer's name, description, and workgroup easily enough. To do so, follow these steps:

1. Press Winkey+Break. (Alternatively, display the Start menu, right-click the My Computer item, and choose Properties from the context menu.) Windows displays the System Properties dialog box.

2. Click the Computer Name tab. Windows displays the Computer Name page (shown in Figure 11.4), which shows the description, computer name, and workgroup name.

FIGURE 11.4

You can change the computer's name on the Computer Name page of the System Properties dialog box.

3. In the Computer Description text box, enter the description for the computer.

4. To change the computer name or workgroup, click the Change button. Windows displays the Computer Name Changes dialog box (shown in Figure 11.5).

FIGURE 11.5

Use this Computer Name Changes dialog box to change the computer's name or workgroup.

5. Change the name in the Computer Name text box if necessary.

6. Change the name in the Workgroup text box if necessary.

7. Click the OK button. Windows closes the Computer Name Changes dialog box, considers the changes, and (if you changed the name or workgroup) displays another Computer Name Changes dialog box (shown in Figure 11.6) telling you that you need to restart the computer for the changes to take effect.

FIGURE 11.6

When you change the computer's name or workgroup, Windows displays this Computer Name Changes dialog box telling you that you'll need to restart the computer.

8. Click the OK button. Windows closes the second Computer Name Changes dialog box, returning you to the System Properties dialog box. The Computer Name page now displays a warning telling you that changes will take effect after you restart the computer.

9. Click the OK button. Windows closes the System Properties dialog box. If you need to restart your computer, Windows displays the System Settings Change dialog box (shown in Figure 11.7).

FIGURE 11.7

If you need to restart the computer to make the changes stick, Windows displays the System Settings Change dialog box to remind you.

10. Choose the Yes button if you want Windows to restart your computer straight away. Choose the No button if you want to take any other actions and then restart the computer yourself.

Converting a Disk to NTFS

If you need to use Windows' security features, compression (discussed next), or quota management (discussed later in this chapter), your volumes need to be NTFS rather than FAT. Windows provides a tool for converting a disk from FAT or FAT32 to NTFS, so you can convert your volumes at any time. This is a one-way process, in that you can't convert the disk back to FAT unless you reformat it (which involves removing all the data from the disk), so it's not something to try idly or on a whim.

The best time to convert a disk from FAT to NTFS is when you install Windows XP. The second-best time is when you need to format the disk, because formatting overwrites all the contents of the drive anyway. But if you want to maintain a dual-boot system with Windows 9x until you're sure that Windows XP suits you, you'll need to keep one or more drives formatted with FAT, which means that neither of these options is viable—unless you're prepared to blow away the contents of the FAT disk when you decide to commit to NTFS.

To convert a FAT disk to NTFS without affecting the data on it (other than the file system on which the data is stored), open a command prompt window (Start ➤ All Programs ➤ Accessories ➤ Command Prompt) and issue a convert command. The syntax for the convert command is as follows:

```
convert drive: /FS:NTFS
```

As you'd guess, *drive:* here is the letter of the drive to convert. For example, the following command converts the D drive:

```
convert d: /FS:NTFS
```

The convert command takes a while to run, depending on how big the drive is and how much it contains. There are a couple of other things that you should know about it:

◆ convert needs a modest amount of space for the conversion, so the disk can't be stuffed to the gills with files when you convert it. (If the disk *is* stuffed—which isn't a great idea anyway—you just need to move some of the files off the drive temporarily while you perform the conversion. You can then move the files back onto the drive.)

◆ If you want the files and folders on the converted drive to have no security on them, add the /NoSecurity flag to the command. You won't usually want to do this.

◆ Converting the system volume to NTFS requires two reboots. The conversion happens after the reboot, and Windows then reboots itself again.

Using Compression to Free Up Space

To save disk space, you can *compress* files, folders, or even an entire drive that uses NTFS. (You can't compress a FAT32 drive.) How much disk space you save depends on the types of file you're compressing. Anything that's already compressed—for example, a Zip file or a compressed multimedia file such as an MP3 music file or an MPEG movie—won't compress much, if at all. Files such as Word documents or Excel spreadsheets compress nicely. Uncompressed graphics (for example, TIFF files) compress a treat.

The advantage of compression is, obviously enough, that it saves space so that you can pack more information on your drives. To counterbalance this advantage, compression has two main disadvantages: First, your computer will take longer to access a compressed file, folder, or drive; and second, you cannot encrypt a compressed file or folder.

Given that Windows XP Home doesn't offer encryption (unlike Windows XP Professional), the second disadvantage isn't much of a consideration. But the first disadvantage is real enough: Unless your computer is state-of-the-art fast, it's probably not wise to compress files that you need to play at full speed. For example, multimedia files may not play back without hiccups if you compress them.

Compressing a File or Folder

To compress a file or a folder, follow these steps:

1. Right-click the file or folder and choose Properties from the context menu. Windows display the Properties dialog box for the file or folder.

2. On the General page, click the Advanced button. Windows displays the Advanced Attributes dialog box (shown in Figure 11.8).

FIGURE 11.8

To save space, you can compress a file or folder by selecting the Compress Contents to Save Disk Space check box in the Advanced Attributes dialog box.

3. Select the Compress Contents to Save Disk Space check box.

4. Click the OK button. Windows closes the Advanced Attributes dialog box.

5. Click the OK button. Windows closes the Properties dialog box.

To uncompress a file or folder, repeat this procedure but clear the Compress Contents to Save Disk Space check box.

Compressing a Drive

Compressing individual folders (let alone individual files) is a slow business, and may not save you a large amount of space. You'll usually get better results from compressing a whole drive.

To compress an NTFS drive, follow these steps:

1. Right-click the drive and choose Properties from the context menu. Windows displays the Properties dialog box for the drive.

2. On the General page, select the Compress Drive to Save Disk Space check box.

3. Click the Apply button. Windows displays the Confirm Attribute Changes dialog box (shown in Figure 11.9), asking if you want to apply this change only to the root of the drive or to its subfolders and files as well.

FIGURE 11.9

To compress a drive and its contents, select the Apply Changes to *N*:\, Subfolders and Files option button in the Confirm Attribute Changes dialog box.

4. Select the Apply Changes to *N*:\, Subfolders and Files option button.

5. Click the OK button. Windows closes the Confirm Attribute Changes dialog box, displays the Applying Attributes dialog box, and starts compressing the drive.

 ◆ If Windows displays the Error Applying Attributes dialog box telling you that an error occurred applying the attribute to (in other words, compressing) a file because the file is being used by another process, choose the Ignore button, the Ignore All button, the Retry button, or the Cancel button as appropriate.

6. When compression is complete, click the OK button in the Properties dialog box for the drive. Windows closes the dialog box.

To uncompress the drive, repeat this procedure, but clear the Compress Drive to Save Disk Space check box.

Setting Archiving and Indexing for a File or Folder

Apart from compression, the Advanced Attributes dialog box (shown in Figure 11.10) for a file or folder offers two other options:

File/Folder Is Ready for Archiving check box   Select this check box (or leave it selected) to specify that the file or folder can be archived. Nothing will happen to the folder until you use a program that checks the archiving status of files.

For Fast Searching, Allow Indexing Service to Index This File/Folder check box   Select this check box (or, again, leave it selected, as the case may be) to include this file or folder in any indexing operations you tell Windows to perform. By indexing your files, you can create a database that lets you search more quickly for files matching specified criteria.

FIGURE 11.10

You can set further attributes, including archiving and index-ing options, in the Advanced Attributes dialog box.

When you've finished choosing settings in the Advanced Attributes dialog box, click the OK but-ton. Windows closes the Advanced Attributes dialog box. Then click the OK button. Windows closes the Properties dialog box for the file or folder.

Using Quotas to Apportion Disk Space

As you know, it's not possible to get too thin, to be too rich, or to have too much disk space. Actually, the first two parts of this aren't really true anymore: Most people reckon Cameron Diaz is too thin and Bill Gates is too rich. (But that's their business and is protected by freedom of expression.)

The third part still holds, though: Despite the best efforts of IBM, Seagate, and their competitors, it's almost impossible to have too much disk space these days—unless you're rich (and perhaps thin). However fast the engineers work out ways to pack more information on a platter and stack more platters in a drive, the number and size of files people want to keep grow even faster.

If you're sharing your computer with other members of your family, or with people in your office, you may want to use Windows' quota-management tools to make sure that no one user can hog all the disk space. Quota management may seem a formal and officious thing to implement, but it's easy to do; it can have a salutary effect on users' behavior; and it can help keep your computer running smoothly by preventing it from running out of disk space. Best of all, when you've set quotas on a disk, it appears to the user as if the section of the disk available to them is all the disk space there is. For example, if you have an 80GB drive and set a quota of 20GB per user, each user gets the impression of having a 20GB drive. If you want, you can keep them in ignorance about the rest of the drive. . . .

Quota management is easy—but you need to know three important things in order to get it right:

♦ You can use quotas only on NTFS volumes.

♦ Quotas work on whole volumes, not on individual folders.

♦ If you implement quotas on your system volume, don't prevent users from using more than their allotted quota of disk space. This is because Windows writes information to disk on the system partition when booting. Implementing capped quotas can prevent Windows from booting. You'll get entertaining errors as the Network Service and System try desperately to exceed their quotas to do your bidding.

To set quotas, take the following steps:

1. Right-click the volume for which you want to set quotas and choose Properties from the context menu. Windows displays the Properties dialog box.

2. Click the Quota tab. Windows displays the Quota page (shown in Figure 11.11 with several choices made).

3. Select the Enable Quota Management check box. Windows enables the other controls on the Quota page.

4. If you want to prevent a user from using more than their allotted amount of disk space, select the Deny Disk Space to Users Exceeding Quota Limit check box.

WARNING   *Be aware that denying disk space to a user could cause them to lose work or be forced to delete an existing file in order to save a new file. Think carefully before you use this option; and if you use it, make sure that users understand quotas and their implications before they discover the limitations the hard way.*

FIGURE 11.11

Use quotas to pre-
vent any user from
using up more than
their fair share of
drive space.

5. In the Select the Default Quota Limit for New Users on This Volume area, specify whether to limit disk space for new users:

 ◆ If you don't want to limit disk space, select the Do Not Limit Disk Usage option button.

 ◆ To limit disk space for new users, select the Limit Disk Space To option button and enter an appropriate number of megabytes (MB), gigabytes (GB), terabytes (TB), petabytes (PB), or exabytes (EB) in the drop-down list. (You can also enter a number of kilobytes—KB—but any amount of disk space smaller than a megabyte makes no sense.)

NOTE *By offering terabytes, petabytes, and exabytes, Windows is showing it's ready for the future. A terabyte (1TB) is 1024GB, a petabyte (1PB) is 1024TB, and an exabyte (1EB) is 1024PB. At this writing, terabytes are the province of serious servers, petabytes are the province of server farms, and exabytes are provinces of server farms.*

 ◆ If you limit disk space, use the Set Warning Level To text box and drop-down list to specify the limit at which Windows warns the user that they're about to run out of disk space. This limit should be a little less than the amount of disk space they're limited to—enough less that the user will need to create several files of the size they usually work with between triggering the warning and reaching the limit. For this setting, you may want to accept the default that Windows offers or manually set a bigger cushion of your own. You can use decimal places with the same unit in the Set Warning Level To text box or select the next smaller item in the drop-down list so that you can work with whole numbers.

6. In the Select the Quota Logging Options for This Volume area, select the Log Event when a User Exceeds Their Quota Limit check box or the Log Event when a User Exceeds Their Warning Level check box if you want Windows to log these events.

7. Click the Quota Entries button. Windows displays the Quota Entries window (shown in Figure 11.12). The first time you display this window, the only quota it lists is the one for your user identity or the Administrators group.

FIGURE 11.12

Once you've enabled quotas, use the Quota Entries window to set quotas for each user.

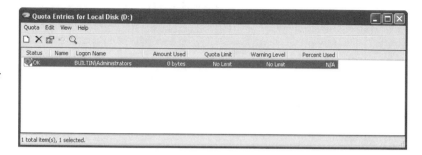

8. Choose Quota ➢ New Quota Entry or click the New Quota Entry button. Windows displays the Select Users dialog box.

9. Enter the username in the Enter the Object Names to Select list box and click the OK button. Windows displays the Add New Quota Entry dialog box (shown in Figure 11.13).

FIGURE 11.13

Use the Add New Quota Entry dialog box to specify the quota limits for the user.

10. Set a disk space quota and warning level as described in step 5.

11. Click the OK button. Windows closes the Add New Quota Entry dialog box and adds the quota entry to the Quota Entries window.

    ◆ To change an existing quota entry, double-click it in the Quota Entries window. Windows displays the Quota Settings dialog box for the user. Change the quota settings or warning level and click the OK button.

    ◆ To delete a quota entry, right-click it in the list box and choose Delete from the context menu. Alternatively, select the quota entry and choose Quota ➢ Delete or click the Delete Quota Entry button on the toolbar. Windows displays a Disk Quota dialog box confirming the deletion. Click the Yes button.

12. Create further quota entries as appropriate, then choose Quota ➢ Close. Windows closes the Quota Entries window and displays the Properties dialog box.

13. Click the Apply button to make Windows apply the quotas, or click the OK button to make Windows apply the quotas and close the Properties dialog box.

If disk quotas are not currently enabled, when you click the Apply button or the OK button to apply the quotas, Windows displays the Disk Quota dialog box (shown in Figure 11.14). This dialog box warns you that when you enable quotas, Windows needs to rescan the volume to update disk usage statistics, and that this process can take several minutes. Click the OK button to enable quotas.

FIGURE 11.14

If the quota system isn't enabled for the volume, Windows displays the Disk Quota dialog box warning you that it will need to rescan the volume.

When you've set a quota on a volume, Explorer shows the user the amount of space that remains to them on the volume, not the actual amount of space available on the volume. When a user reaches their warning level, they see a message telling them that they're running out of space.

If you chose to deny disk space to users exceeding their quota limit, they'll see a message such as that shown in Figure 11.15 when they take an action that will exceed their quota limit. Notice that the message isn't that the user is over quota—it's simply that there isn't enough space on disk.

FIGURE 11.15

When a user takes an action that will exceed their quota limit, Windows tells them there's not enough space on the disk.

TIP   If you need to apply the same quotas to several volumes, choose Quota ➢ Export to export quotas from one volume to a file. From another volume, choose Quota ➢ Import to import the quota settings file.

Disk Maintenance

Like cars, hard disks can take a fair amount of abuse these days, but the better you treat them, the better performance they give you and the longer they last. Unlike cars, hard disks thrive on running all the time; but like cars, they don't appreciate fragmentation or crashes—and they appreciate a little cleaning-up from time to time.

This section details the steps you can take to keep your disks in good order.

Defragmenting Your Disks

As you know, data is stored on your hard disk in physical areas called sectors that are mapped into logical areas called clusters. Each cluster contains a relatively small amount of information so that Windows can use the clusters efficiently. As a result, most files occupy more than one cluster. These clusters can be located just about anywhere on the partition of the drive that contains the volume. Ideally, all the data in a file is stored in contiguous clusters, so that the hard disk's heads can read the data without having to move too far. The further the hard disk's actuator arm has to move to allow the heads to read the clusters that make up the file, the slower the file is to load.

When files are stored in widely spread-out clusters, the volume is said to be *fragmented*. To improve disk performance, you *defragment* (or *defrag*) it using a disk *defragmenter* (or *defragger*). A defragmenter rearranges the data on the disk so that each file occupies contiguous clusters wherever possible.

NOTE *Related to defragmenters but more specialized are tools such as the Microsoft Office optimizer, which defragments a specific set of files and arranges them in a location on the hard drive that the disk heads can quickly access.*

Depending on how fragmented a volume is, and how big it is, defragmentation can take anything from a few minutes to a few hours. You *can* work on your computer while defragmentation is going on, but you'll find the computer responding more slowly than usual, and any files that you create, move, or copy may slow down the defragmentation process. Because of this, the best time to defragment a volume is when you're going to leave your computer for a few hours—for example, when you hear the siren song of the mall, an extended lunch hour, or an endless meeting.

See pages 77–78 of the *Essential Skills* section for a visual guide to defragmenting a disk.

To start Disk Defragmenter, choose Start ➤ All Programs ➤ Accessories ➤ System Tools ➤ Disk Defragmenter. Alternatively, right-click the drive icon in an Explorer window, choose Properties from the context menu, display the Tools page in the Properties dialog box, and click the Defragment Now button. Figure 11.16 shows Disk Defragmenter. The list box shows the volumes on your computer, their session status (whether they're being analyzed or defragmented), file system, capacity, amount of free space, and percentage of free space.

FIGURE 11.16

Use Disk Defragmenter to defragment your drives.

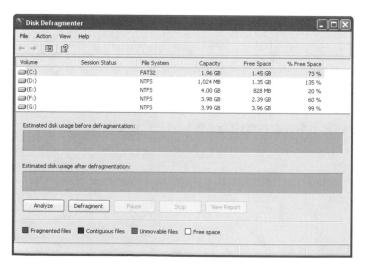

NOTE   You can also run Disk Defragmenter from a Computer Management window. Doing so can be handy if you're working with Computer Management already, but otherwise it conveys no particular benefits. But you need to know about this because, once you access Disk Defragmenter in a Computer Management session, Disk Defragmenter stays active. Now, you can run only one instance of Disk Defragmenter at a time, so if you start Disk Defragmenter while Computer Management is running, Windows displays a Disk Defragmenter message box telling you that "This version of Disk Defragmenter does not support running more than one instance." If you've forgotten about the Computer Management session, this message box seems to come out of the blue. (If you're not running Computer Management, this message box may mean that another Computer Administrator user is running Disk Defragmenter.)

Typically, you'll want to start by analyzing a volume. Select it in the list box and click the Analyze button. Disk Defragmenter examines the volume and displays the Disk Defragmenter dialog box (shown in Figure 11.17) with its recommendations.

FIGURE 11.17

The Disk Defragmenter dialog box tells you the result of the analysis and makes a recommendation.

To see the detail of what Disk Defragmenter found on the volume, click the View Report button. Disk Defragmenter displays the Analysis Report dialog box, of which Figure 11.18 shows an example. The Volume Information list box contains everything from the volume size, cluster size, and used space through pagefile fragmentation and Master File Table (MFT) fragmentation. The Most Fragmented Files list box lists the most fragmented files. You can sort this list by any of the columns—Fragments, File Size, or File Name—by clicking the appropriate column heading.

FIGURE 11.18

The Analysis Report dialog box provides a large amount of information about the volume and the most fragmented files it contains.

From the Analysis Report dialog box, you can use the Print button to print a copy of the analysis report or the Save As button to save it to a file. More likely, though, you'll want to click the Defragment button to defragment the drive (if Disk Defragmenter recommends doing so) or the Close button to close the dialog box.

If you click the Defragment button in the Analysis Report dialog box or the Disk Defragmenter dialog box, Windows closes the dialog box and starts defragmentation. While defragmentation is running, the status bar provides information on the percentage completed and the file currently being moved. (Unfortunately, Disk Defragmenter doesn't offer a full-screen graphical view of the process like Windows 9*x* defragmenters did.) You can use the Pause button and Stop button to pause or stop defragmentation.

When defragmentation is complete, Disk Defragmenter displays another Disk Defragmenter dialog box telling you so. Click the View Report button to display the Defragmentation Report dialog box containing a report (similar to the Analysis Report dialog box's report) on the volume's status, or click the Close button to close the dialog box.

How often you need to run Disk Defragmenter depends on how actively you use your computer and how often you create, modify, or delete files. Under normal usage, running Disk Defragmenter anything from once a week to once every couple of months will keep your files adequately defragmented. Experiment with Disk Defragmenter to establish a schedule that works for you. If Disk Defragmenter says that a volume doesn't need defragmenting, decrease the frequency with which you run Disk Defragmenter.

Cleaning Up Your Disks with Disk Cleanup

Most Windows programs create temporary files that they use to store information temporarily when you're running them. Some programs remember to get rid of these files when you exit them. Others forget. And if your computer loses power or crashes, even the well-behaved programs don't have a chance to get rid of temporary files.

Windows' Disk Cleanup feature provides an effective way to remove from local drives not only these temporary files but also temporary Internet files, downloaded program files, offline Web pages, and the contents of the Recycle Bin. (Disk Cleanup does not work on network drives.)

See page 79 of the *Essential Skills* section for a visual guide to running Disk Cleanup.

Close all programs you're running, then start Disk Cleanup by choosing Start ➢ All Programs ➢ Accessories ➢ System Tools ➢ Disk Cleanup. (Alternatively, right-click a drive and choose Properties so that Windows displays the Properties dialog box. Then click the Disk Cleanup button on the General page.) If your computer has multiple hard drive volumes, Disk Cleanup displays the Select Drive dialog box. (If your computer has a single hard drive volume, Disk Cleanup goes ahead and calculates how much space you will be able to free up on the drive.) In the Drives drop-down list, select the drive you want to clean up, then click the OK button. Disk Cleanup examines the disk (which may take a few minutes) and then displays the Disk Cleanup dialog box (shown in Figure 11.19).

As you can see in the figure, the Disk Cleanup page of the Disk Cleanup dialog box lists the items you can remove and how much space you can recover by doing so. Which of the following items appear in the list depends on the drive's contents:

Downloaded Program Files   ActiveX controls and Java applets downloaded by Internet Explorer so that it could display pages that needed them. If you delete these files, Internet Explorer may need to download the controls and applets again when you next access pages that need them, which may slow down your browsing a bit. You can click the View Files button to have Windows display an Explorer window containing the files.

FIGURE 11.19

Disk Cleanup presents a list of the items you can remove to clean up your disk.

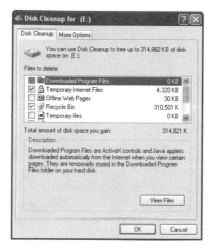

Temporary Internet Files   These files are the components of Web pages that Internet Explorer has downloaded and has stored on your hard drive so that it can retrieve them quickly when you access the same sites again. Deleting these files means that Internet Explorer will need to download them again the next time you access one of the sites, which will slow down your browsing. Again, you can click the View Files button to have Windows display an Explorer window containing these files—but be warned that there are usually thousands of them, and that the format in which they appear is less than informative.

Offline Web Pages   This item appears only if you use offline favorites in Internet Explorer. These files hold the information for the cached copies of your offline favorites. If you use offline favorites extensively, these files may take up a lot of space. If you delete these files, you won't be able to view your offline favorites until you synchronize them again—and synchronizing them will probably reclaim most of the disk space that deleting these files freed up.

Recycle Bin   These files are the contents of the Recycle Bin. As usual, make sure that you want to get rid of these files before you tell Disk Cleanup to delete them. You can click the View Files button to have Windows display an Explorer window showing the contents of the Recycle Bin.

Temporary Files   These files are temporary storage files that should have been deleted by the program that created them. You can delete with impunity any temporary files that aren't currently being used. (Disk Cleanup leaves alone any temporary files still in use.)

WebClient/Publisher Temporary Files   These files are temporary storage files kept by the WebClient/Publisher service. Deleting these files may affect WebClient/Publisher performance, but it can't lose you any information.

Compress Old Files   To free up some space, you can tell Windows to compress files that you haven't used for a while. If you select this check box, select the Compress Old Files item, then click the Options button that appears in the Disk Cleanup dialog box and use the Compress Old Files dialog box (shown in Figure 11.20) that Windows displays to specify when to compress files. (The default setting is 50 days.)

FIGURE 11.20

If you choose to have Windows compress old files to free up space on your hard drive, specify in the Compress Old Files dialog box how long the files should remain unaccessed before Windows compresses them.

Catalog Files for the Content Indexer These files are leftover catalog files from indexing. There's no downside to deleting them—they don't contain the current index.

Select the check boxes for those items you want to delete and click the OK button. Disk Cleanup displays a Disk Cleanup for *N*: dialog box to confirm that you want to perform the actions (for example, deleting the files). Click the Yes button. Disk Cleanup performs the cleanup.

Checking a Disk for Errors

Once you've cleaned unnecessary files off your hard disk, it's a good idea to check it for errors. Errors typically occur when sectors go bad, which can happen through natural selection (some disks age more quickly in parts) or unnatural intervention (such as physical damage resulting from the disk being bumped or receiving an electrical spike).

To check a disk for errors, follow these steps:

1. Close all programs that are on the disk or that might be accessing the disk. (In practice, it's best to close all programs for the time being.) Close any files open from the disk.

2. In an Explorer window, right-click the drive and choose Properties from the context menu. Windows displays the Properties dialog box for the drive.

3. Click the Tools tab. Windows displays the Tools page of the Properties dialog box.

4. Click the Check Now button. Windows displays the Check Disk dialog box (shown in Figure 11.21).

FIGURE 11.21

In the Check Disk dialog box, specify whether to automatically fix errors in the file system and whether to detect bad sectors and attempt to recover their contents.

5. If you want Windows to repair file-system errors, select the Automatically Fix File System Errors check box.

6. If you want Windows to scan for bad sectors and attempt to recover information from them, *and* repair file-system errors, select the Scan for and Attempt Recovery of Bad Sectors check box.

7. Click the Start button to run Check Disk. Windows displays the Checking Disk dialog box while it performs the checks.

- ◆ If you see a Checking Disk dialog box such as that shown in Figure 11.22 telling you that "the disk check could not be performed because the disk check utility needs exclusive access to some Windows files on the disk" and asking whether you want to schedule the disk check to take place the next time you restart the computer, select the Yes button. This dialog box typically appears when you're checking a system volume: Because Windows is constantly using the volume, Check Disk can't get exclusive access to it.

FIGURE 11.22

The Checking Disk dialog box tells you that it can't get exclusive access to the disk and asks if you want to run the check the next time you restart the computer.

8. When Check Disk has finished, it displays a message box telling you that the disk check is complete.

9. Click the OK button. Check Disk closes and returns you to the Properties dialog box.

10. Click the OK button. Windows closes the Properties dialog box.

Scheduling Your Maintenance Tasks with the Scheduled Task Wizard

Windows includes a Scheduled Task Wizard that runs you through the process of scheduling the running of just about any program that you want to run at a particular time. This is particularly useful for tedious maintenance tasks—though of course you can also use the Scheduled Task Wizard to schedule regular games of FreeCell or DOOM should you feel the need.

See pages 80–82 of the *Essential Skills* section for a visual guide to scheduling a task.

CREATING A SCHEDULED TASK

To create a scheduled task, open the Scheduled Tasks folder by choosing Start ➢ All Programs ➢ Accessories ➢ System Tools ➢ Scheduled Tasks. (Alternatively, choose Start ➢ Control Panel, click the Performance and Maintenance link, and click the Scheduled Tasks link.) Start the Scheduled Task Wizard by double-clicking the Add Scheduled Task item. Then follow the screens that the Wizard presents through these steps:

- ◆ Choose the program to run.

- ◆ Enter a name for the task. If you want, this can be the name of the program, or you can enter a descriptive name—whatever works for you.

- ◆ Specify the frequency with which to perform the task: Daily, Weekly, Monthly, One Time Only, When My Computer Starts, or When I Log On.

- ◆ Specify the time of day, the frequency, and the days of the week for the task. For example, you might choose to run Disk Defragmenter at 2:00 A.M. every Friday.

◆ Specify the user under whose name to run the task and the password (if applicable) for that user. Usually, you'll want the task to be run under your own name. But you might want to use another username only for maintenance tasks. That way, you could let other users know they shouldn't use the computer when that user was logged on, so that the maintenance tasks wouldn't slow down their use of the computer (and vice versa).

SETTING ADVANCED PROPERTIES FOR A SCHEDULED TASK

The Scheduled Task Wizard gives you access to most of a task's properties, but not to all of them. To set further properties than the Wizard offers—for example, to set multiple schedules for the same task—use the task's Properties dialog box.

On the last page of the Scheduled Task Wizard, you can select the Open Advanced Properties for This Task when I Click Finish check box if you want to have the Wizard open the task's Properties dialog box automatically. Alternatively, double-click the task in the Scheduled Tasks folder (which resides under Control Panel). Windows displays the task's Properties dialog box.

The Properties dialog box for the task has three pages: Task, Schedule, and Settings:

◆ The Task page shows the program assigned to the task, the folder in which the task starts, and the username under which the task runs. There's also a Comments text box in which you can add comments to the task. For example, you might note any changes to the task and why you've made them. Clear the Enabled (Scheduled Task Runs at Specified Time) check box to prevent a task from running.

◆ The Schedule page shows the current schedule or schedules for the task. Select the Show Multiple Schedules check box if you need to set up more than one schedule for a task. (Alternatively, you can set up multiple separate tasks doing the same thing at different times. But using multiple schedules for the same task is neater and usually more efficient.) To specify an end date or a duration for the task, click the Advanced button and work in the Advanced Schedule Options dialog box.

◆ The Settings page contains three group boxes of advanced settings not offered by the Scheduled Task Wizard:

Scheduled Task Completed group box   For a one-time task, select the Delete the Task if It Is Not Scheduled to Run Again check box if you want Windows to delete the task automatically once it has run successfully. To prevent a task from running for an inordinately long time, select the Stop the Task if It Runs for *NN* Hours *NN* Minutes check box and specify appropriate values in the two text boxes.

Idle Time group box   This group box contains three self-explanatory options for making sure the task runs when the computer is idle rather than when it is in use: the Only Start the Task if the Computer Has Been Idle for At Least *NN* Minutes check box and text box; the If the Computer Has Not Been Idle That Long, Retry for Up to *NN* Minutes check box and text box; and the Stop the Task if the Computer Ceases to Be Idle check box.

Power Management group box   If you don't want to drain your portable's battery by running the task on battery power, select the Don't Start the Task if the Computer Is Running on Batteries check box and the Stop the Task if Battery Mode Begins check box. If you want Windows to wake your computer from its questionably deserved slumber in order to perform the task, select the Wake the Computer to Run This Task check box.

CHANGING A SCHEDULED TASK

To change the details of a scheduled task, double-click the task in the Scheduled Tasks folder and work in the task's Properties dialog box. (See the previous section for details of the settings you can change.)

PREVENTING A SCHEDULED TASK FROM RUNNING

To prevent a scheduled task from running, clear the Enabled (Scheduled Task Runs at Specified Time) check box on the Task page of the Properties dialog box for the task.

To delete a scheduled task, right-click it in the Scheduled Tasks folder and choose Delete from the context menu. (Alternatively, select the task and click the Delete This Item link in the Folder Tasks list.) Select the Yes button in the confirmation message box.

Managing Disks with Disk Management

Formatting disks and converting their file system is all very well—but what if you need to create or delete a partition? For these tasks, Windows provides a Computer Management snap-in called Disk Management.

Starting Disk Management

Take the following steps to start Disk Management:

1. Choose Start ➤ Control Panel. Windows displays Control Panel.

    ◆ Alternatively, click the Start button to display the Start menu, right-click the My Computer item, and choose Manage from the context menu. Windows opens the Computer Management window. Go to step 5.

2. Click the Performance and Maintenance link. Windows displays the Performance and Maintenance screen.

3. Click the Administrative Tools link. Windows displays the Administrative Tools screen.

4. Double-click the Computer Management shortcut. Windows opens a Computer Management window.

5. Expand the Storage item in the console tree if it's not already expanded.

6. Click the Disk Management item. Computer Management starts the Disk Management snap-in, which displays information about your disks. Figure 11.23 shows an example.

FIGURE 11.23

Use Disk Manage-
ment to manage
your disks.

As you can see in the figure, the top section of the right-hand pane lists the volumes currently defined on the system, giving the following information about each volume:

◆ The letter for the volume (for example, C:)

◆ The volume's layout—whether it's a full disk or a partition

◆ The type (basic or dynamic)

◆ The file system (FAT32, NTFS, CDFS, UDF, and so on)

◆ The status—for example, Healthy (Boot) for a boot volume in good condition

◆ The capacity in megabytes, gigabytes, or larger units

◆ The amount of free space

◆ The percentage of the volume free

◆ Whether fault tolerance is used on the volume

◆ The overhead consumed by fault tolerance (if it's used). You can't see this column in the figure, because it's off the right side of the screen.

Below this list, Disk Management shows a graphical representation of each physical disk attached to the computer and how it's broken down. For example, in the figure, Disk 0 (the first hard disk—computer counting begins at 0) has a FAT32 C: drive, three NTFS drives, and a chunk of free space. Then there's a CD-ROM drive that shows up as CD-ROM 0 and a DVD drive that shows up as CD-ROM 1.

That bit about basic disks and dynamic disks may have raised your eyebrows a bit—especially since Disk Management shows that your computer has basic disks. But don't worry—the term refers to the disk's configuration rather than to its capabilities. If you bought the largest and fastest hard drive on the block, it'll still be the largest and fastest until the engineers release something better, no matter that it uses the basic disk configuration.

A *basic disk* is one configured to support primary partitions, extended partitions, and logical drives (within extended partitions). A *dynamic disk* is one configured so that you can use fault tolerance or create multi-disk volumes on the fly. You can't create dynamic disks in Windows XP Home, but because Windows XP Home borrows the Disk Management tool from Windows XP Professional and Windows XP Server, Disk Management shows the disk type for Windows XP Home too.

Fault tolerance is a feature typically implemented only in servers or high-end workstations. It uses multiple disks to avoid the possible loss of information when disk problems occur. Windows 2000 Server and Windows XP Professional implement software fault tolerance through Redundant Array of Inexpensive Disks (RAID). Fault tolerance involves *overhead*—extra space used to keep extra copies of information so that it isn't lost if hardware fails.

Creating a Partition

If you have free space available, you can create a partition in it. Below is an example of creating a new logical drive using that free space shown back in Figure 11.23. The options available to you will depend on your disk configuration.

1. Right-click the free space and choose New Logical Drive from the context menu. Computer Management starts the New Partition Wizard, which displays an introductory page.

2. Click the Next button. The Wizard displays the Select Partition Type page (shown in Figure 11.24).

FIGURE 11.24

On the Select Partition Type page of the New Partition Wizard, specify which type of partition to create (if there's a choice).

3. Select the partition type (you may not have a choice, as in the figure) and click the Next button. The Wizard displays the Specify Partition Size page (shown in Figure 11.25).

FIGURE 11.25

On the Specify Partition Size page of the New Partition Wizard, specify the size of the partition.

4. In the Partition Size in MB text box, enter the size of partition you want to create. The Wizard suggests using all the space available, which you may well not want to do. The readout above the text box shows the minimum and maximum sizes possible.

5. Click the Next button. The Wizard displays the Assign Drive Letter or Path page (shown in Figure 11.26).

FIGURE 11.26

On the Assign Drive Letter or Path page of the New Partition Wizard, specify the drive letter to use for the partition.

6. Leave the Assign the Following Drive Letter option button selected and specify the letter in the drop-down list.

   ◆ Instead of assigning a drive letter, you can select the Mount in the Following Empty NTFS Folder option button and specify the folder in the text box. This option tends to be of more use for servers than for home or home-office computers.

◆ Instead of doing either of the above, you *can* avoid assigning a drive letter or path by selecting the Do Not Assign a Drive Letter or Drive Path option button. The only reason to do this is if you're planning to assign letters (or paths) later after creating other partitions. In order to access the partition through the Windows interface (for example, from Explorer or from an application), you'll need to assign a drive letter or path to it sooner or later—and it may as well be sooner.

7. Click the Next button. The Wizard displays the Format Partition page (shown in Figure 11.27).

FIGURE 11.27

On the Format Partition page of the New Partition Wizard, specify the file system and label for the partition.

8. Leave the Format This Partition with the Following Settings option button selected and choose settings:

◆ Choose the file system (preferably NTFS, but FAT32 or FAT if necessary) in the File System drop-down list.

◆ Leave the Allocation Unit Size drop-down list set to Default unless you've got a very good reason to change it.

◆ Enter the label for the volume in the Volume Label text box. (The Wizard suggests New Volume, but you should be able to come up with something more descriptive. Again, you have 20 characters for the label on an NTFS volume and 11 characters for that on a FAT or FAT32 volume.)

◆ Select the Perform a Quick Format check box if you've checked the disk for errors recently and found none. If not, it's better to perform a full format, including the check for errors.

◆ Select the Enable File and Folder Compression check box if you want to use compression on the volume.

9. Click the Next button. The Wizard displays the Completing the New Partition Wizard page (shown in Figure 11.28).

10. Click the Finish button. The Wizard closes, creates the partition, and formats it. You'll need to wait for the formatting to finish before you can use the volume.

FIGURE 11.28

On the Completing the New Partition Wizard page of the New Partition Wizard, double-check the choices you made.

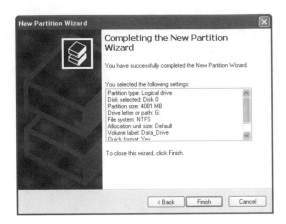

Deleting a Partition

To delete a partition and dispose of all its data, right-click the partition and issue the Delete command from the context menu. For example, if it's a logical drive, choose the Delete Logical Drive item on the context menu. Disk Management displays a Delete Drive dialog box such as that shown in Figure 11.29. Click the Yes button to proceed.

FIGURE 11.29

Disk Management double-checks that you're sure you want to delete a drive.

Changing the Drive Letter

Disk Management also lets you change the drive letter for a volume other than your system volume or boot volume. This capability comes in handy if you get your drive letters in a tangle. Be aware, though, that changing the drive letter will confuse any program that has learned the path to files on this drive.

To change the drive letter, follow these steps:

1. Right-click the drive whose letter you want to change and choose Change Drive Letter and Paths from the context menu. Disk Management displays the Change Drive Letter and Paths dialog box (shown in Figure 11.30).

2. To change the drive letter, select it (if it's not already selected) and click the Change button. Disk Management displays the Change Drive Letter or Path dialog box (shown in Figure 11.31).

3. Make sure the Assign the Following Drive Letter option button is selected, then select the letter in the drop-down list.

FIGURE 11.30

Use the Change Drive Letter and Paths dialog box to change the drive letter for a drive.

FIGURE 11.31

Specify the drive letter or path in the Change Drive Letter or Path dialog box.

4. Click the OK button. Disk Management displays the Confirm dialog box (shown in Figure 11.32), warning you that changing the drive letter might prevent programs from running.

FIGURE 11.32

Confirm the change in the Confirm dialog box.

5. Click the Yes button. If files on the drive are open, Disk Management displays the Disk Management dialog box shown in Figure 11.33 telling you that you can continue to use the old drive letter until you reboot and asking if you want to continue.

FIGURE 11.33

Read the small print in the Disk Management dialog box and signal your willingness to proceed.

6. Click the Yes button. Disk Management makes the change.

7. Change other drive letters if necessary, then restart your computer so that you can start using the new drive letter assignments.

Exiting Disk Management

When you've finished working in Disk Management, choose File ➢ Exit to close the Computer Management window.

Up Next

This chapter has discussed how to manage your disks and drives, from actions such as formatting and compressing them to setting quotas in order to prevent users from grabbing more than their fair share of disk space. It has also covered how to look after your disks by defragmenting them, checking them for errors, and running Disk Cleanup; and how to use Disk Management to create partitions, delete them, and assign drive letters to them.

The next chapter discusses how to work with the Registry to tweak your computer's configuration in ways that Microsoft failed to provide in the user interface.

Chapter 12

Working with the Registry

THIS CHAPTER COVERS HOW to work with one of the most mentioned but least understood components of Windows—the Registry, the giant repository of Windows' knowledge and wisdom about your computer.

The chapter starts by discussing what the Registry is, what it does, why you might want to mess with it, and what the dangers are of doing so. It then details the step you *must* take before you make any changes to the Registry: backing up the Registry so that you can restore it if something goes wrong. After that, the chapter shows you how to use Registry Editor to examine the contents of the Registry, find what you're looking for, and make changes. It concludes by showing you how to goose the Registry so that you can crash your computer with two keystrokes.

This chapter covers the following topics:

◆ Understanding what the Registry is and what it does

◆ Running Registry Editor

◆ Backing up your Registry

◆ Restoring the Registry from backup

◆ Restoring the Last Known Good Configuration

◆ Registry subtrees and data types

◆ Finding and changing information in the Registry

◆ Crashing your computer manually

What Is the Registry and What Does It Do?

Put simply, the *Registry* is a hierarchical database of all the settings required by your installation of Windows and the programs you've installed. These settings include information on the hardware installed on your computer and how it's configured; all the programs and their file associations; profiles for each user and group; and property settings for folders and files.

The Registry stores the information needed to keep your computer running. Windows itself stores a huge amount of information in the Registry, and each program you install stores information there too. You can store information in the Registry yourself if you want to, though unless you're creating programs, there's not much reason to do so.

The number of entries in the Registry depends on the number of users of the computer and the software installed, but between 50,000 and 100,000 entries is normal. This multitude of entries makes browsing through the Registry practical only for those with serious amounts of time weighing on their hands. Even searching through the Registry can be a slow process, because many of the entries contain similar information.

The Registry was introduced in Windows 95, and all 32-bit desktop versions of Windows have used it. In Windows 3.*x*, information was stored in initialization files—INI files for short. For example, Windows configuration information was stored in files such as WIN.INI and SYSTEM.INI. Most programs typically created configuration files of their own.

Centralizing all the information in the Registry has two main advantages. First, all the information is in a central location. (Actually, it's in a couple of locations. More on this a little later in the chapter.) And second, you can back up the Registry (though most users forget or fail to do so) and restore it.

Not surprisingly, this centralization has the concomitant disadvantage that damage to the Registry can cripple Windows completely.

Why Work with the Registry?

Paradoxically enough, you *don't* work with the Registry—most of the time. In theory, you should never need to mess with the Registry.

That's why Windows provides no direct way from the user interface to view the Registry and change its contents. If you want to explore and change the Registry, you need to deliberately run the Registry Editor program, which is tucked away in a safe place where no casual user should stumble across it.

Most of the information that's stored in the Registry, you'll never need to change. Those relatively few pieces of information that Windows is happy for you to change are accessible through the Windows user interface, which provides you with an easier—if more restrictive—way of changing them than working in the Registry. For example, the settings in Control Panel applets store most of their information in the Registry, so you *could* edit the Registry and change the information there. But for all conventional purposes, you'll do better to work through those Control Panel applets and let them set the values in the Registry for you. Control Panel is designed to be easy to use, while the Registry isn't. Control Panel shows you your options in (mostly) intelligible ways; the information in the Registry is arcane when not incomprehensible. And Control Panel seldom screws up in translating your choices into hex and binary, whereas the Registry will happily accept input that will instruct Windows to disable itself.

That said, sometimes you may need to access the Registry to change a vital piece of information that you cannot change through the user interface. Sometimes you'll need to access the Registry because something has gone wrong, and you need to change an entry manually. But more often, you'll hear about a cool tweak that you can perform by entering a new value in the Registry or by changing an existing value.

You can also use the Registry to store information of your own that you want to have available to Windows or to the programs you use. You might want to do this if you write your own programs, or if you use a macro language to create automated procedures in a program—for example, if you use VBA to automate tasks in Word, Excel, or Outlook. (You *could* also use the Registry to store odd information, such as names and addresses—but there are far better ways of spending your life.)

Preparing to Access the Registry

Before you do anything to the Registry, you need to understand this:

If you mess up the Registry, you may disable parts of Windows' functionality. You may even disable Windows itself so that it cannot boot.

So before you do *anything* to the Registry, back it up by exporting it as discussed in the section after next. In fact, even if you don't make any changes to the Registry, it's a good idea to keep a backup of your Registry in case a program, Windows itself, or (more likely) a piece of malware makes a change for the worse.

Running Registry Editor

To work with the Registry, you use Registry Editor. Windows provides no Start menu item for Registry Editor, though you can of course create your own Start menu item or Desktop shortcut if you want.

Unless you create a Start menu item or shortcut, the easiest way to run Registry Editor is to choose Start ➤ Run (or press Winkey+R), enter **regedit** in the Run dialog box, and click the OK button. Windows starts Registry Editor (shown in Figure 12.1).

NOTE *If you've worked with the Registry in Windows 2000 or in Windows NT, you'll recall that those OSes included two Registry Editors—*REGEDIT.EXE *and* REGEDT32.EXE. *Both were functional, but* REGEDT32.EXE *offered a few more features than* REGEDIT.EXE. *Good news: Windows XP includes just one Registry Editor,* REGEDIT.EXE, *but there's a stub for* REGEDT32.EXE, *so you can start the same Registry Editor by using either name.*

FIGURE 12.1

Launch Registry Editor by choosing Start ➤ Run and entering **regedit** in the Run dialog box.

Backing Up Your Registry

Before you do anything else with Registry Editor—and that includes exploring the subtrees and keys of the Registry, let alone changing any values—back up your Registry.

To back up the Registry, export it by taking the following steps from Registry Editor:

1. Select the My Computer item in Registry Editor.

    ◆ If you want to back up only a subtree of the Registry, select the subtree instead of the My Computer item.

2. Choose File ➤ Export. Registry Editor displays the Export Registry File dialog box (shown in Figure 12.2). As you can see in the figure, this dialog box is a common Save As dialog box with an extra section tacked on at the bottom to house the Export Range group box.

FIGURE 12.2

In the Export Registry File dialog box, specify that you want to export all of the Registry.

3. In the Export Range group box, make sure the All option button is selected.

    ◆ If you chose a subtree in step 1, the Export Registry File dialog box appears with the Selected Branch option button selected and the subtree's name entered in the Selected Branch text box.

4. Specify the filename and location for the file as usual.

    ◆ Registry files tend to be large—on the order of 20–30MB—so don't try to save yours to a floppy. If you have a CD recorder, save the Registry file to disk, then burn it to CD.

5. Click the Save button. Windows closes the Export Registry File dialog box and saves the Registry file.

Restoring Your Registry

To restore your Registry (or part of it) from a Registry file you've exported, follow these steps:

1. From Registry Editor, choose File ➤ Import. Windows displays the Import Registry File dialog box, which is a renamed Open dialog box.

2. In the Files of Type drop-down list, select the Registration Files item or the Registry Hive Files item as appropriate.

3. Select the Registry file to import.

4. Click the Open button. Registry Editor imports the Registry file and adds it to the Registry.

Restoring the Registry to Its Last Known Good Configuration

If you do to the Registry anything so horrible that Windows won't boot anymore, you may need to restore the Registry to its Last Known Good Configuration in order to get Windows going again. The *Last Known Good Configuration* is the one with which Windows last booted successfully. Restoring the Last Known Good Configuration loses any changes you've made to your Windows configuration since the last boot—including whichever change has disabled Windows.

To restore the Registry to the Last Known Good Configuration, take the following steps:

1. If Windows is still running (and if you need to restore the Registry, Windows may well *not* be running), choose Start ➤ Turn Off Computer. From the Turn Off Computer screen, choose the Restart option. If Windows isn't running, power up your computer as usual.

2. When Windows restarts (or starts) and displays the Please Select the Operating System to Start screen, press the F8 key. Windows displays the Windows Advanced Options menu.

3. Select the Last Known Good Configuration item and press the Enter key. Windows displays the Please Select the Operating System to Start menu but adds the words *Last Known Good Configuration* at the bottom of the screen in blue.

4. Select the operating system to start, and then press the Enter key. Windows starts and displays the Welcome screen.

Working in the Registry

Now that your Registry is safely backed up, it's time to examine how the Registry works and how you can change it.

As mentioned earlier in this chapter, the Registry is a hierarchical database. It's hierarchical in that its contents are arranged into a hierarchy of folders organized into five main areas called *subtrees* or *root keys*. You'll also sometimes hear them called *predefined keys*, though the term tends to be confusing because the Registry contains thousands of keys that are predefined—at least, from the user's point of view. As you can see in Figure 12.1 above, the name of each subtree begins with the letters HKEY.

The Five Subtrees of the Registry

These are the five subtrees and the types of information they contain:

HKEY_CLASSES_ROOT This subtree contains an exhaustive list of the file types that Windows recognizes, the programs associated with them, and more.

HKEY_CURRENT_USER This subtree contains information on the current user and their setup. For example, when you're logged on, all your Desktop preferences are listed in this subtree.

HKEY_LOCAL_MACHINE This subtree contains information on the hardware and software setup of the computer.

HKEY_USERS This subtree contains information on the users who are set up to use the computer, together with a DEFAULT profile that's used when no user is logged on to the computer.

HKEY_CURRENT_CONFIG This subtree contains information on the current configuration of the computer—the hardware with which the computer booted.

Keys, Subkeys, and Value Entries

In Registry Editor, expand the HKEY_CURRENT_USER subtree by clicking the plus (+) sign next to it or by double-clicking its name. Registry Editor displays the items contained within the subtree—an apparently endless list of folderlike objects, many of them containing further objects. Figure 12.3 shows the HKEY_CURRENT_USER subtree with some of its subkeys expanded.

Within each subtree, there are keys, subkeys, and value entries. A *key* is (as it were) one of the folders within the subtree. Just as a subfolder is a folder within a folder, a *subkey* is a key within a key. Also as with "folder" and "subfolder," many people say "key" rather than "subkey" except when they need to be specific; this chapter does the same.

FIGURE 12.3

Each subtree contains keys, subkeys, and value entries.

Each key or subkey can contain subkeys and value entries. The term *value entry* sounds like a management-consultant way of saying "value," but in fact it's not: A value entry is the current definition of a key, and consists of a name, a data type, and the value assigned to the key.

For example, consider the `MinAnimate` key and value entry that you can see in Figure 12.3 in the `HKEY_CURRENT_USER\Control Panel\Desktop\WindowMetrics\` subkey. As you can see in the Data column, the value of `MinAnimate` is 1. This value entry controls whether Windows animates windows when you minimize, maximize, or restore them. (The animation zooms the window from its displayed size and position down to its button on the Taskbar, and vice versa, instead of popping it off or back on the screen instantly.) A value of 0 indicates that the animation is off, a value of 1 that the animation is on.

`MinAnimate` is interesting in that it's an example of a key added to the Registry in Windows XP in order to implement functionality already in Windows. In earlier versions of Windows, including Windows NT and Windows 2000, this key wasn't included in the Registry, though its functionality was implemented in Windows. These versions of Windows automatically animated windows that you minimized, maximized, or restored.

This animation was (and remains) pure eye candy—and like much eye candy, this animation didn't appeal to everyone. On a slow computer, or one with an underpowered graphics card, it was particularly irritating, as Windows seemed to be running arthritically. To switch off this animation, you needed to create the `MinAnimate` value entry in the Registry and assign it the value 0, then restart Windows. (You could've also implemented this change by using a utility such as TweakUI, which created and adjusted the `MinAnimate` value entry transparently for you.)

Windows XP lets you control this setting via the Animate Windows when Minimizing and Maximizing check box on the Visual Effects page of the Performance Options dialog box (which you reach by clicking the Settings button in the Performance group box on the Advanced page of the System Properties dialog box). When this check box is selected, `MinAnimate` has the value 1; when the check box is cleared, `MinAnimate` has the value 0.

Registry Data Types

As you can see in Figure 12.3, the `MinAnimate` value entry is of type `REG_SZ`. REG means Registry, as you'd guess; SZ means string, indicating that the value entry contains a string of text (text characters, as opposed to, say, binary data). The `\WindowMetrics\` key also contains value entries of another data type, `REG_BINARY`. You get no prize for guessing that these are binary data.

Strings and binary data are the most widely used of the data types in the Registry. Next comes `REG_DWORD`, a double-word value entry. Figure 12.4 shows the `HKEY_CURRENT_USER\Control Panel\Desktop\` key, which contains some double-word value entries as well as string and binary value entries.

The other two most widely used data types are `REG_MULTI_SZ`, multi-string entries, and `REG_EXPAND_SZ`, expandable strings. Table 12.1 provides a roundup of the five most widely used data types.

TABLE 12.1: THE FIVE MOST WIDELY USED REGISTRY DATA TYPES

TYPE	TYPE DISPLAYED	EXPLANATION
String	REG_SZ	Text
Multi-String	REG_MULTI_SZ	Text, but with multiple text values

Continued on next page

TABLE 12.1: THE FIVE MOST WIDELY USED REGISTRY DATA TYPES *(continued)*

TYPE	TYPE DISPLAYED	EXPLANATION
Expandable String	REG_EXPAND_SZ	Text, but expandable
Binary	REG_BINARY	A binary value, displayed as hexadecimal
DWORD	REG_DWORD	Double-word: A 32-bit binary value displayed as an 8-digit hexadecimal value

FIGURE 12.4

The HKEY_CURRENT_USER\ Control Panel\ Desktop\ key contains a variety of different data types.

You can create and edit value entries with any of these data types. We'll get to that a bit later in the chapter, after discussing where the Registry is stored and how to find information in it.

TIP   Beyond these five widely used data types, the Registry can contain many different data types, such as REG_DWORD_BIG_ENDIAN (a value stored in reverse order of double-word value), REG_DWORD_LITTLE_ENDIAN (another type of double-word value), REG_FULL_RESOURCE_DESCRIPTOR (a hardware-resource list), REG_QWORD (a quadruple-word value), and REG_FILE_NAME (three guesses). You shouldn't need to mess with any of these unless you get into programming Windows—in which case, you'll need a book more specialized than this one.

Where the Registry Is Stored

Most of the Registry is stored in several different files on your hard drive. (Part of the Registry is created automatically when Windows boots and discovers which devices are attached to your computer.) These files are binary and are called *hives* (think bees, not allergies) or *hive files.*

Perhaps surprisingly, the hives aren't hidden files, so you don't even need to tell Windows to display hidden files before you can see them. But you do have to go through Windows' veil of secrecy over the files by clicking the Show the Contents of This Folder link.

Hive files containing computer-related information are stored in the `\Windows\system32\config\` folder, where `\Windows\` is your Windows folder. Hive files containing user-specific information are stored in the `\Documents and Settings\Username\` folder for each user.

These are the main hive files:

SYSTEM   This file contains information about the computer's hardware and about Windows. This information goes into the `HKEY_LOCAL_MACHINE\SYSTEM\` key.

NTUSER.DAT   This file contains information about the user's preferences. Windows XP keeps an `NTUSER.DAT` file for each user in the `\Documents and Settings\Username\` folder. This information goes into the `HKEY_CURRENT_USER` subtree.

SAM   This file contains the user database. This information goes into the `HKEY_LOCAL_MACHINE\SAM\` key.

SECURITY   This file contains information on security settings. This information goes into the `HKEY_LOCALMACHINE\SECURITY\` key.

SOFTWARE   This file contains information on the software installed on the computer. This information goes into the `HKEY_LOCAL_MACHINE\SOFTWARE\` key.

DEFAULT   This file contains information about the default user setup. This information goes into the `HKEY_USERS\DEFAULT\` key.

Each of the hive files has a log file named after it: `DEFAULT.LOG`, `SOFTWARE.LOG`, `NTUSER.DAT.LOG`, and so on. These log files note the changes to the hive files so that, if a change is applied that crashes the system, Windows can read the log, identify the problem change, and undo it.

Having read this, you're probably longing to lift the lid off a hive so that you can see what's inside it. Perhaps if you use Notepad or another text editor, you can get a peek inside in the same way you did with that Word document in Chapter 7—

Don't.

Taking a text editor to a hive file would be like taking one of those old-fashioned can openers (you know, the ones that leave those nice jagged edges) to your favorite black box of electronic wizardry: clumsy, messy, and ultimately fruitless. In any case, Windows keeps the hive files open the whole time it's running so that it can write information to them and retrieve information from them whenever it needs, so they're locked. All you'll get for your pains is a message box telling you something like "The process cannot access the file because it is being used by another process." Translation: Windows needs this file. Hands off.

Let's look at what you *can* profitably do with the Registry: find keys and value entries or information in it, change values, and create (and delete) keys and value entries of your own.

Finding Information in the Registry

There are two ways to find information in the Registry: by digging through the Registry looking for it, or by using the Find function.

Digging through the Registry takes minimal explanation, because it's very similar to browsing in Explorer in Explore mode. You can expand and collapse keys as you would drives and folders in Explorer, and you can use type-down addressing to reach the next key or entry matching the letters you type. But because of the number of keys and value entries the Registry contains, you'll usually do better by searching through it rather than browsing.

If you know the name of a key, the name of a value entry, or the data contained in a value entry, you can search for it. For example, if you wanted to find where FTP sites were listed, you might search for **FTP Sites**. If you wanted to find out what the entry for the Microsoft Office AutoCorrect file was called, you might search for **.ACL**, the extension of the AutoCorrect file. Choose Edit ➢ Find (or press Ctrl+F). Registry Editor displays the Find dialog box (shown in Figure 12.5). You can restrict the search by selecting only the check boxes for the items you're looking at—Keys, Values, or Data—in the Look At group box. And you can search for only the entire string by selecting the Match Whole String Only check box. Selecting this check box prevents Find from finding the string you're looking for inside other strings—it makes Find find only whole strings that match the string in the Find What text box.

FIGURE 12.5

Use the Find dialog box in Registry Editor to find the keys, values, or data you want to manipulate.

Because of the volume of information that Windows stores in the Registry, the first match you find may not be the key (or value entry, or value) you need. For example, if you use your company's name as the Find item when looking for the `RegisteredOrganization` key for Windows, you may find another key, such as the registered organization for Internet Explorer. Close examination of the key will usually tell you whether you've found the key you were looking for. If not, press the F3 key or choose Edit ➢ Find Next to find the next instance.

Editing a Value Entry

To edit a value entry in the Registry, navigate to it and double-click it. (Alternatively, select it and choose Edit ➢ Modify.) Windows displays an Edit dialog box appropriate to the type of data the value entry contains.

String values and expandable string values are the easiest values to edit. In the Edit String dialog box (shown in Figure 12.6), enter the text of the string in the Value Data text box, then click the OK button.

FIGURE 12.6

You can edit both string values and expandable string values in the Edit String dialog box.

Multi-string values are relatively simple to edit. In the Edit Multi-String dialog box (shown in Figure 12.7), enter all the data for the value entry on separate lines, and then click the OK button.

FIGURE 12.7

Editing a multi-string value in the Edit Multi-String dialog box

Double-word values are the next-easiest values to edit. In the Edit DWORD Value dialog box (shown in Figure 12.8), enter the data in the Value Data text box, then choose the Hexadecimal option button or the Decimal option button as appropriate in the Base group box. (When you're editing a built-in double-word value, you shouldn't need to change the existing Base setting.) Click the OK button.

FIGURE 12.8

Editing a double-word value in the Edit DWORD Value dialog box

Binary values are brutes to change, and you probably won't want to mess with them for fun. In the Edit Binary Value dialog box (shown in Figure 12.9), edit the data in the Value Data text box with great care, and then click the OK button.

FIGURE 12.9

Editing a binary value in the Edit Binary Value dialog box is hard work.

Adding a Key or a Value Entry

You can add a key or a value entry to the Registry either automatically or manually.

To add a key or value entry to the Registry automatically, double-click a REG file that you've received. For example, some programs sold via download use Registry keys to implement a license: You pay for the program and download it. The company then e-mails you a license and a REG file. To add the registration data to your Registry, double-click the REG file. Windows adds the necessary keys and value entries to the Registry.

To add a key or a value entry to the Registry manually, follow these steps

1. Right-click the key in which you want to create the new key or value entry, choose New from the context menu, and choose the appropriate item from the submenu: Key, String Value, Binary Value, DWORD Value, Multi-String Value, or Expandable String Value. Registry Editor creates a new key named `New Key #1` or `New Value #1` (or the next available number) and displays an edit box around it.

2. Type the name for the key or value entry.

3. Press the Enter key or click elsewhere in the Registry Editor window. Registry Editor assigns the name you specified to the key or value entry.

If you created a value entry, double-click it. Registry Editor displays the Edit dialog box appropriate to its type. Enter the data for the value entry as described in the previous section.

Deleting a Key or a Value Entry

Just as you can create keys and value entries, you can delete them. Generally speaking, it's a bad idea to delete any keys other than those you've created. Windows itself and Windows programs protect some keys in the Registry, but you'll find a surprising number that aren't protected and that you can therefore delete freely.

To delete a value entry, right-click it and choose Delete from the context menu. Registry Editor displays the Confirm Value Delete dialog box or the Confirm Key Delete dialog box (shown in Figure 12.10). Click the Yes button to confirm the deletion.

FIGURE 12.10

Confirm a deletion in the Confirm Key Delete dialog box (shown here) or the Confirm Value Delete dialog box.

If the key or value entry is locked against deletion, Registry Editor displays an error message box.

Copying a Key Name

If you're describing to someone how to find particular information in the Registry, you'll need to get the key name right. But you don't need to type it painstakingly—you can copy it instead.

To copy a Registry key name, select it in the left pane in Registry Editor and choose Edit ➤ Copy Key Name. You can then paste it from the Clipboard into a program.

An Example: Changing Your Windows Name and Organization

As mentioned at the beginning of the chapter, Microsoft reckons you should seldom (or preferably never) need to make changes to the Registry directly. But you'll probably run into tips and tweaks, online or in magazines, that promise to improve Windows' performance, compatibility, or behavior with a judicious change or two.

For example, say you misspelled your name or your organization's name during setup. Or perhaps you've bought a computer loaded with Windows from someone else. Either way, when you display the General page of the System Properties dialog box, there's the misspelling or the wrong name laughing at you.

You'll want to change the name or organization name so that they're correct. There's no way to do so through the Windows user interface, but by navigating to the `HKEY_LOCAL_MACHINE\SOFTWARE\Microsoft\WindowsNT\CurrentVersion\` key and changing the `RegisteredOwner` and `RegisteredOrganization` value entries as appropriate, you can fix the problem in a minute or two.

Using Registry Favorites to Quickly Access Keys

If you find yourself using the Registry a lot, there's another feature you should know about: Registry favorites. To access the keys you need to work with frequently, you can create favorites in Registry Editor much as you can in Explorer and Internet Explorer.

To create a favorite, follow these steps:

1. Select the key to which you want the favorite to refer.

2. Choose Favorites ➢ Add to Favorites. Registry Editor displays the Add to Favorites dialog box (shown in Figure 12.11).

FIGURE 12.11

Use the Add to Favorites dialog box to create favorites to provide quick access to keys you access frequently.

3. In the Favorite Name text box, enter the name for the favorite. (By default, Registry Editor suggests the key name, but you may well want to change this to more descriptive text.)

4. Click the OK button. Registry Editor adds the favorite to your Favorites menu.

To access a favorite, display the Favorites menu and choose the favorite from the list.

To remove a favorite from the Favorites menu, choose Favorites ➢ Remove Favorite. Windows displays the Remove Favorites dialog box. Choose the favorite in the Select Favorite list box and click the OK button.

EXPERT KNOWLEDGE: CRASHING YOUR COMPUTER ON CUE

Most people want their computer to crash seldom or (preferably) never. But if you want to test what happens when it crashes (for example, to see how memory dumping works), you'll be relieved to know that you don't have to wait for your software to disagree horribly with itself: Windows XP includes a built-in way of crashing itself. You just have to add the right Registry entry, set the appropriate value, and then press a couple of keys.

Here's what to do:

1. Back up your Registry. (Yes, really back it up this time.)

2. Open Registry Editor (for example, choose Start ➢ Run, enter **regedit**, and press the Enter key).

3. Navigate to the `HKEY_LOCAL_MACHINE\SYSTEM\CurrentControlSet\Services\i8042prt\Parameters\` key.

4. Right-click in the right pane and choose New ➢ DWORD Value from the context menu. Registry Editor creates a new value called `New Value #1` and displays an edit box around the new value's name.

5. Enter the name **CrashOnCtrlScroll** and press the Enter key.

6. Double-click the `CrashOnCtrlScroll` value. Registry Editor displays the Edit DWORD Value dialog box.

7. Enter **1** in the Value Data text box. In the Base group box, leave the Hexadecimal option button selected.

8. Click the OK button. Registry Editor closes the Edit DWORD Value dialog box.

9. Close Registry Editor.

10. Restart your computer and log back on.

11. Hold down the Ctrl key on the right side of the keyboard and press the Scroll Lock key twice. Windows goes down as if sandbagged, and any memory dumping you've set occurs.

Up Next

This chapter has discussed what the Registry is; what it does; why you *must* back it up before messing with it; how to mess with it; and why you shouldn't mess with it most of the time. It's also shown you how to crash your (or someone else's) computer on cue. Use this power only for good.

The next chapter discusses how to install, configure, and manage printers.

Chapter 13

Installing, Configuring, and Managing Printers and Fonts

WITH THE PROMISE OF the paperless office seemingly destined to remain eternally unfulfilled, printing continues to be vital to the average home office, and only marginally less vital to the average home.

This chapter discusses how to install, configure, and manage printers and fonts. Chapter 33 discusses how to share a printer via your network and how to connect to a shared printer.

This chapter covers the following topics:

◆ The basics of Windows printing

◆ Installing a local printer

◆ Configuring a printer

◆ Removing a printer

◆ Printing a document

◆ Managing your print jobs

◆ Printing offline

◆ Creating multiple entries for the same printer

◆ Printing to a file

◆ Working with fonts

The Basics of Windows Printing

As you'll see in a minute, installing a printer is straightforward enough, with Wizards to help you left, right, and center. But before we get into that, let's go over the basics of printing in Windows. First, there's a bit of terminology you ought to understand. Then there are three ways of installing a printer, the first of which this chapter discusses. (Chapter 33 discusses the other two ways.) And there's a little you should know about how an item you print makes its way from the program to the printer.

The Terminology of Windows Printing

Just as the windows in Windows are most likely substantially different from those in your home, Windows terminology for printing is a little different than regular terminology. Here are the terms that you need to know before you consult the Help files or call for tech support:

◆ A *printer* is the hardware device that actually prints the page—in other words, what people normally mean when they say "printer." This doesn't go without saying because Microsoft sometimes refers to a printer as a *print device*. If so, what does Microsoft mean by *printer* at those times? Read on. . . .

◆ When the hardware device is called a *print device*, a *printer* is the software that controls the *print device*. Normally, it's clearer to call this software a printer driver.

◆ A *print job* (or just plain *job*) is an item sent to a printer for printing.

◆ A *network printer*, *shared printer*, or *printer connection* is a printer that's being shared by another computer or by a print server and that you can connect to across the network.

◆ A *print server* is a device (typically a hardware device) that relays print jobs to a printer.

This book uses the terms *printer* for the hardware device and *print driver* for the software that drives it.

Three Ways of Installing a Printer

These are the three ways of installing a printer:

Local printer attached to the computer   The simplest way of installing a printer is to install it *locally*—in other words, attach it directly to the computer. The printer is usually attached directly to the computer with a cable to the parallel port or USB port. There are also more specialized arrangements, such as infrared printer connections for laptop users too impatient to plug into a docking station.

Networked printer attached to a server   The next way of installing a printer is to install it as a *networked*—shared—printer attached to a server. The server in this case doesn't have to be literally a server. It can be just another client computer that's sharing a printer directly attached to it. Alternatively, it can be a literal server running a server operating system. The client computer connects to the networked printer through a network (cabled, wireless, or—rarely—infrared).

Networked printer attached to a print server   You can also share a printer attached to a print server. A print server is essentially a specialized computer designed for sharing and managing printers. The advantage of using a print server over a networked computer is that you don't need to keep a computer running all the time in order to use the printer.
Figure 13.1 illustrates these printer configurations.

How Does a Print Job Get Printed?

Provided your printer works as it should, you don't need to know how the printing process works. But if anything goes wrong with printing, understanding the basic process can be a great help in troubleshooting the problem.

FIGURE 13.1

The three basic configurations for printers: a local printer attached directly to the computer; a networked printer shared by another computer; and a networked printer attached to a print server

Local Printer

Networked Printer Shared by a Computer

Networked Printer Attached to a Print Server

Here's what typically happens in the print process:

◆ You issue a Print command for a document you've got open in a program. For example, you're working on a workbook in Excel and you get a worksheet into shape to print. You press Ctrl+P, choose options in the Print dialog box, and click the OK button.

◆ The program tells Windows that it needs to print the document.

◆ The printer driver (the print software, or what Microsoft sometimes calls the *printer*) kicks in. The printer driver grabs the information that the program is emitting about what needs to be printed. The printer driver *spools* the printing information, saving it to disk all at once and then feeding it to the printer (the hardware print device) at a speed the printer and its cable can handle. Printer cables transfer data very slowly compared to the wiring inside the computer, and if the printer didn't spool the data, the program would be stuck transferring the information to the printer bit by bit. (This isn't entirely true—some programs are intelligent enough to print in the background while allowing you to continue working in the foreground. But generally speaking, spooling lets you continue your work much more quickly.)

There's one other part to this: Each print job is typically spooled into a *print queue* rather than just fed into the printer. Documents in the print queue are normally printed in the order in which they are submitted, but you can assign different priorities to different users' print jobs if you want. If you have Computer Administrator privileges, you can also manage the print queue, promoting, demoting, pausing, and deleting print jobs.

All straight? Then let's install that printer.

Installing a Local Printer

If your printer was connected to the computer when you installed Windows XP, Setup sets it up during the setup routine. If you connect it afterward, you'll need to set it up by using the hardware Wizards.

In most cases, Windows detects the addition of the printer when you connect the printer to the computer's parallel or USB port and switch the printer on. If Windows has a driver for the printer, it loads the driver and notifies you that the printer is ready for use. If Windows doesn't have a driver for the printer, it starts the Found New Hardware Wizard to walk you through the process of identifying the printer and installing the right driver for it. See "Using the Hardware Wizards" in Chapter 14 for information on using the Found New Hardware Wizard.

If Windows doesn't detect your local printer, use the Add Printer Wizard to install the printer. See pages 71–74 of the *Essential Skills* section for a visual walkthrough of installing a printer manually, or take the following steps:

1. Choose Start ➤ Control Panel. Windows displays Control Panel.

2. Click the Printers and Other Hardware link. Windows displays the Printers and Other Hardware screen.

3. Click the Add a Printer link in the Pick a Task list. (Alternatively, click the Add a Printer link in the Tasks list on the Printers and Faxes screen.) Windows starts the Add Printer Wizard, which displays its Welcome page.

4. Click the Next button. The Wizard displays the Local or Network Printer page (shown in Figure 13.2).

FIGURE 13.2

On the Local or Network Printer page of the Add Printer Wizard, select the Local Printer Attached to This Computer option button.

5. Make sure the Local Printer Attached to This Computer option button is selected.

6. If you want to have the Wizard search for the printer, select the Automatically Detect and Install My Plug and Play Printer check box. If you prefer to identify your printer yourself, clear this check box.

7. Click the Next button. If you chose to have the Wizard search, it does so. If not, the Wizard displays the Select a Printer Port page (shown in Figure 13.3).

FIGURE 13.3

On the Select a Printer Port page of the Add Printer Wizard, select the port to which the printer is connected.

8. Make sure the Use the Following Port option button is selected, then select the port in the drop-down list. The default setting is LPT1, which is typically the port for the parallel port on your computer.

9. Click the Next button. The Wizard displays the Install Printer Software page (shown in Figure 13.4).

FIGURE 13.4

On the Install Printer Software page of the Add Printer Wizard, specify the make and model of your printer or provide a driver from another location.

10. To use a driver that Windows includes, select the printer's manufacturer in the Manufacturer list box. Then select the printer model in the Printers list box and go to step 12.

11. To provide a driver that you have (for example, on a CD or floppy), follow these steps:

- Click the Have Disk button. The Wizard displays the Install from Disk dialog box.

- In the Copy Manufacturer's Files From text box, enter the path and filename of the drive file. You can type in this information, but usually it's easier to click the Browse button and use the resulting Locate File dialog box (a common Open dialog box) to select the file, then click the Open button. The Wizard closes the Locate File dialog box and enters the path and filename in the text box in the Install from Disk dialog box.

- Click the OK button. The Wizard closes the Install from Disk dialog box and displays the Install Printer Software page, which lists the printer for which the driver is designed.

12. Click the Next button. The Wizard displays the Name Your Printer page (shown in Figure 13.5).

FIGURE 13.5

On the Name Your Printer page of the Add Printer Wizard, specify the name for the printer. If this is your second or subsequent printer (as in this example), choose whether to make it your default printer.

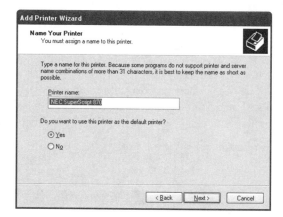

13. In the Printer Name text box, adjust the default name that the Wizard suggests for the printer. Keep the name relatively short, because some programs have problems with printer names that are longer than 31 characters including the server's name.

14. If this is the first printer you've installed, Windows automatically makes it your default printer. If you've already installed another printer, Windows includes the Do You Want to Use This Printer As the Default Printer? list on the Name Your Printer page. Select the Yes option button or the No option button as appropriate.

15. Click the Next button. The Wizard displays the Printer Sharing page (shown in Figure 13.6).

16. If you don't want to share the printer with other users via the network, leave the Do Not Share This Printer option button selected. If you do want to share the printer, select the Share Name option button and adjust the name that the Wizard suggests for the printer in the text box.

NOTE   Other users of this computer will be able to use the printer even if you choose not to share the printer on the network.

FIGURE 13.6

On the Printer Sharing page of the Add Printer Wizard, choose whether to share the printer with other network users.

17. Click the Next button. The Wizard displays the Print Test Page button, which invites you to print a test page to confirm that the printer is installed and working properly.

18. Select the Yes option button or the No option button as appropriate.

19. Click the Next button. The Wizard displays the Completing the Add Printer Wizard page (shown in Figure 13.7), which lists the choices you made.

FIGURE 13.7

The Completing the Add Printer Wizard page of the Add Printer Wizard

20. Double-check the list of choices, and click the Finish button if you're satisfied. The Wizard installs the printer. If you chose to print a test page, the Wizard prints it. If the page prints okay, click the OK button to close the dialog box the Wizard displays about the test page. The Wizard then closes itself.

Configuring a Printer

This section discusses how to configure a printer—everything from setting a printer as your default to telling it what kind of separator pages to print.

Setting a Printer As Your Default

As you saw, the Add Printer Wizard makes the first printer you install on your computer your default printer and invites you to set each subsequent printer you install as the default printer instead of the incumbent. But you can also change the default printer at any time. To set a printer as your default, right-click it on the Printers and Faxes screen and choose Set As Default Printer from the context menu.

To set properties for a printer, display its Properties dialog box by taking either of the following actions:

- Right-click the printer on the Printers and Faxes screen and choose Properties from the context menu.

- Select the printer on the Printers and Faxes screen and click the Set Printer Properties link on the Tasks list.

The following sections discuss the standard options in the Properties dialog box for a printer. Depending on the type of printer you're using and the printer driver you installed for it, you may see other pages than these. For example, for a color printer you'll see a Color Management page, on which you can associate color profiles with the printer so that you get approximately the colors you want. For an inkjet printer, you may see a Utilities page or a Maintenance page that offers options such as Nozzle Check and Head Cleaning.

General Page Options

The General page of the Properties dialog box (shown in Figure 13.8) for a printer contains the following options:

Printer Name text box This text box contains the name you entered for the printer during setup or a default name that Windows provided on the basis of the printer driver used. You can change the name by typing in the text box.

Location text box In this text box, you can enter any location information about the printer. This information is more useful when you're sharing a printer on the network than when the printer is used only by your computer.

Comment text box In this text box, you can enter further information about the printer. This information too is primarily useful when you're sharing the printer on the network, but you might also use it to note that the printer is loaded with a special type of paper.

Features list box This list box provides information about the printer's capabilities, such as whether it can print in color, print double-sided, staple, and so on.

Printing Preferences button Click this button to make Windows display the Printing Preferences dialog box, on whose pages you can choose options for layout, paper selection, and print quality. Different settings are available for different printers.

Print Test Page button Click this button to print a test page to the printer to make sure it's handling text and graphics correctly.

FIGURE 13.8

The General page of the Properties dialog box for a printer

FIGURE 13.8

The General page of the Properties dialog box for a printer

Sharing Page Options

The Sharing page of the Properties dialog box for a printer contains options for sharing the printer on the network. "Sharing a Printer" in Chapter 33 discusses how to use these options.

Ports Page Options

The Ports page of the Properties dialog box for a printer (shown in Figure 13.9) contains options for creating, deleting, and configuring ports.

FIGURE 13.9

The Ports page of the Properties dialog box for a printer

CREATING A PRINTER PORT

Windows automatically provides you with three printer ports (LPT1 through LPT3) and four serial ports (COM1 through COM4), so normally you'll need to add a port only if your printer or other output device requires a specialized port setup or if you need to use a TCP/IP port.

To create a new port, install the device and then follow these steps:

1. Click the Add Port button. Windows displays the Printer Ports dialog box (shown in Figure 13.10).

FIGURE 13.10

Use the Printer Ports dialog box to create a new local port or TCP/IP port.

2. To create a new local port, select the Local Port item in the Available Port Types list box, then click the New Port Type button. Windows displays the Installing Print Monitor dialog box, which you use to select the printer initialization file containing the port monitor installation information. Windows then installs the port.

3. To create a new standard TCP/IP port for a network printer, select the Standard TCP/IP Port item in the Available Port Types list box, then click the New Port button. Windows starts the Add Standard TCP/IP Printer Port Wizard, which walks you through the process of adding a TCP/IP port and then returns you to the Printer Ports dialog box.

4. Click the Close button. Windows closes the Printer Ports dialog box, returning you to the Ports page of the Properties dialog box for the printer.

DELETING A PRINTER PORT

Windows doesn't let you delete any of the system ports that come built in, but you can delete any custom ports that you create.

To delete a port, select it in the Print to the Following Ports list box and click the Delete Port button. Windows displays the Delete Port dialog box (shown in Figure 13.11). Click the Yes button.

FIGURE 13.11

Windows confirms any port deletions you attempt.

CONFIGURING A PRINTER PORT

Windows offers only one configuration setting for a parallel port: the number of seconds allowed to elapse before Windows decides the printer has taken a hike. To set this timeout, follow these steps:

1. Select the port in the Print to the Following Ports list.

2. Click the Configure Port button. Windows displays the Configure LPT Port dialog box (shown in Figure 13.12).

FIGURE 13.12

You can adjust the timeout interval for a parallel port in the Configure LPT Port dialog box.

3. In the Transmission Retry text box, enter the number of seconds.

4. Click the OK button. Windows closes the Configure LPT Port dialog box.

NOTE   For TCP/IP port monitors, Windows offers further configuration options.

USING BIDIRECTIONAL SUPPORT

If the Enable Bidirectional Support check box is available, you can select it to allow the printer to send status information. For example, the printer can notify you that it's running out of ink or paper.

USING PRINTER POOLING

If you have two or more identical printers, you can *pool* them to create a single logical printer capable of twice the throughput. Set up the printers as usual, then select the Enable Printer Pooling check box for each printer. In the Print to the Following Ports list box, select the appropriate ports. You can then print to the printer pool, and Windows will use the first printer that's available.

Advanced Page Options

The Advanced page of the Properties dialog box (shown in Figure 13.13) for a printer contains a slew of options for everything from setting availability times for printers to adding separator pages between print jobs.

SETTING AVAILABILITY OPTIONS

By default, Windows sets the printer to be always available, selecting the Always Available option button. This setting is useful for many home or office situations, but you may want to limit availability in some situations. For example, you might want to prevent people from printing at night if that might disturb the household.

To limit availability, select the Available From option button and use the two time text boxes to specify the range of time the printer should be available.

FIGURE 13.13

The Advanced page of the Properties dialog box for a printer

SETTING THE PRIORITY

To set the priority for the printer, adjust the setting in the Priority text box. You can set priorities from 1 (the lowest priority) to 99 (the highest priority). Each job printed by this printer entry gets the same priority, so there's no point in setting priorities unless you're using multiple printer entries.

CHANGING THE DRIVER

You can change the printer driver to another currently installed printer driver by using the Driver drop-down list. To install a new printer driver, click the New Driver button. Windows starts the Add Printer Driver Wizard, which walks you through the process of installing the driver.

CHOOSING SPOOLING OPTIONS

As you'll remember from "How Does a Print Job Get Printed?" earlier in this chapter, the print driver saves information to the hard disk and from there sends it along to the printer. This process, spooling, lets you continue your work without having to wait while the program you're working in forces every byte of the print job down the cable to the printer.

By default, Windows selects the Spool Print Documents so Program Finishes Printing Faster option button and its suboption, the Start Printing Immediately option button. If starting printing immediately seems to be causing problems, you can try selecting the Start Printing after Last Page Is Spooled option button to give the printer a chance to get its virtual paws on all the information it needs. If this doesn't help, you can cut out spooling by selecting the Print Directly to the Printer option button—but be warned that printing this way is very slow.

CHOOSING OTHER OPTIONS

The next four options defy easy grouping:

Hold Mismatched Documents check box Select this check box (which is cleared by default) if you want Windows to make sure the spooled document matches the printer setup before sending the document to the printer. If the document doesn't match the printer setup, Windows holds the document in the print queue.

Print Spooled Documents First check box   Select this check box (which is cleared by default) if you want spooled documents to print before partially spooled documents that carry a higher priority. This setting improves printer efficiency but is relevant only if you use printer priorities.

Keep Printed Documents check box   Select this check box (which is cleared by default) if you want to keep the spooled files on disk so that you can resend them to the printer from the print queue if necessary. Use this option only if you're having difficulty printing documents correctly—for example, if you're reconfiguring your printer and don't want to waste time and effort by resending the print job from the program. Obviously enough, the spooled files consume disk space.

Enable Advanced Printing Features check box   Clear this check box (which is selected by default) if you want to disable advanced printing features (such as booklet printing) in order to troubleshoot printing problems.

SETTING PRINTING DEFAULTS

To set default properties for the printer, click the Printing Defaults button and choose options in the resulting Printing Defaults dialog box.

CHANGING THE PRINT PROCESSOR

To use a different print processor or a different data type, click the Print Processor button and choose settings in the resulting Print Processor dialog box. Don't mess with this setting unless you're sure what you're doing.

USING SEPARATOR PAGES

To make Windows print a *separator page* between print jobs, click the Separator Page button. Windows displays the Separator Page dialog box (shown in Figure 13.14). Use the Browse button and the resulting Separator Page dialog box (a common Open dialog box) to locate the separator page file, and then click the OK button. Windows closes the Separator Page dialog box.

FIGURE 13.14

In the Separator Page dialog box, specify the separator page file to use.

NOTE   *Windows includes several separator page files, which have the SEP extension. You can also create custom separator files of your own by using a text editor such as Notepad.*

Device Settings Page Options

The Device Settings page of the Properties dialog box (of which Figure 13.15 shows an example) contains settings specific to your printer. For example, for many printers you can change the paper assigned to the paper trays or choose options for manual feed.

FIGURE 13.15

The Device Settings page of the Properties dialog box for a printer

Removing a Printer

To remove a printer, select it on the Printers and Faxes screen in Control Panel and click the Delete This Printer link in the Tasks list. Windows displays a Printers dialog box asking if you're sure (shown in Figure 13.16).

FIGURE 13.16

Windows double-checks to make sure you want to remove the printer.

Click the Yes button. Windows closes the Printers dialog box and removes the printer.

Printing a Document

The conventional way of printing a document is by issuing a Print command from the program that created it or from a program designed to handle its file type, choosing any relevant options (which pages to print, or the resolution to use) in the Print dialog box, and then clicking the Print button or OK button. But Windows also lets you print directly to the printer from Explorer if you so choose.

You can print a document from Explorer by dragging it and dropping it on the printer (or a shortcut to the printer). But usually you won't have the printer (or a shortcut to it) handy enough for this technique to be useful—though of course you can create shortcuts to a printer wherever you need them, such as on the Desktop.

Many programs support printing directly from Explorer and so include a Print command on the context menu for the document. To print a document, right-click it and choose Print from the context menu.

Managing Your Print Jobs

Once you've sent a document to the printer, you can just wait for Windows to print it: If you're the only person using this printer, and if there's no problem, it should print more or less right away. But if you're printing many documents, or if you're sharing one or more printers with people who are printing many documents, you may find yourself needing to manage print jobs. This section discusses how to do so.

Pausing and Resuming Printing

To pause printing of all documents on the printer, right-click the printer on the Printers and Faxes screen in Control Panel and choose Pause Printing from the context menu. Alternatively, select the printer and click the Pause Printing link in the Tasks list.

To resume printing, right-click the printer and choose Resume Printing from the context menu. Alternatively, select the printer and click the Resume Printing link in the Tasks list.

Canceling Printing of All Documents on the Printer

To cancel printing of all documents on the printer, right-click it on the Printers and Faxes screen and choose Cancel All Documents from the context menu. Windows displays a confirmation dialog box. Select the Yes button.

Managing Print Jobs by Using the Print Queue

Pausing or canceling all print jobs in the queue is quick and effective. But often you'll want to pause or cancel only some of the print jobs. Other times, you'll want to rearrange the order of the print jobs so that important ones print first.

To manage print jobs, open the print queue by using one of the following methods:

♦ If the notification area is displaying a printer icon, double-click it.

♦ Double-click the printer on the Printers and Faxes screen in Control Panel, or select the printer and click the See What's Printing link in the Tasks list.

Figure 13.17 shows an example of the print queue for a printer.

FIGURE 13.17

Use the print queue to see what's printing, to cancel a print job, or to manage print jobs.

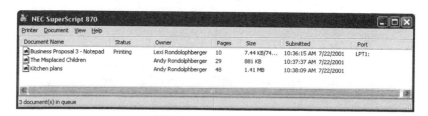

From the print queue, you can take the following actions:

Cancel a print job Right-click the job in the print queue and choose Cancel from the context menu. Alternatively, choose Document ➤ Cancel.

Pause a print job Right-click the job in the print queue and choose Pause from the context menu. Alternatively, choose Document ➤ Pause.

Resume a paused print job Right-click the paused job in the print queue and choose Resume from the context menu. Alternatively, choose Document ➤ Resume.

Restart a paused or failed print job Right-click the paused or failed job in the print queue and choose Restart from the context menu. Alternatively, choose Document ➤ Restart.

Change priorities or time restrictions for a print job Right-click the job and choose Properties from the context menu. Windows displays the Document Properties dialog box for the print job. On the General page (shown in Figure 13.18), drag the Priority slider to set the priority for the job, or use the controls in the Schedule text box to set or remove time scheduling. Click the OK button. Windows closes the Document Properties dialog box.

FIGURE 13.18

On the General page of the Document Properties dialog box for a print job, you can change the priority and schedule for the print job.

Printing Offline

If you're working offline, or if you want to queue up a number of print jobs and let them all rip at once, put the printer offline. To do so, right-click the printer on the Printers and Faxes screen and choose Use Printer Offline from the context menu. You can then print to the printer as if your computer were connected to it, but instead of sending the data to the printer, Windows holds it in the print queue and saves it to disk.

When you've reconnected to the printer (or when you want to print, if you didn't disconnect), right-click the printer on the Printers and Faxes screen and choose Use Printer Online. Windows starts sending the print jobs to the printer.

Creating Multiple Entries for the Same Printer

If you want to use the same printer regularly in different ways, you can create two or more entries for it on the Printers and Faxes screen and set different properties for each. For example, you might set one printer entry to have a higher priority than the other, and then use that printer entry yourself while assigning the lower-priority printer entry to other users.

To create a new entry for the printer, install it again using the technique described earlier in this chapter. When you install the printer again like this, the Add Printer Wizard displays the Use Existing Driver page (shown in Figure 13.19). Given that the driver is the same, leave the Keep Existing Driver option button selected and click the Next button.

FIGURE 13.19

On the Use Existing Driver page of the Add Printer Wizard, specify whether to keep the existing driver for the printer you're reinstalling or replace it.

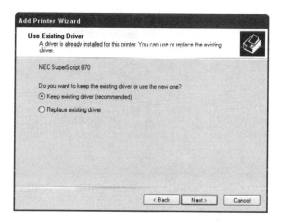

On the Name Your Printer page, assign the printer a name that reflects the role you plan for it. For example, if you create a new entry for a printer so that you can use it to print to a file, include that information in the printer's name (and perhaps add it to the printer's Location and Comment fields as well).

After installing the printer, set properties for it to play the role you intend.

Printing to a File

Sometimes you may want to print a document to a file that you can send to someone else for printing or (less commonly) that you can use in another program. For example, if you need to have a document printed on a high-resolution device in your local print shop, you can print the document to a file, put the file on a portable medium, and take it along to the print shop. That way, the print shop doesn't need to have a copy of the program that created the document, the way it would need one if you just copied the document onto a removable disk or recordable CD and took that along to the print shop instead.

You can print to a file in either of two ways: by selecting the Print to File check box in the Print dialog box from a program, or by configuring the printer to always print to a file. The former technique is useful for printing to a file occasionally. The latter technique is useful for always printing to a file with a particular printer entry.

Printing to a File from the Print Dialog Box

To print to a file from the Print dialog box, follow these steps:

1. Issue a regular Print command as usual. (For example, choose File ➤ Print or press Ctrl+P.) Windows displays the Print dialog box.

2. Select the Print to File check box.

3. Choose any other appropriate printing options as usual for the program.

4. Click the OK button or the Print button, depending on the program. Windows displays the Print to File dialog box (shown in Figure 13.20).

FIGURE 13.20

In the Print to File dialog box, enter the filename (and, if necessary, the path) for the print file.

5. Enter the filename for the print file. If you want to specify the folder in which the print file is saved, enter the path to the folder before the filename. Otherwise, Windows saves the print file in the program's current folder.

6. Click the OK button. Windows closes the Print to File dialog box and the Print dialog box and prints the document to the file. Windows gives the file the PRN extension.

Setting a Printer to Always Print to a File

You can also set up a printer so that it prints to a file every time and doesn't let the user print to a physical printer. This capability is useful when you always need to create print files on a particular printer and don't want to risk actually printing a document by forgetting to select the Print to File check box in the Print dialog box, or if the printer in question is never available from your computer.

To make a printer always print to a file, select the FILE port in the Print to the Following Ports list box on the Ports page of the Properties dialog box for the printer. Windows clears any other port selected for the printer (unless you've selected the Enable Printer Pooling check box). When you click the OK button and Windows closes the Properties dialog box, Windows displays a disk on the printer icon to indicate that the printer is set up for printing to a file (shown in Figure 13.21).

FIGURE 13.21

A disk on the printer icon means that the printer is set up for printing to a file.

NEC SuperScript - FILE
0
Ready

Working with Fonts

Windows comes with a number of fonts that you can use to enhance your Windows display and your documents. You can add extra fonts as you need them, either by installing software that includes fonts (such as Corel WordPerfect Office or Microsoft Office) or by installing fonts directly.

A *font* is the name given to a typeface. A *typeface* is a set of characters. Normally, the characters in a typeface have similar characteristics, so that they look as though they belong together, but this isn't an absolute requirement.

Three Categories of Fonts

Windows supports three different categories of fonts:

Outline fonts   *Outline fonts* are the newest types of fonts. Windows renders outline fonts by using line and curve commands, which means that it can scale them to any size without distorting them and can rotate them. Windows supports three different types of outline fonts: TrueType fonts (which Windows has used for many years), OpenType fonts (a more recent extension of True-Type), and Type 1 fonts (which are created by Adobe Systems for use with PostScript printers and devices). Outline fonts use the TTF extension.

Vector fonts   *Vector fonts* are an older type of font that are included in Windows XP for backward compatibility. Vector fonts are rendered from a mathematical model and are mostly used with plotters. Windows includes three vector fonts: Modern, Roman, and Script. Vector fonts use the FON extension.

Raster fonts   *Raster fonts* are another older technology that Windows XP includes for backward compatibility. In a raster font, each character consists of a bitmap image that's displayed on the screen or printed on paper. Windows includes five raster fonts: Courier, MS Sans Serif, MS Serif, Small, and Symbol. Like vector fonts, raster fonts use the FON extension.

Displaying the Fonts Window

To work with fonts, display the Fonts window by taking the following steps:

1. Choose Start ➤ Control Panel. Windows displays Control Panel.

2. Click the Appearance and Themes link. Windows displays the Appearance and Themes screen.

3. In the See Also list, click the Fonts link. Windows displays the Fonts window (shown in Figure 13.22).

Viewing the List of Fonts

By default, Windows displays the Fonts window in Large Icons view. You can switch the window to List view by choosing View ➤ List or clicking the List button on the toolbar, or to Details view by choosing View ➤ Details or clicking the Details button on the toolbar.

The Fonts window also offers a List Fonts by Similarity view, which you can invoke by choosing View ➤ List Fonts by Similarity or clicking the Similarity button on the toolbar. Figure 13.23 shows an example of List Fonts by Similarity view. In the List Fonts by Similarity To drop-down list, select the font you're interested in. The Fonts window then lists the other fonts installed on the computer in descending order of similarity to that font, using terms such as Very Similar, Fairly Similar, and Not Similar. (You can click the Similarity To column heading to display the list in ascending order of similarity.)

FIGURE 13.22

Use the Fonts window to add, remove, and view fonts.

FIGURE 13.23

Use the Fonts window's List Fonts by Similarity view to see which fonts are similar to a specified font.

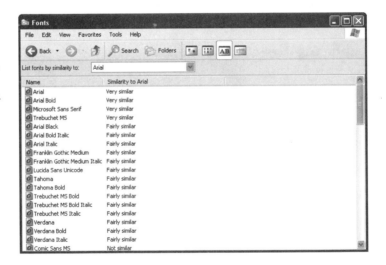

List Fonts by Similarity view is useful for getting an idea of which font is likely to complement another font. To simplify a long list of fonts, you can choose View ➤ Hide Variations. This command tells Windows to hide bold and italic variations on a font. So instead of seeing Times New Roman, Times New Roman Bold, Times New Roman Bold Italic, and Times New Roman Italic, you see only Times New Roman. This option makes it easier to get an overview of the different fonts you have available.

To display the full list of fonts once more, choose View ➤ Hide Variations again.

EXPERT KNOWLEDGE: AVOIDING RASTER FONTS AND VECTOR FONTS

If you want to make sure you don't use raster fonts and vector fonts in your documents, you can tell Windows to stop showing them to you. Take the following steps:

1. In the Fonts window, choose Tools ➤ Folder Options. Windows displays the Folder Options dialog box.

2. Click the TrueType Fonts tab. Windows displays the TrueType Fonts page.

3. Select the Show Only TrueType Fonts in the Programs on My Computer check box.

4. Click the OK button. Windows displays the System Settings Change dialog box, telling you that you must restart your computer in order to implement the system change.

5. Click the Yes button if you want Windows to restart your computer for you. If not, click the No button to dismiss the System Settings Change dialog box, then restart the computer at your convenience.

Viewing and Printing a Font

To get an idea of what a font looks like, double-click its entry in the Fonts window. Windows displays the font in Font Viewer, which shows information on the font type, its file size, and copyright information, together with various sizes of the canonical sentence involving the quick brown fox and the lazy dog and the full set of numbers. Figure 13.24 shows an example of Font Viewer.

FIGURE 13.24

Font Viewer displays information about the font and examples of it.

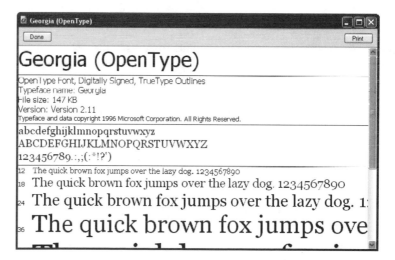

To print the information displayed, click the Print button. Windows displays the Print dialog box. Choose the printer and any options, then click the Print button. Windows closes the Print dialog box and prints the information.

To close Font Viewer, click the Done button.

Installing a Font

To install a font, take the following steps from the Fonts window:

1. Choose File ➤ Install New Font. Windows displays the Add Fonts dialog box (shown in Figure 13.25 with a font selected for installation).

FIGURE 13.25

Use the Add Fonts dialog box to add further fonts to your computer.

2. Use the Drives drop-down list and the Folders list box to navigate to the drive and folder that contain the font you want to install. (If necessary, click the Network button and use the Map Network Drive dialog box to map a network drive.)

3. In the List of Fonts list box, select the font or fonts you want to install.

    ◆ Click the Select All button to select all the fonts in the List of Fonts list box.

4. Make sure that the Copy Fonts to Fonts Folder check box at the bottom of the Add Fonts dialog box is selected. This option causes Windows to copy the fonts you're installing to the Fonts folder, where you can manage them centrally. This is usually the best way to install fonts, especially when you're installing them from a removable medium (such as a CD). But if the fonts you're installing are already located on your hard drive, and you don't want to make copies of them in the Fonts folder, you can clear this check box. Windows then creates a pointer to the folder that contains the font.

5. Click the OK button. Windows installs the font or fonts and closes the Add Fonts dialog box, returning you to the Fonts window.

TIP   You can buy commercial font packages from most major software outlets and from many smaller vendors. But first, go to Microsoft's Web site (www.microsoft.com) and see if Microsoft is offering any fonts for free download. Then check out the free fonts that are available from a number of sites online: You may find a wide enough selection that you don't need to buy any fonts.

Deleting a Font

To delete a font, right-click it in the Fonts window and choose Delete from the context menu. (Alternatively, select the font and press the Delete key or choose File ➤ Delete.) Windows displays the Windows Fonts Folder dialog box (shown in Figure 13.26) to confirm the deletion.

FIGURE 13.26

Windows displays the Windows Fonts Folder dialog box to confirm that you want to delete a font.

Click the Yes button. Windows closes the Windows Fonts Folder dialog box and deletes the font.

EXPERT KNOWLEDGE: UNLOADING FONTS INSTEAD OF DELETING THEM

If you load your Fonts folder to the gunwales with hundreds or thousands of fonts, don't be surprised if Windows handles like a supertanker rather than a speedboat. Loading a huge number of fonts increases the amount of memory Windows needs and generally slows down the speed with which it can handle other tasks.

So it's a good idea not to load too many fonts at a time. But you don't have to delete fonts that you temporarily don't want to load. Instead, you can move them to another folder and store them there until you need them again. At that point, move the fonts back to the Fonts folder, and you can use them again in your programs.

If you work with many fonts, consider grouping them into a number of different folders so that you can quickly load the set of fonts you need for a particular type of document.

Up Next

This chapter has discussed how to install, configure, and manage printers and fonts.

The next chapter discusses how to manage hardware and power, including how to install, update, and roll back device drivers.

Chapter 14

Managing Hardware, Drivers, and Power

THIS CHAPTER DISCUSSES HOW to install hardware on your computer and how to install, update, and roll back device drivers, the software that makes hardware function. It also covers how to configure power management on your computer and how to install an uninterruptible power supply.

Windows XP greatly simplifies the software end of the process of adding hardware. If the hardware is hot pluggable, Windows locates and loads the correct driver automatically. If the hardware is conventional, you use the Found New Hardware Wizard (if Windows finds the hardware) or the Add Hardware Wizard (if you have to tell Windows that the hardware is there) to install the software for the device. The chapter shows you how to use these Wizards and notes special considerations for installing common types of hardware.

NOTE   *Chapter 13 discusses how to install, configure, and manage printers. Chapter 28 discusses how to install, configure, and use scanners and digital cameras. Chapter 30 discusses how to install, configure, and use games controllers.*

This chapter covers the following topics:

◆ What hardware can you use with Windows XP?

◆ Using hot-pluggable devices

◆ Using the Found New Hardware Wizard and Add Hardware Wizard

◆ Working with hardware devices

◆ Disabling and uninstalling a device

◆ Adding specific hardware items

◆ Configuring power management and installing a UPS

What Hardware Can You Use with Windows XP?

One of Microsoft's goals in designing Windows XP was to make it capable of picking up the hardware compatibility mantle of Windows 98 and Windows Me, each of which supported an impressive range of hardware both (relatively) ancient and modern. As a result, Windows XP supports a very full range of hardware right out of the box, and it includes compatibility-tested drivers for many products. A *driver* is a piece of software that enables it and Windows to communicate with each other.

By using the Windows Update feature to keep your copy of Windows up to date, and by downloading new drivers from hardware manufacturers' Web sites as necessary, you can also add the latest hardware to Windows XP. The devices you're more likely to have problems with are legacy devices more than a few years old, particularly those from smaller companies or from companies that have gone out of business.

To check whether a hardware item is compatible with Windows XP, open Help and Support Center (Start ➢ Help and Support), click the Compatible Hardware and Software link on the Home page, and use the search options on the Compatible Hardware and Software page.

Using Hot-Pluggable Devices

Hardware devices that use USB, FireWire, and PC Card connections are *hot pluggable*—you can plug in and unplug the device while Windows is running without any adverse effects. Windows automatically loads and unloads drivers for hot-pluggable devices as needed.

NOTE   Limited users and Guest users can install hot-pluggable devices. In most cases, only Computer Administrator users can install devices that are not hot pluggable.

Installing a Hot-Pluggable Device

When you plug in a hot-pluggable device for the first time, Windows displays a pop-up from the notification area to let you know that it has noticed the device. Figure 14.1 shows an example.

FIGURE 14.1

Windows displays a notification-area pop-up message when it notices you've plugged in a hot-pluggable device.

Windows then automatically looks for a driver to let Windows and the device communicate with each other. It first checks in its capacious driver cache, which contains a wide variety of preinstalled drivers. If it draws a blank there, and if your computer is connected to the Internet, it checks the Windows Update site for a driver for the device; if it finds a driver, it downloads it and installs it. If Windows is able to find a suitable driver in either the driver cache or Windows Update, it unpacks and installs the driver, displaying a pop-up identifying the device as it does so. Figure 14.2 shows an example of such a pop-up.

FIGURE 14.2

If Windows can find a driver for the hot-pluggable device, it loads it.

FIGURE 14.3

Windows lets you know when the device is ready to use.

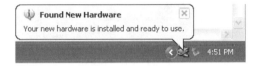

When the driver is installed and working, Windows displays a pop-up telling you that the hardware is ready to use. Figure 14.3 shows an example of such a pop-up.

If Windows can't find a driver for the device, it starts the Found New Hardware Wizard, so that you can supply the driver for the device manually. See "Using the Found New Hardware Wizard" later in this chapter for a walkthrough of using the Found New Hardware Wizard.

Removing a Hot-Pluggable Device

Removing a USB device or FireWire device is as simple as unplugging it. Windows notices that you've removed the device and unloads its driver.

To remove a PC Card device, you're supposed to use the Safely Remove Hardware feature. See "Using PC Cards" in Chapter 15 for coverage of this feature. But often you can simply unplug the PC Card without causing any problems.

Plugging a Hot-Pluggable Device In Again

When you plug a hot-pluggable device in again, Windows notices it and loads the driver without displaying any pop-up.

Using the Found New Hardware Wizard

For devices that aren't hot pluggable, or for hot-pluggable devices for which Windows can't find a suitable driver, you use Windows' two hardware Wizards, the Found New Hardware Wizard and the Add Hardware Wizard.

When Windows discovers some hardware new to it (or that Windows thinks it doesn't know about), it starts the Found New Hardware Wizard. Figure 14.4 shows the first page of the Found New Hardware Wizard.

As you can see in the figure, the Wizard lists the type of hardware it has found—in this case, Multimedia Controller. If the Wizard can't identify the type of hardware, it displays *Unknown device*.

FIGURE 14.4

Windows displays the first page of the Found New Hardware Wizard when it discovers new hardware. Choose whether to install the software for the hardware automatically or specify the details of the software you want to install.

The What Do You Want the Wizard to Do? list gives you two options:

Install the Software Automatically option button   Select this option button (which is usually selected by default) if you want the Wizard to try to install the software needed for the hardware. This is usually a good option: The Wizard often manages to set up the hardware, and if it doesn't, you can easily return to this stage and try the second option. Click the Next button. The Wizard searches for the software and installs it automatically.

Install from a List or Specific Location option button   Select this option button if you want to specify a particular driver for the hardware. Then follow the procedure described in the next section.

If the Found New Hardware Wizard *doesn't* find the software it needs, it displays the Cannot Install This Hardware page (shown in Figure 14.5).

FIGURE 14.5

The Found New Hardware Wizard displays the Cannot Install This Hardware page if it can't find the software needed for the device. Click the Back button if you want to return to the start of the Wizard so that you can try the procedure manually.

At this point, you have three choices:

◆ If you want to give up on installing the software for this hardware completely (or at least for the foreseeable future), make sure the Don't Prompt Me Again to Install This Software check box is selected. Then click the Finish button. The Wizard closes itself and makes a note not to find this piece of hardware again.

◆ If you want to give up on installing the software for the time being, clear the Don't Prompt Me Again to Install This Software check box. Then click the Finish button. Each time you restart Windows (or run the Add Hardware Wizard), the Found New Hardware Wizard will offer to install the hardware. These offers get old fast, but you may sometimes want to leave the installation of hardware for a day or two while you dig out the driver disk, download a new driver manually, or run Windows Update to see if it can find a driver.

◆ To try to identify the necessary software yourself, click the Back button to return to the start of the Wizard. Then follow the steps below.

Installing a Driver from a Specific Location

To install a driver from a specific location, take the following steps:

1. On the first page of the Found New Hardware Wizard, select the Install from a List or Specific Location option button.

2. Click the Next button. The Found New Hardware Wizard displays the Please Choose Your Search and Installation Options page (shown in Figure 14.6).

FIGURE 14.6

On the Please Choose Your Search and Installation Options page of the Found New Hardware Wizard, choose whether to search for a driver or specify a particular one.

3. Choose whether to let the Wizard search for a driver or to specify a specific driver:

◆ To let the Wizard search, leave the Search for the Best Driver in These Locations option button selected. Then select the Search Removable Media (Floppy, CD-ROM) check box if you want the Wizard to search your floppy and CD-ROM drives. (Insert a floppy or CD at this point if appropriate.) Alternatively, or additionally, select the Include This

Location in the Search check box and use the text box, drop-down list, or Browse button to specify the location to search.

◆ To specify a driver yourself, select the Don't Search. I Will Choose the Driver to Install option button.

4. Click the Next button.

◆ If you chose to search for a driver, the Wizard searches for one, installs it (if it finds one), and displays the Completing the Found New Hardware Wizard page.

◆ If you chose to specify a driver, the Wizard displays the Hardware Type page (shown in Figure 14.7).

FIGURE 14.7

On the Hardware Type page of the Found New Hardware Wizard, choose the type of hardware you're installing.

5. In the Common Hardware Types list box, select the type of hardware you're installing. The list is extensive, but if the device doesn't fit any of the descriptions, select the Show All Devices item.

TIP   If you're installing a driver from a floppy or a CD, it's not crucial that you get the hardware type right. The function of this page is to display the appropriate list of manufacturers and devices on the Select the Device Driver You Want to Install for This Hardware page of the Wizard.

6. Click the Next button. The Found New Hardware Wizard displays the Select the Device Driver You Want to Install for This Hardware page. Figure 14.8 shows this page with all devices shown.

7. If Windows has a driver for the device, you can select it by selecting the manufacturer in the Manufacturer list box and the device in the Model list box. But usually the Found New Hardware Wizard will have identified the driver if Windows has it already, so you'll be visiting this page of the Wizard only if you need to install a driver that Windows *doesn't* have. Click the Have Disk button. Windows displays the Install from Disk dialog box (shown in Figure 14.9).

FIGURE 14.8

On the Select the Device Driver You Want to Install for This Hardware page, select the manufacturer and device, or use the Have Disk button to identify the driver by its file.

FIGURE 14.9

Use the Install from Disk dialog box to provide a driver of your own.

8. If you have the driver on a floppy or a CD, insert it in the appropriate drive and select the drive in the Copy Manufacturer's Files From drop-down list. If you have the driver on a local drive or network drive, click the Browse button, use the resulting Locate File dialog box (a common Open dialog box) to locate the driver file, and click the Open button to enter its name and path in the Copy Manufacturer's Files From text box.

9. Click the OK button. The Wizard displays the Select the Device Driver You Want to Install for This Hardware page (shown in Figure 14.10) with the name of the hardware model or models identified by the driver.

10. Select the driver and click the Next button. If Windows doesn't think the driver is correct for the device, it displays the Update Driver Warning dialog box (shown in Figure 14.11), warning you that the hardware may not work and that your computer might become unstable or stop working. Click the Yes button if you're sure you want to install this driver. Otherwise, click the No button and select another driver.

NOTE *If the Wizard can't find hardware information in the location you specified, it displays the Select Device message box telling you that the location you specified doesn't contain information about your hardware. The Wizard then displays the Install from Disk dialog box again so that you can specify a different location for the file. If you get to this stage, you're probably stuck. You can click the Cancel button to close the Install from Disk dialog box and return to the Select the Device Driver You Want to Install for This Hardware page so that you can select a built-in driver, but that's about it. Click the Cancel button to cancel the Wizard.*

FIGURE 14.10

When you specify the driver to use, the Wizard displays the Select the Device Driver You Want to Install for This Hardware page.

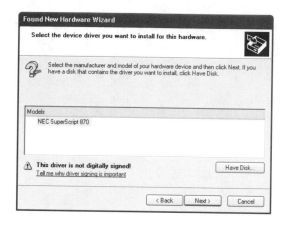

FIGURE 14.11

The Update Driver Warning dialog box warns you if you've chosen a driver that appears not to match your device.

11. The Wizard checks to make sure that the driver you're installing has passed the Windows Logo testing to verify its compatibility with Windows XP. (See the next Note for an explanation of Windows Logo testing.) If the driver has passed Windows Logo testing, all is well; if it hasn't passed, the Wizard displays the Hardware Installation dialog box (shown in Figure 14.12) warning you of the problem and strongly discouraging you from installing the driver. If you're sure the driver is okay, click the Continue Anyway button. If you have any doubts about the driver, click the STOP Installation button.

NOTE *Windows Logo testing isn't testing a logo, as its name implies, but rather a Windows compatibility test. When a product passes the test, the manufacturer is allowed to display the Designed for Microsoft Windows logos on the product. Drivers that pass Windows Logo testing are digitally signed by Microsoft to verify their compatibility. The Wizard checks for the digital signature and raises Cain if it's not there.*

FIGURE 14.12

If the driver you're installing hasn't passed Windows Logo testing, the Wizard displays the Hardware Installation dialog box to warn you.

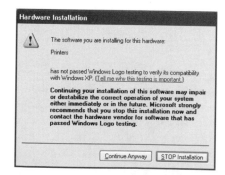

12. If Windows finds no problem with the driver, it installs it and displays the Completing the Found New Hardware Wizard page.

13. Click the Finish button. The Wizard closes itself, and the hardware is ready for use.

If the Found New Hardware Wizard is unable to install the device, it displays the Cannot Install This Hardware page telling you what the problem was. Figure 14.13 shows an example in which the driver file ("the third-party INF"—*inf* is short for *initialization file*) didn't contain digital signature information.

FIGURE 14.13

The Found New Hardware Wizard displays the Cannot Install This Hardware page if it runs into a problem installing the device.

NOTE *Help and Support Center contains a system for referring searches for drivers that don't come with Windows or with the hardware device. When you plug in a new hardware device, and Windows finds that it doesn't have a driver for it and you can't supply a driver, Windows invites you to send information about the hardware to Microsoft. Once you've sent the information, you can take a variety of actions depending on what information is available. For example, you might be able to view a list of compatible devices (if any), search for information on compatible devices or Knowledge Base articles about the hardware, or find a link to the vendor's Web site.*

Running the Add Hardware Wizard

If Windows doesn't find the new hardware you install, run the Add Hardware Wizard so that you can add the hardware manually. As you'll see, there's considerable overlap between the Add Hardware Wizard and the Found New Hardware Wizard, so don't be surprised if some of the steps in this list duplicate those in the previous section.

To run the Add Hardware Wizard, take the following steps:

1. Choose Start ➤ Control Panel. Windows displays Control Panel.

2. Click the Printers and Other Hardware link. Windows displays the Printers and Other Hardware screen.

3. Click the Add Hardware link in the See Also pane. Windows starts the Add Hardware Wizard, which displays the Welcome to the Add Hardware Wizard page.

4. Click the Next button. The Wizard searches for new hardware and displays the The Following Hardware Is Already Installed on Your Computer page (shown in Figure 14.14).

FIGURE 14.14

On the The Following Hardware Is Already Installed on Your Computer page of the Add Hardware Wizard, select the Add a New Hardware Device item.

NOTE   *If the Add Hardware Wizard doesn't find any hardware it didn't already know about, it displays the Is the Hardware Connected? page, which asks whether you've already connected the hardware to the computer. Select the Yes, I Have Already Connected the Hardware option button or the No, I Have Not Added the Hardware Yet option button as appropriate. If you select the Yes, I Have Already Connected the Hardware option button, the Wizard displays the The Following Hardware Is Already Installed on Your Computer screen. If you select the No, I Have Not Added the Hardware Yet option button, the Wizard displays the Cannot Continue the Add Hardware Wizard screen, which offers to turn off the computer for you so that you can connect the hardware and try the Add Hardware Wizard again.*

5. If the device you want to install is listed in the Installed Hardware list box, select it. If it's not, select the Add a New Hardware Device item in the list box—the last item in the list.

6. Click the Next button. The Wizard displays the The Wizard Can Help You Install Other Hardware page (shown in Figure 14.15), offering to search for the hardware.

FIGURE 14.15

The Add Hardware Wizard offers to search for the hardware, but usually you'll do better to select it manually.

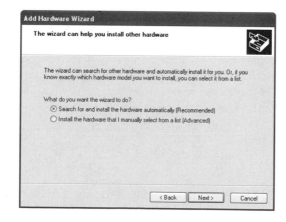

7. Select the Install the Hardware That I Manually Select from a List option button.

8. Click the Next button. The Wizard displays the From the List Below, Select the Type of Hardware You Are Installing page (shown in Figure 14.16).

FIGURE 14.16

On the From the List Below, Select the Type of Hardware You Are Installing page, select the category of hardware that you're installing.

9. In the Common Hardware Types list box, select the type of hardware you're installing. Again, if the device doesn't fit any of the descriptions, leave the Show All Devices item selected (as it is by default).

10. Click the Next button. If you chose the Show All Devices item, the Wizard displays the Select the Device Driver You Want to Install for This Hardware page (shown in Figure 14.17). If you chose a specific type of hardware, the Wizard leads you off on a byway of options appropriate to that type of hardware.

11. If Windows has a driver for the device, select it by selecting the manufacturer in the Manufacturer list box and the device in the Model list box. If you have a new driver, click the Have Disk button and use the resulting Install from Disk dialog box to specify the location of the driver.

FIGURE 14.17

On the Select the Device Driver You Want to Install for This Hardware page of the Add Hardware Wizard, select the device driver.

12. Click the Next button. The Wizard displays the The Wizard Is Ready to Install Your Hardware page, listing the hardware that's lined up for installation.

13. Click the Next button. The Wizard installs the hardware and displays the Completing the Add Hardware Wizard page (shown in Figure 14.18).

FIGURE 14.18

The Completing the Add Hardware Wizard page of the Add Hardware Wizard lists the hardware that the Wizard has successfully installed.

14. Click the Finish button. The Add Hardware Wizard closes itself. The hardware should be ready for use.

Working with Hardware Drivers

Without a functional driver, Windows can't use any piece of hardware. And using the wrong driver or a badly written driver can make Windows unstable or even make it crash.

Hardware manufacturers frequently release new versions of drivers for their hardware to improve performance, to banish bugs, or both. If you want to keep your hardware running to the best of its capacity, check the manufacturers' sites and the Windows Update site for updated drivers. In theory, Windows Update should be able to supply you with the latest drivers for most of your hardware. In practice, you can probably get the latest drivers more quickly by haunting the hardware manufacturers' Web sites and newsgroups.

To view, change, or uninstall the driver for a device, display the Driver page of the Properties dialog box for the device. The easiest way to display the Properties dialog box for the device is to go through Device Manager.

Opening Device Manager

To display the Device Manager window, take the following steps:

1. Press Winkey+Break or click the Start button, right-click the My Computer item, and choose Properties from the context menu. Windows displays the System Properties dialog box.

2. Click the Hardware tab. Windows displays the Hardware page.

3. Click the Device Manager button. Windows displays the Device Manager window (shown in Figure 14.19).

FIGURE 14.19

Use Device Manager to access hardware devices you want to configure.

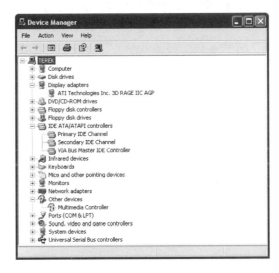

As you can see in the figure, Device Manager presents a categorized tree of the devices on the computer in its default view. Any device that isn't working or has a problem is marked with a question-mark icon, like the Multimedia Controller that appears in the figure. When all is well with a category of device, Device Manager presents the category collapsed. In the figure, the Display Adapters category and the IDE ATA/ATAPI Controllers category are expanded to show their entries.

You can change the view by displaying the View menu and choosing Devices by Type (the default view), Devices by Connection, Resources by Type, or Resources by Connection from the menu. You can display hidden devices by choosing View ➤ Show Hidden Devices.

If you leave Device Manager open while you plug in a hot-pluggable device, you may need to refresh the listing in Device Manager to make it list the device. To do so, choose Action ➤ Scan for Hardware Changes.

To check or set properties for a device, double-click its entry in Device Manager (or right-click the entry and choose Properties from the context menu). Windows displays the Properties dialog box for the device.

Checking the Details of a Driver

The Driver page of the Properties dialog box for a device shows some details of the driver: the provider of the driver (the company that supplied the driver to your computer), the date, the version, and the *digital signer*—the owner of the digital certificate applied to the driver. Figure 14.20 shows an example of the Driver page of the Properties dialog box for a graphics card driver.

To display further information, click the Driver Details button. Windows displays the Driver File Details dialog box, which displays further information: the filenames and paths of the driver files, the provider (the company that originally provided the driver), the file version, the copyright information, and the digital signer (again). Figure 14.21 shows an example of the Driver File Details dialog box.

FIGURE 14.20

The Driver page of the Properties dialog box shows some information about the driver.

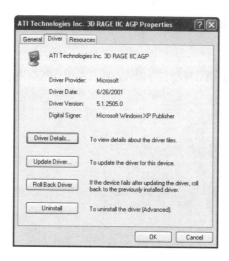

FIGURE 14.21

The Driver File Details dialog box contains further information about the driver, including the filenames and paths of the driver files.

Updating a Driver

To update a driver, you use the Hardware Update Wizard. You'll have no problems with the Hardware Update Wizard, because it's essentially another manifestation of the Found New Hardware Wizard and the Add Hardware Wizard that you met earlier in the chapter.

To run the Hardware Update Wizard, click the Update Driver button on the Driver page of the Properties dialog box for the device. See pages 92–95 of the *Essential Skills* section for a visual guide to using the Hardware Update Wizard to update a driver.

Rolling Back a Driver

If a new driver you've installed doesn't work, or doesn't improve things, revert to the previous driver by using the driver rollback feature. To use the rollback feature, click the Roll Back Driver button on the Driver page of the Properties dialog box for the device. See page 96 of the *Essential Skills* section for a visual guide to rolling back a driver.

Disabling a Device

If you want to stop using a device temporarily, you can disable it. For example, you might want to disable a device that you think is making Windows unstable.

To disable a device, right-click it in Device Manager and choose Disable from the context menu. Windows displays a confirmation message box such as that shown in Figure 14.22. Click the Yes button. Windows closes the message box and disables the device.

FIGURE 14.22

Windows displays a confirmation message box when you instruct it to disable a device.

Uninstalling a Device

If you want to stop using a device permanently and remove it from your computer, uninstall it first. To do so, right-click the device in Device Manager and choose Uninstall from the context menu. Windows displays the Confirm Device Removal dialog box, of which Figure 14.23 shows an example. Click the OK button. Windows closes the dialog box and uninstalls the device.

FIGURE 14.23

Windows displays the Confirm Device Removal dialog box for confirmation when you uninstall a device.

NOTE   *You can also uninstall a device by clicking the Uninstall button on the Driver page of the Properties dialog box for the device.*

Adding Specific Hardware Items

The following sections discuss considerations for adding particular hardware items that need configuration beyond the driver. Many hardware items do not.

The easiest place to start configuring most hardware items is Device Manager.

Adding a CD Drive

The Properties dialog box for a CD-ROM has two settings on its Properties page (shown in Figure 14.24):

CD Player Volume slider   Drag the slider to set the volume you want the CD player to deliver when playing audio CDs. This setting controls the output of the CD drive. You can control the output volume from your sound card by using Volume Control (discussed in Chapter 27).

Enable Digital CD Audio for This CD-ROM Device check box   Select this check box if you want to use digital output rather than analog output from the CD drive for audio CDs. Digital output typically gives you higher audio quality, especially when you're copying audio CDs to your hard drive. (Chapter 27 discusses how to copy audio CDs to your hard drive.) Most newer CD-ROM drives and just about all DVD drives support digital output, but some older CD-ROM drives don't. If digital output doesn't work for you, clear this check box to return to analog output.

FIGURE 14.24

On the Properties page of the Properties dialog box for a CD-ROM drive, you can set the CD's volume and specify whether to use digital CD audio.

Adding a DVD Drive

Because DVD drives can play CDs, it should come as no surprise that the Properties dialog box for a DVD drive contains the same Properties page as the Properties dialog box for a CD drive. (See the previous section for a discussion of the two controls this Properties page contains.)

The Properties dialog box for a DVD drive also contains a DVD Region page (shown in Figure 14.25), which displays the DVD encoding region currently set for the DVD player. To change the region, select the country you want in the list box and click the OK button.

FIGURE 14.25

The DVD Region page of the Properties dialog box for a DVD drive displays the current encoding region.

Adding a Removable Drive

The first time you plug in a removable drive or local drive and Windows finds pictures or audio files on it, Windows displays the Removable Disk dialog box or Local Disk dialog box to let you specify whether you want to set a default action to take with files of this type. Figure 14.26 shows an example of the Removable Disk dialog box for a CompactFlash card in a PC Card adapter. The CompactFlash card contains picture files, so the Removable Disk dialog box contains actions that Windows can take with picture files: Print the Pictures, View a Slideshow of the Images, Copy Pictures to a Folder on My Computer, Open Folder to View Files, or Take No Action.

FIGURE 14.26

In the Local Disk dialog box or Removable Disk dialog box (shown here), you can specify which action you want Windows to take for a particular content type when you add a local disk or removable disk.

Select the action you want to take. If you want Windows to take this action for every disk you add that contains this type of file, select the Always Do the Selected Action check box. Then click the OK button. Windows closes the Local Disk dialog box or Removable Disk dialog box and takes the action you specified.

EXPERT KNOWLEDGE: DVD ENCODING REGIONS

In case you've managed to avoid the question of DVD encoding regions: As far as DVDs are concerned, the world is divided into eight regions or *locales*. Region 1 is the U.S., Canada, and U.S. Territories. Region 2 is Europe, Japan, South Africa, and the Middle East. Region 3 is Southeast Asia, East Asia, and Hong Kong. Region 4 is Australia, New Zealand, the Pacific Islands, South America, Central America, Mexico, and the Caribbean. Region 5 is Eastern Europe, Mongolia, North Korea, the Indian subcontinent, and Africa. Region 6 is China. Region 7 is "reserved" (for off-world use, perhaps). And Region 8 is for international vessels such as airplanes and cruise ships.

DVD players are encoded to play only DVDs for their region. Almost all DVDs are encoded for the region in which they're intended to be sold. (There are also *all-region DVDs* that'll play in any region.) So to play a DVD, you need a player with a matching region code.

Most consumer-electronics DVD players are coded for one region only. Some players—typically more expensive ones—can play discs for two, more, or all regions. Other players can be *chipped*—modified—to play DVDs with different regional encoding or even to play any regional encoding. Chipping is legal but typically costs a proportion of the cost of a cheap DVD player.

PC DVD drives are a little more flexible. With most drives, you can switch region a certain number of times on a DVD drive before it goes into a locked state in which you can no longer change the region. The DVD Region page of the Properties dialog box for the DVD drive displays the number of times you can change the region again. Use them sparingly.

Why do DVDs have regional encoding anyway? In theory, it's to let the movie studios control the release of the movie in different countries. For example, U.S.–made movies are usually released in the U.S. several months before they're released in Europe, and DVDs and videos of the movie are often released in the U.S. while the movie is still running in Europe. Regional encoding prevents most of the Europeans from viewing the movie on DVD until it's released with Region 2 encoding.

In practice, regional encoding also enables the distributors to charge different prices for DVDs in different countries without being undercut by imported DVDs from the least expensive regions. For example, at this writing, DVDs in Region 2 are substantially more expensive than those in Region 1, and the European Union is investigating whether this constitutes price-fixing.

Adding a Modem

Windows automatically loads the driver for a USB modem, a PCI modem, or a PC Card modem if it can find the driver. It sometimes loads the driver for a serial modem too, but other times, it fails to notice that you've added it. If this happens, run the Add Hardware Wizard manually and specify the details of the modem.

SPECIFYING YOUR LOCATION

The first time you go to use a modem, Windows displays the Location Information dialog box (shown in Figure 14.27) demanding your location information unless you've given it already.

Specify the details: your country and region; your area code or city code; any carrier code you need to enter; any number you dial to access an outside line; and whether the phone system uses tone dialing (the norm for most modern exchanges) or pulse dialing. Then click the OK button. Windows closes the Location Information dialog box.

FIGURE 14.27

Sooner or later, Windows prompts you for information about your location. Supply it once, and you should be free from all future demands.

SPECIFYING PHONE AND MODEM OPTIONS

After you close the Location Information dialog box, Windows displays the Phone and Modem Options dialog box with the Dialing Rules page foremost. Figure 14.28 shows this page of the dialog box.

FIGURE 14.28

Edit your locations on the Dialing Rules page of the Phone and Modem Options dialog box.

Windows provides you with a default location named My Location with the area code you specified in the Location Information dialog box. Rename this location to something descriptive (for example, *Home* or the name of the city or town): Click the Edit button and enter the new name in the Location Name text box on the General page of the Edit Location dialog box that Windows displays.

Click the OK button. Windows closes the Edit Location dialog box. Click the OK button. Windows closes the Phone and Modem Options dialog box.

NOTE *For a laptop or other computer you take traveling, you'll probably want to create other locations as well. Chapter 15 discusses how to do this.*

Adding a Video Card

When you install a new video card, Windows may detect it on boot-up and display the Found New Hardware Wizard so that you can install the correct driver for it. Other times, you may have to change the video driver manually by using the Hardware Update Wizard.

After installing the driver for the new video card, you usually need to restart Windows. When you log back in, Windows displays the Display Properties dialog box so that you can test and apply the screen resolution and color quality you want. See "Choosing Video Settings" in Chapter 3 for a discussion of how to choose a suitable screen resolution and color depth. See pages 39–40 of the *Essential Skills* section for a visual guide to changing the screen resolution.

Adding a Monitor

Adding a monitor tends to be simplicity itself, involving only a couple of cables. But Windows identifies many monitors simply as Plug and Play Monitor, assigning them a generic driver. This driver works well enough for undemanding programs, but to get the best performance, use the Hardware Update Wizard to install the latest driver for your specific type of monitor.

If you're seeing corrupt images on your monitor, or if the mouse pointer doesn't respond properly to conventional stimuli, or if DirectX isn't working, you may need to change the graphics hardware acceleration on your computer or disable write combining. (*Write combining* is a method of shunting more information from the video card to the monitor at once. It can cause screen corruption by providing the monitor with more information than it can handle.) To do so, take the following steps:

1. Right-click open space on the Desktop and choose Properties from the context menu. Windows displays the Display Properties dialog box.

2. Click the Settings tab. Windows displays the Settings page.

3. Click the Advanced button. Windows displays the Monitor and Graphics Card Properties dialog box.

4. Click the Troubleshoot tab. Windows displays the Troubleshoot page (shown in Figure 14.29).

5. Move the Hardware Acceleration slider one notch at a time from Full (or wherever you find it) toward None until the problems disappear. At each setting, click the Apply button, and check your computer to see what effect the change has had.

6. Alternatively, or additionally, try clearing the Enable Write Combining check box to prevent screen corruption. Click the Apply button and see what effect the change has had.

7. When the screen seems to be behaving as it should, click the OK button. Windows closes the Monitor and Graphics Card Properties dialog box, returning you to the Display Properties dialog box.

8. Click the OK button. Windows closes the Display Properties dialog box.

FIGURE 14.29

If you see corrupt images on the screen, try reducing hardware acceleration or disabling write combining on the Troubleshoot page of the Monitor and Graphics Card Properties dialog box.

Setting Up and Using Multiple Monitors

Like Windows 98 Second Edition, Windows Me, and Windows 2000 Professional, Windows XP lets you attach multiple monitors to your computer to increase the amount of Desktop space available to you. This feature can make both work and play much easier—but it can also lead you to loading your desk with more monitors than it can comfortably provide a footing for.

This discussion of using multiple monitors concerns only desktop computers to which you can add one or more extra graphics cards. But Windows XP includes a feature called DualView that lets you use multiple monitors with portable computers and graphics cards with multiple outputs. Chapter 15 discusses DualView.

WARNING   *Setting up multiple monitors can be a tricky and frustrating business. With some combinations of motherboards and graphics cards, you need to install the graphics cards in the right sequence in order to get them to work. Others work fine immediately. Others never work. Before you try to implement multiple monitors, check the Hardware Compatibility List (HCL) at the Microsoft Web site,* www.microsoft.com, *for details of the graphics cards that are known to work in multiple-monitor configurations with Windows XP.*

To use multiple monitors, you need to make sure that your graphics cards work together (some graphics cards don't) and that your computer's motherboard supports multiple monitors (some motherboards don't). In most cases, you'll want to use an AGP graphics card and one or more PCI graphics cards, but two or more PCI graphics cards without an AGP card can provide a satisfactory solution as well. The monitors, by contrast, don't need to know about each other—each gets its own input, so each can believe it's the only monitor in town if it wants to. So any monitors should do. You can mix CRTs and LCDs provided that the graphics cards in question can handle the monitor to which they're connected.

NOTE   In the 1990s, large monitors were so expensive that it was much cheaper to buy two, three, or even four small monitors than one large one. That's now changed, at least with cathode-ray tube monitors (LCD monitors are still prohibitively expensive). 19-inch monitors are reasonably affordable, and even 21-inch and 22-inch monitors are worth thinking about if you need a serious amount of Desktop space. But there's no reason why you shouldn't have a monster monitor and a couple of satellite monitors if you want—or even two or more monsters. . . .

To set up multiple monitors, power down your computer and insert the new graphics card. (You *can* install multiple graphics cards and monitors at a time, but unless you're very lucky and everything works, you'll be looking at some doubly confusing troubleshooting.) Connect the second monitor, then power everything on. Don't be surprised if the boot-up display appears on the second monitor rather than your primary one. After you log in to Windows, it should discover the new hardware, which will trigger a Found New Hardware notification-area pop-up followed by the Found New Hardware Wizard. If Windows affects not to have noticed the new hardware, run the Add Hardware Wizard manually to add the graphics card and monitor.

Next, display the Settings page of the Display Properties dialog box. For each monitor you want to use (hint: all of them), select the monitor and then select Extend My Windows Desktop onto This Monitor. Once you've done that, let Windows know where the monitors are positioned in relation to each other by dragging the monitor icons into their relative positions. If you get confused as to which monitor is which, click the Identify button to have Windows flash up the number of each monitor on the monitor. Then set the screen resolution, color depth, and refresh rate for each monitor as usual (see Chapter 4 for details).

Once you close the Display Properties dialog box, you should have a substantially enlarged Desktop. By default, the Taskbar appears on your primary monitor (the one that shows the boot sequence), but you can drag it to any of the other monitors as you see fit.

Maximizing a window maximizes it for the monitor it's currently (or mostly) on. You can extend a "normal" window across two or more monitors by dragging its window border to the appropriate size.

Configuring Power Management

If you have a laptop computer and use it on the road, power management tends to be an exciting part of your computing life. You've probably developed strategies to maximize your battery life while traveling, such as dimming the screen or slowing down the processor when you can accept poorer performance in the interests of longevity. (Chapter 15 discusses the features that Windows XP offers for portable computers.)

If you have a desktop computer, power management tends to be a much less stimulating topic, because leaving your computer running usually isn't a problem. But to keep your computer healthy, to keep your (or your employer's) electrical bill to a minimum, and perhaps to contribute to keeping the polar icecaps in place, it's a good idea to configure power management on your computer.

Windows XP offers a variety of power-management settings, from power schemes and hibernation to attaching an uninterruptible power supply (UPS) to your computer. The following sections discuss these options.

To configure power management, open the Power Options Properties dialog box as follows:

1. Right-click the Desktop and choose Properties from the context menu. Windows displays the Display Properties dialog box.

2. Click the Screen Saver tab. Windows displays the Screen Saver page.

3. Click the Power button. Windows displays the Power Options Properties dialog box.

NOTE *Because the Power Options Properties dialog box displays different pages depending on how your computer is configured, the following sections show the Power Options Properties dialog box from different computers.*

Choosing a Power Scheme

First, choose a power scheme and adjust it as necessary:

1. Display the Power Options Properties dialog box as discussed in the previous section. By default, the Power Schemes page (shown in Figure 14.30) is displayed.

FIGURE 14.30

Choose basic power-management options on the Power Schemes page of the Power Options Properties dialog box.

2. In the Power Schemes drop-down list, select the power scheme that seems best to describe your computer's role: Home/Office Desk, Portable/Laptop, Presentation, Always On, Minimal Power Management, or Max Battery. The Presentation scheme never turns off the monitor and is intended for computers left to run kiosk-style presentations (for example, at a trade show). The Always On scheme is useful for a computer that's acting as a server. The Minimal Power Management scheme aims to get the maximum performance out of a computer without worrying about conserving power.

3. The Settings for Power Scheme group box contains adjustable settings for the power scheme. Which settings there are depends on which of your computer's components are designed for power management. For most computers, Windows offers the Turn Off Monitor drop-down list and the Turn Off Hard Disks drop-down list. If your computer offers power features for standby and hibernation, the Settings for Power Scheme group box displays a System Standby drop-down list and a System Hibernates drop-down list as well.

NOTE *If you adjust the settings for a power scheme, you can save your custom power scheme by clicking the Save As button and specifying the name for the scheme in the Save Scheme dialog box that Windows displays.*

4. Click the Apply button to apply the power scheme to your computer.

Choosing Advanced Power Options

The Advanced page of the Power Options Properties dialog box (shown in Figure 14.31) offers various advanced power-management options. Which of these options you see depends on the hardware configuration of your computer.

Always Show Icon on the Taskbar check box   Select this check box to make Windows display a power icon in the System Tray. This option is most useful for laptop computers, as you can see at a glance whether the computer is plugged in (Windows displays a plug icon) or running on battery power (a battery icon).

FIGURE 14.31

If necessary, choose further power-management options on the Advanced page of the Power Options Properties dialog box.

Prompt for Password when Computer Resumes from Standby check box   Select this check box if you want Windows to make you enter your password when you wake the computer from a standby state.

When I Press the Power Button on My Computer drop-down list   In this drop-down list, select the action you want Windows to take when you press the Power button on your computer when Windows is running. The options are Do Nothing, Ask Me What to Do, Sleep, Hibernate, and Shut Down.

When I Press the Sleep Button on My Computer drop-down list   In this drop-down list, select the action you want Windows to take when you press the Sleep button on your computer. As for the Power button, the options are Do Nothing, Ask Me What to Do, Sleep, Hibernate, and Shut Down.

Enabling and Disabling Hibernation

Hibernation suspends your computer in its current state with programs and documents open. When you tell your computer to hibernate, it writes all the data held in RAM to a hibernation file on the hard disk. This way, even if the computer's battery runs out, all your information is safe. (If the battery *does* run out, hibernation saves you no time over shutting the computer down.)

The more RAM you have, the longer it takes for your computer to enter hibernation and to emerge from it again. But using hibernation is usually substantially faster than shutting down the computer and restarting it, especially as hibernation allows you to keep your programs and documents open, so that you can restart your work where you left off.

To enable hibernation, select the Enable Hibernation check box on the Hibernate page of the Power Options Properties dialog box (shown in Figure 14.32).

FIGURE 14.32

Use the Hibernate page to enable and disable hibernation.

Enabling and Disabling Advanced Power Management

If your computer supports Advanced Power Management (APM), Windows displays an APM page in the Power Options Properties dialog box. On this page, you can toggle APM on and off by selecting and clearing the Enable Advanced Power Management Support check box.

NOTE   *For portable computers, Windows includes an Alarms page in the Power Options Properties dialog box. These options are discussed in the next chapter.*

Configuring Windows to Use an Uninterruptible Power Supply

One of the great benefits of a laptop computer is that its battery protects it from data loss when a power outage occurs. To get similar protection in a desktop computer, you need to attach a separate device—an uninterruptible power supply (UPS). A UPS is about the most important hardware add-on purchase you're likely to make for your computer, so this section discusses in some depth which features you should look for in a UPS.

Like backup media, a UPS is seldom if ever included in a PC bundle.

WHAT IS A UPS?

A *UPS* is essentially a large battery of above-average intelligence that sits between your computer and the electricity supply and ensures a steady power stream to your computer to protect it from blackouts, brownouts, and surges. Different UPSes do this in two different ways.

The simpler way is for the device to monitor power fluctuations and kick in when the power supply falls outside acceptable thresholds. Technically, this type of device is called a *standby power supply (SPS)* rather than a UPS, but you'll often hear SPSes described as UPSes, because consumers will pay more money for them that way.

The more complicated—and better—way is for the device to feed power to the computer continuously, charging itself when the power supply is running within acceptable parameters. This device is technically a UPS. This way of supplying power is better because the UPS delivers conditioned power to the computer all the time, protecting it better from fluctuations and avoiding the critical moment of changeover from mains power to battery power that can be a drawback with an SPS.

CHOOSING A UPS

If you're looking for a UPS, keep these features in mind:

Operating system support   Make sure the UPS is designed for use with Windows XP. With operating system support and an appropriate system management port (discussed next), the UPS can warn Windows XP when the electricity supply has failed. Windows can then shut itself down automatically if the computer is unattended. (More on this in a moment.)

System management port   Make sure the UPS has an appropriate system management port for your computer. Many UPSes use a serial port connection. Others use a USB connection.

Indicators for line voltage and battery power   The UPS should have an indicator to indicate when the incoming power to the UPS is okay, and another indicator to indicate when the devices attached to the UPS are running on battery power. (Many UPSes also sound an alarm when battery power is being used.)

Multiple power outlets   Make sure the UPS has enough outlets for all the devices you want to plug into it directly.

Enough power and battery life   Before buying the UPS, work out how much power and battery life you need it to have. Make a list of the computers and devices you'll need to have plugged into the UPS, then use a power-supply template such as that on the American Power Conversion Corp. Web site (www.apc.com) to calculate the number of volt-amps (VA) you'll need to keep the equipment running. (You can simply add up the voltages listed on the equipment, but be aware that the power-supply rating on your computer equipment shows the maximum power rather than typical power usage.) Then decide the amount of time you'll need to shut down the computers once the power alarm goes off. Generally speaking, the more power and battery life you need, the more the UPS will cost. If you just want a few minutes to allow you to shut down Windows under control (or to have Windows shut itself down), a modest and inexpensive UPS may fit the bill.

TIP   *Unless you're convinced that you'll need to print during a power outage, don't plan to plug your printer into your UPS. Printers are power hogs. Laser printers are such power hogs that they can kill a UPS.*

INSTALLING A UPS

Once you've bought a UPS and lugged it home, power down your computer and install the UPS. Bring up the computer again, log on to Windows, and display the UPS page of the Power Options Properties dialog box (shown in Figure 14.33).

FIGURE 14.33

The UPS page of the Power Options Properties dialog box

To let Windows know about your UPS, take these steps:

1. Click the Select button. Windows displays the UPS Selection dialog box (shown in Figure 14.34 with American Power Conversion chosen in the Select Manufacturer drop-down list).

FIGURE 14.34

Use the UPS Selection dialog box to specify which UPS you're using and the port it's connected to.

2. In the Select Manufacturer drop-down list, choose the manufacturer of your UPS. If the manufacturer isn't listed, choose the Generic item.

3. If the manufacturer was listed, specify the model of UPS in the Select Model list box, and select the port in the On Port drop-down list. Click the Finish button. Windows closes the UPS Selection dialog box, returning you to the Power Options Properties dialog box.

4. If the manufacturer wasn't listed, select the Custom item in the Select Model list box. Then click the Next button. Windows displays the UPS Interface Configuration dialog box (shown in Figure 14.35). Consult your documentation, then choose settings for Power Fail/On Battery, Low Battery, and UPS Shutdown as appropriate. Then click the Finish button. Windows closes the UPS Interface Configuration dialog box, returning you to the Power Options Properties dialog box.

FIGURE 14.35

If Windows doesn't list the manufacturer of your UPS, use the UPS Interface Configuration dialog box to configure signal polarities for the UPS.

5. In the Power Options Properties dialog box, click the Configure button. Windows displays the UPS Configuration dialog box (shown in Figure 14.36).

FIGURE 14.36

Use the UPS Configuration dialog box to choose settings for the UPS.

6. Select or clear the Enable All Notifications check box as appropriate. Adjust the value in the Seconds between Power Failure and First Notification text box and the Seconds between Subsequent Power Failure Notifications text box to suit your needs. For example, if your electricity supply suffers from mini-outages of a few seconds each, you might choose to increase the Seconds between Power Failure and First Notification setting to a value such as 20 or 30 seconds so that the UPS raises the alarm only for a more serious outage than usual.

7. In the Critical Alarm group box, specify what actions Windows should take when the UPS sends Windows a critical alarm, warning Windows that the UPS is almost out of battery power.

    Minutes on Battery before Critical Alarm check box and text box   Select this check box if you want Windows to sound an alarm after the specified number of minutes running on battery power.

    When the Alarm Occurs, Run This Program check box and text box   If you want Windows to run a program when an alarm occurs, select this check box and specify the program in the text box. For example, you might want to run a custom shutdown utility or use a program to send a warning to users of connected computers.

    Next, Instruct the Computer To drop-down list   In this drop-down list, choose Shut Down or Hibernate as appropriate.

    Finally, Turn Off the UPS check box   Leave this check box selected (as it is by default) to have Windows turn off the UPS (and stop the alarm).

8. Click the OK button. Windows closes the UPS Configuration dialog box.

9. Click the Apply button. Windows applies your UPS settings. The Status group box shows status information on your UPS, and the Details group box shows the UPS's type. Figure 14.37 shows an example.

10. Click the OK button. Windows closes the Power Options Properties dialog box.

FIGURE 14.37

When you've configured the UPS, the Status group box on the UPS page of the Power Options Properties dialog box shows you the UPS' estimated runtime and capacity.

Up Next

This chapter has discussed how to install, uninstall, and disable hardware; update, roll back, and remove drivers; and manage power, including configuring a UPS.

The next chapter discusses the considerations for using Windows on a portable computer.

Chapter 15

Using Windows on a Portable Computer

THIS CHAPTER DISCUSSES HOW to use Windows XP on a portable computer. It starts by discussing how to use the power-management features specific to portables to prolong your battery life and warn you when it's running out. It continues by showing you how to use the Safely Remove Hardware feature for PC Cards and how to use hardware profiles to manage different hardware configurations. It mentions how to use ClearType for better readability on some LCD screens, and DualView for connecting an extra display to some portables. Last, it shows you how to use locations in dial-up networking and points you to information on connecting your portable to your desktop computer so that you can transfer files between them.

This chapter covers the following topics:

- Using the power-management features for portable computers
- Safely removing PC Cards
- Using ClearType
- Using DualView
- Using hardware profiles for different hardware configurations
- Using locations for dial-up networking
- Transferring files between a desktop computer and a portable

Preamble and Apologia

Before we get started with this chapter, a word or two of explanation on why this chapter is relatively short. Portable computers are growing more capable and more popular by the year if not by the month, and if you have a portable, you may well feel portables deserve more coverage.

Here's why this chapter is relatively short:

◆ First, many of the features that apply to portable computers also apply to desktop computers and have been covered in other chapters. The chapter mentions these features and refers to the chapters in which they're covered. For example, the last chapter discussed power management, which applies to both desktop computers and portable computers. This chapter discusses some additional power-management options that apply only to laptops. Some of the topics that *are* discussed in this chapter aren't entirely specific to portable computers, but because they mostly apply to portable computers, they're discussed here.

◆ Second, Windows XP Home doesn't have one of the killer features for portable computers that Windows XP Professional has: offline folders. Offline folders let you create copies of folders that are located on another PC and work with them when you're not connected to that PC. For example, you can make copies of your desktop computer's data folders on your portable computer, then work with them on your portable computer wherever you happen to be. When you return to your desktop computer, you synchronize the offline copies (on the portable) with the folders on the desktop computer, so that the folders on the desktop computer contain all the changes you've made.

You'll have no problem using Windows XP Home on a portable computer that's your main computer. But you'll find it difficult—at least, more difficult than it should be—to use a portable computer running Windows XP Home as a satellite to your main computer. You may even get the impression that Microsoft would like you to use Windows XP Professional instead for a portable with this type of role.

Using the Power-Management Features for Portables

In addition to the power-management features discussed in the previous chapter, Windows XP provides six power-management features for portable computers. Three of these features are configurable from the Power Options Properties dialog box; the other three are implemented behind the user interface. As you'll remember from the previous chapter, the easiest way to display the Power Options Properties dialog box is to click the Power button on the Screen Saver page of the Display Properties dialog box—and the easiest way to display *that* dialog box is to right-click the Desktop and choose Properties from the context menu.

Choosing Power Settings for Running on Batteries

On the Power Schemes page of the Power Options Properties dialog box for a portable computer, you can choose different power settings for when the computer is plugged in and when it is running on batteries. Figure 15.1 shows an example of the Power Schemes page for a portable computer.

FIGURE 15.1

On the Power Schemes page of the Power Options Properties dialog box, specify power settings for when the computer is running on batteries.

You shouldn't need much advice on how to choose settings for when the computer is running on battery power: The sooner you let the computer turn off one of the power-draining components, such as the monitor or the hard disk, the longer your battery will last. That said, don't set a minimal timeout (1 or 2 minutes, say) for the monitor if you tend to work on the computer on documents that require pauses for thought—having the monitor black out when you're constructing a formula or a sentence can be very distracting.

Setting Battery Alarms

If Windows XP recognizes your computer as a portable that can run off a battery, it includes the Alarms page in the Power Options Properties dialog box (shown in Figure 15.2).

FIGURE 15.2

You can set a low battery alarm and a critical battery alarm on the Alarms page of the Power Options Properties dialog box.

To set battery alarms, take the following steps:

1. Use the controls in the Low Battery Alarm group box to specify the battery level and the action for a low battery alarm. To use the alarm, select the Activate Low Battery Alarm when Power Level Reaches check box and drag the slider to a suitable level.

   ◆ By default, the alarm displays a message box warning you of the low battery level. To change what the alarm does, click the Alarm Action button. Windows displays the Low Battery Alarm Actions dialog box (shown in Figure 15.3).

FIGURE 15.3

Use the Low Battery Alarm Actions dialog box to specify the action that you want Windows to take when the battery reaches the low battery threshold.

   ◆ In the Notification group box, select the Sound Alarm check box or the Display Message check box as appropriate.

   ◆ In the Alarm Action group box, select the When the Alarm Goes Off, the Computer Will check box if you want the computer to take an action when the alarm is triggered. In the drop-down list, choose Stand By, Hibernate, or Shut Down as appropriate. Select the Force Stand By or Shutdown Even if a Program Stops Responding check box if you want to make sure that a hung program or driver doesn't prevent Windows from shutting the computer down or putting it into Sleep mode.

   ◆ In the Run a Program group box, select the When the Alarm Occurs, Run This Program check box if you want to run a program automatically when the alarm is triggered. Click the Configure Program button. Windows displays the Low Battery Alarm Program dialog box (shown in Figure 15.4), in which you can create a task as described in "Creating a Scheduled Task" in Chapter 11.

   ◆ Click the OK button. Windows closes the Low Battery Alarm Actions dialog box.

2. In the Critical Battery Alarm group box, specify the criteria for a critical battery alarm—the alarm that Windows raises when your battery is very close to running out of power. The options for the critical battery alarm are the same as those for the low battery alarm.

3. Click the Apply button. Windows applies your alarm settings.

FIGURE 15.4

To configure a program to run automatically when the battery alarm goes off, work in the Low Battery Alarm Program dialog box.

Power Meter

For portable computers that it recognizes, Windows also includes the Power Meter page in the Power Options Properties dialog box (shown in Figure 15.5). This page shows the current power source and the percentage of battery power remaining. (In the figure, the battery is in poor health.)

FIGURE 15.5

Use the Power Meter page in the Power Options Properties dialog box to see how much battery power you've got left.

Processor Power Control

Windows XP supports processor power control. If the computer has a processor that supports running at multiple speeds, such as an Intel SpeedStep processor, Windows can use the computer's power-management features to run at full speed when on AC power and at a lesser speed when running on battery power (to deliver longer battery life at somewhat lesser performance).

Dimming and Turning Off the Display

Slowing down the processor saves some battery power, but in most portables, the display consumes far more power than the processor. To save power, Windows XP automatically turns off the display when the user closes the lid of the computer.

Similarly, Windows XP automatically decreases the brightness of LCD screens when they're running on battery power. This reduces the amount of power needed, and so prolongs battery life, but it can make it hard to work on screens that aren't too bright in the first place. To restore the screen to its full brightness, use a hardware command (these vary depending on the laptop and its manufacturer).

Hibernation when Battery Runs Low

If the portable computer's battery runs low, and the user doesn't respond to warnings, Windows XP puts the laptop into hibernation rather than letting it run out of power and crash.

Safely Removing PC Cards

You can install PC Card devices by inserting them like any other hot-pluggable devices. (See "Using Hot-Pluggable Devices" in Chapter 14 for brief details—but basically, you just plug in hot-pluggable devices.) But before removing a PC Card device, you're supposed to stop it by using the Safely Remove Hardware feature. *Supposed*? Yes—you can often get away without using this feature, though it's never a good idea to do so. Usually, Windows handles the unannounced removal of hot-pluggable hardware gracefully. Sometimes, though, removing hardware without using Safely Remove Hardware causes the computer to lock up or become unstable.

You can use the Safely Remove Hardware feature in two ways: the quick way and the slow way. Guess which we'll start with? Right.

The Quick Way of Using Safely Remove Hardware

To use Safely Remove Hardware the quick way, follow these steps:

1. Click the Safely Remove Hardware icon in the notification area. Windows displays a pop-up menu of devices (shown in Figure 15.6).

2. Select the device you want to remove. Windows stops the device and displays a Safe to Remove Hardware pop-up (shown in Figure 15.7).

3. Remove the device.

FIGURE 15.6

Click the Safely Remove Hardware icon in the notification area and select the device to stop in the pop-up menu.

FIGURE 15.7

Windows displays a Safe to Remove Hardware pop-up when it's safe to remove the device.

The Slow Way of Using Safely Remove Hardware

To use Safely Remove Hardware the slow way, follow these steps:

1. Right-click the Safely Remove Hardware icon in the notification area. Windows displays the Safely Remove Hardware dialog box (shown in Figure 15.8).

FIGURE 15.8

You can also use the Safely Remove Hardware dialog box to stop the device.

2. Select the device you want to remove.

   ◆ If you want to display more information about the device's components, select the Display Device Components check box. (This check box is selected in the figure.) Confusion about the components of a device is the main reason for using the slow way.

3. Click the Stop button. Windows displays the Stop a Hardware Device dialog box (shown in Figure 15.9).

FIGURE 15.9

In the Stop a Hardware Device dialog box, confirm that you want to stop the PC Card device.

4. Click the OK button. Windows stops the device and displays a Safe to Remove Hardware pop-up (as in Figure 15.7 above).

5. Remove the device.

6. Click the Close button. Windows closes the Safely Remove Hardware dialog box.

Using ClearType

Unless your portable is one of the very few portables that doesn't have an LCD screen, it's worth trying the ClearType resolution-enhancement technology to see if it makes fonts look better. Some people find ClearType a help; others find it produces an irritatingly smeary effect unless they peer closely at it. Your mileage will vary depending on your screen and your eyesight.

To enable ClearType, display the Display Properties dialog box and click the Effects button on the Appearance page. Windows displays the Effects dialog box. Select the Use the Following Method to Smooth Edges of Screen Fonts check box and select ClearType in the drop-down list. (See "Choosing Desktop Effects" in Chapter 4 for more details.)

Using DualView

DualView is a great new feature in Windows XP that enables you to extend your Desktop onto an external display connected to your portable's external graphics port. DualView exploits the capability of the graphics cards in almost all portables to send two signals at once: a digital signal to the portable's LCD screen, and an analog signal to the external graphics port. Normally, the portable sends the same signal both internally and externally, which is useful for giving presentations but not much else. By contrast, DualView uses the external port and monitor as an extension of your Desktop, much as in a multi-monitor setup.

DualView works with only some graphics cards, but if you have an external monitor, it shouldn't cost you more than a few seconds' effort to connect it to the external graphics port and see what happens. On some portables, the external graphics port is switched off to conserve battery power, so you'll need to turn it on, typically by using custom configuration software supplied by the manufacturer or poking in the BIOS. You'll then need to set your computer to send signals to both ports; most portables have a built-in key combination to do this.

If you find that DualView works for your portable, configure it as you would a desktop multi-monitor setup (as described in the previous chapter).

Using Hardware Profiles

Windows' *hardware profiles* let you create different hardware configurations for the same computer. Hardware profiles are useful for computers that you regularly use with two or more different hardware configurations. You can set up different hardware configurations with a desktop computer by dint of diligent plugging and unplugging of a set of hardware, but it's much easier to achieve the same effect with a laptop that you use both docked and undocked or that has swappable components—and that's what hardware profiles are usually used for.

NOTE *Hardware profiles can seem forbidding until you start using them, at which point most people find them surprisingly easy. Even if you don't have a docking station and need a profile only for something as simple as using your portable with an external monitor (with perhaps a higher resolution than your portable's screen) or an external mouse, profiles can save you a lot of time and effort.*

Creating a Hardware Profile

To create a hardware profile, take the following steps:

1. Press Winkey+Break or click the Start button, right-click the My Computer item, and choose Properties from the context menu. Windows displays the System Properties dialog box.

2. Click the Hardware tab. Windows displays the Hardware page.

3. Click the Hardware Profiles button. Windows displays the Hardware Profiles dialog box (shown in Figure 15.10). By default, Windows starts you off with a profile named Profile 1, which it lists in the Available Hardware Profiles list box. It displays (Current) next to the current profile, so you should see Profile 1 (Current) before you create a new profile.

FIGURE 15.10

In the Hardware Profiles dialog box, create profiles for the different configurations your computer uses.

4. In the Available Hardware Profiles list box, select the profile you want to copy.

5. Click the Copy button. Windows displays the Copy Profile dialog box (shown in Figure 15.11).

FIGURE 15.11

In the Copy Profile dialog box, specify the name for the copy you're making of the profile.

6. Enter the name for the copy of the profile in the To text box. Windows suggests a default name of Profile N, where N is the next unused number, but you'd be wise to opt for something more descriptive.

7. Click the OK button. Windows closes the Copy Profile dialog box and creates the profile.

8. Set properties for the profile:

   ◆ Select the profile in the Available Hardware Profiles list box.

◆ Click the Properties button. Windows displays the Properties dialog box for the profile. Figure 15.12 shows an example of the Properties dialog box.

FIGURE 15.12

Use the Properties dialog box for a profile to set options.

◆ If this is a portable computer, select the This Is a Portable Computer check box. Windows enables the options in the group box. Select the appropriate option button: The Docking State Is Unknown, The Computer Is Docked, or The Computer Is Undocked.

◆ In the Hardware Profiles Selection group box, select the Always Include This Profile As an Option when Windows Starts check box if you want Windows always to present this profile in the start-up menu of profiles. If you don't select this check box, Windows includes the profile in the start-up menu of profiles only if it determines that the profile is relevant to the hardware configuration it has detected.

◆ Click the OK button. Windows closes the Properties dialog box for the profile and applies your changes to it.

9. Create further profiles as necessary. (Or delete one or more profiles by using the Delete button.)

10. To rename a profile (for example, the `Profile 1` profile), select it in the Available Hardware Profiles list box and click the Rename button. Windows displays the Rename Profile dialog box. Enter the new name for the profile in the To text box and click the OK button. Windows closes the Rename Profile dialog box and renames the profile.

11. Use the up-arrow button and down-arrow button to sort the profiles in the Available Hardware Profiles list box into the order in which you want Windows to present them. If you want to use a profile as the default, put it at the top of the list.

12. In the Hardware Profiles Selection group box in the Hardware Profiles dialog box, choose the Wait until I Select a Hardware Profile option button or the Select the First Profile Listed if I Don't Select a Profile in *NN* Seconds option button as appropriate. If you choose the latter, enter the number of seconds in the text box. (The default is 30 seconds, which makes for slow booting.)

13. Click the OK button. Windows closes the Hardware Profiles dialog box, returning you to the System Properties dialog box, and applies your changes.

14. Click the OK button. Windows closes the System Properties dialog box.

Choosing a Hardware Profile

Once you've set up hardware profiles as described in the previous section, Windows displays the Hardware Profile/Configuration Recovery Menu screen when the computer reboots. (If you're using a multiboot configuration, the Hardware Profile/Configuration Recovery Menu screen appears after you choose the Windows XP entry from the Please Select the Operating System to Start menu—as you'd expect if you think about it.)

Use the ↓ key and ↑ key to select the profile from the menu, and then press the Enter key. Windows starts the computer with that profile.

Setting Up the Hardware in the Profile

Once you've started Windows with the profile you want, make the hardware changes and install drivers to suit the profile. These changes apply only to the current profile.

Using Dial-up Networking from Multiple Locations

If you travel with your portable computer, you'll probably want to create multiple locations for dial-up networking. To do so, display the Phone and Modem Options dialog box by taking the following steps:

1. Choose Start ➤ Control Panel. Windows displays Control Panel.

2. Click the Network and Internet Connections link. Windows displays the Network and Internet Connections screen.

3. Click the Phone and Modem Options link in the See Also pane. Windows displays the Phone and Modem Options dialog box.

Creating a New Location

To create a new location, follow these steps:

1. Click the New button on the Dialing Rules page of the Phone and Modem Options dialog box. Windows displays the New Location dialog box with the General page foremost (shown in Figure 15.13).

2. Enter the name for the location in the Location Name text box.

3. In the Country/Region drop-down list, specify the country or region in which you'll use this location.

4. Enter the area code for the location in the Area Code text box.

5. In the Dialing Rules group box, specify access numbers for outside lines and carrier codes for long-distance calls and international calls as appropriate.

FIGURE 15.13

Create the new location on the General page of the New Location dialog box.

6. If you need to disable call waiting, select the To Disable Call Waiting, Dial check box and enter the appropriate code in the text box, either by typing or by selecting one of the standard codes from the drop-down list.

7. If the location uses pulse dialing, select the Pulse option button. (The Tone option button is selected by default.)

8. If necessary, create area code rules for dialing from the new location:

   ◆ Click the Area Code Rules tab. Windows displays the Area Code Rules page (shown in Figure 15.14).

FIGURE 15.14

You can create area code rules for dialing from the new location by using the Area Code Rules page of the New Location dialog box.

◆ Click the New button. Windows displays the New Area Code Rule dialog box (shown in Figure 15.15).

FIGURE 15.15

Use the New Area Code Rule dialog box to create area code rules.

◆ Enter the area code in the Area Code text box.

◆ In the Prefixes group box, select the Include All the Prefixes within This Area Code option button or the Include Only the Prefixes in the List Below option button as appropriate. If you choose the latter, click the Add button and use the resulting Add Prefix dialog box to specify the prefixes (separated by spaces or commas).

◆ In the Rules group box, select the Dial check box if these numbers require an extra number; if so, enter it in the text box. Select the Include the Area Code check box if necessary.

◆ Click the OK button. Windows closes the New Area Code Rule dialog box and enters the rule in the Area Code Rules group box on the Area Code Rules page.

9. If you need to use a credit card to pay for the call from the location, specify it by following the steps below.

◆ Click the Calling Card tab. Windows displays the Calling Card page of the New Location dialog box (shown in Figure 15.16).

◆ To use one of the card types listed in the Card Types list box, select its option button and enter the details in the Account Number text box and the Personal ID Number (PIN) text box.

◆ To add a calling card, click the New button. Windows displays the New Calling Card dialog box (shown in Figure 15.17). Enter the details of the calling card on the four tabs of this dialog box, then click the OK button. Windows adds the new calling card to the list in the Card Types list box on the Calling Card page of the New Location dialog box.

FIGURE 15.16

On the Calling Card page of the New Location dialog box, specify the calling card to use for calls from this location.

FIGURE 15.17

Use the New Calling Card dialog box to add the details of a new calling card.

10. Click the OK button. Windows closes the New Location dialog box and adds the new location to the Phone and Modem Options dialog box.

Editing a Location

To edit a location, select it in the Locations list box on the Dialing Rules page of the Phone and Modem Options dialog box and click the Edit button. Windows displays the Edit Location dialog box, which is a renamed version of the New Location dialog box. Make the necessary changes and then click the OK button. Windows closes the Edit Location dialog box and applies your changes to the location.

Using a Location

To use a location, select it in the Phone and Modem Options dialog box and click the OK button. Windows closes the Phone and Modem Options dialog box and uses the location you chose for calls you dial.

Transferring Files between a Desktop Computer and a Portable

The easiest way to transfer files between a desktop computer and a portable is to put a network card in each of them and connect them either via a network or directly via a crossover cable. Chapter 32 discusses how to network your computers.

If you don't want to buy network cards and can tolerate low transfer speeds, connect the computers by using a serial cable or a parallel cable. See "Setting Up a Direct Connection" in Chapter 32 for details of how to do this.

Up Next

This chapter has discussed considerations for using Windows XP on a portable computer: using the power-management features for portables; using the Safely Remove Hardware feature for PC Cards; using ClearType if it suits you; using DualView if you can; using hardware profiles for different hardware configurations; and using dial-up networking locations.

The next chapter discusses how to troubleshoot, optimize, and dual-boot Windows.

Chapter 16

Troubleshooting, Optimizing, and Dual-Booting Windows

YOU'VE READ A NUMBER of times already in this book that Windows XP is much more reliable than Windows 9x—and it's quite true. But things still sometimes go wrong with Windows XP: a program hangs; you start getting bizarre error messages about some strangely named component not having done something it should; or Windows starts to slow down, behave oddly, or become unstable.

This chapter discusses how to use the tools that Windows provides for dealing with untoward occurrences such as these. It also discusses some steps you may want to take to optimize Windows in the hope of keeping it running smoothly and as swiftly as your hardware permits. And it shows you how to set up a dual-boot arrangement so that you can use both Windows XP and another operating system on your computer.

This chapter covers the following topics:

- ◆ Dealing with program hangs
- ◆ Using Event Viewer to identify problems
- ◆ Optimizing performance
- ◆ Setting environment variables
- ◆ Enabling error reporting
- ◆ Setting start-up and recovery options
- ◆ Restoring your system with System Restore
- ◆ Restoring the Last Known Good Configuration
- ◆ Repairing a Windows installation using Recovery Console
- ◆ Creating a dual-boot setup

Dealing with Program Hangs

When a program hangs, it'll usually be very obvious. The program stops responding to direct stimuli (keystrokes and mouse commands issued in its window) and indirect stimuli (for example, commands issued via the Taskbar or via another program). If you move another program window in front of the hung program's window and then move it away, the hung program's window fails to redraw correctly, leaving either parts of the window that you've moved or a blank, undrawn area on the screen.

Ending a Program

Sometimes Windows notices when a program has hung and displays the End Program dialog box automatically so that you can choose whether to end the program. Other times, you'll need to use Task Manager to tell Windows to end the program. To do so, take the following steps:

1. If you have Task Manager running already, switch to it. If not, press Ctrl+Alt+Delete. Windows displays Task Manager with the Applications page foremost.

2. Select the task you want to end.

3. Click the End Task button. If Windows can end the task easily, it does so. Otherwise, Windows displays the End Program dialog box, of which Figure 16.1 shows an example.

FIGURE 16.1

If Windows can't close the program easily, it displays the End Program dialog box to let you end it forcibly.

4. Click the End Now button. Windows ends the program. You lose any unsaved data in the program.

5. After clearing up the debris and virtual shrapnel left by the program, Windows displays a message box such as that shown in Figure 16.2, inviting you to tell Microsoft about the problem, with the implication that doing so will help them prevent such problems from recurring in the future.

6. Click the Send Error Report button or the Don't Send button as appropriate. (To see details on what information you'll be sending to Microsoft, click the Click Here link before dismissing the dialog box.)

You can turn off or tweak this error reporting if you want. See "Enabling and Disabling Error Reporting" later in this chapter.

FIGURE 16.2

Windows displays a dialog box such as this one when you've used the End Program dialog box to end a program. Choose whether to send Microsoft information on the problem.

NOTE *By default, Task Manager appears with its Always on Top attribute on, so that it always appears as the topmost window on the Desktop, no matter which program window is active. Always having Task Manager on top makes it easy to keep track of Task Manager, but it means that Task Manager often blocks dialog boxes or error messages in the programs you're using, particularly at low screen resolutions such as 800×600. If you find Task Manager useful and often keep it open to see what's happening with your programs, choose Options ➤ Always on Top to remove the check mark from the Always on Top menu item and make the Task Manager window behave like a normal program window. (To turn Always on Top back on, repeat the command.) Also on the Options menu are two other items that are both on by default: Minimize on Use, and Hide when Minimized.*

Ending a Process or a Process Tree

Instead of ending a program, you can end a process. A *process* is the executing environment in which program components called *threads* operate. Many programs run as a single process much of the time, but others involve multiple processes.

There are two problems with ending a process. First, doing so may make your computer unstable, so it's a last resort. Second, you need to know which process does what. Now, as you saw in Chapter 3, you can use the Go to Process command from a program on the Applications page of Task Manager to identify the process on the Processes page. This command can be useful for learning the name under which the main process for a program is executing, but it's not much use for ending a process, because usually you'll do much better to end the program itself from the Applications page. Ending the program takes out all the processes associated with the program. So the only reason to end a process directly is if it doesn't have its associated program listed on the Applications page. This is the case for a system process, but it's not a good idea to end a system process unless you're certain what it's doing. But if you overload Windows, it can sometimes get confused about which programs are running and lose a program's listing from the Applications page while keeping its process or processes going.

If this happens, you can end a process by selecting it on the Processes page and clicking the End Process button. Windows displays the Task Manager Warning dialog box shown in Figure 16.3 warning you that ending the process may make your system unstable or lose you data. If you're prepared to risk such consequences, click the Yes button. Windows terminates the process.

To end all the processes associated with a process, right-click the process and choose End Process Tree from the context menu. Windows displays the Task Manager Warning dialog box shown in Figure 16.4 with a variation of its message about the possible undesirable results of stopping processes. Click the Yes button if you want to continue. Windows stops the processes.

FIGURE 16.3

Windows displays this Task Manager Warning dialog box when you tell it to end a process.

FIGURE 16.4

Windows displays this Task Manager Warning dialog box when you tell it to end a process tree.

Using Event Viewer to Identify Problems

If your computer seems to be behaving strangely, you can use Event Viewer to try to pinpoint the source of the problem.

Take the following steps to open Event Viewer:

1. Choose Start ➢ Control Panel. Windows displays Control Panel.

2. Click the Performance and Maintenance link. Windows displays the Performance and Maintenance screen.

3. Click the Administrative Tools link. Windows displays the Administrative Tools screen.

4. Double-click the Event Viewer shortcut. Windows starts Event Viewer (shown in Figure 16.5).

FIGURE 16.5

Use Event Viewer to identify problems and to learn what's happening behind the scenes in your computer.

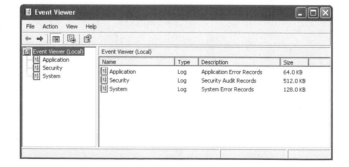

As you can see in the figure, Event Viewer contains three logs: the Application Log, the Security Log, and the System Log.

NOTE   Event Viewer automatically opens the current logs. You can also open old logs by choosing Action ➤ Open Log File. Event Viewer displays a common Open dialog box with two peculiarities: a Log Type drop-down list and a Display Name text box. Navigate to the log and select it. Then select the appropriate type of log—Application, Security, or System—in the Log Type drop-down list. The Display Name text box automatically displays Saved Type Log, where Type is the log type selected (for example, Saved Application Log for an Application Log). You can change this description as necessary. Click the Open button. Event Viewer opens the log file and adds it to the left pane. (You can also rename it here by using standard Windows editing techniques, such as selecting the name and pressing the F2 key.)

The System Log

The System Log contains information about Windows processes. The System Log uses the following three types of events:

Error events   A notification that an error has occurred. Errors can be anything from mildly serious (for example, "The device U.S. Robotics 56K FAX EXT disappeared from the system without first being prepared for removal") to seriously serious (for example, a system error described only by forbidding error codes).

Warning events   A notification that something has gone wrong, but not disastrously so. For example, you might see a warning that "The browser was unable to retrieve a list of servers from the browser master on the network." This isn't bad—it just means that the browser (a service that finds out which resources are available on the network) has to find another browser master (a computer that's coordinating information on available resources).

Information events   Events worth noting in the System Log but that are not considered errors and do not merit warnings. For example, when you start Windows, it starts the event log service, and logs this as an Information event. Other examples include Windows' starting to use a network adapter that it has detected is connected to the network, or that the browser has forced an election on the network because a master browser was stopped.

The System Log is stored in the `SYSEVENT.EVT` file in the `\Windows\System32\Config\` folder.

The Application Log

The Application Log contains information about programs running on the computer. Like the System Log, the Application Log supports three types of events: Error events, Warning events, and Information events. Program developers specify the events that their programs raise and which event type each event has.

The Application Log is stored in the `APPEVENT.EVT` file in the `\Windows\System32\Config\` folder.

The Security Log

The Security Log contains information on security-related events. In Windows XP Home, these events are limited to Account Logon actions, Logon/Logoff actions, Policy Change actions (initiated by the System object), and System Events (such as the loading of authentication packages). Windows XP Home audits these events automatically. (In Windows XP Professional, you can enable auditing on files and folders, which lets you track which users take which actions on those files and in those folders.)

The Security Log is stored in the (you've guessed it) SECEVENT.EVT file in the \Windows\ System32\Config\ folder.

Viewing an Event Log

To view one of the three event logs, select it in the left pane of the Event Viewer window. Event Viewer displays the events in the log in the right pane. Figure 16.6 shows an example of viewing the System Log.

FIGURE 16.6

Use Event Viewer to find out which events have occurred on your system.

To view the details of an event, double-click it (or right-click it and choose Properties from the context menu). Windows displays the Event Properties dialog box (shown in Figure 16.7). The dialog box shows the date, time, type, user (if appropriate), computer, source, category, and ID number of the event. The Description text box displays the description of the event, and the Data text box displays any data for it. You can toggle the display of the data between bytes and words by clicking the Bytes option button or the Words option button. With the dialog box open, you can use the Previous Event button (the up-arrow button) and the Next Event button (the down-arrow button) to display the details for the previous event or next event, or the Copy Event Details to Clipboard button (the button below the Next Event button) to copy the details of the event to the Clipboard.

FIGURE 16.7

Use the Event Properties dialog box to view the properties for an event.

Managing the Event Logs

As you can imagine, event logs grow in size, particularly when many events occur that need logging. Windows offers features to keep the size of your event logs under control.

To manage the event logs, follow these steps:

1. Right-click the event log in question and choose Properties from the context menu. Windows displays the Properties dialog box for the log. Figure 16.8 shows the General page of the Properties dialog box for the Application Log.

2. In the Maximum Log Size text box, you can specify the maximum size to which the file can grow. The default size is 512KB, but you can set any size from 64KB upward. Having the log file grow to a couple of megabytes shouldn't be a problem unless you're backing it up from another machine, but there's no particular reason to keep a large amount of log-file data.

FIGURE 16.8

Use the General page of the Properties dialog box for an event log to specify a maximum size for the log file and which events to overwrite.

3. In the When Maximum Log Size Is Reached area, select one of the option buttons to specify what Windows should do when the log file reaches its maximum size:

Overwrite Events As Needed option button   Select this option button to have Windows delete the oldest event to make room for the newest event, thus keeping the log file around its maximum size.

Overwrite Events Older than *NN* Days option button   Select this option button (the default setting) to make Windows overwrite events older than a particular number of days in order to make room for new events. If you archive your log files, set the number of days in the text box to match your frequency of archiving. The default setting is 7 days. Be aware that if the log file reaches its maximum size within the allotted number of days and contains no events older than that number of days, Windows stops writing events to the log file. (This isn't usually a good idea.)

Do Not Overwrite Events option button   Select this option button if you want to prevent Windows from overwriting any events. This means that you'll need to clear the event log manually. Until you clear the log, Windows writes no more events to the log once it has reached its maximum size.

4. If your computer is connected to the network via a modem and is receiving event information from other computers (or is transmitting event information to other computers), select the Using a Low-Speed Connection check box. This option reduces the amount of information transmitted.

5. Click the OK button. Windows applies your changes and closes the Properties dialog box for the event log.

FILTERING THE EVENT LOG

Your event logs can fill up quickly, especially when there's something wrong with your system or with a program. To find particular events, you can use the Filter page of the Properties dialog box to apply filters.

1. Right-click the event log in question and choose Properties from the context menu. Windows displays the Properties dialog box for the log.

2. Click the Filter tab. Windows displays the Filter page (shown in Figure 16.9).

3. In the Event Types group box, select the check boxes for the types of events you want to see. Clear the other check boxes.

4. Use the controls on the lower two-thirds of the page to specify the details of the events you want to see.

5. Click the OK button. Windows applies your choices and closes the Properties dialog box.

FIGURE 16.9

Use the Filter page of the Properties dialog box for a log to filter the types of events displayed.

CLEARING THE EVENT LOG

To clear a log, right-click it in Event Viewer and choose Clear Log from the context menu. Alternatively, display its Properties dialog box and click the Clear Log button on the General page.

Event Viewer displays an Event Viewer dialog box asking if you want to save the log before clearing it. Click the Yes button or the No button as appropriate.

Optimizing Performance

This section discusses steps you can take to optimize the performance of your computer and of Windows. These steps range from getting more RAM (if you need it), through setting suitable performance options for your computer, to specifying the size and location of the paging file. You should also defragment your disk or disks as discussed in "Defragmenting Your Disks" in Chapter 11.

RAM: Do You Have Enough?

If your computer's performance seems disappointing, make sure that your computer has plenty of RAM to run Windows itself plus all the programs that may be running in the background. As mentioned earlier in the book, 128MB is usually enough for running a single-user session at reasonable speed, and 256MB is usually enough for several user sessions running conventional programs. If you want multiple users to be able to open large programs or large files at the same time, you might need 384MB or 512MB.

If your computer is light on RAM, consider adding more. At this writing, RAM prices have reached an all-time low, and you can get 256MB of SDRAM for less than $100.

There are various ways of finding out how much RAM you have on your computer. Normally, when the computer starts, you'll see the boot routine take a quick count of the RAM. (Some computers hide this part of the boot process behind a custom splash screen.)

Once Windows is running, the easiest way to find out the amount of RAM is to display the System Properties dialog box (press Winkey+Break, or right-click the My Computer item on the Start menu and choose the Properties item from the context menu) and look at the Computer section of the General page.

Choosing Performance Options

Next, make sure that Windows is configured to give the best performance possible for your needs.

As mentioned in Chapter 1, getting the best performance out of Windows XP on a computer that isn't screamingly fast is partly a question of choosing the right balance between visual delight and speed: the more graphics and visual effects that Windows XP is using, the slower their display will be, and the heavier the demands placed on the processor as well as the graphics subsystem.

You also need to give the foreground program as much of a boost as possible, make sure that memory usage is optimized for programs rather than system cache, and set an appropriate size for your paging file.

To set performance options, follow these steps:

1. Press Winkey+Break. Alternatively, choose Start ➤ Control Panel, click the Performance and Maintenance link, and then click the System link. Windows displays the System Properties dialog box.

2. Click the Advanced tab. Windows displays the Advanced page (shown in Figure 16.10).

FIGURE 16.10

The Advanced page of the System Properties dialog box is the starting place for setting performance options.

3. Click the Settings button in the Performance group box. Windows displays the Performance Options dialog box.

4. On the Visual Effects page of the Performance Options dialog box (shown in Figure 16.11), select one of the option buttons:

◆ Select the Let Windows Choose What's Best for My Computer option button to have Windows apply the mixture of settings it deems most appropriate to your computer's speed and your graphics card's capabilities.

◆ Select the Adjust for Best Appearance option button to turn on all the effects.

◆ Select the Adjust for Best Performance option button to turn off all the effects.

◆ Select the Custom option button if you want to apply a custom set of effects. Then select the check boxes for the effects you want to use. Most of the effects are self-explanatory—for example, the Animate Windows when Minimizing and Maximizing check box controls whether Windows animates windows when minimizing and maximizing them. (In fact, this item isn't precisely named, as the effect is applied to windows that are being restored as well as minimized or maximized—but no matter.) The fewer visual effects you use, the better the performance you'll enjoy, but the plainer and less subtle the Windows interface will seem.

FIGURE 16.11

You can improve performance by turning off unnecessary visual effects on the Visual Effects page of the Performance Options dialog box.

5. Click the Advanced tab. Windows displays the Advanced page of the Performance Options dialog box (shown in Figure 16.12)

6. In the Processor Scheduling group box, make sure that the Programs option button is selected. The Programs option button causes Windows to give priority to the foreground program—the active program—giving you faster response time in it. (Select the Background Services option button only if you're using this computer as a sort of server and are not running programs on it.)

FIGURE 16.12

On the Advanced page of the Performance Options dialog box, make sure that processor scheduling and memory usage are optimized for applications.

7. In the Memory Usage group box, make sure the Programs option button is selected so that Windows manages memory to give the maximum performance boost to the foreground program. Select the System Cache option button only if you want to optimize the system cache performance at the expense of program performance.

8. If necessary, change the size of the paging file by following the instructions in the next section.

9. Click the OK button. Windows applies your changes and closes the Performance Options dialog box.

10. Click the OK button. Windows closes the System Properties dialog box.

Specifying the Size and Location of the Paging File

The *paging file* is space reserved on the hard disk for Windows to use as virtual memory. *Virtual memory* involves storing memory information on the hard disk so that more information can be loaded into memory (both real and virtual) at the same time. Windows juggles virtual memory automatically, swapping information between the RAM and the paging file, so its use should be imperceptible to you. (You'll hear the hard drive working, of course; but then the hard drive works so much when Windows is running that you'll hear it even when no virtual memory swapping is taking place.)

Being able to load more information into memory at a time is good, but because the hard drive is much slower to access than RAM, storing memory information in virtual memory makes your computer run more slowly than it would if it were to store all memory information in RAM. Even if you have a huge amount of memory, Windows XP still requires you to use virtual memory. Given that RAM is at a new historic low price at this writing, making 512MB or 768MB of memory borderline affordable, this is a bit disappointing—but that's the way it is.

Windows automatically creates the paging file on the drive that Windows itself is installed on, going on the general assumption that this is a convenient place to have it. It may not be, and you may want to move the paging file.

The paging file takes up anything from about 100MB to a gigabyte or more. By default, the paging file is initially set to 1.5 times the amount of RAM in the computer: a 96MB paging file for a computer with 64MB RAM; 192MB for 128MB RAM; 384MB for 256MB RAM; and so on. So if you have a small drive or partition, you may want to move the paging file off it when you start running low on disk space. You can also split the paging file between different partitions if you're running low on space on all the partitions.

You might also want to move your paging file to a faster drive than the drive it's currently on. For example, if you had a small but screamingly fast SCSI drive in your computer as well as a slower but much larger EIDE drive, you might want to move the paging file to the SCSI drive to improve performance. (This would work for a large and fast SCSI drive as well—but you'd probably have installed Windows on that drive in the first place, so the paging file would already be there.) Similarly, you may be able to improve performance by moving the paging file to an otherwise unused EIDE drive, should you have one hanging around.

The paging file is called PAGEFILE.SYS. It's a hidden and protected operating system file, so if you feel the urge to look at it, you'll need to select the Show Hidden Files and Folders option button and clear the Hide Protected Operating System Files check box on the View page of the Folder Options dialog box in order to see it. (To display the Folder Options dialog box, choose Tools ➢ Folder Options in an Explorer window.)

NOTE   *If you look for the paging file, you may also see the hibernation file,* HIBERFIL.SYS. *(Your computer will have a hibernation file only if your computer supports hibernation.) By default, the hibernation file is stored on the same drive as the paging file, and is approximately the same size as the amount of RAM your computer contains. For example, if the computer has 256MB RAM, the hibernation file will be about 256MB as well. That's because Windows writes the contents of RAM to the hibernation file before entering hibernation—RAM doesn't store information when it's powered down.*

As you've undoubtedly guessed, you shouldn't delete the paging file (even if you can see it). In fact, Windows XP won't let you delete it—if you try to do so, it prevents you with an Error Deleting File or Folder message box telling you that the file "is being used by another person or program" and suggesting that you close any programs that might be using the file (but not any people!) and try again. You *can* delete the paging file by booting another operating system and attacking it from there, but there's little point in doing so—you can manage the paging file easily enough by following the procedure described next.

To specify the size and location of the paging file, follow these steps:

1. Click the Change button in the Virtual Memory group box on the Advanced page of the Performance Options dialog box. Windows displays the Virtual Memory dialog box (shown in Figure 16.13).

2. In the Drive list box, select the drive (or one of the drives) that contains the paging file.

3. In the Paging File Size for Selected Drive list box, specify the size of the file:

    ◆ If you want Windows to manage the paging file's size, select the System Managed Size option button.

◆ If you want to manage the paging file's size yourself, select the Custom Size option button. Enter appropriate values in the Initial Size text box and the Maximum Size text box, based on the Recommended readout and the Currently Allocated readout in the Total Paging File Size for All Drives group box. Click the Set button.

◆ To remove the paging file from this drive, select the No Paging File option button. Click the Set button.

4. Specify paging file sizes for the other drives as appropriate by repeating steps 2 and 3.

5. Click the OK button. Windows closes the Virtual Memory dialog box and returns you to the Advanced page of the Performance Options dialog box.

6. Click the OK button. Windows closes the Performance Options dialog box and returns you to the Advanced page of the System Properties dialog box.

You'll need to restart Windows before your changes to the paging file take effect.

FIGURE 16.13

In the Virtual Memory dialog box, you can specify the size of the paging file and the drive on which to locate it.

EXPERT KNOWLEDGE: WHAT HAPPENS WHEN YOU RUN OUT OF VIRTUAL MEMORY?

The main point of having virtual memory, of course, is to prevent you from running out of physical memory—as far as possible. But what happens if you run out of virtual memory as well?

Between the memory used by Windows itself, the memory any running program occupies, and the memory taken up by whatever data files you've got open, RAM itself goes quickly enough. It's easy to chew up 128MB of RAM on a single-user session. And if a couple of other users have sessions running in the background, perhaps with a few large graphics files open for editing between them, 256MB can disappear faster than a sixteen-inch pepperoni pizza waylaid by teenagers.

Continued on the next page

EXPERT KNOWLEDGE: WHAT HAPPENS WHEN YOU RUN OUT OF VIRTUAL MEMORY? *(continued)*

Of course, Windows doesn't allocate the RAM just like that to itself, the programs, and the files. Instead, it monitors your memory usage the whole time, doling out RAM and virtual memory as it judges best to keep itself running (the first priority) and the programs you're using in the foreground responding smoothly. As you work, Windows is constantly shunting pages of memory from RAM to the paging file on the hard disk and vice versa, trying to keep ahead of the game.

If you want to get a rough picture of what's happening in memory and the page file, open Task Manager (right-click the Taskbar and choose Task Manager from the context menu). Look at the PF Usage readout and the Page File Usage History graph on the Performance page to see how much memory is being used. That reading is in megabytes or gigabytes. Then look at the Physical Memory (K) group box, which lists the total memory, available memory, and system cache. These figures are in kilobytes, so you'll need to divide by 1024 to get exact megabytes, but dividing by 1000 will give you figures close enough for government work.

The illustration below shows the computer struggling. You can see that the CPU usage has been high but has dropped a bit. Memory usage is massive and has been steadily increasing. And there's only a pathetic amount of physical memory unused and available: less than 1 percent of the total.

Then display the Processes page and look at what's going on there. Select the Show Processes from All Users check box so that you see all the processes that are going on. Then choose View ➤ Select Columns to display the Select Columns dialog box. Select the Virtual Memory Size check box and click the OK button. Task Manager adds the VM Size column to the columns displayed. You can then sort the running processes by the Mem Usage column or by the VM Size column to see how much memory and virtual memory each is taking up. The illustration below (which doesn't show processes from all users) explains why the computer in the above illustration was struggling: Two processes have absurdly large virtual machines. Also, check out the Commit Charge readout at the bottom of the Taskbar window. There's a runt's helping of memory left, and that's all.

Continued on the next page

EXPERT KNOWLEDGE: WHAT HAPPENS WHEN YOU RUN OUT OF VIRTUAL MEMORY? *(continued)*

For more precise monitoring of performance, use the Performance tool, as discussed in "Monitoring Performance with the Performance Tool" later in this chapter.

If you watch the readouts in Task Manager, you'll see that Windows tries to keep some RAM available for as long as possible. When most of the RAM is gone, the amount of virtual memory consumed grows faster to accommodate your memory demands. But if you keep using up more memory (for example, by opening large files), and you've set a maximum size for your paging file, you'll eventually run out of virtual memory as well as RAM.

When you run out of virtual memory, Windows XP displays the Windows – Virtual Memory Minimum Too Low pop-up in the notification area (shown below), telling you that it is increasing the size of your virtual memory paging file and that, while this is happening, requests for memory may be denied. Windows is serious about denying requests for memory—it starts responding glacially slowly, and you'll probably be less frustrated if you leave it alone until it has finished increasing the size of the paging file. Click the pop-up to dismiss it, then sit back for a minute or two. Again, if you have Task Manager open, you can see Windows increasing the size of the paging file—the size of the second Commit Charge figure on the Processes page will increase to show the new amount of memory available.

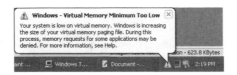

Once Windows has grabbed more memory for the paging file, and has written as much data to disk as it must in order to get things moving again, it'll become more responsive—but probably only a *bit* more responsive. You can try to start using Windows normally again at this point, but in most cases you'll be

Continued on the next page

EXPERT KNOWLEDGE: WHAT HAPPENS WHEN YOU RUN OUT OF VIRTUAL MEMORY? *(continued)*

better off reducing the amount of memory you're using. This could mean closing some programs; closing some big files; using the Users page of Task Manager to log someone off and close their programs (losing any unsaved data if necessary); or shutting down Windows and restarting it. (Restarting Windows will also terminate any other user sessions and lose any unsaved data they contain.)

When Windows is struggling for memory, you'll see the Applications page of Task Manager list programs as *Not Responding* when in fact they *are* responding but are doing so very slowly. You can use the End Task button to kill any program that really isn't responding, but it's usually better to wait a few seconds (or a few minutes) to see if the program comes back to life when Windows is able to feed it more memory.

If you start any memory-hungry program when Windows is struggling for memory, Windows may clobber the program without notifying you. Again, it's better to wait until Windows has stabilized itself and the programs that are currently running before you try to run any more programs.

Setting Environment Variables

From the Advanced page of the System Properties dialog box, you can click the Environment Variables button to display the Environment Variables dialog box (shown in Figure 16.14).

FIGURE 16.14

You can examine user variables and system variables in the Environment Variables dialog box.

Environment variables have largely been superseded by Registry values, so you probably won't need to do much in this dialog box. You *can* use the New buttons, the Edit buttons, and the Delete buttons to create, edit, and delete user variables and system variables, but you shouldn't need to do so. And you *can* find out some information about Windows and your system from the System Variables list box—but most of this information is more easily found elsewhere. For example, you'll find processor information in the System Info applet, which you can access from the Help and Support Center window.

Click the OK button or the Cancel button to close the Environment Variables dialog box when you've finished gazing at the wonders it offers.

Enabling and Disabling Error Reporting

If you've ever complained about software crashing on Windows, or about Windows itself crashing, you should like Windows XP's error-reporting features, which by default are set up to enable error reporting on Windows itself and programs running on it. You can turn off error reporting if it doesn't suit you, or you can choose to include or exclude specific programs from error reporting. For example, if you're developing a program, and it keeps crashing because you haven't programmed it right, you'd probably want to exclude it from error reporting on the grounds that Microsoft hadn't even heard of it yet (and they might not want to hear of it until you improve it).

To configure error reporting, follow these steps:

1. Click the Error Reporting button on the Advanced page of the System Properties dialog box. Windows displays the Error Reporting dialog box (shown in Figure 16.15).

FIGURE 16.15

Use the Error Reporting dialog box and the linked dialog boxes to configure error reporting to your taste.

2. To turn off error reporting entirely, select the Disable Error Reporting option button. Otherwise, leave the Enable Error Reporting option button selected (as it is by default).

   ◆ If you turn off error reporting, it's best to leave the But Notify Me when Critical Errors Occur check box selected so that Windows lets you know when something goes badly wrong.

3. In the Enable Error Reporting list, select or clear the Windows Operating System check box and the Programs check box as appropriate.

4. To specify which programs to include or exclude, select the Programs check box. Then click the Choose Programs button. Windows displays the Choose Programs dialog box (shown in Figure 16.16).

5. In the Report Errors for These Programs area, select the All Programs option button (the default setting) or the All Programs in This List option button as appropriate.

6. If you selected the All Programs in This List option button, select or clear the check boxes in the list box to indicate the programs you're interested in. Use the upper Add button and the resulting Add Program dialog box to add programs to this list.

FIGURE 16.16

Use the Choose Programs dialog box to specify programs to include or exclude from error reporting.

7. To exclude specific programs from error reporting, use the lower Add button and its Add Program dialog box to build a list of programs for exclusion in the Do Not Report Errors for These Programs list box. Select and clear the check boxes for the programs you add to the list as appropriate.

8. Click the OK button. Windows closes the Choose Programs dialog box.

9. Click the OK button. Windows closes the Error Reporting dialog box.

Setting Start-up and Recovery Options

Windows XP includes several start-up options that you should know about if you're running a dual-boot setup. (If you're not, just ignore these options: They don't apply to you at the moment.) And it lets you specify what it should do when it encounters a system failure—an error bad enough to crash the system.

To set start-up and recovery options, follow these steps:

1. Click the Settings button in the Startup and Recovery group box on the Advanced page of the System Properties dialog box. Windows displays the Startup and Recovery dialog box (shown in Figure 16.17).

2. If you have a dual- or multiple-boot system, choose options in the System Startup group box:

   ◆ In the Default Operating System drop-down list, select the operating system that you want to boot by default.

   ◆ If you want Windows to display the boot list of operating systems for a number of seconds before booting one, so that you can boot an operating system other than the default one, select the Time to Display List of Operating Systems check box and enter a suitable value in the text box. You can enter any value from 0 seconds to 999 seconds. The default value is 30 seconds, but most people find a shorter value more useful—long enough to give you time to select the operating system (or just tap a key) without needing pro-sports reflexes, but short enough to pass quickly if you just want to boot the default operating system.

TIP   You can edit the boot options file, BOOT.INI, manually by clicking the Edit button in the System Startup group box. The section "Creating a Dual-Boot Setup" at the end of this chapter discusses how to edit the boot options file.

FIGURE 16.17

Use the System Startup options in the Startup and Recovery dialog box to specify the default operating system to boot and for how long Windows should display the boot list of operating systems. Use the System Failure options to specify what Windows should do if it suffers a system failure.

3. Whether you're using a single-boot system or a multiple-boot system, leave the Time to Display Recovery Options when Needed check box selected, and enter an appropriate number of seconds in its text box. When Windows is rebooting after a failed boot, it displays the Recovery Options menu so that you can restart it in Safe mode if you want.

4. Choose options in the System Failure group box:

   Write an Event to the System Log check box   Select this check box (which is selected by default) if you want Windows to write an event to the System Log. ("The System Log" earlier in this chapter shows you how to view and interpret the System Log.)

   Send an Administrative Alert check box   Select this check box (which is selected by default) if you want Windows to display an Alert dialog box when a system failure occurs. Having a visual indication of narrowly averted or impending disaster can concentrate the mind wonderfully.

   Automatically Restart check box   Select this check box (which is selected by default) if you want Windows XP to automatically reboot if there's a system failure. (Windows reboots after writing that event to the System Log and sending an administrative alert, of course—if you left those check boxes selected.)

TIP   It should go without saying that these recovery options aren't a panacea. Any crash serious enough to be called a system failure will almost invariably result in the loss of any unsaved data sitting around in the programs affected. Besides, despite sitting stably on the New Technology bedrock of Windows NT and 2000, Windows XP still suffers occasional lockups, particularly with misbehaved hardware drivers. If your system hangs (freezes), you'll probably need to reboot it manually, because the auto-reboot functionality will be frozen as well. After rebooting, you'll find that no event was written to the System Log and no administrative alert was sent, because Windows was just as blindsided by the hang as you were.

Write Debugging Information group box   In the drop-down list, select the type of debugging information that you want Windows to write in the event of a crash. Your choices are None, Small Memory Dump, Kernel Memory Dump, and Complete Memory Dump. The None choice turns off the writing of debugging information. A Small Memory Dump creates a file with a name built of the prefix `MINI`, the date in MMDDYY format, a hyphen, the number of the dump, and the DMP extension. For example, the first dump on Christmas Day 2001 is named `MINI122501-01.DMP`. The dump file is stored in the directory specified in the Small Dump Directory text box and contains the smallest possible amount of memory information to be useful for debugging. With each crash, Windows creates a new file. A Kernel Memory Dump dumps only the kernel memory into a file called `MEMORY.DMP` by default and needs between 50 and 800MB of space for the paging file on the boot volume (not on another volume). A Complete Memory Dump, as its name suggests, dumps all the information contained in system memory when the crash occurred. Again, this goes into a file named `MEMORY.DMP` by default. To create a complete memory dump, you need to have a paging file on the boot volume (again, not on another volume) of at least the size of your computer's RAM plus 1MB (for example, a paging file of at least 97MB if your computer has 96MB RAM). Choose the location and name for the dump file in the text box in the Write Debugging Information group box, and select the Overwrite Any Existing File check box if appropriate. (This check box isn't available for Small Memory Dump, because this option creates a sequence of files automatically.)

NOTE   A small memory dump happens instantaneously. A kernel dump takes a bit longer. A complete memory dump takes anything from a few seconds to a minute or two. For a kernel dump or a complete dump, Windows displays a Blue Screen of Death with a percentage counter as it writes the contents of memory to disk. When this is done, the computer reboots (if you've left the Automatically Restart check box selected).

5. Click the OK button. Windows closes the Startup and Recovery dialog box.

TIP   To check how the memory dump works, or to experience a crash in action, try using the `CrashOnCtrlScroll` Registry key as discussed in the "Crashing Your Computer on Cue" sidebar in Chapter 12. On some computers, this produces a dump followed by a reboot. On other computers, it produces a custom Blue Screen of Death and nothing beyond it.

Monitoring Performance with the Performance Tool

As you saw earlier in the chapter, you can monitor performance to some extent by using Task Manager—and if any program gets out of hand, you can shut it down without much difficulty from there. But if you want to see more precisely what's happening on your computer, use the Performance tool instead.

To run Performance, take the following steps:

1. Choose Start ➢ Control Panel. Windows displays Control Panel.

2. Click the Performance and Maintenance link. Windows displays the Performance and Maintenance screen.

3. Click the Administrative Tools link. Windows displays the Administrative Tools screen.

4. Double-click the Performance shortcut. Windows starts Performance (shown in Figure 16.18).

FIGURE 16.18

If Task Manager doesn't give you the detail you need on your computer's performance, use the Performance tool to monitor performance.

1. New Counter Set Button
2. Clear Display Button
3. View Current Activity Button
4. View Log Data Button
5. View Graph Button
6. View Histogram Button
7. View Report Button
8. Add Button
9. Delete Button
10. Highlight Button
11. Copy Properties Button
12. Paste Counter List Button
13. Properties Button
14. Freeze Display Button
15. Update Data Button
16. Help Button

In grayscale, this looks like a spider taking a polygraph test, but in color, it's easy enough to read. As you can more or less see in the figure, Performance starts you off in Graph view tracking three counters: Pages/Sec, Avg. Disk Queue Length, and % Processor Time (listed in the list box at the bottom of the window).

You can add further counters by taking the following steps:

1. Click the Add button. Windows displays the Add Counters dialog box (shown in Figure 16.19).

FIGURE 16.19

Use the Add Counters dialog box to add to Performance the counters that you want to track.

2. Either select the Use Local Computer Counters option button or select the Select Counters from Computer option button and choose your computer in the drop-down list. It doesn't matter which. Performance is designed to allow administrators to monitor computers remotely, but you can't use this capability with Windows XP Home.

3. In the Performance Object drop-down list, select the category of item you want to monitor. For example, you might select Memory. Windows displays a list of the counters available for that performance object in the left list box.

4. With the Select Counters from List option button selected (as it is by default), select the first counter in the left list box and click the Add button to add it to the Performance window.

   ◆ Click the Explain button to display a window explaining the meaning of the current counter.

5. Add further counters by repeating steps 3 and 4.

6. Click the Close button. Windows closes the Add Counters dialog box.

To remove a counter from Performance, select it in the list box at the bottom of the Performance window and press the Delete key or click the Delete button.

To highlight a counter with a thick black line, select the counter in the list box and click the Highlight button.

TIP   Once you've set up a view in Performance that shows the items you want to track, you can add it to your favorites by choosing Favorites ➢ Add to Favorites, specifying the name for the favorite in the resulting Add to Favorites dialog box, and clicking the OK button.

When you've finished using Performance, choose File ➢ Exit. Windows closes Performance.

Using the System Restore Feature

Windows' System Restore feature provides a way of recovering from the consequences of installing the wrong hardware driver (or a buggy driver) or a dysfunctional piece of software.

How System Restore Works

System Restore uses a system of *restore points* that include information about the state of the computer's software configuration when the restore point was created. Windows creates some restore points automatically at quasi-regular intervals and before you install some drivers and programs, and you can create restore points manually whenever you want to. For example, you might choose to create a restore point manually before you install a new driver or program, just in case Windows doesn't create a restore point and things turn out for the worse.

If your computer starts misbehaving, you can return your computer to one of the restore points before whatever change precipitated the trouble. You run System Restore and specify the restore point. Windows then restores the computer's software configuration using the information stored in the restore point.

System Restore is very impressive technology, but it can't fix every problem. It affects only your system files (as opposed to your data files), so rolling back the computer to an earlier state doesn't delete any data files that you've created or downloaded in the meantime. Likewise, returning to a restore point doesn't reinstate any data files that you've deleted since that point in time.

Adjusting the Amount of Space System Restore Takes Up

As you'd guess, System Restore stores the restore-point information in files on your hard disk. The more restore points Windows creates automatically and you create manually, the more space they take up. Windows automatically reserves space on each hard drive volume for System Restore files. System Restore needs at least 200MB in order to do any good. By default, it claims anywhere between 12 percent and 20 percent of each drive.

That's a serious investment of space, and you don't really need to use System Restore on any drive but the one that contains your Windows files and program files. Once you've gotten your computer fixed up with the hardware and software you need, and everything seems to be working to your satisfaction, you may want to reduce the amount of space devoted to System Restore. To do so, take the following steps:

1. Press Winkey+Break; or click the Start button, right-click the My Computer item on the Start menu, and choose Properties from the context menu. Windows displays the System Properties dialog box.

2. Click the System Restore tab. Windows displays the System Restore page. Figure 16.20 shows two examples of the System Restore page, because the page shows different controls depending on whether your computer has one hard drive (as in the left example) or multiple hard drives (as in the right example). Windows displays *Monitoring* for a drive you're monitoring and *Turned Off* for a drive on which you've turned off System Restore.

3. If you have only one hard drive, drag the Disk Space to Use slider to specify the amount of space to use for System Restore.

FIGURE 16.20

On the System Restore page of the System Properties dialog box, you can turn off System Restore or adjust the amount of space it takes up.

4. If you have multiple hard drives, follow these steps for each drive:

   ◆ Select the drive in the Available Drives list box and click the Settings button. Windows displays the Settings dialog box for the drive. Figure 16.21 shows an example of the Settings dialog box for a system drive (on the left) and an example for a nonsystem drive (on the right).

   ◆ For a nonsystem drive, you can turn off System Restore by selecting the Turn Off System Restore on This Drive check box.

   ◆ Drag the Disk Space to Use slider to specify the amount of space to use for System Restore.

   ◆ Click the OK button. If you chose to turn off System Restore, Windows displays a confirmation dialog box warning you that you won't be able to undo harmful changes on the drive. Click the Yes button. Windows closes the Settings dialog box.

FIGURE 16.21

If you have multiple drives, use the Settings dialog box to choose settings for each drive. The Settings dialog box on the left is for a system drive. The Settings dialog box on the right is for a nonsystem drive.

NOTE   If you're desperate enough to trade recoverability for space, you can turn off System Restore by selecting the Turn Off System Restore check box or the Turn Off System Restore on All Drives check box. But usually it's a much better idea to keep using System Restore but devote less space to it.

5. Click the OK button. Windows closes the System Properties dialog box.

Setting System Restore Points

Windows automatically creates restore points called *system checkpoints* periodically—usually one or two a day. It also creates restore points automatically when you install certain types of software.

 You can create system checkpoints manually by running System Restore (Start ➤ All Programs ➤ Accessories ➤ System Tools ➤ System Restore), selecting the Create a Restore Point option button, and following the prompts. See pages 83–84 of the *Essential Skills* section for a visual walkthrough of setting system restore points.

Restoring Your System to a Restore Point

 To restore your computer to a restore point, run System Restore (Start ➤ All Programs ➤ Accessories ➤ System Tools ➤ System Restore), select the Restore My Computer to an Earlier Time option button, and follow the prompts. See pages 85–86 of the *Essential Skills* section for a visual guide to restoring your system to a system restore point.

After restoring your system to the restore point, check your system to make sure that it's running properly. If the restoration didn't produce the effect you wanted, run System Restore again. You can either choose a restore point further in the past or undo your last restoration.

Restoring the Last Known Good Configuration

System Restore can work wonders—provided that your system can boot Windows. But if your system can't boot Windows, you need to take other measures. Your first step should be to try restoring the Last Known Good Configuration, as discussed in "Restoring the Registry to Its Last Known Good Configuration" in Chapter 12. Failing that, try using Recovery Console as described in the next section.

Repairing a Windows Installation Using Recovery Console

If using the Last Known Good Configuration does you no good, or if you want to go nuclear without taking conventional recovery steps, try Recovery Console. Recovery Console gives you a command prompt skeleton of Windows XP that you can use to perform basic file maintenance (for example, replacing a corrupted system file) or to issue repair commands for getting Windows running again.

To start Recovery Console, take the following steps:

1. Boot from your Windows XP CD as if you were installing Windows XP from scratch. Wait while Setup loads all the files required for setup.

2. On the Welcome to Setup screen, press **R**. Setup displays the Recovery Console, which presents you with a numbered list of the operating systems that it has identified on the computer. The operating systems are identified by the drive and folder that contains them rather than by type, so make sure you select the right one if the computer has multiple operating systems installed.

3. Type the number of the operating system you want to recover and press the Enter key. (To cancel out of Recovery Console, press the Enter key without typing a number.) Setup prompts you for the Administrator password for the account.

4. Type the password for a Computer Administrator account and press the Enter key. (If your account doesn't use a password, just press the Enter key.) Setup displays a command prompt to the system root folder for the operating system.

The command prompt doesn't look very exciting, but it gives you the entrée to the operating system that you need to fix Windows XP. Recovery Console supports regular DOS commands. For example, you can use the COPY command to copy files from a floppy or from a CD (for example, the Windows XP CD) to replace files.

Recovery Console also supports commands for taking the following actions:

Partitioning the disk   Invoke the DISKPART command to display a partitioning screen that you can use to create and delete partitions.

Creating a new boot sector   Use the FIXBOOT command to create a new boot sector on a partition you specify and make that partition active.

Repairing the master boot record   Use the FIXMBR command to repair the master boot record on the drive. (If you don't know what the master boot record is, you probably shouldn't be using this command.)

Listing the devices and services on your computer   Use the LISTSVC command to list the devices and services on your computer.

Enabling and disabling devices   Use the ENABLE command and the DISABLE command to enable or disable a specific device or service. (Use the LISTSVC command to list the devices or commands that you can enable or disable.)

Logging on to a different operating system   Use the LOGON command to log on to another operating system so that you can repair it.

Returning to the system root folder   Use the SYSTEMROOT command to return to the system root folder.

To exit Recovery Console and restart your computer, issue the EXIT command and press the Enter key.

Creating a Dual-Boot Setup

If you want to run not only Windows XP but also another operating system on your computer, you'll probably want to create a dual-boot setup or multiboot setup. Windows XP includes a boot loader that makes dual-booting relatively simple—provided that either the other operating system cooperates or you install Windows XP after the other operating system.

EXPERT KNOWLEDGE: EXTRACTING A COMPRESSED FILE FROM A CABINET FILE

If Windows won't boot because it has corrupted a vital system file (or you've somehow managed to delete a vital system file), you'll need to replace the system file in order to get Windows working again.

The best place to get a replacement system file is your Windows CD. If you don't have a second PC handy on which to extract the file from the compressed cabinet file that contains it, you can use the DOS-based EXTRACT command from Windows 9x to extract the file.

The basic syntax for the EXTRACT command is as follows, where *cabinet* is the name of the cabinet file and *filename* is the name of the file to extract:

```
EXTRACT cabinet filename
```

To display a directory listing of the contents of the CAB file, use the following syntax, where *cabinet* is the name of the cabinet file:

```
EXTRACT /D cabinet
```

Creating a Dual-Boot Setup with Another Version of Windows

To create a dual-boot setup with another version of Windows, follow the procedure described in "Performing a New Installation of Windows XP" in Chapter 2. Setup automatically creates a dual-boot setup with the previous version of Windows. When you boot your computer, Windows displays the Please Select the Operating System to Start screen, from which you specify which of the operating systems should boot.

Choosing System Start-up Options for Booting Windows

When you've created a dual-boot setup as described in the previous section, you can specify which of the operating systems the boot loader boots by default. You can also edit the boot menu (which is stored in the BOOT.INI file) to change the order in which the operating systems are listed and the way in which they are listed. You may also need to remove boot menu items that have become superfluous or confusing.

To choose system start-up options, take the following steps:

1. Press Winkey+Break. Alternatively, choose Start ➤ Control Panel, click the Performance and Maintenance link, click the Other Control Panel Options link, and click the System link. Windows displays the System Properties dialog box.

2. Click the Advanced tab. Windows displays the Advanced page.

3. Click the Settings button in the Startup and Recovery group box. Windows displays the Startup and Recovery dialog box (shown in Figure 16.17, earlier in the chapter).

4. In the Default Operating System drop-down list, select the operating system that you want to boot by default.

5. If you want Windows to display the boot list of operating systems for a number of seconds before booting one, so that you can boot an operating system other than the default one, select the Time to Display List of Operating Systems check box and enter a suitable value in the text box. You can enter any value from 0 seconds to 999 seconds. The default value is 30 seconds.

6. If you want to change the names and descriptions of the items on the boot menu, click the Edit button. Windows opens the `BOOT.INI` file in a Notepad window. Figure 16.22 shows an example of a `BOOT.INI` file open in Notepad.

FIGURE 16.22

You can edit the `BOOT.INI` file to change the list of entries displayed and the order in which they're listed.

◆ Edit the descriptions of the operating systems as necessary within the double quotation marks. For example, you might add to the name of an operating system a note about when it should be used:

```
multi(0)disk(0)rdisk(0)partition(1)\WINDOWS-"Windows XP Home -
   ➥ test configuration" /fastdetect
```

WARNING   *Don't change any of the disk, volume, or partition information. Doing so may prevent Windows from booting.*

◆ To change the number of seconds the boot menu is displayed, change the `timeout=` value. (It's usually easier to do this in the Startup and Recovery dialog box.)

◆ Similarly, you *can* change the `default=` line to change the default operating system, but it's usually much easier to use the Default Operating System drop-down list in the Startup and Recovery group box.

◆ Press Ctrl+S or choose File ➢ Save to save the `BOOT.INI` file, then press Alt+F4 or choose File ➢ Exit to close it.

7. Click the OK button. Windows closes the Startup and Recovery dialog box.

8. Click the OK button. Windows closes the System Properties dialog box.

EXPERT KNOWLEDGE: *MULTI(), RDISK(), AND /FASTDETECT*

Unless you feel a compelling need to create BOOT.INI manually, you don't need to know what the components of the boot menu items mean. But if that's a curious look on your face, read on....

- ◆ multi() specifies the hard disk controller of the disk on which the operating system in question is installed. Numbering starts at zero (because it's computer-counting).

- ◆ disk() specifies the hard disk on which the operating system is installed. disk() is used only when scsi() is used; otherwise, it's included in the boot menu item but has no function. Again, numbering begins at zero.

- ◆ rdisk() specifies the hard disk on which the operating system is installed. Once again, numbering begins at zero.

- ◆ partition() specifies the partition on which the operating system is installed. Just to be confusing, numbering starts at 1.

If Windows XP or Windows 2000 is installed on a FAT32 partition, there's also a signature() component to the boot menu item. This specifies the disk controller.

If the operating system is installed on a SCSI disk without an active BIOS, the boot menu item has a scsi() component that specifies the hard disk controller.

The /fastdetect switch turns off the detection of serial mice. You can also use this switch with a specific COM port to turn off detection on that port—for example, /fastdetect=COM1.

Setting Up a Dual-Boot with Linux

The Windows XP boot loader handles previous installations of Windows deftly, but it's not designed to work with Linux (or indeed OS/2, Solaris, BeOS, or other non-Microsoft operating systems). If you want to dual-boot Windows XP and Linux, you need to take a different approach.

You can install Linux either before installing Windows XP or after installing Windows XP. In either case, you'll need to keep your partitions straight so that the later installation doesn't overwrite the earlier installation. When installing Linux after Windows XP, make sure that you don't install Lilo (the *Linux Loader*) on the master boot record (MBR). Doing so overwrites the Windows XP boot loader, which prevents Windows XP from starting at all.

This means that (obviously enough) you shouldn't use an automated installation routine that's designed to take over the whole disk for Linux. For most installations of Linux, you'll need to choose a custom installation. For example, for Red Hat, specify a Custom System on the Install Type screen, and partition the drive manually with Disk Druid (or fdisk if you're feeling bold). On the Lilo Configuration screen, select the First Sector of Boot Partition option button instead of the Master Boot Record option button in the Install Lilo Boot Record On list. Also, make sure the Create Boot Disk check box is selected.

If you don't mind leaving a floppy disk dangling around your floppy drive, you can also boot Lilo off a floppy. Windows XP boots regularly when the floppy drive is empty.

EXPERT KNOWLEDGE: SERIOUS MULTIBOOTING

The methods discussed in this section work well enough for setting up a dual-boot arrangement or a multiboot arrangement with a modest number of operating systems. But if you need to install serious numbers of operating systems on the same computer, it's worth investing in a heavy-duty boot manager such as System Commander from V Communications (www.v-com.com). System Commander lets you install more than 100 operating systems on the same computer. (You'll have a hard time finding that many different operating systems, but you can also install multiple copies of the same operating systems to get the numbers up.)

Up Next

This chapter has discussed how to use Windows' tools to identify problems on your computer and troubleshoot them. It has also discussed how to set up a dual-boot arrangement so that you can run Windows XP and another operating system on the same computer.

That's the end of Part II of the book. Part III discusses communications, the Internet, and the Web.

Part III

Communications, the Internet, and the Web

Chapter 17

Connecting to the Internet

THESE DAYS, AN INTERNET connection is almost a must-have for anyone with a computer—and indeed Windows XP's setup routine heavily encourages you to connect your computer to the Internet by any viable means that it can find.

This chapter discusses how to connect to the Internet with Windows XP and how to secure your Internet connection. Along the way, it discusses the different types of Internet connection and the benefits they offer; what dial-up networking is, how it works, and how to configure it; and how to work with digital certificates so that you can establish the authenticity of a document or transaction.

This chapter covers the following topics:

◆ Choosing an Internet connection type and ISP

◆ Creating an Internet connection

◆ Establishing an Internet connection

◆ Using multiple modems on a dial-up connection

◆ Securing your Internet connection

◆ Using digital certificates

NOTE *One topic that isn't covered in this chapter is how to share your Internet connection with other computers in your household or office. Chapter 33 discusses the Internet Connection Sharing feature. (This chapter does cover how to share your Internet connection with other users of this computer.)*

Choosing an Internet Connection Type and ISP

This section provides a brief summary of the options you should be considering if you don't have an Internet connection or you need to improve on your existing connection.

Unless you're very unusual, you'll want an Internet connection as fast as you can a) get and b) afford. You'll also want your ISP to provide the features you need.

In the old days (say, three or four years ago), shopping around for an ISP used to involve minute comparisons of the details of the services that competing dial-up ISPs offered: This ISP offered you three more mailboxes than that ISP, but that ISP had more points of presence nationwide. These days, such comparisons hold if you're looking for a dial-up connection, but you're more likely to want a high-speed connection—if one is available. If one is, selecting an ISP is more likely to involve choosing among as few as two or three providers of high-speed access. In some cases, your only choice may be between your incumbent high-speed provider and poky old dial-up.

Trying to move with the times, this section starts by discussing the connection types in descending order of speed, starting with the type that's by far the fastest but also the one you're least likely to be able to get.

Fiber

The fastest affordable Internet connection available in the U.S. is optical fiber, which can deliver speeds of around 100Mbps—the same speed as the Fast Ethernet networks used in many companies and on many campuses. This bandwidth is typically shared, so you usually won't be able to download at the full 10+MB per second it offers, but you'll find it plenty fast enough.

If you can get fiber, go for it. Unfortunately, the chances of your being able to get it are minimal at this writing. Some new housing communities in high-tech areas (such as Silicon Valley, Silicon Island, Silicon Prairie—hmm, there's a theme here) are being built with fiber to the home, and some apartment buildings in major cities are being refitted with fiber. But if you live anywhere else, you're apt to be straight out of luck.

As you'd expect, fiber tends to be more expensive than other technologies, but when it's run to the home (rather than to a business), it's usually more or less affordable—especially if you need the speed it delivers.

Cable Modem

If cable modem access is available where you live, go for it. After fiber, cable provides the fastest affordable residential access—up to several megabits (millions of bits) per second.

Cable has three main drawbacks:

♦ First, the bandwidth is shared with your neighbors, so if everyone gets online at the same time, the speed drops. Ask the cable company what the network's capacity is, how many people share that capacity, and what the minimum bandwidth they guarantee you is. (They may not guarantee *any* minimum bandwidth.) If you find the speed dropping to unacceptable levels, lobby the cable company vociferously to add bandwidth to your loop. Get your neighbors to lobby too—if you can pry them away from their computers.

♦ Second, many cable companies implement an *upload speed cap*, which limits the amount of data you can upload per second, typically to prevent you from running a Web server or FTP server. If you're neither going to be running a server nor sharing many files via P2P technologies, this shouldn't be a problem, but make sure that you know what the company's policy is before you sign up.

♦ Third, because the wire is shared, your computer is essentially networked with your neighborhood, so it's vital that you use a firewall to secure it. Also, be sure to turn off file-sharing on any computer that's connected to the Internet via a cable modem.

Digital Subscriber Line (DSL)

If digital subscriber line (DSL) connectivity is available and affordable where you live, get it. DSL typically offers between 384Kbps and 1.5Mbps downstream (to the consumer) and slower upstream (to the ISP) speeds. At this writing, the Baby Bells are vying with the cable companies for high-speed customers, so the cost of DSL is reasonable—from $20 to $50 per month for good service, including an account with their ISP.

Because DSL is always on, your computer is continuously connected to the Internet, so there's a threat of your computer being attacked across the wire. With DSL, the threat is significantly lower than with cable (because the wire isn't shared in most U.S. implementations), but you'll still need a firewall.

EXPERT KNOWLEDGE: 31 FLAVORS OF DSL

DSL comes in a variety of flavors—not as many as Baskin-Robbins, which can manage one flavor for each day of the month, but more than enough for one flavor for each day of the week. These are the main types of DSL you're likely to encounter:

Asymmetric DSL (ADSL)   ADSL delivers faster speed downstream (downloading data to your computer) than upstream (uploading data). ADSL is currently the most widely used form of DSL for residential connections. ADSL can manage up to 6.1Mbps downstream and 640Kbps upstream, but most reasonable-priced offerings give 384Kbps to 1.544Mbps downstream and 128Kbps to 384Kbps upstream. The disadvantage to ADSL is that it requires a device called a *splitter* to be installed at the consumer end of the line to split the line between data use and voice use. Installing the splitter is a professional job and so requires a (technical term) *truck roll*—in theory, only one per installation, but enough to greatly increase the cost and time needed for deployment.

Consumer DSL (CDSL)   CDSL is a new implementation of DSL by Rockwell that's designed (as its name suggests) for the consumer market and to be easier to install than ADSL: It doesn't need a splitter at the consumer end of the line. It delivers 1Mbps downstream and slower speeds upstream.

DSL Lite (G.Lite)   DSL Lite wins the competition for the most names, as it's also known as *splitterless ADSL* and *Universal ADSL*. As you'd guess from the first of those alternative names, DSL Lite doesn't require a splitter to be installed at the consumer end of the line. It delivers from 1.544Mbps to 6Mbps downstream and from 128Kbps to 384Kbps upstream.

Rate-adaptive DSL (RADSL)   RADSL adjusts its speed to the capabilities of the phone line. It requires a splitter and can deliver from 640Kbps to 2.2Mbps downstream and from 272Kbps to 1.088Mbps upstream.

Symmetrical DSL (SDSL)   SDSL delivers the same data rate (1.544Mbps) upstream and downstream, making it suitable for businesses (or individuals) who need to transmit a lot of data—for example, running a Web server. SDSL requires a splitter and is usually considerably more expensive than ADSL.

That's probably more DSLs than you really want details on—and we haven't even mentioned x2/DSL, HDSL, IDSL, or UDSL....

It's likely that your provider will offer only one flavor of DSL for residential service. That flavor is likely to be ADSL.

Unlike with cable, you're not on the same local network as your neighbors, so the bandwidth isn't shared, and you should be able to get the minimum guaranteed rate (sometimes referred to as the *committed information rate* or *CIR*) any time of the day or night.

The main disadvantage of DSL is that it works only within a relatively short distance from the telephone company's central office, which means in effect that it's confined to urban locations. Some non-telco DSL providers are more aggressive with the distance than the telcos, but you'll typically have to pay more, and you'll get a lower-speed connection. If you live out in the sticks, you're almost certainly beyond the range of DSL.

Integrated Services Digital Network (ISDN)

If you can't get cable or a DSL, your next choice should be ISDN (Integrated Services Digital Network). An ISDN is a digital line that's not as fast as a DSL but is more widely available, especially for people outside major metropolitan areas. ISDN's *basic rate interface (BRI)* provides two *bearer channels* that deliver 64Kbps each, plus a 16Kbps signaling channel, so it delivers decent speeds when both bearer channels are open. The signaling channel is more formally called a *data channel*, and you'll sometimes hear BRI referred to as *2B+D*—two bearer channels plus one data channel.

Check the prices before you order ISDN: It's traditionally been a business service, and it can be expensive, with most companies levying per-minute charges for each channel.

The good news about ISDN (apart from its wide availability) is that most implementations are symmetrical, so you get the same speed upstream as downstream.

Satellite Solutions

If you're too rural to get ISDN, or if ISDN is too slow for you, consider one of the satellite solutions available, such as DirecPC. These solutions typically offer speeds of around 400Kbps downstream, so they can be good if you need to download large chunks of data (such as audio or video files).

Satellite solutions used to have one major drawback: The satellite provided only downlink capabilities, so you had to use your phone line to send data to your ISP to tell them which information to deliver by satellite. Less-expensive satellite solutions still use this method, but if you pay more, you can send your outgoing data via satellite as well, making satellite much more attractive.

But there are several caveats:

◆ First, the satellite dish and installation can be pricey. (Watch for special offers.)

◆ Second, check the plan or pricing scheme carefully. Make sure it provides enough hours each month so that you don't start incurring expensive extra hours every month on your normal level of usage.

◆ Third, some satellite services have a *fair access policy (FAP)* by which they reserve the right to throttle back your download speed if you continuously run it full bore—in other words, you can have your 400Kbps (or whatever speed the provider offers), but you can't have it all the time. This can put a serious crimp into your ability to download a massive amount every day via a satellite hookup. So read your sign-up agreement carefully for details of the fair access policy, and be especially wary of clauses that allow the service provider to modify the terms of the contract without your explicit consent.

Wireless Services

If you need mobility with your Internet connection, check out the wireless services available. At this writing, you *can* hook up a laptop to a mobile phone, but the resulting data rates are too slow for anything but checking e-mail—and you're paying your usual call rates for the mobile phone. More promising is the Ricochet service from Metricom (www.metricom.com), which delivers always-on 128Kbps access in a number of metropolitan locations and airports across the U.S. and is more or less affordable.

Criteria for Choosing an ISP

If the connection type you chose isn't the only game in town, you may have a choice of ISPs as well. If you're using dial-up, you'll probably have plenty of choice. This section suggests the main criteria to use when evaluating the offerings of competing ISPs.

How many e-mail accounts do you get?   These days, a single e-mail account gets you about as far as a single tire on a car. Many ISPs offer five or so e-mail accounts for residential accounts—one for each member of the nuclear family, including the dog. You may want more than this, particularly if you use your computer for business. The better ISPs give you as many e-mail accounts as you need. Other ISPs charge you for additional mailboxes.

How much connect time are you allowed?   (Dial-up connections only) Some ISPs and some plans allow unlimited connection time. Others allow you a certain number of hours per month and charge extra for each hour or part of an hour beyond that.

Does your ISP provide a full suite of newsgroups?   Almost all ISPs provide newsgroups, but some filter out newsgroups they consider offensive or that have exceptionally high volumes of traffic.

How much Web space and traffic are you allowed?   Make sure that your ISP provides enough space for your Web site: Some ISPs offer 10MB, some 20MB, some 50MB. If you plan to get a lot of visitors to your Web site, check the amount of traffic that the ISP permits before charging you extra. Some ISPs permit unlimited traffic, but others charge beyond a certain limit (usually measured in gigabytes per month).

How many dial-up points of presence does it have?   First, make sure that the local point of presence (POP) is within your unrestricted calling area. Second, if you're traveling, you'll want to be able to connect at local rates. Make sure that your ISP has POPs in enough geographical areas or the right geographical areas. Your ISP might also have an 800 number that you can use when traveling; it'll probably have a per-minute charge, but it should cost less than calling long-distance with hotel surcharges.

Can you use multilink?   (Dial-up connections only) Multilink lets you connect with two or more modems at the same time to get faster throughput. You'll need a second phone line to use multilink, and many ISPs who support multilink charge extra for it.

How good is the service?   This question is best asked of people who are already using the service. If they report slow browsing and e-mail outages, look elsewhere.

Does the ISP support Windows XP?   Sooner or later, just about every ISP will support Windows XP, but many may not do so at first. Some require you to use their proprietary software, which typically offers a customized front end to the Web but in many cases proves less flexible than using Internet Explorer or another browser.

Can you access your e-mail via the Web?   This feature can be useful when you're traveling without your PC. Many ISPs don't support it.

Creating an Internet Connection

This section discusses how to create an Internet connection manually. For a visual guide to creating a dial-up Internet connection, see pages 43–45 of the *Essential Skills* section.

NOTE   If you have an always-on DSL connection, your computer should already be connected to the Internet, and you shouldn't need to follow this procedure. (For other types of broadband, such as cable modems, follow this procedure unless Windows tells you that you don't need to.) If you have a CD from your ISP that promises to set up your Internet connection for you, use that instead of following this procedure.

To create an Internet connection, take the following steps:

1. Choose Start ➢ Connect To ➢ Show All Connections. Windows displays the Network Connections folder.

    ◆ If you haven't created a network connection, the Connect To item doesn't appear on the Start menu. Choose Start ➢ Control Panel. Windows displays Control Panel. Click the Network and Internet Connections link. Windows displays the Network and Internet Connections screen. Click the Network Connections link. Windows displays the Network Connections folder.

2. Click the Create a New Connection link in the Network Tasks list. Windows starts the New Connection Wizard, which displays its Welcome to the New Connection Wizard page.

    ◆ If you haven't identified the country (or region) and area code that you're in, or your phone and modem options, Windows prompts you for them. See the sections "Specifying Your Location" and "Specifying Phone and Modem Options" in Chapter 14 for details.

3. Click the Next button. The Wizard displays the Network Connection Type page (shown in Figure 17.1).

4. Select the Connect to the Internet option button (if it's not selected by default).

5. Click the Next button. The Wizard displays the Getting Ready page (shown in Figure 17.2).

FIGURE 17.1

On the Network Connection Type page of the New Connection Wizard, select the Connect to the Internet Connection option button.

FIGURE 17.2

On the Getting Ready page of the New Connection Wizard, tell the Wizard how you want to connect to the Internet.

6. Select the Set Up My Connection Manually option button.

◆ If you select the Choose from a List of Internet Service Providers (ISPs) option button, the Wizard displays the Completing the New Connection Wizard page when you click the Next button. On that page, you have the choice to set up Internet access using MSN Explorer (for the U.S. only) or to select from a list of other ISPs listed on the Microsoft Internet Referral Service.

◆ If you select the Use the CD I Got from an ISP option button, the Wizard displays the Completing the New Connection Wizard page when you click the Next button. It then essentially tells you to run the ISP's CD to set up your connection.

7. Click the Next button. The Wizard displays the Internet Connection page (shown in Figure 17.3).

FIGURE 17.3

On the Internet Connection page of the New Connection Wizard, specify whether you'll be connecting via a dial-up modem or via broadband.

8. Select the Connect Using a Dial-up Modem option button, the Connect Using a Broadband Connection That Requires a User Name and Password option button, or the Connect Using a Broadband Connection That Is Always On option button as appropriate.

9. Click the Next button.

◆ If you selected the Connect Using a Dial-up Modem option button or the Connect Using a Broadband Connection That Requires a User Name and Password option button, the Wizard displays the Connection Name page (shown in Figure 17.4).

FIGURE 17.4

On the Connection Name page of the New Connection Wizard, enter the name by which you want to know the connection.

◆ If you selected the Connect Using a Broadband Connection That Is Always On option button, the Wizard displays the Completing the New Connection Wizard page, telling you that your connection should already be configured and ready to use. Click the Finish button and find out whether the Wizard is right.

10. Enter the name by which you want to know the connection. The Wizard suggests using your ISP's name, but there's no need to do so if you find another name more suitable.

11. Click the Next button.

   ◆ If you selected the Connect Using a Dial-up Modem option button, the Wizard displays the Phone Number to Dial page (shown in Figure 17.5). Take the next two steps.

FIGURE 17.5

On the Phone Number to Dial page of the New Connection Wizard, specify the phone number of the dial-up connection.

   ◆ If you selected the Connect Using a Broadband Connection That Requires a User Name and Password option button, the Wizard displays the Internet Account Information page. Go to step 14.

12. Enter the phone number for your ISP, including any area code or long-distance number.

13. Click the Next button. The Wizard displays the Internet Account Information page (shown in Figure 17.6).

FIGURE 17.6

On the Internet Account Information page of the New Connection Wizard, enter your username and password and choose options for the connection.

14. Enter your username in the User Name text box, and your password in the Password text box and the Confirm Password text box.

15. If you want other users of this computer to be able to connect to this Internet connection by using this username and password, leave the Use This Account Name and Password when Anyone Connects to the Internet from This Computer check box selected (as it is by default). If you want users to have to enter a username and password to establish an Internet connection, clear this check box.

16. If you want this connection to be the default Internet connection for this computer, leave the Make This the Default Internet Connection check box selected (as it is by default). Otherwise, clear this check box.

NOTE *Windows displays a white check mark in a black circle on the icon for the default Internet connection in the Network Connections window. To stop this connection from being the default connection, right-click its icon and choose Unset As Default Connection from the context menu. (To set it as the default connection again, right-click again and choose Set As Default Connection.)*

17. If you want to use Windows XP's Internet Connection Firewall (ICF) to protect your computer and others that connect to the Internet via your computer from attack via this Internet connection, leave the Turn On Internet Connection Firewall for This Connection check box selected (as it is by default). If you don't want to use ICF, clear this check box. See "Securing Your Internet Connection" later in this chapter for more information about firewalls in general and ICF in particular.

18. Click the Next button. The New Connection Wizard displays the Completing the New Connection Wizard page (shown in Figure 17.7).

FIGURE 17.7

On the Completing the New Connection Wizard page of the New Connection Wizard, specify whether you want a shortcut for the connection on the Desktop.

19. Select the Add a Shortcut to This Connection to My Desktop check box if you want the Wizard to create a shortcut on the Desktop for each user.

20. Click the Finish button. The New Connection Wizard finishes creating the connection and closes itself.

You can then connect as described in the next section.

Establishing a Connection

See pages 46–47 of the *Essential Skills* section for a visual guide to using a dial-up connection. To establish a connection, take the following steps:

1. If you created a shortcut for the connection on your Desktop, double-click it. If not, choose Start ➤ Connect To and choose the connection from the submenu. Windows displays the Connect dialog box for the connection (shown in Figure 17.8).

FIGURE 17.8

The Connect dialog box

2. If necessary, enter your username in the User Name text box and your password in the Password text box. You won't need to enter these if whoever set up the connection chose to store the username and password in the connection.

◆ If you want Windows to store the username and password, make sure the Save This User Name and Password for the Following Users check box is selected. Then select the Me Only option button or the Anyone Who Uses This Computer option button as appropriate.

3. Click the Dial button (for a dial-up connection) or the Connect button (for a broadband connection). Windows dials the connection or attempts to connect and displays the Connecting dialog box to keep you informed of its progress. If it receives an answer, it checks your username and password and, all being well, logs you in.

4. When the connection is established, Windows displays a notification-area pop-up giving the connection name and the connection speed.

If you chose to have the connection display an icon in the notification area, Windows places the icon there.

Viewing the Status of a Connection

The two monitor screens on the icon in the System Tray show light blue as data is transferred. When no data is being transferred, they appear dark. When a short burst of information is transferred, they flicker blue briefly; when sustained data transfer is taking place, both stay blue.

To view brief statistics for the connection, hover the mouse pointer over the icon. Windows displays a pop-up showing the connection name, the speed, and the number of packets sent and received, as shown on the left side of Figure 17.9.

To get a closer reading of what's happening on the connection, double-click the icon in the System Tray. Windows displays the Status dialog box for the connection. The General page of the Status dialog box (of which the right side of Figure 17.9 shows an example) gives the connection status, duration, speed, and details including the number of bytes of information sent and received and the number of errors.

FIGURE 17.9

Two ways of checking what's happening on a connection: Hover the mouse pointer over the System Tray icon to get a quick readout (left), or double-click the System Tray icon to display the Status dialog box with more details.

As you can see in the figure, the General page of the Status dialog box contains three buttons. Click the Properties button to display the Properties dialog box for the connection. Click the Disconnect button to disconnect the connection and close the Status dialog box. Click the Close button to close the Status dialog box without disconnecting the connection.

The Details page of the Status dialog box for a connection displays information about the server type, transport protocol, authentication, compression, PPP multilink framing, and IP addresses for the server and the client.

EXPERT KNOWLEDGE: WHEN DOES UNEXPECTED DATA TRANSFER INDICATE A PROBLEM?

As mentioned a page or so ago, the monitor screens on the System Tray icon for a dial-up connection appear light blue as data is transferred and black when no data is being transferred. By watching this icon, you can see at a glance whether the connection is transferring data. By displaying the Status dialog box for the connection, you can see details of the flow of bytes in and out.

When you're browsing the Web, or when you're downloading files, data is being transferred—obviously enough. When you're uploading files, you'll usually know about it. When you're in a conference with

Continued on next page

EXPERT KNOWLEDGE: WHEN DOES UNEXPECTED DATA TRANSFER INDICATE A PROBLEM?
(continued)

NetMeeting, packets will be zipping back and forth. If you make phone calls over your Internet connection, it'll be busy in both directions. (And if you stream video, you'll be giving your connection a fair workout.)

At other times, when you're not obviously doing things on the Internet or Web, you'd expect the connection not to be transferring data. But often it will be—sometimes for a long period at a stretch. What's going on? Has someone cracked your security screen? And are they busily downloading your Quicken or Money files?

They may have, and they may be. But before you yank the modem or network connection out of the computer, make sure you know why your computer might be uploading or downloading data without your knowledge. Here are some of the reasons for apparently unexplained activity:

◆ TCP/IP sends acknowledgment packets while receiving data so that the computer sending the information knows that it has been received. So when you're downloading information, there will always be some outbound packets. The normal ratio is about one outbound packet for every eight inbound packets. If your connection to the computer that's sending the packets is unreliable, and some inbound packets are being lost, you may see a higher ratio of outbound to inbound packets.

◆ If you set your e-mail program to check your mail server regularly, it will do so until you tell it to stop. Checking e-mail shows up as a brief flicker on the screens when you don't have mail to send or retrieve. Sustained downloading can indicate that someone has attached a huge PowerPoint presentation or a dozen uncompressed 4.3 megapixel digital pictures of their dog.

◆ If you run Windows Messenger, it keeps sending packets to tell the service that you're still online (or that you're Away, when it decides you're so). Other IM programs do much the same thing.

◆ If you run a P2P file-sharing program such as Napster, audioGnome, or one of the Gnutella clients, you'll see a bunch of activity taking place on your connection even when you're not downloading or uploading a file, searching, or chatting. Gnutella is the worst offender in this regard, because its searches are not coordinated through a central network of servers but through the peer computers with which each Gnutella client is connected. So your computer ends up relaying a lot of packets of information for search requests—plus the packets for the responses to those requests, of course.

◆ Windows Update automatically downloads update files in the background when it discovers that they're available and your computer needs them. As mentioned earlier in the book, Windows Update uses bandwidth-throttling techniques that try to prevent the download from interfering with your activity across the connection. These techniques increase the time it takes to download a file, and work better on fast connections than on slow ones. So apparently suspicious activity that goes on for a long time may be nothing worse than Windows Update downloading an update.

As you can see, there are a lot of activities that could legitimately be using your Internet connection without your direct involvement. At the same time, you could have been hacked. Read the section "Securing Your Internet Connection" later in this chapter to learn how you can prevent that from happening.

Disconnecting a Connection

There are three easy ways to disconnect a network connection. Which you find most convenient depends on whether you have the connection configured to display an icon in the System Tray and whether you have its Status dialog box open:

◆ If you have the Status dialog box for the connection open, click the Disconnect button.

◆ If the connection has a status icon in the System Tray, right-click that icon and choose Disconnect from the context menu.

◆ If neither of the above is the case, choose Start ➤ Connect To ➤ Show All Connections. Windows displays the Network Connections window. Then right-click the icon for the connection and choose Disconnect from the context menu.

Whichever method you choose, Windows closes the connection. If the Status dialog box or a status icon was displayed, Windows removes it from the screen.

If the connection fails, or if Windows disconnects it when the screen saver or Welcome screen kicks in after a period of inactivity, Windows displays the Reconnect dialog box, which is a renamed version of the Connect dialog box shown earlier in Figure 17.8. Connect as described earlier in this chapter.

NOTE   *If your Internet connection is running when you log out, Windows displays a dialog box asking you if you want to close the connection.*

Connecting Automatically to the Internet

If you set any of your Internet-enabled programs to connect to the Internet automatically (or they set themselves to do so), Windows displays the Dial-up Connection dialog box shown in Figure 17.10 when a program tries to connect via a connection that's not open. Click the Connect button to let the program connect. If you want the program to be able to use the connection without your intervention, select the Connect Automatically check box first.

FIGURE 17.10

Windows displays the Dial-up Connection dialog box when a program tries to connect to the Internet via a connection that's not open.

Using Multiple Modems on a Dial-up Connection

If your ISP supports multilink and you have two phone lines and two modems, you can use multilink to improve your aggregate connection speed and increase the amount of data you can transmit. Connecting with two multilinked modems of the same speed doesn't quite double the speed you get, because there's some overhead in coordinating them, but it can still net you a considerable increase in speed.

To use multilink, take the following steps:

1. Install and configure both modems as described in Chapter 14.

2. Set up a dial-up connection as described earlier in this chapter using the first modem.

3. In the Network Connections window, right-click the icon for the dial-up connection and choose Properties from the context menu. Windows displays the Properties dialog box for the connection with the General page foremost (shown in Figure 17.11).

FIGURE 17.11

On the General page of the Properties dialog box for the connection, select the modems you want to use for the connection and specify the phone numbers to use.

4. In the Connect Using list box, select the check boxes for the modems you want to use for the connection. Use the up-arrow button and down-arrow button to arrange the modems into the order in which you want them to connect.

5. By default, Windows selects the All Devices Call the Same Numbers check box. To change this, clear this check box, select the modem that needs to dial a different number in the Connect Using list box, and enter the other number in the Phone Number list box.

6. Click the Options tab. Windows displays the Options page of the Properties dialog box (shown in Figure 17.12).

FIGURE 17.12

On the Options page of the Properties dialog box for the connection, specify which devices to dial.

7. In the Multiple Devices drop-down list, select the Dial All Devices item (the default) if you want to have both (or all) lines open all the time. Select the Dial Devices Only As Needed item if you want Windows to dial the second and subsequent lines only when the first is at or near capacity.

8. If you choose the Dial Devices Only As Needed item, you can specify settings for when Windows dials another line and when it drops the connection by clicking the Configure button and working in the resulting Automatic Dialing and Hanging Up dialog box (shown in Figure 17.13) that Windows displays.

FIGURE 17.13

In the Automatic Dialing and Hanging Up dialog box, specify criteria for when to dial additional lines and when to drop them.

9. Click the OK button. Windows closes the Properties dialog box and applies your choices.

Securing Your Internet Connection

As you read earlier in the chapter, Windows XP includes a personal firewall that you can use as a first line of defense for your computer or your network. (That's the first line of defense seen from an inside perspective.) You may also want to consider adding a third-party firewall, either software or hardware—or even both.

But we're getting ahead of ourselves. What *is* a firewall, and what does it do?

What Is a Firewall?

A *firewall* is a device used to secure the connection between one computer or network and another computer or network. For example, a home user would typically use a firewall to secure the connection between their computer (or their home network) and the Internet. An IT department might use various firewalls to secure the connections between a corporate network and the Internet, or between two corporate networks that are linked together.

A firewall can be implemented in hardware, in software, or in a combination of the two. Loosely speaking, hardware firewalls are more expensive than software firewalls, but because the hardware is dedicated to its job (as opposed to having to run an operating system, manipulate spreadsheets, and play Quake on command), it tends to be more reliable and effective than a software firewall.

A firewall monitors the packets of information being sent and received from the computers inside the network. Depending on the configuration of the firewall, it may pass all the packets it receives (both ingoing and outgoing) to a proxy server that checks whether the packets are safe, dangerous, or indeterminable, or it may check them itself. Actually, the firewall doesn't check whether the packets are *safe* or *dangerous*—it checks whether they're packets that are allowed to pass the firewall. If the packets are allowed, it passes them on. If they're not allowed, it stops them in their tracks.

NOTE   In case you're wondering—the term firewall *comes not from building but from automobiles, in which the firewall is the fireproof shielding between the engine compartment and the passenger compartment designed to protect you from having foot flambé when the engine decides to combust externally for a change. (The analogy with networking is a bit strange, but the term sounds cool, and so it has stuck.) You may also hear a firewall called a* security-edge gateway, *though the term isn't used nearly as often as* firewall. *(Security-edge gateway just isn't snappy enough.)*

Do You Need to Use a Firewall?

The brief and simple answer to this question is: Yes, you should use a firewall. Every computer connected directly to the Internet should use a firewall. That goes in spades for any computer that provides Internet connectivity to other computers—for example, a networked computer that shares an Internet connection via Windows' Internet Connection Sharing feature.

As usual, though, life tends to be a little more complicated than that. In some circumstances, you may decide not to use a firewall—for example, because you consider the threats to your computer to be minimal, or because a firewall interferes with the functionality of a program, or because you're using virtual private networking. But before you decide not to use a firewall, you should at least consider the threats to your security and balance them against such problems as a firewall may cause you.

Generally speaking, if you have a persistent connection to the Internet (for example, a connection through a cable modem or a DSL), a firewall is vital. Because your computer is connected to the Internet all the time, and because it most likely has a static IP address, a hacker or cracker can poke and prod at it at will to see if your computer is easy to break into. Often crackers will run what's called a *port scan* on a number of computers they're eyeing. The port scan explores the TCP/IP ports open for communication on the computer and sees if there are any obvious vulnerabilities. A port scan is an automated routine that can be run quickly with minimal effort.

If you have a dial-up connection to the Internet, and your ISP assigns your computer an IP address dynamically each time you connect, you're unlikely to have the same IP address from one session to the next. (It's possible, but it probably won't happen before you win that lottery for which you've been buying tickets for half your life.) The changing IP address, and the fact that the computer will be offline at least some of the time, make it a little less vulnerable to attack. Your computer is still vulnerable all the time that it's online, but if you're working at it while it's online, you're in a reasonable position to detect signs of suspicious activity (though you may be too late to do anything about them).

Enabling and Disabling Internet Connection Firewall (ICF)

Internet Connection Firewall (ICF) is a software firewall rather than a hardware firewall. Technically, ICF is a *stateful* firewall: It monitors all the communications that pass it, checking the source, the destination, and the content of each packet that passes it.

How does ICF know which incoming packets are legitimate and which aren't? Basically, ICF watches the outgoing packets and builds a table from the information. It then compares incoming packets against the entries in the table, letting pass the packets for which there's a matching outbound entry and jettisoning all other packets.

As you saw earlier in this chapter, Windows encourages you to enable ICF when you set up your Internet connection. You can also enable and disable ICF manually at any time by taking the following steps:

1. Choose Start ➢ Connect To ➢ Show All Connections. Windows displays the Network Connections window.

2. Right-click the Internet connection and choose Properties from the context menu. Windows displays the Properties dialog box for the connection.

3. Click the Advanced tab. Windows displays the Advanced page (shown in Figure 17.14).

4. Select or clear the Protect My Computer and Network by Limiting or Preventing Access to This Computer from the Internet check box.

5. Click the OK button. Windows starts or stops ICF and closes the Properties dialog box.

FIGURE 17.14

Enable the Internet Connection Firewall (ICF) on the Advanced page of the Properties dialog box for the Internet connection.

NOTE   You can also specify advanced settings for Internet Connection Firewall. Chapter 33 discusses how to choose these settings and those for Internet Connection Sharing.

Using Digital Certificates

In the physical world, we're used to proving our identity in various ways, such as brandishing a driver's license when the cops pull us over for weaving, producing a credit card and corresponding signature to pay for goods, or presenting a passport at Immigration Control at the airport.

In the virtual world, we need to prove our identity without a piece of paper or plastic. Up until around the turn of the millennium, this was largely done at the personal level by using the mechanisms adapted from the real world for the telephone over the previous couple of decades. Online merchants accepted your credit card (linked to your physical address, of course) as proof of identity. Credit card companies already knew about your credit card and demanded your social security number, mother's maiden name, and perhaps a code phrase of your choosing. But these methods, while still workable, are growing increasingly clumsy as more of the world gets wired and its less-honest elements latch on to the possibilities on offer. (For example, identity theft is growing apace.)

Digital certificates are starting to be accepted as a way of authenticating the provenance of an item, be it a piece of code that Internet Explorer needs to install in order to perform an especially clever piece of 3-D animation, or simply establishing that an e-mail is from the person or company it claims to be from.

If you trust the source of, say, an ActiveX control to produce a control that's safe and beneficial to use, you may want to install it. If you know nothing about the source of the control or suspect it to be malignant, you'll want to avoid it at all costs. Similarly, you may need to prove your identity to others—for example, in order to execute a transaction.

This section discusses what digital certificates are, what they mean in the real world, how to get hold of them, and how to import them, export them, and examine them. If this seems a bit theoretical and useless, hold your horses: In the next chapter, you'll see how you can use digital certificates in

Internet Explorer to control the content you accept or reject, and in Chapter 20 you'll learn how to use digital certificates to apply digital signatures to messages you send.

What Is a Digital Certificate?

A *digital certificate* is essentially a piece of code that uniquely identifies its holder. You use your digital certificate to prove your identity.

This being a big world, various technologies support digital certificates. Microsoft's technology is called Authenticode; it requires Internet Explorer 4 or later to work. Competing formats include Marimba Channel Signing and Netscape Object Signing; as you'd expect, they don't work with Microsoft programs.

Getting a Digital Certificate

There are several types of digital certificates: those you create yourself, those you get from your company or organization, and those you get from a commercial certification authority. As you might imagine, a digital certificate you create yourself is of little use to people beyond you and those who trust you, whereas a certificate from a commercial certification authority should be good enough for anyone short of the INS. A certificate issued by your company falls in the middle: The company will have gotten the certificate from the commercial certification authority, which means the commercial certification authority has established, to its satisfaction, that the company is trustworthy. Who the company chooses to trust with the certificate introduces another link of complication into the chain of trust.

The following sections briefly examine these different ways of getting a digital certificate. After that, we'll look at how you install the certificates.

CREATING A DIGITAL CERTIFICATE OF YOUR OWN

The quickest and easiest way of getting a digital certificate is to create one yourself. There are various utilities for creating digital certificates, including one, SELFCERT.EXE, that ships with most versions of Microsoft Office. Creating a digital certificate yourself won't make anybody else trust you, but it will help you work with digital certificates.

GETTING A DIGITAL CERTIFICATE FROM YOUR COMPANY

Your second option is to get a digital certificate from a digital certificate server that your company has. The details of this procedure will vary from company to company. The key point is that the certificates the company provides via its digital certificate server are generated in the same fashion as the digital certificates distributed by the commercial certification authorities discussed in the next section. The difference is that the company distributes the certificates from a pool that it has been allocated, without needing to apply to the certification authority for each certificate as it's needed.

GETTING A DIGITAL CERTIFICATE FROM A COMMERCIAL CERTIFICATION AUTHORITY

Your third choice is to get a digital certificate from a commercial certification authority, such as VeriSign (www.verisign.com), BankGate (www.bankgate.com), Thawte Consulting (www.thawte.com), or GlobalSign NV-SA (www.globalsign.net).

If you're planning to use the digital certificate with Microsoft products (as seems likely if you're reading this), run Outlook Express and click the Get Digital ID button on the Security page of the Options dialog box. Alternatively, look for the list that Microsoft usually provides on its Web site (www.microsoft.com) of certificate authorities that provide certificates for use with Microsoft products. (Try searching for **certificate authorities** and see what you find.)

Several different types of certificate are available, depending on what you want to do—prove your personal identity, distribute software, prove your corporate identity, and so on. Each involves an online enrollment form, a pledge of good conduct, and a check with a suitable agency—a credit service such as Equifax or TRW for an individual certificate, Dun & Bradstreet Financial Services (if the company has a Dun & Bradstreet number) for a company, and so on. Almost all involve payment.

If all goes well, you typically receive an e-mail containing an URL and a PIN. You access the URL, enter the PIN, and get the digital ID, which you install to your computer. This installation means that you have the digital certificate: It's been assigned to you by the certification authority, you've downloaded it, and you've got it as a file on your computer. (You should also create a backup of your digital certificate on a floppy disk or a CD and slot it away somewhere secure, such as a bank deposit box.)

Installing a Digital Certificate

Getting the digital certificate is the first step. You then need to install it so that Internet Explorer knows where it is.

NOTE *You may find that the digital certificate is automatically stored where it needs to be on the computer on which you created or downloaded it. For example, the* SELFCERT.EXE *certificate-generator program automatically registers the certificates it creates on the computer on which it creates them. So if you created a digital certificate for yourself, you shouldn't need to install it on the same computer.*

Here's how to install a digital certificate:

1. Start or activate Internet Explorer.

2. Choose Tools ➤ Internet Options. Windows displays the Internet Options dialog box.

3. Click the Content tab. Windows displays the Content page.

4. In the Certificates group box, click the Certificates button. Windows displays the Certificates dialog box, shown in Figure 17.15.

5. Click the Import button. Windows starts the Certificate Import Wizard.

6. Click the Next button. Windows displays the File to Import stage of the Certificate Import Wizard dialog box.

7. In the File Name text box, enter the name of the certificate file you want to import. Either type the name of the certificate by hand, or click the Browse button. Windows displays the Open dialog box. Locate the certificate as usual. (Make sure the Files of Type drop-down list in the Open dialog box is set to the appropriate type of certificate, so that the certificate's file shows up in the dialog box.) Click the Open button. Windows closes the Open dialog box and enters the certificate name and path in the File Name text box.

FIGURE 17.15

Internet Explorer provides the Certificates dialog box for managing digital certificates.

8. Click the Next button. Windows displays the Certificate Store page of the Certificate Import Wizard dialog box, shown in Figure 17.16.

FIGURE 17.16

On the Certificate Store page of the Certificate Import Wizard, choose the certificate store in which to store the certificate you're importing.

9. Specify whether to store the certificate in the default certificate store for that type of certificate or in a certificate store of your own choosing. By default, Internet Explorer suggests a certificate store it deems appropriate. You may need to change this store.

◆ To do so, select the Place All Certificates in the Following Store option button. Then click the Browse button. Windows displays the Select Certificate Store dialog box, shown on the left in Figure 17.17. Choose the certificate store (for example, Personal) and click the OK button.

◆ To specify a particular location within a certificate store, select the Show Physical Stores check box and then click the plus (+) sign next to the store in question. Windows displays its subfolders. Select the folder you want, and then click the OK button. Internet Explorer closes the Select Certificate Store dialog box and displays your selection in the Certificate Store text box in the Certificate Import Wizard.

FIGURE 17.17

Use the Select Certificate Store dialog box to specify the certificate store in which you want to store the certificate. The screen on the left shows the categories of stores; the screen on the right shows the physical stores displayed.

10. Click the Next button to finish setting up the import procedure. The Wizard displays the Completing the Certificate Import Wizard dialog box, shown in Figure 17.18, to confirm the choices you've made. The list box shows the certificate store that you or the Wizard chose, the type of content you're putting in it (a certificate, a certificate trust list, a certificate revocation list, and so on), and the name of the file from which the content is being drawn.

FIGURE 17.18

The Certificate Import Wizard displays the choices you've made for importing the certificate. Make sure they still look appropriate and then click the Finish button.

11. If you (or the Wizard) decide to import the certificate into the root certificate store, Internet Explorer displays the Root Certificate Store dialog box, asking you to confirm that you want to add the certificate to the root store. If placing this certificate in the root certificate store is correct, click the Yes button. Otherwise, click the No button.

12. If you're ready to go, click the Finish button. The Certificate Import Wizard imports the certificate (or whatever) and displays a message box confirming that the operation was successful.

Now that you've imported the certificate, it shows up in the Certificates dialog box on the appropriate page.

Exporting a Certificate

You may need to export a certificate for backup or so that you can install it on another computer. To export a certificate, select it in the Certificates dialog box and click the Export button. Windows starts the Certificate Export Wizard, which walks you through the process of exporting the certificate. If you choose to export the private key with the certificate, be sure to protect it with a password.

Removing a Certificate

Usually, digital certificates bear a distinct relation to other people's phone numbers—you just keep accumulating them in one store or another (read: one phone book or organizer or another) until you die. But sometimes you'll need to remove a digital certificate from the store—perhaps because a once-trusted associate has turned rogue, or an esteemed competitor has gone belly-up, or another event has occurred that obviates your need for that digital certificate's services.

To remove a digital certificate from the digital certificate store in Internet Explorer, follow these steps:

1. Display the Certificates dialog box by clicking the Certificates button on the Content page of the Internet Options dialog box.

2. Display the page that contains the digital certificate in question, and then select the certificate you want to remove.

3. Click the Remove button. Windows displays a Certificates dialog box warning you of the consequences of deleting the digital certificate and asking you to confirm the deletion:

   ◆ Figure 17.19 shows the warning you get when removing a certification authority.

FIGURE 17.19

Windows displays this Certificates dialog box to warn you of the consequences of removing a certificate authority's certificate.

   ◆ Figure 17.20 shows the warning you get when removing one of your personal certificates.

FIGURE 17.20

Windows displays this Certificates dialog box to warn you of the consequences of removing one of your personal certificates.

4. Click the Yes button to delete the certificate. Click the No button if the warning has persuaded you to relent.

Examining a Certificate

So far, we've discussed how to go about getting, installing, and exporting digital certificates. This section discusses how to examine a certificate that identifies someone else.

Often, you'll want to examine a certificate because Internet Explorer asks you whether you want to trust the person, company, or organization that the certificate is supposed to identify. The next couple of pages show an example of this. But if you want to follow along on your PC, and you haven't got a handy Web site that will raise a certificate question, open the Certificates dialog box, select a certificate, and click the View button. (Alternatively, just double-click the certificate.) To open the Certificates dialog box: From Internet Explorer, choose Tools ➢ Internet Options, and then click the Certificates button on the Content page of the Internet Options dialog box.

When there's a problem with a certificate for a site you're visiting, Internet Explorer brings it to your attention, typically by displaying a Security Alert dialog box. Internet Explorer recommends that you view the certificate to determine whether you want to trust the certifying authority. Clicking the View Certificate button displays the certificate in the Certificate dialog box.

The General page of the Certificate dialog box explains any problem that Windows has identified with the certificate. Figure 17.21 shows an example of the Certificate dialog box for a certificate with a problem (left) and an example of the Certificate dialog box for a certificate that seems to be okay. When there's a problem, you'll see explanations such as "This certificate cannot be verified up to a trusted certification authority" or "Windows does not have enough information to verify this certificate." This page also displays some basic information about the certificate: to whom the certificate is issued, by whom it was issued, and the period for which it's valid.

FIGURE 17.21

Use the Certificate dialog box to examine the properties of a certificate and learn of any problems that Windows has identified with it.

When there isn't a problem with the certificate, this page displays a list of the purposes for which the certificate is intended: for example, "Protect e-mail messages," "Ensure the identity of a remote computer," "Protect software from tampering after publication," or "Ensure software came from software publisher." When you're examining a certificate, make sure that the stated purposes cover the bases you're expecting. If Internet Explorer thinks the certificate is valid, the Issuer Statement button will be enabled. Clicking this button is supposed to make Windows displays a statement by the issuer. (At this writing, it doesn't always work.)

The Details page of the Certificate dialog box, shown in Figure 17.22, contains about a score of specifics on the certificate. If the information in a field overflows the list box, click the field. Windows displays its value in the text box below. To restrict the view to a subset of the fields available, select one of the following choices in the Show drop-down list: Version I Fields Only (which displays the X.509 basic certificate fields); Extensions Only (the X.509 extension fields); Critical Extensions Only (fields that ensure safe operation when security is needed, such as the Key Usage Restriction field and the SpcSpAgencyInfo field); or Properties Only (the Thumbprint Algorithm field, the Thumbprint field, the Friendly Name field, and the Description field).

FIGURE 17.22

The Details page of the Certificate dialog box contains a host of details about the certificate.

From the Details page, you can edit some of the properties of a certificate by clicking the Edit Properties button. The next section, "Editing the Properties of a Certificate," discusses this.

On the Certification Path page (shown in Figure 17.23), you can follow the chain of certificates up from the current holder to the issuing authority to find one that's trustworthy. To check one of the links in the chain, select it in the Certification Path list box and click the View Certificate button (if it's available). Windows displays the Certificate dialog box for the certificate in question. You can then pursue the certification path for that certificate if you choose, or click the OK button to dismiss the second (or subsequent) Certificate dialog box and return to the previous one.

If on examination and reflection you decide the certificate is okay, you can install it on your computer by clicking the Install Certificate button on the General page of the Certificate dialog box and letting the Certificate Import Wizard shepherd you through the process as discussed earlier in this section. Alternatively, you can click the Yes button in the Security Alert dialog box to proceed without installing the certificate; or you can click the No button in the Security Alert dialog box if you choose not to proceed.

When you finish exploring the certificate, click the OK button. Internet Explorer closes the Certificate dialog box.

FIGURE 17.23

The Certification Path page of the Certificate dialog box displays the path by which the certificate has been issued from the issuing authority to the current holder.

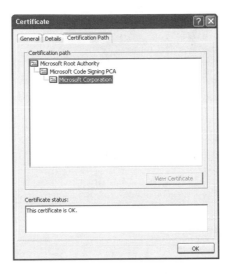

EDITING THE PROPERTIES OF A CERTIFICATE

On the Details page of the Certificate dialog box, clicking the Edit Properties button displays the Certificate Properties dialog box, shown in Figure 17.24. In this dialog box, you can change the friendly name and description for the certificate, and specify the purposes for which the certificate can be used. The *friendly name* is a name that humans can read easily; it shows up in the Certificates dialog box in the Friendly Name column and also appears as a property on the Details page of the Certificate dialog box. The description is a text description to accompany the friendly name; it appears on the Details page of the Certificate dialog box.

FIGURE 17.24

You can edit the properties of a certificate in the Certificate Properties dialog box.

In the Certificate Purposes group box, choose the purposes for which you want to use the certificate by selecting one of the three option buttons:

◆ The Enable All Purposes for This Certificate option button enables all the purposes for which the certificate is valid.

◆ The Disable All Purposes for This Certificate option button prevents use of the certificate.

◆ The Enable Only the Following Purposes option button lets you select the check boxes for the purposes you want. Note that the list box displays only the purposes you can edit, not necessarily the full set of purposes for the certificate.

Click the OK button. Windows closes the Certificate Properties dialog box and applies your choices.

SPECIFYING ADVANCED PURPOSES

You can designate the purposes that you want Windows to list as advanced for certificates. To do so, take the following steps:

1. Click the Advanced button in the Certificates dialog box. Windows displays the Advanced Options dialog box (shown in Figure 17.25).

FIGURE 17.25

In the Advanced Options dialog box, specify the purposes that you want Windows to list as advanced.

2. In the Certificate Purposes group box, select the check boxes that you want to designate as advanced.

3. In the Export Format group box, you can select the default format for Windows to use when you drag a certificate to a folder. For some formats, you can choose whether to include all certificates in the certification path.

4. Click the OK button. Windows closes the Advanced Options dialog box, applies your choices, and returns you to the Certificates dialog box.

Up Next

This chapter has discussed how to choose an Internet connection type and ISP (if you have the choice); how to create an Internet connection; how to start and stop it; and how to secure it by implementing Windows XP's built-in firewall. It has also covered what digital certificates are, where to get them, and how to import them, export them, and examine them.

The next chapter discusses how to use Internet Explorer to surf the Web.

Chapter 18

Surfing the Web with Internet Explorer

THIS CHAPTER DISCUSSES HOW to browse the Web with Internet Explorer, the Web browser built into Windows, and how to configure Internet Explorer's most important settings, including the security settings. At the end of the chapter, there's a short introduction to MSN Explorer, Microsoft's Internet service. The chapter assumes that you have already configured an Internet connection as discussed in the previous chapter.

This chapter covers the following topics:

◆ Starting Internet Explorer

◆ Using the Internet Explorer interface

◆ Opening and saving documents

◆ Creating and using favorites

◆ Changing your home page and Quick Links

◆ Dealing with common error messages

◆ Managing your temporary Internet files

◆ Controlling your history

◆ Choosing security options

◆ Using Content Advisor to screen out objectionable content

◆ Managing your AutoComplete information

◆ Choosing advanced options

◆ Browsing offline

◆ A quick introduction to MSN Explorer

Starting Internet Explorer

These are the easiest ways of starting Internet Explorer:

◆ Choose Start ➤ Internet.

◆ Click the Launch Internet Explorer Browser shortcut on your Quick Launch toolbar (if you have the Quick Launch toolbar displayed).

◆ Double-click an URL or another file type associated with Internet Explorer.

EXPERT KNOWLEDGE: HOW TO STOP INTERNET EXPLORER, NETSCAPE, AND OPERA FROM DUELING FOR DOMINANCE

As you no doubt know, Internet Explorer isn't the only browser in town. Netscape (www.netscape.com) and Opera (www.operasoft.com) are competitive browsers that are yours for the download.

If you have two or more Web browsers installed on your computer, they'll bicker for your attentions like puppies or MP3 players. Each time you run a different browser, it'll prompt you to make it your default browser. The default browser gets pole position, including possession of the coveted Internet shortcut at the top of the Start menu and the associations for the many Internet file types (for example, HTM, HTML, URL, and so on). The illustrations below show Opera (on the left) and Internet Explorer (on the right) competing for attention.

To prevent Internet Explorer from asking to be your default browser, clear the Always Perform This Check when Starting Internet Explorer check box before dismissing the Internet Explorer dialog box. Alternatively, choose Tools ➤ Internet Options. Internet Explorer displays the Internet Options dialog box. Click the Programs tab. Internet Explorer displays the Programs page. Clear the Internet Explorer Should Check to See whether It Is the Default Browser check box. Click the OK button. Internet Explorer closes the Internet Options dialog box and applies the settings.

To prevent Opera from bugging you about making it the default browser, select the Do Not Show This Dialog Again check box before dismissing the Opera dialog box shown above. Alternatively, choose File ➤ Preferences. Opera displays the Preferences dialog box. Select the Default Browser category. Clear the Check if Opera Is Default Browser on Startup check box. In the File Types group box, select the file types that you want to associate with Opera. In the Protocols group box, select the protocols that you want to associate with Opera. Click the OK button. Opera closes the Preferences dialog box and applies the settings.

To suppress Netscape's ambitions to be your default browser and commandeer file types, choose Edit ➤ Preferences. Netscape displays the Preferences dialog box. Expand the Advanced category and select the Desktop Integration item. In the File Types group box, select the file types you want to associate with Netscape. In the Internet Shortcuts group box, select the Internet shortcuts you want to associate with Netscape. And clear the Check that Windows Is Set Up to Match These Preferences Each Time Netscape Starts Up check box. Click the OK button. Netscape closes the Preferences dialog box and applies the settings.

Using the Internet Explorer Interface

Figure 18.1 shows the main features of the Internet Explorer window.

FIGURE 18.1

The main features of the Internet Explorer window

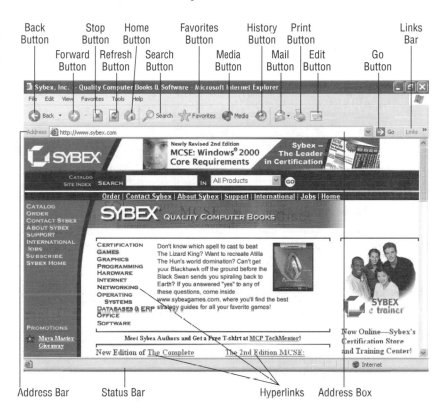

The status bar shows information on the current operation (for example, *Connecting to site www.sybex.com*) or information on any hyperlink the mouse pointer is currently pointing to.

As you can see in the figure, Internet Explorer provides three toolbars for navigating the Web and Internet. When you start Internet Explorer, the Address bar is displayed as the lower layer of the toolbar, with the Links bar reduced to just a button at the right end of the Address bar.

Unlocking the Toolbars and Menu Bar

By default, the toolbars are locked, so to move them, you need to unlock them. To do so, right-click the menu bar or any displayed toolbar and choose Lock the Toolbars from the context menu. Internet Explorer removes the check mark from the Lock the Toolbars item on the context menu, unlocks the toolbars and menu bar, and displays handles at their left ends so that you can move and resize them.

You can then customize the size and position of the three toolbars by dragging the handles. For example, you can drag the toolbar handles of the Links bar to the left from their default position to display more of the Links bar and less of the Address bar. Alternatively, you could drag the Links bar down to display it below the Address bar.

Using the Toolbar Buttons

Here's how to use the buttons on the toolbar in Internet Explorer:

◆ Click the Back button to move to the previous page you were on. To move back more than one page in a single jump, click the downward-arrow button on the Back button to display a list of pages that you can go back to.

◆ Click the Forward button to move forward to a page you were on before you clicked the Back button. To move forward more than one page, click the downward-arrow button on the Forward button to display a list of pages that you can go forward to.

NOTE *Until there is a page to go forward or back to, the Back button and the Forward button are dimmed and unavailable.*

◆ Click the Stop button to stop Internet Explorer from pursuing a jump that's in progress. (For example, if the jump has stalled or if the page is loading very slowly, you might want to stop it.)

◆ Click the Refresh button to have Internet Explorer reload the current page. You might want to do this if part of the page fails to transfer properly, or if you think the page may have changed since you loaded this instance of it.

◆ Click the Home button to jump to your home page. (You'll learn about home pages in a minute or two.)

◆ Click the Search button to display Search Companion, which offers natural-language searching of the Web.

◆ Click the Favorites button to display the Favorites Explorer bar. ("Creating and Using Favorites" later in this chapter discusses favorites.)

◆ Click the Media button to display the Media bar (shown in Figure 18.2), which gives you quick access to WindowsMedia.com.

◆ Click the History button to display the History Explorer bar, which you can use to navigate to a site you've visited recently.

◆ Click the Mail button to display a menu of mail and news commands. For example, choosing the Read Mail item from this menu launches or activates your default e-mail client.

◆ Click the Print button to print the current page. (Internet Explorer doesn't display the Print dialog box—it goes right ahead and prints the page.)

◆ Click the Edit button to open the current page for editing in your default HTML editor. (You can change your default HTML editor on the Programs page of the Internet Options dialog box.)

FIGURE 18.2

The Media bar provides quick access to the information and entertainment that WindowsMedia.com offers. Click a heading to display or hide the information it contains.

Using Keyboard Shortcuts

Internet Explorer supports many of the same keyboard shortcuts as Explorer. For example, you can press the F4 key to display the Address drop-down list and select the current entry in the Address bar. Refer back to Table 6.2 for a list of keyboard shortcuts for Explorer.

Opening a Web Page or a Document

Each Web site or Web page is identified by an address called a *Uniform Resource Locator*, or *URL* for short. (URL is usually pronounced "earl," but it's also sometimes spelled out as "U-R-L.") For example, the URL for the Microsoft Web site is `http://www.microsoft.com`. By pointing your browser at this URL, you can access the Microsoft Web site.

See pages 48–50 of the *Essential Skills* section for a visual guide to browsing the Web with Internet Explorer.

Opening a Web Page or a Document the Easy Way

The easiest way to open an URL is to click in the Address box on the Address bar, type in the address of the document, and press Enter to accept it. You don't need to include the `http://` prefix: Internet Explorer adds that automatically if you enter a valid URL. Similarly, to access an FTP site, you don't need to enter the `ftp://` prefix: Just enter the address, and Internet Explorer adds the prefix. (Occasionally this prefix-adding doesn't work. In that case, enter the prefix manually.)

If the URL starts with www. (after the http:// prefix) and ends with .com, you can enter those parts of the address automatically by pressing Ctrl+Enter. For example, to access the Sybex Web site, www.sybex.com, you could type **sybex** and press Ctrl+Enter to have Internet Explorer enter http://www.sybex.com.

WARNING   Internet Explorer's AutoComplete feature does its best to make a complete URL out of whatever you enter. If you enter part of an URL, AutoComplete adds http://www to it and then tries the .com, .edu, and .org domain suffixes (in that order). Be warned that if you give Internet Explorer this much latitude in constructing URLs, you may get some sites you didn't bargain for. The canonical example of this is www.whitehouse.com, a pornographic site, which people access accidentally when trying to reach the White House (government) site (www.whitehouse.gov).

If the address you're typing matches an address you've visited within Internet Explorer's memory, Internet Explorer displays a drop-down list of URLs. If one of them is right, use the ↓ key to select it, and then press the Enter key. If not, finish typing the new URL and then press the Enter key or click the Go button.

You can also open a document stored on a local drive or network drive in the same way by using type-down addressing in Internet Explorer, just as you can in Explorer. Type the drive letter (for example, D:), and Internet Explorer displays a drop-down list of the folders on the drive. Type down to select one of them (or use the ↓ key and the ↑ key) to select one, and Internet Explorer displays a drop-down list of the contents of that folder. This can be a quick way of accessing a document provided you know its name and location. For general digging through directories, browse as usual using an Explorer window or an Internet Explorer window.

TIP   If you don't like the AutoComplete feature, turn it off. Choose Tools ➤ Internet Options and clear the Use Inline AutoComplete check box on the Advanced page of the Internet Options dialog box.

Opening a Web Page or a Document the Formal Way

There's also a more formal (and almost invariably slower) way of opening a Web page or a document on a local drive, a network drive, or an intranet. This way is useful for opening documents because it lets you browse through folders, so you don't need to know the exact name and location of the document. A more dubious benefit is that opening an URL or a document this way doesn't add the URL or filename to the Address drop-down list, so it's a little more private. (However, the Address drop-down list does suggest it in AutoComplete items.)

Here's the formal way of opening a Web page or document:

1. Choose File ➤ Open. Internet Explorer displays the Open dialog box (shown in Figure 18.3).

FIGURE 18.3

To open a document on the Web, choose File ➤ Open, enter the address in the Open text box, and click the OK button.

2. In the Open text box, enter the address for the document or file you want to open, using any of the following three methods:

   ◆ Type the name of the document or file into the Open text box.

   ◆ To open a document or file you've accessed recently, click the down-arrow button at the right end of the Open text box and select the file from the drop-down list.

   ◆ Click the Browse button. Internet Explorer displays the Microsoft Internet Explorer dialog box (a common Open dialog box in disguise). Select the file and click the Open button. Internet Explorer enters the file's name and path in the Open text box in the Open dialog box. To open a file of a file type not explicitly associated with Internet Explorer, select All Files in the Files of Type drop-down list.

3. Click the OK button in the Open dialog box. Internet Explorer closes the Open dialog box and opens the file.

Internet Explorer includes built-in support for a large number of file formats, including HTML pages, text files, several types of graphics files (such as GIF, JPEG, and PNG), and Adobe Acrobat files. When you encounter a file type that needs an add-on program or a plug-in, Internet Explorer warns you and seeks permission to download and install the add-on or plug-in.

Jumping to a Hyperlink

Many Web documents contain *hyperlinks,* which are jumps to other locations. Hyperlinks are typically displayed as underlined text, graphical objects, or pictures. (For example, Figure 18.1 contains a large number of hyperlinks, several of which are labeled.)

When you move the mouse pointer over a hyperlink, the mouse pointer takes on the shape of a hand with a finger pointing upward. To jump to the hyperlinked location, click the hyperlink.

Returning to a Previous Document

Because you'll often access dead ends or pages that don't offer the information you need, you'll often want to return to the previous document you accessed. There are several ways to move back to a document you've visited before:

   ◆ Click the Back button on the toolbar, or use its drop-down list, as described earlier in the chapter. Alternatively, press Alt+← to move back one page. (To move forward, use the Forward button or press Alt+→.) This technique works well when you're browsing in a single window. If you're using multiple windows (as discussed in the next section), each will have a different sequence of sites visited, so it may be more difficult to find the one you want.

   ◆ Click the down arrow at the right end of the Address box and choose the document from the drop-down list. This drop-down list gives you quick access to a good number of the sites you've visited.

◆ Choose one of the items listed in the View ➢ Go To menu (for example, View ➢ Go To ➢ Back, View ➢ Go To ➢ Home Page, or View ➢ Go To ➢ *one of the listed sites*).

◆ Click the History button (or choose View ➢ Explorer Bar ➢ History) to display the History Explorer bar (shown in Figure 18.4). This pane contains a complete list of the pages you've visited and the documents you've opened recently, organized into folders by day and site. Use the View context menu to sort the history sites by date, site, or most visited, or by order visited today; or use the Search feature to search the history sites by keyword. Then click the shortcut for the item you want to return to. You can also copy the shortcut to another folder, create a favorite from it, or delete it.

FIGURE 18.4

Use the History Explorer bar to return to a previous document.

TIP By default, Internet Explorer stores history for 20 days. You can change the number of days to anything from 0 to 999 by adjusting the number in the Days to Keep Pages in History text box on the General page of the Internet Options dialog box (Tools ➢ Internet Options). When you set this number to 0, Internet Explorer doesn't keep pages from one day to the next, but you can still access pages on the same day. See the section "Keeping Control of Your History" for information on how to prune and clear your history.

Opening Multiple Internet Explorer Windows

Given the amount of information on the Web, you'll often want to have several Internet Explorer windows open at once so that you can see multiple Web pages at the same time without having to move back and forth from one to the other. All Internet Explorer windows share your connection (whether modem, cable, DSL, or network) and slow each other down.

You can open multiple windows in several ways:

◆ To open another copy of the page displayed in the current window, press Ctrl+N or choose File ➢ New ➢ Window.

◆ To open a hyperlinked location in a new browser window, so that the current window still displays the current page, right-click the hyperlink and choose Open in New Window from the context menu.

◆ To start a new instance of Internet Explorer, click its shortcut on the Quick Launch toolbar or choose Start ➢ Internet.

◆ Some Web sites will open a new browser window for you. This tends to happen when you've chosen to display a page that doesn't involve their site. Keep an eye on the number of browser windows you have open, because there may be more than you have opened yourself—and some of them may be showing items that you haven't specifically chosen to see.

To close a window, click its Close button (the × button), choose File ➢ Close, or press either Alt+F4 or Ctrl+W.

TIP   If you want to open each link you follow in a new window instead of in the same window, clear the Reuse Windows for Launching Shortcuts check box on the Advanced page of the Internet Options dialog box (Tools ➢ Internet Options).

Making a Page Easier to Read

One of the problems with viewing Web pages is that they tend to look different when displayed in different browsers. Because Internet Explorer is so widely used, commanding between half and three-quarters of the total browser market for Windows and the Mac, this is less of a problem with Internet Explorer than with Netscape or Opera. A bigger problem for Internet Explorer users is that Web designers design pages for optimal viewing at a certain screen resolution (for example, 800×600). When you view them at a different resolution, they can be hard to read.

Depending on how the Web designer has created the page, you can do a couple of things to make it easier to read. The first thing to try is adjusting the text size displayed. Choose View ➢ Text Size and choose one of the items from the Text Size submenu: Largest, Larger, Medium, Smaller, or Smallest. (The size currently used appears with a dot next to it on the menu.)

NOTE   When you change the text size by using the View ➢ Text Size submenu, your choice carries through to subsequent pages you visit in this browser window or other browser windows you launch from it. Other browser windows already displayed when you issue the command are not affected.

If all goes well, Internet Explorer increases or decreases the text size when you issue this command. But if the text size doesn't change—perhaps because the Web site designer has used Cascading Style Sheets (CSS) to specify exact sizing and placement of the text and other elements on the page—you need to take the following steps:

1. Choose Tools ➢ Internet Options. Internet Explorer displays the Internet Options dialog box.

2. Click the Accessibility button on the General page. Internet Explorer displays the Accessibility dialog box (shown in Figure 18.5).

3. Choose options in the Formatting group box:

   ◆ Select the Ignore Colors Specified on Web Pages check box to ignore colors.

   ◆ Select the Ignore Font Styles Specified on Web Pages check box to override font styles.

   ◆ Select the Ignore Font Sizes Specified on Web Pages check box to override font sizes.

FIGURE 18.5

If choosing a different text size doesn't change the page, use the Accessibility dialog box to override the Web designer's settings.

4. Click the OK button. Internet Explorer closes the Accessibility dialog box and applies your choices.

TIP   If you have persistent difficulty in reading other people's Web pages, try creating a style sheet of your own that uses font sizes you find comfortable to read. (Consult a Web design book for advice on creating a style sheet.) In the Accessibility dialog box, select the Format Documents Using My Style Sheet check box, then specify the style sheet in the Style Sheet text box by clicking the Browse button and navigating to the file that contains it.

If you're generally dissatisfied with how Web pages look in Internet Explorer, change the default font size and font color to see if that improves things. Choose Tools ➤ Internet Options. Internet Explorer displays the Internet Options dialog box. To change the font size and color, click the Fonts button and use the resulting Fonts dialog box to select a typeface and size that please you. To change the color, click the Colors button to display the Colors dialog box (shown in Figure 18.6):

◆ To change the text and background colors, clear the Use Windows Colors check box and use the Text button and Background button to select colors.

◆ To change the colors of links, use the Visited button and the Unvisited button.

◆ To make Internet Explorer display a link over which you're hovering the mouse pointer in a different color, select the Use Hover Color check box and use the Hover button to pick the color. The hover color is especially useful for identifying which link you're about to select on a busy page that presents several links close to each other.

FIGURE 18.6

Use the Colors dialog box to change the color of fonts and links. You can also apply a hover color to make Internet Explorer colorize the link over which the mouse pointer is hovering.

Saving a Document

Although you cannot create new documents in Internet Explorer, you can use Internet Explorer to save documents to your computer. For example, you might want to save a copy of a Web page or intranet page to your hard disk so that you can examine it in detail when your computer is offline.

To save the current page, choose File ➤ Save As. Internet Explorer displays the Save Web Page dialog box. Choose a location for the file as usual, specify a filename, and click the Save button. Internet Explorer closes the Save As dialog box and saves the file.

NOTE   *Instead of saving a page like this, you can have Internet Explorer create an offline favorite for it—a copy of the page that you can access when your computer isn't connected to the Internet. See "Creating and Using Favorites" for details.*

Printing a Document

To print the Web page you're viewing, click the Print button on the toolbar. Internet Explorer prints the page without displaying the Print dialog box.

To display the Print dialog box so that you can choose printing options, choose File ➤ Print. Internet Explorer displays the Print dialog box. Choose options as usual. For example, the Options page of the Print dialog box offers options for printing frames (layout areas of Web pages), printing all linked documents, and printing a table of links.

Downloading Files

Apart from surfing the Internet, you'll probably find yourself using Internet Explorer for downloading a lot of files: drivers, patches, updates, programs, games, screen savers, audio, video, or whatever. Internet Explorer lets you download files seamlessly via both HTTP and FTP. Most of the time, you don't need to worry about whether the download is happening via HTTP or FTP. (The exception is when you're accessing a password-protected FTP server. More on this in a minute.)

Here's what usually happens when you download a file: You click a link to download a file. If the extension on the file indicates that the file is of a file type registered on your computer, Internet Explorer displays a File Download dialog box (of which Figure 18.7 shows an example) offering you the choice between opening the file from its current location, saving it to disk, canceling the download, or getting more information. (If the file appears to be of a file type that isn't registered on your computer, Internet Explorer doesn't offer to open it from its current location.) Click the Open button to open the file, the Save button to save it to a file on your computer, or the Cancel button to cancel the download. Clicking the More Info button opens an Internet Explorer Help window to a topic explaining about downloading files and the risk of viruses.

FIGURE 18.7

In the File Download dialog box, choose whether to open the file from its current location or save it to disk.

The File Download dialog box also contains the Always Ask before Opening This Type of File check box, which is selected by default. If you *always* want to perform the same operation with this type of file—always open this type of file from its current location, or always save this type of file to disk—clear this check box, and Internet Explorer will not prompt you for files of this file type that you download in the future. This check box isn't available for executable files (such as EXE files or COM files).

TIP   To avoid having Internet Explorer prompt you about opening a file you're downloading and that you want to save, right-click its link (instead of clicking it) and choose Save Target As from the context menu.

Sometimes you'll want to open the file from its current location. For example, the setup routines for some programs involve opening them from the Web so that they can examine your computer and download only the components they need rather than a huge file that contains all the components. But usually, if Internet Explorer offers you this choice, you'll want to download the file and save it locally.

If the file you're downloading is of a file type registered to play, Internet Explorer starts it playing rather than giving you the opportunity to save it to disk. For example, if you click a link for an audio stream, Internet Explorer starts it playing. For copyright reasons, most companies and individuals that stream audio and video try to prevent the listener or viewer from saving the file. This is because streaming a file is legally analogous to broadcasting, whereas distributing savable files is legally analogous to copying them.

If you choose to save the file, Internet Explorer displays the Save As dialog box so that you can choose a drive, folder, and filename for it. Once you've specified these, the download continues as usual. The Download window (of which Figure 18.8 shows an example) displays the progress of the download, with a percentage-complete readout in its title bar that shows on the Taskbar button for the window as well.

FIGURE 18.8

Internet Explorer displays the progress of the download in the Download window.

When the download finishes, Internet Explorer changes the Download window title to Download Complete and provides three command buttons. Click the Open button to open the downloaded file in the associated program, if there is one. (Bear in mind that you may well want to virus-check the downloaded file before opening it.) Click the Open Folder button to open an Explorer window showing the folder containing the downloaded file. Or click the Close button to close the Download

Complete window. If you regularly find yourself clicking the Close button, select the Close This Dialog Box when Download Completes check box if you want Internet Explorer to close the Download window automatically when it has received the whole file.

You can download multiple files at the same time by setting multiple downloads in motion. All downloads share your Internet connection, so running multiple downloads will make each take longer than it would if it were the only download running—unless you have a fast Internet connection that is being held back by slow (or busy) servers at the other end *and* each of your downloads is coming from a different server. On the other hand, you may want to run multiple downloads concurrently if you're planning to take a break from your computer.

*TIP   If you download many files over an unreliable dial-up connection, consider getting a download manager that can resume downloads from the point at which they get broken off. Download managers include RealDownload (*www.real.com*) and Go!Zilla (*www.gozilla.com*)*.

EXPERT KNOWLEDGE: SUPPLYING AN FTP USERNAME AND PASSWORD IN INTERNET EXPLORER

Internet Explorer handles accessing FTP servers via anonymous logon transparently. But if the FTP server requires you to supply a username and password, you need to enter it in the Address bar as follows:

```
ftp://username:password@ftpserver/url
```

As you can see, this makes for tricky typing. If you access password-protected FTP servers frequently, consider getting a dedicated graphical FTP client such as WS_FTP Pro (www.ipswitch.com) or CuteFTP (www.globalscape.com).

Creating and Using Favorites

Internet Explorer lets you designate URLs as *favorites*, which allows you to access them quickly using the Favorites menu or the Favorites Explorer bar. (Other Web browsers such as Netscape call favorites *bookmarks*.) Regular favorites are simply shortcuts to sites, but Internet Explorer can also create *offline favorites*, cached copies of pages that you can access when your computer isn't connected to the Internet.

NOTE   Because they're stored on your hard drive (or another local drive or network drive) and don't need to be downloaded, offline favorites load very quickly. But to counteract this advantage, they have several disadvantages: They may not be up to date (because a Web page may have changed since you last synchronized its offline favorite), they take up disk space, and (if the Web site tries to prevent web-crawling) they may not synchronize properly.

To use favorites, you create them as described in the next section, then access them from the Favorites menu or the Favorites Explorer bar (shown in Figure 18.9).

FIGURE 18.9

Internet Explorer provides the Favorites Explorer bar for accessing your favorites quickly.

Adding a Page to Your Favorites

To add the current URL (the page that Internet Explorer is currently displaying) to your list of favorites, follow these steps:

1. Choose Favorites ➤ Add to Favorites. Internet Explorer displays the Add Favorite dialog box (shown in Figure 18.10).

FIGURE 18.10

To add an URL to your list of favorites, choose Favorites ➤ Add to Favorites. Internet Explorer displays the Add Favorite dialog box.

2. In the Name text box, enter the name by which to identify the favorite. You will often need to change the default name, which will be the title of the page, to something shorter, more descriptive, or more memorable.

3. If you want to have the favorite available offline (when your computer is not attached to the network or the Internet), select the Make Available Offline check box. Then choose a schedule and details by using the Offline Favorite Wizard as follows:

◆ Click the Customize button. Internet Explorer starts the Offline Favorite Wizard. The first time you run the Wizard, you'll see an introductory page. Select the In the Future, Do Not Show This Introduction Screen check box and click the Next button.

◆ On the next page of the Offline Favorite Wizard, shown in Figure 18.11, choose whether you want to download just this page or pages linked to it. To download just this page, leave the No option button selected (this is the default). To download linked pages, select the Yes option button (as shown in the figure) and specify the depth of links you want to download by entering a number in the Download Pages *NN* Links Deep from This Page text box. Then click the Next button.

FIGURE 18.11

On the next screen of the Offline Favorite Wizard, decide whether to download just this page or the pages linked to it as well.

WARNING *Don't set too deep a level of links to download. Setting more than one level can quickly fill up your hard drive and monopolize your Internet connection with synchronization. If you want to try this feature, experiment cautiously, setting a minimal level of links at first for any given favorite. (Bear in mind that each favorite is likely to need a different level of links.)*

◆ On the next page of the Offline Favorite Wizard, shown in Figure 18.12, decide how you want to synchronize this favorite. You can choose among the Only when I Choose Synchronize from the Tools Menu option button, the I Would Like to Create a New Schedule option button (which lets you create a custom synchronization schedule for the favorite), and the Using This Existing Schedule option button (which lets you use an existing schedule from the drop-down list). The Using This Existing Schedule option button (which doesn't appear in the figure) isn't available until you create a schedule. Click the Next button to proceed.

FIGURE 18.12

On the next screen of the Offline Favorite Wizard, decide how you want to synchronize this favorite.

◆ If you chose to create a custom synchronization schedule for the favorite, Internet Explorer displays the Offline Favorite Wizard page shown in Figure 18.13. Specify the interval (in days) and the time for the update at the top of the dialog box. Enter a name in the Name text box. If you want your computer to connect to the network or Internet automatically if it is not connected when the time for the synchronization arrives, select the If My Computer Is Not Connected when This Scheduled Synchronization Begins, Automatically Connect for Me check box. Click the Next button.

FIGURE 18.13

If you chose to create a custom synchronization schedule for the favorite, specify the details on the next screen.

◆ On the final page of the Offline Favorite Wizard (shown in Figure 18.14), choose the Yes, My User Name and Password Are option button and specify your username and password (twice) if the site requires you to enter a password when accessing it. Click the Finish button to finish scheduling the update.

FIGURE 18.14

On the final screen of the Offline Favorite Wizard, enter your username and password if the site requires you to log on.

4. Choose where you want to create the favorite. You can create the favorite either at the top level, so that it appears directly on the Favorites menu (and in the Favorites Explorer bar), or in a folder.

   ◆ To create the favorite in a different folder, click the Create In button in the Add Favorite dialog box. Internet Explorer displays an additional part of the dialog box (shown in Figure 18.15).

FIGURE 18.15

Use the additional part of the Add Favorite dialog box to specify where to create the favorite.

◆ Select an existing folder or create a new folder. To create a new folder beneath the currently selected folder, click the New Folder button, enter the name in the Folder Name text box in the resulting Create New Folder dialog box, and click the OK button.

5. Click the OK button. Internet Explorer closes the Add Favorite dialog box and creates the favorite. If you chose to make this favorite an offline favorite, you'll see the Synchronizing dialog box as Internet Explorer performs the initial synchronization.

Thereafter, Internet Explorer will synchronize the favorite automatically if you set up a schedule. If not, or to force an immediate synchronization, choose Tools ➤ Synchronize. Internet Explorer displays the Items to Synchronize dialog box, which offers both a compact view and an expanded view (shown in Figure 18.16) that you can access by clicking the Details button. Select the items you want to synchronize, and then click the Synchronize button.

FIGURE 18.16

Use the Items to Synchronize dialog box to force a synchronization.

You'll see the Synchronizing dialog box (shown in Figure 18.17) as Internet Explorer synchronizes the pages. The dialog box closes automatically when synchronization is complete.

FIGURE 18.17
Internet Explorer
displays the Syn-
chronizing dialog
box while it synchro-
nizes your pages.

NOTE *Internet Explorer keeps the list of offline favorites in the* \Windows\Offline Web Pages\ *folder. You can examine them here if you want—but usually you'll find it easier to work with them via the Favorites menu, the Favorites Explorer bar, or the Organize Favorites dialog box (Favorites ➤ Organize Favorites). All users can see this folder, but each user sees only the offline favorites that belong to them.*

Choosing Further Options for Offline Favorites

The Offline Favorite Wizard offers you a good range of options for your offline favorites—but it doesn't offer you several key options. For the extra options, you need to edit the properties of the offline favorite after creating it.

TIP *You can turn a regular favorite into an offline favorite by editing its properties as described here.*

Right-click the favorite in the Favorites Explorer bar, on the Favorites menu, or in the Organize Favorites dialog box and choose Properties from the context menu. Internet Explorer displays the Properties dialog box for the favorite. Figure 18.18 shows an example of this Properties dialog box for an offline favorite.

NOTE *The Properties dialog box for a regular favorite displays only two pages—the General page and the Web Document page. When you select the Make This Page Available Offline check box to turn the favorite into an offline favorite, the dialog box displays the Schedule page and Download page as well.*

Click the Download tab. Internet Explorer displays the Download page (shown in Figure 18.19). Then select options as follows:

◆ In the Download Pages *NN* Links Deep from This Page text box, enter the number of links to pursue from this page. (This option is available in the Offline Favorite Wizard.) Valid numbers are 0, 1, 2, and 3. 0 downloads no pages linked to this one; 1 downloads the pages directly linked; 2 downloads all the pages linked to those; and 3 downloads all the pages linked to *those*. As in the movie-buff game Six Degrees of Kevin Bacon, each increment of the number increases the area covered almost exponentially. (A setting of 6 here—were Internet Explorer to offer it—might net you enough of the Web to fill the average hard disk.)

FIGURE 18.18

Use the Properties dialog box for an offline favorite to adjust its synchronization schedule or the amount of information to download. This dialog box also contains the check box for turning a regular favorite into an offline favorite.

◆ If you set 1, 2, or 3 in the previous step, the Follow Links outside of This Page's Web Site check box is available. (If you set 0, this check box is unavailable because it doesn't apply.) Select this check box if you want Internet Explorer to follow links to other sites. Leave this check box cleared (as it is by default) if you don't. Use this option with great caution—for example, monitor the first synchronization session to get an idea of whether it's reasonable to go outside the favorite's Web site.

WARNING *Be aware that the Follow Links outside of This Page's Web Site option can cause Internet Explorer to try to download large amounts of information. For example, if you set a value of 3 in the Download Pages NN Links Deep from This Page text box and select the Follow Links outside of This Page's Web Site check box for an offline favorite of a book on Sybex's Web site, Internet Explorer will end up trying to download substantial chunks of the Amazon.com Web site, the FatBrain.com Web site, and so on.*

FIGURE 18.19

On the Download page of the Properties dialog box for an offline favorite, you can specify whether to follow links outside this page's Web site and whether to limit the amount of hard disk space this offline favorite can consume.

◆ To cap the amount of space this offline favorite and its associated pages can consume, select the Limit Hard-Disk Usage for This Page To check box and enter a value in the Kilobytes text box. Internet Explorer suggests 500KB by default, but you'll often want to increase this. If you want to download a large amount of a particular Web site but make sure that you don't end up downloading half the Web (so to speak), set a value of between 5MB (5120KB) and 20MB (20,480KB). The maximum value you can set is 32,767KB, or a hair under 32MB.

Then click the Advanced button. Internet Explorer displays the Advanced Download Options dialog box (shown in Figure 18.20). Specify which items to download by selecting or clearing the Images check box, the Sound and Video check box, and the ActiveX Controls and Java Applets check box. Not downloading sound and video saves you the most bandwidth (if the pages contain them), but if you really want to pare down the content, clear the Images check box as well.

FIGURE 18.20

Use the Advanced Download Options dialog box to specify which items Internet Explorer should download for offline favorites.

Select the Only to HTML Pages check box if you want Internet Explorer to follow only links to HTML pages. By selecting this check box, you can avoid having Internet Explorer waste time downloading items such as Zip files—but the links to these will of course be nonfunctional when you're browsing offline.

Click the OK button. Internet Explorer closes the Advanced Download Options dialog box. Then click the OK button. Internet Explorer closes the Properties dialog box for the offline favorite.

EXPERT KNOWLEDGE: GETTING NOTIFIED BY E-MAIL WHEN A WEB SITE CHANGES

If you need to keep close track of a site, you can get Internet Explorer to automatically send you an e-mail when the site changes. To do this, you need to set the site up as an offline favorite as described in the previous section.

Right-click the favorite and choose Properties from the context menu. Internet Explorer displays the Properties dialog box for the favorite. On the Download page, select the When This Page Changes, Send E-mail To check box. Then enter your e-mail address in the E-mail Address text box and the address of your *outgoing* mail server (the SMTP server) in the Mail Server (SMTP) text box. (Internet Explorer needs this information in order to send the message.) Then click the OK button. When the site changes, you'll receive a message titled *Internet Explorer Notice* and the name of the favorite.

Chances are, you won't want to do this for more than a few key offline favorites, because many sites change frequently, and you've probably got better things to do than constantly deleting Web site–change messages from your Inbox.

Organizing Your Favorites into Folders

Internet Explorer automatically sorts your favorites alphabetically on the Favorites menu, which works well enough for a short list of favorites. But if you use the Web vigorously, you'll soon build a collection of favorites that will overrun the Favorites menu. You'll need to organize these favorites into folders.

To organize your favorites, take the following steps:

1. Choose Favorites ➤ Organize Favorites. Internet Explorer displays the Organize Favorites dialog box (shown in Figure 18.21). Alternatively, if you have the Favorites Explorer bar displayed, click the Organize button at the top of it.

FIGURE 18.21

Use the Organize Favorites dialog box to organize your favorites into folders.

2. Organize your favorites into folders by using the following techniques:

   ◆ To move a favorite to a folder, either drag it to the folder in the list box (this is difficult if your Favorites menu is long) or select the favorite and click the Move to Folder button. Internet Explorer displays the Browse for Folder dialog box. Select the folder, and click the OK button. Internet Explorer closes the Browse for Folder dialog box and moves the favorite.

   ◆ To change the order of the list, drag a favorite or a folder up or down the list box.

   ◆ To rename a favorite or a folder, select it and click the Rename button. Type the new name over the existing name and press the Enter key.

   ◆ To delete a favorite or a folder, select it and click the Delete button. Internet Explorer displays the Confirm Folder Delete dialog box. Click the Yes button. Internet Explorer closes the dialog box and deletes the favorite or folder.

   ◆ To create a new folder, click the Create Folder button. Internet Explorer creates a new folder called New Folder at the bottom of the list box and selects its name. Type in the new name for the folder and press the Enter key.

3. Click the Close button. Internet Explorer closes the Organize Favorites dialog box.

Changing a Favorite so that It's Available Offline

To make one of your designated favorites available even when you're not online, take the following steps.

1. Choose Favorites ➤ Organize Favorites. Internet Explorer displays the Organize Favorites dialog box.

2. Select the favorite in the panel on the right side of the dialog box so that its details appear in the pane on the lower left of the dialog box.

3. Select the Make Available Offline check box. (This check box appears when you select a favorite in the list box.) When you select the check box, Internet Explorer displays a Properties button below the check box.

4. Click the Properties button. Internet Explorer displays the Properties dialog box for the favorite.

5. Click the Schedule tab. Internet Explorer displays the Schedule page of the Properties dialog box (shown in Figure 18.22).

FIGURE 18.22

Designate the synchronization schedule on the Schedule page of the Properties dialog box for the favorite.

6. Select the appropriate synchronization options.

7. Click the OK button. Internet Explorer closes the Properties dialog box.

8. Click the Close button. Internet Explorer closes the Organize Favorites dialog box.

EXPERT KNOWLEDGE: USING NETSCAPE BOOKMARKS IN INTERNET EXPLORER

To use a bookmark list that you've put together in Netscape, export it from Netscape: Choose Bookmarks ➤ Manage Bookmarks. Netscape displays the Manage Bookmarks window. Choose File ➤ Export Bookmarks. Netscape displays the Export Bookmark File dialog box, which is a common Save As dialog box. Specify the location and filename for the file and click the Save button. Netscape closes the Export Bookmark File dialog box and saves the file.

Then, in Internet Explorer, choose File ➤ Import and Export. Internet Explorer starts the Import and Export Wizard. Follow the Wizard's prompts to import the file.

Using the Explorer Bars

Internet Explorer provides a handful of Explorer bars that provide some additional functionality and an alternate way of accessing certain features. The drawback to using these Explorer bars is that they take up a chunk of your browsing area. Some people find these bars useful; others find them a waste of screen space. But you should know about them so that you can use them if you'll benefit from doing so. You've already met a couple of them in this chapter.

To display an Explorer bar, choose View ➤ Explorer Bar and choose the bar's name from the submenu, or (where appropriate) press the key combination listed below. To hide the bar again, repeat the command or click the Close button (the × button) on the bar. Most of the Explorer bars appear at the left side of the Internet Explorer window; you can display only one of these Explorer bars at once. The Tip of the Day Explorer bar and the Discussion Explorer bar (which grafts itself onto Internet Explorer when you install Microsoft Office XP or Microsoft Office 2000) appear across the bottom of the window.

These are the main Explorer bars:

Search Explorer bar (Ctrl+E) This bar provides tools for searching for a Web page, a person's address, a business, or a map. The contents of the Search Explorer bar change depending on which item you're searching for. You can customize your search settings by clicking the Customize button and working in the Customize Search Settings dialog box.

Favorites Explorer bar (Ctrl+I) This bar lists your favorites, essentially duplicating the Favorites menu in a more visible way.

History Explorer bar (Ctrl+H) This bar displays a list of the Web sites you've visited and the documents you've opened recently.

Folders Explorer bar This bar displays a tree showing your Desktop and the folders accessible from it: My Documents, My Computer, My Network Places, and Recycle Bin. This bar can be useful for opening documents in Internet Explorer. For general file-management tasks, you'll normally be better off using an Explorer window.

Media Explorer bar This bar provides quick access to WindowsMedia.com's music, radio, movies, and entertainment, together with play controls.

Tip of the Day Explorer bar   This bar displays tips. Use it to quickly view all tips by clicking the Next Tip link; implement or memorize the good ones; and then turn this bar off to reclaim the space it wastes.

Customizing Your Home Page and Quick Links

Apart from favorites, Internet Explorer provides several features for quickly accessing particular sites. These features include your home page, your search page, and Quick Links buttons.

Your *home page* is the page that Internet Explorer automatically opens when you start Internet Explorer and when you click the Home button on the toolbar. You'll usually want to change your home page from the default setting (MSN) to the site you want to see first in every Internet Explorer session.

EXPERT KNOWLEDGE: CREATING A CUSTOM HOME PAGE LOCALLY

One of the problems with most home pages is that, even with the fastest of connections, they take a few seconds to load. If you want to see what's new on the home page, that may be well and good. But if you just want to use the home page as a jumping-off point for sites further afield, the delay may be annoying.

To avoid this delay, create a custom home page and store it on your hard drive. It needs to contain no more than a little HTML—though you can make it as complex as you like.

The Links bar provides Quick Links to regularly updated Microsoft sites, such as Free Hotmail and the Windows site. (The names of these Quick Links vary a little in different versions of Internet Explorer. Your hardware provider may also have customized the Quick Links.) You can access any of these sites by clicking its button on the Links bar.

To customize the Quick Links bar, navigate to a site that you like, then drag the page icon from the beginning of the Address box to the Quick Links bar. Drop the icon in an open space on the bar. Internet Explorer creates a link for it.

See page 51 of the *Essential Skills* section for a visual guide to changing your home page, or take the following steps:

1. Navigate to your target page.

2. Choose Tools ➤ Internet Options. Internet Explorer displays the Internet Options dialog box with the General page foremost.

3. Click the Use Current button in the Home Page group box on the General page.

   ◆ You can also type the address into the Address text box, but it's usually easier to display the site first.

   ◆ Alternatively, click the Use Blank button to make Internet Explorer start with a blank page. (A blank page displays immediately but doesn't get you far.)

4. Click the OK button. Internet Explorer closes the Internet Options dialog box.

WARNING   Installing Microsoft programs may reset your home page to its default setting without warning you. In case this happens, create a favorite for your start page so that you will be able to access it quickly in order to restore it as your home page.

Customizing the Toolbar

You can customize the Internet Explorer toolbar by adding, removing, or rearranging buttons, and changing the presentation of the labels on the buttons you display.

To customize the toolbar, take the following steps:

1. Choose View ➤ Toolbars ➤ Customize. (Alternatively, right-click the toolbar and choose Customize from the context menu.) Internet Explorer displays the Customize Toolbar dialog box (shown in Figure 18.23).

FIGURE 18.23

Use the Customize Toolbar dialog box to customize the Internet Explorer toolbar so that it contains the buttons you need.

2. To add a button to the toolbar, select it in the Available Toolbar Buttons list box and click the Add button. Internet Explorer adds the button to the Current Toolbar Buttons list box:

    ◆ Use the Move Up button or Move Down button to move the new button to the position in which you want it.

    ◆ Internet Explorer adds the button above the currently selected item in the Current Toolbar Buttons list box. To place the button you're adding in a particular position so that you don't need to move it with the Move Up button and Move Down button, select the current item above which you want the button to appear, then select the button and click the Add button.

3. To remove a button from the toolbar, select it in the Current Toolbar Buttons list box and click the Remove button.

4. To rearrange the buttons on the toolbar, use the Move Up button and Move Down button to change their order.

5. To change the text labels, choose one of the items in the Text Options drop-down list:

    ◆ Show Text Labels makes the text label appear beneath the graphic on each button.

◆ Selective Text on Right makes the text labels appear on some buttons (such as Search, Favorites, and History) to the right of the graphic. Other buttons display no text label. When a button has no text label, Internet Explorer displays a ScreenTip when you hover the mouse pointer over the button so that you can identify it easily.

◆ No Text Labels removes the text labels from the buttons.

6. In the Icon Options drop-down list, select Small Icons or Large Icons to suit your preference. For example, choose small icons and no text labels to pack more buttons onto the toolbar.

7. Click the Close button. Internet Explorer closes the Customize Toolbar dialog box and applies your changes to the toolbar.

You can rearrange the toolbars and menu bar by dragging them by their handles (the raised line at the left end of the toolbar). For example, you might drag the bars so that they occupy two rows across the screen rather than their default three. You can also toggle off the display of the toolbars by right-clicking the menu bar or any displayed toolbar and choosing Standard Buttons, Address Bar, or Links as appropriate. You can toggle off the display of the status bar by choosing View ➢ Status Bar.

TIP   To get the maximum display area in the Internet Explorer window, press the F11 key or choose View ➢ Full Screen, then right-click the toolbar and choose Auto Hide from the context menu. Press the F11 key again to toggle Full Screen view off.

To restore your toolbar buttons to their default state, removing any customizations, click the Reset button in the Customize Toolbar dialog box.

Dealing with Common Error Messages

When you're surfing the Web, you'll often see a couple of error messages: *Server too busy*, and *The page cannot be displayed*.

The first message typically means that the Web server the browser contacted was too busy right then handling other requests to deal with your request for information. Click the Refresh button on the toolbar to try the link again. Often, you'll get straight through on the second attempt; but if the server is truly busy, you may need to retry a number of times, or wait until later.

The second message typically means either that the address you are trying to access doesn't exist or that the address is temporarily unavailable (for example, because the server that hosts the address is offline or not working). If you know that the address exists, try it later, when the server may be back online. If not, and if you typed in the URL, double-check each character to make sure you didn't miss or add anything. Then try it again.

Configuring Internet Explorer

This section discusses the most important options that Internet Explorer offers for controlling how it runs. You can configure most aspects of its behavior—everything from the font size Internet Explorer uses to display text, to security, to improving performance over a slow Internet connection.

Internet Explorer has a plethora of options, so this section doesn't discuss all of them. Instead, it concentrates on the options that will make the most difference in your daily surfing.

All these options live in the Internet Options dialog box. Start by choosing Tools ➤ Internet Options. Internet Explorer displays this dialog box.

Cleaning Up Temporary Internet Files

Every time you view a page on the Internet or on an internal network, the information on the page is transferred to your computer. That's no surprise—that's why download times matter so much to the surfing experience. But it's not so obvious that this information is written into temporary files on your hard drive. This enables you to view the information more quickly the next time you access the page, as Internet Explorer has to download only new items if the page has changed. Over a high-speed network, that may not make a big difference, but over the average Internet connection, it can save anything from a few seconds to a minute or two.

The disadvantages to having the files on your hard drive are, first, that they take up space, and second, that you can have embarrassing or dangerous information stored on your computer without your knowledge. So it's a good idea to clear out your temporary files periodically.

To clean up temporary Internet files, click the Settings button in the Temporary Internet Files group box on the General page of the Internet Options dialog box. Internet Explorer displays the Settings dialog box (shown in Figure 18.24).

FIGURE 18.24

Use the Settings dialog box to keep your temporary Internet files under control.

In the Check for Newer Versions of Stored Pages list, select an option button to determine how frequently Internet Explorer should check for newer versions of stored pages: Every Visit to the Page, Every Time You Start Internet Explorer, Automatically, or Never. The first, second, and fourth of these options are self-explanatory. The default setting, Automatically, causes Internet Explorer to build its own schedule for updating each stored page. If you return to a page the same day and during the same Internet Explorer session as your previous visit, Internet Explorer does not check for a new version of the page (unless you issue a Refresh command). If your last visit was in an earlier session or on an earlier day, Internet Explorer updates the page. Subsequently Internet Explorer monitors the page and tries to establish a schedule that approximately reflects the page's frequency of change. Internet Explorer isn't psychic and can't intuit the frequency of changes, so the schedule it establishes may result in you seeing an out-of-date version of the page.

In the Temporary Internet Files Folder group box, check the amount of disk space Internet Explorer is using for temporary files. If you have space to burn and you're not concerned about having potentially embarrassing information stored, devote anything up to several gigabytes to temporary files, because storing more of them may speed up your browsing.

From the Settings dialog box, you can take three other actions:

◆ Move the folder to another folder or drive if necessary by clicking the Move Folder button and using the resulting Browse for Folder dialog box to designate the folder. If you do this, you need to restart Internet Explorer.

◆ Display an Explorer window showing your temporary files by clicking the View Files button. You probably won't need to do this unless you want to delete an objectionable item (for example, a graphics file) that you know Internet Explorer has downloaded.

◆ Display an Explorer window listing the objects installed—for example, ActiveX controls—by clicking the View Objects button. From this window, you can check an object's properties by right-clicking it and choosing Properties from the context menu; remove it by right-clicking it and choosing Remove from the context menu; or update it by right-clicking it and choosing Update from the context menu.

When you've chosen suitable settings, click the OK button. Internet Explorer closes the Settings dialog box.

To clear out your current temporary files, click the Delete Files button in the Temporary Internet Files group box. Internet Explorer displays the Delete Files dialog box (shown in Figure 18.25). To delete all your offline content, select the Delete All Offline Content check box. Usually, you'll want to keep the offline content but get rid of everything else. Click the OK button. Internet Explorer closes the Delete Files dialog box and deletes your temporary files.

FIGURE 18.25

Use the Delete Files dialog box to delete your temporary Internet files.

To delete your cookies, click the Delete Cookies button in the Temporary Internet Files group box on the General page of the Internet Options dialog box. Internet Explorer displays the Delete Cookies dialog box to confirm that you want to delete all your cookies. Click the OK button. Internet Explorer closes the Delete Cookies dialog box and deletes your cookies.

Keeping Control of Your History

As you saw earlier in the chapter, Internet Explorer's History feature tracks where you've been. History is a great feature for retracing your steps to find a site you forgot to bookmark, but it's also a threat: Those who study your history can repeat your movements step by step—which, depending on what you've been doing, could be a threat to your business' security, to your family's good name, or to the recipient's blissful ignorance of that perfect Christmas present you bought well ahead of time.

If you perceive a security threat, reduce the Days to Keep Pages in History text box entry in the History group box on the General page of the Internet Options dialog box to a minimum—perhaps

0 days. Then click the Clear History button to clear your current history. Click the OK button in the confirmation message box that appears.

If clearing your history would raise suspicions, you can delete a particular shortcut or a Web location by right-clicking it and choosing Delete from the context menu.

Choosing Security Options

The History feature touches on security, but Internet Explorer has a bunch of explicit security features as well. Click the Security tab in the Internet Options dialog box. Internet Explorer displays the Security page (shown in Figure 18.26).

FIGURE 18.26

Choose security options on the Security page of the Internet Options dialog box.

The Select a Web Content Zone to Specify Its Security Settings box at the top of the page contains four categories of sites. The easiest way to explain them is in reverse order:

- Restricted Sites (sites you've specifically designated as potentially dangerous)

- Trusted Sites (sites you've specifically designated as trusted not to damage your computer or your data)

- Local Intranet (local sites not specifically designated as restricted or trusted)

- Internet (everything else)

You can set a different level of security for each category by selecting the category, clicking the Default Level button so that Internet Explorer displays the Security Level for This Zone slider, and then dragging the slider up or down. If you understand the specifics of security, you can also specify a custom level for a zone by selecting the category and clicking the Custom Level button. Internet Explorer displays the Security Settings dialog box (shown in Figure 18.27). Select settings for the different categories, then click the OK button. Internet Explorer closes the Security Settings dialog box and implements your settings.

FIGURE 18.27

If you understand
security issues, you
can use the Security
Settings dialog box
to implement cus-
tom security settings.

By default, the Internet category has a Medium security level designed to let you browse effectively while protecting you from harmful content. Local Intranet has a Medium-Low level; Trusted
Sites has a Low level; and Restricted Sites has a High level.

To change your list of Local Intranet sites, Trusted Sites, or Restricted Sites, select the category
and click the Sites button. Internet Explorer displays the Local Intranet dialog box, the Trusted Sites
dialog box, or the Restricted Sites dialog box (shown in Figure 18.28). To add a site to the list, enter
its URL in the Add This Web Site to The Zone text box and click the Add button; to remove a site
from the list, select it in the Web Sites list box and click the Remove button. Click the OK button to
close the dialog box.

FIGURE 18.28

Use the Restricted
Sites dialog box
(shown here), the
Trusted Sites dialog
box (not shown), or
the Local Intranet
dialog box (not
shown) to adjust
your list of restricted
sites, trusted sites, or
local intranet sites.

NOTE   *The security zone for the current site appears in the status bar.*

Choosing a Level of Privacy

For the Internet zone, you can choose the level of privacy to use. Click the Privacy tab. Internet
Explorer displays the Privacy page of the Internet Options dialog box (shown in Figure 18.29).

FIGURE 18.29

Use the Privacy page of the Internet Options dialog box to specify your privacy preferences for the Internet zone.

Drag the slider in the Settings group box to specify the level of security to use. Beside the slider, Internet Explorer displays specifics for that level of privacy.

If you prefer to have the boundaries of your privacy designed by other people, you can download privacy settings files from privacy organizations. Then click the Import button and use the resulting Privacy Import dialog box to import the file, which applies the preferences it contains.

Handling Cookies

A key aspect of privacy is handling *cookies*, the text files that Web sites place on your computer in order to track your dealings with their site. For example, if you visit an e-commerce site and fill out a form to buy a product, the information you enter in the form is typically stored in a cookie so that the Web site can maintain the information in the fields if you need to go back to a previous page. Only the Web site that creates a cookie can read it; other Web sites cannot. Most cookies are *persistent*, lasting from one session to another so that their information can be used when you revisit a site in a later session, but there are also *temporary cookies* or *session cookies* that last only until the end of the current Internet Explorer session.

To specify custom cookie handling, take the following steps:

1. Click the Advanced button on the Privacy page of the Internet Options dialog box. Internet Explorer displays the Advanced Privacy Settings dialog box (shown in Figure 18.30 with some settings chosen).

FIGURE 18.30

Use the Advanced Privacy Settings dialog box to specify custom handling of cookies.

2. Select the Override Automatic Cookie Handling check box.

3. In the First-Party Cookies list, choose the Accept option button, the Block option button, or the Prompt option button as appropriate. *First-party cookies* are those that come from the Web site you're viewing.

4. In the Third-Party Cookies list, choose the Accept option button, the Block option button, or the Prompt option button as appropriate. *Third-party cookies* are those that come from Web sites associated with the one you're viewing. They're often used for advertising or marketing, so you might want to block them.

5. If you want to use session cookies no matter what your settings in the First-Party Cookies list and the Third-Party Cookies list, select the Always Allow Session Cookies check box. Session cookies are temporary cookies maintained during a session to facilitate communication with Web sites. Internet Explorer deletes session cookies when you close it.

6. Click the OK button. Internet Explorer closes the Advanced Privacy Settings dialog box and applies your choices.

That custom cookie handling you just set applies to all Web sites. If you want to be more specific about which sites can and cannot place cookies on your computer, click the Edit button in the Web Sites group box. Internet Explorer displays the Per Site Privacy Actions dialog box (shown in Figure 18.31).

FIGURE 18.31

You can use the Per Site Privacy Actions dialog box to specify which Web sites may use cookies and which Web sites are blocked.

To allow or block cookies from a Web site, enter the domain name in the Address of Web Site text box and then click the Allow button or the Block button as appropriate. Use the Remove button to remove a blocked or allowed site from the Managed Web Sites list box, or use the Remove All button to clear the list.

Click the OK button. Internet Explorer closes the Per Site Privacy Actions dialog box and applies your choices.

Internet Explorer monitors cookies and displays messages such as that shown in Figure 18.32 when there's a problem that you might want to know about. You'll probably want to accept Internet Explorer's offer to turn off this warning, but watch for the privacy icon in the status bar.

FIGURE 18.32

Internet Explorer displays this Privacy dialog box to alert you to restricted cookies.

When Internet Explorer displays the privacy icon in the status bar, you can double-click it to display a Privacy Report dialog box (shown in Figure 18.33). Use the Show drop-down list to toggle between Restricted Web Sites and All Web Sites. Click the Settings button if you want to move to the Privacy page of the Internet Options dialog box (for example, to block a new offender). Or click the Close button to close the Privacy Report dialog box.

FIGURE 18.33

In the Privacy Report dialog box, you can see which sites are being blocked from sending you cookies.

NOTE   To delete all your cookies, click the Delete Cookies button in the Temporary Internet Files group box on the General page of the Internet Options dialog box and then click the OK button in the Delete Cookies dialog box that Internet Explorer displays. Bear in mind that deleting all cookies denies you any benefit those cookies offered.

Screening Out Objectionable Content

The Content Advisor feature enables you to set up content screening based on the ratings of the Recreational Software Advisory Council rating service for the Internet (RSACi). Content Advisor is very useful if children or easily offended friends or relatives may be using your computer.

To set up Content Adviser, take the following steps:

1. Click the Content tab of the Internet Options dialog box. Internet Explorer displays the Content page.

2. Click the Enable button in the Content Advisor group box. Internet Explorer displays the Content Advisor dialog box.

3. On the Ratings page, select the item in the Category list box and drag the Rating slider to a suitable level (shown in Figure 18.34). Each of the items has five levels, ranging from 0 (none of the offensive item) to 4 (lots of it). For example, the Violence levels are No Violence (0), Fighting (1), Killing (2), Killing with Blood and Gore (3), and Wanton and Gratuitous Violence (4). The Language levels are Inoffensive Slang (0), Mild Expletives (1), Moderate Expletives (2), Obscene Gestures (3), and Explicit or Crude Language (4).

FIGURE 18.34

Choose rating levels for Language, Nudity, Sex, and Violence on the Ratings page of the Content Advisor dialog box.

4. Click the Approved Sites tab. Internet Explorer displays the Approved Sites page (shown in Figure 18.35).

FIGURE 18.35

Use the Approved Sites page of the Content Advisor dialog box to specify sites that should be always viewable or never viewable no matter what rating they carry.

5. Set up your list of approved and disapproved sites by taking the following steps:

   ◆ In the Allow This Web Site text box, enter the URL of the Web site you want to make always viewable or never viewable.

   ◆ Click the Always button or the Never button as appropriate. Internet Explorer adds the site to the List of Approved and Disapproved Web Sites list box and marks it with the corresponding icon.

   ◆ To remove a Web site from the List of Approved and Disapproved Web Sites list box, select it and click the Remove button.

6. Click the General tab. Internet Explorer displays the General page (shown in Figure 18.36).

FIGURE 18.36

Choose general options on the General page of the Content Advisor dialog box.

7. Choose options as appropriate:

   ◆ Select the Users Can See Sites That Have No Rating check box if you want users to be able to view Web sites that don't use ratings. This check box is cleared by default, because unrated Web sites may well have offensive content.

   ◆ Leave the Supervisor Can Type a Password to Allow Users to View Restricted Content check box selected (as it is by default) if you want to be able to let other users view restricted sites by your entering a password. If not, clear this check box.

   ◆ To change the supervisor password, click the Change Password button and specify the new password in the resulting Change Supervisor Password dialog box.

TIP   If you don't find RSACi adequate, you can add other rating systems to Internet Explorer by using the controls in the Rating Systems group box on the General page of the Content Advisor dialog box. The Advanced page contains controls for adding a ratings bureau and PICSRules to Content Advisor. You're unlikely to need to use these options for home or home-office computing.

8. Click the OK button. Internet Explorer closes Content Advisor. The first time you close Content Adviser, Internet Explorer displays the Create Supervisor Password dialog box (shown in Figure 18.37).

FIGURE 18.37

Create a supervisor password in the Create Supervisor Password dialog box.

Create Supervisor Password
To prevent unauthorized users from changing Content Advisor settings, provide a password.
Content Advisor settings can be changed or turned on or off only by people who know the password.
Password:
Confirm password:
Provide a hint to help you remember your password. Set the hint so that others cannot use it to easily guess your password.
Hint:
OK   Cancel

9. Enter the password in the Password and Confirm Password text boxes, then click the OK button. Internet Explorer displays a Content Advisor message box (shown in Figure 18.38) telling you that Content Advisor has been installed and to close Internet Explorer.

FIGURE 18.38

When Internet Explorer warns you that Content Advisor has been enabled, click the OK button and exit the program.

10. Click the OK button. Internet Explorer closes the Content Advisor dialog box and returns you to the Internet Options dialog box, where the Enable Ratings button has changed to the Disable Ratings button.

11. Click the OK button. Internet Explorer closes the Internet Options dialog box.

12. Exit all Internet Explorer windows, then reopen one.

To adjust the settings for Content Advisor, click the Settings button in the Content Advisor group box on the Content page of the Internet Options dialog box. Internet Explorer displays the Supervisor Password Required dialog box. Enter your password and click the OK button to display the Content Advisor dialog box, then change the settings and click the OK button.

To disable ratings again, click the Disable button in the Content Advisor group box on the Content page of the Internet Options dialog box. Internet Explorer displays the Supervisor Password Required dialog box. Enter your password and click the OK button. Internet Explorer displays a Content Advisor message box telling you that Content Advisor has been turned off.

When users hit a site that contains unapproved content, they see a Content Advisor dialog box such as the one shown in Figure 18.39. If you're the user, you can enter the supervisor password and choose the Always Allow This Web Site to Be Viewed option button (to make a lasting exception for the site), the Always Allow This Web Page to Be Viewed option button (to make a lasting exception for the page but not the site), or the Allow Viewing Only This Time option button (to make a temporary exception). Then click the OK button. Internet Explorer closes the Content Advisor dialog box and displays the site. (A user without the supervisor password will need to click the Cancel button and will not be able to reach the site.)

FIGURE 18.39

Content Advisor in action

Managing Your AutoComplete Information

AutoComplete is a great feature that can save you a lot of fuss with passwords and often-repeated information. But it can also severely compromise your digital persona and your finances, so you need to understand what it does and how it works so that you can use it appropriately.

Briefly put, AutoComplete automatically fills in URLs and entries on forms for you. To do so, it needs to watch as you enter URLs and information on forms, and store that information. Then, when you start typing an URL or access a form it recognizes, it can fill in the information for you. For example, the first time you access your Hotmail account via Internet Explorer, AutoComplete can learn your username and password, and offer to fill them in for you in the future.

You can see the downside to this: Internet Explorer is storing sensitive or secret information, which means that other people who use your computer can more easily masquerade as you. There's also a risk that your computer could be hacked to give up this information, though this risk is less severe than the direct risk from people who can physically access your computer.

To configure AutoComplete, follow these steps:

1. Click the AutoComplete button in the Personal Information group box on the Content page of the Internet Options dialog box to display the AutoComplete Settings dialog box (shown in Figure 18.40).

FIGURE 18.40

Choose AutoComplete options in the AutoComplete Settings dialog box.

2. In the Use AutoComplete For group box, specify the items for which you want to use Auto-Complete:

   ◆ The Web Addresses check box controls whether AutoComplete tracks the URLs you access and suggests matching URLs in the Open dialog box and the Address box.

   ◆ The Forms check box controls whether AutoComplete tracks your entries in forms other than usernames and passwords.

   ◆ The User Names and Passwords on Forms check box controls whether AutoComplete tracks the usernames and passwords you enter in forms. This is the most sensitive information, so you may want to clear this check box. If you leave it enabled (as it is by default), leave the Prompt Me to Save Passwords check box selected so that Internet Explorer gets your consent each time it's about to store a password of yours. (This way, you can use AutoComplete for less sensitive passwords but not for high-security passwords.)

3. If you want to clear your form information or passwords stored to date, click the Clear Forms button or the Clear Passwords button in the Clear AutoComplete History group box and click the OK button in the Internet Options confirmation dialog box that Internet Explorer displays.

4. Click the OK button. Internet Explorer closes the AutoComplete Settings dialog box.

Specifying Programs for Internet Services

The Programs page of the Internet Options dialog box (shown in Figure 18.41) lets you specify which program Windows should use for Internet-related tasks such as editing HTML and reading newsgroups. Use the six drop-down lists to specify the programs to use. By default, Internet Explorer chooses Outlook Express for E-mail and Newsgroups, NetMeeting for Internet Call, and Address Book for Contact List.

FIGURE 18.41

On the Programs page of the Internet Options dialog box, you can manually configure the programs that you want Windows to use for the assorted Internet services.

Advanced Options

The Advanced page of the Internet Options dialog box (shown in Figure 18.42) contains a formidable number of options organized in a number of categories. The following sections discuss the key options.

FIGURE 18.42

Choose advanced options on the Advanced page of the Internet Options dialog box.

WARNING   Because many of the options on the Advanced page control important behavior on the part of Internet Explorer, don't change them unless you understand exactly what they do and what the results can be. If you think you've chosen some unwise settings, you can click the Restore Defaults button to restore the default settings.

BROWSING CATEGORY

These are the key options in the Browsing category:

Automatically Check for Internet Explorer Updates check box   This check box controls whether Internet Explorer checks for any available updates. It's a good idea to select this check box even if you use Windows Update regularly: Because Internet Explorer handles a wide range of duties and has extensive contact with the Internet, any vulnerabilities can prove painful.

Enable Offline Items to Be Synchronized on a Schedule check box   Make sure this check box is selected if you want to create offline favorites.

Notify when Downloads Complete check box   Leave this check box selected (as it is by default) if you want Internet Explorer to prompt you when it finishes downloading a file. Clear this check box if you find the notification annoying.

Reuse Windows for Launching Shortcuts check box   When selected (as it is by default), this check box causes Internet Explorer to display the page for a hyperlink you click in the current window. Clear this check box if you want Internet Explorer to display the linked page in a new window by default.

Underline Links option buttons   Select the Always option button (the default), the Hover option button, or the Never option button to specify whether and when Internet Explorer should underline links. (*Hover* means that you position the mouse pointer over the link.)

Use Inline AutoComplete check box   This check box controls whether Internet Explorer offers AutoComplete suggestions when you're typing an address or URL in the Address box or in Explorer. Most people find AutoComplete helpful, but its suggestions can be embarrassing if you've been visiting URLs or viewing documents you shouldn't have.

Use Passive FTP check box   Select this check box if you want to use passive FTP—FTP in which your computer does not need to supply its IP address. Because of this, passive FTP is normally more secure than regular FTP. Depending on your network settings, you may need to use passive FTP—for example, if you have a vigilant firewall. Generally speaking, stick with regular FTP unless you find it doesn't work, in which case, try passive FTP.

Use Smooth Scrolling check box   This check box (which is selected by default) controls whether Internet Explorer scrolls the contents of its window in a smooth and gentle fashion or in jerks (as most Windows programs do). If you're used to regular Windows behavior, or if you find the smooth scrolling sick-making, try clearing this check box.

MULTIMEDIA CATEGORY

These are the key options in the Multimedia category:

Play Animations in Web Pages check box   This check box controls whether Internet Explorer plays animations. If your computer or connection is slow, you may want to turn animations off.

Play Sounds in Web Pages check box   This check box controls whether Internet Explorer plays sounds. Because sound files can be big, consider clearing this check box to speed up your downloads.

Play Videos in Web Pages check box   This check box controls whether Internet Explorer plays videos. Video files can be huge, so if you have a slow connection, consider turning videos off to speed up your browsing.

Show Pictures check box   This check box controls whether Internet Explorer displays pictures. If your Internet connection is really slow (for example, if you're surfing via a cell-phone hookup), you may want to turn pictures off—but the Web is so graphical nowadays that some pages may be tough going without their pictures.

SECURITY CATEGORY

You should understand most of the items in the Security category:

Check for Publisher's Certificate Revocation check box   Select this check box to have Internet Explorer check that a software publisher's digital certificate is still valid before accepting it. Checking a certificate slows down the installation of add-on software but offers you a little extra protection against bad software.

WARNING   Surprisingly, even some major software publishers have been known to let their certificates lapse. If you select the Check for Publisher's Certificate Revocation check box, you may occasionally have to override warnings that a certificate is out of date in order to install add-ons you need.

Check for Server Certificate Revocation check box   This check box (which is cleared by default) controls whether Internet Explorer checks an Internet site's certificate to make sure it hasn't been revoked.

Do Not Save Encrypted Pages to Disk check box   Select this check box (which is cleared by default) to prevent Internet Explorer from saving encrypted Web pages to disk.

Empty Temporary Internet Files Folder when Browser Is Closed check box   This check box (which is cleared by default) controls whether Internet Explorer deletes all temporary files each time you close Internet Explorer. If you're concerned about security, select this check box.

Enable Integrated Windows Authentication check box   Leave this check box selected if you want to use Integrated Windows Authentication.

Enable Profile Assistant check box   Leave this check box selected (as it is by default) if you want to use Internet Explorer's Profile Assistant for providing information requested by Web sites. The Profile Assistant manages the requests for information and lets you specify which information to share with each Web site and whether to respond automatically to future requests from that site. Clear this check box to turn off the Profile Assistant. (See "Editing Your Profile for Address Book" in Chapter 19 for coverage of Profile Assistant.)

Use SSL 2.0 check box and Use SSL 3.0 check box   Leave these check boxes selected (as they are by default) if you want to use the Secure Sockets Layer Level 2 (SSL 2) and Secure Sockets

Layer Level 3 (SSL 3) protocols for securing the transmission of information. As you'd guess from the number, SSL 3 is supposed to be more secure than SSL 2. At this writing, SSL 2 is almost universally used, but SSL 3 is starting to supplant it.

Use TLS 1.0 check box   Select this check box (which is cleared by default) if you want to use Transport Layer Security (TLS) to secure the transmission of information. TLS is not widely used.

Warn about Invalid Site Certificates check box   This check box (which is selected by default) controls whether Internet Explorer warns you if a digital certificate is invalid. Keep this check box selected.

Warn if Changing Between Secure and Not Secure Mode check box   This check box (which is selected by default) controls whether Internet Explorer warns you when you are switched from a secure (encrypted) connection to a server to an insecure connection. Keep this check box selected until you've got the hang of secure connections. When the warnings become an irritant, clear this check box.

Warn if Forms Submittal Is Being Redirected check box   This check box (which is selected by default) controls whether Internet Explorer warns you when a form you've submitted is being redirected to a different destination than its apparent destination. Many forms contain sensitive information, so keep this check box selected.

Browsing Offline

Once you've set up offline favorites as described earlier in the chapter, you're ready to browse them offline.

If your computer isn't currently connected to the network or Internet, you'll automatically be offline. If your computer is connected to the network or Internet, choose File ➤ Work Offline to start working offline. Internet Explorer displays an indicator on the status bar—a network cable with a red cross on it and a gray cloud above it—to show you're currently offline. (Choose File ➤ Work Offline again to switch back to online mode.)

As long as you stay within the material you have available offline, you'll be able to surf as usual. Because the pages are stored on your hard drive, the surfing will probably be quicker than when you have to download them. When you hit a link that leads to a page that's not available, or you enter an address that's not available, Internet Explorer displays the Web Page Unavailable while Offline dialog box (shown in Figure 18.43). Click the Connect button to connect to the Internet or the Stay Offline button to cancel the connection request.

FIGURE 18.43

If you try to go to an URL that's not available, Internet Explorer offers you the choice of connecting to the network or staying offline.

A Quick Introduction to MSN Explorer

This short section discusses MSN Explorer, Microsoft's latest effort to take a bite out of AOL's pie and make a larger chunk of the Web its own.

MSN Explorer provides a highly graphical interface that integrates e-mail (via MSN and Hotmail), instant messaging (via Windows Messenger), discussion groups (the MSN Communities), online shopping (from big names including Amazon.com, RadioShack, and Nordstrom), and music and entertainment (via WindowsMedia.com). MSN Explorer also delivers personalized news and information; provides an online calendar facility; gives you a location to store your own Web pages, including photos; and offers MoneyCentral, an area for managing your finances (if you care to do so online).

Figure 18.44 shows the e-mail component of the MSN Explorer interface. As you can see in the figure, the toolbar provides quick access to the main areas of MSN with large and colorful buttons, while the panel on the left gives access to the calendar, stock tracking, Web sites you're a member of, your photo albums, and a search facility.

FIGURE 18.44

MSN Explorer provides a colorful and graphical interface to MSN and Microsoft's services.

To get started with MSN Explorer, choose Start ➢ All Programs ➢ MSN Explorer. MSN Explorer walks you through a setup routine that involves the following steps:

◆ Specifying how MSN Explorer should connect to the Internet—via modem, via DSL or your LAN, or having you establish the connection manually

◆ Identifying a Hotmail or MSN e-mail address that you already have or getting a new e-mail address

◆ Providing a good bit of personal information, including your name (or an approximation of it), a street address, your occupation, and your date of birth

◆ Choosing a secret question in case you lose your password and need to request it

◆ Reading and accepting the MSN Internet Access Member Agreement

◆ Choosing an e-mail name (if you didn't already have one) and specifying whether to list yourself in Internet directories and whether to receive notifications of "new services and opportunities"

TIP   *If you never use MSN Explorer, you might want to remove it from your computer to free up a few megabytes of disk space. To do so, use the Windows Components Wizard as discussed in Chapter 5.*

Up Next

In this chapter, you've learned the key skills to surfing the Web with Internet Explorer, to using favorites, and to configuring Internet Explorer for speed, comfort, and security. You've also read a word or two about MSN Explorer and what it offers.

The next chapter discusses how to use Address Book to store contact information.

Chapter 19

Using Address Book

WINDOWS COMES WITH AN ADDRESS book program, unimaginatively named Address Book, for storing contact information: names of people, companies, and organizations; their phone numbers, addresses, and e-mail addresses; their birthdays and anniversaries; and even the details of their digital IDs.

Address Book doesn't advertise itself aggressively, and as a result even many experienced Windows users don't make the most of its capabilities. While Address Book isn't as powerful as Microsoft's desktop information management program, Outlook—let alone professional contact management programs such as ACT! and GoldMine—it provides more than enough features for efficient contact management for many home or home-business users. (In other words, try it before you reject it. It's free.)

As you'd expect given Windows XP's multiuser focus, each person with a user account on the PC can maintain a separate list of contacts. Address Book also offers a Shared Contacts folder so that each user can share contact information with other users. You can group contacts to manage them efficiently, and you can use group addresses for easy multiple (or mass) mailings.

Address Book is integrated with Outlook Express, so you can quickly create e-mail messages to contacts in Address Book. Conversely, you can create new contacts from the information contained in e-mail addresses.

This chapter discusses the main actions you'll need to perform with Address Book, from adding contacts to your address book to exporting a list of your contacts for use with another contact management program.

This chapter covers the following topics:

◆ Starting Address Book

◆ Adding and deleting contacts

◆ Sharing contacts with other users

◆ Editing your profile

◆ Importing and exporting information

◆ Using folders and groups to organize your contacts

◆ Sending mail to a contact

◆ Finding a contact in Address Book or in Internet directories

Starting Address Book

You can start Address Book from the Start menu (Start ➤ All Programs ➤ Accessories ➤ Address Book) or in various ways from Outlook Express: Click the Addresses button, choose Tools ➤ Address Book, or press Ctrl+Shift+B. You can also access Address Book via the Select Recipients dialog box that Outlook Express displays when you click the To button or the Cc button from the New Message window.

To make Address Book more quickly accessible from the Desktop, copy or move its shortcut from the Accessories submenu. Alternatively, create a new shortcut to the Address Book executable file, WAB.EXE.

When you start Address Book, it displays your main identity. When you first open Address Book, you probably won't have any entries in it. Figure 19.1 shows Address Book with a number of entries already entered in it.

FIGURE 19.1

Address Book with a number of contacts entered

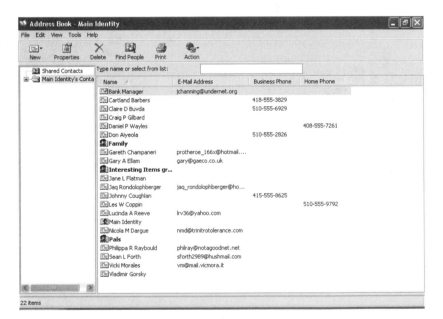

Adding a Contact to Your Address Book

The most conventional way to add a contact to your Address Book is as follows.

1. In the Folders and Groups pane, make sure you have selected your identity's contacts or the Shared Contacts folder as appropriate.

2. Click the New button on the toolbar and choose New Contact from the drop-down menu. (Alternatively, choose File ➤ New Contact or press Ctrl+N.) Address Book displays the Properties dialog box for a new contact, with the Name page foremost (see Figure 19.2).

FIGURE 19.2

Use the Properties dialog box to create a new contact.

3. On the Name page, enter the contact's name, title, nickname, and e-mail addresses:

- Once you've entered the contact's first, middle, and last names, Address Book automatically builds entries for the Display drop-down list. Its default format is First Middle Last—for example, Randall A Chaucer—but you can choose a different format (Chaucer Randall A or Chaucer, Randall A) in the Display drop-down list. You can also type something completely different—for example, a description such as **Bank Manager**.

- You can use the Nickname field in two ways. First, you can use it to hold a nickname associated with the contact but that you don't want to use instead of their actual first name. But even if the contact doesn't have a nickname, you can use this field as a unique identifier within Address Book and Outlook Express. You can type a nickname in the To field or Cc field in a new message in Outlook Express and issue a Check Names command. Outlook Express fills in the corresponding e-mail address. For example, if you entered **Law** as the nickname for your attorney in Address Book, you could enter **Law** as the address in Outlook Express. (If two or more contacts have the same nickname, Outlook Express displays the Check Names dialog box so that you can pick the one you want.)

- You can enter multiple e-mail addresses for a contact. By default, the first e-mail address you enter is set as the default address. If you add multiple e-mail addresses and want to use one other than the first as the default, select the address to use as the default and click the Set As Default button. Address Book adds an envelope icon to the left of the listing and the text *(Default E-mail)* to its left.

- If you need to send plain-text e-mail rather than formatted or HTML e-mail to the contact, select the Send E-mail Using Plain Text Only check box. If you're not sure whether a contact can receive formatted e-mail, select this check box. That way, the contact will be able to read your message.

4. On the Home page and the Business page, enter home-related information and business-related information for the contact. Almost all the fields and controls on these pages are self-explanatory, but these three deserve comment:

   ◆ Select the Default check box on either the Home page or the Business page to specify that this is the default address to use for the contact. Selecting the Default check box on one page clears it on the other page if it is selected there.

   ◆ Clicking the View Map button on either page causes your browser to look up the address on the Expedia Maps service (`maps.expedia.com`) and display a map of the area to you.

   ◆ The Business page includes a text box for the contact's IP telephone address, which is useful if you use IP telephony.

5. On the Personal page, enter any personal information known for the contact:

   ◆ Address Book creates all contacts as being of "Unspecified" gender. With luck, you should be able to improve on this.

   ◆ To add a child, click the Add button. Address Book adds an entry named New Child and displays an edit box around it. Type in the appropriate name and press the Enter key. (If you need to change the child's name afterward, select the child and click the Edit button.)

6. If you have other information about the contact, enter it in the Notes text box on the Other page. This page also contains the Group Membership text box, which lists any of your Address Book groups the contact belongs to.

7. If you have conferencing information for the contact, enter it on the NetMeeting page. This page also contains a Call Now button that you can click to place a NetMeeting call to the contact.

8. To import a digital ID for the contact, display the Digital IDs page, click the Import button, and follow through the import procedure. You can also export a digital certificate from here, view its properties, and choose which digital certificate to use as the default for a contact. (Chapter 17 discusses digital IDs.)

9. Click the OK button to close the Properties dialog box. Your contact appears in Address Book.

Deleting a Contact

To delete a contact, right-click it and choose Delete from the context menu. Address Book displays a dialog box asking you to confirm the deletion. Click the Yes button.

Moving a Contact from One Identity to Another

You can move a contact from one identity to another by dragging it from the list box to the appropriate folder in the Folders and Groups pane. For example, to move a contact from your main identity to the Shared Contacts folder, drag the contact to the Shared Contacts folder and drop it there.

EXPERT KNOWLEDGE: CREATING A CONTACT RECORD FROM AN E-MAIL MESSAGE

When you're reading e-mail in Outlook Express, you can add a sender to your Address Book by right-clicking the message in the Inbox and choosing Add Sender to Address Book from the context menu. (Alternatively, select the message and choose Tools ➢ Add Sender to Address Book.) Outlook Express adds the name and e-mail address directly to Address Book. So when you do this, it's usually a good idea to display Address Book and immediately add all the information you know about the contact—before you forget.

From a message window, you can create contacts from the sender, a Cc addressee, or everyone on the addressee list of the message (except any Bcc addressees). Choose Tools ➢ Add to Address Book ➢ Sender; Tools ➢ Add to Address Book ➢ Everyone on To List; or one of the e-mail addresses listed on the Add to Address Book submenu. Alternatively, double-click the From listing, one of the To listings other than yourself, or one of the Cc listings.

Outlook Express displays the Properties dialog box for the contact with a Summary page added and displayed (shown below). At this point, the information is minimal. Click the Name page of the dialog box and start improving the information while it's fresh, or just click the Add to Address Book button if you're in a hurry.

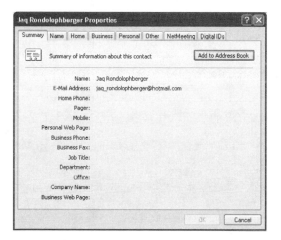

Editing Your Profile for Address Book

Address Book creates a profile called Main Identity for each user with a user account on the PC. When you start Address Book, it displays the Main Identity profile for the user account under which you logged on to Windows.

Address Book is integrated with the Profile Assistant tool in Internet Explorer. To enable Address Book to provide Internet Explorer with the information it needs for Web sites that request data such as your e-mail address or a digital certificate, you need to create a profile for yourself and associate it with the Main Identity. To do so, follow these steps:

1. Choose Edit ➤ Profile. Address Book displays the Address Book – Choose Profile dialog box (shown in Figure 19.3).

FIGURE 19.3

In the Address Book – Choose Profile dialog box, choose whether to create a new entry for your profile or to use an existing entry.

2. Choose whether to use an existing entry for your profile or to create a new entry. If you choose the Select an Existing Entry from the Address Book to Represent Your Profile option button, choose the profile from the list box.

3. Click the OK button. Address Book closes the Address Book – Choose Profile dialog box. If you chose to create a new entry, Address Book displays the Properties dialog box for an identity named Main Identity. Fill in the information as you would for any other contact (though perhaps with more care), and change the name from Main Identity to your name.

When Profile Assistant receives a request for information from a Web site, Profile Assistant tells you the URL or IP address of the site requesting the information, the types of information requested, how the site claims it will use the information (invariably for good—*your* good—of course), and whether the connection to the site is secured with SSL. You can choose which information to give the site. If the connection is secure, you can view the certificate for the site to help you decide.

Importing Information into Your Address Book

If you already have information in a data source (for example, in an organizer or in a database), you can import it into Address Book. Address Book can handle formats that include Windows address books, the vCard business-card format, Address Books in Works, Exchange, Microsoft Internet Mail for Windows 3.1, Eudora (Pro and Light), Netscape and Netscape Communicator, and the LDAP Data Interchange Format. If your data is in a different format (for example, a spreadsheet or an organizer), the best way of exporting and importing the information is to use a *comma-separated values file* (CSV file for short)—a file in which the fields are separated by commas.

WARNING   With some data sources, Address Book may fail to preserve divisions between address books—for example, it may lump entries from multiple separate address books into the same category in Address Book. Make sure you keep your data source until you've checked your imported data carefully in case Address Book messes things up and you need to import it all again.

Importing a Windows Address Book

Importing a file in Windows address book (WAB) format is a straightforward process: Choose File ➤ Import ➤ Address Book (WAB), use the Select Address Book to Import From dialog box to identify the file, and click the Open button. Then dismiss the message box telling you that the address book has been imported.

Importing a vCard

Importing a record stored in a vCard business card is equally straightforward. Choose File ➤ Import ➤ Business Card (vCard), use the Import Business Card (vCard) dialog box to select the file, and click the Open button. Address Book displays the Properties dialog box for the contact so that you can check that the information is in the right slots and add any other data you want. Then click the OK button. Address Book closes the Properties dialog box and files away the information.

Importing Information Stored in Another Format

Importing address information stored in another format tends to be a more involved process, because you usually need to map the fields in the data source to the fields in Address Book.

EXPERT KNOWLEDGE: EXPORTING YOUR ADDRESS INFORMATION FIELDS IN THE BEST ORDER

If the program from which you're exporting the address information lets you name the fields and specify their order, use this order and these names: First Name, Last Name, Middle Name, Name, Nickname, E-mail Address, Home Street, Home City, Home Postal Code, Home State, Home Country, Home Phone, Home Fax, Mobile Phone, Personal Web Page, Business Street, Business City, Business Postal Code, Business State, Business Country, Business Web Page, Business Phone, Business Fax, Pager, Company, Job Title, Department, Office Location, and Notes. Using this sequence makes the information snap into the fields in Address Book without any remapping.

Here's an example using a comma-separated values (CSV) file:

1. Choose File ➤ Import ➤ Other Address Book. Address Book displays the Address Book Import Tool dialog box (see Figure 19.4).

2. In the list box, choose the appropriate format. The example uses Text File (Comma Separated Values).

FIGURE 19.4

In the Address Book Import Tool dialog box, select the type of information you want to import and then click the Import button.

3. Click the Import button. Address Book displays the first CSV Import dialog box, which lets you select the file to import.

4. Either type in the name and path or click the Browse button to display the Open dialog box, specify the location and name as usual, and click the Open button.

5. Click the Next button. Address Book displays the second CSV Import dialog box (see Figure 19.5).

FIGURE 19.5

In the second CSV Import dialog box, check and change the field mapping, and then click the Finish button.

6. Check that each field in the data source (the first column) is *mapped* (matched) to an appropriate field in Address Book (the second column) and that each text field that you want to import has its check box selected:

   ◆ To change the mapping of a field, select it and click the Change Mapping button. Address Book displays the Change Mapping dialog box (see Figure 19.6). In the drop-down list, select the target Address Book field, select the Import This Field check box, and click the OK button.

FIGURE 19.6

Use the Change Mapping dialog box to change the mapping of a field as necessary.

   ◆ If your data source doesn't have column headings, you'll have to look at it to see which field contains which information. If possible, open it in a spreadsheet program such as Excel, because doing so separates the information into separate columns, making it easier to read. If you don't have a spreadsheet program, open the data source in Notepad and count the commas. (If you have Word, open the data source in Word and convert it to a table.)

7. Click the Finish button to perform the import:

    ◆   If any of the information you're importing does not match the expected field, Address
        Book displays the Error Importing Contact dialog box, of which Figure 19.7 shows an
        example. Click the OK button to proceed or the Cancel button to cancel the whole
        import procedure. Select the Don't Show Me Error Messages Anymore check box if you
        want to suppress further error messages when proceeding.

FIGURE 19.7

By default, Address Book displays the Error Importing
Contact dialog box to warn
you when it encounters data it
thinks is unsuitable for a field.

8. When Address Book has finished importing the data, it displays a message box telling you so.
    Close this dialog box and then click the Close button to close the Address Book Import Tool
    dialog box.

Double-check the resulting Address Book entries for duplicates and errors before you use them.

Exporting Information from Your Address Book

As you'd expect, you can also export information from Address Book so that you can import it into
an organizer, database, or spreadsheet.

If the recipient program can read the WAB format, use that. Choose File ➢ Export ➢ Address
Book (WAB), specify the filename and location in the Select Address Book File to Export To dialog
box, and click the Save button. Address Book exports the information and displays a message box
telling you that it has done so. Click the OK button to dismiss the message box, and you're done.

To export a single record, save it as a vCard. Choose File ➢ Export ➢ Business Card (vCard),
specify the filename and location in the Export As Business Card (vCard) dialog box, and click the
Save button.

To export your address book in a format other than WAB, use a CSV file as follows:

1. Choose File ➢ Export ➢ Other Address Book. Address Book displays the Address Book
    Export Tool dialog box (shown in Figure 19.8).

2. In the list box, select the Text File (Comma Separated Values) entry.

3. Click the Export button. Address Book displays the first CSV Export dialog box.

4. In the Save Exported File As text box, enter the name under which to save the exported file.
    Either type in the name and path or click the Browse button, use the resulting Save As dialog
    box to specify the location and filename, and click the Save button.

FIGURE 19.8

Choose the Text File (Comma Separated Values) item in the Address Book Export Tool dialog box.

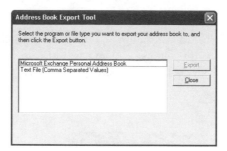

5. Click the Next button. Address Book displays the second CSV Export dialog box (shown in Figure 19.9).

FIGURE 19.9

In the second CSV Export dialog box, select the fields you want to export and then click the Finish button.

6. Select the fields you want to export. By default, the CSV Export dialog box does not select the check boxes for the First Name, Last Name, and Middle Name fields, because it lumps the names together into a single field (called Name), which it selects. If you need to have the individual fields as well, select their check boxes too.

7. Click the Finish button. Address Book exports the address book and displays a message box telling you that it has completed the export procedure. Click the OK button to dismiss the message box, then click the Close button to close the Address Book Export Tool dialog box.

You can now import the CSV file into your organizer, database, or spreadsheet.

Organizing Your Contacts into Folders and Groups

To prevent your contact list from growing to the length of the San Andreas fault, you can divide your contacts up among a number of folders. For example, in a home situation, you might create a folder to contain family members, one for friends, one for local businesses, another for emergency contacts, and so on. You can also create groups to help administer your contacts.

Normally, a folder actually contains a contact, while a group contains only a pointer to a contact. You *can* create contacts that reside only within groups, but usually you'll want to use groups mostly to organize contacts rather than contain them.

Creating a Folder

As you saw earlier in this chapter, Address Book starts you off with a Shared Contacts folder (shared with all the other users of the computer) and a Main Identity's Contacts folder (of which each user has one to her- or himself). Under each of these, you can add as many folders as you need to sort your contacts into logical containers.

To create a new folder, follow these steps:

1. Right-click the folder that will contain it (Shared Contacts or Main Identity's Contacts) in the Folders and Groups pane and choose New ➤ New Folder from the context menu. (Alternatively, select the folder and choose File ➤ New Folder, or press Ctrl+R.) Address Book displays a Properties dialog box.

2. Enter the name for the folder in the Folder Name text box.

   ◆ Address Book displays the folders in alphabetical order. To implement a specific order of your own, add numbering to the beginning of the folder names. To force a single folder to float to the top of the list without numbering, put a space at the beginning of its name.

3. Click the OK button. Address Book creates the folder.

You can then move contacts to the folder by dragging them from their current location and dropping them on the folder.

Deleting a Folder

To delete a folder, right-click it in the Folders and Groups pane and choose Delete from the context menu, then select the Yes button in the confirmation message box.

Deleting a folder deletes all the contacts it contains and is not undoable. Consider backing up Address Book before deleting a folder.

Creating a Group

To create a group, follow these steps:

1. Click the New button on the toolbar and choose New Group from the drop-down list (or choose File ➤ New Group or press Ctrl+G). Address Book displays the Properties dialog box for the group with the Group page displayed. Figure 19.10 shows an example.

2. Enter the name for the group in the Group Name text box. This is the name that appears in the Folders and Groups pane.

3. Click the Select Members button to display the Select Group Members dialog box.

FIGURE 19.10

Use the Properties dialog box for a group to define the group and add contacts to it.

4. In the left-hand list box, select the contacts to add to the group and then click the Select button to transfer them to the group:

   ◆ Double-click a contact to add it to the Members list box.

   ◆ Use Shift+click and Ctrl+click to select multiple contacts at once.

   ◆ To remove a contact from the right-hand list box, right-click the contact and choose Remove from the context menu.

5. Click the OK button. Address Book closes the Select Group Members dialog box. The Group Members list box in the Properties dialog shows the members you added.

TIP   To add a contact to the group but not to Address Book, enter the contact's name and e-mail address in the Name text box and E-mail text box in the Properties dialog box and click the Add button. To add a contact to both the group and Address Book, click the New Contact button and create the contact as usual in the Properties dialog box for the contact.

6. If you have details to add for the group (such as an address, phone number, or notes), click the Group Details tab to display the Group Details page, then enter the information there.

7. Click the OK button. Address Book closes the Properties dialog box for the group.

NOTE   You can check which groups a contact belongs to on the Other page of the contact's Properties dialog box.

Removing a Contact from a Group

To remove a contact from a group, select the group in the Folders and Groups pane, then right-click the contact in the list box and choose Delete from the context menu. Address Book displays the confirmation dialog box shown in Figure 19.11 to let you know that you're removing the contact from the group rather than deleting them. Click the Yes button.

FIGURE 19.11

When you remove a contact from a group, Address Book checks to make sure you understand you're not deleting the contact.

Deleting a Group

To delete a group, select it in the Folders and Groups pane and click the Delete button. Address Book displays the confirmation message box shown in Figure 19.12, reminding you that getting rid of the group does not delete its members. Click the Yes button if you want to proceed.

FIGURE 19.12

Address Book double-checks to make sure you want to delete a group.

Changing the Fields Displayed

By default, Address Book displays the Name, E-mail Address, Business Phone, and Home Phone columns. You can change any of these fields except the Name field or E-mail Address field by right-clicking its column heading and choosing a different field from the context menu of fields that appears (see Figure 19.13).

FIGURE 19.13

To change a displayed field, right-click its column heading and choose a replacement from the context menu.

Using Views

Address Book offers four views for scrutinizing your contacts: Details view (the default view), Large Icon view, Small Icon view, and List view. You'll recognize these views from the views in Windows Explorer—they're essentially the same. (Unfortunately—or perhaps otherwise—there's no Thumbnails view, so you can't assign a different picture to each contact.) Details view tends to be the most useful, because it puts the most information on-screen at the same time, but you may want to use Small Icon view or List view occasionally so that you can see a larger number of contacts at once.

To change view, choose View ➤ Large Icon, View ➤ Small Icon, View ➤ List, or View ➤ Details as appropriate.

Sorting Your Contacts

By default, Address Book sorts your contacts alphabetically by first name. If you're on a first-name basis with them, or have relatively few contacts, this works fine. If not, you'll probably need to sort your contacts into a different order sooner or later.

To sort the contacts by one of the columns displayed, click the column heading once for an ascending sort (alphabetical order) or twice for a descending sort (reverse alphabetical order).

To sort by last name, choose View ➤ Sort By ➤ Last Name. To restore the default first-name sorting, choose View ➤ Sort By ➤ First Name.

Sending Mail to a Contact

To send e-mail to a contact, right-click the contact's name and choose Action ➤ Send Mail from the context menu. Address Book activates Outlook Express and starts a new message to the contact you chose.

If the contact has no e-mail address, Address Book displays an exclamation message box alerting you to the problem (see Figure 19.14) and doesn't activate Outlook Express.

FIGURE 19.14

Here's what happens when you try to e-mail a contact who doesn't have an e-mail address in Address Book.

Finding a Forgotten Contact in Address Book

To access a contact whose name you remember in Address Book, you can type down through the list box until you reach the entry you want. If you can't remember the contact's name but can remember other information about the contact, use the Find feature to locate the contact as follows:

1. Click the Find People button on the toolbar, or choose Edit ➤ Find People, or press Ctrl+F, to display the Find People dialog box (shown in Figure 19.15).

FIGURE 19.15

Use the Find People dialog box to find a contact whose full name you can't remember.

2. In the Look In drop-down list, make sure Address Book is selected if you want to search Address Book. (The alternatives are to search information repositories such as Active Directory and online directory services.)

3. In the Name, E-mail, Address, Phone, and Other text boxes, enter such information as you can remember about the person:

    ◆ The Name, E-mail, Address, and Phone text boxes cause Address Book to search *all* name fields, all e-mail addresses, all address fields, and all phone fields for the contact.

    ◆ Each piece of information doesn't have to be complete: For example, you might enter only part of the last name in the Name text box and only an area code in the Phone text box.

    ◆ The more specific the information you enter, the fewer matches you'll get. If you enter information the contact record doesn't contain, you won't find the contact.

4. Click the Find Now button to perform the search. If it finds matches, the Find People dialog box displays a lower section containing them (see Figure 19.16). If not, it displays a message box saying that it found no matches.

5. Click the Properties button to open the Properties dialog box for the contact. Click the Delete button to delete the contact. Or click the Close button to close the Find People dialog box.

FIGURE 19.16

If it finds matches, the Find People dialog box displays them. You can work directly from the results.

Searching Internet Directories for People

If Address Book doesn't have the contact you need, you can search Active Directory or an Internet directory as follows:

1. Click the Find People button on the toolbar, or choose Edit ➤ Find People. Address Book displays the Find People dialog box.

2. In the Look In drop-down list in the Find People dialog box, select one of the directories: Active Directory, Bigfoot Internet Directory Service, VeriSign Internet Directory Service, WhoWhere Internet Directory Service, or one of the other directory services listed. The Find People dialog box reduces the number of fields on its People page to just the Name text box and the E-mail text box but displays an Advanced page as well (shown in Figure 19.17).

FIGURE 19.17

Use the Advanced page of the Find People dialog box to define criteria when searching for people on directory services.

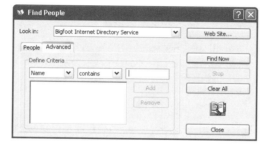

3. Use the Define Criteria group box on the Advanced page to define criteria for your search:

   ◆ In the first drop-down list, choose Name, E-mail, First Name, Last Name, or Organization as appropriate.

   ◆ In the second drop-down list, choose the appropriate condition: Contains, Is, Starts With, Ends With, or Sounds Like. (The Sounds Like item can give you some peculiar results, but it's worth trying when all else fails.)

   ◆ In the text box, enter the text for the criterion. For example, you might specify **Last Name Starts With Rob** to find people with last names such as Robson, Roberts, or Robertson.

   ◆ Click the Add button to add the criterion to the list box. Then define other criteria as necessary by repeating these steps.

4. Click the Find Now button to execute the search.

NOTE   *If the Web Site button is available, you can click it to open an Internet Explorer window showing the directory's Web site, which may offer further search options.*

EXPERT KNOWLEDGE: ADDING AND CONFIGURING DIRECTORY SERVICES

If you often need to search for people on directory services, you can add to Address Book's preconfigured list of directory services to increase your chances of finding whom you're looking for. You can also remove directory services that you don't find useful. And if you use more than one directory service to check names when sending e-mail, you can change the order in which Address Book and Outlook Express check the directory services.

To add a directory service:

1. Choose Tools ➢ Accounts. Address Book displays the Directory Service page of the Internet Accounts dialog box.

2. Click the Add button. Address Book starts the Internet Directory Server Name feature of the Internet Connection Wizard.

3. Enter the address of the directory server (for example, ldap.yahoo.com for the Yahoo directory server) in the Internet Directory (LDAP) Server text box.

4. If you have to log on to your LDAP server before you can use it, select the My LDAP Server Requires Me to Log On check box. When you click the Next button, the Internet Connection Wizard displays the Internet Directory Server Logon panel. Enter your account name and password, and select the Log On Using Secure Password Authentication check box if necessary.

5. Click the Next button. The Internet Connection Wizard displays the Check E-mail Addresses panel. Select the Yes option button if you want to use this directory service to check e-mail addresses. (The No option button is selected by default. This isn't a good idea for conventional e-mail use.)

6. Click the Next button to proceed to the Congratulations panel of the Internet Connection Wizard. Click the Finish button. The Wizard closes itself.

Address Book adds the directory service to the list on the Directory Service page of the Internet Accounts dialog box under a name based on its address. To give the directory service a descriptive name, select the directory service and click the Properties button to display its Properties dialog box (shown below). Enter the descriptive name in the upper text box and click the OK button.

Continued on next page

EXPERT KNOWLEDGE: ADDING AND CONFIGURING DIRECTORY SERVICES *(continued)*

On the General page of the Properties dialog box, you can also change whether you log on to the LDAP server, your account name and password, whether you use Secure Password Authentication, and whether Outlook Express checks names against the server when sending e-mail. The Advanced page offers further options, including the maximum number of matches to return from the directory service and whether to use a search base (a grouping) in the directory service.

To change the order in which Outlook Express uses the directory servers when checking names against them, click the Set Order button in the Internet Accounts dialog box. In the resulting Directory Services Order dialog box, use the Move Up button and Move Down button to arrange the accounts into the appropriate order, and then click the OK button.

Up Next

This chapter has discussed how to use Address Book for storing and managing contact information. As you've seen, Address Book is limited compared to professional contact management packages, but it provides enough capabilities for most home and home-office use. And the price is right.

You'll hardly have been able to miss that many of Address Book's features are designed for use with the e-mail capabilities of Outlook Express. Discussing Address Book ahead of Outlook Express sometimes feels like putting the cart before the horse—but discussing Outlook Express before Address Book tends to be even worse. And there's no comfortable way for the horse and cart to proceed side-by-side in the narrow pages of a book....

In the hopes of putting the cart back in its natural place, the next chapter discusses how to use Outlook Express for e-mail. The chapter after that discusses how to use Outlook Express for reading news.

Chapter 20

E-mail with Outlook Express

THIS CHAPTER DISCUSSES HOW to use the e-mail features of Outlook Express, the powerful e-mail and newsreader program built into Windows. (The next chapter discusses how to use the newsreader features.)

This chapter covers the following topics:

◆ Setting up e-mail with Outlook Express

◆ Configuring Outlook Express

◆ Creating and sending e-mail messages

◆ Reading e-mail messages

◆ Replying to an e-mail message

◆ Managing your e-mail messages

◆ Filtering your messages

◆ Using multiple e-mail accounts

◆ Creating and using identities

Before you can do anything with Outlook Express, you need to configure it to work with your ISP, so that's the first order of business. After that, the chapter shows you how to create and send e-mail messages; read e-mail messages; send and receive attachments; and use the multiple identities (personalities or roles) that Outlook Express supports to maintain multiple e-mail accounts—for example, one for business use and one for personal use. Along the way, you'll learn how to filter your e-mail, how to block e-mail from certain people, and how to implement e-mail security.

Information You Need to Get Started

To work through this chapter, you'll need to have a modem or network connection to the Internet and an account with an ISP or e-mail provider. You'll need to know the following information: your logon name and password, your e-mail address, your incoming mail server and its type (POP, IMAP, or HTTP), your outgoing mail server, and whether to use Secure Password Authentication (SPA).

For the next chapter, you'll also need to know the name for your ISP's news server, whether you need to log on to it, and (if you do log on) whether you need to use Secure Password Authentication. So if you're asking your ISP for information, include those questions.

Starting Outlook Express

In Windows XP's default configuration, the easiest way to start Outlook Express is to choose Start ➤ E-mail.

Alternatively, create a shortcut to Outlook Express on your Quick Launch toolbar, on your Desktop, or in another handy location. If you want to run Outlook Express automatically each time you start Windows—not a bad idea, given how vital e-mail is these days—put a shortcut to Outlook Express in your Startup group.

This might seem the logical time for a screen shot of Outlook Express—but you won't see it at once the first time you run Outlook Express. Instead, you get to do some configuration.

Setting Up E-mail with Outlook Express

The first time you start Outlook Express, you'll need to set it up to work with your Internet connection and ISP. Follow these steps:

1. Choose Start ➤ E-mail. Windows starts the Internet Connection Wizard, which displays the Your Name page (shown in Figure 20.1).

2. In the Display Name text box, enter your name the way you want it to appear in outgoing messages. (For example, you might choose to use your full name with middle initial, or you might prefer to use your diminutive and your last name. Or you might choose an alias.)

FIGURE 20.1

The first time you run Outlook Express, the Internet Connection Wizard springs into action to configure your e-mail account. The Wizard starts by asking your name.

Internet Connection Wizard

Your Name

When you send e-mail, your name will appear in the From field of the outgoing message. Type your name as you would like it to appear.

Display name:

For example: John Smith

[< Back] [Next >] [Cancel]

3. Click the Next button. The Wizard displays the Internet E-mail Address page (shown in Figure 20.2).

4. Enter your e-mail address in the E-mail Address text box.

5. Click the Next button. The Wizard displays the E-mail Server Names page (shown in Figure 20.3):

   ◆ In the My Incoming Mail Server Is a XXX Server drop-down list, choose POP3, IMAP, or HTTP, as appropriate for your ISP. (If you're curious about these acronyms and their implications, see the next sidebar.)

   ◆ In the Incoming Mail (POP3, IMAP or HTTP) Server text box, enter the name of your ISP's incoming mail server.

   ◆ In the Outgoing Mail (SMTP) Server text box, enter the name of your ISP's outgoing mail server.

◆ If you entered a Hotmail address on the Internet E-mail Address page, the Wizard pre-
fills the E-mail Server Names page with Hotmail information, as shown in Figure 20.4.
You shouldn't need to change these settings.

FIGURE 20.4

The Internet Con-
nection Wizard
automatically enters
server information if
you specified a Hot-
mail address.

6. Click the Next button. The Wizard displays the Internet Mail Logon page (shown in
Figure 20.5).

FIGURE 20.5

On the Internet
Mail Logon page of
the Internet Connec-
tion Wizard dialog
box, specify your
account name and
password.

7. Enter your account name in the Account Name text box and your password in the Password
text box.

8. Select the Remember Password check box if you think it's wise. (Using this option saves you
time typing your password when you retrieve your mail, but it means that anyone who can
access your user account on the computer can check your mail, too.)

9. Select the Log On Using Secure Password Authentication (SPA) check box if you need to use SPA.

10. Click the Next button. The Wizard displays its Congratulations page, telling you that you've successfully entered all the information needed to set up your e-mail account.

11. Click the Finish button. The Wizard closes itself and launches Outlook Express. If you just set up a Hotmail account, Outlook Express offers to display a list of available folders for the account. Click the Yes button.

EXPERT KNOWLEDGE: POP3, IMAP, HTTP, AND SMTP

POP3, IMAP, HTTP, SMTP—that's a pretty dish of acronyms to set before a king. What do they mean, and how much should you worry about them?

To answer the second question first, you shouldn't worry about them too much beyond giving Outlook Express the correct information. Usually you won't have a choice of server types—your ISP will support either POP3 or IMAP for incoming mail and will use SMTP for outgoing mail. If you use Hotmail, or a similar Web-based e-mail service that can work with Outlook Express, both your incoming mail server and your outgoing mail server will be HTTP.

But you're waiting for an answer to the first question: What do these terms mean?

HTTP Hypertext Transfer Protocol, the protocol on which much of the Web is based. (You'd guessed that one already, hadn't you?)

SMTP Simple Mail Transfer Protocol, the protocol used for sending e-mail. SMTP is part of the TCP/IP protocol suite (which is largely responsible for the running of the Internet).

POP3 Post Office Protocol, the common-or-garden Internet mail-server protocol for storing and passing on mail. POP3 works well and is very widely used, but it doesn't have advanced features that IMAP has. POP3's major limitation is that when you check your mail, you have to download all the messages waiting for you. You can leave copies of all your messages on the server, but each time you download them, you download everything waiting for you. (Tech moment: POP3 actually uses SMTP to move the messages from the one server to another, or from the server to the client.)

IMAP Internet Mail Access Protocol, a newer protocol than POP3 and one that has more features. IMAP offers strong authentication and supports Kerberos security, but from the average user's point of view its big advantage is that it's smart enough to allow you to manage your mail on the server. You can download just the headers of the messages so that you can decide which you want to download, delete messages off the server without reading them, and shuttle them between different folders on the server. These capabilities make IMAP especially useful for checking mail from multiple computers—for example, when traveling.

From the user's point of view, IMAP offers many advantages over POP3. (The only disadvantage is that you may have to do more configuration with IMAP than with POP3, depending on how smart your mail client is.) Unfortunately, many ISPs aren't enthusiastic about implementing IMAP because doing so would probably result in a huge amount more mail lying around on their servers than is currently on them (which is already more than enough). Given that spam hasn't exactly decreased, and that legitimate (nonspam) advertising e-mail messages seem to be getting not only more frequent but also larger, *and* that more people are using e-mail and sending more messages, you can understand their concern.

Getting a Hotmail Account

If you don't have an e-mail account (but you do have an Internet connection), Web-based e-mail such as Hotmail can be attractive. As their name suggests, Web-based e-mail services let you access your e-mail from any Web browser, so you can easily check your e-mail from just about any computer—from a friend's computer, from an Internet café, or (perhaps most popular) from a computer at work.

Hotmail's one of the biggest free e-mail services, but it's far from being the only game in town. Other free e-mail services you might want to consider include those offered by Yahoo (www.yahoo.com), Bigfoot (www.bigfoot.com), and Netscape (www.netscape.com). HushMail (www.hushmail.com) is noted for its security features for inter-HushMail messages (messages to non-HushMail users don't have the security), but it's also widely used for conventional e-mail.

Because it's owned and operated by Microsoft, Hotmail offers strong interoperability with Outlook Express. Accessing your e-mail through a Web browser is great for using assorted computers, but it's much more convenient to use Outlook Express's features for downloading Hotmail to your Inbox on your regular computer. Some other Web-based e-mail services offer similar functionality; others are browser-only.

If you don't have an e-mail account and decide Hotmail would be a good place to have one, point your Web browser at the Hotmail Web site (www.hotmail.com) and follow the sign-up procedure. This procedure is straightforward, but the following points are worth noting:

♦ Because more than 50 million Hotmail accounts have been created (though many have been abandoned by their users, and many others have been closed by Hotmail), snappy usernames are in short supply. Be prepared to get creative with underscores to get something resembling the name you want.

♦ Hotmail passwords can include only letters and numbers—they can't include symbols—so you'll have to work harder to create a secure password. Make the effort, because you don't want anyone breaking into your Hotmail account. (Hotmail may be free, but it shouldn't be easy.)

♦ Hotmail encourages you to list yourself in the Hotmail Member Directory and register yourself in the Internet White Pages. These aren't quite the Internet equivalent of being listed or unlisted in the phone book, but they come close enough for a conventional comparison. Some people want to be listed; others don't. It's up to you.

♦ Worse, Hotmail encourages you to flood your Inbox by signing up for receiving Special Offers and newsletters. You don't have to be all that cynical to see these Special Offers as junk mail. Some of the newsletters can be worthwhile—if you really want to read them.

♦ The Hotmail user agreement is vigorous enough to be worth reading carefully. For example, Hotmail users agree not to send spam from their accounts—and to pay Microsoft $5 for each piece of spam they send if actual damages for spamming can't be reasonably calculated.

♦ The Inbox Protector feature lets you specify filtering for messages so that you can keep some unwanted messages out of your Inbox. This feature is only partly effective, but it's better than nothing, and is well worth using.

To help remind people to keep up their Hotmail accounts, Hotmail axes any user accounts that aren't used within 10 days of sign-up or that, after that first use, are left unused for more than 60 days.

The Outlook Express Screen

Once you've configured Outlook Express, and thereafter when you start it, it displays your Start page, as shown in Figure 20.6.

FIGURE 20.6

The Start page provides links to the main features of Outlook Express

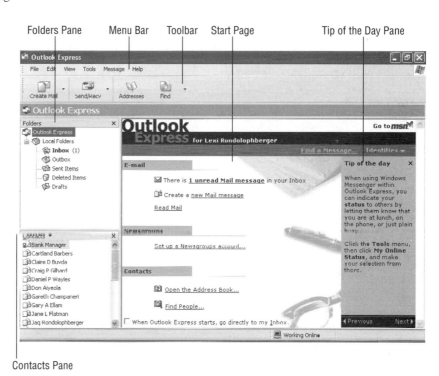

TIP *If you have a small monitor, you may want to get rid of the Tip of the Day pane by clicking the close button in its upper-right corner to give yourself more room on the Start page.*

If you prefer to start your Outlook Express session in the Inbox rather than on the Start page, select the When Outlook Express Starts, Go Directly to My Inbox check box at the bottom of the Start page. Thereafter, when you start Outlook Express, it displays the Inbox first.

If the Internet Connection Wizard didn't persuade you to enter your password and have Outlook Express remember it, you'll need to log on when you launch Outlook Express. Figure 20.7 shows an example of the Logon dialog box you'll see. This Logon dialog box is for Hotmail.

If the tediousness of having to log on each time lulls your fears about the inadvisability of saving your password, select the Remember Password check box before clicking the OK button in the Logon dialog box.

FIGURE 20.7

If you didn't save your password, you'll need to enter it in the Logon dialog box in order to log on to the mail servers.

Choosing Options for Outlook Express

At this point, you *could* start sending e-mail straight away, but it's a good idea to configure Outlook Express first. This section discusses the configuration options that Outlook Express offers.

Because of its complexity, Outlook Express has a host of options, many of which it's a good idea to know about. Because there are so many options, you may prefer not to read through this section in full at this point—it's uncomfortably long unless you're sitting very easy and in no hurry. That's fine; go ahead and start using e-mail, and see how the default settings suit you. Just know that if you want to change an aspect of Outlook Express's behavior, you probably can. Return to this section, find the appropriate option, and set it.

To configure Outlook Express, choose Tools ➤ Options. Outlook Express displays the Options dialog box. Then choose settings as appropriate.

General Page Options

The General page of the Options dialog box (shown in Figure 20.8) contains three sets of options.

FIGURE 20.8

The General page of the Options dialog box

GENERAL AREA

The General area of the General page contains four options:

When Starting, Go Directly to My "Inbox" Folder check box   This check box performs the same function as the When Outlook Express Starts, Go Directly to My Inbox check box on the Start page. Select it if you want Outlook Express to start in your Inbox; clear it to make Outlook Express start with the Start page.

Notify Me if There Are Any New Newsgroups check box   Leave this check box selected (as it is by default) if you want Outlook Express to notify you of new newsgroups on the news server you're using. This option is a double-edged sword: It may be good to learn about new newsgroups that might interest you, but new newsgroups are created so often that leaving this option selected means that Outlook Express will offer you new newsgroups every time you fire up the newsreader. This gets old fast.

Automatically Display Folders with Unread Messages check box   Leave this check box selected (as it is by default) if you want Outlook Express to automatically display e-mail folders and newsgroup folders that contain messages you haven't read. Most people find this option helpful. If you don't, clear this check box.

Automatically Log On to Windows Messenger check box   Leave this check box selected (as it is by default) if you want to start Windows Messenger automatically when you start Outlook Express. If Messenger is already running, this option does nothing.

SEND/RECEIVE MESSAGES AREA

The Send/Receive Messages area of the General page contains four options:

Play Sound when New Messages Arrive check box   Leave this check box selected (as it is by default) to have Outlook Express automatically play a sound when it receives a new message. Clear this check box if you prefer to be uninterrupted; the Outlook Express status bar will still indicate any new messages that come in.

Send and Receive Messages at Startup check box   Leave this check box selected (as it is by default) if you want Outlook Express to send any pending mail and receive any incoming mail when you start it. Clear this check box if you want to choose when to send and receive mail.

Check for New Messages Every NN Minutes check box and text box   Leave this check box selected (as it is by default) if you want Outlook Express to check for messages at regular intervals. Specify the interval in the text box (the default is 30 minutes). Clear this check box if you prefer to check for messages manually.

TIP   *If you run Windows Messenger, it alerts you to incoming messages on your Hotmail account.*

If My Computer Is Not Connected at This Time drop-down list   If you leave the Check for New Messages check box selected, use this drop-down list to specify what you want Outlook Express to do if your computer isn't connected to the Internet when Outlook Express needs to send and receive mail. Your options are Do Not Connect, Connect Only when Not Working

Offline, and Connect Even when Working Offline. Use the second option when your computer is disconnected from its Internet connection (for example, if it's a laptop and you're on the move). Use the third option for dial-up Internet connections

DEFAULT MESSAGING PROGRAMS AREA

The Default Messaging Programs area of the General page notes whether Outlook Express is your default mail handler and news handler. In the figure, Outlook Express is both; but if it's not, you can click the Make Default button to make it the default.

Read Page Options

The Read page of the Options dialog box (shown in Figure 20.9) contains three areas.

FIGURE 20.9

The Read page of the Options dialog box

READING MESSAGES AREA

The Reading Messages area of the Read page contains the following options:

Mark Message Read after Displaying for *NN* Seconds check box and text box   Leave this check box selected (as it is by default) if you want Outlook Express to mark a message as having been read when you've displayed it for the specified number of seconds in the Preview pane. Adjust the number of seconds if you want to be able to browse quickly through messages in the Preview pane without Outlook Express marking them as read. Clear this check box if you prefer to mark messages as read manually.

Automatically Expand Grouped Messages check box   Select this check box (which is cleared by default) if you want Outlook Express to automatically expand threads of messages in newsgroups. Clear this check box to have Outlook Express display just the original message.

Automatically Download Message when Viewing in the Preview Pane check box   Leave this check box selected (as it is by default) if you want Outlook Express to download the body of a message when you select its header in the message list. Most people find this option useful. If you don't, clear this check box and press the spacebar to display the body for the selected header.

Show ToolTips in the Message List for Clipped Items check box   Leave this check box selected (as it is by default) to have Outlook Express display a tooltip over a message header when the header is too long to fit in its column. To display the tooltip, hover the mouse pointer over the header.

Highlight Watched Messages drop-down list   Select the color you want to use for watched conversations. (More on this later in the chapter.)

NEWS AREA

The News area of the Read page contains two options:

Get *NN* Headers at a Time check box and text box   These controls let you choose between downloading the specified number of headers from the newsgroup (if there are that many; otherwise you get however many there are) and downloading all the messages. If you frequent very busy newsgroups, keep this check box selected (as it is by default), and reduce the number in the text box if necessary.

Mark All Messages As Read when Exiting a Newsgroup check box   Select this check box (which is cleared by default) if you want Outlook Express to mark all messages in a newsgroup as read when you exit the newsgroup. Clear this check box to have Outlook Express mark the messages as read only when you've read them. This check box is useful if you tend to browse newsgroups that have a high volume of traffic with many posts that you don't want to read or manually mark as read but that you want Outlook Express to know that you've dealt with.

FONTS AREA

This area contains two buttons:

◆ The Fonts button displays the Fonts dialog box, in which you can choose font settings for reading messages. For example, you might increase the font size or choose a different font.

◆ The International Settings button displays the International Read Settings dialog box, in which you can specify whether to use default encoding for all incoming messages. You shouldn't need to do this unless you find yourself coming up against apparently garbled messages that use different language encoding.

Receipts Page Options

The Receipts page of the Options dialog box (shown in Figure 20.10) also contains three areas.

REQUESTING READ RECEIPTS AREA

The Requesting Read Receipts area of the Receipts page contains only one option, but it's an important one: the Request a Read Receipt for All Sent Messages check box.

FIGURE 20.10

The Receipts page of the Options dialog box

Select this check box (which is cleared by default) if you want to try to get a notification of when the recipient opens ("reads") the message. Whether you receive a receipt depends on whether the recipient has chosen to send receipts. It may also depend on their ISP's server software, though these days it's more likely to work than it did a few years ago.

If you want to request receipts only on certain messages you send, leave this check box cleared and choose Tools ➤ Request Read Receipt from the New Message window when composing a message for which you want a receipt. Similarly, if you want to request receipts on all but a few messages you send, select this check box and choose Tools ➤ Request Read Receipt from the New Message window to turn off the request on any given message.

A read receipt appears as a regular message in your Inbox, with the subject *Read:* and the original subject (for example, *Read: Dinner at 8?* for a message with the subject "Dinner at 8?") and details of when the message was sent and when it was read.

RETURNING READ RECEIPTS AREA

The Returning Read Receipts area of the Receipts page contains three option buttons and a check box for specifying how Outlook Express deals with requests you receive for read receipts.

Select the Never Send a Read Receipt option button, the Notify Me for Each Read Receipt Request option button (the default setting), or the Always Send a Read Receipt option button as appropriate to your needs. If you select the Always Send a Read Receipt option button, you can select the Unless It Is Sent to a Mailing List and My Name Is Not on the To or Cc Lines of the Message check box to prevent you from sending read receipts to mailing lists. Sending these receipts will annoy everyone on the group if they're not filtered out by software or by humans, so this check box is selected by default (and comes highly recommended).

If you select the Notify Me for Each Read Receipt Request option button, you get to choose whether to send the receipt. When you open a message with a request for a read receipt, Outlook Express displays the Outlook Express dialog box shown in Figure 20.11. Click the Yes button or the No button as appropriate to the message and your temper.

FIGURE 20.11

This Outlook Express dialog box appears when you read a message that has a request for a read receipt.

SECURE RECEIPTS AREA

The Secure Receipts area of the Receipts page contains only the Secure Receipts button. If you want to receive secure receipts for digitally signed messages you send, click the Secure Receipts button. Outlook Express displays the Secure Receipt Options dialog box (shown in Figure 20.12), which contains similar options to the Returning Read Receipts area, except for secure receipts. Choose the options you want and click the OK button.

FIGURE 20.12

Use the Secure Receipt Options dialog box to choose whether to request and send secure receipts.

Send Page Options

Like the previous three pages, the Send page of the Options dialog box (shown in Figure 20.13) contains three areas. There's definitely a trend developing here....

FIGURE 20.13

The Send page of the Options dialog box

SENDING AREA

The Sending area of the Send page contains the following options:

Save Copy of Sent Messages in the "Sent Items" Folder check box   Leave this check box selected (as it is by default) to have Outlook Express save a copy of each message you send in the Sent Items folder. Clear this check box if you don't want to keep copies of messages you send.

Send Messages Immediately check box   Leave this check box selected (as it is by default) if you want Outlook Express to send messages immediately rather than put them in your Outbox until you issue a Send and Receive command.

Automatically Put People I Reply To in My Address Book check box   Leave this check box selected (as it is by default) if you want Outlook Express to create Address Book entries for any person whose message you reply to who doesn't already have an entry. This option can be a labor saver, but it can also pack your Address Book with useless entries consisting of just an e-mail address. If you prefer to add Address Book entries manually (for example, if you send replies to people you don't want in your Address Book), clear this check box.

Automatically Complete E-mail Addresses when Composing check box   Leave this check box selected (as it is by default) if you want Outlook Express to attempt to help you out by suggesting e-mail addresses from your Address Book to match addresses you type in the To, Cc, and Bcc fields in message windows. This option can be helpful, but it doesn't suit everyone. If it annoys you, turn it off so that you can type the addresses in peace.

Include Message in Reply check box   Leave this check box selected (as it is by default) to include the message in the reply. Clear this check box to create blank replies.

Reply to Messages Using the Format in Which They Were Sent check box   Leave this check box selected (as it is by default) to have Outlook Express create replies in the same format—plain text or HTML—as the message. This option is intended to help prevent you from sending HTML messages to people who prefer text, and vice versa, and is usually a good idea. Clear this check box to send all messages in the format you specify in the Mail Sending Format area.

MAIL SENDING FORMAT AREA

In this area, select the HTML option button or the Plain Text option button to specify which format to use for mail you send. This setting is overridden by the Reply to Messages Using the Format in Which They Were Sent option if you selected its check box.

If you want to tweak the settings for the format you choose, click the HTML Settings button or the Plain Text Settings button. The HTML Settings dialog box (shown in Figure 20.14) contains the following settings:

Encode Text Using drop-down list   If necessary, change this setting from Quoted Printable (the default setting) to None or Base 64. (You shouldn't need to change this setting.)

Allow 8-Bit Characters in Headers check box   Select this check box (which is cleared by default) if you want Outlook Express to display foreign character sets, double-byte character sets, and extended ASCII characters in the header without encoding. If you don't know what these character sets are, leave this check box cleared, and Outlook Express encodes these characters in the header.

EXPERT KNOWLEDGE: SHOULD YOU USE PLAIN TEXT OR HTML? AND WHAT ABOUT STATIONERY?

When the Internet was young, all e-mail was plain text, because that was all that e-mail programs were designed to send. Plain-text messages were as plain as the term suggests, but they were small, and they traveled quickly through Internet servers and the wires. Then HTML mail was developed.

The advantages of HTML formatting (also called rich-text formatting) are clear: You can add to your messages not only formatting (such as colors, bulleted lists, and paragraph styles) but also hyperlinks, graphics, and background colors. By using HTML formatting, you can create messages that pack far greater punch than plain-text messages. From the recipient's point of view, the mail can look more or less like a Web page, full of color, light, and impact.

Provided, of course, that the recipient can receive HTML mail. If they can receive only plain-text e-mail, they'll receive a plain-text version of your message plus a text version containing all the HTML codes. If the message contained pictures, they'll come through as attachments, and the recipient will need to view them separately. The resulting message will look pretty sorry, and all your effort in formatting it will be wasted. So it's not a great idea to send HTML mail to someone who can receive only plain-text messages.

These days, many (perhaps most) e-mail programs can receive HTML mail and display it accurately; but quite a few cannot. If you receive HTML mail from someone, you can be sure that their e-mail client can handle HTML, so you're safe sending them an HTML reply. And if you know the recipient is using Outlook Express, you can feel free to send HTML mail. But if you know that someone is using plain-text e-mail, don't send them HTML mail if you can avoid it. Simple enough—but if you're used to sending HTML mail, it's easy to forget that some people won't be able to read it, especially when you're sending messages to multiple recipients.

So—much of the time, you're probably safe in sending HTML mail. But think before you add gratuitous formatting to your messages. Just because you can add, say, a picture or a background color to your messages doesn't mean that you should. Use these features only if they will enhance the recipient's reading or understanding of your message. This applies in spades to colorful stationery, which tends to be more appropriate to personal settings than business settings. For example, if you wrote to your bank, you'd probably use regular paper (or letterhead) rather than a colorful greeting card. Likewise, if you send your bank e-mail, use no stationery or simple stationery rather than inappropriately colorful stationery.

Send Pictures with Messages check box   Leave this check box selected (as it is by default) if you want Outlook Express to send pictures or background images included in the message with the message. Clear this check box if you don't want to send pictures (Outlook Express includes a reference to the picture instead) or if the recipients will already have access to the pictures.

Indent Message on Reply check box   Leave this check box selected (as it is by default) if you want Outlook Express to indent the text of a message to which you're replying. Usually, indenting the original message is a good idea, because it enables the recipient to distinguish it from your reply. If you clear this check box, Outlook Express left-aligns the original message.

Automatically Wrap Text at *NN* Characters, when Sending text box   This option is available only if you choose the None setting in the Encode Text Using drop-down list. Set the number of characters at which to wrap the lines of text in outgoing messages. This is so that they don't wrap when displayed in text-only e-mail clients or when indented in replies. As a standard line length for text-only e-mail clients is 80 characters, the default setting of 76 characters allows for an indent of three or four characters on a reply before wrapping occurs. To allow two indentations without wrapping, choose a setting of 72 characters.

FIGURE 20.14

The HTML Settings dialog box contains settings for specifying whether to send pictures with messages and whether to indent messages to which you're replying.

The Plain Text Settings dialog box (shown in Figure 20.15) lets you choose between sending messages in MIME format and Uuencode format. (See the next sidebar for a quick explanation of MIME and Uuencode.) If you choose MIME, you can specify text encoding and whether to allow 8-bit characters in headers, just as you could in the HTML Settings dialog box. For either MIME or Uuencode, you can specify the number of characters for text wrapping. The Plain Text Settings dialog box offers a different indentation option:

Indent the Original Text with *Character* **when Replying or Forwarding check box**   Leave this check box selected (as it is by default) if you want to indent original text in replies and forwarded messages. Select a character—>, |, or :—in the drop-down list. Clear this check box if you want original text to appear flush left.

FIGURE 20.15

The Plain Text Settings dialog box contains settings for plain-text (non-HTML) messages.

NEWS SENDING FORMAT AREA

The News Sending Format area of the Send page essentially duplicates the Mail Sending Format area, except that its controls apply to news rather than mail. Select the HTML option button or the Plain Text option button as appropriate, and use the HTML Settings button or the Plain Text Settings button to set options for that format.

EXPERT KNOWLEDGE: MIME AND UUENCODE

MIME is the acronym for Multipurpose Internet Mail Extension, an Internet specification for sending multimedia and multipart messages. MIME is widely used, and you should use it unless you have a good reason not to. S/MIME is the abbreviation for Secure MIME, a MIME extension that adds RSA security to MIME. S/MIME is a good choice for secure e-mail.

Uuencoding is a method of converting a binary file (for example, a graphic or an audio file) into a text file so that it can be sent in a text-only message. Uuencode is the utility for uuencoding, and there's a corresponding utility called Uudecode for decoding the resulting text (usually after transfer) back to the binary file. Uuencode and Uudecode essentially enabled the transfer of binary files via e-mail and newsgroups, but they've largely been superseded by MIME. You'll still find uuencoded files in Usenet newsgroups and on systems that need to maintain backward compatibility with old standards.

Compose Page Options

The Compose page of the Options dialog box (shown in Figure 20.16) contains three sets of options for composing mail and news.

FIGURE 20.16

The Compose page of the Options dialog box lets you choose fonts, stationery, and business cards for your mail and news messages.

COMPOSE FONT AREA

This area contains four controls:

Mail text box and Font Settings button   This text box displays the font and font size currently selected for mail. Click the Font Settings button to display the Font dialog box, in which you can change the font, font size, style, and effects (for example, underline, strikeout, and color).

News text box and Font Settings button   This text box displays the font and font size currently selected for news. Again, you can click the Font Settings button to display the Font dialog box to change the settings.

STATIONERY AREA

The Stationery area contains controls for specifying the stationery to use for HTML messages for mail and news. To use stationery, select the Mail check box or the News check box, then click the Select button. Outlook Express displays the Select Stationery dialog box. Select the stationery item to use, and click the OK button.

Click the Create New button to start the Stationery Setup Wizard, which walks you through the process of creating custom stationery.

Click the Download More button to open a browser window showing the Outlook Express area on the Microsoft Web site, which offers more stationery files.

BUSINESS CARDS AREA

The Business Cards area contains controls for specifying a business card to include as a vCard with mail and news messages you send. To include a business card, select the Mail check box or the News check box as appropriate, then choose the business card from the drop-down list, which contains the contacts in your Address Book. To edit the business card, click the Edit button. Outlook Express displays the Properties dialog box with the details for the contact.

Signatures Page Options

The Signatures page of the Options dialog box (shown in Figure 20.17 with a couple of signatures added) contains three sets of options for creating signatures and adding them to your messages. A *signature* is text that usually gives your name (or assumed name), e-mail address or other immediately relevant contact information, and sometimes an epigram or quote. Use a signature only if it will benefit recipients of your messages.

TIP Signatures are best kept short. Try not to be one of those people who become so delighted by the possibilities of signatures that they include far too much text.

These options are best explained through the process of creating and using signatures.

FIGURE 20.17

The Signatures page of the Options dialog box lets you create signatures to add to your outgoing messages.

To create signatures and add them to your messages, follow these steps:

1. Click the New button. Outlook Express adds to the Signatures list box a signature named Signature #1 (or the next available number), selects it, and positions the insertion point in the Edit Signature Text text box.

    ◆ Outlook Express makes the first signature you create the default signature.

2. Type the text for the signature.

    ◆ If you have multiple accounts and want to use the signature for only one of them, click the Advanced button. Outlook Express displays the Advanced Signature Settings dialog box. Select the check box for the account, and click the OK button. Outlook Express closes the Advanced Signature Settings dialog box and applies the signature to that account.

    ◆ Instead of creating a signature in Outlook Express, you can create one in a text file (for example, by using Notepad) and then tell Outlook Express to use it. To use a file, select the File option button, click the Browse button, use the resulting Open dialog box to select the file, and click the Open button. Outlook Express enters the path and filename in the File text box.

    ◆ To make the signature your default signature, click the Set As Default button. (Outlook Express automatically makes the first signature you create the default, so you need take this action only with subsequent signatures.)

3. Click the Rename button. Windows displays an edit box around the signature's name in the Signatures list box. Type the name for the signature and press the Enter key.

4. To delete a signature, select it in the Signatures list box and click the Remove button.

5. Select the Add Signatures to All Outgoing Messages check box if you want to do just that.

    ◆ If you select this check box, select or clear the Don't Add Signatures to Replies and Forwards check box. By default, this check box is selected, preventing Outlook Express from adding signatures to replies and forwarded messages.

    ◆ If you choose not to add signatures to all your outgoing messages, you can apply a signature to an individual message from the New Message window.

Security Page Options

The Security page of the Options dialog box (shown in Figure 20.18) contains options for securing Outlook Express. These options work closely with those you set for Internet Explorer (discussed in Chapter 18).

Virus Protection Area

The Virus Protection area of the Security page contains the following options:

Select the Internet Explorer Security Zone to Use list   Select the Internet Zone option button or the Restricted Sites Zone option button.

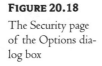

FIGURE 20.18

The Security page
of the Options dia-
log box

Warn Me when Other Applications Try to Send Mail As Me check box   Select this check box
(which is cleared by default) if you want Outlook Express to warn you when other programs try
to send mail under your identity. This setting offers some protection against viruses that send
mail in your name, but it may also cause you to thwart some legitimate operations.

**Do Not Allow Attachments to Be Saved or Opened That Could Potentially Be a Virus check
box**   Select this check box (which is cleared by default) if you want Outlook Express to refuse
documents of file types that might contain viruses. This setting offers you some protection
against viruses, but it may cause Outlook Express to discard some harmless documents because
their file type is suspect. In many cases, you'll be better off using good, up-to-date anti-virus software than using this setting.

SECURE MAIL AREA

The Secure Mail area of the Security page contains three command buttons and two check boxes for
specifying how to handle secure mail—messages that are either encrypted to protect their contents or
signed with a digital certificate to verify the sender.

To send an encrypted message, you need to have added the recipient's certificate to your Address
Book. Likewise, anyone who wants to send you an encrypted message needs to have your public key.

Tell Me More button   Click this button to display the Sending Secure Messages topic in the
Outlook Express Help file.

Digital IDs button   Click this button to display the Certificates dialog box (discussed in
Chapter 18).

Get Digital ID button   Click this button to open a browser window containing information
from the Microsoft Web site on where to obtain a digital certificate.

Encrypt Contents and Attachments for All Outgoing Messages check box   Select this check box if you want to try to encrypt all the messages and attachments you send. As mentioned a moment ago, you need to have the recipient's certificate in your Address Book in order to send an encrypted message or attachment. If you select this option and send messages or attachments to people whose digital certificates you don't have, Outlook Express warns you of the problem and offers you the choice of sending the item without encryption or canceling sending it.

Digitally Sign All Outgoing Messages check box   Select this check box if you want to digitally sign all the messages you send.

To choose advanced security settings, click the Advanced button. Outlook Express displays the Advanced Security Settings dialog box (shown in Figure 20.19).

FIGURE 20.19

The Advanced Security Settings dialog box

The Advanced Security Settings dialog box offers the following options:

Warn on Encrypting Messages with Less than This Strength drop-down list   Select the minimum acceptable level of encryption for messages: 40 bits, 56 bits, 64 bits, 128 bits, or 168 bits. (See the next sidebar for an explanation of the bit-ness of encryption—but basically, the higher the number, the more secure.) Outlook Express then warns you if you're about to send a message with a lower level of encryption.

Always Encrypt to Myself when Sending Encrypted Mail check box   Leave this check box selected (as it is by default) if you want Outlook Express to encrypt with your digital certificate the copy of the message that it puts in your Sent Mail folder. (If you don't encrypt this copy, you won't be able to read it.)

Include My Digital ID when Sending Signed Messages check box   Leave this check box selected (as it is by default) to send your digital certificate with a digitally signed message so that the recipient can use the public key to read it. (If the recipient already has your public key, you don't need to send the digital certificate again.)

Encode Message before Signing (Opaque Signing) check box   Select this check box (which is cleared by default) if you want to encode your digitally signed messages in order to keep the signature secure. If you use this option, the recipient's e-mail program must support S/MIME. Otherwise, they won't be able to read the message.

Add Senders' Certificates to My Address Book check box   Leave this check box selected (as it is by default) to have Outlook Express automatically add certificates from messages you receive to Address Book. This option is usually a good way to build your collection of certificates so that you can gradually send secure messages to more people (assuming you want to do so).

Check for Revoked Digital IDs list   Select the Only when Online option button or the Never option button to specify when to check that digital IDs you receive are current and haven't been revoked.

Click the OK button. Outlook Express closes the Advanced Security Settings dialog box and returns you to the Options dialog box.

EXPERT KNOWLEDGE: SHOULD YOU USE ENCRYPTION? AND IF SO, HOW MUCH?

Internet e-mail is inherently insecure, because it passes through a shared medium (the Internet). The standard analogy used to illustrate the insecurity of Internet e-mail is that of a postcard sent through the mail: At any point, anyone who can get a hold of it can read its contents. Conversely, anyone looking for that particular postcard would have a hard time finding it among all the other mail being sent unless they were able to intercept it close to its source or its destination.

So the standard advice goes that you shouldn't write anything in an unencrypted e-mail that you wouldn't mind the whole world reading, because anyone who reads the e-mail could publish it worldwide almost instantly by posting it on a Web site or to a newsgroup. (The recipient could also do this, but presumably you trust them enough to read the content of the message.)

There's much truth in this, but (at this writing, at least) most people send unencrypted e-mail all day long without suffering any adverse consequences. But if you want to make sure that nobody who intercepts a message can read it, you need to secure the message by using encryption.

As you saw a page or so ago, Outlook Express offers various strengths of encryption: 40 bit, 56 bit, 64 bit, 128 bit, and 168 bit. Which should you use?

Very generally speaking, the more bits, the more secure the encryption, and the more processing power it takes to encode and decode. The weakest encryption strengths, 40 bit and 56 bit, are those the U.S. government allows software firms to export. (Unlike with beer, export-strength encryption is weaker than the normal article.) 64-bit encryption is a little more exciting than 40-bit and 56-bit, but probably not enough so to be worth using if you're concerned about security. 128-bit encryption is considered strong encryption and should be enough for most civil purposes, but if you're trying to make the NSA and Echelon think that you have material worth cracking, you might want to step up to the 168-bit level—which Outlook Express suggests you use in the first place.

Of course, if you want to be truly secure, you need to make sure that nobody else can access your computer to attempt to hack it. Unplug the modem and seal the computer in a lead-lined room in an underground bunker....

Connection Page Options

The Connection page of the Options dialog box (shown in Figure 20.20) contains refreshingly few options:

Ask before Switching Dial-up Connections check box   Leave this check box selected (as it is by default) if you want Outlook Express to check with you before switching from a connection that isn't working to another connection. If you have only one dial-up connection, you don't need to worry about this setting.

Hang Up after Sending and Receiving check box   Select this check box (which is cleared by default) if you want Outlook Express to hang up your dial-up connection once it has finished sending and receiving mail when you issue a Send and Receive command. This setting is most useful with pay-as-you-go Internet connections.

Change button   Click this button to display the Connections page of the Internet Properties dialog box (discussed in Chapter 18).

FIGURE 20.20

The Connection page of the Options dialog box

Maintenance Page Options

The Maintenance page of the Options dialog box (shown in Figure 20.21) contains a double-handful of options for keeping Outlook Express running smoothly without silting up your hard disk.

These are the options on the Maintenance page:

Empty Messages from the "Deleted Items" Folder on Exit check box   Select this check box (which is cleared by default) to have Outlook Express empty all the deleted messages in your Deleted Items folder when you exit Outlook Express. By default, Outlook Express keeps the deleted messages until you empty the Deleted Items folder manually.

FIGURE 20.21

The Maintenance
page of the Options
dialog box

Purge Deleted Messages when Leaving IMAP Folders check box   Select this check box (which is cleared by default) to have Outlook Express dispose of all messages you've marked as deleted when you close an IMAP folder. If your server doesn't use IMAP, you don't need to worry about this option.

Compact Messages in the Background check box   Leave this check box selected (as it is by default) to have Outlook Express squeeze extra space out of messages in the background as you're working. If you clear this check box, you can compact messages by clicking the Clean Up Now button. The next three controls are available only when this check box is selected.

> **Delete Read Message Bodies in Newsgroups check box**   Select this check box (which is cleared by default) if you want Outlook Express to delete all the message bodies of messages you've read when you quit Outlook Express. This option saves a lot of space, but it means that you'll need to download a message again if you want to reread it.

> **Delete News Messages *NN* Days after Being Downloaded check box and text box**   Leave this check box selected (as it is by default) and specify the number of days in the text box if you want Outlook Express to automatically delete messages after a set time. Clear this check box if you want to keep old messages for reference.

> **Compact Messages when There Is *NN* Percent Wasted Space text box**   In this text box, specify the percentage of wasted space at which Outlook Express should compact messages.

Clean Up Now button   Click this button to display the Local File Clean Up dialog box, which provides actions for compacting and deleting messages. The section "Compacting and Cleaning Up Messages" later in this chapter discusses these actions.

Store Folder button   Click this button to display the Store Location dialog box, which you can use for changing the folder in which your message store is located. The section "Moving Your Message Store" later in this chapter discusses this process.

Troubleshooting area If you're having problems communicating with a mail or news server, you can select the Mail check box, the News check box, the IMAP check box, or the HTTP check box to make Outlook Express log the commands used for that server. (All these check boxes are cleared by default.) The log file may help cast light on the problem. The log files have the extension LOG and are named after the account they log. For example, the HTTP mail log is called `HTTPMail.log`, and the news log for the account `news.demon.com` would be called `news.demon.com.log`. You'll find these files in the message store folder.

Reading E-mail Messages

To read e-mail, click the Read Mail link on the Start page. Outlook Express displays your Inbox. Figure 20.22 shows a sparsely populated Inbox.

As you can see in the figure, Outlook Express displays icons to indicate information about the message headers:

◆ The Attachment icon means that the message has one or more files attached to it. (You'll learn how to work with attachments later in this chapter.)

◆ The Unread Message icon indicates that a message has not been read.

TIP   You can mark a message as unread or read by right-clicking its header and choosing Mark As Unread or Mark As Read, as appropriate, from the context menu.

FIGURE 20.22

The Inbox

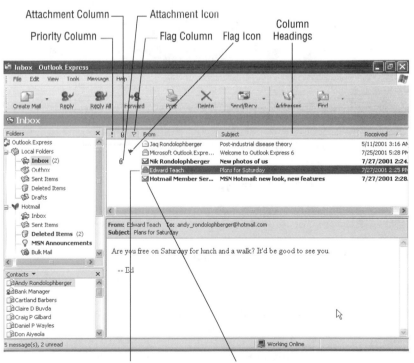

Attachment Column — ⌐ Attachment Icon

Priority Column ⌐   Flag Column Flag Icon   Column Headings

Read Message Icon   Unread Message Icon

◆ The Read Message icon indicates that a message has been read.

◆ A flag is a mark you can set on a message to indicate that you need to deal with it. To set or remove a flag, click in the Flag column beside the message's header.

◆ If a message is marked as high priority, it displays a red exclamation point in the Priority column.

To read a message in the Preview pane, click it in the message headers listing. Outlook Express displays it in the Preview pane.

To read a message in a separate window, double-click its message header listing. Outlook Express displays the message in a separate window, as shown in Figure 20.23.

To sort your messages by one of the column headings, click the heading once for an ascending sort (alphabetical order) or twice for a descending sort (reverse-alphabetical order).

To view a subset of your messages, choose View ➤ Current View ➤ Hide Read Messages or View ➤ Current View ➤ Hide Read or Ignored Messages. To restore the view to all messages, choose View ➤ Current View ➤ Show All Messages.

If you have multiple messages from the same conversation (on the same topic, with the same subject), choose View ➤ Current View ➤ Group Messages by Conversation to group the messages. Issue the command again to ungroup the messages.

To ignore a conversation that's going on, select one of the messages and choose Message ➤ Ignore Conversation.

FIGURE 20.23

Instead of reading a message in the Preview pane, you can display it in a separate window if you prefer.

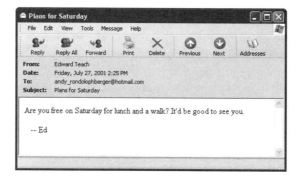

Sending E-mail

You can generate e-mail in Outlook Express by creating new messages, replying to messages you've received, or forwarding either messages you've received or messages you've created and sent before.

Composing a New Message

To create a new message, take the following steps:

1. Click the Create Mail button on the toolbar to create a new message. Outlook Express opens a message window containing a new message. Figure 20.24 shows an example.

   ◆ To create a message using Outlook Express's stationery, click the Create Mail button's drop-down list button and choose the type of stationery from the drop-down menu.

◆ To create a message to a contact, double-click the contact in the Contacts pane, or right-click the contact in the Contacts pane and choose Send E-mail from the context menu.

FIGURE 20.24

Create your message in the New Message window.

2. If you have multiple e-mail accounts, choose the account from which you want to send the account by using the drop-down list at the right end of the From text box.

3. Enter the e-mail address of the recipient or recipients in the To text box and the names of cc: recipients in the Cc: text box. Separate multiple addresses with semicolons. You can either type each address in or choose it from Address Book as follows:

◆ Click the To button. Outlook Express displays the Select Recipients dialog box (shown in Figure 20.25).

◆ In the Type Name or Select from List list box, select the name and click the To: button, the Cc: button, or the Bcc: button to add the selected name to the appropriate box of message recipients.

FIGURE 20.25

Use the Select Recipients dialog box to designate the recipients for the message.

    ◆ Add further names to the To:, Cc:, and Bcc: lists as applicable, and then click the OK button. Outlook Express closes the Select Recipients dialog box and adds the recipients to the appropriate boxes in the New Message window.

4. Click in the Subject text box and enter the Subject line for the message. The more descriptive, informative, and concise the Subject line is, the more useful it will be to the recipients of the message—and the more likely they will be to read the message.

5. In the message box, enter the text of the message:

    ◆ You can enter and edit the text using the standard Windows commands (such as cut-and-paste, and drag-and-drop) and format the text (if you're sending a formatted message) by using the buttons on the Formatting toolbar, shown in Figure 20.26.

    ◆ To switch the message from plain text to rich text (HTML) or vice versa, choose Format ➣ Rich Text (HTML) or Format ➣ Plain Text.

FIGURE 20.26

Use the Formatting toolbar to format your messages if necessary.

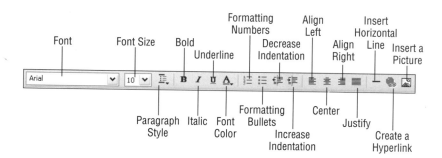

    ◆ To insert a horizontal line, click the Insert Horizontal Line button on the toolbar.

    ◆ If you type a recognizable hyperlink, Outlook Express automatically converts it to a hyperlink. To insert a hyperlink manually, select the text to include in the hyperlink and click the Create a Hyperlink button on the toolbar. Outlook Express displays the Hyperlink dialog box (shown in Figure 20.27). Choose the type of hyperlink from the Type drop-down list (for example, http for a regular connection, https for a secure connection), enter the URL in the URL text box, and click the OK button. Outlook Express closes the Hyperlink dialog box and inserts the hyperlink in the message.

FIGURE 20.27

You can use the Hyperlink dialog box to insert a hyperlink manually.

◆ To insert a picture, click the Insert a Picture button. Outlook Express displays the Picture dialog box (shown in Figure 20.28). Enter the path and filename for the picture in the Picture Source text box (use the Browse button and the resulting Picture dialog box if necessary to select the picture). In the Alternate Text text box, enter text to be displayed in case the recipient cannot view the picture. Choose alignment and border thickness options in the Layout group box and horizontal and vertical spacing options in the Spacing group box, then click the OK button. Outlook Express closes the Picture dialog box and inserts the picture in the message.

FIGURE 20.28

Use the Picture dialog box to insert a picture. Always specify alternate text in case the recipient cannot view the picture.

6. To override for this message your default setting for requesting read receipts, choose Tools ➤ Request Read Receipt.

7. To override for this message your default setting for encrypting messages, choose Tools ➤ Encrypt.

8. To override for this message your default setting for digitally signing messages, choose Tools ➤ Digitally Sign.

◆ If you turn on digital signing and want to request a secure receipt, choose Tools ➤ Request Secure Receipt.

9. You're now ready to send the message. Read through the message quickly to make sure it conveys what you want it to and that you haven't written anything rash or ambiguous. Spell-check the message if necessary. Then click the Send button or choose File ➤ Send to send the message on its way.

If you try to send an encrypted message without having a digital certificate with which to encrypt it for yourself, Outlook Express displays the Security Warning dialog box shown in Figure 20.29. Choose the Yes button to send the message, or choose the No button to cancel sending the message so that you can change the encryption setting or find your digital certificate.

FIGURE 20.29

Outlook Express displays this Security Warning dialog box if you try to send an encrypted message when you don't have a digital certificate.

If you try to send an encrypted message to someone whose digital certificate you don't have, Outlook Express displays the Outlook Express Mail dialog box shown in Figure 20.30. Click the Don't Encrypt button to send the message without encryption. Click the Cancel button to cancel sending the message.

FIGURE 20.30

You'll see this Outlook Express Mail dialog box if you try to send an encrypted message to someone whose digital certificate you don't have.

Replying to an E-mail Message

To reply to a message from the Inbox, click the Reply button on the toolbar, or right-click the message header and choose Reply to Sender from the context menu. Alternatively, press Ctrl+R.

To reply to a message from a message window, click the Reply button on the toolbar in the message window.

If you weren't the only recipient of a message, you can use the Reply to All feature to reply quickly to all the recipients of that message (and to cc: everyone on the Cc: list, if the message has one). From the Inbox, click the Reply All button on the toolbar, or right-click and choose Reply to All from the context menu. Alternatively, press Ctrl+Shift+R. From a message window, click the Reply All button on the message window's toolbar.

Outlook Express opens a message window for the reply. Compose your reply, add any extra recipients, and send the message as usual.

When you reply to a message, Outlook Express adds RE: to the Subject line so that the recipient can easily see that the message is a reply.

Adding a vCard to Your Outgoing Messages

You can include a *vCard*—a virtual business card—with your outgoing messages either automatically or manually. Usually it's better to include vCards manually when necessary so that you don't barrage your friends and colleagues with useless vCards. vCards are small, but they travel as attachments to messages, so they can make attachments folders silt up.

To send a vCard with every message, select the Mail check box in the Business Cards area of the Compose page of the Options dialog box (Tools ➤ Options), then choose the appropriate contact entry from the context menu.

To send a vCard manually, specify the vCard as described in the previous paragraph, but then clear the Mail check box in the Business Cards area. You can then choose Insert ➤ My Business Card from a message window to add the vCard to a message.

Adding vCards You Receive to Address Book

When you receive a vCard as an attachment, you can quickly add it to Address Book by taking the following steps:

1. Click the icon for the vCard in the message window and choose Open from the pop-up menu. Outlook Express displays the Open Attachment Warning dialog box (shown in Figure 20.31).

   ◆ Alternatively, select the message in your Inbox and click the icon for the vCard in the Preview pane header.

FIGURE 20.31

In the Open Attachment Warning dialog box, select the Open It option button to add vCard you receive as an attachment to Address Book.

2. Select the Open It option button

3. Click the OK button. Outlook Express displays the Properties dialog box for the vCard.

4. Click the Add to Address Book button to make the contact information editable, and then edit it as usual.

Forwarding a Message

You can easily forward a message to someone else. To forward a message from the Inbox, click the Forward button on the toolbar or right-click the message header and choose Forward from the context menu. Alternatively, press Ctrl+F.

To forward a message from a message window, click the Forward button on the toolbar in the message window.

Outlook Express opens a message window for the forwarded message. Choose recipients, enter your contribution to the message, and send it as usual.

When you forward a message, Outlook Express adds FW: to the Subject line so that the recipient can easily see that the message was forwarded.

Sending and Receiving Attachments

In addition to sending and receiving e-mail messages, you can send and receive files as attachments to messages. Attachments are a great way of sharing files and getting information from point A to point B.

Sending Attachments

To send a file as an attachment, start a message as usual (or reply to a message, or forward a message), then click the Attach button on the toolbar. Outlook Express displays the Insert Attachment dialog box (shown in Figure 20.32).

FIGURE 20.32

Use the Insert Attachment dialog box to attach a file to an e-mail message.

Select the file or files to attach, and click the Attach button. Outlook Express closes the Insert Attachment dialog box and displays the Attach box on the message (shown in Figure 20.33) with details of the attachment. You can then complete and send the message as usual.

TIP   If the attachment you're sending is much larger than 1MB, it may be rejected by a mail server on the way. If this happens (or to prevent this from happening), select the Break Apart Messages Larger than NN KB check box on the Advanced page of the Properties dialog box for the mail account and specify a value of 1MB (1024KB) or smaller in the text box. Outlook Express then breaks up the message into parts, and the recipient can recombine the parts. See the "Configuring an Individual Account" section later in the chapter for details.

FIGURE 20.33

When you've attached one or more files to a message, the message displays the Attach box.

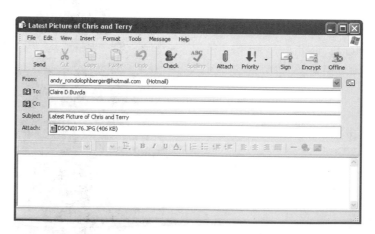

EXPERT KNOWLEDGE: RESIZING PICTURES YOU SEND VIA E-MAIL

Large graphics files can be slow to transmit. Windows XP lets you resize (or, more accurately, down-resolve) a graphics file to produce a smaller file size that will transmit more quickly.

To use this feature, take the following steps:

1. Open an Explorer window to the folder containing the file.

2. Select the file, then click the E-mail This File link in the File and Folder Tasks list. (Alternatively, right-click the file and choose Send To ➤ Mail Recipient from the context menu.) Windows displays the Send Pictures via E-mail dialog box (shown below).

3. Click the Show More Options link. Windows displays a hidden part of the Send Pictures via E-mail dialog box. The illustration below shows the expanded version of the dialog box.

4. In the Make My Pictures This Size list, select the Small option button, the Medium option button, or the Large option button as appropriate. (Each size lists the resolution used.)

5. Click the OK button. Windows creates a new version of the file using the specified resolution, starts a new message, and attaches the file.

6. Finish the message and send it as usual.

Receiving Attachments

When someone sends you a file with an attachment, the message header in your Inbox displays an Attachment icon, as you saw earlier in this chapter. If you open the message in a message window, it displays an Attach box.

To save an attachment:

1. Select the message header.

2. Choose File ➢ Save Attachments. Outlook Express displays the Save Attachments dialog box (shown in Figure 20.34).

FIGURE 20.34

Use the Save Attachments dialog box to save the attachments from an e-mail message to a folder of your choosing.

3. For each attachment, specify a destination location in the Save To text box (use the Browse button and the resulting Browse for Folder dialog box if necessary), then click the Save button.

4. Check the detached file with virus-checking software before you open it.

WARNING   *Never open attachments from anyone you don't know without virus-checking them first. E-mail has become a prime vector of computer viruses and macro viruses, and any attachment could be infected with a virus. Because some viruses hijack e-mail clients and send messages with infected attachments to some or all of the addresses in their address books, it's best to check all attachments (or at least all unexpected attachments), no matter how well you know the sender.*

If you receive an attachment that has been broken into multiple parts, select all the messages in the Inbox, right-click one of them, and select the Combine and Decode command.

TIP   *For extra security, you may want to avoid using the Preview pane, because the act of displaying the message in the Preview pane can run a script that can trigger a virus. (To stop using the Preview pane, choose View ➢ Layout. Outlook Express displays the Window Layout Properties dialog box. Clear the Show Preview Pane check box in the Preview Pane area, and click the OK button.) However, because the Preview pane helps you process your e-mail quickly, and because most viruses travel as attachments, most people choose to continue using the Preview pane.*

Managing Your E-mail Messages

To keep your Inbox in order, you'll need to manage your messages carefully, by deleting messages, moving them to folders, and being able to locate messages for reference. You may also need to move your message store, and you should certainly back it up to safeguard against data loss.

Deleting a Message

To delete a message from the Inbox, select it and click the Delete button on the toolbar or press the Delete key. Doing so moves the message to the Deleted Items folder. To delete everything in the

Deleted Items folder, right-click the folder, choose Empty "Deleted Items" Folder from the context menu, and click the Yes button in the confirmation message box that appears.

Compacting and Cleaning Up Messages

If you send and receive many messages, and subscribe to a number of newsgroups, the messages and posts can take up a lot of space on your hard disk. To reduce the amount of space taken up, or the amount of information stored, follow these steps:

1. Choose Tools ➤ Options. Outlook Express displays the Options dialog box.

2. Click the Maintenance tab. Outlook Express displays the Maintenance page.

3. Click the Clean Up Now button. Outlook Express displays the Local File Clean Up dialog box (shown in Figure 20.35).

FIGURE 20.35

In the Local File Clean Up dialog box, select the action you want to take to free up more disk space.

4. In the Local File(s) For text box, make sure the right account is selected. If it's not, click the Browse button, select the account in the resulting Outlook Express dialog box, and click the OK button.

5. Click the button for the action you want to take:

- ◆ The Compact button compresses the files, removing any wasted space, but keeps all the messages. This action saves you the least disk space—the amount shown in the Wasted Space readout in the File Information group box—but is worth performing if you have a huge number of messages.

- ◆ The Remove Messages button deletes the bodies of downloaded messages but keeps the headers. Because the bodies tend to be bulkier than the headers (especially for messages that have attachments), this action can recover a good amount of space.

- ◆ The Delete button deletes all the messages (both headers and bodies). This action reclaims even more space, but it doesn't leave much behind.

◆ The Reset button deletes all the messages (again, both headers and bodies) *and* resets the folder so that it will download the message headers again. This action is best saved for when an account has become corrupted.

6. Click the Close button. Outlook Express closes the Local File Clean Up dialog box and returns you to the Options dialog box.

7. Click the OK button. Outlook Express closes the Options dialog box.

Moving a Message to a Folder

You can move a message to a folder in several ways:

◆ From the Inbox, click the message header and drag it to the appropriate folder in the Folders pane.

◆ From the Inbox, right-click the message and choose Move to Folder from the context menu, or choose Edit ➢ Move to Folder. Outlook Express displays the Move dialog box (shown in Figure 20.36). Select the folder and click the OK button.

◆ From a message window, choose File ➢ Move to Folder. Outlook Express displays the Move dialog box. Proceed as described in the previous paragraph.

FIGURE 20.36

Use the Move dialog box to move a message to a folder.

TIP You can also copy a message to a folder (instead of moving it) by using the Copy to Folder command instead of the Move to Folder command.

Moving Your Message Store

By default, Outlook Express puts your *message store* (the folder in which the messages are kept) in a folder deeply buried under the folder for your account on the computer. The folder for your account is named with your username, a period, and the computer name. For example, if your username is Jaq Rondolophberger and the computer's name is ZWEIFEL, the folder for your account is named `Jaq Rondolophberger.ZWEIFEL`. The folder for your account lives in the `\Documents and Settings\` folder.

If you need to, you can move your Outlook Express message store to a different folder. For example, you might want to move the message store to a different drive if the current drive were getting full.

To move the message store, follow these steps:

1. Choose Tools ➤ Options. Outlook Express displays the Options dialog box.

2. Click the Maintenance tab. Outlook Express displays the Maintenance page.

3. Click the Store Folder button. Outlook Express displays the Store Location dialog box (shown in Figure 20.37).

FIGURE 20.37

Use the Store Location dialog box to move your message store to a different folder or drive.

4. Click the Change button. Outlook Express displays the Browse for Folder dialog box.

5. Select the folder for the new location and click the OK button. Outlook Express moves the folder and returns you to the Store Location dialog box.

6. Click the OK button. Outlook Express displays a dialog box telling you that the store location will not be changed until you exit and restart Outlook Express.

7. Click the OK button. Outlook Express closes the Store Location dialog box and returns you to the Options dialog box.

8. Click the OK button. Outlook Express closes the Options dialog box.

9. If you want to move your message store immediately, exit Outlook and restart it.

Backing Up a Mail Folder

If you want to be able to restore your e-mail in the event of a catastrophic computer failure, back up your mail folders regularly by copying them to an archivable medium such as a removable disk (for example, a Zip disk) or a recordable CD.

Your mail folders have a DBX extension and live in the message store. If your message store is in the default location, the easiest way of getting to it is to display the Store Location dialog box as discussed in the previous section, copy the path to the folder, switch to an Explorer window, paste the path into the Address bar (display it if it's not displayed), and click the Go button.

TIP   Compact the mail folders before backing them up (unless you've recently compacted them).

Finding a Message

To find a particular message, take the following steps:

1. Click the Find a Message link on the Start page, or choose Edit ➤ Find ➤ Message. Outlook Express displays the Find Message window (shown in Figure 20.38 with a search performed and a message found).

FIGURE 20.38

Use the Find Message window to find a particular message by specifying information it contains.

2. Enter such information as you can muster about the message in the From, To, Subject, and Message text boxes; specify dates in the Received Before and Received After boxes if possible; and select the Message Has Attachment(s) check box or the Message Is Flagged check box if applicable to narrow the field further.

3. Click the Find Now button. The Find Message window displays the messages it finds in a list box at the bottom of the window, as shown in the figure.

4. Double-click a message to open it.

If you're sure that the message you're looking for is in the current folder, choose Edit ➤ Find ➤ Message in This Folder. Outlook Express displays the Find dialog box (shown in Figure 20.39), which offers simpler searching capabilities.

FIGURE 20.39

Use the Find dialog box to perform simple searches.

Filtering Your E-mail

Business queries, love letters, spam, messages from your family, and solicitations for mass-mailing software and pornography—these days, you never know exactly what to expect in your Inbox, though most people can count on an increasing number of messages arriving.

To help you manage the mayhem, Outlook Express lets you create rules for filtering e-mail and news. By creating a rule that defines certain conditions, you can take action when a matching message arrives. That action can be anything from moving or copying the message to a particular folder, to forwarding the message automatically to people, to deleting it unread. For example, you could create a rule that deleted any message that contained the word *marketing*.

Better yet, with Outlook Express you can block specific senders, no matter what kind of message they try to send you. Read on.

Creating Rules for Filtering E-mail

Your first priority in filtering should be to filter the e-mail you receive. By filtering e-mail, you can move messages to different folders or even delete them without your ever seeing them.

To create a rule for filtering e-mail, take the following steps:

1. Choose Tools ➢ Message Rules ➢ Mail. Outlook Express displays the New Mail Rule dialog box. Figure 20.40 shows the New Mail Rule dialog box with a rule underway.

FIGURE 20.40

Use the New Mail Rule dialog box to create rules for filtering e-mail.

2. In the Select the Conditions for Your Rule list box, select the condition or conditions under which you want the rule to operate. For example, you might choose the Where the From Line Contains People condition in order to take action on messages from a particular e-mail account. (You get to specify which people in a moment.) You might also choose the Where the Subject Line Contains Specific Words condition to filter the subject line for particular words.

3. In the Select the Actions for Your Rule list box, select the action that you want Outlook Express to take when the condition is met. For example, you might choose the Move It to the Specified Folder action to move the message to a particular folder. (Again, you get to specify which folder in a moment.)

4. In the Rule Description list box, Outlook Express has built the general rule. Now click one of the underlined values to edit it.

   ◆ Continuing the example, you'd click the Contains People link. Outlook Express displays the Select People dialog box (shown in Figure 20.41). Enter a name in the text box and click the Add button to add it to the list box. Or click the Address Book button to display the

Rule Addresses dialog box, select the names, move them to the Rule Addresses list box, and click the OK button. Outlook Express closes the Rule Addresses dialog box and updates the Contains condition in the Rule Description list box to reflect the names you chose.

FIGURE 20.41

Use the Select People dialog box to specify which people the rule should work on.

◆ You'd then click the And link in the Rule Description list box. (This link appears when you've created two or more criteria that can be complementary.) Outlook Express displays the And/Or dialog box (shown in Figure 20.42). Select the Messages Match All of the Criteria option button if you want messages to meet each condition for the rule to kick in, or select the Messages Match Any One of the Criteria option button to have one condition suffice. (The example uses the Messages Match All of the Criteria option button.) Click the OK button. Outlook Express closes the And/Or dialog box and updates the Rule Description list box.

FIGURE 20.42

In the And/Or dialog box, choose whether messages must match all the criteria (an And condition) or any one of the criteria (an Or condition).

◆ You'd then click the Contains Specific Words link. Outlook Express displays the Type Specific Words dialog box (shown in Figure 20.43 with several words added). Type one word at a time into the text box, then click the Add button to add them. Click the OK button. Outlook Express closes the Type Specific Words dialog box and updates the Where the Subject Line Contains condition to contain the words.

FIGURE 20.43

In the Type Specific Words dialog box, enter the words for which you want to filter.

◆ You'd then click the Specified link. Outlook Express displays the Move dialog box. Select the folder in the folder structure as usual (create a new folder if necessary) and click the OK button. Outlook Express closes the Move dialog box and returns you to the New Mail Rule dialog box.

TIP   You can also create a rule that applies if a message does not *contain the specified information—for example, if a message does not come from a specified sender. Click the Options button in the selection dialog box (the Select People dialog box, the Type Specific Words dialog box, or another selection dialog box). Outlook Express displays the Rule Condition Options dialog box. Choose options as appropriate, and then click the OK button to return to the selection dialog box.*

5. In the Name of the Rule text box, enter a memorable name for the rule. Figure 20.44 shows the completed rule from the example.

FIGURE 20.44

The rule with information entered

6. Click the OK button. Outlook Express closes the New Mail Rule dialog box, creates the rule, and displays the Message Rules dialog box (shown in Figure 20.45).

FIGURE 20.45

Manage your mail rules on the Mail Rules page of the Message Rules dialog box.

7. Click the Apply Now button. Outlook Express displays the Apply Mail Rules Now dialog box (shown in Figure 20.46).

FIGURE 20.46

In the Apply Mail Rules Now dialog box, choose which rules to apply to which folder.

8. In the Select Rules to Apply list box, select the rules you want to apply.

9. By default, the rule is applied to the folder you were working in when you created it. If necessary, use the Browse button and the resulting Apply to Folder dialog box to designate a different folder, and click the OK button. If the folder has subfolders to which you want to apply the rules, select the Include Subfolders check box.

10. Click the Apply Now button to apply the rules you chose. Outlook Express displays a message box telling you that it has applied the rules to the folder.

11. Click the OK button. Outlook Express closes the message box.

12. Click the Close button. Outlook Express closes the Apply Mail Rules Now dialog box and returns you to the Message Rules dialog box.

13. If you're using multiple mail rules, use the Move Up and Move Down buttons to arrange the rules in the best order.

14. Click the OK button. Outlook Express closes the Message Rules dialog box.

Next, if possible, send yourself a message that meets the condition. (For example, if you created the rule described, you could send yourself a message with *FREE Sex* in the Subject line.) Make sure the filter catches the message. If not, adjust the filter until it works.

Blocking a Sender

To quickly block a sender from the Inbox, choose Message ➤ Block Sender to add the sender of the current message to your blocking list. Outlook Express displays the Outlook Express dialog box shown in Figure 20.47, offering to remove from the current folder all messages from that sender. Click the Yes or No button as appropriate.

FIGURE 20.47

When you block a sender, Outlook Express offers to remove from the current folder all messages sent by that sender.

To unblock a sender that you've blocked:

1. Choose Tools ➤ Message Rules ➤ Blocked Senders List. Outlook Express displays the Blocked Senders page of the Message Rules dialog box (shown in Figure 20.48).

FIGURE 20.48

To unblock a sender, use the Blocked Senders page of the Message Rules dialog box.

2. Select the sender and click the Remove button. Outlook Express displays a confirmation message box.

3. Click the Yes button. Outlook Express closes the message box and unblocks the sender.

4. Click the OK button. Outlook Express closes the Message Rules dialog box.

Adding Another Mail Account

If you have multiple mail accounts, you can check them all from a single identity or by using multiple identities (as described in "Using Identities to Keep Multiple E-mail Accounts Separate" later in the chapter). If you check multiple accounts from a single identity, messages to all accounts except your Hotmail account end up in the same Inbox, where you can deal with them as if they had all been addressed to the same account. Outlook Express maintains a separate set of folders for Hotmail, so you can keep that separate from your main Inbox.

Which you find more convenient will probably depend on whether you're using the accounts for different purposes (for example, business and personal use) and need to be able to keep the messages for each separate or whether you have (as it were) legacy mailboxes that you can't afford to get rid of because too many of your contacts are still using them (and can't be persuaded to change the e-mail address they have stored for you).

To add another mail account to Outlook Express, take the following steps:

1. Choose Tools ➢ Accounts. Outlook Express displays the Internet Accounts dialog box with the Mail page foremost (shown in Figure 20.49).

FIGURE 20.49

Use the Internet Accounts dialog box to create new accounts and set properties for existing accounts.

2. Click the Add button and choose Mail from the resulting pop-up menu. Outlook Express starts the Internet Connection Wizard.

3. Enter the details for the account just as you did with your first account in "Setting Up E-mail with Outlook Express" at the beginning of this chapter.

Removing a Mail Account

To remove a mail account, select the account in the Internet Accounts dialog box and click the Remove button. Outlook Express displays an Internet Accounts dialog box (shown in Figure 20.50) to confirm that you want to delete the account. Click the Yes button.

FIGURE 20.50

Outlook Express displays this Internet Accounts dialog box to double-check that you mean to delete the account.

Configuring an Individual Account

You may have thought there were plenty of configuration options earlier in the chapter when you configured Outlook Express—but Outlook Express also lets you configure individual accounts. For example, you might need to change the server used for incoming or outgoing mail; you might want to change the name for the account so that it's easier to recognize when Outlook Express is checking it; or you might want to use a particular digital certificate for one account but not for others.

To change the properties of an account, choose Tools ➢ Accounts. Outlook Express displays the Internet Accounts dialog box with the Mail page foremost. Select the account and click the Properties button. Outlook Express displays the Properties dialog box for the account.

The next sections discuss the options on the pages of the Properties dialog box. The number of pages in the Properties dialog box varies depending on the type of account: It has four pages for an HTTP account, five for a POP3 account, and six for an IMAP account.

General Page Properties

The General page of the Properties dialog box (shown in Figure 20.51) for a mail account contains the following settings:

Mail Account area   Enter the descriptive name for the mail account in the text box. This is the name that you see when Outlook Express is accessing the account or otherwise dealing with it.

User Information area   Enter or adjust your name, organization, e-mail address, and reply address in the four text boxes. The name and e-mail address will be filled in already with the information you entered while setting up the account. Specify the organization if you want to use one. Enter a reply address only if you want replies to your e-mail to be automatically sent to a different e-mail address than the address entered in the E-mail Address text box.

Select the Include This Account when Receiving Mail or Synchronizing check box if you want Outlook Express to check this account for new messages each time you check for new messages.

FIGURE 20.51

The General page of the Properties dialog box for a mail account

Servers Page Properties

The Servers page of the Properties dialog box (shown in Figure 20.52) for a mail account contains the following settings:

Server Information area   Enter or adjust the information for the incoming mail server and the outgoing mail server. If you entered this information correctly when setting up the account, you should need to change it only if your ISP changes server type or server name.

Incoming Mail Server area   Enter or adjust your account name and password. Select the Remember Password check box if you want Outlook Express to store your password; clear it if you don't. If this server requires you to use Secure Password Authentication, select the Log On Using Secure Password Authentication check box.

FIGURE 20.52

The Servers page of the Properties dialog box for a mail account

Outgoing Mail Server area   If you need to log on to your outgoing mail server, select the My Server Requires Authentication check box. If you need to use different settings than those for your incoming mail server, click the Settings button. Outlook Express displays the Outgoing Mail Server dialog box (shown in Figure 20.53). Select the Log On Using option button. Enter your account name and (if you wish) your password. Select or clear the Remember Password check box and the Log On Using Secure Password Authentication check box as appropriate. Then click the OK button. Outlook Express closes the Outgoing Mail Server dialog box and returns you to the Properties dialog box.

FIGURE 20.53

If you need to log on to your outgoing mail server, you can use the Outgoing Mail Server dialog box to set the account name and password to use.

Connection Page Properties

The Connection page of the Properties dialog box (shown in Figure 20.54) for a mail account lets you instruct Outlook Express to use a specific dial-up connection or LAN connection for connecting to the account.

To use a specific connection, select the Always Connect to This Account Using check box and select the connection in the drop-down list. Clicking the Settings button displays the Properties dialog box for the connection. Clicking the Add button starts the New Connection Wizard so that you can create a new connection.

FIGURE 20.54

The Connection page of the Properties dialog box for a mail account

Security Page Properties

The Security page of the Properties dialog box (shown in Figure 20.55) for a mail account contains the following settings:

Signing Certificate area   To specify a digital certificate to use for signing messages from this account, click the Select button. Outlook Express displays the Select Default Account Digital ID dialog box. Select the certificate and click the OK button. Outlook Express closes the Select Default Account Digital ID dialog box and enters the name of the certificate in the text box in the Signing Certificate area.

Encrypting Preferences area   To specify an encryption certificate and algorithm, use the Select button and the resulting Select Default Account Digital ID dialog box to enter the name of the certificate in the text box. If necessary (and it shouldn't be), change the algorithm in the Algorithm drop-down list.

Advanced Page Properties

The Advanced page of the Properties dialog box (shown in Figure 20.56) for a mail account contains a full house of advanced options. This page is not available for HTTP connections such as Hotmail.

Server Port Numbers area   If necessary, change the port number in the Outgoing Mail (SMTP) text box from the default setting (25) to another port specified by your ISP. Likewise, change the port number in the Incoming Mail (POP3) text box if your ISP uses a different port. Also if necessary, select the This Server Requires a Secure Connection (SSL) check box. Again, your ISP will let you know if you need to apply this setting.

FIGURE 20.55

The Security page of
the Properties dialog
box for a mail
account

Server Timeouts area   If Outlook Express is timing out when you feel it shouldn't be, drag the slider to increase the length of the server timeout interval.

Sending area   Select the Break Apart Messages Larger than *NN* KB check box and enter an appropriate value in the text box if you want Outlook Express to automatically divide large files you attach to a message into a number of smaller parts. This option is useful for making sure that large files don't get rejected by mail servers.

Delivery area   This area of the dialog box is displayed only for POP3 servers. Select the Leave a Copy of Messages on Server check box (which is cleared by default) if you want to leave a copy of messages on the server while downloading the full set of messages. This option is useful when you need to check your mail from a computer other than your usual one but later download the same messages to your usual computer, so as to have the full set of messages on your usual computer. Don't use this option on your usual computer, because the number of messages on the server will build up as you receive more mail, and Outlook Express will download all of them each time you check mail. To reduce this problem, if you leave a copy of messages on the server, you can select the Remove from Server after *NN* Days check box and use the text box to specify the number of days after which Outlook Express should instruct the server to delete the messages you've downloaded. You can also select the Remove from Server when Deleted from "Deleted Items" check box to make Outlook Express tell the server to delete the messages you've downloaded after you've deleted them *and* removed them from your Deleted Items folder (for example, by emptying the Deleted Items folder).

IMAP Page Properties

The IMAP page of the Properties dialog box (shown in Figure 20.57) for a mail account appears only for accounts that use an IMAP server. It contains the following options:

Folders area   In the Root Folder Path text box, enter the name of the root folder—the folder that contains all your folders. For a Unix server, this is usually the `Mail` folder in the folder named

FIGURE 20.56

The Advanced page of the Properties dialog box for a mail account

with your username. For example, if your username is ppiper, your root folder path would usually be ~ppiper/Mail. (Don't add a forward slash (/) to the path, because this invalidates the name.) For a Cyrus IMAP server, the root folder is the Inbox.

Leave the Check for New Messages in All Folders check box selected if you want Outlook Express to check all folders (including hidden folders) for new messages

Special Folders area   If you want to store Outlook Express's Sent Items folder and Drafts folder on the IMAP server, leave the Store Special Folders on IMAP Server check box selected (as it is by default) and enter the appropriate paths in the Sent Items Path text box and the Drafts Path text box.

When you've finished adjusting properties in the Properties dialog box, click the OK button. Outlook Express closes the Properties dialog box and returns you to the Internet Accounts dialog box. Click the Close button to return to Outlook Express.

FIGURE 20.57

The IMAP page of the Properties dialog box for an IMAP mail account

Using Identities to Keep Multiple E-mail Accounts Separate

To enable you to check multiple e-mail accounts, Outlook Express provides support for *identities*—different personalities, either for the same person or for different people. By using identities, you can maintain separate online personae for your business and personal selves, or for different activities that you undertake online. Your Outlook Express identities work for Address Book as well.

NOTE *In Windows 9x installations that didn't use user profiles, identities were useful for implementing a separate account for each member of the family or household. In Windows XP, it's much better to have each user log on using a separate username, which gives them access to (as it were) their own copy of Outlook Express.*

Outlook Express starts you off with an identity called Main Identity that you get to use by default. After that, it's up to you to create and use identities as you need them.

Creating an Identity

To create an identity, follow these steps:

1. Choose File ➤ Identities ➤ Add New Identity. Outlook Express displays the New Identity dialog box (shown in Figure 20.58).

FIGURE 20.58

Use the New Identity dialog box to create a new identity.

2. In the Type Your Name text box, enter the name for the identity. (This won't necessarily be your name—it might equally well be something like Business or Personal.)

3. If you want to use a password to secure the identity, select the Require a Password check box. Outlook Express displays the Enter Password dialog box (shown in Figure 20.59). Enter the password in both text boxes and then click the OK button.

FIGURE 20.59

Create a password for your new identity in the Enter Password dialog box.

4. Click the OK button. Outlook Express closes the New Identity dialog box and displays the Identity Added dialog box (shown in Figure 20.60), inviting you to switch to the new identity.

FIGURE 20.60

Outlook Express offers to switch you to the new identity immediately.

5. Click the Yes button or the No button as appropriate. If you select Yes, Outlook Express starts the Internet Connection Wizard so that you can set up the e-mail account for the identity. Do so as usual.

When you've created the account, Outlook Express switches you to the new identity. You'll see that everything looks as normal, except that the title bar and the Outlook Express bar bear the name you gave the identity to remind you who you currently are. Figure 20.61 shows an example. Similarly, when you're using your main identity, Outlook Express displays *Main Identity*.

FIGURE 20.61

When you're logged in under another identity, Outlook Express displays the identity name in the title bar and the Outlook Express bar.

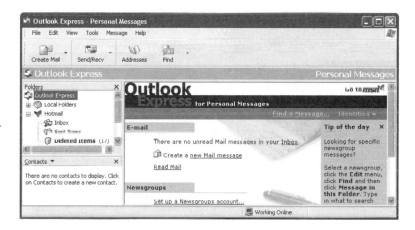

TIP   You can also use the Identities drop-down list on the Start page to work with identities. This drop-down list contains a Switch Identities item, an Add New Identity item, a Manage Identities item, and a Log Off Current Identity item and provides an alternative way to issue these commands.

Managing Identities

To manage your identities, follow these steps:

1. Choose File ➢ Identities ➢ Manage Identities. Outlook Express displays the Manage Identities dialog box (shown in Figure 20.62).

2. To specify which identity Outlook Express should use when you start it, select the Use This Identity when Starting a Program check box and choose the identity in the drop-down list.

3. In the Use This Identity when a Program Cannot Ask You to Choose an Identity drop-down list, select the identity that you want Outlook Express to use for automatic processes.

FIGURE 20.62

Use the Manage Identities dialog box to manage your identities.

4. To delete an identity you've created, make sure you're currently using another identity. Then select the victim in the Identities list box and click the Remove button. Outlook Express displays a Warning dialog box (shown in Figure 20.63). Click the Delete button. You can't delete your main identity.

5. Click the Close button. Outlook Express closes the Manage Identities dialog box.

FIGURE 20.63

Outlook Express displays this Warning dialog box when you ask it to delete an identity.

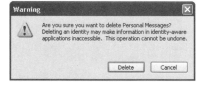

Switching Identities

To switch from one identity to another, follow these steps:

1. Close any message windows that you've been working in.

2. Choose File ➢ Switch Identity. Outlook Express displays the Switch Identities dialog box (shown in Figure 20.64).

FIGURE 20.64

Use the Switch Identities dialog box to switch between your different identities.

3. In the list box, select the identity you want to switch to.

4. If the identity requires a password, enter it in the Password text box.

5. Click the OK button. Outlook Express closes the Switch Identities dialog box and switches you to the identity you chose.

Logging an Identity Off

By default, Outlook Express starts as the identity you chose in the Manage Identities dialog box. But if you like, you can force it to ask you at start-up which identity to use. To do so, log off your current identity.

To log off your current identity, close any messages you have open and then take the following steps:

1. Choose File ➢ Switch Identity. Outlook Express displays the Switch Identities dialog box.

2. Click the Log Off Identity button. Outlook Express displays the Log Off Current Identity dialog box (shown in Figure 20.65).

FIGURE 20.65

Outlook Express displays the Log Off Current Identity dialog box to confirm that you want to log off the current identity.

3. Click the Yes button. Outlook Express logs you off and closes itself.

The next time you start Outlook Express, it displays the Identity Login dialog box (shown in Figure 20.66). Select the identity, enter the password if necessary, and click the OK button.

FIGURE 20.66

When you log an identity off from Outlook Express, Outlook Express displays the Identity Login dialog box the next time you start it.

Customizing the Columns Displayed in the Inbox

By default, the Inbox displays six columns: Priority, Attachment, Flag, From, Subject, and Received. For most purposes, these are the most widely useful columns. Outlook Express offers five more columns—Account, Size, Sent, To, and Watch/Ignore—that you can add if you want. You can also remove the default columns, specify widths for all the columns you display, and change the order in which they appear.

NOTE *You can also customize the Hotmail Inbox. This Inbox displays a different set of columns: Attachment, Mark for Offline, From, Subject, and Received. You can add a Size column and a Watch/Ignore column.*

To customize the columns displayed in the Inbox, take the following steps:

1. Right-click a column heading and choose Columns from the context menu, or choose View ➤ Columns. Outlook Express displays the Columns dialog box (shown in Figure 20.67).

FIGURE 20.67

Use the Columns dialog box to change the columns displayed in the Inbox.

2. In the list box, clear the check box for any column that you don't want to have appear. Select the check box for any column you want to add. For any column you display, you can specify a suitable width in the The Selected Column Should Be *NN* Pixels Wide text box.

3. To rearrange the order of the columns, select a column and use the Move Up or Move Down button.

4. Click the OK button. Outlook Express closes the Columns dialog box and implements your changes to the Inbox.

Customizing the Inbox Layout and the Toolbar

In addition to changing the columns displayed, you can customize the layout of your Inbox, displaying only the elements you want, arranging the Preview pane where you need it, and customizing the toolbar. Take the following steps:

1. Choose View ➤ Layout. Outlook Express displays the Layout page of the Window Layout Properties dialog box (shown in Figure 20.68).

2. In the Basic area, select the check boxes for the components you want to see, and clear the check boxes for the components you want to hide. Most of the items you've seen already, but there are a couple you haven't:

◆ The Outlook bar is a vertical bar that you can display at the left side of the Inbox to provide navigation between the main Outlook Express folders (the Inbox, the Outbox, the Sent Items folder, the Deleted Items folder, and the Drafts folder). In Outlook itself, which has many more features, the Outlook bar is a useful navigational tool, but in Outlook Express, it's seldom necessary.

◆ The Views bar is a horizontal bar that appears below the toolbar and provides a drop-down list of different views: Show All Messages, Hide Read Messages, or Hide Read Or Ignored Messages. Figure 20.69 shows the Outlook bar and the Views bar.

3. To customize the toolbar, click the Customize Toolbar button. Outlook Express displays the Customize Toolbar dialog box. This dialog box works the same as the Customize Toolbar dialog box for Internet Explorer. Use the methods discussed in "Customizing the Toolbar" in Chapter 18 to customize it to your liking.

FIGURE 20.68

Use the Layout page of the Window Layout Properties dialog box to display the elements you want and place the Preview pane in a suitable position.

FIGURE 20.69

The Inbox with the Outlook bar and the Views bar displayed

4. In the Preview Pane area, choose options for the Preview pane:

◆ Clear the Show Preview Pane check box if you don't want to use the Preview pane.

◆ If you do use the Preview pane, choose the Below Messages option button or the Beside Messages option button to determine its placement.

◆ Select the Show Preview Pane Header check box if you want to have the Preview pane header displayed. (The Preview pane header is the gray strip at the top of the Preview pane that shows information about the current message.)

5. Click the OK button. Outlook Express closes the Window Layout Properties dialog box and applies your choices.

Up Next

This chapter has discussed how to set up Outlook Express and how to use its mail features to send and receive e-mail, with and without attachments; manage your e-mail effectively; filter your e-mail by creating custom rules; check multiple accounts; use multiple identities to keep them separate if you need to; and customize the Inbox.

The next chapter discusses how to use Outlook Express' newsreader features to read and participate in newsgroups.

Chapter 21

Reading News with Outlook Express

THIS CHAPTER DISCUSSES HOW to use the newsreader features of Outlook Express to read messages posted to Internet newsgroups and to post messages yourself. It assumes that you've already read (and perhaps taken to heart) the previous chapter, setting up Outlook Express and creating as many identities as you need. In this chapter, you'll need to do a little more setup, configuring Outlook Express to access the right news server.

This chapter covers the following topics:

- What is news?
- The dangers of newsgroups
- Setting up Outlook Express to read news
- Reading messages in newsgroups
- Posting to a newsgroup
- Filtering news
- Working offline

What Is News?

News in this context refers to Internet newsgroups, a very loose agglomeration of discussion areas based on the Network News Transport Protocol (NNTP for short). A *newsgroup* consists of the messages (and sometimes attachments) that people post to the list. These messages, often referred to as *posts*, are available to anyone who chooses to take part in the group.

Internet newsgroups encompass most every topic under the sun, the moon, and the earth. In the olden days of the early 1990s, newsgroups were divided up into a relatively formalized informal structure based around a dozen or so hierarchies of newsgroups with names such as `alt` (alternative topics), `biz` (business topics), `comp` (computer topics), and assorted others, with many groups in subgroups under each hierarchy. Nowadays, in concert with the near-anarchy into which the Web has grown, newsgroups are often named capriciously, so the best way to find a newsgroup covering topics you're interested in is to search for keywords (or get a recommendation from a friend).

The Dangers of Newsgroups

Before you dive into Internet newsgroups, there are several things that you should keep in mind—even if you're fully up to speed on the dangers of the Internet and the Web in general.

First, Internet newsgroups are public. In most cases, anyone who can get online can post to them. If you dip into the right newsgroups (or maybe the *wrong* newsgroups), you'll sooner or later run into the full range of online humanity—the good, the bad, the ambivalent, the mediocre, and of course the resoundingly ugly.

Some of these people post things that most people would much rather they didn't. Sooner or later (probably sooner), you're likely to run into such posts.

TIP   *In addition to public, free-for-all newsgroups, there are also members-only newsgroups that you may be lucky enough to be invited to join. If so, behave yourself.*

Second, much of the information you find in newsgroups is incomplete, inaccurate, wrong, misinformation, disinformation, lies, or even advertising. Chances are, you don't believe even a quarter of what you read on the Web; you'd be wise to apply an even greater standard of disbelief to newsgroups.

Third, newsgroups tend to get archived. (For an example of an archive, point your Web browser at Google's Deja.com, `groups.google.com/`, where you can search through a truly frightening number of postings recent and ancient.) This archiving means that every throwaway posting has a good chance of remaining available more or less forever—or at least long enough to severely embarrass the poster. Before you dash off an inflammatory post, remember that it may stick around to haunt you for years.

Fourth, spammers use *bots* (robot programs) to harvest e-mail addresses from newsgroups, both for direct use and for selling to other people. (Perhaps you've already received spam offering you *2 million valid e-mail addresses for only $29.99*? Right—many of those e-mail addresses have been harvested from newsgroups.) This harvesting means that if you expose your real e-mail address, you're likely to get spam almost immediately from the current crop of spammers.

Many people who post to newsgroups change their e-mail addresses in a way that will defeat bots but enable humans to establish the real e-mail address with a minimal application of sentience. For example, if your e-mail address is `peterpiper@pacbell.net`, you might post with an address of `peterpiper@removethis.pacbell.net` and add a note saying "remove `removethis` from the address when replying." This type of custom addition to an address is enough to defeat most bots while remaining manageable for anyone with even minimal command of English.

Fifth, many of the more specialized newsgroups tend to attract an expert audience that doesn't tolerate off-topic or ill-considered questions well. Before posting, be sure to read the Frequently Asked Questions list (the FAQ) for the newsgroup, and check through its archives to make sure that the topic of your posting a) is on topic for the newsgroup, and b) hasn't been answered five times already in the last three months.

Still raring to get to those newsgroups? Okay, read on.

Setting Up Outlook Express to Read Newsgroups

To get Outlook Express set up to read newsgroups, follow these steps:

1. Open Outlook Express and display your Start page.

2. Click the Set Up a Newsgroups Account link. Outlook Express starts the Internet Connection Wizard, which displays the Your Name page (shown in Figure 21.1) and enters on it the name for your current identity.

NOTE   *If Outlook Express detects an existing news account, it displays a dialog box asking whether you want to create a new Internet news account or use an existing account. The steps shown here apply to creating a new account.*

FIGURE 21.1

Enter the name you'll use for newsgroups on the Your Name page of the Internet Connection Wizard.

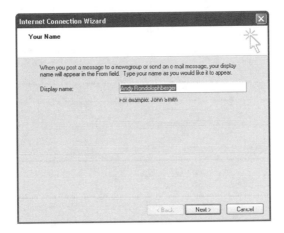

3. Enter the name you want to use for your news messages. Depending on whether you'll be posting personally or professionally, you may want to use a pseudonym or a variation of your name, at least for some of your identities.

4. Click the Next button. The Wizard displays the Internet News E-mail Address page (shown in Figure 21.2).

FIGURE 21.2

On the Internet News E-mail Address page of the Internet Connection Wizard, consider adding an antispam section to your e-mail address to prevent easy harvesting.

5. The Wizard suggests this identity's current e-mail address in the E-mail Address text box. You may well want to use a different address to throw off spammers, as discussed in the previous section. If so, enter it now.

6. Click the Next button. The Wizard displays the Internet News Server Name page (shown in Figure 21.3).

FIGURE 21.3

Enter the name of your Internet news server on the Internet News Server Name page of the Internet Connection Wizard.

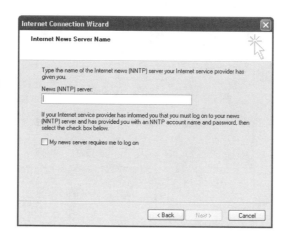

7. Enter the name of your news server in the News (NNTP) Server text box.

8. If you need to log on to the news server, select the My News Server Requires Me to Log On check box.

9. Click the Next button. If you didn't select the check box in the previous step, the Wizard displays its Congratulations page. Go to step 11.

10. If you did select the My News Server Requires Me to Log On check box, the Wizard displays the Internet News Server Logon page (shown in Figure 21.4). Enter your account name and password. Select the Remember Password check box if you think it's wise. Select the Log On Using Secure Password Authentication (SPA) check box if you need to use SPA. Then click the Next button. The Wizard displays the Congratulations page.

11. Click the Finish button. The Wizard closes. Outlook Express displays the Outlook Express dialog box shown in Figure 21.5 prompting you to download the current list of newsgroups from the news account.

12. Click the Yes button or the No button as appropriate. You'll need to download the list of newsgroups at some point—so if this is a convenient time, go ahead. Depending on the speed of your Internet connection, downloading the list will take a few minutes. Skip ahead to the section "Downloading the List of Newsgroups."

FIGURE 21.4

On the Internet News Server Logon page of the Internet Connection Wizard, enter the logon information for your news server.

FIGURE 21.5

Outlook Express prompts you to download the list of newsgroups from the new news account.

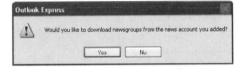

Configuring Outlook Express for newsgroup access like this adds newsgroup items to your Start page. Your Start page now contains links for Create a New News Message, Read News, and Subscribe to Newsgroups. An item for the news server you added appears in the Folders pane. Figure 21.6 shows an example of the changes to the Start page.

FIGURE 21.6

Your Start page now has links for news, and the Folders pane contains an entry for the news server you added.

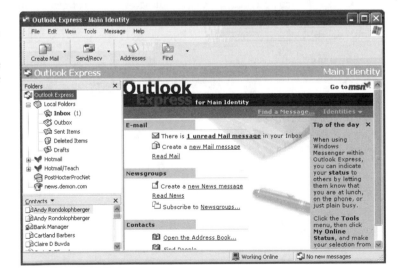

Adding Another News Account

You can add another news account at any time by running the Internet Connection Wizard again. To do so, follow these steps:

1. Choose Tools ➤ Accounts. Outlook Express displays the Internet Accounts dialog box.

2. Click the Add button and choose News from the pop-up menu. Outlook Express starts the Internet Connection Wizard for news.

Changing the Properties for a News Account

You can change the properties for a news account you've set up by working in its Properties dialog box. For example, you might want to change the name that Outlook Express displays for the news account to something snappier, or you might need to change your password or connection information.

To display the Properties dialog box for the account, take either of the following actions:

◆ Right-click the news account in the Folders pane and choose Properties from the context menu.

◆ Choose Tools ➤ Accounts. Outlook Express displays the Internet Accounts dialog box. On the News page, select the account and click the Properties button.

General Page Properties

The General page of the Properties dialog box (shown in Figure 21.7) for a news account contains the following options:

News Account area   In the text box, enter the name that you want displayed for the news account. Changing the name doesn't affect the server.

User Information area   Enter or adjust your name, organization, e-mail address, and reply address in the four text boxes. Select the Include This Account when Checking for New Messages check box if you want Outlook Express to check this account's newsgroups for new messages each time you check for new messages. (Doing so tends to slow down checking for mail.)

FIGURE 21.7

The General page of the Properties dialog box for a news account contains the name for the news account, user details, and a check box for specifying whether to check the account when checking for new messages.

Server Page Properties

The Server page of the Properties dialog box (shown in Figure 21.8) for a news account contains the connection information for the server that you entered during setup. Change this information if necessary to connect to the server. (For example, your ISP might start requiring you to log on or to use Secure Password Authentication.)

FIGURE 21.8

Change your server information on the Server page of the Properties dialog box for a news account if necessary.

Connection Page Properties

The Connection page of the Properties dialog box (shown in Figure 21.9) for a news account lets you specify which connection to use for connecting to the account. In many cases, you won't need to change the settings on this page.

FIGURE 21.9

On the Connection page of the Properties dialog box for a news account, you can specify the connection to use for the account.

Advanced Page Properties

The Advanced page of the Properties dialog box (shown in Figure 21.10) contains the following options:

Server Port Number area   If necessary, change the port number in the News (NNTP) text box from the default setting (119) to another port specified by your ISP. Also if necessary, select the This Server Requires a Secure Connection (SSL) check box. Again, your ISP will let you know if you need to apply this setting.

Server Timeouts area   If Outlook Express is timing out when you feel it shouldn't be, drag the slider to increase the length of the server timeout interval.

Descriptions area   Select the Use Newsgroup Descriptions check box if you want Outlook Express to download newsgroup descriptions. Doing so can be informative but slows down the downloading of the list of newsgroups.

Posting area   Select the Break Apart Messages Larger than *NN* KB check box and enter an appropriate value in the text box if you want Outlook Express to automatically divide large files you post into a number of smaller parts. (This setting is primarily useful if you're posting large attachments, but it will also help protect the denizens of the newsgroups if you start posting million-word theses on a regular basis.) Select the Ignore News Sending Format and Post Using check box and select the HTML option button or the Plain Text option button if you want Outlook Express to override the format in which you compose your messages.

FIGURE 21.10

The Advanced page of the Properties dialog box for a news account provides options for server connections, downloading newsgroup descriptions, and posting messages.

When you've finished choosing options in the Properties dialog box, click the OK button. Outlook Express closes the Properties dialog box and applies your choices.

Downloading the List of Newsgroups

As mentioned in the previous section, Outlook Express encourages you to download the list of newsgroups from the news server you've just added. If you prefer not to do so right away, you can download the list the first time you issue the Tools ➤ Newsgroups command.

Outlook Express displays the Downloading Newsgroups dialog box (shown in Figure 21.11) while downloading the list of newsgroups. The number of newsgroups available depends on the ISP. Some ISPs offer as many newsgroups as they can get (usually a figure upward of 50,000), whereas others provide only the newsgroups that they think their customers want (or should want).

FIGURE 21.11

Outlook Express displays the Downloading Newsgroups dialog box to keep you abreast of its progress.

When Outlook Express has finished downloading the list of newsgroups, it displays the list in the Newsgroup Subscriptions box. The next section covers how to subscribe to newsgroups.

Subscribing to Newsgroups

At this point, you're ready to start reading news. You can do this either by subscribing to newsgroups that interest you or simply by opening newsgroups that might interest you and browsing through them.

To subscribe to a newsgroup, follow these steps:

1. Click the Subscribe to Newsgroups link on your Start page, or choose Tools ➤ Newsgroups, or press Ctrl+W. Outlook Express displays the Newsgroup Subscriptions dialog box (shown in Figure 21.12 with two groups subscribed).

FIGURE 21.12

Subscribe to newsgroups in the Newsgroup Subscriptions dialog box.

2. In the list box, select a newsgroup that you want to subscribe to, and click the Subscribe button to subscribe:

♦ The Newsgroup Subscriptions dialog box has three pages: All, Subscribed, and New. Typically, you'll want to start on the All page, so that you can access all the newsgroups. Once you've subscribed to the newsgroups you're interested in, use the Subscribed page to access them quickly, and use the New page to check out new newsgroups from time to time.

♦ To filter the thousands of newsgroups down to a manageable number, enter search text in the Display Newsgroups Which Contain text box. For example, if you're interested in PC-compatible computer systems, you could enter `comp.sys.ibm.pc` to display the set of newsgroups that contain that string of text, as shown in the figure.

♦ Select the Also Search Descriptions check box if you want to search the newsgroup descriptions for the terms in the Display Newsgroups Which Contain text box. (Many of the newsgroups lack descriptions, however, so this step may not get you far.)

♦ Outlook Express places an icon to the left of newsgroups you're subscribed to, as you can see with the `comp.sys.ibm.pc.hardware.networking` and `comp.sys.ibm.pc.hardware.video` newsgroups in the figure.

♦ To unsubscribe from a newsgroup you're subscribed to, select the newsgroup and click the Unsubscribe button.

♦ To download the latest newsgroups, click the Reset List button. You'll see the Downloading Newsgroups dialog box again.

3. When you've assembled your list of newsgroups, click the OK button. Outlook Express closes the Newsgroup Subscriptions dialog box and returns you to your Start page, where the Folders pane lists the newsgroups you subscribed to under the news server (shown in Figure 21.13).

FIGURE 21.13

Outlook Express displays the newsgroups you've subscribed to in the Folders pane.

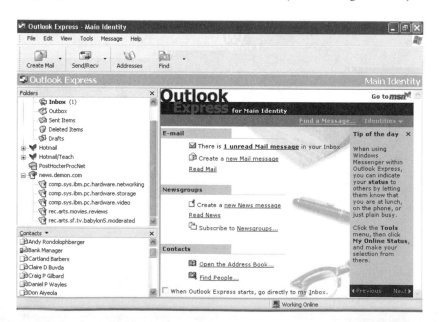

To read a newsgroup without subscribing to it, select its name in the Newsgroup Subscriptions dialog box and click the Go To button. Outlook Express displays the newsgroup.

Reading Newsgroup Messages

To read the messages in a newsgroup you've subscribed to, double-click the newsgroup in the Folders pane to display it. Outlook Express downloads the first batch of headers for the newsgroup—up to 300, at the default setting, if there are that many—and displays them in the Header pane.

Click a message to display it in the Preview pane, as shown in Figure 21.14. Alternatively, double-click a message to display it in a separate window. If a message has an attachment, you can open it by using the same techniques as for e-mail messages with attachments.

FIGURE 21.14

As with e-mail, you can read newsgroups in the Preview pane or in a separate window.

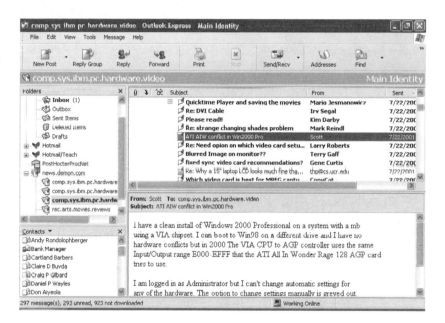

TIP   When a large file has been posted in multiple parts, you can reconstitute it by downloading the messages for each part, selecting the messages, right-clicking one of them, and issuing the Combine and Decode command.

Where posters have replied to a message using the same Subject line, the messages are *threaded*—linked together in a sequence—as you see in Figure 21.15. You can expand a collapsed thread by clicking the + sign next to it, and collapse an expanded sign by clicking its – sign. Each generation of a threaded message is indented more than the previous generations.

The status bar shows you the current status of your subscription to the newsgroup: how many messages there are in the newsgroup, how many you've read, and how many more you haven't downloaded yet. For example, the status bar in Figure 21.15 displays *297 message(s), 292 unread, 923 not downloaded.*

FIGURE 21.15

Threaded messages

To download message headers you haven't downloaded yet, choose Tools ➤ Get Next 300 Headers. To display another newsgroup, double-click it in the Folders pane.

Posting to a Newsgroup

You can post to a newsgroup either by creating a new post or by replying to a post:

◆ Click the New Post button on the toolbar to start a new post. Don't use stationery for a post to an Internet newsgroup, because chances are that many people won't be able to see it— they'll probably have to download it as an attached graphic, which improves nobody's temper. Outlook Express starts a new post to the newsgroup, as shown in Figure 21.16.

FIGURE 21.16

Creating a new post to the alt.beer newsgroup

◆ To reply to the newsgroup, click the Reply Group button on the toolbar. Outlook Express creates a reply message to the group, quoting the text of the original post (shown in Figure 21.17). Reduce this text to the minimum needed for context, because surplus quoted text is a killer in highly trafficked newsgroups.

FIGURE 21.17

Creating a reply
to a posting in the
alt.beer newsgroup

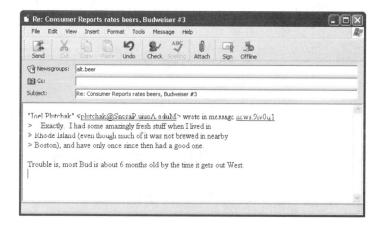

Once you've written your post, set it aside for 10 minutes. Then read it carefully to make sure its meaning is clear, that there's nothing offensive in it, and that you're not about to annoy people by writing in all capitals (doing so is considered to be shouting). Make changes as necessary, and spell-check it if appropriate. Then click the Send button to send the post.

You may also want to reply only to the author of the post (particularly if you don't want to broadcast your response to the post) or to forward the post to someone else:

◆ To reply only to the author of the post, click the Reply button on the toolbar. Outlook Express creates a regular reply for you, as if you were replying to an e-mail message.

◆ To forward a post, click the Forward button on the toolbar. Outlook Express creates a regular forwarded message.

Posting an Attachment

To attach a file to a post, follow the same procedure as for an e-mail message:

1. Click the Attach button or choose Insert ➤ File Attachment. Outlook Express displays the Insert Attachment dialog box.

2. Select the file.

3. Click the Attach button. Outlook Express attaches it to the post.

If you're posting large attachments, make sure that you've selected the Break Apart Messages Larger than *NN* KB check box on the Advanced page of the Properties dialog box for the news account and entered an appropriate value in the text box. What's appropriate will depend on the size of the files you're posting and the sensitivity (or otherwise) of the news server. For example, if you're posting your latest compositions in MP3 format, consider breaking the files down into segments of 100KB or so by using this option.

Creating Rules for Filtering News

In the previous chapter, you learned how you can filter e-mail to perform preordained maneuvers on messages that match certain criteria. As you'd guess, you can filter news messages as well.

Here's the brief version of what to do (for more specifics, look at the section titled "Creating Rules for Filtering E-mail" in the previous chapter):

1. Choose Tools ➢ Message Rules ➢ News. Outlook Express displays the New News Rule dialog box (shown in Figure 21.18).

FIGURE 21.18

Use the New News Rule dialog box to create rules for handling news.

2. In the Select the Conditions for Your Rule list box, select the conditions to apply to the messages.

3. In the Select the Actions for Your Rule list box, select the actions to take when the conditions are met.

4. In the Rule Description list box, click the links to edit them as appropriate.

5. In the Name of the Rule text box, enter a memorable name for the rule.

6. Click the OK button to close the New News Rule dialog box. Outlook Express displays the Message Rules dialog box.

7. Click the Apply Now button to display the Apply News Rules Now dialog box.

8. Select the rule in the Select Rules to Apply list box.

9. Use the Browse button and the resulting Apply to Folder dialog box to apply the rule to a different newsgroup if necessary.

10. Click the Apply Now button to apply the rule. Outlook Express displays a message box telling you when the rule has been applied.

11. Click the OK button to close the message box.

12. Click the Close button to close the Apply News Rules Now dialog box.

13. Click the OK button to close the Message Rules dialog box.

Working Offline

If you don't have a permanent Internet connection, you can work offline with newsgroups. Briefly, you download the headers for the newsgroups, mark those you want to download, and then download them when you go back online.

To work offline, follow these steps:

1. When you're ready to go offline, choose File ➢ Work Offline. Outlook Express stops working online and switches to offline mode. The status bar displays *Working Offline*.

2. Browse the headers for the newsgroups you subscribe to. Mark any messages you want to download:

   ◆ To mark a message for downloading, right-click it and choose Download Message Later from the context menu. Outlook Express marks the message with an arrow to indicate that it will be downloaded.

   ◆ To mark a thread for downloading, right-click one of the messages in it and choose Download Conversation Later from the context menu. Outlook Express marks the messages with arrows.

3. When you're ready to go back online, choose File ➢ Work Online or double-click the *Working Online* indicator on the status bar.

4. With the newsgroup selected, choose Tools ➢ Synchronize Newsgroup. Outlook Express displays the Synchronize Newsgroup dialog box (shown in Figure 21.19).

FIGURE 21.19

In the Synchronize Newsgroup dialog box, specify which items to download.

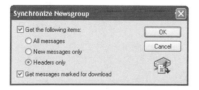

5. Leave selected the Get Messages Marked for Download check box. To download further headers, select the Get the Following Items check box and the Headers Only option button.

6. Click the OK button. Outlook Express downloads the items you specified.

7. Choose File ➢ Work Offline to go offline again to read the items.

Up Next

In this chapter, you've seen how to use Outlook Express' newsreader features to read Internet news-groups and to post to newsgroups. Along the way, you've learned what newsgroups are, and you've been lectured a bit about the unpleasant things that may happen to you in newsgroups if you don't pay attention.

The next chapter discusses how to use Windows Messenger for instant messaging.

Chapter 22

Instant Messaging with Windows Messenger

THIS CHAPTER DISCUSSES HOW to use Windows Messenger, the instant-messaging software built into Windows XP.

Windows Messenger (hereafter plain *Messenger* except where we need to be formal) provides solid instant-messaging capabilities: You can keep a list of online buddies, see at a glance which of them are online, and communicate instantly with them via text-based chat, voice, and even video (if you have the hardware). You can also transfer files to them and receive files from them.

Messenger has some very nice features. For example, one of the problems in instant messaging is that you can't see when someone is typing a reply to your message. If you send another message while they're trying to reply to you, the conversation can get out of gear. Messenger has an indicator that tells you when one of the people you're chatting with is typing, so that you can choose whether to wait or to go ahead.

Sad to say, Messenger also has a major downside, in that you need to have a Microsoft .NET Passport in order to use Messenger. (In case you haven't run into it yet, Microsoft .NET Passport is a sort of electronic identity.) If you have a Hotmail account, you can use that as your .NET Passport, but there's no other way around the requirement.

This chapter covers the following topics:

◆ Configuring Windows Messenger

◆ Adding and removing contacts

◆ Chatting with one or more people

◆ Using emoticons in your messages

◆ Adding voice and video to a conversation

◆ Blocking and unblocking users

◆ Transferring files via Messenger

Why Instant Messaging Is Hot

Instant messaging (IM) is hot because it's a great way to keep in touch with people. The big advantage to IM is that the communication—the conversation, if you will—takes place in real time. If someone is online at the same time you are, you can communicate with them. Like other IM software, Messenger notifies you when your contacts come online (and notifies your contacts when *you* go online), so you know who's available to chat. The disadvantage to IM, of course, is that the person or people with whom you're communicating need to be online at the same time as you. If they're not online (or are pretending not to be online), you can't communicate with them.

NOTE   *At this writing, Microsoft and AOL are continuing their face-off over instant messaging, with AOL refusing to give users of IM software other than its own AOL Instant Messenger (AIM) software access to AIM users. This means that if you use Windows Messenger, and your buddy uses AIM, you can't send them instant messages—you'll need to install AIM instead. On the plus side, AIM is free, doesn't require that you have an AOL account, and works well. On the minus side— well, nobody wants to be compelled to run a particular software package or sign up for a particular network identity, do they?*

Starting Messenger

To start Messenger, choose Start ➤ All Programs ➤ Windows Messenger. Alternatively, if Messenger is displaying an icon in the notification area, double-click it.

If you haven't added a .NET Passport to your Windows XP user account, Messenger displays a Click Here to Sign In link in its window. Clicking this link starts the .NET Passport Wizard, which shepherds you through the process of adding an existing .NET Passport to Windows XP or getting a new .NET Passport and adding that to Windows. Once you've done that, Messenger signs you in.

Once you've started Messenger, it displays an icon in your notification area. Click this icon to display a menu of actions you can take with Messenger.

When Messenger appears on your screen, chances are that it tells you that you don't have anyone in your contacts list and suggests you click the Add button to start adding contacts. (If you've just set Messenger up, your lack of contacts should be no surprise.) Figure 22.1 shows Messenger with a modest number of contacts added. As you can see in the figure, Messenger tells you the number of new messages you have in your Hotmail account (if you have one).

FIGURE 22.1

Messenger with a number of contacts added

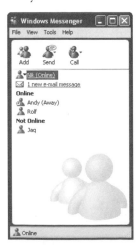

You're probably itching to add some contacts and get on with messaging. But before you do that, configure Messenger by choosing options as described in the next section.

Configuring Messenger

Messenger comes with a raft of configuration options. You don't need to set all of them at once (but this section covers them all in case you want to), but you should know about them before using Messenger. At the very least, you should edit your public profile so that you know what information other people can access about you.

Choose Tools ➤ Options to display the Options dialog box, then configure your choice of the options described in the following sections.

Personal Page Options

The Personal page of the Options dialog box (shown in Figure 22.2) contains a couple of important settings and a couple of trivial ones.

FIGURE 22.2

On the Personal page of the Options dialog box, set your display name and edit your Passport public profile.

My Display Name text box   Enter the name you want Messenger to display for you.

Always Ask Me for My Password when Checking Hotmail or Opening Other .NET Passport-Enabled Web Pages check box   Select this check box (which is cleared by default) if you want to enter your Passport password manually each time it's required by a Web site. Entering the password manually improves your security, but you may find yourself needing to enter the password too often for speedy or comfortable browsing.

Change Font button   Use this button and the resulting Set My Message Font dialog box to specify the font you want to use in IM windows.

Show Graphics (Emoticons) in Instant Messages check box   Clear this check box (which is selected by default) if you want to prevent Messenger from displaying emoticons (for example, ☺).

Phone Page Options

The Phone page of the Options dialog box (shown in Figure 22.3) lets you specify your country or region code and your home, work, and mobile phone numbers.

FIGURE 22.3

On the Phone page of the Options dialog box, specify your country or region code and enter the phone numbers you want Messenger to know.

Preferences Page Options

The Preferences page of the Options dialog box (shown in Figure 22.4) contains a slew of options that affect Messenger's behavior:

Run This Program when Windows Starts check box   Leave this check box selected (as it is by default) if you want Windows to launch Messenger every time you log on to Windows. Clear this check box if you prefer to run Messenger manually when you need it.

Allow This Program to Run in the Background check box   Leave this check box selected (as it is by default) if you want Messenger to be able to run in the background and lurk in your notification area when you're not actively using it. Keeping Messenger running in the background lets you know instantly when one of your contacts comes online or sends you a message, but it also means that you need to keep your Internet connection open all the time. If you don't want Messenger to run in the background, clear this check box, and Messenger will exit when you close its window.

Show Me as "Away" when I'm Inactive for *NN* Minutes check box and text box   Leave this check box selected (as it is by default) if you want Messenger to change your status to Away after the specified period of inactivity. (Adjust the number of minutes in the text box as necessary. The default setting is 10 minutes, which is too short for many busy people.) Clear this check box if you don't want Messenger to monitor you in this way.

Display Alerts near the Taskbar when Contacts Come Online check box   Leave this check box selected (as it is by default) if you want Messenger to pop up an alert above the notification area when one of your contacts comes online.

Display Alerts near the Taskbar when an Instant Message Is Received check box   Leave this check box selected (as it is by default) if you want Messenger to pop up an alert above the notification area when you receive an instant message.

Play Sound when Contacts Sign In or Send a Message check box   Leave this check box selected (as it is by default) if you want Messenger to play a sound when contacts of yours sign in or send you a message. This audio alert is especially useful if you turn off the two visual alerts. If you use this option, you can click the Sounds button to customize the sounds displayed. Windows displays the Sound and Audio Devices Properties dialog box. In the Program Events list box on the Sounds page, scroll down to the Windows Messenger category, and assigns sounds that you like to the Contact Online event (when a contact signs in), the New Alert event (when Messenger displays an alert), the New Mail event, and the New Message event. Then click the OK button. Windows closes the Sound and Audio Devices Properties dialog box.

File Transfer text box   Specify the folder in which you want Messenger to put files that you receive from your contacts. The default setting is your \My Documents\My Received Files\ folder.

FIGURE 22.4

On the Preferences page of the Options dialog box, customize Messenger's behavior.

Privacy Page Options

The Privacy page of the Options dialog box (shown in Figure 22.5) is where you maintain your Allow List (people who can see your online status and can send you messages) and your Block List (people who can do neither).

To move a contact from one list to another, select them in the appropriate list box and click the Allow button or the Block button.

TIP   By default, Messenger allows all other users to contact you and view your status until you block them. If you want to use Messenger privately, consider blocking all other users until you decide to allow them. To do so, select the All Other Users item in the My Allow List and click the Block button to move it to the My Block List.

FIGURE 22.5

Use the Privacy page of the Options dialog box to keep your Allow List and your Block List up to date.

To see which users have added you to their contacts lists, click the View button. Messenger displays the Which Users Have Added You? dialog box, which provides an unadorned list of names. You can right-click a name and choose Add to Contacts from the context menu to add the person to your list of contacts, or choose Properties from the context menu to display a Properties dialog box giving information about the person.

To have Messenger notify you when another user adds you to their contact list, leave the Alert Me when Other Users Add Me to Their Contact Lists check box selected (as it is by default).

Connection Page Options

On the Connection page of the Options dialog box, you can specify proxy server settings if you connect to the Internet through a proxy server (for example, through a company network). If not, leave these settings alone.

Running the Audio and Video Tuning Wizard

If you have speakers (or headphones) and a microphone, you can use them to make voice calls via Messenger. If you have a webcam or another live video camera, you can make video calls as well. To set Messenger up for making voice and video calls, make sure your sound and video hardware is plugged in and working, and then run the Audio and Video Tuning Wizard by taking the following steps:

1. Choose Tools ➤ Audio and Video Tuning Wizard. Messenger starts the Audio and Video Tuning Wizard, which displays its first page. This instructs you to make sure that your camera, speakers, and microphone are plugged in and turned on, and to close any other programs that might be using them.

2. Click the Next button. The Wizard displays its second page (shown in Figure 22.6).

3. In the Camera drop-down list, select the video camera to use.

4. Click the Next button. The Wizard grabs the video feed from the camera and displays it on its third page (shown in Figure 22.7).

FIGURE 22.6

On the second page of the Audio and Video Tuning Wizard, choose the video camera to use for video calls.

FIGURE 22.7

On the third page of the Audio and Video Tuning Wizard, adjust your video camera to show the image you want.

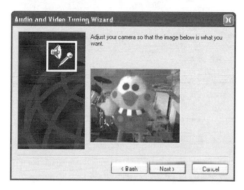

5. Adjust the picture until it shows what you want it to.

6. Click the Next button. The Wizard displays its fourth page with tips on positioning your microphone and speakers.

7. Move your microphone or your speakers if necessary.

8. Click the Next button. The Wizard displays its fifth page (shown in Figure 22.8).

FIGURE 22.8

On the fifth page of the Audio and Video Tuning Wizard, choose which microphone and speakers to use.

9. In the Microphone drop-down list, select the microphone to use.

10. In the Speakers drop-down list, select the output device (for example, a sound card) connected to the speakers.

11. If you're using headphones, select the I Am Using Headphones check box, which tells the Wizard to turn off echo cancellation. (You don't need this, because with headphones, the echoes should be confined to your head.)

12. Click the Next button. The Wizard displays its sixth page (shown in Figure 22.9).

FIGURE 22.9

On the sixth page of the Audio and Video Tuning Wizard, test your speakers or headphones.

13. Click the Click to Test Speakers button to play a sound for a volume check. Drag the Speaker Volume slider to adjust the volume as necessary. Click the Stop button (which replaces the Click to Test Speakers button) to stop the sound.

14. Click the Next button. The Wizard displays its seventh page (shown in Figure 22.10).

FIGURE 22.10

On the seventh page of the Audio and Video Tuning Wizard, set your microphone volume.

15. Speak into your microphone for 20 to 30 seconds at normal volume. (If you want, read the sample text shown, but it's instructive rather than magical, so declaim poetry or curse fluently if you prefer.) The Audio and Video Tuning Wizard adjusts the Microphone Volume slider to an appropriate level.

16. Click the Next button. You should see the eighth and final page of the Wizard, telling you that you've completed the Wizard. (If you had a microphone problem, you'll see instead a dialog box telling you that instead. Fix the problem and try setting the microphone volume again.)

17. Click the Finish button. The Wizard closes and applies the settings it helped you choose.

Signing Out and Signing Back In

Messenger automatically signs you in when you start it. But you can sign out manually, leaving Messenger running, by choosing File ➤ Sign Out.

NOTE   The first time you sign out, if you have things going on, Messenger displays a dialog box explaining that signing out will close all your conversations and stop any file transfers. Click the OK button to proceed. After that, Messenger doesn't give you any warning when you sign out.

To sign back in as the same user, click the Click Here to Sign In As *Username* link in the Windows Messenger window. Messenger signs you in. To sign in using a different Passport, click the Or, Click Here to Sign In As Someone Else link, choose File ➤ Sign In, or click the Messenger icon in the notification area and choose Sign In from the menu it displays. Messenger displays the .NET Messenger Service dialog box (shown in Figure 22.11). Enter your sign-in name and password, then click the OK button.

FIGURE 22.11

Signing back in to Messenger Service

Adding a Contact

You can add a contact to your list of contacts in several ways: by using their e-mail address or Passport sign-in name; by searching for them in a directory; by adding them when they contact you; or by reciprocating when they add you as a contact.

Adding a Contact by E-mail Address or Passport Sign-In

If you know a contact's e-mail address or Passport sign-in name, you can add them to your contacts list as follows:

1. Click the Add button in the Messenger window (or choose File ➤ Add a Contact). Messenger displays the How Do You Want to Add a Contact? page of the Add a Contact Wizard (shown in Figure 22.12).

FIGURE 22.12

On the How Do You Want to Add a Contact? page of the Add a Contact Wizard, specify whether to add a contact by e-mail address or Passport sign-in name or to search for them.

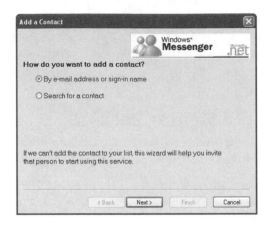

2. Leave the By E-mail Address or Sign-In Name option button selected, as it is by default.

3. Click the Next button. Messenger displays the Please Type Your Contact's Complete E-mail Address page.

4. Enter the e-mail address and click the Next button. Messenger searches for a matching user. If it finds one, it displays a Success screen telling you that it has added the contact to your list. If Messenger doesn't find a match, it offers to send a message to the user inviting them to try Messenger. Take up this request if you like.

Adding a Contact by Searching for Them

You can also add a contact to your contacts list by searching for them:

1. Click the Add button in the Messenger window (or choose File ➤ Add a Contact). Messenger displays the How Do You Want to Add a Contact? page of the Add a Contact Wizard.

2. Select the Search for a Contact option button.

3. Click the Next button. Messenger displays the Type Your Contact's First and Last Name page (shown in Figure 22.13).

4. Enter the person's first name and last name. If you're sure of their country or region, specify that in the Country/Region drop-down list.

   ◆ By default, Messenger searches in the Hotmail Member Directory. You may be able to choose another search location, such as your Address Book, in the Search for This Person At drop-down list.

5. Click the Next button. Messenger displays a Search Results page showing possible matches.

6. Select the right person and click the Next button. Messenger then walks you through the process of having the .NET service send an e-mail to the person and tell them how to install Messenger and contact you. You can add your own message to this e-mail, but Messenger won't give you the person's e-mail address so that you can contact them directly.

FIGURE 22.13

To add a contact to your list in Messenger, you can search for them by name.

Adding a Contact when Someone Adds You to Their Contacts List

You can also add a contact quickly by adding a person who adds you to *their* contacts list (unless you've configured Messenger not to notify you when this happens).

When someone adds you to their contacts list, Messenger displays the Windows Messenger dialog box shown in Figure 22.14 asking whether you want to allow this person or block them. Select the Allow This Person to See when You Are Online and Contact You option button or the Block This Person from Seeing when You Are Online and Contacting You option button as appropriate. If you want to add the person to your contacts list, leave the Add This Person to My Contact List check box selected. If not, clear it. Then click the OK button. Messenger closes the dialog box and takes the actions you specified.

FIGURE 22.14

Messenger displays this Windows Messenger dialog box when someone adds you to their contacts list. Specify whether to allow the contact or block them.

Removing a Contact from Your Contacts List

To remove a contact from your contacts list, select their entry and press the Delete key (or choose File ➤ Delete Contact). Alternatively, right-click the contact and choose Delete Contact from the context menu. Messenger deletes the contact without confirmation.

Chatting

To chat with a Messenger user, double-click the user's entry in the Online list, or right-click the user's entry in the Online list and choose Send an Instant Message from the context menu.

Messenger opens a Conversation window of chat with the user. Figure 22.15 shows an example. Type a message into the text box and press the Enter key (or click the Send button) to send it.

FIGURE 22.15

Starting a conversation in Messenger

The other user receives a screen pop (of which Figure 22.16 shows an example) telling them that you've sent them a message and a minimized Conversation window. The user can display the Conversation window by clicking the screen pop (if they're quick enough to catch it before it disappears) or by clicking the Conversation window's button on the Taskbar.

FIGURE 22.16

Messenger displays a screen pop like this when someone sends you a message.

Figure 22.17 shows chat getting started in a Conversation window. Note the readout at the bottom that tells you that the other protagonist in the chat is typing a message. This alert helps you avoid sending overlapping messages and having the conversations spiral off into multiple threads.

Adding More People to a Conversation

To add a third or fourth person to your current conversation, choose File ➤ Invite ➤ To Join This Conversation. From the submenu, select one of your contacts from the context menu. Alternatively, select the Other item, specify the user's e-mail address in the Invite to This Conversation dialog box, and click the OK button. Messenger adds the user to the conversation if they're online.

FIGURE 22.17

Chatting in a Conversation window. The readout at the bottom warns the user that the other participant is typing a message.

Including Emoticons in Your Messages

To include *emoticons* (also called *smileys* or *glyphs*) in your messages, type in the appropriate text sequence. Table 22.1 lists the possibilities. Note that where the main protagonist is a letter, you can type it either uppercase or lowercase. For example, both (**d**) and (**D**) produce a martini-glass icon—so use whichever capitalization you find easier to type.

TABLE 22.1: TEXT SEQUENCES FOR PRODUCING EMOTICONS

EMOTICON	TYPE	ALTERNATIVE	EMOTICON	TYPE
🙂	:)	:-)		(X)
😀	:d	:-D or :-> or :>		(Z)
😮	:O	:-O		(P)
😛	:P	:-P		(B)
😉	;)	;-)		(D)
🙁	:(	:-(or :-< or :<		(T)
😖	:-S	:S		(@)
😐	:|	:-|		(C)
	(Y)			(I)
	(N)			(H)
	(L)			(S)
	(U)			(*)
	(K)			(8)
	(G)			(E)
	(F)			(M)

When you send a sequence that contains the text sequence for an emoticon, Messenger converts the text sequence and displays the emoticon on both your screen and that of the person (or people) you're chatting with.

To prevent Messenger from displaying emoticons, choose Edit ➢ Show Emoticons so that Messenger removes the check mark from the Show Emoticons item on the menu. You'll then see the characters intended to make up the emoticon still as text. To allow Messenger to display emoticons again, issue the command again.

Setting Font, Style, and Color for Text You Send

If you want to be distinctive, you can change the font, style, and color for text you send to others and that you see on your screen. For the text you see in the Messenger windows, you can change the size as well. (You can't change the size of the text that others see, and they can't change the size that you see.)

To set the font, style, color, and size, choose Edit ➢ Change Font. Messenger displays the Change My Message Font dialog box. Choose settings you like and click the OK button to apply them.

Adding Voice to a Conversation

If both participants have functioning audio hardware, you can add voice to a Messenger conversation between two people. (You can't use voice in a conversation that has three or four people.)

As usual for Internet telephony, the audio that's transmitted is converted from its (spoken) analog form to a digitized version, transmitted digitally, and then converted back to analog output at the sound card, headphones, or speakers on the other end. As a result, the quality tends to suffer compared to a regular phone call, in which the audio stays analog the whole way. That said, you can get intelligible audio quality over a connection as slow as 21.6Kbps, acceptable quality in the 40–53Kbps range, and good quality over faster connections.

NOTE   *If you haven't run the Audio and Video Tuning Wizard, Messenger runs it the first time you click the Talk button.*

To add voice to your current conversation, click the Start Talking heading in the right pane in the Conversation window. Messenger displays a Speakers volume control and a Microphone Mute check box (shown in Figure 22.18) and notifies the person you're chatting with that you want to have a voice conversation. They get to accept this or decline it. If they accept, Messenger establishes the connection.

To hang up the voice portion of the call, click the Stop Talking heading.

Adding Video to a Conversation

If one or both participants have video hardware installed, you can add video to a Messenger conversation between two people. (As with voice, you can't use video in a conversation that has three or four people.)

To add video to a conversation, click the Start Camera heading. Messenger displays a camera panel on your computer with a picture-in-picture picture of the video you're sending, and invites your victim to take part in the video conversation. If they accept, they receive a larger version of the picture. Figure 22.19 shows a conversation with incoming video.

FIGURE 22.18

When you add voice to a Messenger conversation, the Conversation window displays a Speakers volume control and a Microphone Mute control.

FIGURE 22.19

You can also add video to a Messenger conversation.

To toggle your picture-in-picture picture on and off, click the Options button and choose Show My Video As Picture-in-Picture from the menu.

To stop transmitting or receiving video, click the Stop Camera heading.

Blocking and Unblocking Users

To block somebody from chatting with you, take one of the following actions:

◆ In a Conversation window with the person you want to block, click the Block button or choose File ➢ Block.

◆ In a Conversation window with multiple people, click the Block button and choose the person from the pop-up menu, or choose File ➢ Block and choose the person from the submenu.

◆ From the Windows Messenger window, right-click the person and choose Block from the context menu.

When you block a user from a Conversation window, Messenger displays the Windows Messenger dialog box shown in Figure 22.20 telling you that the blocked user will not be able to contact you or see your online status. When you unblock a user, Messenger displays a similar dialog box telling you that the other user *will* be able to do these things. In either case, you get an OK button to proceed with the blocking or unblocking, a Cancel button to cancel it, and a Don't Show Me This Message Again check box that you can select to prevent Messenger from telling you what you already know.

FIGURE 22.20

When you block a user, Messenger displays a dialog box to make sure you understand the consequences of your action. Select the Don't Show Me This Message Again check box to prevent Messenger from displaying this dialog box again.

To unblock a user, take one of the following actions:

◆ In a Conversation window, choose File ➢ Unblock.

◆ In a Conversation window with multiple participants, choose File ➢ Block and select the blocked user from the submenu.

◆ In the Windows Messenger window, right-click the blocked user and choose Unblock from the context menu.

Changing Your Status

To let people know what you're up to, you can change the status that Messenger displays for you. To do so, click your icon in the Windows Messenger window and choose Online, Busy, Be Right Back, Away, On the Phone, Out to Lunch, or Appear Offline from the pop-up menu. You can also set your status by choosing File ➢ My Status and selecting the status from the submenu.

When you change your status to Appear Offline, Messenger displays the Windows Messenger dialog box shown in Figure 22.21 warning you that your instant message windows and Conversation windows will be closed and your file transfers will be canceled. Click the OK button if this is okay, or click the Cancel button to cancel the status change.

FIGURE 22.21

You can change your status to Appear Offline, but doing so closes your instant message and conversation windows and cancels your file transfers.

Transferring Files

Messenger provides an easy way to transfer files quickly to other Messenger users who are currently online.

Sending a File

To send a file to someone via Messenger, follow these steps:

1. Choose File ➤ Send a File To and select either an existing user or the Other item from the submenu. Messenger displays the Send a File To dialog box, which is an Open dialog box in disguise.

   ◆ If you select the Other item, Messenger displays the Send a File dialog box (shown in Figure 22.22). Enter the person's e-mail address, select the service in the Service drop-down list (if applicable), and click the OK button.

FIGURE 22.22

Use the Send a File dialog box to send a file to a Messenger user who isn't one of your contacts.

2. ◆ To send a file to a user you're chatting with in a Conversation window, click the Send a File heading or choose File ➤ Send a File. You don't need to identify the user because Messenger knows it already. (If you're chatting with multiple people, Messenger displays the Send a File submenu listing the people in the conversation.)

2. Navigate to the file, select it, and click the Open button. Messenger contacts the user, asking them if they want to accept or decline the file.

   ◆ You can cancel the transfer by pressing Alt+Q or clicking the Cancel link.

3. If the user accepts the file, Messenger displays a progress readout in the Conversation window. When the file transfer is complete, Messenger lets you know that too. Figure 22.23 shows an example of a successful file-transfer session.

NOTE   If the user does not accept the transfer, or if it fails, Messenger tells you that the user declined the file or the file could not be sent.

Receiving a File

Receiving a file via Messenger is even easier than sending one. Here's what happens:

1. If you're using pop-ups, Messenger displays a pop-up telling you that someone is trying to send you a file. (Messenger identifies the user and the file by name.)

2. Click the pop-up to display the Conversation window. (If you're already in a messaging session with this user, you'll go directly to this step.)

FIGURE 22.23

Messenger keeps you informed at each step of sending a file.

3. To accept the file, click the Accept link (or press Alt+T). To decline the file, click the Decline link (or press Alt+D).

4. If you choose to accept the file, Messenger displays a Windows Messenger dialog box warning you that files may contain harmful viruses or scripts and advising you to make sure that the file you're receiving is from a trustworthy source. Click the OK button to dismiss this dialog box. You can select the Don't Show Me This Message Again check box before dismissing the dialog box if you're fully aware of malware tricks and you carefully check every file you receive before running it.

5. Messenger transfers the file, stores it in the folder specified on the Preferences page of the Options dialog box, and displays a link that you can click to open the file. Figure 22.24 shows the anatomy of a successful file-transfer session from the recipient's point of view.

To access your received files folder, choose File ➤ Open Received Files.

FIGURE 22.24

Likewise, Messenger keeps you well informed when you're receiving a file.

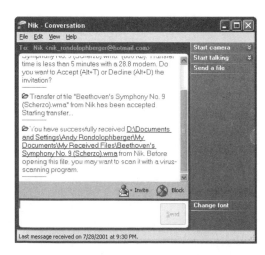

Up Next

This chapter has discussed how to use Messenger for everything from instant text messaging to making audio and video calls to sending and receiving files.

You can also use Messenger to send—and respond to—requests for Remote Assistance. Chapter 24 discusses these capabilities. Before that, the next chapter discusses how to use the faxing and telephony features that Windows XP provides.

Chapter 23

Faxing and Telephony

THIS CHAPTER DISCUSSES HOW to send faxes and make telephone calls in Windows. Windows XP Home provides strong fax features—not as strong as those in Windows XP Professional (which lets you share faxing with other networked computers), but strong enough for most home or home-office use—and two programs for taking care of your telephony and dial-up needs.

This chapter covers the following topics:

- ◆ Installing and configuring the fax components
- ◆ Sending and receiving faxes in Windows
- ◆ Annotating faxes you've received
- ◆ Using Phone Dialer
- ◆ Using HyperTerminal

Sending Faxes in Windows

Despite the best efforts of Internet fax services that aim to take the telephone and the paper out of faxing, regular, station-to-station, paper faxing remains an essential part of daily office life, especially in home offices that need to share paper-based documents with their clients. But you can save time and effort (not to mention paper) by sending and receiving faxes directly from your computer—and you can keep incoming faxes away from inquisitive eyes around your house or office. If you don't have a fax machine, you shouldn't even need to buy one.

Sending faxes in Windows isn't difficult, though Windows' faxing components are annoyingly piecemeal instead of being integrated into a single, slick interface. This is because the components are borrowed from Windows XP Professional and Windows XP Server (which have a better excuse for needing multiple components to provide the flexibility for company-duty faxing and fax-management solutions) and then disguised a bit.

These are the Windows faxing components and what they do:

- Fax Services is the umbrella term for Windows' faxing components. The next four items are essentially manifestations of different aspects of Fax Services, which itself lurks mostly unseen in the background.

- The Fax Configuration Wizard is a user-friendly utility for configuring faxes. As long as you want to use the same settings for all your faxes, the Fax Configuration Wizard is pretty much a one-stop configuration solution.

- The Send Fax Wizard walks you through the steps of sending a fax. The most convenient way to invoke the Send Fax Wizard is by issuing a Print command for the document you want to fax.

- Fax Console is a program for manipulating the faxes you send and receive. It has an Inbox and an Outbox, an Incoming folder, and a Sent Items folder. It also offers features for configuring how Fax Services handles incoming and outgoing faxes.

- Fax Cover Page Editor is a program for creating custom cover pages for your faxes. It's not exciting (but then, neither are most cover pages), but it's effective.

To get faxing in Windows, you'll probably want to take these steps in approximately this order:

1. Install Fax Services by running the Windows Component Wizard. (For reasons best known to Microsoft, Fax Services isn't included in default installations.)

2. Configure Fax Services.

3. Send a few faxes, and use Fax Console to see what happened to them.

4. Receive a fax or two.

Let's take it from the top.

Installing Fax Services

To install Fax Services, make sure you've got your Windows CD (or that you know where your installation source files are). Then follow these steps:

1. Choose Start ➢ Control Panel. Windows displays Control Panel.

2. Click the Add or Remove Programs link. Windows displays the Add or Remove Programs window.

3. Click the Add/Remove Windows Components button. Windows displays the Windows Components Wizard dialog box (shown in Figure 23.1).

4. Select the Fax Services check box. If other check boxes are already selected, leave them be unless you want to uninstall the component in question. (An already selected check box indicates that the component is already installed, not that you're about to install it.)

FIGURE 23.1

In order to send faxes, use the Windows Components Wizard to install Fax Services.

5. Click the Next button. You'll see the Windows Components Wizard: Configuring Components page as Windows configures things.

6. If Windows displays the Insert Disk dialog box demanding your Windows CD, insert it. Alternatively, identify the hard disk or network location in which Windows can find the Windows installation files. (If the CD is already in the drive, or if the installation source files are still where they used to be, Windows finds them automatically and doesn't prompt you.)

7. When the Wizard finishes, click the Finish button. The Wizard closes itself, returning you to the Add or Remove Programs window.

8. Click the Close button. Windows closes the Add or Remove Programs window.

That's the first step: You've got Fax Services installed. Now you need to configure it.

Configuring Fax Services

Windows provides a Fax Configuration Wizard to help you configure Fax Services. Take the following steps:

1. Choose Start ➢ All Programs ➢ Accessories ➢ Communications ➢ Fax ➢ Fax Console. The first time you run Fax Console, Windows runs the Fax Configuration Wizard, which displays its Welcome screen.

   ◆ If your computer doesn't currently have a fax/modem installed, Windows prompts you to install one. If you click the Yes button, it starts the Add New Hardware Wizard, which displays its Install New Modem page. Install the modem as described in Chapter 14.

2. Click the Next button. The Wizard displays the Sender Information page (shown in Figure 23.2).

3. Enter your fax information: name, fax number, e-mail address, phone numbers, and so on.

4. Click the Next button. The Wizard displays the Select Device for Sending or Receiving Faxes page of the Wizard (shown in Figure 23.3).

FIGURE 23.2

The Fax Configuration Wizard walks you through configuring Fax Services and entering user information.

FIGURE 23.3

On the Select Device for Sending or Receiving Faxes page, tell Fax Services which device to use for sending faxes.

5. In the Please Select the Fax Device drop-down list, choose the fax device (for example, a modem) to use for sending faxes.

6. Leave the Enable Send check box selected (as it is by default) if you want to send faxes using this fax device.

7. If you want to receive faxes on this fax device, select the Enable Receive check box. Then select the Manual Answer option button or the Automatically Answer after *NN* Rings option button. If you select the latter, specify the number of rings in the text box.

8. Click the Next button. The Wizard displays the Transmitting Subscriber Identification (TSID) page of the Wizard.

9. Enter a TSID for your computer. The TSID can be up to 20 characters long and can contain any information you can fit into them. Conventional practice is to use the TSID to identify yourself or your business, or to give your incoming fax phone number.

10. Click the Next button. The Wizard displays the Called Subscriber Identification (CSID) page of the Wizard.

   ◆ If you didn't select the Enable Receive check box, you get to skip this step and the next step.

11. Enter the CSID you want Fax Services to transmit when it answers a fax. Like the TSID, the CSID can be up to 20 characters long. As with the TSID, conventional practice is to use the CSID to identify yourself or your business, or to give your fax number so that the sender of the fax can see they've got the right number, business, or person.

12. Click the Next button. The Wizard displays the Routing Options page of the Wizard (shown in Figure 23.4).

FIGURE 23.4

On the Routing Options page, specify whether Fax Services should print the fax or save it to a folder.

13. By default, Fax Services stores incoming faxes in Fax Console's Inbox. Specify if you want Fax Services to print the fax or save it to another folder as well as the Inbox:

   ◆ To print the fax, select the Print It On check box and select a printer in the drop-down list. (Remember that automatically printing every fax you receive on a shared printer removes the privacy advantages of receiving a fax via computer.) If you don't have a printer set up for this computer, the Print It On check box isn't available.

   ◆ To save the fax to a folder, select the Store a Copy in a Folder check box and use the Browse button and the resulting Browse for Folder dialog box to identify the folder.

14. Click the Next button. The Wizard displays the Completing the Fax Configuration Wizard page, which contains a summary of the options you chose. Check the configuration summary. To change anything, use the Back button to navigate to the appropriate page of the Wizard. When all looks to be right, click the Finish button. The Wizard closes itself, applies the settings you chose, and opens Fax Console.

Once you've used the Fax Configuration Wizard to configure faxing, you should be all set to send and receive faxes (as described in the next sections). You can rerun the Fax Configuration Wizard at any stage by choosing Tools ➤ Configure Fax from Fax Console. You can also change the fax settings more directly from Fax Console as described later in this chapter.

We'll examine Fax Console later in the chapter. First, here's how to send a fax.

Sending a Fax

To send a fax, follow these steps:

1. Create or open the document you want to fax.

2. Issue a Print command as usual. (For example, press Ctrl+P.)

3. In the Print dialog box, select the Fax item for the fax you want to use.

4. If necessary, choose preferences for the fax. Click the Preferences button. Windows displays the Fax Properties page of the Printing Preferences dialog box. In this dialog box, you can specify a different page size or orientation, but more often you'll want to change the setting in the Image Quality drop-down list. The standard setting is Normal (200×200 dpi). To send documents faster but with a more grainy effect, choose Draft (200×100 dpi).

5. Click the Print button in the Print dialog box. Windows starts the Send Fax Wizard, which displays the Welcome to the Send Fax Wizard page.

6. Click the Next button. The Wizard displays the Recipient Information page of the Send Fax Wizard (shown in Figure 23.5).

FIGURE 23.5

Specify the recipient or recipients of the fax on the Recipient Information page of the Send Fax Wizard.

7. Enter the name of the recipient (or recipients) in the To text box.

◆ If the recipient doesn't have an entry in Address Book and you don't want to add them, enter their name or company in the To text box, and enter the fax number in the Fax

Number text box. By default, Fax Services dials the number as you entered it. If you want to use dialing rules (having Windows add any country, region, area, or long-distance codes the number needs based on your location), select the Use Dialing Rules check box and use the Location drop-down list to specify your location.

◆ To select a recipient from Address Book, click the Address Book button. In the Address Book dialog box, select the recipient from the appropriate contacts list. Click the To button to add the recipient to the Message Recipients list box. Click the OK button.

◆ If the recipient's Address Book entry contains no fax number, the Wizard discards the recipient and displays a Send Fax Wizard message box telling you it has done so. If this happens, open Address Book and add the missing fax number, then select the recipient again from the Send Fax Wizard.

◆ If the recipient's Address Book entry contains both a business fax number and a home fax number, the Wizard displays the Choose Fax Number dialog box (shown in Figure 23.6). Select the Business Fax option button or the Home Fax option button (or, if it's available, the Other Fax option button) and click the OK button.

FIGURE 23.6

If the recipient has both business and home fax numbers, the Wizard displays the Choose Fax Number dialog box so that you can select the appropriate number.

◆ To change the fax number for a recipient you've entered by using Address Book, select the recipient in the list box and click the Edit button. The Wizard displays the Check Fax Number dialog box (shown in Figure 23.7), in which you can change the information as necessary.

FIGURE 23.7

Use the Check Fax Number dialog box to change a fax number you've entered from Address Book.

8. When you've finished adding recipients, click the Next button. The Wizard displays the Preparing the Cover Page page (shown in Figure 23.8).

FIGURE 23.8

Use the options on the Preparing the Cover Page page of the Wizard to specify the type of cover page to include (if any).

9. To include a cover page, select the Select a Cover Page Template with the Following Information check box. (If you don't want to include a cover page, leave this check box cleared.) Then specify the information to use:

◆ The first time you send a fax from this installation of Fax Services for this user identity, it's a good idea to check the sender information that Fax Services is planning to supply to the recipient. Click the Sender Information button. The Wizard displays the Sender Information dialog box (shown in Figure 23.9). Check that the information is appropriate. Modify it if necessary. To enter a temporary change for this fax but not store the change for future use, select the Use the Information for This Transmission Only check box.

FIGURE 23.9

Check your sender information in the Sender Information dialog box before sending a fax.

◆ In the Cover Page Template drop-down list, choose the template to use. The preview box on the right side of the Wizard shows an approximation of how the template looks.

◆ Enter the subject for the fax in the Subject Line text box and any note in the Note text box.

10. Click the Next button. The Wizard displays its Schedule page (shown in Figure 23.10).

FIGURE 23.10

On the Schedule page of the Send Fax Wizard, specify the fax priority and when you want to send the fax.

11. In the When Do You Want to Send This Fax? list, select the appropriate option button. The default setting is the Now option button. Select the When Discount Rates Apply option button if you want Windows to wait until it thinks telephone rates will be discounted (for example, in the evening). Select the Specific Time in the Next 24 Hours option button and enter a time in the text box if you want the fax to be sent at a particular time. (For example, you might choose to send a fax so that it arrived early in the morning but outside the recipient's sleeping hours.)

NOTE *Looking at the Schedule page of the Send Fax Wizard, you may find yourself wondering where the Wizard gets its knowledge of when discount rates apply. Does it (for example) have a hotline to the decision-makers at your local telco? Or does it apply some standardized information that might be wholly wrong for your location? In fact, it does neither. You specify the discount times in Fax Console, as discussed a little later in the chapter.*

12. In the What Is the Fax Priority? list, select the High option button, the Normal option button, or the Low option button as appropriate. High-priority faxes get sent before low-priority ones if they're due to be sent at the same time. Usually priorities become important only when you stack up faxes for later transmission.

13. Click the Next button. The Send Fax Wizard displays the Completing the Send Fax Wizard page (shown in Figure 23.11), which lists the choices you've made.

14. Review the details of the fax. To look at how the fax will appear, click the Preview Fax button. Use the Back button to adjust any details. When you're ready, click the Finish button. The

Send Fax Wizard closes and either starts sending the fax or queues it for transmission, depending on the options you chose.

FIGURE 23.11

Review your choices on the Completing the Send Fax Wizard page.

If you chose to send the fax immediately, Fax Services displays the Fax Monitor dialog box (shown in Figure 23.12 at its expanded size) so that you can see what's happening. Click the More button and the Less button (which replace each other as appropriate) to toggle between the small and expanded sizes of this dialog box. Click the Disconnect button to disconnect the current connection, the Answer Now button (not shown in the figure) to answer an incoming fax call manually, the Clear List button to clear the list of fax events, or the Hide button to hide the Fax Monitor dialog box.

FIGURE 23.12

The Fax Monitor dialog box lets you see what's happening on your fax modem.

If you're sending a lot of faxes, you may want to select the Keep This Dialog Visible at All Times check box to make Fax Services display the Fax Monitor dialog box all the time, whether it's sending faxes or not. You can also display the Fax Monitor dialog box at any time by choosing Tools ➢ Fax Monitor from Fax Console.

EXPERT KNOWLEDGE: FAXING AN EXISTING DOCUMENT FROM THE SEND TO MENU

When you're faxing a document you've just created, or that you've opened to review or edit before faxing it, starting the Send Fax Wizard from the Print dialog box is convenient. But if you want to fax an existing document, you can save time by faxing it from the Send To menu.

To create an entry for Fax Services on the Send To menu, follow these steps:

1. Open an Explorer window to the SendTo folder. You'll find it under \Documents and Settings*Username*\. If you haven't already turned on the display of hidden files in Explorer, you'll need to do so (choose Tools ≻ Folder Options, click the View tab, select the Show Hidden Files and Folders option button, and click the OK button).

2. Open Control Panel, click the Printers and Other Hardware link, and click the Printers and Faxes link.

3. Drag the Fax icon from the Printers and Faxes window to the SendTo folder. Windows displays a Shortcut dialog box telling you that you cannot move or copy the Fax item and suggesting you create a shortcut instead. (Alternatively, right-drag the Fax icon to the folder and choose Create Shortcut from the context menu.)

4. Click the Yes button. Windows creates the shortcut and names it Shortcut to Fax (or whatever your fax was named).

5. Rename the shortcut if you want. (For example, you might want to rename it **Fax**.)

Once you've done this, you'll be able to right-click a document and choose Send To ≻ Fax from the context menu to start the Send Fax Wizard.

Managing Faxes from Fax Console

If you've been following along through the chapter, you probably have Fax Console open by now. If not, choose Start ≻ All Programs ≻ Accessories ≻ Communications ≻ Fax ≻ Fax Console. Windows opens Fax Console (shown in Figure 23.13).

As you can see in the figure, Fax Console is a regular Microsoft Management Console snap-in. The left list box shows the fax printer (which may represent one fax device, two, or more), and under it four folders: an Incoming folder, an Inbox folder, an Outbox folder, and a Sent Items folder.

FIGURE 23.13

Use Fax Console to monitor the state of your faxes and to pause or delete outgoing faxes.

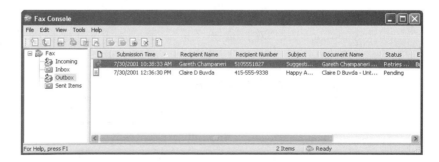

Fax Console supports a variety of actions, most of which you can take either from the context menu for a fax or from the toolbar. Figure 23.14 shows the toolbar with labels.

FIGURE 23.14

The Fax Console toolbar

These are the key actions that you may want to take from Fax Console:

View a fax you've received   Display the Inbox and double-click the fax, select the fax and click the View button, or right-click the fax and choose View from the context menu. Fax Console opens the fax in Windows Picture and Fax Viewer.

Print a fax you've received   Display the Inbox, select the fax, and click the Print button, or right-click the fax and choose Print from the context menu.

Pause an outgoing fax   Display the Outbox, select the fax, and click the Pause button, or right-click the fax and choose Pause from the context menu.

Resume an outgoing fax   Display the Outbox, select the fax, and click the Resume button, or right-click the fax and choose Resume from the context menu.

Delete an outgoing fax   Display the Outbox, select the fax, and click the Delete button. Alternatively, select the fax and press the Delete key, or right-click the fax and choose Delete from the context menu.

Update your sender information   Choose Tools ➢ Sender Information and work in the Sender Information dialog box.

Add a personal cover page to a fax   Choose Tools ➢ Personal Cover Pages. Fax Console displays the Personal Cover Pages dialog box.

Display the Fax Monitor dialog box   Choose Tools ➢ Fax Monitor.

Configure your fax printer   Choose Tools ➢ Fax Printer Configuration and work in the resulting Properties dialog box for the fax printer, as discussed in the next section.

Configuring Your Fax Printer

By this time, you should already have configured your fax printer by using the Fax Configuration Wizard. As mentioned earlier, you can rerun the Fax Configuration Wizard at any time from Fax Console by choosing Tools ➢ Configure Fax. But you can also set the same properties, and others, by working directly in the Properties dialog box for the fax printer. To do so, choose Tools ➤ Fax Printer Configuration from Fax Console.

The following sections discuss the options in the Properties dialog box for a fax printer.

GENERAL PAGE OPTIONS

The General page of the Properties dialog box for a fax printer (shown in Figure 23.15) contains the following options:

Name text box   (Actually, *unnamed* text box would be more appropriate.) In this text box, enter the name by which you want to refer to the fax. The default name is *Fax*, which is succinct but uninformative.

Location text box   If you feel the need, enter details of the location of the fax in this text box. (The location is more relevant with shared faxes, but Windows XP Home doesn't support fax sharing.)

Comment text box   Enter any comment about the fax printer in this text box. For example, you might note which phone line it uses.

Features group box   This group box summarizes known information about the fax. This group box is mostly designed for printers, and for many fax modems the only relevant information is Maximum Resolution.

FIGURE 23.15

The General page of the Properties dialog box for a fax printer

SHARING PAGE OPTIONS

The Sharing page actually has no options for Windows XP Home, because Windows XP Home doesn't support fax sharing. (Windows XP Professional does.)

DEVICES PAGE OPTIONS

The Devices page of the Properties dialog box for a fax printer (shown in Figure 23.16) contains the following options:

Device Name list box This list box lists the fax devices installed on your computer and their current Send and Receive settings. To toggle the Send setting or the Receive setting, right-click the fax device and choose Send ➤ Enable, Send ➤ Disable, Receive ➤ Enable, or Receive ➤ Disable from the context menu.

Device **group box** This group box lists the TSID, CSID, and Rings before Answer setting for the fax device selected in the Device Name list box.

FIGURE 23.16

The Devices page of the Properties dialog box for a fax printer

To change the properties for a device, select it in the Device Name list box and click the Properties button. Fax Console displays the Properties dialog box for the device. Then choose settings as discussed in the following sections.

Send Page Options

The Send page of the Properties dialog box for a fax device (shown in Figure 23.17) contains the following options:

Enable Device to Send check box Select this check box to enable sending on the fax device. Clear this check box to disable sending. (For example, you might choose to use one fax device for outgoing faxes only and another for receiving faxes.)

TSID text box You can change your TSID in this text box.

Include Banner check box Leave this check box selected (as it is by default) to have Fax Services include a banner of information along the top edge of the faxes you send.

Number of Retries text box Specify the number of retries in this text box. You can set any value from 0 to 99.

Retry After text box   Specify the retry interval (in minutes) in this text box.

Discount Rate Start text box and Discount Rate Stop text box   Use these text boxes to specify the times that Fax Services should treat as discount rates. (As mentioned earlier in the chapter, you can schedule faxes for transmission at discount-rate times.)

FIGURE 23.17

The Send page of the Properties dialog box for a fax device

Receive Page Options

The Receive page of the Properties dialog box for a fax device (shown in Figure 23.18) contains the following options:

Enable Device to Receive check box   Select this check box to enable receiving on the fax device. Clear this check box to disable receiving.

CSID text box   You can change your CSID in this text box.

Answer Mode list   Use the Manual option button or the Automatic after *NN* Rings option button and text box to specify whether you want the fax device to answer incoming faxes automatically or to engage it manually yourself.

When a Fax Is Received group box   Use the Print It On check box and/or the Save a Copy in Folder check box to specify any action you want Fax Services to take with the fax apart from placing it in the Inbox. (See step 13 in "Configuring Fax Services" earlier in this chapter for more information.)

Cleanup Page Options

The Cleanup page of the Properties dialog box for a fax device (shown in Figure 23.19) contains the Automatically Delete Failed Faxes after *NN* Days check box and text box. If you want Fax Services to dispose of failed faxes, select this check box (which is cleared by default) and specify their stay of execution.

FIGURE 23.18

The Receive page of the Properties dialog box for a fax device

FIGURE 23.19

The Cleanup page of the Properties dialog box for a fax device

TRACKING PAGE OPTIONS

The Tracking page of the Properties dialog box for a fax printer (shown in Figure 23.20) contains the following options:

Please Select the Fax Device to Monitor drop-down list   Select the fax device for which you want to set tracking options.

Notification Area group box   Select or clear the Show Progress when Faxes Are Sent or Received check box, the Notify of Success and Failure for Incoming Faxes check box, and the Notify of Success and Failure for Outgoing Faxes check box to specify for which items Fax Services should display alerts in the notification area.

Fax Monitor group box Select or clear the Sent check box and the Received check box to specify when you want Fax Services to display the Fax Monitor dialog box. Most people find it useful to see this dialog box whenever a fax is being sent or received.

FIGURE 23.20

The Tracking page of the Properties dialog box for a fax printer

To specify when Fax Services plays sounds, click the Configure Sound Settings button and work in the resulting Sound Settings dialog box (shown in Figure 23.21).

FIGURE 23.21

Use the Sound Settings dialog box to specify when Fax Services should play sounds.

ARCHIVES PAGE OPTIONS

The Archives page of the Properties dialog box for a fax printer (shown in Figure 23.22) lets you specify whether and where to archive incoming faxes and successfully sent faxes.

When you've finished choosing options, click the OK button. Fax Console closes the Properties dialog box and applies your choices.

Creating Custom Cover Pages with Fax Cover Page Editor

Instead of using Fax Services' canned cover pages, you can use custom cover pages that you create by using Fax Cover Page Editor. (You can also tweak the canned cover pages to suit your needs, or create new cover pages based on them.) Fax cover pages consist of text and graphics in your choice of layout (with some constraints) and use the COV extension.

FIGURE 23.22

The Archives page of the Properties dialog box for a fax printer

Start Fax Cover Page Editor by choosing Start ➤ All Programs ➤ Accessories ➤ Communications ➤ Fax ➤ Fax Cover Page Editor. Alternatively, if you have Fax Console open, you can start Fax Cover Page Editor by choosing Tools ➤ Personal Cover Pages, then clicking the New button in the Personal Cover Pages dialog box that Fax Console displays.

When you launch Fax Cover Page Editor, it automatically creates a new, blank cover page. Figure 23.23 shows Fax Cover Page Editor with a new cover page underway.

FIGURE 23.23

Use Fax Cover Page Editor to create custom cover pages for your faxes.

Fax Cover Page Editor offers a lot of features that we don't have the space to cover in depth here. But these are the basic steps to follow to put together a cover page:

1. If necessary, create a new page: Press Ctrl+N or choose File ➤ New.

2. If necessary, adjust the paper size or orientation in the Page Setup dialog box (File ➤ Page Setup).

3. If you want to use the grid to help you position items more precisely and evenly, display it: Choose View ➤ Grid Lines.

4. Insert the fields for the text on the cover page by using the Insert menu. For example, choose Insert ➤ Recipient ➤ Name to insert the field for the recipient's name and Insert ➤ Sender ➤ Fax Number to insert the field for the sender's fax number.

5. Arrange the fields by using the commands on the Layout menu:

   ◆ To select one of the items on a cover page, click it. Alternatively, press the Tab key to move from the selected item to the next. Press Shift+Tab to select the previous item.

   ◆ You can select multiple items in a couple of ways. Either select the first item, hold down the Ctrl key, and then select the remaining items. Or click outside one corner of the group and drag the selection border until it extends around the items.

   ◆ To align selected objects, choose Layout ➤ Align Objects and choose Left, Right, Top, or Bottom from the submenu.

   ◆ To space selected objects evenly, choose Layout ➤ Space Evenly ➤ Across or Layout ➤ Space Evenly ➤ Down.

   ◆ To change the order in which items are stacked on top of each other, select an object and choose Layout ➤ Bring to Front or Layout ➤ Send to Back.

TIP *To copy an item (except the Note field), select it, hold down the Ctrl key and the Shift key, and drag it to where you want the copy to appear.*

6. Change the font of a selected field by choosing Format ➤ Font and working in the Font dialog box. Alternatively, use the toolbar buttons.

7. Change the alignment of text in a selected field by choosing Format ➤ Align Text and selecting Left, Center, or Right from the submenu.

8. Change lines and shading by choosing Format ➤ Line, Fill and Color and working in the Line, Fill and Color dialog box. (Before you ask—your color choices are limited to black, white, and shades of gray.)

9. Add any decorative elements (such as shapes or lines) by using the buttons on the Drawing toolbar.

10. Use Print Preview (File ➤ Print Preview) to make sure your cover page looks the way you want it to.

11. Save the cover page by choosing File ➤ Save and specifying the name and location in the Save As dialog box.

    ◆ If you want the cover page to be available to all users of this computer, save it in the `\Documents and Settings\All Users\Application Data\Microsoft\Windows NT\MSFax\ Common CoverPages\` folder. (You'll need to have selected the Show Hidden Files and Folders option button on the View page of the Folder Options dialog box from Explorer to get to this folder.)

    ◆ If you want the Personal Cover Pages dialog box to list this cover page automatically, save it in the `\Fax\Personal Cover Pages\` folder under your `\My Documents\` folder.

    ◆ Otherwise, save the cover page in any folder that suits you and add it to the Personal Cover Pages list as described in the next section.

ADDING AN EXISTING COVER PAGE TO THE PERSONAL COVER PAGES DIALOG BOX

For most purposes, it's easiest to keep your personal cover pages where Microsoft wants you to keep them—in the `\Fax\Personal Cover Pages\` folder under your `\My Documents\` folder. But you can also keep them in other folders if you prefer.

If you do, you can add cover pages to the list in the Personal Cover Pages dialog box as follows:

1. From Fax Console, choose Tools ➤ Personal Cover Pages. Windows displays the Personal Cover Pages dialog box (shown in Figure 23.24).

FIGURE 23.24

Use the Personal Cover Pages dialog box to manage your personal cover pages.

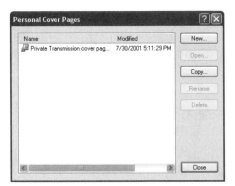

2. Click the Copy button. Windows displays the Copy Cover Page to List of Personal Cover Pages dialog box, which is a common Open dialog box by another name.

3. Navigate to and select the cover page file.

4. Click the Open button. Windows closes the dialog box and copies the cover page to the Personal Cover Pages dialog box.

Editing and Annotating a Fax

After you receive a fax, you may want to annotate it or censor it before passing it along to a family member or colleague (or, if you're brave or foolish, both). To do so, double-click the fax file to open it in a Windows Picture and Fax Viewer window. Then annotate it as described in the "Annotating an Image" section in Chapter 7. For example, you might want to draw a frame around a key section of the fax and attach a text box with commentary to it; you might want to draw a solid rectangle over a part of the fax that you want to keep secret; or you might want to add freehand doodles to the fax to convey a sense of freshness or informality. With Windows Picture and Fax Viewer's annotation features, the world is pretty much your lobster—at least, as far as annotating faxes goes.

Making and Receiving Calls with Phone Dialer

Phone Dialer is a telephony program with which you can make voice calls, video calls, and video-conference calls. You can make calls either via regular dial-up (station to station) or via the Internet.

Phone Dialer has been a part of Windows for several years now, and it's included in a standard Windows XP Home installation (in other words, you don't need to install it separately the way you do Fax Services). But you could be forgiven for assuming that Windows XP Home is somehow embarrassed by (or scared of) Phone Dialer, because it provides no shortcut for it on the Start menu. This is perhaps partly because Windows Messenger (discussed in the previous chapter) is muscling in on Phone Dialer's territory to some extent, and perhaps partly because Microsoft is so heavily committed to Internet telephony as to deprecate dial-up. But given that most people don't yet have always on broadband connections, dial-up telephony remains important for many people, and Phone Dialer is a useful and capable if fundamentally unexciting program.

All of which is essentially a preamble to saying that you need to create your own shortcut to Phone Dialer. You'll find its executable, DIALER.EXE, in the \Program Files\Windows NT\ folder.

EXPERT KNOWLEDGE: PHONE DIALER VERSUS NETMEETING

Windows offers two separate programs for telephonic communication over regular phone lines and Internet connections: Phone Dialer (discussed in this section) and NetMeeting (discussed in Chapter 25). To get the most out of your calls, you need to understand the strengths and weaknesses of each program.

Both Phone Dialer and NetMeeting can make voice calls, video calls, and conference calls. With either program, each type of call can be dialed direct or made via an Internet connection.

That's about as far as the similarities go. The differences are significant and worth understanding. Phone Dialer is essentially a telephony program, while NetMeeting is essentially a collaboration and file-sharing program.

NetMeeting offers chat, whiteboarding, file sharing, and remote control of not only individual programs but also of the whole Windows Desktop. Phone Dialer offers none of these.

Phone Dialer can handle audio conferences and video conferences involving more than two people. (NetMeeting can handle audio and video for only two people at a time.) To compensate, Phone Dialer keeps each video window to a tiny size, while NetMeeting lets you adjust the size of the video you send.

To get the most out of Phone Dialer, you need a modem or an Internet connection; a sound card, microphone (or handset), and speakers; and a video camera (if you want to send video; you can receive video calls without a camera).

Obviously enough, you need to have Phone Dialer open in order to use it to place a call. Less obviously, you need to have Phone Dialer open in order to receive a call. So if you use Phone Dialer for telephony, it's a good candidate for adding to your Startup group so that Windows starts it automatically when you log on.

To start Phone Dialer, double-click that shortcut you just created. Alternatively, choose Start ➤ Run, enter **dialer** in the Run dialog box, and click the OK button. Figure 23.25 shows Phone Dialer. The left pane lists the directories and numbers available to you, broken down into these categories: Internet Directories, My Network Directory (a directory on the local network), Speed Dial (your list of Speed Dial entries), and Conference Room (any ongoing conferences).

FIGURE 23.25

Phone Dialer lets you make voice and video calls over regular phone lines and over the Internet.

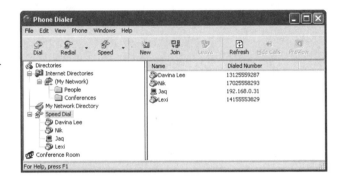

Configuring Phone Dialer

Before you start using Phone Dialer, perform some basic configuration. Take the following steps:

1. Choose Edit ➤ Options. Phone Dialer displays the Options dialog box.

2. On the Lines page (shown in Figure 23.26), make any necessary phone line choices:

   Preferred Line for Calling group box   Select the Phone option button or the Internet option button as appropriate. (You can specify phone or Internet for each call you make, but you'll save time by choosing your normal setting here.)

   Line Used For group box   In the Phone Calls drop-down list, the Internet Calls drop-down list, and the Internet Conferences drop-down list, you can specify the line you prefer to use. The default setting for each is Auto-Select, which lets Phone Dialer decide which line to use. The setting you're most likely to want to change is Phone Calls, which lists each modem you have. It also offers a choice called H323 Line, which is an Internet telephony line.

FIGURE 23.26

On the Lines page of the Options dialog box, choose which lines to use for which types of call.

3. On the Audio/Video page (shown in Figure 23.27), select options as appropriate:

Use the Telephone Handset Connected to This PC for All Calls check box   Select this check box to use a handset for all your calls. If Windows doesn't detect a handset, this check box is not available.

Enable Acoustic Echo Cancellation check box   Select this check box to have Phone Dialer try to cancel out echoes.

Devices Used for Calling group box   In the Line drop-down list, select the Phone Calls item, the Internet Calls item, or the Internet Conferences item. Then make selections for this type of call in the Audio Record drop-down list, the Audio Playback drop-down list, and the Video Recording drop-down list. Select the Video Playback check box if you want to receive video playback on this type of call. For Internet conferences, the Devices Used for Calling group box also displays a Maximum Video Windows text box. In this, enter the maximum number of video windows you want to have open at any time. The default setting is 6, which is plenty for most people. You may want to reduce this number to get better video performance.

4. Click the OK button. Phone Dialer closes the Options dialog box.

FIGURE 23.27

Choose audio and video options on the Audio/Video page of the Options dialog box.

Placing a Call

To place a call with Phone Dialer, follow these steps:

1. Click the Dial button or choose Phone ➤ Dial. Phone Dialer displays the Dial dialog box (shown in Figure 23.28).

FIGURE 23.28

Use the Dial dialog box to place a call.

2. Enter the phone number, IP address, or DNS name in the text box. (Once you've used Phone Dialer, you can choose a recent number, address, or name from the drop-down list.)

3. In the Dial As group box, select the Phone Call option button for a regular (dialed) phone call. Select the Internet Call option button to call via the Internet.

4. If you want to create a Speed Dial entry for this number, address, or name, select the Add Number to Speed Dial List check box.

5. Click the Place Call button to place the call. Phone Dialer displays the active call window and the preview window (shown in Figure 23.29).

FIGURE 23.29

The active call window appears when you place a call.

6. If the person you've called picks up the call, the active call window displays *Connected*.

7. Carry on the call as normal. Use the microphone and volume controls to adjust the microphone volume and speaker (or headphone) volume if necessary.

   ◆ If your telephony setup supports hold, the active call window displays a Hold button. Click this button to toggle the active call on and off hold.

8. Click the Disconnect button to end the call.

9. Click the Close button to close the active call window.

Receiving Incoming Calls

When someone calls you—either via the phone or via the Internet—Phone Dialer displays the active call window as shown in Figure 23.30, flashing the message *Incoming call* and sounding a ringing tone. Click the Take Call button to accept the call or the Reject Call button to reject the call.

FIGURE 23.30

When you get an incoming call, Phone Dialer displays the active call window and sounds a ringing tone.

Keeping a Speed Dial List

Like most smart phones, Phone Dialer lets you create and maintain a Speed Dial list of numbers that you call frequently.

ADDING AN ENTRY TO YOUR SPEED DIAL LIST

You can add entries to your Speed Dial list in several ways:

◆ This is the formal way:

1. Choose Edit ➤ Add to Speed Dial List. Phone Dialer displays the Speed Dial dialog box (shown in Figure 23.31).

2. In the Display Name text box, enter the name under which you want the Speed Dial listed.

3. In the Number or Address text box, enter the telephone number, the IP address, or the DNS name.

4. In the Dial As group box, select the Phone Call option button, the Internet Call option button, or the Internet Conference option button as appropriate.

5. Click the OK button. Phone Dialer closes the Speed Dial dialog box.

FIGURE 23.31

Create Speed Dial entries for numbers you need to call frequently.

- When you're using the Dial dialog box to place a call, select the Add Number to Speed Dial List check box.

- When you're on a call, click the Add to Speed Dial icon. Phone Dialer displays the Speed Dial dialog box with the telephone number, IP address, or DNS name entered in both the Display Name text box and the Number or Address text box. Change the contents of the Display Name text box if necessary, then click the OK button.

DIALING A SPEED DIAL NUMBER

You can dial a Speed Dial entry in several easy ways:

- Click the down-arrow on the Speed button and select the entry from the drop-down menu.

- Choose Phone ➢ Speed Dial and select the entry from the submenu.

- Expand the Speed Dial list in the left pane and double-click the entry.

EDITING YOUR SPEED DIAL LIST

You can edit your Speed Dial list to change the order in which the entries are listed, to change a particular entry, or to add or remove entries.

To edit your Speed Dial list, select Edit ➢ Speed Dial List or click the down-arrow on the Speed button and choose Edit Speed Dial List. Phone Dialer displays the Edit Speed Dial List dialog box (shown in Figure 23.32).

FIGURE 23.32

Use the Edit Speed Dial List dialog box to edit your Speed Dial entries, rearrange their order, and weed out entries you seldom call.

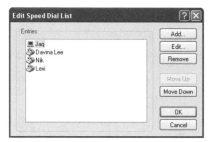

Edit your list as follows:

- Use the Move Up button and Move Down button to move a selected entry up or down the list.

- Click the Remove button to remove a selected entry.

- Click the Edit button to display the selected entry for editing in the Speed Dial dialog box.

- Click the Add button to display the Speed Dial dialog box. Specify the details for the entry and click the OK button.

When you've finished editing the list, click the OK button. Phone Dialer closes the Edit Speed Dial List dialog box.

Adding an Internet Directory to Phone Dialer

To add an Internet directory to Phone Dialer, follow these steps:

1. Choose Edit ➢ Add Directory. Phone Dialer displays the Add Directory Server dialog box (shown in Figure 23.33).

FIGURE 23.33

Use the Add Directory Server dialog box to add a directory server to Phone Dialer.

2. Enter the name of the directory server in the text box.

3. Click the Add button. Phone Dialer closes the Add Directory Server dialog box and adds the directory server to your Internet Directories list.

NOTE *The My Network Directory list in Phone Dialer lets you access a directory of the network you're currently logged on to. This feature is primarily aimed at Windows XP Professional users rather than Windows XP Home users, because to use it, you need to be logged on to a network domain—which Windows XP Home users normally will not be.*

Closing Phone Dialer

When you close Phone Dialer, it displays the Confirm Phone Dialer Exit dialog box (shown in Figure 23.34) to warn you that when you close it, you won't be able to accept Internet calls or receive notice of incoming calls. Click the Yes button to close Phone Dialer. If you don't want to see the Confirm Phone Dialer Exit dialog box again, select the Don't Ask Me Again check box before dismissing the dialog box.

FIGURE 23.34

When you close Phone Dialer, it displays the Confirm Phone Dialer Exit dialog box until you tell it not to.

Using HyperTerminal

HyperTerminal is a dial-up communications program that you can use for connecting to other computers or BBSes via terminal emulation. Because so much communication takes place via the Internet nowadays, you may need to use HyperTerminal only occasionally. But when you need it, it's straightforward and effective.

To use HyperTerminal, follow these steps:

1. Start HyperTerminal by choosing Start ➤ All Programs ➤ Accessories ➤ Communications ➤ HyperTerminal. When you start HyperTerminal, it assumes you want to create a new connection, and displays the Connection Description dialog box (shown in Figure 23.35).

   ◆ The first time you run HyperTerminal, it displays the Default Telnet Program? dialog box, asking whether you want to make HyperTerminal your default Telnet program. Choose the Yes button or the No button as appropriate. To prevent HyperTerminal from displaying this dialog box each time you start it, select the Don't Ask Me This Question Again check box before dismissing the dialog box.

FIGURE 23.35

When you start HyperTerminal, it displays the Connection Description dialog box so that you can create a new connection.

2. Enter the name for the connection in the Name text box, select an icon in the Icon list box, and click the OK button. HyperTerminal displays the Connect To dialog box (shown in Figure 23.36).

FIGURE 23.36

Enter the connection information in the Connect To dialog box.

3. Specify the country or region, enter the area code and phone number, and make sure the right dial-up device is selected in the Connect Using drop-down list. Then click the OK button. HyperTerminal displays the Connect dialog box (shown in Figure 23.37).

FIGURE 23.37

In the Connect dialog box, check the phone number and your current location. Then click the Dial button.

4. Check the phone number:

   ◆ To change the phone number, click the Modify button and change the country or region, area code, or phone number on the Connect To page of the Properties dialog box (shown in Figure 23.38).

FIGURE 23.38

Use the Connect To page of the Properties dialog box to change the phone number or to set redialing for a busy number.

   ◆ To make HyperTerminal redial a busy connection automatically, click the Modify button. HyperTerminal displays the Properties dialog box for the connection. Then select the Redial on Busy check box on the Connect To page.

5. Check your location in the Your Location drop-down list. Change it if necessary.

   ◆ If you need to create a dialing rule, click the Dialing Properties button. Windows displays the Phone and Modem Options dialog box.

6. Click the Dial button. HyperTerminal dials the number and, if it answers, establishes a connection.

What happens next depends on the computer you've dialed. For example, you may be prompted to enter a username and password in order to log in.

TIP   *If you need to specify which type of terminal HyperTerminal should emulate for a connection, choose File ➢ Properties to display the Properties dialog box for the connection. On the Settings page, choose the type of emulation you want. You can also specify the type of behavior you want for the function keys, arrow keys, Ctrl key, and Backspace key.*

You may then want to take some of the following actions from the main HyperTerminal window:

♦   To upload a file, choose Transfer ➢ Send File. In the Send File dialog box, specify the filename and the protocol to use. (Use the default choice, Zmodem with Crash Recovery, unless you know you need to use another protocol.) Then click the Send button.

♦   To download a file, choose Transfer ➢ Receive File. In the Receive File dialog box, specify the folder in which to place the downloaded file and the protocol to use for receiving it. Then click the Receive button.

♦   To capture text in your HyperTerminal session, select Transfer ➢ Capture Text. In the Capture Text dialog box, specify the file in which to store the text. Then click the Start button. To pause capturing, choose Transfer ➢ Capture Text ➢ Pause. To resume paused capturing, choose Transfer ➢ Capture Text ➢ Resume. To stop capturing to this file, choose Transfer ➢ Capture Text ➢ Stop.

♦   To upload a text file, choose Transfer ➢ Send Text File. In the Send Text File dialog box, select the file to send and then click the Open button.

When you've finished your session, log off the remote computer. Then hang up the connection by clicking the Disconnect button on the toolbar or by choosing Call ➢ Disconnect.

If you've made any changes to the connection, save them by choosing File ➢ Save.

Once you've created some connections, the Accessories menu off the Start menu displays a HyperTerminal submenu as well as the HyperTerminal program item. This HyperTerminal submenu lists the connections you have created. To open one of them, and open HyperTerminal, select the connection from the submenu.

TIP   *To make HyperTerminal listen for an incoming call, choose Call ➢ Wait for a Call. To stop HyperTerminal from listening, choose Call ➢ Stop Waiting.*

Up Next

In this chapter, you've learned how to use Windows XP's fax capabilities for sending, receiving, and managing faxes, and how to use Phone Dialer and HyperTerminal for basic telephony.

The next chapter discusses how to use the Remote Desktop Connection feature to remotely control a computer running Windows XP Professional (for example, your computer at the office) and how to use the Remote Assistance feature to give and receive help across the Internet.

Chapter 24

Remote Desktop Connection and Remote Assistance

THIS CHAPTER DISCUSSES TWO of the remote-connection technologies built into Windows XP:

◆ Remote Desktop Connection lets you connect to a remote computer running Windows XP Professional from a computer that's running Windows XP Home or Windows XP Professional or another version of Windows with Remote Desktop Connection installed. For example, if your computer at work runs Windows XP Professional and your computer at home runs Windows XP Home, you could connect from your home computer to your work computer. Once connected, you can work on the remote computer as if you were sitting at it (provided your Internet or network connection is fast enough—otherwise everything happens much more slowly).

◆ Remote Assistance provides a secure way to get help from a friend or other helper at a distance (or to give them help). You invite the helper to connect remotely to your computer, which lets them view your screen and see what the problem is. You decide whether to chat with them (via text or voice) and implement their suggestions—which keeps you secure—or to let them control your computer remotely and take the actions they deem necessary (which is not secure).

NOTE *Windows XP Professional also supports Remote Desktop Web Connection, a version of Remote Desktop Connection that lets you connect to a computer running Windows XP Professional from a remote computer using just Internet Explorer. Windows XP Home doesn't support Remote Desktop Web Connection.*

This chapter covers the following topics:

◆ Remote Desktop Connection terminology and basics

◆ Configuring Remote Desktop Connection

◆ Connecting via Remote Desktop Connection

◆ Working via Remote Desktop Connection

◆ Enabling Remote Assistance

◆ Receiving help via Remote Assistance

◆ Giving help via Remote Assistance

EXPERT KNOWLEDGE: REMOTE DESKTOP CONNECTION IS TERMINAL SERVICES

Remote Desktop Connection is the snappy new name for the Terminal Services Client, a feature from the black lagoon days of Windows NT 4. A couple of years after releasing NT Server 4, Microsoft loosed NT Server 4 Terminal Server Edition, a version of NT Server with a multiuser technology called Terminal Server added to it. In Windows 2000 Server, Terminal Server was integrated into the server and renamed Terminal Services, but the underlying technology remained the same.

Here's what happens with Terminal Services. The user has a local computer as usual, but they don't run programs on it. Instead, they run a smallish program called Terminal Services Client that lets them run programs on a server but have the output displayed on the local computer. The server does all the heavy lifting, so as long as the server is big and fast, the local computer can be small, underpowered, or outdated. All it needs to do is send keystrokes and mouse clicks to the server and display the output it receives back across the wire. Given a fast server and a fast network, performance can be quite snappy, so there's no problem from the users' end.

With Terminal Services, corporations can save big money by continuing to use ancient hardware (we're talking 486s and early Pentiums here) several years past their sell-by date for running modern programs. For example, some early Pentium computers had 250MB hard drives. Office 2000 needs about 340MB to get comfortably settled, even before you create any data files. Sure, you can put a bigger hard drive in an old PC like this, but why bother if you don't have to?

Terminal Services also greatly reduces administration: Instead of needing to install—and maintain—programs on each client, administrators can install them on the servers instead. And they can lock down the lame old clients so that users can't waste good company time trying to configure their Desktops… but that's another story.

So much for the history of Terminal Services. With Windows XP, Terminal Services has been renamed Remote Desktop and integrated into the Professional version as well as the Server version. (You could look at this another way and say that Windows XP Home and Windows XP Professional, with their capabilities to support multiple concurrent user sessions, are in fact a cut-down version of Windows XP Server running both the server and the client sessions on the same computer.) Terminal Services Client has been renamed Remote Desktop Connection.

As you'll see in this chapter, Remote Desktop Connection is installed automatically in Windows XP. But on the Windows XP CD, you also get a copy of Remote Desktop Connection that works on previous versions of Windows as well. To install Remote Desktop Connection on an earlier version of Windows, run the SETUP.EXE program on the CD and follow the Perform Additional Tasks link, then click the Set Up Remote Desktop Connection link.

Using Remote Desktop Connection

This section discusses what Remote Desktop Connection is, what it does, and how to use it.

What Is Remote Desktop Connection For?

Remote Desktop Connection lets you connect via a dial-up connection, via a local area network connection, or across the Internet and take control of somebody's computer (or your own).

Remote Desktop Connection is designed to let you access and control one computer (say, your work computer) from another computer (say, your home computer or your laptop). It's great for catching up with the office when you're at home, or for grabbing the files that you forgot to load on your laptop before you dived into the taxi for the airport.

You can also use Remote Desktop Connection for other purposes, such as helping a friend or family member find their way out of a computing problem from a distance. It's not really designed for this, though, and you'd do better to use Windows XP's Remote Assistance feature, which is designed for precisely that. Similarly, Remote Desktop Connection is not good for collaboration, because only one user can be working with the computer at a time. For collaboration, visit the next chapter, which discusses the NetMeeting collaboration package.

Remote Desktop Connection Terminology and Basics

Remote Desktop Connection terminology is a little confusing. Here are the terms:

◆ The *home computer* is the computer on which you're working. The home computer needs to have Remote Desktop Connection installed. Remote Desktop Connection is installed by default in Windows XP Home.

◆ The *remote computer* is the computer that you're accessing from the home computer. The remote computer needs to have Remote Desktop installed. Remote Desktop is separate from Remote Desktop Connection and is included in Windows XP Professional and the (forthcoming, at this writing) versions of Windows XP Server. Remote Desktop is not included in Windows XP Home.

So the typical scenario is for the home computer to be running Windows XP Home and the remote computer to be running Windows XP Professional. You can also access one Windows XP Professional computer from another Windows XP Professional computer.

NOTE *You can access more than one remote computer at a time from the same home computer. Unless you have impressive bandwidth, though, this results in slow sessions.*

In order for you to be able to connect to another computer via Remote Desktop Connection, any active session (whether local or connected via another Remote Desktop Connection) on that computer needs to be disconnected. Both you and the other user receive warnings about this. If you choose to proceed, the remote computer displays the Welcome screen while your Remote Desktop Connection session is going on. There's no easy way for anyone looking at that computer to tell that you're remotely connected to it.

If a user comes back and starts using the remote computer while your Remote Desktop Connection session is going on, your session will be terminated.

In lay terms, Remote Desktop Connection works as follows:

◆ Keystrokes and mouse clicks are transmitted from the home computer to the remote computer via the display protocol. The remote computer registers these keystrokes and clicks as if they came from the keyboard attached to it.

◆ Programs run on the remote computer as usual. (Programs aren't run across the wire—that would be desperately slow.)

◆ Screen display information is passed to the home computer, again via the display protocol. This information appears on the display as if it came from the video adapter (only rather more slowly, and usually in a window).

Sound can be passed to the home computer as well, so that you can hear what's happening at the remote computer. Transferring sound like this enhances the impression of controlling the remote computer, but sound takes so much bandwidth that transferring it isn't a good idea on slow connections. The default Remote Desktop Connection setting is to transfer sound, but you may well want to switch it off.

Setting the Remote Computer to Accept Incoming Connections

The first step in getting Remote Desktop Connection to work is to set the remote computer to accept incoming connections. Remember that this is the computer that's remote from you and that's running Windows XP Professional (or Server).

To set your remote computer to accept incoming connections, take these steps:

1. Display the System Properties dialog box in whichever way you find easiest. For example, press Winkey+Break. Or click the Start button to display the Start menu, right-click the My Computer link, and choose Properties from the context menu.

2. Click the Remote tab. Windows displays the Remote page (shown in Figure 24.1).

3. To allow users to connect to your computer, select the Allow Users to Connect Remotely to This Computer check box.

4. To specify which users may connect via Remote Desktop Connection, click the Select Remote Users button. Windows displays the Remote Desktop Users dialog box (shown in Figure 24.2). The list box shows any users currently allowed to connect to the computer. Below the list box is a note indicating that you (identified by your username) already have access—as you should have.

5. Click the Add button. Windows displays the Select Users dialog box.

6. Select a user or group, and then click the OK button. Windows adds them to the list in the Remote Desktop Users dialog box.

FIGURE 24.1

On the Remote page of the System Properties dialog box for the remote computer, select the Allow Users to Connect Remotely to This Computer check box to tell your computer to accept incoming calls.

FIGURE 24.2

You can use the Remote Desktop Users dialog box to restrict Remote Desktop use to specified users.

7. Add further users or groups as necessary.

8. To remove a user or a group, select them in the list box and click the Remove button.

9. Click the OK button. Windows closes the Remote Desktop Users dialog box.

10. Click the OK button in the System Properties dialog box. Windows closes the dialog box and applies your changes.

The remote computer is all set. Leave it up and running and return to the home computer.

NOTE *There's one other thing that you might need to do on the remote computer—but it's something that you'll almost certainly have done already: Apply a password to any user account that will be used to access the computer via Remote Desktop Connection. (See "Requiring a Password for an Account" in Chapter 9 for details of how to apply a password to an account.)*

Choosing Settings for Remote Desktop Connection

Next, choose settings for Remote Desktop Connection on the home computer. Remote Desktop Connection has a modestly large number of settings, but many of them are set-and-forget. Even better, you can save sets of settings so that you can quickly apply them for accessing different remote computers (or the same remote computer under different circumstances, such as when the cable modem is working and when it's flaked out on you).

To choose settings for Remote Desktop Connection, follow these steps:

1. Choose Start ➤ All Programs ➤ Accessories ➤ Communications ➤ Remote Desktop Connection. Windows starts Remote Desktop Connection and displays the Remote Desktop Connection window in its reduced state (shown in Figure 24.3).

FIGURE 24.3

The Remote Desktop Connection window appears first in its reduced state.

2. Click the Options button. Windows displays the rest of the Remote Desktop Connection window.

3. The General page of the Remote Desktop Connection window (shown in Figure 24.4) offers these options:

   Computer drop-down list   Enter the name or the IP address of the computer to which you want to connect; or select it from the drop-down list; or click the Browse for More item from the drop-down list to display the Browse for Computers dialog box, then select the computer in that.

   User Name text box   Enter the username under which you want to connect to the remote computer. Windows enters your username by default.

   Password text box   If you want to store your password (for the remote computer) for the connection, enter it in this text box and select the Save My Password check box. If you don't enter your password here, you get to enter it when logging on to the remote computer.

   Domain text box   If the remote computer is part of a domain, enter the domain name here. If the computer is part of a workgroup, you can leave this text box blank.

   Save My Password check box   Select this check box if you want to save your password with the rest of the Remote Desktop Connection information. This can save you time and effort, but it compromises your security a bit.

   Connection Settings group box   Once you've chosen settings for a connection, you can save the connection information by clicking the Save As button and specifying a name for the connection in the Save As dialog box that Windows displays. Remote Desktop Connection connections are saved as files of the file type Remote Desktop File, which by default is linked to the RDP extension, in the \My Documents\Remote Desktops\ folder. You can open saved connections by clicking the Open button and using the resulting Open dialog box.

NOTE *You'll see a file named* DEFAULT.RDP *in the* \My Documents\Remote Desktops\ *folder. Windows automatically saves your latest Remote Desktop Connection configuration under this name when you click the Connect button. But by explicitly saving your settings under a name of your choice, you can easily maintain different configurations for different Remote Desktop Connection settings.*

FIGURE 24.4

The General page of the expanded Remote Desktop Connection window

4. The Display page of the Remote Desktop Connection window (shown in Figure 24.5) offers three display options:

Remote Desktop Size group box Drag the slider to specify the screen size you want to use for the remote Desktop. The default setting is Full Screen, but you may want to use a smaller size so that you can more easily access your Desktop on the home computer. When you display the remote Desktop full screen, it takes over the whole of the local Desktop, so that you can't see your local Desktop. (To get to your local Desktop, you use the connection bar, discussed in a moment or two.)

Colors group box In the drop-down list, select the color depth to use for the connection. Choose a low color depth (for example, 256 colors) if you're connecting over a low-speed connection. This choice will be overridden by the display setting on the remote computer if you ask for more colors than the remote computer is using.

Display the Connection Bar when in Full Screen Mode check box Leave this check box selected (as it is by default) if you want Windows to display the connection bar when the remote Desktop is displayed full screen. The connection bar provides Minimize, Restore/Maximize, and Close buttons for the remote Desktop. (When the remote Desktop is displayed in a window, that window has the control buttons, so the connection bar isn't necessary.)

FIGURE 24.5

Choose display settings on the Display page of the Remote Desktop Connection window.

5. The Local Resources page of the Remote Desktop Connection window (shown in Figure 24.6) offers the following options:

    Remote Computer Sound group box   In the drop-down list, specify what you want Windows to do with sounds that would normally be generated at the remote Desktop. The default setting is Bring to This Computer, which transfers the sounds to the home computer and plays them there. This setting helps sustain the illusion that you're working directly on the remote Desktop, but it's heavy on bandwidth, so don't use it over low-speed connections. Instead, choose the Do Not Play setting or the Leave at Remote Computer setting. The Leave at Remote Computer setting plays the sounds at the remote computer and is best reserved for occasions when you need to frighten somebody remotely or pretend to be in your office.

    Keyboard group box   In the drop-down list, specify how you want Windows to handle Windows key combinations that you press (for example, Alt+Tab or Ctrl+Alt+Delete). Select the On the Local Computer item, the On the Remote Computer item, or the In Full Screen Mode Only item (the default) as suits your needs.

    Local Devices group box   Select the Disk Drives check box, the Printers check box, and the Serial Ports check box if you want these devices on your home computer to be available from the remote computer. This means that you can save documents from the remote computer to local drives, print them on your local printer, or transfer them via devices attached to serial ports (for example, a PDA). Local disk drives appear in the Other category in Explorer windows, named *Driveletter on COMPUTERNAME*. Local printers appear with *from COMPUTERNAME* in parentheses after them.

FIGURE 24.6

On the Local Resources page of the Remote Desktop Connection window, specify how Windows should handle sound, keyboard shortcuts, and devices on the home computer.

6. The Programs page of the Remote Desktop Connection window (shown in Figure 24.7) lets you specify that Windows run a designated program when you connect via Remote Desktop Connection. Select the Start the Following Program on Connection check box, then enter the program path and name in the Program Path and File Name text box. If you need to specify the folder in which the program should start, enter that in the Start in the Following Folder text box.

FIGURE 24.7

If you need to have a program run on the remote Desktop when you connect, specify it on the Programs page of the Remote Desktop Connection window.

7. The Experience page of the Remote Desktop Connection window (shown in Figure 24.8) contains the following options:

Choose Your Connection Speed to Optimize Performance drop-down list In this drop-down list, select one of the four listed speeds to apply a preselected set of settings to the five check boxes on this page. The choices in the drop-down list are Modem (28.8Kbps), Modem (56Kbps), Broadband (128Kbps–1.5Mbps), LAN (10Mbps or Higher), and Custom.

Desktop Background check box This check box controls whether Remote Desktop Connection transmits the Desktop background. Because Desktop backgrounds are graphical, transmitting them is sensible only at LAN speeds. (If you clear this check box, Remote Desktop Connection uses a blank Desktop background.)

Show Contents of Window while Dragging check box This check box controls whether Remote Desktop Connection transmits the contents of a window while you're dragging it, or only the window frame. Don't use this option over a modem connection, because the performance penalty outweighs any benefit you may derive from it.

Menu and Window Animation check box This check box controls whether Remote Desktop Connection transmits menu and window animations (for example, zooming a window you're maximizing or minimizing). Don't use this option over a modem connection—it's a waste of bandwidth.

Themes check box This check box controls whether Remote Desktop Connection transmits theme information or uses "classic" Windows–style windows and controls. Transmitting theme information takes a little bandwidth, so you can improve performance over a very slow connection by clearing the Themes check box. But bear in mind that Windows will look different enough to unsettle some inexperienced users.

Bitmap Caching check box This check box controls whether Remote Desktop Connection uses bitmap caching to improve performance by reducing the amount of data that needs to be sent across the network in order to display the screen remotely. Caching could prove a security threat, so you *might* want to turn it off for security reasons. But in most cases, you're better off using it.

8. If you want to save the settings you've chosen under a particular name so that you can reload them at will, click the Save As button on the General page of the Remote Desktop Connection window.

Connecting via Remote Desktop Connection

Once you've chosen settings as outlined in the previous section, you're ready to connect. If you're connecting via the Internet (rather than a local network) and you have a dial-up connection, make sure it's up and running.

Click the Connect button in the Remote Desktop Connection window. Windows attempts to establish a connection to the computer you specified.

FIGURE 24.8

On the Experience page of the Remote Desktop Connection window, you can customize which graphical information Remote Desktop Connection transmits in order to balance performance against looks.

If Windows is able to connect to the computer, and you didn't specify your username or password in the Remote Desktop Connection window, it displays the Log On to Windows dialog box (shown in Figure 24.9). Enter your username and password and click the OK button to log in. Windows then displays the remote Desktop. (If you chose to provide your password on the General page of the Remote Desktop Connection window, you shouldn't need to enter it again.)

FIGURE 24.9

Windows displays the Log On to Windows dialog box for the remote computer.

If you left a user session active on the computer, Remote Desktop Connection drops you straight into it—likewise if you left a user session disconnected and no other user session is active. But if another user *is* active on the remote computer when you submit a successful logon and password, Windows displays the Logon Message dialog box shown in Figure 24.10 to warn you that logging on will disconnect the user's session. Click the Yes button if you want to proceed. Click the No button to withdraw stealthily.

If you click the Yes button, the active user gets a Request for Connection dialog box such as that shown in Figure 24.11, which tells them that you (it specifies your name) are trying to connect to the computer, warns them that they'll be disconnected if you do connect, and asks if they want to allow the connection.

FIGURE 24.10

Windows displays the Logon Message dialog box when you're about to bump a user off the remote computer by logging on.

FIGURE 24.11

Windows displays the Request for Connection dialog box to tell the active user of your incoming session.

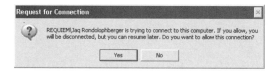

The active user then gets to click the Yes button or the No button as appropriate to their needs and inclinations. If Windows doesn't get an answer within 30 seconds or so, it figures they're not there, disconnects their session, and lets you in.

If the active user clicks the Yes button in the Request for Connection dialog box, Windows logs them off immediately and logs you on. But if the active user clicks the No button, you get a Logon Message dialog box such as that shown in Figure 24.12 telling you that they didn't allow you to connect. Windows displays this Logon Message dialog box for a few seconds, and then closes it automatically, returning you to the Remote Desktop Connection window.

If Windows is unable to establish the connection with the remote computer, it displays one of its Remote Desktop Disconnected dialog boxes to make you aware of the problem. Figure 24.13 shows two examples of the Remote Desktop Disconnected dialog box.

The first example of the Remote Desktop Disconnected dialog box tells you that the client couldn't connect to the remote computer and suggests that you try again later. The second example tells you that the remote computer couldn't be found and suggests checking that the computer name or IP address are correct. This should indeed be your first move—but if that doesn't work, that's about all you can do. If the remote computer has been shut down (or has crashed); or if its network or Internet connection has gone south; or if someone has reconfigured the computer not to accept Remote Desktop Connection connections, or has revoked your permission to connect—if any of these has happened, you're straight out of luck, and no amount of retyping the computer name or IP address will make an iota of difference.

FIGURE 24.12

Windows displays this Logon Message dialog box when the active user decides not to let you interrupt their session on the computer.

FIGURE 24.13

If Windows is unable to connect, you'll see a Remote Desktop Disconnected dialog box.

Working via Remote Desktop Connection

Once you've reached the remote Desktop, you can work more or less as if you were sitting at the computer. The few differences worth mentioning are discussed briefly in this section.

USING CUT, COPY, AND PASTE BETWEEN THE LOCAL AND REMOTE COMPUTERS

You can use Cut, Copy, and Paste commands to transfer information between the local computer and the remote computer. For example, you could copy some text from a program on the local computer and paste it into a program on the remote computer.

COPYING FROM REMOTE DRIVES TO LOCAL DRIVES

You can copy from remote drives to local drives by working in Explorer. The drives on your local computer appear in Explorer windows on the remote computer marked as *Driveletter on COMPUTER-NAME*. The drives on the remote computer appear as regular drives. You can copy and move files from one drive to another as you would with local drives.

PRINTING TO A LOCAL PRINTER

You can print to a local printer from the remote Desktop by selecting the local printer in the Print dialog box just as you would any other printer.

Printer settings are communicated to the remote Desktop when you access it. If you add a local printer during the remote session, the remote Desktop won't be able to see it. To make the printer show up on the remote Desktop, log off the remote session and log back on.

Returning to Your Local Desktop

If you chose to display the connection bar, it hovers briefly at the top of the screen, then slides upward to vanish like a docked toolbar with its Auto-Hide property enabled. To pin the connection bar in position, click the pin icon at its left end. (To unpin it, click the pin icon again.) To display the connection bar when it has hidden itself, move the mouse pointer to the top edge of the screen, just as you would do to display a docked toolbar hidden there.

The connection bar provides a Minimize button, a Restore/Maximize button, and a Close button. Use the Minimize button and the Restore button to reduce the remote Desktop from full screen to an icon or a partial screen so that you can access your local Desktop. Maximize the remote Desktop window to return to full-screen mode when you want to work with it again. Use the Close button as discussed in the next section to disconnect your remote session.

Disconnecting the Remote Session

You can disconnect the remote session in either of the two following ways:

◆ On the remote Desktop, choose Start ➤ Disconnect. Windows displays the Disconnect Windows dialog box (shown in Figure 24.14). Click the Disconnect button.

FIGURE 24.14

You can disconnect the remote session by issuing a Start ➤ Disconnect command and clicking the Disconnect button in the Disconnect Windows dialog box.

◆ Click the Close button on the connection bar (if the remote Desktop is displayed full screen) or on the Remote Desktop window (if the remote Desktop is not displayed full screen). Windows displays the Disconnect Windows Session dialog box (shown in Figure 24.15). Click the OK button.

FIGURE 24.15

The Disconnect Windows Session dialog box appears when you click the Close button on the connection bar. Click the OK button to end your remote session while leaving the programs running.

Windows disconnects the remote session but leaves the programs running for the time being. You can then log on again and pick up where you left off.

Logging Off the Remote Session

To log off and end your user session, click the Start button on the remote Desktop and choose Log Off from the Start menu. Windows displays the Log Off Windows dialog box (shown in Figure 24.16). Click the Log Off button.

FIGURE 24.16

To log off from the remote computer, choose Start ➤ Log Off and click the Log Off button in the Log Off Windows dialog box.

When someone else bumps you off the remote Desktop (by logging on locally or remotely), Windows displays the Remote Desktop Disconnected dialog box shown in Figure 24.17, telling you that the remote session "was ended by means of an administration tool."

FIGURE 24.17

This Remote Desktop Disconnected dialog box appears when you log off and when someone logs you off the remote computer.

If the network connection between the home computer and the remote computer is broken, the home computer displays a Remote Desktop Disconnected dialog box such as that shown in Figure 24.18.

FIGURE 24.18

This Remote Desktop Disconnected dialog box indicates that the network connection between the home computer and the remote computer was broken.

Using Remote Assistance

Remote Desktop Connection is great for accessing your Desktop from a distance. But what if you need someone to access your home computer remotely in order to help you fix a problem?

Remote Assistance lets you permit a designated helper to connect to your computer, see what's going on, and help you out of trouble. The helper—a friend or an administrator; whomever you choose—can control the computer directly if you give them permission, or you can simply chat with them and apply yourself such of their advice as you deem fit.

To use Remote Assistance, both your computer and your helper's must be running Windows XP. You send an invitation via e-mail or via Windows Messenger, or save it as a file (for example, to a network location designated for Remote Assistance request files, or on a floppy or CD that you then pop in the snail mail). When your helper responds, you decide whether to accept their help.

Each of the three methods of requesting Remote Assistance has its advantages and disadvantages. An e-mail invitation lets you include details of the Windows problem with which you need help—but you don't know when the recipient will check their e-mail. A Messenger invitation will be received immediately (because you can't send an invitation to someone who isn't online), but you can't include details of the problem. A file invitation, like an e-mail invitation, lets you include details of the problem, but you have no idea of when you'll receive a response to it (if ever).

On the other end of the wire, you can offer help via Remote Assistance. All you need is for someone to send you an invitation.

Security Considerations

Like all remote-control technologies, Remote Assistance has serious security implications that you need to consider before using it.

If you give another person control of your computer, they can take actions almost as freely as if they were seated in front of the computer. You can watch these actions, and you can take back control of the computer at any time, but you may already be too late: It takes less than a second to delete a key file, and little longer to plant a virus or other form of malware.

Even if you *don't* give your helper control, and simply chat, keep your wits about you when deciding which of their suggestions to implement. Malicious or ill-informed suggestions can do plenty of damage if you apply them without thinking. Never take any actions that could compromise your security or destroy your data. Above all, treat any incoming files with the greatest of suspicion and virus-check them using an up-to-date anti-virus program before using them.

One particular problem is that you can't tell that the person at the other computer is who they claim to be. For this reason alone, always protect your Remote Assistance connections with a strong password known only to the person from whom you're requesting help. That way, if someone else is at their computer or has identity-jacked them, they won't be able to respond to the Remote Assistance invitation you send.

Enabling Remote Assistance

Remote Assistance is enabled by default. To find out if Remote Assistance is enabled on your computer, take the following steps:

1. Display the System Properties dialog box (for example, by pressing Winkey+Break or clicking the System link on the Performance and Maintenance screen of Control Panel).

2. Click the Remote tab. Windows displays the Remote page (shown in Figure 24.19).

3. Check the status of the Allow Remote Assistance Invitations to Be Sent from This Computer check box. If this check box isn't selected, select it.

4. Click the OK button. Windows closes the System Properties dialog box.

FIGURE 24.19

You can turn Remote Assistance on and off on the Remote page of the System Properties dialog box.

Setting Limits for Remote Assistance

To set limits for Remote Assistance, take the following steps:

1. Click the Advanced button in the Remote Assistance group box on the Remote page of the System Properties dialog box. Windows displays the Remote Assistance Settings dialog box (shown in Figure 24.20).

FIGURE 24.20

Set limits for Remote Assistance in the Remote Assistance Settings dialog box.

2. In the Remote Control group box, clear the Allow This Computer to Be Controlled Remotely check box if you don't want your helpers to be able to control the computer. (This check box is selected by default.) Even when this check box is selected, you need to approve each request for control of the PC manually.

3. In the Invitations group box, use the two drop-down lists to specify an expiration limit for Remote Assistance invitations that your computer sends out. The default setting is 30 days; you might want to shorten this period considerably for security.

4. Click the OK button. Windows closes the Remote Assistance Settings dialog box, returning you to the System Properties dialog box.

5. Click the OK button. Windows closes the System Properties dialog box. You're now ready to start sending out invitations for Remote Assistance.

Sending a Remote Assistance Invitation via E-mail

To send a Remote Assistance invitation as an e-mail message via your existing e-mail account, follow these steps:

1. Choose Start ➢ All Programs ➢ Remote Assistance. Windows opens a Help and Support Center window to the Remote Assistance topic.

2. Click the Invite Someone to Help You link. Help and Support Center displays the Remote Assistance—Pick How You Want to Contact Your Assistant screen (shown in Figure 24.21).

3. In the Or Use E-mail area, enter your putative assistant's e-mail address in the Type an E-mail Address text box. Either type in the address or click the Address Book button and use Address Book to specify the address.

4. Click the Invite This Person link. Help and Support Center displays the Provide Contact Information screen (shown in Figure 24.22).

FIGURE 24.21

On the Remote Assistance—Pick How You Want to Contact Your Assistant screen of Help and Support Center, specify which type of Remote Assistance invitation to send.

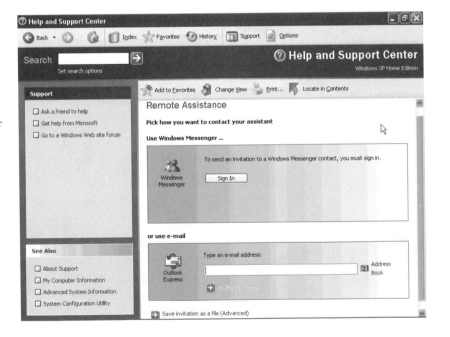

FIGURE 24.22

On the Provide Contact Information screen of Remote Assistance, check your name and enter a message detailing the problem you're having.

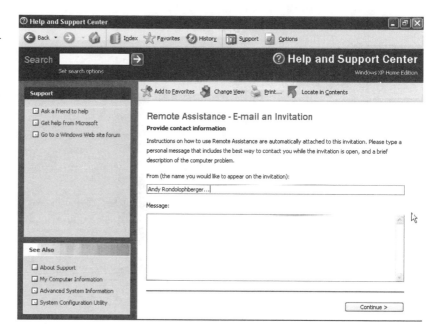

5. Change the name in the From text box if you want.

6. In the Message text box, enter a description of the problem and any blandishments necessary to get the help you want.

7. Click the Continue button. Help and Support Center displays the Set the Invitation to Expire screen (shown in Figure 24.23).

8. In the Set the Invitation to Expire area, specify the time limit for the recipient to accept the invitation. Choose a number in the first drop-down list and a time period—Minutes, Hours, or Days—in the second drop-down list.

9. To set a password, make sure the Require the Recipient to Use a Password check box is selected, then enter the password in the Type Password text box and the Confirm Password text box.

10. Click the Send Invitation button. Help and Support Center creates a file named `rcBuddy.MsRcIncident` containing the invitation and sends it via your default e-mail client with a message explaining how to use it. Help and Support Center then displays a screen telling you that the invitation has been sent successfully.

   ◆ If Help and Support Center can't send the file—for example, if your ISP's mail server is down—it invites you to save the file and send it manually.

   ◆ If you've set Outlook Express to warn you if other programs attempt to send mail in your name, Outlook Express will display an Outlook Express dialog box such as that shown in Figure 24.24, warning you that a program (Help and Support Center) is trying to send a message. Click the Send button.

FIGURE 24.23

On the Set the Invitation to Expire screen of Remote Assistance, set the expiration period for the invitation and enter a password.

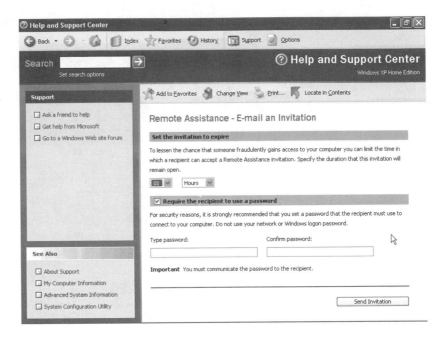

FIGURE 24.24

Outlook Express may warn you that Help and Support Center is trying to send a message on your behalf.

Sending an Invitation via Windows Messenger

To send an invitation via your existing Messenger account, follow these steps:

1. Start Messenger as usual, or activate it from the notification area.

2. Choose Tools ➣ Ask for Remote Assistance and choose either a contact name or the Other item from the submenu.

   ◆ If you choose Other, Messenger displays the Send an Invitation dialog box. Enter the person's e-mail address in the text box and click the OK button.

   ◆ You can also send an invitation to an existing contact by right-clicking them in the Online list and choosing Ask for Remote Assistance from the context menu.

3. Messenger opens an Instant Message window with the specified user and displays a note saying that you've invited the user to start Remote Assistance.

◆ To cancel the invitation, click the Cancel link in the Instant Message window, or press Alt+Q.

4. Wait for a response, then proceed as described in "Receiving Remote Assistance," later in this chapter.

Saving an Invitation As a File

Saving an invitation as a file works in essentially the same way as sending an invitation as an e-mail message, except that instead of specifying an e-mail address, you click the Save Invitation As a File link, create the invitation, and then specify a filename and location in the Save File dialog box. For example, your company might designate a network folder as a drop-box for Remote Assistance requests. Administrators would then examine the contents of the folder and respond to the requests accordingly. Alternatively, you could save the file to a floppy disk or other mobile medium and mail it to a helper.

Viewing the Status of Your Invitations

To view the status of the Remote Assistance invitations you've sent (or saved), display the Remote Assistance screen in Help and Support Center.

Click the View Invitation Status link. Windows displays the Remote Assistance—View or Change Your Invitation screen. Figure 24.25 shows an example.

FIGURE 24.25

On the View or Change Your Invitation screen, you can view the Remote Assistance invitations you've sent, "expire" them, resend them, or delete them.

From here, you can view the details of an invitation by clicking the Details button, kill off an open invitation by clicking the Expire button, resend an invitation by clicking the Resend button, or delete an invitation by clicking the Delete button.

Receiving Remote Assistance

The following sections describe what happens when you receive a response to your Remote Assistance request.

E-MAIL INVITATION

When a helper responds to an e-mail invitation, Windows displays a Remote Assistance dialog box such as that shown in Figure 24.26, telling you that the person has accepted the invitation and asking if you want to let them view your screen and chat with you. Click the Yes button to start the Remote Assistance session.

FIGURE 24.26

You'll see this Remote Assistance dialog box when your helper has accepted your e-mail invitation and is ready to get down to business.

NOTE *If you don't take any action for a few minutes, Windows assumes you're not in the market for Remote Assistance and times out the connection.*

WINDOWS MESSENGER INVITATION

When an invitee responds to a Messenger request for Remote Assistance, Windows displays a Remote Assistance window such as that shown in Figure 24.27.

FIGURE 24.27

You'll see a Remote Assistance window such as this when an invitee responds to a Messenger request for Remote Assistance.

FILE INVITATION

When a helper responds to a Remote Assistance request saved in a file, Windows displays a Remote Assistance window telling you that the person has accepted the invitation and asking if you want to let them view your screen and chat with you. Click the Yes button to start the Remote Assistance session.

RECEIVING ASSISTANCE

Once the Remote Assistance session is established, Remote Assistance displays the Remote Assistance window shown in Figure 24.28, which provides a chat pane and control buttons.

FIGURE 24.28

During a Remote Assistance session, this Remote Assistance window provides a chat pane and control buttons.

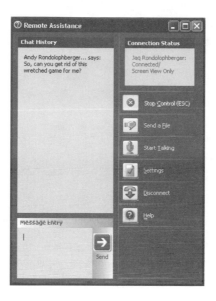

Chatting with Your Helper

You can chat both via text and by using voice (if both computers are set up for audio):

◆ Type a message in the Message Entry text box and press the Enter key or click the Send button to send it.

◆ To start voice transmission, click the Start Talking button. Your helper then sees a dialog box asking if they want to use a voice connection. If they click the Yes button, Remote Assistance establishes the voice connection. Talk as usual, and then click the Stop Talking button when you want to stop using the voice connection.

NOTE   *The first time you use the talk feature, Remote Assistance runs the Audio and Video Tuning Wizard if you haven't run it before.*

◆ To choose voice settings, click the Settings button. Windows displays a Remote Assistance Settings dialog box. Choose the Standard Quality option button or the High Quality option button as appropriate. Alternatively, click the Audio Tuning Wizard button (if it's available) to run the Audio and Video Tuning Wizard to optimize your speaker and microphone settings. Close the Remote Assistance Settings dialog box when you've finished.

Giving Your Helper Control of Your Computer

If your helper requests control of your computer, Windows displays the Remote Assistance dialog box shown in Figure 24.29. Click the Yes button or the No button as appropriate.

You can regain control by pressing the Esc key, by pressing Alt+C, or by clicking the Stop Control button.

FIGURE 24.29

When your helper requests control of the computer, decide whether you trust them.

Disconnecting Your Helper

To disconnect your helper, click the Disconnect button. Remote Assistance closes the connection and restores your Desktop to its full complement of colors (if you chose to optimize performance for your helper).

When your helper disconnects themselves, Windows displays a Remote Assistance dialog box telling you so. Click the OK button to close this dialog box, then close the Help and Support Center window.

Responding to a Remote Assistance Invitation

This section discusses how to respond to a Remote Assistance invitation that someone sends you. As you'd expect, the specifics vary depending on whether it's an e-mail invitation, a Messenger invitation, or a file invitation.

E-MAIL INVITATION

When someone sends you a Remote Assistance invitation via e-mail, you receive an e-mail message with the Subject line "YOU HAVE RECEIVED A REMOTE ASSISTANCE INVITATION FROM *USERNAME*." The message comes with explanatory text augmenting whatever message text the requester entered, and an attached file with a name such as rcBuddy.MsRcIncident.

Open the file by double-clicking it. Alternatively, in Outlook Express, click the Attachment icon, select the file from the drop-down menu, select the Open It button in the Open Attachment Warning dialog box, and click the OK button. Windows displays a Help and Support Center window such as that shown in Figure 24.30, giving the details of the Remote Assistance invitation: who it's from, and when it expires.

FIGURE 24.30

Double-click the file you receive to open the Remote Assistance invitation.

Enter the password (if the window is displaying a Password text box) and click the Yes button to start the help session. Windows tries to contact the remote computer.

WINDOWS MESSENGER INVITATION

When someone sends you a Remote Assistance invitation via Messenger, you see a Conversation window such as that shown in Figure 24.31. Click the Accept link (or press Alt+T) to accept it or click the Decline link (or press Alt+D) to decline it.

FIGURE 24.31

Receiving a Remote Assistance invitation in Messenger

If the user chose to specify a password, you'll need to enter it in a Help and Support Center window after the user accepts the incoming Remote Assistance connection.

FILE INVITATION

If you find a file invitation waiting for you, or receive one on a physical medium, double-click the file to open it. The rest of the procedure is the same as for an e-mail invitation, discussed in the section before last.

PROVIDING REMOTE ASSISTANCE

If Windows is able to contact the remote computer, and if the user accepts the Remote Assistance connection, Windows displays the Remote Assistance window (shown in Figure 24.32). As you can see, this features a chat pane, a view pane that shows the user's Desktop, and assorted command buttons.

Chatting with the User

To chat with the user via text, click the Show Chat button to display the chat pane if it's not currently displayed. Type a message in the Message Entry text box and press the Enter key or click the Send button to send it.

To hide the chat pane so that you can see more of the remote screen, click the Hide button.

FIGURE 24.32

When you're supplying the assistance in a Remote Assistance session, you can view the screen and chat with the user.

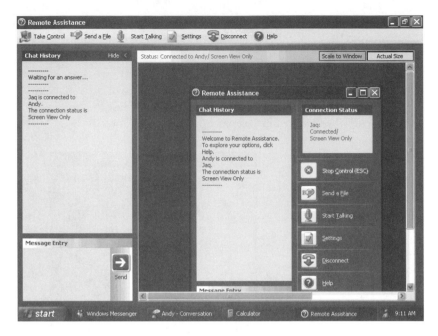

To chat via voice, click the Start Talking button. Remote Assistance displays a dialog box asking the person at the other end whether they want to use voice. If they click the Yes button, Remote Assistance activates the audio hardware. Click the Stop Talking button to stop using voice to chat.

Scaling the Display

You can scale the remote display to fit the area available on your screen by clicking the Scale to Window button, and restore it to its actual size by clicking the Actual Size button. Depending on the resolution you and the remote user have set, scaling the display may make the fonts illegible, but viewing the whole screen at once may make it easier for you to see what's happening on the computer than being able to see only a partial screen and having to scroll to see its outer reaches.

Taking Control of the Remote Computer

To request control of the remote computer, click the Take Control button. Windows displays a Remote Assistance dialog box on the remote screen asking the user if they want to give you control. If they click the Yes button, you get a Remote Assistance dialog box telling you so. When you dismiss this dialog box, you have control of the computer and can take any action with it as if you were working directly on it. To release control, click the Release Control button or press the Esc key.

WARNING *Avoid pressing the Esc key when taking keyboard actions on the remote computer. Even combinations that use the Esc key will release control.*

Transferring Files to and from the Remote Computer

To transfer a file to the remote computer, click the Send a File button. Windows displays a Remote Assistance dialog box. Use the Browse button to locate the file, and then click the Send File button to send it. The remote user then gets to decide whether to keep the file and in which folder to save it. (If you have control of the computer, you can make these decisions.)

To transfer a file from the remote computer to your computer, have the user click the Send a File button in their Remote Assistance window. Alternatively, if you have control of the computer, you can do this yourself.

Disconnecting from the Remote Computer

To disconnect from the remote computer, click the Disconnect button. Then close the Remote Assistance window manually. Unless you expect you'll need to reconnect to the remote computer to help the user further during the time remaining before the Remote Assistance invitation expires, delete the invitation file before you forget.

If the person you're helping disconnects the connection, Windows displays a Remote Assistance dialog box telling you so.

Up Next

This chapter has discussed how to use Remote Desktop Connection to connect your computer to a remote computer running Windows XP Professional (or Server) and work on it as if you were sitting at it. It has also discussed how to use the Remote Assistance feature to request, receive, and provide assistance from a distance.

The next chapter continues the theme of remote control. It discusses how to use NetMeeting, the powerful remote-control and collaboration package that comes built into Windows but is hidden in the morass of Windows system files.

Chapter 25

Sharing and Conferencing with NetMeeting

THIS CHAPTER DISCUSSES NETMEETING, the collaboration, file-sharing, and videoconferencing package built into Windows. NetMeeting is great for sharing files, collaborating, and videoconferencing for two reasons: First, Windows is widely used, and NetMeeting comes with almost every version of Windows. And second, NetMeeting is powerful and effective—and it can be very secure.

This chapter covers the following topics:

◆ Configuring NetMeeting

◆ Making and receiving calls with NetMeeting

◆ Hosting a meeting with NetMeeting

◆ Sharing files via NetMeeting

◆ Chatting via NetMeeting

◆ Sharing programs via NetMeeting

What Can You Do with NetMeeting?

These are the basic things you can do with NetMeeting:

◆ Transfer files from one computer to another

◆ Chat with other users

◆ Share audio and video

◆ Share a program—or your entire Desktop—with another user

◆ Remotely control a program on another user's computer

◆ Remotely control another user's computer

◆ Remotely control your own computer (This is essentially the same as controlling another user's computer, but with slight security differences.)

◆ Share ideas via a whiteboard (Microsoft Paint)

EXPERT KNOWLEDGE: USING NETMEETING SECURELY

NetMeeting is a very powerful program with wide-ranging features. If you use these features correctly and carefully, NetMeeting can be highly secure and can deliver great benefits to your computing life. But if you use them casually or carelessly, as you can easily do if you don't understand how they work, you can compromise the security of your computer and the integrity of your documents—and lay yourself open to identity fraud in the process.

For security, *never* use NetMeeting's audio-conferencing and videoconferencing features, because audio and video prevent you from using NetMeeting's security features. Stick with data-only calls and require security for each call so that you can use certificates to make sure of the identity of each participant in your calls or meetings. Assign a different password to each meeting you set up and communicate it securely to each participant.

Even on secure calls, never use any of NetMeeting's features that give someone else control of your computer. These features can be lethal to your computer, even if the guilty party is only playing around rather than being actively bent on inflicting damage. (These features are useful for remote control of your own PC by yourself—provided you can trust yourself, of course.)

If you do seem to lose control of your computer, disconnect the network or Internet connection first, then power down your PC—if necessary, by switching it off rather than shutting down Windows. After restarting Windows (or your computer), run a comprehensive virus scan for anything unpleasant that the attacker may have installed to give them control of your PC.

NetMeeting's audio- and video-sharing features are of interest primarily to people who either are on the same local area network (or campus area network) or have enviably fast Internet connections. Over dial-up, ISDN, DSL, or cable connections, NetMeeting's audio-sharing features can be tolerably useful, like Internet telephony programs. Over anything but the most robust connection, video sharing (or videoconferencing) tends to be disappointing, unless you can muster enthusiasm for a small window and a single-digit frame rate.

NetMeeting lets you share audio or video with only one other user at a time, so neither is of any use if you're conferencing with multiple people. Chat, on the other hand, can be shared among pretty much any number of people since it is text based and takes up very little bandwidth.

A bigger problem is that while NetMeeting can encrypt data (including chat and whiteboarding), it cannot encrypt audio and video, so any call involving audio or video is insecure.

Setting Up and Configuring NetMeeting

NetMeeting is installed by default in a regular installation of Windows XP, but it's not set up and configured until the first time you run it. Neither does Windows XP advertise NetMeeting's presence: XP doesn't even give NetMeeting a shortcut on the Communications submenu of the Start menu.

On hearing that, you may feel you should begin by creating a shortcut for NetMeeting. But it does that itself if you give it half a chance, as you'll see in a moment.

TIP   Microsoft tends to update NetMeeting independently of releases of Windows. Because the various versions of Net-Meeting don't always entirely agree with each other, it's a good idea to make sure you're using the latest version of NetMeeting that's available. You'll find the number in the About Windows NetMeeting dialog box (Help ➢ About Windows NetMeeting). If you're using the Windows Update feature, Windows XP should offer to download new versions of NetMeeting automatically. If you're not using Windows Update, visit the Microsoft Web site (www.microsoft.com) and see if there's a later version available; if there is, download it and install it. Doing so will optimize your chances of being able to communicate with other people.

Setting Up NetMeeting

The first time you run NetMeeting, you need to set it up. (Each user needs to set NetMeeting up separately. It doesn't install for all users the way most programs do.) As usual, there's a Wizard to walk you through the process.

To set NetMeeting up, take the following steps:

1. Choose Start ➢ Run (or press Winkey+R). Windows displays the Run dialog box.

2. Type **conf** in the Open text box and click the OK button. NetMeeting starts its setup and configuration routine and displays an introductory NetMeeting dialog box extolling its wonders.

3. Click the Next button. NetMeeting displays the second NetMeeting dialog box (shown in Figure 25.1).

FIGURE 25.1

In the second Net-Meeting dialog box, enter such personal information as you want made public.

4. Enter whatever information you find appropriate in the First Name text box, the Last Name text box, and the E-mail Address text box. All three are required fields, but you can supply bogus information if you so choose—there's no check to make sure that, say, the e-mail address is valid. The Location text box and Comments text box aren't required, but you can fill them in if doing so amuses you or will provide information useful to others.

5. Click the Next button. NetMeeting displays the third NetMeeting dialog box (shown in Figure 25.2).

FIGURE 25.2

In the third Net-
Meeting dialog box,
specify whether you
want to log on to a
directory server
automatically.

6. If you want NetMeeting to log you on to a directory server when you start NetMeeting, leave the Log On to a Directory Server when NetMeeting Starts check box selected and choose the server in the Server Name drop-down list. If you don't want to log on automatically, clear the check box. (You can log on manually at any time that suits you.) If you don't want Net-Meeting to list your name in the directory when you log on (automatically or manually), select the Do Not List My Name in the Directory check box; otherwise, leave it cleared, as it is by default.

7. Click the Next button. NetMeeting displays the fourth NetMeeting dialog box (shown in Figure 25.3).

FIGURE 25.3

In the fourth Net-
Meeting dialog box,
specify your connec-
tion speed.

8. Select the option button that most closely matches your connection speed: 14400 bps Modem; 28800 bps or Faster Modem; Cable, xDSL or ISDN; or Local Area Network. This setting controls how NetMeeting tries to handle heavy data streams such as audio and video, so choose accurately.

9. Click the Next button. NetMeeting displays the fifth NetMeeting dialog box, which lets you specify where NetMeeting should place shortcuts.

10. Select or clear the check boxes to tell NetMeeting whether to put one of its shortcuts on your Desktop and/or on your Quick Launch toolbar. If you use the Quick Launch toolbar, that is

typically the most useful place to have the shortcut. You might also choose to let NetMeeting put a shortcut on the Desktop so that you can drag it to a convenient position on the Start menu. (This is quicker than creating a shortcut for NetMeeting manually.)

11. Click the Next button. NetMeeting displays the first Audio Tuning Wizard dialog box, which asks you to turn off all audio programs.

NOTE   *The Audio Tuning Wizard used by NetMeeting is a younger sibling of the Audio and Video Tuning Wizard discussed in "Running the Audio and Video Tuning Wizard" in Chapter 22. See that section for more details. NetMeeting runs the Audio Tuning Wizard even if you've already run the Audio and Video Tuning Wizard for Messenger or another program.*

12. If you're planning ever to use NetMeeting's audio features, close all sound-producing or audio-recording programs. If you have a microphone, make sure it's plugged in, not muted, and (if it has a switch) switched on.

13. Click the Next button. NetMeeting displays the second Audio Tuning Wizard dialog box.

NOTE   *If you have multiple sound cards in your computer, or if your webcam has a microphone in it, you'll see another Audio Tuning Wizard dialog box that lets you select which devices to use for recording and playback.*

14. Click the Test button. The Audio Tuning Wizard starts playing a sound sample. Adjust the volume as necessary to get the signal comfortably audible. Then click the Next button to display the third Audio Tuning Wizard dialog box.

15. Speak into your microphone for 20 to 30 seconds at normal volume. The Audio Tuning Wizard adjusts the Record Volume slider to an appropriate level.

16. Click the Next button. You should see the fourth Audio Tuning Wizard dialog box, telling you that all is well. (If you had a microphone problem, you'll see instead a dialog box telling you that instead. Fix the problem and try setting the microphone volume again.)

17. Click the Finish button. NetMeeting closes the Wizard and then starts itself.

NetMeeting is now adequately configured for basic use—but you'll do well to change some settings immediately, as discussed in the next section.

Configuring NetMeeting

As usual with Windows programs, most of NetMeeting's options appear in the Options dialog box. Choose Tools ➢ Options to display the Options dialog box and choose options as discussed in the following subsections.

GENERAL PAGE OPTIONS

These are the options on the General page of the Options dialog box (shown in Figure 25.4):

My Directory Information group box   Enter in the First Name text box and Last Name text box the name by which you want NetMeeting and other users to know you. In the E-mail Address text box, enter the e-mail address you want to appear. These fields will already be populated with the information you entered while setting up NetMeeting. As mentioned earlier, you don't have to enter anything in the Location text box and Comments text box, but feel free to do so if you want to.

Directory Settings group box   In the Directory drop-down list, choose the directory server you want to use. To prevent NetMeeting from listing you in the directory—for example, if you want to lurk on a public server—you can select the Do Not List My Name in the Directory check box. Select the Log On to a Directory Server when NetMeeting Starts check box if you want Net-Meeting to automatically log you on to a directory server when you start it.

Run NetMeeting in the Background when Windows Starts check box   Select this check box (which is cleared by default) if you want to start NetMeeting automatically with each session of Windows. This option is useful only if you use NetMeeting almost all the time.

Show the NetMeeting Icon on the Taskbar check box   Select this check box if you want to have a NetMeeting icon in your notification area (*not* on the Taskbar—the option is misnamed).

FIGURE 25.4

The General page of the Options dialog box

Network Bandwidth Dialog Box

If you need to check or change your bandwidth setting, click the Bandwidth Settings button on the General page of the Options dialog box to display the Network Bandwidth dialog box (shown in Figure 25.5). Choose the setting that most closely corresponds to the speed of your network connection, and then click the OK button.

FIGURE 25.5

Use the Network Bandwidth dialog box to check or change your bandwidth setting.

Advanced Calling Options Dialog Box

If you need to place your NetMeeting calls through a gatekeeper computer or through a gateway, click the Advanced Calling button on the General page of the Options dialog box to display the Advanced Calling Options dialog box (shown in Figure 25.6). You're unlikely to need to use these options unless you're using NetMeeting at work—in which case you should really be using Windows XP Professional, because it offers better security.

FIGURE 25.6

If your NetMeeting calls need to go through a gateway, choose the appropriate options in the Advanced Calling Options dialog box.

To choose the right security options, you need to understand the basics of NetMeeting security. By default, any NetMeeting call you place is not secure, which means that (in theory) it can be eavesdropped on by anyone determined enough. You may feel that you have no especial secrets from the world, but you probably wouldn't welcome eavesdroppers on any phone calls you make—perhaps more as a point of privacy than because of any useful information they might pick up. If you want privacy, NetMeeting's security features are easy enough to turn on.

NetMeeting offers some good security features:

◆ You can use passwords to restrict access to meetings. You should always use this feature so that you can keep out uninvited would-be participants. You specify the password when setting up the meeting.

◆ You can encrypt the data transferred during a meeting. If you're doing anything remotely sensitive, turn these features on.

◆ You can use authentication certificates to check the identity of callers. For business settings, this feature is great, because many business users have authentication certificates. But many home users of NetMeeting won't have authentication certificates and won't be willing to get them.

Unfortunately, NetMeeting's security is limited in that it cannot encrypt audio and video: If you want to videoconference or transmit audio, you need to place an insecure call. (This is why NetMeeting calls are not secure by default: NetMeeting is built to try to transmit audio and video until you prevent it from doing so.)

Anyway… to use a gateway, select the Use a Gatekeeper to Place Calls check box and enter the gatekeeper computer's IP address or name in the Gatekeeper text box. You can then select the Log On Using My Account Name check box or the Log On Using My Phone Number check box as appropriate, and enter the account name in the Account Name text box or the phone number in the Phone Number text box.

To use a gateway, select the Use a Gateway to Call Telephones and Videoconferencing Systems check box and enter the gateway's IP address or name in the Gateway text box.

SECURITY PAGE OPTIONS

The Security page of the Options dialog box (shown in Figure 25.7) offers choices that are important for keeping your NetMeeting meetings secure and private. But before you choose them, you need to know the basics of NetMeeting security. See the adjacent sidebar for a quick briefing.

FIGURE 25.7

Choose security options on the Security page of the Options dialog box.

These are the options on the Security page of the Options dialog box:

I Prefer to Receive Secure Incoming Calls. Accept Only Secure Calls when I'm Not in a Meeting check box   Select this check box if you want to receive only secure calls when you're not in a meeting. (When you are in a secure meeting, NetMeeting automatically rejects insecure incoming calls.)

I Prefer to Make Secure Outgoing Calls check box   Select this check box to use NetMeeting's security features for all your outgoing calls. (If you prefer, you can choose manually to make some calls secure and other calls not secure.) Remember that any call that includes audio or video is not secure.

Certificate group box   In this group box, choose the type of security you want to use. The default setting is the Use Privacy (Encryption) Only option button. Leave this option button selected if you want to use NetMeeting's security features to encrypt data but don't want to authenticate meeting participants. If you do want to use authentication, select the Use This Certificate for Privacy and Authentication option button. Then click the Change button to display the Select Certificate dialog box, choose the certificate to use, and click the OK button.

AUDIO PAGE OPTIONS

The Audio page of the Options dialog box (shown in Figure 25.8) contains the following options.

FIGURE 25.8

Choose audio options on the Audio page of the Options dialog box.

NOTE   *If your computer does not have a sound card, the Audio page does not appear in the Options dialog box.*

Enable Full-Duplex Audio so I Can Speak while Receiving Audio check box   Select this check box to enable full-duplex audio—input and output at the same time. The only problem here is if your sound card doesn't support full-duplex audio; in this case, this check box will be dimmed and unavailable. Most modern sound cards do support full-duplex audio. If yours doesn't, you'll need to upgrade if you want to use this feature

Enable Auto-Gain Control check box   Select this check box if you want NetMeeting to work with your sound card and audio driver to automatically adjust the microphone volume to a workable level. Provided your sound card supports auto-gain, it's a good idea to use it, because you'll then be able to vary your speaking volume and your distance from your microphone without becoming uncomfortably loud or inaudible. If your sound card doesn't support auto-gain, this check box will be dimmed and unavailable.

Automatically Adjust Microphone Volume while in a Call check box   This option picks up where the previous option leaves off: If your sound card doesn't support auto-gain, select this check box so that NetMeeting can adjust the microphone volume to keep you audible during a call. Even if your sound card does support auto-gain, there's no harm in keeping this check box selected, as it is by default.

Enable DirectSound for Improved Audio Performance check box   Select this check box if you want to use DirectSound to improve audio performance. If your system doesn't support Direct-Sound, this option will be dimmed and unavailable.

Silence Detection group box   Use the two option buttons and the slider in this group box to specify how you want silence detection to be adjusted. The default setting is to have the Adjust Silence Detection Automatically (Recommended) option button selected, which gives NetMeeting control over detecting when silence has broken out. If you find that NetMeeting's silence detection gives you unsatisfactory results, such as chopping off your voice when you're speaking softly, select the Let Me Adjust Silence Detection Myself option button and move the slider to an appropriate position.

In addition to the options described above, the Audio page of the Options dialog box has two command buttons: a Tuning Wizard button and an Advanced button. As you'd imagine, clicking the Tuning Wizard button runs the Audio Tuning Wizard, which you can use to help you adjust your audio and microphone levels.

Clicking the Advanced button displays the Advanced Compression Settings dialog box (shown in Figure 25.9), in which you can specify a codec (a coder/decoder) for compressing and decompressing the audio you transfer with NetMeeting. Usually you won't need to do this, because the standard codec does a good job for normal use. Select the Manually Configure Compression Settings check box (it's cleared by default) and select the appropriate codec in the Preferred Codec for Audio Compression drop-down list.

FIGURE 25.9

Use the Advanced Compression Settings dialog box if you need to configure your audio compression settings manually.

VIDEO PAGE OPTIONS

The Video page of the Options dialog box (shown in Figure 25.10) contains the options for video-conferencing. As mentioned earlier, NetMeeting supports video only on two-person meetings and only on insecure connections—so if you want to conference with multiple people at the same time, or if you want to use only secure connections, you'll probably want to turn these features off.

Anyway, these are the options open to you:

Automatically Send Video at the Start of Each Call check box   Select this check box if you want NetMeeting to send video at the start of every call. Unless you're heavy into videoconferencing, you won't want to select this check box. And if you don't have a video camera, this check box won't be available to you.

TIP   *If you choose not to send video automatically, you can start to send video at any time during a two-person, non-secure call by clicking the Start Video button.*

FIGURE 25.10

Choose videoconfer-encing options—or turn them all off—on the Video page of the Options dialog box.

Automatically Receive Video at the Start of Each Call check box   Select this check box if you want NetMeeting to automatically receive incoming video. Clear this check box if you have no interest in video or if your bandwidth is too meager to manage it.

Send Image Size group box   If you'll be sending video, specify the image size to send by selecting the Small option button, the Medium option button, or the Large option button. As you'd expect, unless you establish a very fast connection with the other participant in the meeting, you're trading off image size against frame rate: You can have postage stamp–sized video with a decent frame rate or more easily visible video with a lower and jerkier frame rate.

Video Quality group box   If you'll be receiving video, set the I Prefer to Receive slider to the balance between Faster Video and Better Quality that most pleases you. (Chances are, you'll need to experiment with this setting.)

Video Camera Properties group box   In this group box, you can select the video camera you want to use in the The Video Capture Device I Want to Use Is drop-down list and use the Source button and the Format button (if they're available) to configure it.

Show Mirror Image in Preview Video Window check box   Select this check box if you want NetMeeting to display a mirror image of the video you're sending in the preview window instead of displaying it the right way around.

Those are all the options that NetMeeting offers in the Options dialog box. Click the OK button. NetMeeting closes the Options dialog box and applies the settings you chose.

SETTING YOUR RECEIVED FILES FOLDER

Next, specify your *received files folder*—the folder in which NetMeeting places files other people send you. By default, NetMeeting uses a folder named `\Received Files\` under the `\Program Files\` folder. You'll probably want to use a folder in a handier location—for example, under your `\My Documents\` folder, where you can keep files away from other users of this computer.

To specify the received files folder, follow these steps:

1. From the main NetMeeting window, press Ctrl+F or choose Tools ➢ File Transfer. NetMeeting displays the File Transfer window.

2. Choose File ➢ Change Folder. NetMeeting displays the Browse for Folder dialog box.

3. Navigate to and select the folder you want to use.

4. Click the OK button. NetMeeting closes the Browse for Folder dialog box and records your choice.

Placing and Receiving Calls

Once you've got NetMeeting set up, you'll probably want to start making calls. Here's how to proceed.

Finding Out Who's Available

First, you'll need to find out who's available. One way of finding out who's available is to use a directory server. If you have a Hotmail account or a Passport account, you can use the Windows Messenger service (discussed in Chapter 22). Another way of finding out who's available is to use chat, e-mail, or even a conventional phone call. Chat is often the quickest method, and it has the added advantage that whoever you're communicating with can easily check their current IP address.

Placing a Call

NetMeeting gives you several ways to place a call. We'll start with the way that gives you most control over the call.

Follow these steps:

1. Choose Call ➢ New Call or press Ctrl+N from the main NetMeeting window. NetMeeting displays the Place a Call dialog box (shown in Figure 25.11).

FIGURE 25.11

The Place a Call dialog box gives you the most control over the call you're placing.

2. In the To text box, enter the designator of the person or computer you're calling. This can be an e-mail address (for example, jaq_rondolophberger@hotmail.com), an IP address (for example, 206.13.31.12), a telephone number, or a computer name.

   ◆ Once you've placed a few calls, you'll be able to choose previous recipients from the To drop-down list.

3. In the Using drop-down list, choose Automatic, Network, or Directory as appropriate. Automatic puts the onus on NetMeeting to decide whether to connect via the network or via a directory.

4. If you want to place a secure, data-only call, select the Require Security for This Call (Data Only) check box. You can't use this option for voice and video.

5. Click the Call button to place the call.

A quicker way of placing a call, but one that does not let you specify security (NetMeeting goes by your choice on the Security page of the Options dialog box) or choose between Automatic, Network, or Directory placement, is to enter the address in the Place Call text box of the NetMeeting window and press Enter or click the Place Call button. If you're calling someone you've called before, you'll be able to choose the address from the Place Call drop-down list instead.

While the phone is ringing at the other end, NetMeeting displays the NetMeeting dialog box shown in Figure 25.12.

FIGURE 25.12

NetMeeting displays this Net-Meeting dialog box while waiting for the other party to pick up.

If the other person accepts the call (or if they've set up NetMeeting to accept calls automatically, and it does so), their name and your name will appear in the Name list box, as in Figure 25.13. If you've chosen to send or receive audio or video at the beginning of a nonsecure call, that'll start happening too.

FIGURE 25.13

When the other party picks up the call, you see their name and yours listed in the Name list box.

If the person you're calling does not pick up your call, or if they reject it, NetMeeting displays the NetMeeting dialog box shown in Figure 25.14.

FIGURE 25.14

When the other party does not pick up or rejects your call, you'll see this NetMeeting dialog box.

You can then add further people to the call by calling them using the same procedure.

Keeping a SpeedDial List

Most people tire quickly of typing IP addresses and complex directory entries. To help out, Net-Meeting provides a SpeedDial feature that lets you build a list of the people you want to contact most frequently.

CREATING A SPEEDDIAL ENTRY

To create a SpeedDial entry:

1. Choose Call ➤ Create SpeedDial. NetMeeting displays the Create SpeedDial dialog box (shown in Figure 25.15).

FIGURE 25.15

Create SpeedDial entries for the people you contact most frequently.

2. In the Address text box, enter the address of the person or computer. This can be an IP address, the computer name, or a directory server listing (for example, ils.microsoft.com/ jaq_rondolophberger@hotmail.com).

3. In the Call Using drop-down list, select Directory for a SpeedDial entry that will connect through a directory or Network for a connection through a LAN or over the Internet.

4. In the After Creating the SpeedDial group box, specify where you want NetMeeting to store the new SpeedDial entry:

   ◆ Select the Add to SpeedDial List option button to have it stored in the SpeedDial list on your computer. This SpeedDial list is shared with other users of the computer.

◆ Select the Save on the Desktop option button to have NetMeeting create the SpeedDial entry on your Desktop, where you can keep it to yourself. Having SpeedDial entries on the Desktop also makes them easy to access quickly.

5. Click the OK button. NetMeeting closes the Create SpeedDial dialog box and creates the SpeedDial entry.

TIP By default, NetMeeting stores SpeedDial entries under names based on their addresses, which—whether directory entries, e-mail addresses, or IP addresses—are friendlier for computers than for humans. To make things easier, rename your SpeedDial entries by using conventional Windows renaming techniques. The SpeedDial entries on your Desktop should be easy to find; the ones stored in your SpeedDial list will be in the `\NetMeeting\SpeedDial` *folder, which should be in your* `\Program Files\` *superstructure.*

USING YOUR SPEEDDIAL LIST

SpeedDial entries that you've stored on your Desktop are easy to access: Display the Desktop, and there they should be.

To access the SpeedDial entries stored in your SpeedDial list, choose Call ➤ Directory or click the Find Someone in a Directory button (the button that shows a book icon). NetMeeting displays the Find Someone window. Choose SpeedDial in the Select a Directory drop-down list. NetMeeting displays the SpeedDial list. Figure 25.16 shows an example.

FIGURE 25.16

You can access your SpeedDial list from the Find Someone window.

Select the SpeedDial entry, select the Make This a Secure Call (Data Only) check box if appropriate, and then click the Call button. NetMeeting places the call.

Receiving a Call

Receiving a call is simplicity itself. When someone calls you, NetMeeting displays the NetMeeting – Incoming Call dialog box (shown in Figure 25.17).

FIGURE 25.17

The NetMeeting – Incoming Call dialog box alerts you to an incoming call.

If you want to accept the call, click the Accept button. (Otherwise, obviously enough, click the Ignore button. They won't know whether you've rejected the call or if you just weren't there to take it.)

If the caller is using NetMeeting's security features, the NetMeeting dialog box displays a Details button as well as the Accept button and Ignore button. Figure 25.18 shows an example.

FIGURE 25.18

When the incoming call is using security, a Details button appears on the NetMeeting dialog box.

EXPERT KNOWLEDGE: FINDING OUT YOUR IP ADDRESS

Directory servers work surprisingly well, but the easiest way to establish a connection with another computer is to use its IP address.

If you have a permanent connection to the Internet (for example, if you have a DSL), you probably have a fixed IP address. But if you connect via dial-up, your ISP probably assigns you a free IP address dynamically each time you connect. That means you'll need to find out your IP address before you try to get someone to call you via NetMeeting.

To find out your IP address, choose Help ➢ About Windows NetMeeting. NetMeeting displays the About Windows NetMeeting dialog box (shown below).

The IP Addresses line at the bottom of the About Windows NetMeeting dialog box shows all current IP addresses associated with your computer. In this case, the first IP address is one used by Microsoft applications for local audio and video. The second address is the external IP address of the dial-up adapter. The third address is the internal IP address of the network card. If your computer has multiple network cards or network connections, you will see more IP addresses here.

Click the Details button to expand the NetMeeting dialog box and see details of the certificate the caller is using with NetMeeting. Figure 25.19 shows an example of this.

FIGURE 25.19

Click the Details button to see details of the certificate the caller is using with NetMeeting.

If you want to keep NetMeeting running, but also want to make sure you don't receive any calls, choose Call ➤ Do Not Disturb from the main NetMeeting window. NetMeeting then suppresses any incoming calls. Choose Call ➤ Do Not Disturb again to return to the world of modern communications.

Hosting a Meeting on Your Computer

Placing and receiving calls is easy enough, but for more flexibility, you can host a meeting. Hosting a meeting lets you specify a password, require security, and restrict the actions that the participants can take.

To host a meeting, follow these steps:

1. Choose Call ➤ Host Meeting from the main NetMeeting window. NetMeeting displays the Host a Meeting dialog box (shown in Figure 25.20).

FIGURE 25.20

Use the Host a Meeting dialog box to set up the details of a meeting you plan to host.

2. Enter a name for the meeting in the Meeting Name text box. (You can accept the default name, Personal Conference, but you'll probably want something more descriptive so that those trying to get into the meeting know they're in the right place.)

3. Enter the password for the meeting in the Meeting Password text box. As usual, make the password good—more than six characters long, no recognizable word in any known language, and so on. Unless you establish a small and very secure group of regulars, create a new password for each meeting you host.

4. Choose restrictions for the meeting:

   ◆ Select the Require Security for This Meeting (Data Only) check box. The only reason for not using security is if you must use video or audio—which, you'll remember, are restricted to two participants only, so they're not much use in a group situation.

   ◆ Select the Only You Can Accept Incoming Calls check box if you want to prevent other people from joining the meeting by placing calls to the participants.

   ◆ Select the Only You Can Place Outgoing Calls check box if you want to prevent the participants in the meeting from letting other people into the meeting by calling them once they're connected to the meeting.

5. In the Meeting Tools area, select the check boxes for any of the NetMeeting tools that you want to control yourself. You'll probably want to allow anybody to start chat and file transfer, so leave the Chat check box and the File Transfer check box cleared. But if you want to prevent other people from starting, say, sharing and whiteboarding, select the Sharing check box and the Whiteboard check box.

6. Click the OK button. NetMeeting closes the Host a Meeting dialog box and starts the meeting.

When people join the meeting, you see the NetMeeting – Incoming Call dialog box as usual, and can choose to accept the call or ignore it as usual. If you chose to require security for the meeting, the Details button will appear on the NetMeeting – Incoming Call dialog box, and you will be able to view the information on the certificate the caller is using with NetMeeting.

To end the meeting, click the End Call button or choose Call ➤ Hang Up.

Joining a Meeting

To join a meeting, place a call as usual to the host. Usually, you'll do best to use the Place a Call dialog box so that you can specify a security setting other than your default if necessary.

When your computer has established a connection with the meeting host, NetMeeting displays the Enter Password dialog box (shown in Figure 25.21). Enter the password and click the OK button. If you enter the correct password, the meeting host will see the NetMeeting – Incoming Call dialog box and will be able to accept or ignore the call as usual.

FIGURE 25.21

To join a meeting, you need to supply its password.

If the host accepts the call, and if they've set restrictions on the actions the participants can take, you see the Meeting Properties dialog box, of which Figure 25.22 shows an example. In the figure, the meeting requires security, and the participants can neither accept incoming calls nor place outgoing calls, but all the tools (sharing, chat, whiteboard, and file transfer) are available. Click the OK button. NetMeeting closes the Meeting Properties dialog box.

FIGURE 25.22

The Meeting Properties dialog box shows you the restrictions on the meeting.

NetMeeting then appears as usual. If there are restrictions on the tools you can use, their buttons appear grayed out and disabled. If the call is secure, the words *In a secure call* and a padlock icon are displayed at the bottom of the window.

Using Remote Desktop Sharing to Access Your Own Computer

For those times when you're on the road and need to access your home (or office) computer, Net-Meeting provides a feature called Remote Desktop Sharing. Remote Desktop Sharing is essentially an automatically hosted meeting that will accept only a single connection. (If you want, you can use Remote Desktop Sharing to let someone else access your computer, but it's usually not a good idea; because Remote Desktop Sharing is designed to run without being monitored, you get no warning about incoming connections and no chance to decline them.)

NOTE   *Remote Desktop Sharing uses different technology from Remote Desktop Connection, Remote Desktop Web Connection, and Remote Assistance, but you can do some of the same things with it. (Chapter 24 discusses Remote Desktop Connection and Remote Assistance.)*

You can use Remote Desktop Sharing only when you're *not* running NetMeeting, so you don't need to worry about Remote Desktop Sharing starting when you're using NetMeeting. Depending on your needs, you can set Remote Desktop Sharing to start automatically when you exit NetMeeting or start it yourself manually only when appropriate. Most people find it best to configure Remote Desktop Sharing not to start automatically.

Configuring Remote Desktop Sharing

Before you can use Remote Desktop Sharing, you need to configure it. To do so, you use the Remote Desktop Sharing Wizard as follows:

1. Choose Tools ➢ Remote Desktop Sharing. NetMeeting starts the Remote Desktop Sharing Wizard. The Wizard's first dialog box explains what Remote Desktop Sharing is.

2. Click the Next button. The Wizard displays its second dialog box, which explains that you need to have Computer Administrator privileges to connect to this computer via NetMeeting.

3. Click the Next button. The Wizard displays the Remote Desktop Sharing dialog box shown in Figure 25.23, which suggests you enable a password-protected screen saver in order to protect your computer from the attentions of people who happen to be around when you're not. (You may have enabled a password-protected screen saver already; the Remote Desktop Sharing Wizard doesn't check before asking.)

FIGURE 25.23

It's best to enable a password-protected screen saver to protect your computer from people on site when you're remote.

WARNING   *Whether you use a screen saver or not, everything you do in your Remote Desktop Sharing session will be visible on your monitor—so turn your monitor off if anybody else will be able to see it. Use the screen saver password to prevent anybody else from taking control of your computer locally while you're away.*

4. Choose the Yes, Enable Password-Protected Screen Saver option button or the No, I Will Do This Later option button as appropriate. Then click the Next button. If you chose the Yes option button, the Wizard displays the Screen Saver page of the Display Properties dialog box so that you can choose and enable a screen saver. Click the OK button when you're done, and the Wizard displays the final Remote Desktop Sharing Wizard dialog box, to which it will have taken you directly if you chose the No option button. This dialog box tells you that you've finished setting up Remote Desktop Sharing.

5. Click the Finish button. The Remote Desktop Sharing Wizard closes itself.

Activating and Deactivating Remote Desktop Sharing

To activate Remote Desktop Sharing, choose Call ➢ Exit and Activate Remote Desktop Sharing from the main NetMeeting window. NetMeeting closes itself, places a NetMeeting Remote Desktop Sharing icon in the System Tray, and activates Remote Desktop Sharing.

To deactivate Remote Desktop Sharing, right-click the NetMeeting Remote Desktop Sharing icon in the System Tray and choose Turn Off Remote Desktop Sharing from the context menu.

Accessing Your Computer via Remote Desktop Sharing

To access your computer from another computer via Remote Desktop Sharing, take the following steps:

1. Choose Call ➤ New Call from the main NetMeeting window. NetMeeting displays the Place a Call dialog box.

2. Enter the name or IP address of the host computer in the To text box as usual.

3. In the Using drop-down list, select Automatic, Network, or Directory as appropriate.

4. Select the Require Security for This Call (Data Only) check box. *You must select this check box in order to make a connection to a computer that's running Remote Desktop Sharing*

5. Click the Call button. NetMeeting then places the call as usual.

6. When NetMeeting makes the connection, it displays the Remote Desktop Sharing Password dialog box (shown in Figure 25.24).

7. Enter your username in the User text box, then enter the password in the Password text box and click the OK button. If you get it right, NetMeeting displays the Meeting Properties dialog box (shown in Figure 25.25).

FIGURE 25.24

To make a connection via Remote Desktop Sharing, you need to enter a valid Computer Administrator account name and password for the remote computer.

FIGURE 25.25

NetMeeting displays the Meeting Properties dialog box to let you know the details of the Remote Desktop Sharing meeting you've joined.

8. Click the OK button. NetMeeting closes the Meeting Properties dialog box. You'll then be able to control the remote Desktop.

TIP Choose View ➢ Full Screen or press Alt+Enter to display the remote Desktop at full screen. To revert from full-screen mode to windowed mode, click the Restore button that NetMeeting displays when you enter full-screen mode.

When you end your Remote Desktop Sharing session (by clicking the End Call button or choosing Call ➢ Hang Up), NetMeeting activates the screen saver on the remote computer (assuming a screen saver is enabled).

Changing Your Remote Desktop Sharing Setup

To change your Remote Desktop Sharing setup after you've configured it using the Remote Desktop Sharing Wizard, choose Tools ➢ Remote Desktop Sharing from the main NetMeeting window. Net-Meeting displays the Remote Desktop Sharing Settings dialog box (shown in Figure 25.26). You can then clear the Enable Remote Desktop Sharing on This Computer check box to disable Remote Desktop Sharing or click the Wizard button to run the Remote Desktop Sharing Wizard again. Click the OK button when you've finished.

FIGURE 25.26

Use the Remote Desktop Sharing Settings dialog box to change your Remote Desktop Sharing settings once you've configured Remote Desktop Sharing.

Transferring Files

NetMeeting's file-transfer feature is a favorite of both home and business users. This section discusses how to use it to move files back and forth. Obviously enough, for either operation, you'll need to be connected to one or more other NetMeeting users, so establish a connection first if you're not currently connected.

Sending a File to Another User

To send a file to another user, take the following steps:

1. Click the Transfer Files button in the NetMeeting window. NetMeeting displays the File Transfer window (shown in Figure 25.27 with a file already added). Alternatively, press Ctrl+F or choose Tools ➢ File Transfer.

2. Line up the files you want to transfer. Click the Add Files button (the leftmost button on the toolbar). NetMeeting displays the Select Files to Send dialog box. Navigate to and select the files you want to send, and then click the Add button to add them to the File Transfer window. Repeat this process until you've arranged all the files you want to send. Use the Remove Files button to remove from the list any files that you add by accident.

FIGURE 25.27

Use the File Transfer window to get files from A to B.

Remove Files Button   Send All Button   Stop Sending Button   View Received Files Button   Select the Person You Want to Send Files Drop-Down List

Add Files Button

3. In the Select the Person You Want to Send Files drop-down list, choose the recipient of the files. The default selection is Everyone, which you'll probably want to change.

4. If you want to transfer all the files in the File Transfer window to the recipient, click the Send All button or choose File ➤ Send All. If you want to transfer just some of the files, select them in the File Transfer window and choose File ➤ Send a File.

5. NetMeeting starts to transfer the files one by one. As it does so, the Status column shows the file status: blank until an action is taking place, *Sending* while the file is being sent, *Sent* once the file has successfully been transferred, or *Canceled* if you or the recipient cancel the transfer. Figure 25.28 shows the File Transfer window with file transfer underway.

FIGURE 25.28

The Status column of the File Transfer window tells you how the file-transfer operation is proceeding.

If the recipient cancels the transfer of a file, you'll see the File Transfer message box shown in Figure 25.29 telling you so. NetMeeting then cancels any pending file transfers.

FIGURE 25.29

You'll see this File Transfer message box if the recipient cancels an incoming transfer.

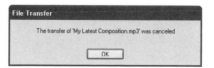

NOTE *To prevent you from wasting time by transferring multiple copies of the same file, NetMeeting lets you send each file listed in the File Transfer window only once. To send a file again (for example, if the transfer fails, or if you have to cancel it), remove the file from the File Transfer window, then add it again.*

Receiving a File from Another User

When another user sends you a file, NetMeeting displays a window such as the one shown in Figure 25.30. The title bar of the window bears the name of the file or as much of it as will fit.

FIGURE 25.30

NetMeeting displays a separate window for each incoming file.

While the file is being transferred, the window offers you an Accept button and a Delete button, together with a dimmed and unavailable Open button. You can click the Accept button to dismiss the window, or simply let it ride until the transfer is complete or you want to deal with it. Because this is a window rather than a dialog box, its presence on-screen does not block any subsequent file transfers; instead, their file-transfer windows will stack up on top of this one, so you can deal with each in turn.

If you don't want to receive the file, click the Delete button. NetMeeting disposes of however much of the file you've received, cancels any subsequent transfers, and closes the file-transfer window.

When the transfer is complete, the Accept button changes into a Close button and the Open button becomes available. Because the file has now arrived and been saved to disk, you can no longer reject it, but you can delete it by clicking the Delete button.

If you're running anti-virus software that monitors each download and automatically warns you of problems, it may be safe to use the Open button to open the file. Clicking this button triggers the Windows program associated with the file type. For example, if the file you've received is an MP3 file, clicking the Open button will activate or launch your default MP3 player or jukebox. But it's safer to try to open the file from a program designed to run it. That way, if the file is a renamed EXE file that your anti-virus software has missed, the program will return an error when it is unable to open it, whereas triggering the Windows association would have run the file.

If you're using anti-virus software that requires manual intervention, don't use the Open button. Instead, click the Close button to close the file-transfer window, and then tell your anti-virus software to scrutinize the file. The files you receive go into your received files folder. To see what you've received, choose File ➤ Open Received Folder from the File Transfer window. NetMeeting opens an Explorer window to your downloads folder.

NOTE   *If you receive two or more files with the same name (for example, two copies of the same file), NetMeeting names the second copy* Copy (1) of *Filename.*

Chatting

Almost as popular as file transfer is chat, because it's a quick and easy way to communicate with one or more people.

To chat with NetMeeting, click the Chat button, choose Tools ➤ Chat, or press Ctrl+T from the main NetMeeting window. NetMeeting displays the Chat window (shown in Figure 25.31). To send a message, enter it in the Message window and press Enter or click the Send Message button. You can send a message to everybody currently in the chat session or restrict it to a particular participant by using the Send To drop-down list.

FIGURE 25.31

NetMeeting includes a straightforward implementation of chat.

NetMeeting provides assorted options for chat, including font formatting on different types of messages, wrapping options for messages, and choices of whether to display the chatter's name, the date, and the time. To select chat options, choose View ➤ Options from the Chat window and work in the Options dialog box that NetMeeting displays.

Whiteboarding

NetMeeting also provides simple whiteboarding tools via its Whiteboard feature. Whiteboard is essentially a cut-down version of Paint with a few multiuser features grafted onto it; if you can use Paint, you'll have no trouble with Whiteboard. It's neither powerful nor pretty, but it can be useful for showing people how to do things from a distance.

To use the Whiteboard feature, click the Whiteboard button or choose Tools ➤ Whiteboard from the main NetMeeting window. NetMeeting displays the Whiteboard window. Figure 25.32 shows an example of using Whiteboard to convey an image, with the remote pointer (View ➤ Remote Pointer) used to indicate a particular part of the screen.

You can save the contents of the whiteboard for posterity if you wish.

Sharing a Program—or Your Desktop

If you want to, you can share one or more programs—or your Desktop—with another NetMeeting user. This can be useful for demonstrating a program, collaborating on a document, or long-distance troubleshooting.

FIGURE 25.32

You can use Net-Meeting's Whiteboard feature for visual illustrations of techniques.

You can even allow another NetMeeting user to control a program or your entire Desktop. Unless you have a lot to gain by doing so, or you trust the other person absolutely *and are completely certain that it's them at the other computer*, there's seldom any reason for using this capability, because it's a huge security risk. If you give someone control of your Desktop, they have free rein to do whatever they want to your system—start programs, rummage through your files, delete anything they want, or install programs or viruses. You can in theory stop them at any point, but you might be too late, and in any case you might not notice something subtle they did.

Seriously—think twice before you share your Desktop. Then think again. Then decide against it.

TIP *Don't share your Desktop to let someone help you through a problem. Use Remote Assistance instead, as discussed in Chapter 24.*

To share your Desktop or a program, click the Share Program button, choose Tools ➤ Sharing, or press Ctrl+S from the main NetMeeting window. (This peculiar usage of the pan-Windows keystroke for the Save command seems ill-advised—but since NetMeeting is Microsoft software, and Microsoft is an 800-pound gorilla, it must be okay in some unfathomable way.) NetMeeting displays the Sharing window (shown in Figure 25.33).

In the list box, select the program you want to share and click the Share button. You can then unshare the program by selecting it and clicking the Unshare button or by clicking the Unshare All button.

NOTE *If the program you share is part of a group, NetMeeting shares the whole group. For example, if you share one of three Explorer windows you have open, NetMeeting shares all three.*

The other user (or users) sees a window titled with your NetMeeting name and *Programs*, as in Figure 25.34. The windows appear on a featureless gray Desktop in the positions in which you currently have them. If you place an unshared window over one of the shared windows, it blocks the other user's view of the shared window, but its contents aren't transmitted. When you're setting up sharing, the NetMeeting window and the Sharing window often block the view of the other windows, so you need to remember to move them out of the way or minimize them once you've arranged the sharing.

FIGURE 25.33

Use the Sharing window to share your Desktop or a program.

FIGURE 25.34

How the other Net-Meeting user (or users) sees the programs you're sharing

To let the other user (or users) control your shared programs, display the Sharing window and click the Allow Control button. Clicking this button makes available the Automatically Accept Requests for Control check box and the Do Not Disturb with Requests for Control Right Now check box, which you can use to automatically accept and to disable requests for control. Once you've clicked the Allow Control button, it changes into a Prevent Control button that you can click to prevent control of the shared programs.

Usually, you'll want to retain manual control over allowing other users control of your programs. When you click the Allow Control button but leave the Automatically Accept Requests for Control check box cleared, NetMeeting displays the Request Control dialog box (shown in Figure 25.35) to alert you to incoming requests for control.

FIGURE 25.35

NetMeeting displays the Request Control dialog box to let you decide whether to grant control or deny it.

If you accept the request for control, the user is able to control the program much as if it were on their own Desktop. You see every action they take, including movements of the mouse pointer. You can regain control temporarily by clicking your mouse in one of the shared windows or regain control permanently by clicking the Prevent Control button in the Sharing window or by unsharing the program.

If you reject the request for control, or do not respond to it within the timeout period, the user requesting control sees a Request Control Failed dialog box such as that shown in Figure 25.36.

FIGURE 25.36

When you reject a request for control or allow it to time out, the requesting user sees a Request Control Failed dialog box.

To share your Desktop and all open programs, select the Desktop item at the top of the Share Programs list box. If you allow control of your Desktop, the other user can take more or less any action that Windows supports—bar anything that closes NetMeeting, of course. Again, you see the actions they take.

NOTE *When you're sharing your Desktop with NetMeeting, you can't change display properties. For example, you can't change your screen resolution or color depth.*

Up Next

This chapter has discussed how to use NetMeeting for audio- and videoconferencing, for file sharing, for whiteboarding, and for chat. It has also shown you how to use Remote Desktop Sharing to access your own Desktop remotely. And it has told you how you can share your programs and Desktop with other NetMeeting users—and why you should do so only with the utmost care.

The next chapter discusses how to publish information to the Web.

Chapter 26

Publishing Information to the Web

THIS CHAPTER DISCUSSES HOW to publish information to the Web. The material isn't difficult (or even long), but there are three questions you need to consider: First, what will you publish? Second, where will you publish it? And third, how will you get it there?

This chapter covers the following topics:

- Understanding copyright issues involved in publishing to the Web
- Performing quality control
- Deciding where to publish your material
- Publishing material to the Web

What Will You Publish?

The first question is what you're going to publish. You'll have your own answer to this question, of course—anything from your family photos to your political opinions, from your recipes to your music and videos.

But before you publish anything, there's one issue you *must* consider: copyright. And there's another issue you really ought to consider: quality control. This section discusses those issues.

Understanding Copyright Issues

Before you publish any material to the Web, make sure you can legally do so. This means either understanding the basics of copyright law or consulting a lawyer. Three guesses as to which is less expensive.

Right. So here's an executive summary:

- If you created an original work yourself, you hold the copyright to it. For example, if you take an original digital photo, write an original story, or compose an original song, you hold the copyright to it. (If the work isn't original, you've probably infringed copyright. For example, taking a digital photo of someone else's work is unlikely to create an original work.) You can post that work to the Web if you want. (And you can try to defend your copyright against anyone who infringes it.)

◆ As the copyright holder, you have five main rights to the work: the Reproduction Right (making copies of the work), the Distribution Right (distributing it), the Modification Right or Derivative Works Right (creating other works based on the work), the Public Performance Right (performing or transmitting the work), and the Public Display Right (displaying the work in a public place). You can exercise these rights yourself or grant them to other people. For example, the author of a book often grants to a publisher the Reproduction Right and the Distribution Right, so that the publisher can print copies of the book and distribute them.

◆ If someone else created the work, you probably need to get explicit permission to publish or distribute it.

◆ Some works are in the *public domain*, a notional area that contains all works that are not protected by copyright and which you can therefore publish and distribute freely. Some works are never protected by copyright, because they're not copyrightable due to their nature (for example, facts, URLs, and names are not copyrightable), because they're not copyrighted (for example, U.S. Government publications under the authorship of the Federal Government are not copyrighted), or because the creator of the work has chosen to put it in the public domain. Other works go out of copyright because the copyright has expired or has been lost.

WARNING   *Some Web site hosting services use their Terms and Conditions to claim copyright of any original material you post. Read the small print before you post anything on these services.*

Those are the bare bones of what you need to know about copyright to avoid committing copyright violations left, right, and center. Here are some resources for understanding copyright:

◆ Brad Templeton's *10 Big Myths about Copyright Explained* site (`www.templetons.com/brad/copymyths.html`) debunks the biggest myths about copyright.

◆ The U.S. Copyright Office (`www.loc.gov/copyright/`) offers a number of resources on copyright, including the Copyright FAQ (`www.loc.gov/copyright/faq.html`) and a Copyright Basics section (`www.loc.gov/copyright/circs/circ1.html`).

◆ The Copyright Clearance Center (`www.copyright.com`) provides a central location for getting permission to reproduce many copyrighted works. (For others, you may need to contact the creator of the work directly.)

◆ Chapter 2 of *Internet Piracy Exposed* (Sybex, 2001; shameless plug: also by me) discusses copyright law in the context of what you can and cannot legally do with material on the Internet.

Performing Quality Control

As you'll have noticed if you've spent more than a few hours surfing, the Web already suffers from a severe lack of quality control. You'll improve your karma if you don't add to this problem.

Historically, the high cost of publishing a work has acted as a strong incentive for the publisher to ensure that the work is of a high enough quality that it will appeal to its intended audience. For example, if a publisher publishes a book that's so bad (or on so unappealing a topic) that nobody buys it, they lose money. If a record company issues an unlistenable CD, they're unlikely to achieve significant sales. And if an artist paints wretched pictures, the chances of their finding a market are slim.

By contrast, the Web is more or less a free-for-all. The cost of publishing to the Web can be extremely low (or can be nothing): You need do little more than create files and post them on a Web site, and anyone with an Internet connection and Web browser can access them. If they don't like what they find at your site, they probably won't return, but the cost to you remains minimal.

But if you want people to look at what you post, make sure that its quality is at least acceptable:

♦ Don't post just anything (or *everything*) you have. Select the best items and post them. If they draw acclaim (or rapture), consider posting more.

♦ Spell-check any text you post. If your grammar isn't the greatest, get someone competent to check it for you. Involve an editor or proofreader if you're looking to be professional and persuasive. (For editors and proofreaders, the unedited and unproofed content on the Web can be painful and gratifying in that it illustrates the need for their often unseen and unsung services.)

♦ Use graphics in moderation—and make sure they contribute to your site. Gratuitous graphics grate on the visitor nearly as badly as artless alliteration.

♦ Produce any audio material to a reasonable standard. Your band's live tapes might not make the cut unmixed, mixed, they might.

♦ Produce any video material to a higher standard. Because downloading video is a serious investment of time and bandwidth over any but the very fastest connections, you'll need to give people a good reason to download your video—and try not to disappoint them.

Above all, beware technologies that make it too easy to post material to the Web. Just because you *can* publish material directly to the Web doesn't mean that you should; in fact, it often means just about the opposite. For example, as you'll see in Chapter 28, Windows XP's Scanner and Camera Wizard offers to copy pictures you download from a digital camera or images you acquire via a scanner directly to the Web. In most cases, this is a very bad idea:

♦ Even if you've edited the photos on the digital camera ruthlessly so that you're sure you're not downloading any duds, you may need to crop the pictures, change their size or resolution, or otherwise manipulate them before posting them to the Web.

♦ Unless you hold the copyright to the documents you are scanning, or the documents are in the public domain or otherwise not copyrighted, you will need to get permission before publishing them to the Web.

Similarly, Windows Movie Maker (also covered in Chapter 28) offers a feature for publishing a movie to a Web server. This feature is more reasonable, in that Windows Movie Maker lets you preview the movie before you publish it. All the same, think twice before uploading huge amounts of scantily reviewed material to the Web.

Where Will You Publish Your Content?

Once you've established that you've got content that you think is worth posting, you need somewhere to publish it. In most cases, your choice will be between your ISP and a free Web hosting service such as MSN.

As discussed in Chapter 17, one of the factors you should evaluate when choosing an ISP is how much Web space they give you and how much traffic they allow your site as part of your monthly fee (or free, as the case may be). Make sure that the ISP allows you plenty of space for as much material as you'll need to post at once (you can always delete some of the fatter files to make room for new material) and that they'll sell you more space and bandwidth for a modest fee should the need arise.

How Will You Publish Your Content?

Windows XP offers two ways of getting material onto your Web site: creating it offline and using FTP to transfer a copy of it, and using WebDAV to create the files directly online.

FTP

The standard way of getting material onto your Web site is to create and assemble the material offline and then upload it to the Web site via FTP. If you're uploading a new version of a page, the upload overwrites the existing page. You can spend as long as you need to creating and saving the content, and because the files you're working with are stored on a local drive, you can access them at full speed.

There are three main methods of transferring material to and from an FTP site:

◆ Create a network place for the site and access it via the My Network Places folder.

◆ Access the site from Internet Explorer and create a favorite for it.

◆ Use an FTP client to access the site.

We'll discuss these methods in a moment or two. But first: WebDAV.

WebDAV

If your ISP supports Web Digital Authoring and Versioning (WebDAV), you can use the new and snappier method of getting material onto your Web site, which is to create it or edit it in situ by using any program that can save directly to a Web folder or to an FTP site.

This method can simplify the process of making minor edits to a page and seeing the effects of the changes. But there are two problems:

◆ First, because even the fastest residential Internet connection is hundreds of times slower than the data-transfer speeds inside even a modest PC, this method makes for painfully slow opening and saving of documents. If there's a problem with the Internet connection, the document you're working on can become corrupted. If this is the only copy you have of the document, you may lose everything in it. Figure 26.1 shows the Windows – Delayed Write Failed dialog box, which gives an example of such unwelcome news.

FIGURE 26.1

Saving files directly to your
Web site doesn't always work—
and when it fails, you can lose
the document involved.

- Second, most ISPs cache Web pages so that they can deliver them more frequently. This means that changes you make to your site may not be propagated through the network until the cache is refreshed. This refresh may take anything from a few minutes to (in extreme cases) a day or two.

These two problems mean that the second way of adding content to a Web site is best left for intranet situations, where you can access the site at full network speeds and perhaps manipulate the refresh process yourself.

Because Windows XP implements WebDAV, XP-aware programs can save directly to FTP sites and Web folders. For example, the ability (mentioned earlier in the chapter) of the Scanner and Camera Wizard and Windows Movie Maker to save material directly to the Web comes courtesy of WebDAV. Similarly, Microsoft Office programs such as Word and Excel can save directly to Web folders—all you need do (in theory) is use the My Network Places list in the Save As dialog box to select the network place, and you're away.

Using Network Places to Access an FTP Site or Web Folder

Network places provide the easiest built-in way to access an FTP site or Web folder for transferring files. A network place essentially puts a pretty face on copying to an FTP site or a Web folder by disguising it to look like a folder on your hard drive. You'll notice the difference, because when you save or copy a file to a network folder, the operation takes place at the speed of your Internet connection rather than at normal blazing computer speeds. But otherwise, the operation is seamless and almost effortless.

CREATING A NEW NETWORK PLACE

Windows provides the Add Network Place Wizard for creating a new network place and adding it to your My Network Places list. Take the following steps:

1. Choose Start ➢ My Network Places. Windows displays the My Network Places window.

   - If your Start menu doesn't include a My Network Places link, choose Start ➢ My Computer, then click the My Network Places link in the Other Places list in the My Computer window.

2. Click the Add a Network Place link in the Network Tasks list. Windows starts the Add Network Place Wizard, which displays its Welcome page.

NOTE *You can also start the Add Network Place Wizard by clicking the Network Place or Site link in the Map Network Drive dialog box (Tools ➢ Map Network Drive).*

3. Click the Next button. The Wizard displays the Where Do You Want to Create This Network Place? page (shown in Figure 26.2).

FIGURE 26.2

On the Where Do You Want to Create This Network Place? page of the Add Network Place Wizard, choose the service you want to use.

4. In the list box, select the Web host or local network location you want to use. In the figure, your choices are limited to MSN Communities or Choose Another Network Location. The next sections discuss these choices.

Creating a Network Place on MSN

To create a network place on MSN, select the MSN Communities item on the Where Do You Want to Create This Network Place? page of the Add Network Place Wizard. Click the Next button. The Wizard walks you through the process of creating a place called My Communities on MSN. This place is linked to your Passport identity.

Creating a Network Place in Another Network Location

To create a network place in another network location, take the following steps:

1. On the Where Do You Want to Create This Network Place? page of the Add Network Place Wizard, select the Choose Another Network Location item.

2. Click the Next button. The Wizard displays the What Is the Address of This Network Place? page (shown in Figure 26.3).

3. In the Type the Address of the Web Site, FTP Site, or Network Location That This Shortcut Will Open text box, enter the location of the network folder, Web folder, or FTP site. For most purposes, you'll want to use one of these three formats:

Network Place	Format
Shared folder on network	`\\server\folder`
Web folder	`http://server/folder`
FTP site	`ftp://ftp.domainname.domain`

FIGURE 26.3

On the What Is the Address of This Network Place? page of the Add Network Place Wizard, specify the folder or FTP site containing the network place.

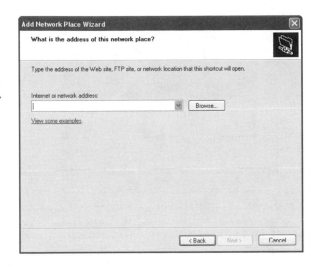

4. Click the Next button. The Wizard checks the type of authentication required and displays the appropriate dialog box:

♦ For an FTP site, the Wizard displays the User Name and Password page (shown in Figure 26.4 with the Log On Anonymously check box cleared). If you log on anonymously to this network place, leave the Log On Anonymously check box selected, as it is by default. If you need to supply a username and password (as is more likely), clear the Log On Anonymously check box and enter your username in the User Name text box. Click the Next button.

FIGURE 26.4

On the User Name and Password page of the Add Network Place Wizard, choose whether to log on anonymously or specify your username.

◆ For a Web folder, the Wizard displays the Enter Network Password dialog box (shown in Figure 26.5). Enter your username and password. Select the Save This Password in Your Password List check box if you think it advisable. Then click the OK button.

FIGURE 26.5

In the Enter Network Password dialog box, enter your username and password for the Web folder.

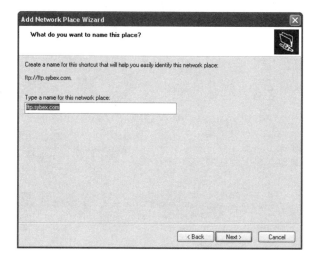

5. The Wizard displays the What Do You Want to Name This Place? page (shown in Figure 26.6).

FIGURE 26.6

On the What Do You Want to Name This Place? page of the Add Network Place Wizard, specify the name you want to use for the network place.

6. Enter the name for the network place. This name is for your benefit, so make it descriptive. By default, Windows suggests a variation on the address for the network place, so you'll often want to change it.

7. Click the Next button. The Wizard displays the Completing the Add Network Place Wizard page.

8. If you want to open the network place immediately, leave the Open This Network Place when I Click Finish check box selected. Otherwise, clear this check box.

9. Click the Finish button. The Add Network Place Wizard closes itself and creates the network place.

ACCESSING A NETWORK PLACE

Once you've created a network place, you can access it from Explorer by using the My Network Places window (Start ➤ My Network Places).

To open a network place, double-click it. If you saved your password for the network place, Windows opens the network place at the full speed of your Internet connection. If the network place is on MSN, Windows automatically logs you in to the network place using your .NET Passport.

If the network place is an FTP site, Windows displays the Log On As dialog box (shown in Figure 26.7). Enter the password. Select the Save Password check box if you want Windows to store your password so that you can access this network place without interruption next time. (Remember that storing a password compromises your security.) Then click the Log On button.

FIGURE 26.7

For an FTP site, you need to enter your password in the Log On As dialog box.

You can add files to the network place by using regular Explorer techniques. For example, you can drag files from another folder and drop them on the icon for a network place to copy them to that network place.

FTP via Internet Explorer

As you saw in Chapter 18, you can use Internet Explorer for FTP. There's no particular advantage to using Internet Explorer when you can use a network place instead, but Internet Explorer works well enough to be worth considering as an alternative.

To transfer files via FTP using Internet Explorer, take the following steps:

1. Choose Start ➤ Internet. Windows launches Internet Explorer.

2. In the Address bar, enter the FTP address, username, and password (if you choose) using the following format:

   ```
   ftp://username[:password]@ftpserver/url
   ```

3. Click the Go button or press the Enter key. If you specified your password (and got it right), Windows connects to the FTP server and displays the folder. If you chose not to specify your password, Windows displays the Login As dialog box, in which you can enter your password and choose whether to save it.

TIP *Once you've connected to the FTP site, create a favorite for it so that you can access it quickly in the future.*

FTP via an FTP Client

Network places provide smooth access to Web folders and FTP sites, but for more powerful FTP capabilities, you may want to invest in a graphical FTP client such as WS_FTP Pro (`www.ipswitch.com`) or CuteFTP (`www.globalscape.com`).

NOTE   Windows includes an FTP client built in—but unfortunately it's a command-line client, which means that in order to use it, you need to use Unix-style commands. If you know these commands, launch the FTP client by choosing Start ➢ Run, entering ftp in the Open text box in the resulting Run dialog box, and clicking the OK button. If you don't know these commands and don't want to learn them, stick with Internet Explorer or a graphical FTP client.

Up Next

This short chapter has discussed the main considerations in publishing material to the Web: what you can legally publish and the importance of performing quality control; where to publish your material; and how to get the material from your computer to the Web host.

This is the end of Part III of the book. Part IV, which begins overleaf, discusses how to enjoy audio, video, and games on Windows XP.

Part IV

Audio, Video, and Games

Chapter 27

Windows Media Player

THIS CHAPTER DISCUSSES HOW to use Windows Media Player, the powerful multimedia player incorporated in Windows XP. A vast improvement on its predecessors of the same name, Windows Media Player not only provides features for enjoying audio and video but also supports copying CDs to your hard disk in WMA format.

This chapter covers the following topics:

- ◆ Configuring Windows Media Player
- ◆ Playing music with Windows Media Player
- ◆ Understanding digital rights management
- ◆ Copying a CD to your hard disk
- ◆ Tuning into Internet radio
- ◆ Backing up and restoring digital licenses
- ◆ Using Volume Control to control output and input
- ◆ Recording and converting sounds with Sound Recorder

Is Windows Media Player Worth Using?

If you've used Windows Media Player in any previous version of Windows except Windows Me, you probably have the greatest skepticism about using Windows Media Player—and rightly so. That's because the versions of Windows Media Player in Windows 95, 98, NT 4, and 2000 were underpowered and near-useless weaklings.

Windows Media Player version 7, the version included with Windows Me, was a totally different animal than the feature-light versions of Windows Media Player that preceded it. Windows Media Player version 8, the version included with Windows XP, goes one better. Windows Media Player 8 has a strong set of features, including better playlist features and the ability to rip and encode to WMA format at a good range of bitrates and to the MP3 format at disappointing bitrates. It's also aware of portable devices such as the Diamond Rio, and it provides full-ish jukebox capabilities. Oh, and it plays videos and DVDs quite competently.

NOTE   *You can also use Windows Media Player to burn audio to CD. Chapter 29 discusses how to burn CDs.*

In short, Windows Media Player is well worth using provided it fulfills your needs. But if you're seriously into audio or video, you'll probably want to use some other programs as well as or instead of Windows Media Player.

Getting Started with Windows Media Player

Start Windows Media Player by choosing Start ➤ All Programs ➤ Windows Media Player. By default, Windows Media Player starts on its Media Guide page, which is essentially a browser window that displays the latest news from the WindowsMedia.com Web site.

Figure 27.1 shows Windows Media Player in its Full mode, with a track playing. By default, the menu bar and window frame hide themselves automatically when Windows Media Player appears in a normal window (in other words, a nonmaximized window), giving Windows Media Player the irregular effect you see here. You can display the menu bar by moving the mouse pointer over the area it occupies or by clicking the Show Menu Bar button at the left end of the gray bar across the top of the window.

FIGURE 27.1

Windows Media Player 8, shown here in its Full mode, provides full-ish capabilities for audio and video and is a huge improvement over the versions of Windows Media Player included in Windows 95, 98, NT, and 2000.

As you can see in Figure 27.1, Full mode takes up a serious chunk of a small screen, even when Windows Media Player isn't maximized and the menu bar and window frame are hidden. For sustained use, you'll be better off using Skin mode, shown in Figure 27.2.

FIGURE 27.2

In Skin mode, Windows Media Player occupies a more reasonable amount of your screen.

EXPERT KNOWLEDGE: DIGITAL RIGHTS MANAGEMENT AND LICENSES

Being able to store audio and video in digital format on a PC, play them back easily, and even transfer them via the Internet or removable media, is great for consumers of audio and video content. But it can be way less than great for creators of audio and video content: These computer capabilities pose a severe threat to their livelihoods by compromising their copyrighted works and robbing them of sales.

In the past, audio and video works have largely been distributed on physical media, such as CDs, cassettes, LPs, video cassettes, and DVDs. The tangible nature and physical presence of such media generally make it clear when a theft has occurred: Physical media can't walk out of stores by themselves. Making unauthorized copies of a work distributed on a physical medium such as a videotape involves cost (for the media for the copies and for any duplicating equipment needed), time (typically real-time copying), and effort. Distributing those copies involves further cost, time, and effort. And the illegality of such pirated works is widely known (and recognized, if not exactly appreciated): Most consumers are aware that it's illegal to distribute (let alone sell) copies of copyrighted works. Besides, copies of works on analog media (such as videotape or audiotape) are lower fidelity than the originals, so the inauthenticity of late-generation copies is clear.

By contrast, any work stored in a digital medium accessible by a PC can be copied in seconds at almost zero cost, and the copies are perfect every time. These perfect copies can be distributed via the Internet, again at negligible cost. And they can be distributed in quantities and over distances unthinkable for physical media. For example, if someone buys a CD in Sioux Falls, makes MP3 files of its tracks, and makes them available on a file sharing service such as GnutellaNet or Freenet, anyone with Internet connectivity anywhere in the world—from Vladivostok to Tierra del Fuego, from Juneau to Java—can download them and then distribute them further.

At this writing, there are several technologies intended to protect the rights of content creators (and their authorized distributors) while allowing consumers to use the content. For example, most DVDs use an encryption system called Content Scrambling System (CSS), which requires an encryption key in order to be decoded. CSS keys were licensed and tightly controlled by the DVD-Copy Control Association (DVD-CCA)—tightly controlled, that is, until Norwegian hackers in the LiVid (Linux Video group) created a utility called DeCSS by reverse engineering some unencrypted code they discovered in a sloppily constructed software DVD player. Now that DeCSS is widely available, CSS-encrypted content can be deciphered by anyone who has the code.

Perhaps the most promising of the technologies designed to protect content is the digital license. A *digital license* is encrypted information that links a particular copy of a downloaded work to a particular computer or individual. For example, in the current model of digital licenses for audio, if you download a track that uses a digital license, you buy or are otherwise granted a license to play the track on the computer on which you downloaded it. If you transfer the track to another computer, it won't play, because the computer lacks the necessary license information.

So far, so good. But in order to be viable enough to become widely accepted, digital licenses need to be not only easy and intuitive to use but also compatible with both generally used technology and with the prevailing laws. For example, the First Sale Doctrine laid out in the Copyright Act allows consumers to sell or give a copy they've legitimately acquired of a copyrighted work to another person. Any copyright-protection technology that prevents consumers from doing this effectively (for example, because any subsequent recipient would not be able to view or listen to the work because it was locked by encryption and a nontransferable license to the first purchaser's computer) would be open to heavy-duty legal challenges.

Continued on next page

Leaving aside such details for the moment… digital licenses are now being used to secure some copyrighted content. Windows Media Player adopts a two-pronged approach to digital licenses for audio content, supporting digital licenses for both tracks you buy and download and tracks you copy from CD. Windows Media Player automatically issues a license for each track you copy from a CD (unless you set it to copy tracks without licensing them).

At this writing, Windows Media Player lets you choose whether to use digital licenses or to be free, easy, and possibly illegal. As long as you use those tracks on the PC with which you created them, there's no problem with using licenses. But if you want to be able to play the tracks from another computer, you've got a problem, because the license ties the associated digital media file to the PC for which the license is issued: You'll need to acquire a new license or transfer a license from the original computer. Similarly, you may not be able to download a copy of a licensed track to a portable player without licensing gymnastics.

Now, simply *playing* a track from another computer should be fine, legally, because it's the same file that you created from the CD. So should be moving the track to another computer that belongs to you and using it on that computer. Only if you create an illegal copy of the track—and particularly if you distribute it—should there be a problem. More on this later in the chapter; but you can see that the implementation of digital licenses tends to be problematic, partly because of the nature of the beast and partly because of the assumption of those who implemented the technology that anything unlicensed will tend to be licentious. There's no good reason for using digital licenses for the tracks you copy from CD unless you can't trust yourself (or other users of your computer) not to take illegal actions with them.

If you choose to use digital licenses for the tracks you copy from CD and the tracks you purchase and download (or download for free), you need to back up your licenses in case you lose them and need to restore them. If your computer crashes, if you reinstall Windows, or if you install another operating system, you'll need to restore your licenses in order to be able to use the tracks.

License files are small, so you can store a good number of them on a floppy disk. If you're not good at keeping your floppy disks in order, or if you want to protect them against local or natural disasters, back them up to an Internet drive instead.

Configuring Windows Media Player

Windows Media Player has a raft of configuration options on the eight or nine pages of its Options dialog box (the DVD page appears only if your computer has a DVD drive and a DVD player installed). The following sections discuss the most important options. If you want some music while you read, go ahead and slot a CD. Windows Media Player should start playing it automatically unless you've disabled Autoplay for music. Then choose Tools ➤ Options. Windows Media Player displays the Options dialog box.

Player Page Options

Almost all of the options on the Player page (shown in Figure 27.3) are worth knowing about:

Automatic Updates group box Select the Once a Month option button (unless you want Windows Media Player to prompt you to upgrade more frequently). Leave the Download Codecs

Automatically check box selected (as it is by default) if you want Windows Media Player to download and install any new codecs it needs to play back audio streams or files. Clear this check box if you prefer to have Windows Media Player prompt you before it installs new codecs.

TIP   You can force Windows Media Player to check for updates by choosing Help ➤ Check for Player Updates, then following the Windows Media Component Setup process that ensues.

Internet Settings group box   The Allow Internet Sites to Uniquely Identify Your Player check box sounds like it's threatening to broadcast your personal information all over the Web. In fact, this check box controls whether Windows Media Player passes an identifier to streaming media servers to enable the servers to monitor the connection and adjust the stream to improve playback quality. For best quality of streaming audio, leave this check box selected, as it is by default. The Acquire Licenses Automatically check box controls whether Windows Media Player tries to automatically get a license when a file requires one. (See the sidebar earlier in this chapter on digital rights management and licenses for a discussion of licenses.)

Player Settings group box   Choose whether to start the player on the Media Guide page, whether to display the player always on top in Skin mode, whether to display the anchor window (a small reference window) when the player is in Skin mode, and whether to let the Windows screen saver kick in while music or video is playing back. The anchor window is more or less useless, but having the player always on top makes it easy to access. The screen saver seldom improves playback, even of music: Visualizations provide better entertainment. Select the Add Items to Media Library when Played check box if you want Windows Media Player to add new tracks to the Media Library when you play them. If you select this check box, you get the choice of selecting the Include Items from Removable Media check box, which controls whether Windows adds tracks from removable media such as CDs or removable disks to the Media Library. (This isn't usually a good idea.)

FIGURE 27.3

The Player page of the Options dialog box

Copy Music Page Options

The Copy Music page of the Options dialog box (shown in Figure 27.4) contains four options that control the "copying" of music from CDs to your hard drive. These options are largely set-and-forget, though you may want to use different music quality settings for different CDs that you copy.

FIGURE 27.4

The Copy Music page of the Options dialog box

These are the options:

Copy Music to This Location group box   This group box contains a label that shows the folder to which Windows Media Player copies music. The default location is your \My Music\ folder, in which Windows Media Player creates folders by artist and, within these, folders by album name. To change the location, click the Change button, use the resulting Browse for Folder dialog box to navigate to and select the location, and then click the OK button.

By default, Windows Media Player names the files by track number and track name (or *song title*, as Windows Media Player refers to it)—for example, 01 Clock without Hands.WMA. To change the naming, click the Advanced button and work in the resulting File Name Options dialog box (shown in Figure 27.5). Select the check boxes for the items you want to include in the filename (track number, song title, artist, album, and so on). Use the Move Up button and Move Down button to shuffle the selected items into order. And use the Separator drop-down list to specify which separator character to use: none, a space, a dash, a dot, or an underline. Then click the OK button. Windows Media Player closes the File Name Options dialog box and applies your choices.

NOTE   *Windows Media Player shares the Media Library among all users, so you don't need to use the* \Shared Documents\ *folder to share music with other users of the computer.*

FIGURE 27.5

Use the File Name Options dialog box to customize the name format that Windows Media Player uses for tracks you copy.

Copy Settings group box   In the File Format drop-down list, select the file format you want to use for the files: Windows Media or MP3. (See the next sidebar for details on how Windows Media and MP3 stack up to each other.) In practice, you'll need to use the Windows Media format unless you add a third-party MP3 encoder to Windows. (If you do add a third-party MP3 encoder, you may well prefer to use its interface for ripping and encoding rather than using Windows Media Player.)

Leave the Protect Content check box selected (as it is by default) if you want to use Windows Media Player's features for personal licensing of CD tracks you copy. See the previous sidebar for a discussion of the advantage (*sic*) and disadvantages of using this feature. Clear this check box if you want more flexibility in what you can do with WMA files.

Use the Copy Music at This Quality slider to specify the quality at which to encode the files you copy. Windows Media Player offers six bitrates (48Kbps, 64Kbps, 96Kbps, 128Kbps, 160Kbps, and 192Kbps) graded from Smallest Size (48Kbps) to Best Quality (192Kbps). Higher bitrates take up more space but sound better. Experiment with this setting on a variety of music and find the bitrate that suits you best:

- If you have plenty of hard disk space for the music you want to copy, choose the 192Kbps bitrate as a hedge against getting a better sound card or speakers in the future.

- If you want to use the files with a portable player with limited memory, use the lowest bitrate that sounds good on the player.

- Microsoft describes the 64Kbps bitrate as "CD Quality." This is optimistic enough to qualify as deluded in most people's terms.

EXPERT KNOWLEDGE: HOW DO MP3 AND WMA STACK UP TO EACH OTHER?

Audiophiles, gearheads, and Microsoft-haters have had a long-running argument about whether MP3 or WMA is better. Impressive amounts of research have been done by interested parties, but the resulting articles and papers have drawn such diametrically opposed conclusions that you'd be forgiven for dismissing them all as propaganda. The argument tends to get polarized into a holy war, and neither the crusaders nor the infidels (or heretics, depending on your point of view) have a monopoly on fact, reason, or logic. In fact, each side often seems to have at best a tenuous grasp on all three. If you want to see Microsoft's side of the story, click the Compare button on the Copy Music page of the Options dialog box.

To really appreciate the nuances of the different sides of the argument, you need to understand a bit about how audio compression works. If you could bear to know some more, try my book *MP3 Complete* (Sybex, 2001).

In the meantime, though, you no doubt want some sensible advice. That's easy enough, because from a lay point of view, the situation is very simple. Here's what you need to know:

◆ Even at the highest quality settings they offer, and on the best equipment, neither MP3 nor WMA sound quite as good as CD-quality audio, which is uncompressed and uses a comprehensive range of samples across the whole area of audio frequencies audible to the human ear. This is because each format uses lossy compression to reduce the size of the audio files. As you'd guess from its name, *lossy compression* involves discarding data from the original in order to compress it. (The opposite of lossy compression is *lossless compression*, which essentially involves squeezing files in such a way that they can be reexpanded to a copy that contains the same information as the original. Zip files use lossless compression, so the files you extract from a Zip file are functionally identical to their originals though not actually the same file.)

◆ Unless you've got amazing ears, very good hi-fi, or perhaps both, the advantages of compression outweigh the disadvantages. In a nutshell, compressed files are small enough to store in large numbers on computers, to carry in small numbers on ultraportable players, and to transfer easily via removable media, networks, or the Internet.

◆ MP3 and WMA use different encoding methods, but the results are roughly comparable in quality.

◆ MP3 is a more widely used file format than WMA. A wide variety of software MP3 players are available for every conceivable computing platform, and you can get hardware MP3 players in an impressive variety of shapes and sizes. Many software MP3 players and some hardware MP3 players can handle WMA files as well as MP3 files.

◆ In June 2001, Thomson Multimedia (www.thomson-multimedia.com) released a demo version of mp3PRO, a new version of MP3 that delivers better sound quality than MP3 at lower bitrates. mp3PRO is more expensive to license than other MP3 encoders, so it's hard to say how quickly or widely it will be integrated into MP3 solutions—but at this writing, it seems a promising technology.

Whether you choose MP3, WMA, or another format will probably boil down to what you want to do with digital audio, how high your standards are, and how much time, effort, and money you're prepared to invest.

Continued on next page

EXPERT KNOWLEDGE: HOW DO MP3 AND WMA STACK UP TO EACH OTHER? *(Continued)*

If all you want to do is rip your CDs and store them on your hard disk so that you can play them back from your computer, Windows Media Player and WMA provide an effective solution. Choose a bitrate that delivers satisfactory audio quality through your sound card and speakers, slot the first CD, and you're away. In this case, it may be a good idea to use Windows' licensing features, because they ensure that you can't inadvertently break the law by using the files on another computer. (You can transfer them to another computer, but because it doesn't have the right license information, it won't be able to play them.)

If you want to use digital audio on a portable player, WMA may not be such a suitable choice. While an increasing number of portable digital-audio players do support WMA as well as MP3, many do not. Even for those players that do support WMA, you may find that MP3 provides more options or easier administration. For example, to use WMA files on a portable player that doesn't support the SDMI specification, you'll need to turn off Windows Media Player's licensing features; by contrast, with MP3 files, you don't need to worry about digital licenses.

Devices Page Options

The Devices page of the Options dialog box (shown in Figure 27.6) lets you configure your CD and DVD drives for playing back and copying CDs and any portable devices for downloading tracks from Windows Media Player.

FIGURE 27.6

The Devices page of the Options dialog box lists your CD drives, DVD drives, and portable devices.

SETTING PROPERTIES FOR A CD DRIVE OR DVD DRIVE

To set properties for a CD drive or DVD drive, select it in the Devices list box and click the Properties button. Windows Media Player displays the Properties dialog box for the drive. Figure 27.7 shows an example of the Properties dialog box for a DVD drive.

In the Playback group box and the Copy group box, choose between the Digital option button and the Analog option button. Digital audio extraction is preferable to analog audio extraction because it maintains a higher-fidelity signal. The main reason not to use digital audio extraction is if your CD drive does not support it or cannot deliver it successfully. If you choose digital audio extraction, you can select the Use Error Correction check box if you want Windows Media Player to use its error-correction features to try to remove errors that occur during playback or copying. Error correction uses a bit more CPU power than regular playback or copying; it slows down copying considerably; and its effect is often undetectable. You may want to try playing your CDs without error correction and turn it on only if you hear odd noises in the playback. Unless you have a savage degree of impatience encoded in your chromosomes, it's a good idea to use error correction for copying music, because any defects in the copied tracks tend to be much more annoying than spending a few extra minutes copying each CD.

NOTE   If Windows Media Player finds, when you insert a CD, that your CD drive doesn't support digital playback, it displays a message telling you so and warning you that visualizations, the graphic equalizer, and SRS WOW will not work. Windows Media Player then switches to analog mode.

Click the OK button. Windows Media Player closes the Properties dialog box for the CD drive.

ADDING A PORTABLE DEVICE

To add a portable device, click the Add button. Windows Media Player opens an Internet Explorer window to the WindowsMedia.com site, which maintains a list of compatible devices and links to the software that you can download to make the devices agree with Windows Media Player. At this writing, Windows Media Player supports a variety of portable players, including later S3 Rio models, some Creative Nomad models, the Compaq iPaq Personal AudioPlayer PA-I, and the Iomega HipZip.

TIP   Most portable devices come with effective software for loading tracks and playlists onto them. Because this software is specifically designed for the portable device, it may offer enhancements that Windows Media Player does not. However, some portable device software packages cannot rip, encode, and load to the portable device in one move, as Windows Media Player can with some of the players it supports.

Performance Page Options

The Performance page (shown in Figure 27.8) of the Options dialog box offers these options:

Connection Speed group box   By default, the Detect Connection Speed (Recommended) check box is selected. This setting usually works well. If you find the results disappointing, try selecting the Choose Connection Speed option button and specifying the speed in the drop-down list.

Network Buffering group box   By default, the Use Default Buffering (Recommended) option button is selected, so Windows Media Player buffers the default number of seconds of audio before starting to play it. (The *buffer* is the quantity of audio that Windows downloads before starting to play an audio stream and holds in reserve so that it can even out any minor interruptions in the audio stream when it's playing.) If you hear interruptions in the audio with the default buffering, note the buffering time the next time you access streaming audio, then try selecting the Buffer For option button and specifying a larger number in the Seconds text box.

Video Acceleration group box   If your video playback in Windows Media Player is unsatisfactory, you can try adjusting the Video Acceleration slider to improve the speed or smoothness.

FIGURE 27.8

If necessary, specify a connection speed on the Performance page of the Options dialog box.

For further video acceleration settings, click the Advanced button. Windows Media Player displays the Video Acceleration Settings dialog box (shown in Figure 27.9). The key settings here are the Digital Video slider, which adjusts the size of the picture, and the Display Full-Screen Controls check boxes in the Video Acceleration group box and the DVD Video group box. The Enable Full-Screen Mode Switch check box in the Video Acceleration group box, which is cleared by default, attempts to expand the video image for viewing at full-screen size in full-screen mode. This capability typically doesn't work with digital video. The Digital Video slider (which, as its name suggests, works only for digital video, not for analog video) kicks in when you expand the Windows Media Player window to a larger size than the original video and Windows Media Player needs to stretch the video to fit. The Large setting allows Windows Media Player to interpolate (add) pixels that are not in the original video in order to stretch the picture. The Small setting keeps the video more faithful to the original but requires more CPU power. For best results, experiment with this setting.

FIGURE 27.9

Choose further video settings in the Video Acceleration Settings dialog box. If you don't have a DVD drive and decoder, you won't see the DVD Video section of the dialog box.

If you have both hardware and software DVD decoders installed, you'll be able to choose the Hardware option button or the Software option button in the Preferred Decoder area. Click the OK button. Windows Media Player closes the Video Acceleration Settings dialog box.

Media Library Page Options

The Media Library page (shown in Figure 27.10) of the Options dialog box contains three crucial settings for keeping control of your Media Library. You may want to stay with the default settings, which are suitable for many people, but you should understand these options.

Access Rights of Other Applications group box   The three option buttons in this group box control whether other programs installed on your computer can access your Media Library. The default setting is the Read-Only Access option button. This setting is useful if you want other programs to be able to read your Media Library (for example, if you use a jukebox other than Windows Media Player to play music sometimes) but not change it. If you want other programs to be able to change your Media Library, select the Full Access option button. If you're sure none of your other programs will need to access your Media Library, select the No Access option button.

Access Rights of Internet Sites group box   The three option buttons in this group box control whether Internet sites can access your Media Library. The default setting is the No Access option button. *Change this setting to the Read-Only Access option button only if you want Internet sites to be able to access your Media Library to collect information about the audio and video you have.* At this writing, there seems no good reason to select the Full Access option button—but no doubt someone will invent a program that requires this.

Media Files group box   Leave the Automatically Add Purchased Music to My Library check box selected if you want Windows Media Player to automatically add to your Media Library all the music you purchase online and download. This check box is selected by default, and leaving it selected is the easiest way of building your Media Library. If you don't want to add all the music you purchase to your Media Library, clear this check box. You can then add music to your Media Library manually after you purchase it.

FIGURE 27.10

You can specify access rights to your Media Library on the Media Library page of the Options dialog box.

Visualizations Page Options

On the Visualizations page (shown in Figure 27.11) of the Options dialog box, you can choose the visualization collection to use for enhancing your listening pleasure.

FIGURE 27.11

Choose a visualization collection on the Visualizations page of the Options dialog box.

Some visualizations have properties that you can set by selecting the entry in the list box and clicking the Properties button to display a Properties dialog box.

You can add other visualizations that you've downloaded by clicking the Add button, using the resulting Open dialog box to identify the visualizations file, and clicking the Open button.

You can remove some visualizations by selecting them and clicking the Remove button. Other visualizations are built in and wish to remain so.

File Types Page Options

On the File Types page (shown in Figure 27.12) of the Options dialog box, you can select and clear check boxes to specify which file types Windows Media Player is associated with. For example, if Windows Media Player has associated itself with the MP3 file type, but you want to use another player for MP3 files, clear the MP3 Format Sound check box.

FIGURE 27.12

Use the File Types page of the Options dialog box to specify the file types to associate with Windows Media Player.

DVD Page Options

If your computer has a DVD drive and a DVD player installed, the Options dialog box includes the DVD page (shown in Figure 27.13). This page offers these options:

Parental Control group box   To implement parental control on DVDs played on the computer, select the Parental Control check box and use the Select a Rating drop-down list to specify the rating to apply.

Language Settings group box   Use the Subtitles drop-down list to specify whether you want subtitles and, if so, in which language. Use the Audio drop-down list and the Menu drop-down list to specify the language to use for movie audio and on-screen menus. The default setting for these two controls is Title Default, which gives you the primary language with which the DVD was encoded.

FIGURE 27.13

If you have a DVD drive, you can choose parental control settings and language settings on the DVD page of the Options dialog box.

Network Page Options

On the Network page (shown in Figure 27.14), you can choose which protocols to use for receiving audio and video streams over a network. Unless you know your protocols well enough not to need advice on configuring them, you probably shouldn't mess with the default selections.

FIGURE 27.14

If you're familiar with network protocols, you can adjust them on the Network page of the Options dialog box. If you're not, leave them alone.

Letting Windows Media Player Know about the Media Files on Your Computer

You've configured Windows Media Player, but you still need to let it know about all the audio and video files on your computer. (If you display the Media Library page before you've searched your computer for media files, Windows Media Player prompts you to search for files.)

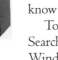

See pages 56–57 of the *Essential Skills* section for a visual guide to letting Windows Media Player know about the media files on your computer.

To let Windows Media Player know about the media files on your computer, choose Tools ➤ Search for Media Files or press the F3 key. In the Search for Media Files dialog box that Windows Media Player displays, specify which drives (and if necessary, which folders) to search, and choose any advanced search options needed. Then click the Search button to set the search going. If you have a hard drive of any size, the search takes a few minutes. Windows Media Player lists the files it found on the Media Library page.

WARNING *The Media Library is shared with all other users of the computer, including the Guest user. Don't put anything in your Media Library that you don't want other users to see or hear.*

Playing Audio Files from Disk

Once you've let Windows Media Player discover the tracks that you have on your computer and list them in the Media Library, you can play any track by navigating to it and double-clicking it (or by selecting it and clicking the Play button).

You can also open a file by choosing File ➤ Open (or pressing Ctrl+O) to display the Open dialog box, navigating to and selecting the file, and clicking the Open button.

Playing Music from the *My Music*\ Folder

If you prefer to locate your music by browsing through your \My Music\ folder or the \Shared Music\ folder rather than by using Windows Media Player, you can launch Windows Media Player and start music playing by selecting a folder of music (or a track) and clicking the Play Selection link in the Music Tasks pane or by clicking the Play All link with no track selected in a folder of music.

To make these links available to other folders, customize each folder and apply one of the music templates: the Music (Best for Audio Files and Playlists) template, the Music Artist (Best for Works by One Artist) template, or the Music Album (Best for Tracks from One Album) template.

Creating Playlists

Playing audio files from disk is easy enough, but you can make it even easier by creating playlists of the audio files you like to play together.

To create a new playlist, follow these steps:

1. Click the New Playlist button on the Media Library page. Windows Media Player displays the New Playlist dialog box.

2. Enter the name for the playlist in the New Playlist dialog box.

3. Click the OK button. Windows Media Player closes the New Playlist dialog box and creates a new playlist in the My Playlists list.

4. Populate the playlist by dragging tracks to it.

To start a playlist playing, double-click it on the Media Library page. To switch from one playlist to another, use the drop-down list in the upper-right corner of Windows Media Player.

Playing a CD

Unless you turn off Autoplay (as discussed in Chapter 6), Windows Media Player automatically starts playing an audio CD you insert in your CD drive. If your computer is connected to the Internet, Windows Media Player attempts to retrieve the CD information by submitting the CD's ID number to the WindowsMedia.com database of information. (According to Microsoft, Windows Media Player doesn't submit any information about you other than the Globally Unique Identifier [GUID] and your IP address, which is required to get the information about the CD back to your computer.)

If Windows Media Player doesn't automatically display the track names, or if it shows them as Unknown Artist – Unknown Album, you'll need to retrieve them manually. Click the Get Names button, and Windows Media Player leads you through a search for the artist and album. The process is clumsy, but it works well enough if WindowsMedia.com has the artist and album listed.

Unfortunately, the WindowsMedia.com database isn't very complete at this writing. It's nothing like as complete as CDDB, the online database of CD information (`www.cddb.org`) that is widely used by MP3 rippers and that contains impressively accurate information for a very wide range of CDs. CDDB works in the same way as WindowsMedia.com: It uses the unique identifying code that each commercially released audio CD contains. By submitting this code, a program can download the CD information: artist name, CD name, and track titles. Most rippers handle this process automatically when you insert a CD.

NOTE *Part of CDDB's wide coverage of CDs is due to its receiving many entries from its users. If a CD you try to look up in CDDB doesn't have an entry, you can submit one. Many MP3 rippers have a built-in mechanism for submitting entries to CDDB.*

If the artist isn't listed, click the Not Found button. Windows Media Player displays a screen that lets you add the CD's information to your local database.

Using the Graphic Equalizer and Sound Effects

Windows Media Player includes a minimalist graphic equalizer for improving the sound that emerges from your speakers or headphones. It's minimalist in that, although it comes with a number of preset equalizations and allows you to adjust 10 bands of frequency to your taste, it does not let you save your custom equalizations or load equalizations automatically with tracks.

The Graphic Equalizer appears on the Now Playing page of Windows Media Player when the Equalizer and Settings panel is displayed. If the Equalizer and Settings panel is not displayed, choose View ➤ Now Playing Tools ➤ Show Equalizer and Settings. Then choose View ➤ Now Playing Tools ➤ Graphic Equalizer to display the Graphic Equalizer if one of the other Now Playing tools is displayed. Figure 27.15 shows the Graphic Equalizer.

FIGURE 27.15

Use the Graphic Equalizer to improve the sound of audio.

The Graphic Equalizer is straightforward to use:

◆ To turn the Graphic Equalizer on and off, click the On/Off button.

◆ To apply a preset equalization, choose it from the Current Preset drop-down list.

◆ To apply custom equalization, drag each frequency-band slider to an appropriate position. The frequency bands start with the lowest frequencies at the left side and progress to the highest frequencies at the right side.

◆ To specify whether the frequency-band sliders move independently or together, click one of the three buttons on the control to the left of the frequency bands. Click the top button to make the sliders move independently. Click the middle button to make the sliders move together in a loose group. Click the bottom button to make the sliders move together in a tight group.

To apply sound effects, click the Select View button and choose SRS WOW Effects from the context menu. Windows Media Player displays the SRS WOW Effects panel (shown in Figure 27.16). From here, you can use the On/Off button to turn the effects on and off, set bass boosting with the TruBass slider, set the wow effect with the WOW Effect slider, or choose a different speaker setting.

FIGURE 27.16

Use the SRS WOW Effects panel to apply sound effects to audio.

Copying (Ripping) a CD

Windows Media Player provides features for what it calls "copying" an audio CD to your hard drive. This doesn't mean copying each file on the CD bit for bit, but rather extracting the audio data from the CD (a process normally called *ripping*) and encoding it to a compressed format called Windows Media Audio (WMA).

As you probably know, CD-quality audio files are huge, taking up about 9MB per minute. (This is why about 74 minutes of audio fits on a 650MB CD.) WMA files can be encoded at various bitrates, including the six bitrates that Windows Media Player offers: 48Kbps, 64Kbps, 96Kbps, 128Kbps, 160Kbps, and 192Kpbs. Windows Media Player's default bitrate is 64Kbps. This bitrate sounds borderline okay to many people and is good if you're trying to pack as much music as possible onto a portable device. But to make the files you copy sound good when you play them back on your PC, increase the bitrate to 128Kbps, 160Kbps, or 192Kbps—the higher the better, especially if you're likely to upgrade your sound card or your speakers before you change your taste in music.

See pages 58–59 of the *Essential Skills* section for a visual guide to copying a CD.

Windows Media Player can encode to MP3 if you add a third-party codec. Click the MP3 Information button on the Copy Music page of the Options dialog box to display an Internet Explorer window containing information on the MP3 Creation Pack for Windows XP and how to get it.

The first time you go to rip a CD with Windows Media Player, it displays the Windows Media Player dialog box shown in Figure 27.17. This dialog box tells you that Windows Media Player is configured to protect your content from "unauthorized use," and that you won't be able to play content that's protected like this on any computer other than this one.

FIGURE 27.17

This Windows Media Player dialog box lets you turn off copy music protection if you claim to understand that the content you're copying is protected by law.

This restriction makes a lot of sense for Microsoft, because it prevents you from violating copyright law in a couple of important ways: by preventing you from using illegal copies of these tracks. (See the nearby Expert Knowledge sidebar for an explanation of what you can and cannot legally do with digital audio.)

But it doesn't protect you from violating copyright law in one important way: by borrowing a CD from someone else and copying it, or by lending someone one of your CDs so that they can copy it.

If you're fine with this restriction, click the OK button. If you're not, select the Do Not Protect Content check box to disable the protection, then click the OK button. This means that you'll be able to use the files you copy on other PCs. It also means that you can commit extra copyright violations either intentionally or unintentionally.

EXPERT KNOWLEDGE: WHAT CAN YOU LEGALLY DO WITH DIGITAL AUDIO?

If you're going to enjoy digital audio, you need to know what you can and cannot do with it. Here's what you can legally do:

◆ Listen to streaming audio from a Web site or an Internet radio station, even if the site or person streaming the audio is doing so illegally.

◆ Record audio from a medium you own (for example, a CD) to a different medium (for example, a cassette) so that you can listen to it at a different time or in a different place.

◆ Download a digital file that contains copyrighted material from a Web site or FTP site *provided that the copyright holder has granted the distributor permission to distribute it.*

◆ Download a digital file from a computer via P2P technology (for example, Napster, audioGnome, or Gnutella) *provided that the copyright holder has granted the distributor permission to distribute it.*

◆ Create digital-audio files (for example, WMA files or MP3 files) of tracks on CDs you own for your personal use.

◆ Distribute a digital-audio file to which you hold the copyright or for whose distribution the copyright holder has granted you permission.

◆ Download (or copy) legal MP3 files or digital-audio files in other supported formats to portable audio devices (such as the Diamond Rio or the Creative Labs Nomad).

◆ Broadcast licensed audio across the Internet.

Here are some of the key things that you cannot legally do with audio:

◆ Download a digital-audio file that contains copyrighted material if the copyright holder has not granted the distributor permission to distribute it.

◆ Distribute a digital-audio file that contains copyrighted material if the copyright holder has not granted you permission to distribute it.

◆ Lend a friend a CD so that she can create digital-audio files from it.

◆ Borrow a CD from a friend and create digital-audio files from it.

◆ Upload digital-audio files from a portable audio player that supports music uploading (such as the I-JAM or the eGo) to another computer. (In this scenario, you're essentially using the portable player to copy the files from one computer to another.)

To copy a CD, follow these general steps:

1. Load the CD in your CD drive.

2. If Windows Media Player starts playing the CD, stop it.

3. Click the Copy from CD tab. Windows displays the Copy from CD page.

4. If Windows Media Player doesn't automatically retrieve the CD information, use the Get Names feature to retrieve the information manually. (If necessary, type in the information.)

5. If necessary, edit the information retrieved. You can edit any of the changeable fields (such as the track names, the artist's name, or the genre) by clicking the field twice (with a pause in between—*not* double-clicking). Windows Media Player displays an edit box around the field. Type the correction and press the Enter key.

6. If necessary, change (or check) the Copy Music at This Quality slider setting on the Copy Music page of the Options dialog box.

7. Select the check boxes for the tracks you want to copy. Use the check box in the column header to change the status of all the individual check boxes at once.

8. Click the Copy Music button. Windows Media Player starts ripping and encoding the music, adding the tracks to the Media Library when they're finished.

If you notice a problem, click the Stop Copy button to stop copying the tracks.

Playing a DVD

Once you've installed a DVD drive and a DVD player, you can play a DVD by putting it in the drive and choosing Play ➤ DVD or CD Audio. Windows Media Player uses the standard Play controls for DVDs and displays a list of the DVD chapters in the playlist area.

NOTE *If you have a DVD drive but no player for it, consult the DVD Troubleshooter for details of compatible players.*

To make the most of your DVDs, you'll probably want to view them full-screen. To do so, choose View ➤ Full Screen or press Alt+Enter. Windows Media Player switches to full-screen view. You can display pop-up controls on-screen by moving the mouse. These disappear after a few seconds when you stop moving the mouse.

To display DVD controls (such as a Variable Play Speed control and a Next Frame control), choose View ➤ Now Playing Tools ➤ DVD Controls.

Tuning Into Internet Radio

See pages 62–63 of the *Essential Skills* section for a visual guide to tuning into Internet radio.

Windows Media Player provides good features for tuning into Internet radio—radio broadcast across the Web via streaming audio servers such as SHOUTcast, icecast, or RealAudio. To listen to Internet radio, click the Radio Tuner tab to display the Radio Tuner page. Figure 27.18 shows the Radio Tuner page with a station playing.

Connecting to an Internet Radio Station

The easiest way to connect to a radio station is to use a preset. Windows Media Player comes with a number of presets built in. You can edit these and create your own presets as you want.

To listen to a preset station, select the category of presets in the Featured Stations list. Then click the preset you want to listen to. Windows Media Player displays information about the station. Click the Play link.

FIGURE 27.18

Use Windows Media Player's Radio Tuner page to listen to radio stations broadcasting across the Internet.

Windows Media Player displays the message *Connecting to media* while it is connecting to the radio station. Next, it displays the word *Buffering* and a percentage-completed readout as it fills the buffer for the signal. When buffering is complete, Windows Media Player starts playing the station.

NOTE   *Windows Media Player sometimes needs to download a codec (a coder/decoder) in order to play back a station. Some codecs may take a minute or two to download—so if you're planning to listen to a broadcast on a station you haven't accessed before, allow time for a codec download. Depending on the settings you've chosen for Windows Media Player, installing a codec may well raise a Security Warning dialog box. Check the publisher's digital certificate if you're in any doubt about the authenticity of the codec.*

Windows Media Player displays a browser window containing information about the radio station. Use this window to learn more about the station and its programming. But if you're listening to radio over a dial-up connection, you may find that this window is taking up bandwidth, especially if it's slow to load or if it runs tickers or animations. If this is happening, close the window so that it doesn't take bandwidth from the signal.

TIP   *If you're using a dial-up connection and the signal keeps stopping and rebuffering, increase the size of the buffer on the Performance page of the Options dialog box.*

Searching for a Radio Station

You can browse for a radio station by following the category links (Country, 80s, Adult Contemporary, and so on) under the Find More Stations heading. Alternatively, click the Find More Stations link and use the screen shown in Figure 27.19 to search by keyword or zip code.

You can also perform an advanced search. To do so, click the Use Advanced Search button to display the Advanced Search panel (shown in Figure 27.20). Specify whichever criteria you want—Genre, Language, Country, State (in the U.S. only), Speed, Band (AM, FM, or the Net), or Keyword, Call Sign, or Frequency—and click the Search button to locate stations that match.

FIGURE 27.19

You can browse for a radio station by genre or search by keyword or zip code.

FIGURE 27.20

Use the Advanced Search panel to use multiple criteria in your search for a radio station.

Creating and Editing Presets

You can edit your presets by changing the My Stations list as you need. You cannot change the Featured Stations list.

To add a station to your My Stations list, expand its heading and click its Add to My Stations link.

To remove a station from your My Stations list, expand its heading in the My Stations list and choose Remove from My Stations.

To change the order in which Windows Media Player lists the stations in your My Stations list, use the red up-arrow and down-arrow buttons to move a station up or down the list.

Applying Skins

You can apply *skins* (custom graphical looks) to Windows Media Player to change its appearance in Skin mode. Windows Media Player comes with a selection of skins built in. To apply a skin, display the Skin Chooser page of Windows Media Player. Select a skin in the list box to see how it looks. When you find one you like, click the Apply Skin button to apply it. See pages 60–61 of the *Essential Skills* section for a visual guide to applying a skin to Windows Media Player.

TIP You can also apply a skin quickly by double-clicking its file in an Explorer window or on your Desktop.

To download extra skins, click the More Skins button on the Skin Chooser page. Windows Media Player opens a browser window of the appropriate page of the WindowsMedia.com Web site, which maintains a gallery of skins, some created by Microsoft and others by users. (You'll also find skins in online software archives such as CNET's Download.com, but WindowsMedia.com is a good place to start.)

When you download a skin package, Windows displays the Windows Media Download dialog box. From this, you can click the View Now button to display the skin or the Close button to dismiss the dialog box.

NOTE *Windows Media Player skins can have the file type Windows Media Player Skin File and the WMS extension, but you'll usually find them compressed into files of the Windows Media Player Skin Package file type. These have the WMZ extension.*

To delete a skin from Windows Media Player, select it in the list box and click the Delete button, then click the Yes button in the Confirm Skin Delete dialog box that Windows Media Player displays.

You can create your own custom skins for Windows Media Player. To do so, download the Windows Media Player Software Development Kit from the Microsoft Web site and follow the tutorials on the Microsoft Developer Network (MSDN; `msdn.microsoft.com/workshop/imedia/windowsmedia/wmpskins.asp`). When you've created a skin, store it in the `\Program Files\Windows Media Player\Skins\` folder, and Windows Media Player will automatically list it on the Skin Chooser page.

Choosing Visualizations

When it's playing audio, Windows Media Player shows visualizations (graphical displays) on the Now Playing page.

To toggle a visualization to full screen, press Alt+Enter or choose View ➤ Full Screen. Press the Esc key (or Alt+Enter again) to toggle off full screen.

To change the visualization, choose View ➤ Visualizations and make a choice from the Ambience, Bars and Waves, Particle, Plenoptic, or Spikes submenu.

Editing MP3 and WMA Tags

WMA files and MP3 files include a *tag*, a virtual container with slots for a number of pieces of information, such as the artist's name, the track name, the album name, the genre, and so on. By using these tags, you can not only keep your music clearly identified, but you can also sort the tracks by any of the pieces of information. For example, you could sort tracks by artist or by album.

To edit the tag on an MP3 file or a WMA file, follow these steps:

1. In an Explorer window, right-click the file and choose Properties from the context menu. Windows displays the Properties dialog box for the file.

2. Click the Summary tab. Windows displays the Summary page. Figure 27.21 shows an example.

    ◆ If the Summary page is displaying an Advanced button, click it to display the Summary page in Advanced view. Windows replaces the Advanced button with a Simple button that you can click to return to Simple view.

3. Edit the tag information as appropriate. You can change any field that has a pen on its icon. You can't change fields such as Duration, Bitrate, and License.

4. Click the OK button. Windows applies the changes to the track's tag and closes the Properties dialog box for the file.

FIGURE 27.21

You can edit the tag information on a WMA file or an MP3 file on the Summary page of the file's Properties dialog box.

Backing Up and Restoring Licenses

If you download tracks secured with digital licenses, or if you use digital licenses on tracks you copy to disk, back up your licenses in case you have disk trouble. Should you lose the licenses, you won't be able to play the tracks.

Backing Up Your Licenses

To back up your licenses, follow these steps:

1. Choose Tools ➤ License Management. Windows Media Player displays the License Management dialog box (shown in Figure 27.22).

FIGURE 27.22

Back up your digital licenses so that you can restore them if you have computer trouble.

2. Check the folder indicated in the Location text box. If necessary, click the Browse button and use the resulting Browse for Folder dialog box to specify a different folder.

◆ For safety, keep the backup on a removable medium, or make a copy of it on an online drive.

3. Click the Backup Now button. Windows Media Player closes the first License Management dialog box, copies the licenses, and displays the second License Management dialog box (shown in Figure 27.23).

FIGURE 27.23

This License Management dialog box appears when the licenses have been safely backed up.

4. Click the OK button. Windows Media Player closes the second License Management dialog box.

Restoring Your Licenses

To restore your licenses from backup, follow these steps:

1. Choose Tools ➤ License Management. Windows Media Player displays the License Management dialog box.

2. Click the Restore Now button. Windows Media Player displays the License Management dialog box shown in Figure 27.24, warning you that the restoration needs Internet access and that Windows Media Player will send your GUID to a Microsoft service.

FIGURE 27.24

Windows Media Player displays this License Management dialog box for restoring your licenses.

3. Click the OK button. Windows Media Player contacts the Microsoft site for authorization. If it receives authorization, Windows Media Player copies the licenses and displays the License Management dialog box shown in Figure 27.25 to let you know the operation has succeeded.

FIGURE 27.25

You'll see this License Management dialog box when Windows Media Player has successfully restored your licenses.

4. Click the OK button. Windows Media Player closes the License Management dialog box.

Playing Videos

Playing a video file could hardly be easier:

- To play a video file listed in your Media Library, double-click it.

- To play a video file that's not listed in your Media Library, choose File ➤ Open and use the resulting Open dialog box to select the video to open.

- To change the brightness, contrast, hue, saturation, and size of the image, choose View ➤ Now Playing Tools ➤ Video Settings and work with the resulting Video Settings tools.

Setting Output Volume and Recording Volume

As you saw earlier in the chapter, you can adjust the output volume by moving the Volume slider in Windows Media Player. If you prefer, you can put a Volume control in the notification area (the System Tray) so that it's always at your mouse-tips even when Windows Media Player or your other favorite noise-maker is minimized or hidden behind other windows.

This section starts by showing you how to do that. It then covers the Volume Control program that Windows provides for controlling output volume and recording volume, adjusting the sound balance, choosing input and output, and so on.

Displaying the Volume Control in the Notification Area

For immediate access to a Volume control, you can put one in the notification area. Take the following steps:

1. Choose Start ➤ Control Panel. Windows displays Control Panel.

2. Click the Sounds, Speech, and Audio Devices link. Control Panel displays the Sounds, Speech, and Audio Devices screen.

3. In the Pick a Task list, click the Adjust the System Volume link. Control Panel displays the Volume page of the Sounds and Audio Devices Properties dialog box (shown in Figure 27.26).

4. Select the Place Volume Icon in the Taskbar check box.

FIGURE 27.26

To make Windows display the Volume control in the System Tray, select the Place Volume Icon in the Taskbar check box on the Volume page of the Sounds and Audio Devices Properties dialog box.

5. Click the OK button. Windows closes the Sounds and Audio Devices Properties dialog box and displays the Volume control in the notification area.

TIP By default, Windows applies its default notification-area behavior to the Volume control: Hide When Inactive. You'll probably want to change the Volume control's behavior to Always Show so that it's always available.

To set the volume, click the Volume control. Windows displays a pop-up panel bearing a Volume slider and a Mute check box (shown in Figure 27.27). Drag the slider up and down to set the volume. Windows emits a Ding chord when you release the slider so that you can hear the approximate loudness of that volume. Click anywhere other than the pop-up panel to make the panel disappear.

FIGURE 27.27

Setting volume with the notification-area Volume control

When you mute the sound by selecting the Mute check box on the pop-up panel, Windows displays a red circle and bar beside the Volume control as a visual reminder.

You can double-click the Volume control, or right-click it and choose Open Volume Control from the context menu, to display the Play Control window. And you can right-click the Volume control and choose Adjust Audio Properties from the context menu to display the Volume page of the Sounds and Audio Devices Properties dialog box.

Setting Volume from the Sounds and Audio Devices Properties Dialog Box

If you seldom need to change the volume being output by your computer (for example, if you have a physical volume control strapped to your keyboard or elsewhere within reach), you probably won't want to waste notification-area space on the Volume control. Instead, you can use the Device Volume slider on the Volume page of the Sounds and Audio Devices Properties dialog box to set the volume and the Mute check box to mute the sound.

Setting Speaker Balance

To set speaker balance on the signal output by your sound card (as opposed to setting it via your amplifier), click the Speaker Volume button in the Speaker Settings group box on the Volume page of the Sounds and Audio Devices Properties dialog box. Windows displays the Speaker Volume dialog box (shown in Figure 27.28). Drag the sliders to suitable positions; select the Move All Slide Indicators at the Same Time check box if you want synchronized sliding. Then click the OK button. Windows closes the Speaker Volume dialog box.

FIGURE 27.28

You can set speaker balance on your sound card's output by using the Speaker Volume dialog box.

Setting Advanced Audio Properties

Beyond the speaker balance settings, Windows also offers advanced audio settings. You can specify your speaker layout, the degree of hardware acceleration to use on audio playback, and the sample rate conversion quality to use.

To choose advanced audio settings, click the Advanced button in the Speaker Settings group box on the Volume page of the Sounds and Audio Devices Properties dialog box. Windows displays the Advanced Audio Properties dialog box.

The Speakers page of the Advanced Audio Properties dialog box (shown in Figure 27.29) contains only one setting: the Speaker Setup drop-down list. Choose the appropriate option for your speakers or headphones. Your choices range from Desktop Stereo Speakers through to 7.1 Surround Sound Speakers (seven satellites and a subwoofer).

FIGURE 27.29

Specify your speaker setup on the Speakers page of the Advanced Audio Properties dialog box.

The Performance page of the Advanced Audio Properties dialog box (shown in Figure 27.30) contains two settings:

Hardware Acceleration slider   Drag this slider to set the amount of hardware acceleration you want to use. On most computers, it's best to start with full acceleration and decrease it only if your computer exhibits audio problems.

Sample Rate Conversion Quality slider   Drag this slider to choose a balance between audio quality and CPU usage. Windows starts you off with a setting of Good. Try improving this, and reduce it again only if your computer's performance suffers.

FIGURE 27.30

Choose audio performance settings on the Performance page of the Advanced Audio Properties dialog box.

Click the OK button. Windows closes the Advanced Audio Properties dialog box.

Using the Volume Control Program

Windows' Volume Control program provides close control over audio output and input.

Volume Control can initially be confusing for several reasons:

- First, the window in which it appears isn't even called Volume Control. (See the next objection.)

- Second, Volume Control has separate manifestations for output and input. Depending on the sound card installed on your computer, you'll see different names for each. For example, with most Sound Blaster cards, the output manifestation of Volume Control appears as a window named Play Control, and the input manifestation appears as a window named Record Control. With other sound cards, you'll see other names, such as Master Out and Recording Control.

- Third, Volume Control hides advanced options until you force it to display them.

- And fourth, the set of controls that Volume Control displays changes depending on the capabilities of your sound card.

- Oh, and fifth, you can choose which of the available controls are displayed.

USING PLAY CONTROL

To use Play Control (or whatever your sound card calls it), display its window by taking one of the following actions:

- Choose Start ➤ All Programs ➤ Accessories ➤ Entertainment ➤ Volume Control.

- If Windows is displaying the Volume control in the notification area, double-click it.

- Click the Advanced button in the Device Volume group box on the Volume page of the Sounds and Audio Devices Properties dialog box.

Figure 27.31 shows a typical Play Control window.

FIGURE 27.31

Play Control lets you control the output source and volume for the sound card.

The controls in the Play Control window are intuitive enough to use:

◆ The leftmost set of controls (which appears in Figure 27.31 as Play Control, but which with other sound cards appears with other names such as Master Out) is the master control. Move the Volume slider to control the master volume (doing so manipulates the Volume control in the notification area directly); move the Balance control to change the master left-right balance; and select the Mute All check box to silence all output from the sound card.

◆ Set the volume, balance, and muting for the other controls as appropriate. Which controls appear depends on your sound card, but typically you'll see entries such as Wave, MIDI, Digital, CD Audio, Line In, and Auxiliary.

◆ Select the Mute check box to mute any given output. Select the Mute All check box to mute all the outputs.

◆ To display any advanced options your sound card supports, choose Options ➤ Advanced Controls. The window displays an Advanced button beneath the master Volume controls. Click this button, and Windows displays the Advanced Controls dialog box, which offers bass and treble controls together with any other controls your sound card offers. Figure 27.32 shows an example of the Advanced Controls dialog box.

FIGURE 27.32

Use the Advanced Controls dialog box to set any advanced options your sound card offers.

◆ To change the set of controls displayed, choose Options ➤ Properties. Volume Control displays the Properties dialog box (shown in Figure 27.33). In the Show the Following Volume Controls list box, select the check boxes for the controls you want in the window and clear the check boxes for those you don't want. Then click the OK button. Volume Control closes the Properties dialog box and adjusts the window to show the controls whose check boxes you selected.

TIP   *If your computer has multiple sound cards, you can switch between them by using the Mixer Device drop-down list in the Properties dialog box for Volume Control.*

FIGURE 27.33

In the Properties dialog box, choose the controls you want the Volume Control window to display.

USING RECORD CONTROL

To display the Record Control window (or whatever your sound card calls it), take the following steps:

1. Display Play Control as described in the previous section.

2. Choose Options ➢ Properties. Volume Control displays the Properties dialog box.

3. Select the Recording option button and click the OK button. Volume Control closes the Properties dialog box and displays the Record Control window (shown in Figure 27.34).

FIGURE 27.34

The Record Control window lets you control the input devices, volume, and balance.

As with Play Control, Record Control has a Balance slider and a Volume slider for each input device. Where Play Control has a Mute check box for each device, Record Control has a Select check box. Select the Select check box for the input device you want to use, and choose appropriate volume and balance settings. (With most sound cards, the Select check boxes actually work like a set of option buttons—selecting one Select check box automatically deselects all the other Select check boxes.)

Recording Audio Files with Sound Recorder

If you need to create some simple WAV files, use Sound Recorder, which comes with Windows. Sound Recorder is a simple program with some severe limitations. The worst limitation is that its maximum file length is a mere 60 seconds, so while it's fine for recording sound effects, short memos, and so on, it's no good for, say, recording a song of even modest length.

You can also use Sound Recorder for converting WAV files to some other formats, including MP3. But Sound Recorder is limited in this, too, offering bitrates of only 56Kbps and lower for MP3 files.

Starting Sound Recorder

To start Sound Recorder, choose Start ➤ All Programs ➤ Accessories ➤ Entertainment ➤ Sound Recorder. Figure 27.35 shows Sound Recorder.

FIGURE 27.35

Sound Recorder is useful for recording WAV files.

Recording a Sound File with Sound Recorder

To record a sound file with Sound Recorder, take the following steps:

1. Use Record Control to select the input you want to use. Choose appropriate volume and balance settings.

2. If you currently have a file open in Sound Recorder, choose File ➤ New. Sound Recorder closes the current file, prompting you to save it if it contains unsaved changes, and opens a new file.

3. Get the input ready. For example, bring your microphone within kissing distance of your mouth or throat, or feed in a signal through the Line In jack.

4. Click the Record button.

5. Start the input.

6. Click the Stop button to stop recording. (Sound Recorder automatically stops recording after 60 seconds.)

7. Save the file by choosing File ➤ Save and specifying the name and path in the Save As dialog box.

Once you've recorded a sound, you can take assorted self-explanatory actions with it:

◆ Click the Play button to play back the file.

◆ Drag the slider to move to a specific position in the file.

◆ To add to the end of a sound file you've created, or to record over part of it and add to the end of it, position the slider at the end or at the position at which you want to start recording over its current contents. Then click the Record button.

◆ To truncate the file, place the slider in the appropriate position and choose Edit ➤ Delete before Current Position or Edit ➤ Delete after Current Position as appropriate.

◆ Apply one of the effects by using the Effects menu: Increase Volume (by 25%), Decrease Volume, Increase Speed (by 100%), Decrease Speed, Add Echo, and Reverse.

TIP *Because Sound Recorder doesn't offer an Undo feature, it's a good idea to save the sound file before adding to a file or applying an effect. If you don't like the result, you can then close the file without saving changes.*

Converting a File to Another Format

To convert a WAV file to another format, follow these steps:

1. Open the WAV file.

2. Choose File ➤ Save As. Sound Recorder displays the Save As dialog box.

3. Click the Change button at the bottom of the Save As dialog box. Sound Recorder displays the Sound Selection dialog box (shown in Figure 27.36).

FIGURE 27.36

Use the Sound Selection dialog box to specify the format of the sound file when converting a WAV file to another format.

4. Choose the format in the Format drop-down list.

5. Choose any applicable attributes (for example, the bitrate) in the Attributes drop-down list.

6. Click the OK button. Sound Recorder closes the Sound Selection dialog box and returns you to the Save As dialog box.

7. Specify the filename as usual in the Save As dialog box.

8. Click the Save button. Sound Recorder closes the Save As dialog box, converts the file to the specified format, and saves it under the name you chose.

Up Next

This chapter has concentrated on audio, discussing how to make the most of Windows Media Player for listening to CDs, copying CDs to your hard disk, and tuning into Internet radio. You've also seen the assorted ways of controlling the volume that Windows outputs, and how to record sounds with the distressingly limited tool that Windows provides for the purpose.

It's time to get graphical. The next chapter discusses how to work with pictures and videos.

Chapter 28

Working with Pictures and Videos

WINDOWS XP PROVIDES STRONG FEATURES for working with pictures and videos—everything from easily viewing and rotating a picture to making a video of your own. The chapter starts by discussing the tools that Windows provides for manipulating pictures via Explorer. It then discusses how to install scanners and digital cameras; how to scan documents; and how to retrieve images from a digital camera. After that, it covers how to capture still pictures from a video camera and how to copy your pictures to the Web. It finishes by showing you how to get started at making your own movies with Windows Movie Maker.

This chapter covers the following topics:

◆ Using the Photo Album template image-manipulation features

◆ Installing a scanner or digital camera

◆ Scanning an image

◆ Working with a digital camera

◆ Capturing still pictures from a video camera

◆ Copying your pictures to the Web

◆ Making movies with Windows Movie Maker

Using the Photo Album Template Tools

The most convenient place to work with pictures just so happens to be the \My Pictures\ folder—the folder in which Windows would like you to save all pictures you're not sharing. The next most convenient place is the \Shared Pictures\ folder, which shares the features of the \My Pictures\ folder but is a little slower to access. This folder, of course, is where Windows would like you to save all the pictures you're sharing with other users. However, you can store your pictures in any folder you choose and still use the image-manipulation features that Windows provides.

When Windows detects that all the files in a folder you're opening for the first time are graphics, it applies to it the Photo Album template. This template displays the Picture Tasks list and makes Filmstrip view available. Figure 28.1 shows a folder of pictures in Filmstrip view with the Picture Tasks list displayed.

FIGURE 28.1

The Photo Album template provides the Picture Tasks list and Filmstrip view for manipulating graphics.

The Picture Tasks list provides the following links:

Get Pictures from Camera or Scanner link   Clicking this link starts the Scanner and Camera Wizard, discussed in the section after next.

View As a Slide Show link   Clicking this link makes Windows display a full-screen slideshow of the pictures in the folder. To have a slideshow of just some pictures, select them first. To control the slideshow, use the buttons on the toolbar that Windows displays when you move the mouse.

Order Prints Online link   Clicking this link makes Windows start the Internet Print Ordering Wizard, which walks you through the steps of ordering prints (or T-shirts, sweatshirts, ceramic mugs, and so on) from your choice of a number of online photo services. These services can be convenient, but you may find that your local photo-processing joint or drugstore offers a similar service in a shorter time.

Print This Picture link   Clicking this link makes Windows start the Photo Printing Wizard. See the section "Printing Pictures with the Photo Printing Wizard" later in this chapter for more information.

Set As Desktop Background link   Clicking this link makes Windows apply the picture as your Desktop background. Windows stretches the picture to fit your Desktop. This produces strange effects with portrait-orientation pictures. If that's a problem for you, crop the picture first.

The Filmstrip toolbar contains four buttons for manipulating pictures. Figure 28.2 shows the Filmstrip toolbar with labels. The buttons are self-explanatory to use.

FIGURE 28.2

You can use the buttons on the Filmstrip toolbar to manipulate pictures.

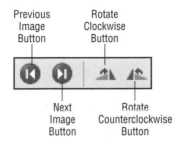

Previous Image Button

Rotate Clockwise Button

Next Image Button

Rotate Counterclockwise Button

You can also move from picture to picture by pressing the ← key and the → key. You can issue the rotation commands from the context menu from the picture or from the File menu.

Installing a Scanner or Digital Camera

To install a scanner or digital camera, connect it to your computer. If Windows notices the scanner or camera, it displays a notification-area pop-up such as that shown in Figure 28.3 and attempts to locate the software for the device. If Windows doesn't have drivers for the scanner, install them manually from the manufacturer's installation media or Web site.

NOTE   You may prefer to use the manufacturer's latest drivers rather than those included with Windows XP, as they may include extra features. To change the driver, follow the procedure described in the section "Installing and Updating Drivers" in Chapter 14.

FIGURE 28.3

If you're in luck, Windows automatically detects your scanner or camera when you plug it in.

If Windows doesn't automatically detect your scanner or camera, use the Scanner and Camera Installation Wizard to identify it. Start the Wizard by taking the following steps:

1. Choose Start ➢ Control Panel. Windows displays Control Panel.

2. Click the Printers and Other Hardware link. Windows displays the Printers and Other Hardware page.

3. Click the Scanners and Cameras Link. Windows displays the Scanners and Cameras page.

4. Double-click the Add an Imaging Device icon. Windows starts the Scanner and Camera Installation Wizard, which displays the Welcome to the Scanner and Camera Installation Wizard page.

To install your scanner or camera, follow the Wizard. This example shows the pages involved in installing a camera:

1. Click the Next button. The Scanner and Camera Installation Wizard displays the Which Scanner or Camera. Do You Want to Install? page (shown in Figure 28.4), which should look familiar from Chapter 14.

FIGURE 28.4

On the Which Scanner or Camera Do You Want to Install? page of the Scanner and Camera Installation Wizard, select the driver or provide one of your own.

2. Use the Manufacturer list and the Model list to specify your camera, or use the Have Disk button and its resulting dialog boxes to give Windows a new driver.

3. Click the Next button. The Scanner and Camera Installation Wizard displays the Connect Your Device to Your Computer page (shown in Figure 28.5).

FIGURE 28.5

On the Connect Your Device to Your Computer page of the Scanner and Camera Installation Wizard, choose which port you want the Wizard to install the camera on.

4. Connect the device, and choose the appropriate port in the Available Ports list. Alternatively, leave the Automatic Port Detection item selected.

TIP *If you have a choice, connect your digital camera to a USB port rather than a serial port. The USB port will transfer pictures at least 10 times faster than the serial port.*

5. Click the Next button. The Scanner and Camera Installation Wizard displays the What Is the Name of Your Device? page, which lets you adjust Windows' name for the device or enter a new name. This is the name under which the device appears in Explorer, so make sure it's descriptive and clear.

6. Click the Next button. The Scanner and Camera Installation Wizard displays the Completing the Scanner and Camera Installation Wizard page.

7. Click the Finish button. The Wizard copies the files, adds the device to the Scanners and Cameras page of Control Panel and to the Scanners and Cameras list in Explorer, and closes itself.

Once you've installed a scanner or a camera, it appears as an entry in the Scanners and Cameras list in My Computer. Double-clicking a scanner or a camera launches the Scanner and Camera Wizard.

TIP   To change the program associated with the scanner or camera, right-click its icon in the My Computer window and choose Properties from the context menu. Windows displays the Properties dialog box for the device. On the Events page, use the Select an Event drop-down list to specify the event you want to affect (for example, Scan Button for a scanner), and then select the program in the Start This Program drop-down list. Alternatively, choose one of the other actions available for the event.

Scanning a Picture

To scan a picture, load it in your scanner and take the following steps:

1. Start the Scanner and Camera Wizard in either of the following ways. The Scanner and Camera Wizard starts and displays its Welcome page.

   ◆ Display your \My Pictures\ folder (for example, by choosing Start ➣ My Pictures) and click the Get Pictures from Camera or Scanner link in the Picture Tasks list.

   ◆ Choose Start ➣ All Programs ➣ Accessories ➣ Scanner and Camera Wizard.

   If you have two or more scanners or cameras, the Wizard displays the Select Device dialog box (shown in Figure 28.6). Select the scanner you want to use and click the OK button. The Scanner and Camera Wizard displays its Welcome page.

FIGURE 28.6

In the Select Device dialog box, choose the scanner you want to use.

2. Click the Next button. The Scanner and Camera Wizard displays the Choose Scanning Preferences page (shown in Figure 28.7 after clicking the Preview button).

FIGURE 28.7

Select your preferences for scanning on the Choose Scanning Preferences page of the Scanner and Camera Wizard.

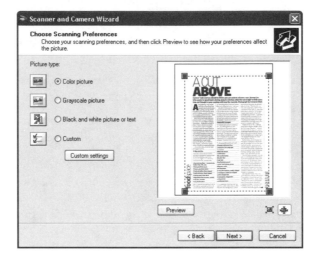

3. In the Picture Type list, select the Color Picture option button, the Grayscale Picture option button, the Black and White Picture or Text option button, or the Custom option button as appropriate. Click the Preview button to scan the image with that picture type and display it in the preview box. (Scanning the image takes a few seconds, so be patient.)

◆ If you select the Custom option button, click the Custom Settings button. The Wizard displays the Properties dialog box. The properties in this dialog box vary depending on your scanner and its features. Figure 28.8 shows an example.

◆ In the Appearance group box, drag the Brightness and Contrast sliders until the sample image looks good to you.

◆ In the Resolution (DPI) text box, specify the resolution you want to use. The Wizard offers values supported by your scanner.

FIGURE 28.8

Use the Properties dialog box to set custom scanning options for the scanner.

◆ In the Picture Type drop-down list, choose the Color Picture item, the Grayscale Picture item, or the Black and White Picture or Text item as appropriate.

◆ Click the OK button. The Wizard closes the Properties dialog box.

4. Adjust the size of the preview image if necessary. Drag the four sizing handles to select the area of the picture you want to scan. Click the Enlarge button (the left button above the Cancel button) to enlarge the selected area to fill the whole page. Click the Show the Entire Image button (the right button) to display the full picture and the sizing handles again.

5. Click the Next button. The Scanner and Camera Wizard displays the Picture Name and Destination page (shown in Figure 28.9).

FIGURE 28.9

On the Picture Name and Destination page of the Scanner and Camera Wizard, specify the location, format, and naming for the picture files.

6. In the Type a Name for This Group of Pictures drop-down list, enter the base name that you want to use for all the images you scan. Windows adds automatically incremented numbers to this name to form a unique name for each image. The default base name is *Picture*.

7. In the Select a File Format drop-down list, select the file format to use for the images. Your choices are BMP, JPG, TIF, or PNG:

◆ BMP (bitmap image) uses no compression, so it produces large files. But this format can be read by a wide variety of old software, so it may be useful for backward compatibility.

◆ JPG (JPEG image; Joint Pictures Experts Group) is the default format. JPG uses lossy compression, so you lose image quality when you use this format, but the results are good for general use. JPG files have a relatively small file size, which is good for saving and transferring the images.

◆ TIF (TIFF image; Tagged Image File Format) uses lossless compression, so it produces medium-large files. TIFFs are widely used, but not as widely as BMPs. Use this format if you want to use Windows Picture and Fax Viewer's image-annotation features.

◆ PNG (PNG image; Portable Network Graphics) is a lossless compression format designed for handling computer-generated images. PNG is generally considered less suitable than JPG for scanned images or photographs.

8. In the Choose a Place to Save This Group of Pictures drop-down list, specify the folder in which to save images. The default location is a folder named with the text in the Type a Name for This Group of Pictures text box and created in your \My Pictures\ folder, but the drop-down list offers other locations (such as your computer's \Shared Pictures\ folder) and naming methods. Alternatively, click the Browse button and use the resulting Browse for Folder dialog box to specify the folder.

9. Click the Next button. The Wizard displays the Scanning Picture page (shown in Figure 28.10) and starts scanning the picture with the settings you specified.

FIGURE 28.10

The Wizard displays the Scanning Picture page while it scans the picture.

10. When the Wizard has finished scanning the picture, it displays the Other Options page (shown in Figure 28.11).

11. Choose any other action you want to take with the pictures:

◆ If you want to copy the pictures to a Web site immediately, select the Publish These Pictures to a Web Site option button. (See "Copying Your Pictures to the Web" later in the chapter for details of this process.)

◆ If you want to order prints of the pictures, select the Order Prints of These Pictures from a Photo Printing Web Site option button. When you click the Next button, the Wizard walks you through the process of selecting a printing company and placing the order.

◆ Otherwise, leave the Nothing. I'm Finished Working with These Pictures option button selected. Click the Next button. The Wizard displays the Completing the Scanner and Camera Wizard page (shown in Figure 28.12).

FIGURE 28.11

On the Other Options page, choose whether to publish the scanned picture to a Web site, order prints of it, or finish working with it.

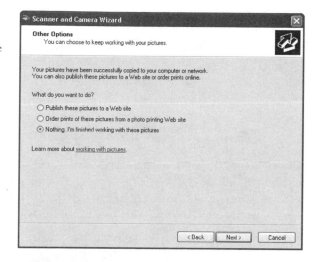

FIGURE 28.12

On the Completing the Scanner and Camera Wizard page of the Wizard, you can click the link to display the picture in an Explorer window.

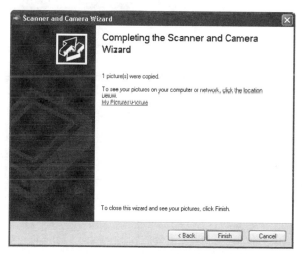

12. To display the picture in an Explorer window, click the link on the page. Otherwise, click the Finish button. The Scanner and Camera Wizard closes itself.

Working with a Digital Camera

This section discusses the three main actions you're likely to want to take with a digital camera: finding out how many pictures it contains, downloading them onto your computer, and deleting the pictures from the camera. It also touches on another action you may want to take: burning the pictures directly to a writable CD.

To work with your digital camera, display its folder by taking the following steps:

1. Choose Start ➤ My Computer. Windows opens an Explorer window to My Computer.

2. In the Scanners and Cameras list, double-click the item for the camera. Windows opens the folder for the camera and establishes communication with it. Figure 28.13 shows an example of a camera's folder with thumbnails downloaded from the camera.

FIGURE 28.13

The folder for a digital camera includes a Camera Tasks list.

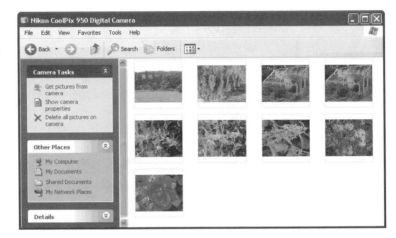

As you can see, the camera's folder includes a Camera Tasks list that contains camera-related actions.

Downloading Pictures from a Still Camera

To download pictures from a still camera, you use the Scanner and Camera Wizard. Take the following steps from the camera's folder:

1. Click the Get Pictures from Camera link. Windows starts the Scanner and Camera Wizard, which displays the Welcome to the Scanner and Camera Wizard page.

2. Click the Next button. The Scanner and Camera Wizard displays the Choose Pictures to Copy page (shown in Figure 28.14). This page displays Downloading Preview placeholders until it has downloaded previews of the pictures from the camera.

3. Select the check boxes for the pictures you want to download. (By default, the Scanner and Camera Wizard selects all the check boxes.) Use the Select All button and Clear All button to toggle selection of all the pictures on and off. Use the Rotate Clockwise button and Rotate Counterclockwise button to rotate an image for better viewing. To find out the size of a picture, click the Properties button (to the right of the Rotate Counterclockwise button). The Wizard displays the Properties dialog box for the picture, which contains the picture's size, name, and image format, and the time and date it was taken.

FIGURE 28.14

On the Choose Pictures to Copy page of the Scanner and Camera Wizard, select the pictures you want to download.

4. Click the Next button. The Wizard displays the Picture Name and Destination page (shown in Figure 28.15). You'll recognize this page as being almost the same as the page in the section earlier in the chapter on scanning pictures.

FIGURE 28.15

On the Picture Name and Destination page, specify the location and naming for the picture files.

5. In the Type a Name for This Group of Pictures drop-down list, enter the base name for all the pictures you download. Again, the default base name is *Picture*.

6. In the Choose a Place to Save This Group of Pictures drop-down list, specify the folder in which to save pictures. The default location is a folder named with the text in the Type a Name for This Group of Pictures text box and created in your \My Pictures\Picture\ folder.

7. Select the Delete Pictures from My Device after Copying Them check box if you want to do just that. This check box is cleared by default.

8. Click the Next button. The Wizard displays the Copying Pictures page (shown in Figure 28.16) while it downloads the pictures.

FIGURE 28.16

The Wizard displays the Copying Pictures page to show you its progress as it downloads the pictures.

9. When the Wizard has finished copying the pictures, it displays the Other Options page (shown in Figure 28.11 earlier in the chapter).

10. Choose any other action you want to take with the pictures:

    ◆ If you want to copy the pictures to a Web site immediately, select the Publish These Pictures to a Web Site option button. (See "Copying Your Pictures to the Web" later in the chapter for details of this process.)

    ◆ If you want to order prints of the pictures, select the Order Prints of These Pictures from a Photo Printing Web Site option button. When you click the Next button, the Wizard walks you through the process of selecting a printing company and placing the order.

    ◆ Otherwise, leave the Nothing. I'm Finished Working with These Pictures option button selected. Click the Next button. The Wizard displays the Completing the Scanner and Camera Wizard page (shown in Figure 28.12 earlier in the chapter).

11. Click the Finish button. The Scanner and Camera Wizard closes itself.

Burning Pictures to CD from the Camera

If you want to burn pictures directly to CD, drag the folder from your digital camera to the CD-R icon and drop it there. Windows copies the files to the queue for the CD, from where you can burn them to CD as usual.

Finding Out How Many Pictures Are on the Camera

To find out how many pictures the camera contains, click the Show Camera Properties link in the Camera Tasks list in the camera's folder. Windows contacts the camera for information and displays the Properties dialog box for the camera, which includes a Pictures Taken readout. Figure 28.17 shows an example of the Properties dialog box.

FIGURE 28.17

Use the Properties dialog box for a camera to find out how many pictures it's taken.

Deleting Pictures from the Camera

As you saw, you can delete pictures from the camera after downloading them—but in many cases you won't want to, especially if your camera has enough storage for a good number of pictures.

To delete pictures, click the Delete All Pictures on Camera link in the Camera Tasks list. Windows displays the Confirm Multiple File Delete dialog box. Click the Yes button. Windows deletes the pictures from the camera.

Capturing Still Pictures from a Video Camera

To capture still pictures from a video camera, connect it to your computer and take the following steps:

1. Choose Start ➢ All Programs ➢ Accessories ➢ Paint. Windows launches Paint.

2. Choose File ➢ From Scanner or Camera. Paint displays the Select Device dialog box (shown in Figure 28.18).

3. Select the device and click the OK button. Paint displays the Capture Pictures from Video dialog box (shown in Figure 28.19) with a feed running from the camera into the left pane.

4. Click the Capture button to capture the current frame. Paint displays a thumbnail of the resulting picture in the right pane.

5. Capture further frames if you want.

6. Choose the thumbnail of the picture you want in the right pane, then click the Get Picture button. Paint closes the Capture Pictures from Video dialog box and displays the captured frame as a new picture in Paint, where you can work with it and save it as usual.

FIGURE 28.18

In the Select Device dialog box, select the video camera from which you want to capture still pictures.

FIGURE 28.19

Use the Capture Pictures from Video dialog box to capture still pictures from a video camera.

Printing Pictures with the Photo Printing Wizard

The Photo Printing Wizard tries to simplify the process of printing pictures by walking you through the process of selecting the pictures and choosing the appropriate paper size and layout.

To print one or more pictures with the help of the Photo Printing Wizard, take the following steps:

1. Click the Print Pictures link in the Picture Tasks list in the \My Pictures\ folder. Windows launches the Photo Printing Wizard, which displays the Welcome to the Photo Printing Wizard page.

   ◆ If you prefer, you can select the pictures you want to print and then click the Print the Selected Pictures link. Alternatively, choose File ➤ Print or right-click a picture and choose Print from the context menu.

2. Click the Next button. The Wizard displays the Picture Selection page (shown in Figure 28.20).

FIGURE 28.20

On the Picture Selection page of the Photo Printing Wizard, select the pictures you want to print.

3. Select the check box for each picture you want to print. Use the Select All button and Clear All button if appropriate.

4. Click the Next button. The Wizard displays the Printing Options page (shown in Figure 28.21).

FIGURE 28.21

On the Printing Options page of the Photo Printing Wizard, choose the printer and the type of paper you want to use.

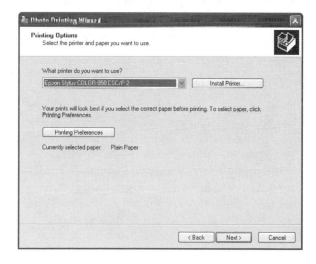

5. In the What Printer Do You Want to Use? drop-down list, select the printer.

6. If the What Type of Paper Do You Want to Use? drop-down list is available, use it to select the paper to use.

   ◆ If necessary, specify further settings by clicking the Printing Preferences button and working in the resulting dialog box.

7. Click the Next button. The Wizard displays the Layout Selection page (shown in Figure 28.22).

FIGURE 28.22

On the Layout Selection page of the Photo Printing Wizard, specify the layout for the paper.

8. In the Available Layouts list box, select the layout to use. The Print Preview box displays an approximation of how it will look.

9. Click the Next button. The Wizard starts sending the pictures to the printer. While it does so, it displays the Please Wait page. When it finishes, it displays the Completing the Photo Printing Wizard page.

10. Click the Finish button. The Wizard closes itself.

Copying Your Pictures to the Web

If you want, you can copy pictures directly from your camera or scanner onto the Web. This is impressive technology, but in most cases it's not a good idea, because usually it's a good idea to check the quality of your pictures or scans (and perhaps manipulate them) before posting them to the Web.

But if you want to use this feature, select the Publish These Pictures to a Web Site option button on the Other Options page of the Scanner and Camera Wizard. Click the Next button. The Wizard displays the Change Your File Selection page, on which you can select the pictures you want to copy to the Web. Click the Next button. The Wizard displays the Where Do You Want to Publish These Files? page, which offers you choices similar to those discussed in Chapter 26 for creating a network place on MSN or on another Web provider's site.

Select the provider and click the Next button. The Wizard walks you through the procedure for copying the pictures to the site. (This procedure varies from site to site.)

Making Movies with Windows Movie Maker

Windows Movie Maker is a basic video-editing program that lets you do the following:

◆ Transfer home movies from a video camera to your computer and edit them there

◆ Break a movie down into clips (shorter segments) to make it more manageable

- Add narration or a soundtrack to a movie
- Capture stills from a scene in the movie
- Add video files to your movies

Starting Windows Movie Maker

To start Windows Movie Maker, choose Start ➤ All Programs ➤ Accessories ➤ Windows Movie Maker.

Recording Video or Audio

The first step in creating a movie is to record video. You can record video and audio together (if your hardware supports it), video only, or audio only.

To record video or audio, take the following steps:

1. Click the Record button. Windows Movie Maker displays the Record dialog box (shown in Figure 28.23). If your source is already feeding data into the computer, the preview box displays the current picture. (For example, a typical webcam will be sending data already.) If not, this box appears blank.

FIGURE 28.23

In the Record dialog box, choose whether to record audio, video, or both, and specify the quality.

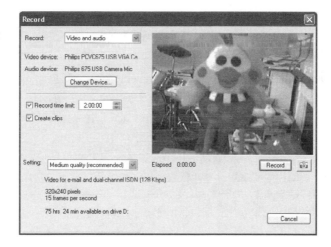

2. In the Record drop-down list, specify what you want to record by choosing Video and Audio, Video Only, or Audio Only.

3. Check the Video Device readout and the Audio Device readout to make sure that Windows Movie Maker has identified the devices you want to use. If it hasn't, change the devices as follows:

    - Click the Change Device button. Windows Movie Maker displays the Change Device dialog box (shown in Figure 28.24).

FIGURE 28.24

If necessary, use the
Change Device dialog
box to select different
audio- and video-
recording devices.

- ◆ Select the camera in the Video drop-down list. If necessary, click the Configure button and use the resulting Properties dialog box to configure the camera.

- ◆ Select the audio input device in the Audio drop-down list.

- ◆ Select the line input device in the Line drop-down list.

- ◆ Click the OK button. Windows Movie Maker closes the Change Device dialog box and enters your choices in the Record dialog box.

4. By default, Windows Movie Maker limits recording time, stopping recording after two hours. To change the limit, enter a different value in the Record Time Limit text box. If you don't want to use a time limit, clear the Record Time Limit check box.

NOTE *The danger of not using a time limit is that you could run out of disk space. Check the readout of available time at the lower-left corner of the dialog box once you've chosen a quality setting to make sure you have enough disk space for limitless recording.*

5. By default, Windows Movie Maker creates clips, breaking up your movie into more manageable segments. If you don't want to record in clips, clear the Create Clips check box.

6. In the Setting drop-down list, choose the quality at which you want to record. Windows Movie Maker offers the following choices:

Low Quality   Low Quality is suitable for Web servers delivering video to clients with dial-up 56Kbps connections. It uses a resolution of 176×144 pixels—a very small window—and a frame rate of 15 frames per second, which gives a jerky result. (30 frames per second gives a smooth transition between frames.)

Medium Quality   Medium Quality is suitable for sending via e-mail and for Web servers delivering video to clients with dual-channel ISDN connections (which give 128Kbps). It uses a resolution of 320×240 pixels and a frame rate of 15 frames per second.

High Quality   High Quality is suitable for Web servers delivering video to clients with fast connections (for example, cable modems, DSLs, or satellite). It uses the same resolution as Medium Quality, 320×240 pixels, but doubles the frame rate to 30 frames per second.

Other   To select from a wider range of qualities, select the Other item. The Record dialog box displays a drop-down list from which you can choose video rates designed for use with connections ranging from 28.8Kbps to 768Kbps. You can also choose video rates designed for color PDA devices.

NOTE *You can create a still image by clicking the Take Photo button, the button to the right of the Record button.*

7. In the Windows Movie Maker window, click the Record button to start recording. (Alternatively, choose File ➤ Record.) Windows Movie Maker starts recording the input from the camera. While it's recording, it flashes the word *Recording* under the picture, and the Elapsed counter shows the time elapsed.

8. Click the Stop button to stop recording. Windows Movie Maker displays the Save Windows Media File dialog box.

9. Specify a filename for the file. If necessary, change the location. (By default, Windows Movie Maker uses your \My Videos\ folder.) Then click the Save button. Windows Movie Maker saves the file, closes the Save Windows Media File dialog box, and displays the Creating Clips dialog box (shown in Figure 28.25) while it creates clips.

FIGURE 28.25

Windows Movie Maker displays the Creating Clips dialog box while it divides the movie into clips.

NOTE *Windows Movie Maker breaks up the video into a number of clips based on when it detects different sequences in the video—for example, pauses in recording. Clips are saved in files called* collections—*collections of clips*—*in the Windows Media Video (WMV) format.*

10. After creating the clips, Windows Movie Maker displays a window showing the collections and clips. Figure 28.26 shows an example.

FIGURE 28.26

Windows Movie Maker displays the collection of clips as thumbnails.

Importing an Audio or Video File

Instead of recording a new audio or video file, you can import an existing one. To import a file, take the following steps:

1. Choose File ➤ Import. Windows Movie Maker displays the Select the File to Import dialog box, which is a common Open dialog box with a Create Clips for Video Files check box added.

2. Navigate to and select the file you want to import.

3. If you want Windows Movie Maker to create clips from a video file you import, leave the Create Clips for Video Files check box selected. If not, clear it.

4. Click the Open button. Windows Movie Maker imports the file and makes clips from it if appropriate.

Saving the Project

To save your movie, choose File ➤ Save Project and specify the name and location in the resulting Save Project dialog box. Windows Movie Maker projects are saved in the Windows Movie Maker Project (MSWMM) format. The default folder is your \My Videos\ folder.

Editing a Movie

To edit a movie, open it by clicking its entry in the Collections pane. You can then take the following actions with the movie's clips.

TIP Once you've chosen the collection you want to work with, you may want to close the Collections pane so that you have more space to work in.

VIEWING A CLIP

To view a clip, select it in the list of clips. (By default, this list is displayed in Thumbnail view, but you can choose View ➤ List or View ➤ Details to use List view or Details view instead.) Windows Movie Maker displays the first frame of the clip in the preview pane.

You can then move through the clip by using the controls below the preview pane. Figure 28.27 shows these controls with labels.

FIGURE 28.27

Use these controls to manipulate a clip.

RENAMING A CLIP

To rename a clip, use one of the standard Windows renaming techniques in the list box: Either click the clip's name twice with a pause in between, or right-click the clip and choose Rename from the context menu. Windows displays an edit box around the name. Type the new name for the clip and press the Enter key or click elsewhere.

SPLITTING A CLIP

To split a clip, navigate to the frame at which you want to split it. Then click the Split Clip button. Windows Movie Maker splits the clip into two. It saves the first part under its previous name and saves the second part under a new name formed by appending (1) (or the next available number) to the clip's original name. For example, if you split a clip named Party Scene, Windows Movie Maker names the second part Party Scene (1).

COMBINING TWO OR MORE CLIPS

To combine two or more clips, select them in the list box, right-click somewhere in the selection, and choose Combine from the context menu. Windows Movie Maker combines the clips under the name of the first clip.

COPYING AND MOVING CLIPS

You can move clips by using drag-and-drop and copy them by using Ctrl+drag-and-drop. You can copy and move clips either within a collection or from one collection to another.

ARRANGING THE CLIPS ON THE STORYBOARD

Once you've got a clip so that it shows what you want it to, drag it into place on the storyboard, the filmstriplike control at the bottom of the window.

To display the preview of a clip on the storyboard, click it. To play a clip, right-click it and choose Play from the context menu. To play the whole sequence of clips on the storyboard, right-click a clip and choose Play Entire Storyboard/Timeline from the context menu.

To remove a clip from the storyboard, select it and press the Delete key.

TRIMMING A CLIP ON THE STORYBOARD

Once you've put a clip on the storyboard, you can trim it so that only part of it is shown in the movie. To do so, follow these steps:

1. Select the clip on the storyboard so that it's displayed in the preview pane.

2. Move to the first frame that you want to include in the movie.

3. Choose Clip ➤ Set Start Trim Point.

4. Move to the last frame that you want to include in the movie.

5. Choose Clip ➤ Set End Trim Point.

6. Play the clip to check that the result is to your liking. If not, set the trim points again.

To remove trimming from a clip, select it and choose Clip ➤ Clear Trim Points.

FADING ONE CLIP INTO ANOTHER

By default, Windows Movie Maker cuts from one clip to the next, as you might expect. To create a fade from one clip to another, take the following steps:

1. Choose View ➤ Timeline. Windows Movie Maker displays the timeline in place of the film-strip (shown in Figure 28.28).

FIGURE 28.28

Use the timeline to implement fading from one clip to another.

2. If necessary, click the Zoom In button or the Zoom Out button to adjust your view of the timeline so that the timeline displays an appropriate length of time for editing the clips.

3. Drag the later clip left so that it overlaps the clip with which you want to fade it. The amount of overlap sets the length of the fade.

Choose View ➤ Storyboard to replace the timeline with the storyboard again.

RECORDING NARRATION

To record narration for your movie, take the following steps:

1. If the timeline isn't displayed, choose View ➤ Timeline to display it.

2. Click the Record Narration button (the button with the microphone at the left end of the timeline) or choose File ➤ Record Narration. Windows Movie Maker displays the Record Narration Track dialog box (shown in Figure 28.29).

3. Check the device in the Device readout. To change it, click the Change button and use the resulting Configure Audio dialog box to specify the device for recording narration.

FIGURE 28.29

In the Record Narration Track dialog box, choose the device for narration, set the recording level, and mute the video soundtrack if necessary.

4. To mute the video soundtrack, select the Mute Video Soundtrack check box.

5. Drag the Record Level slider to set a suitable recording level.

6. Click the Record button and start the narration as Windows Movie Maker plays the clip.

7. When you've finished the narration, click the Stop button. Windows Movie Maker displays the Save Narration Track File dialog box, which is a common Save dialog box in disguise.

8. Specify the filename and location for the file, and then click the Save button. Windows Movie Maker closes the Save Narration Track File dialog box and saves the narration track. It then adds a box for the narration track in the audio track under the pictures in the timeline.

Setting Audio Levels

To set the balance of audio levels between the video track and the audio track, click the Set Audio Levels button at the left end of the timeline (it's the button under the Record Narration button). Windows Movie Maker displays the Audio Levels dialog box (shown in Figure 28.30). Drag the slider to a suitable position, and click the close button to close the Audio Levels dialog box.

FIGURE 28.30

Use the Audio Levels dialog box to set the balance of audio levels between the video track and the audio track.

Saving the Movie

To save the movie you've created, take the following steps:

1. Click the Save Movie button on the toolbar, choose File ➤ Save Movie, or press Ctrl+M. Windows Movie Maker displays the Save Movie dialog box (shown in Figure 28.31).

FIGURE 28.31

In the Save Movie
dialog box, choose
the quality for the
movie and specify
information about it.

2. In the Setting drop-down list, choose the quality you want to use for the movie. The choices are the same as those discussed in step 6 of the section "Recording Video or Audio" earlier in the chapter. The readouts in the Playback Quality group box show you the specifics for the file and how long it will take to download over 28.8Kbps, 56Kbps, and 128Kbps connections.

3. In the text boxes in the Display Information group box, enter the information you want displayed about the movie: its title, the author, the date, any rating, and any description.

4. Click the OK button. Windows Movie Maker closes the Save Movie dialog box and displays the Save As dialog box.

5. Specify the name and folder for the movie, and then click the Save button. Windows Movie Maker closes the Save As dialog box, creates the movie, and saves it (using the Windows Media Video [WMV] file type).

6. While creating the movie (which may take some time), Windows Movie Maker displays the Creating Movie dialog box with a readout of its progress. Processing the movie consumes a lot of CPU power and memory, and your computer may respond slowly until Windows Movie Maker has finished creating the movie.

7. When Windows Movie Maker has finished creating the movie, it displays the Windows Movie Maker dialog box shown in Figure 28.32, asking if you want to watch the movie.

FIGURE 28.32

When Windows Movie Maker
has finished creating the movie,
it invites you to watch it.

8. Click the Yes button or the No button as appropriate. If you click the Yes button, Windows Movie Maker launches or activates Windows Media Player and starts the movie playing in it.

Sharing Your Movies with Others

If your movies are good enough, or if you're proud enough of them, or both, you'll probably want to share them with other people. Windows Movie Maker provides tools for sharing your movies via e-mail and the Web.

TIP   To share a movie via CD, burn it to CD as described in Chapter 29.

SHARING A MOVIE VIA E-MAIL

To share a movie via e-mail, take the following steps:

1. Choose File ➤ Send Movie To ➤ E-mail. Windows Movie Maker displays the Send Movie via E-mail dialog box, which is the Save Movie dialog box (shown earlier in Figure 28.31) with a different name.

2. Choose options and click the OK button. Windows Movie Maker displays the Name the Movie to Send dialog box (shown in Figure 28.33).

FIGURE 28.33

Enter the filename for the movie in the Name the Movie to Send dialog box.

3. Enter the filename in the Enter a File Name text box.

4. Click the OK button. Windows Movie Maker closes the Name the Movie to Send dialog box and displays the Creating Movie dialog box while creating the movie.

5. After creating the movie, Windows Movie Maker displays the E-mail Movie dialog box (shown in Figure 28.34)

FIGURE 28.34

In the E-mail Movie dialog box, select the e-mail program you want to use.

6. Select the e-mail program. Select the Don't Ask Me Again check box if you want Windows Movie Maker to use your default e-mail client in the future. Then click the OK button. Windows Movie Maker starts that e-mail program and creates a message with the movie file as an attachment.

7. Finish creating the message and send it as usual.

SHARING A MOVIE VIA THE WEB

To share a movie via the Web, take the following steps:

1. Choose File ➤ Send Movie To ➤ Web Server. Windows Movie Maker displays the Send Movie to a Web Server dialog box, which is the Save Movie dialog box (shown earlier in Figure 28.31) with a different name.

2. Choose options and click the OK button. Windows Movie Maker displays the Name the Movie to Send dialog box (shown in Figure 28.33 in the previous section).

3. Enter the filename in the Enter a File Name text box.

4. Click the OK button. Windows Movie Maker closes the Name the Movie to Send dialog box and displays the Creating Movie dialog box while creating the movie.

5. After creating the movie, Windows Movie Maker displays the Send to Web dialog box (shown in Figure 28.35).

FIGURE 28.35

In the Send to Web dialog box, specify the Web location to which you want to post the movie.

6. In the Place This Media File group box, select the In My Home Page Directory option button or the In This Folder in My Site option button as appropriate. If you select the In This Folder in My Site option button, enter the folder name in the text box.

7. In the Web Site Host Settings group box, specify the host name, your username, and your password, and choose whether to save the password.

   ◆ The Host Name drop-down list is preloaded with a number of popular Web site hosts, including VideoShare and YesVideo.

   ◆ You can add your own host by clicking the New button and using the resulting Create Web Host Settings dialog box (shown in Figure 28.36) to specify the details of your Web host.

8. Click the OK button. Windows Movie Maker closes the Send to Web dialog box and displays the Sending to Web dialog box as it transfers the movie to the Web host and folder you specified.

FIGURE 28.36

You can use the
Create Web Host
Settings dialog box
to enter details of
your Web host.

Up Next

This chapter has discussed how to use Windows' features for capturing and manipulating still pictures. It has also shown you how to get started creating movies with Windows Movie Maker.

If you want to share your pictures or videos via mail, you may want to burn them to CD. The next chapter discusses how to burn CDs.

Chapter 29

Burning CDs

FROM BEING AN EXOTIC, expensive, and erratically performing technological marvel in the mid 1990s, the recordable CD has progressed to being the most convenient and most cost-effective backup and file-transfer medium for the early 2000s. Recordable CDs now hold up to 700MB of data and can be burned in as little as four minutes. So it should perhaps come as no surprise that Windows XP improves on previous versions of Windows by offering CD writing capability built into the operating system. This chapter discusses how to use those features, how to choose a CD rewriter drive if you don't have one, and how to choose recordable CD media.

This chapter covers the following topics:

♦ Understanding the basics of recording CDs

♦ Choosing a CD rewriter

♦ Choosing recordable CDs

♦ Configuring a recordable CD drive

♦ Burning CDs from Explorer

♦ Burning CDs from Windows Media Player

CD-Recording Basics

To record CDs, you need to have a CD recorder or a CD rewriter. If you have one, you're all set to record CDs. If you don't have one, see the next sidebar for advice on choosing a CD rewriter.

You also need media—blank recordable CDs or rewritable CDs. The next section discusses those.

EXPERT KNOWLEDGE: CHOOSING A CD REWRITER

Because of its value for backup and file transfer, a CD rewriter is almost indispensable nowadays. Many new PCs—including some high-end laptops—have built-in CD rewriters. If your PC doesn't have a CD rewriter and you want to get one, this sidebar explains what you need to know.

You'll notice that this sidebar discusses CD rewriters rather than CD recorders. That's because CD rewriters have become so ubiquitous and come down so far in price that they've essentially replaced plain old CD recorders. (If you missed CD recorders: The difference between CD recorders and CD rewriters is that CD recorders could write only once to any given disc, whereas CD rewriters can write either once or multiple times to the same disc. If you'd like the acronyms, CD-R discs are *Write Once, Read Multiple* media—*WORM* for short—while CD-RW discs are *Write And Read Multiple* or *WARM* media.)

These are the main considerations for choosing a CD rewriter:

Speed CD rewriter speed is measured by the same rating system as regular old read-only CD drives: 1X, 2X, 4X, and so on. Each X represents 150Kbps (the nominal read rate of the first CD drives), so a 4X drive chugs through 600Kbps, an 8X drive handles 1200Kbps (1.2Mbps), a 12X drive manages 1800Kbps (1.8Mbps), a 16X drive burns 2400Kbps (2.4Mbps), a 20X drive blazes through 3000Kbps (3Mbps), and a 24X drive incinerates 3600Kbps (3.6Mbps).

CD rewriter speed keeps on improving. At this writing, 24X drives are just beginning to appear. These can burn a full CD in 4 minutes (other constraints, such as the speed of your system, permitting). 16X drives are more reasonably priced; they can burn a full CD in 5 minutes. 12X drives are starting to look like old technology, though in 2000 they were state of the art; they can burn a full CD in around 6 minutes. 8X drives take about 9 minutes; 6X drives take about 12 minutes; and 4X drives take about 18 minutes.

Those speeds are for the initial writing to the CD. On high-speed drives, the rewriting speeds are typically considerably slower than the writing speeds. For example, a drive might write at 24X but rewrite at 12X, and a 12X drive might rewrite at only 4X. By contrast, slower drives (for example, 4X) may rewrite at the same speed as they write.

CD rewriter speeds are given with the write speed first, the rewrite speed second, and the read speed third. For example, a 24×12×40 drive is one that writes at 24X, rewrites at 12X, and reads at 40X.

As you can see, the higher speed ratings don't translate as directly into a speed gain as the lower speeds do. That's because, no matter how fast the drive is able to burn the CD, there's some overhead in creating the file system on the CD and wrapping up the writing process. So until prices on 24X (or faster) and 16X drives come down, there's little advantage in buying them over buying 12X drives.

CD rewriters almost invariably read data at a faster rate than they write it. Some CD recorders now read up to 32X, making them almost as fast as a dedicated CD drive. Even so, unless you're out of drive bays or ports, look to add a CD recorder to your computer rather than replace your existing CD drive with a CD recorder. That way, you'll be able to duplicate a CD (assuming that you have the right to do so) or install Quake at the same time as listening to music.

Internal or external? Generally speaking, an internal drive will cost you less than an external drive, but you'll need to have a drive bay free in your computer. An external drive will usually cost more, will occupy space on your desk, and will need its own power supply. In addition, most external drives are much noisier than internal drives because they contain their own fans. But if your main computer is a notebook, or if you want to be able to move the drive from computer to computer without undue effort, you'll need an external drive.

Continued on next page

EIDE drives are all internal. SCSI drives can be internal or external. Because the parallel port, the USB ports, and any FireWire ports are external connections, almost all of these drives are external only. (You can find internal FireWire CD-R drives if you look hard enough.)

EIDE, SCSI, parallel port, USB, or FireWire?   If you have a SCSI card in your computer, you'll probably want to get a SCSI CD recorder, because it will typically perform better *and* put much less burden on the processor than an EIDE CD recorder will. SCSI drives are usually more expensive than EIDE drives of the same speed, but if your computer's already got SCSI, the extra cost is probably worth it. If you need to copy CDs, bear in mind that most SCSI CD recorders will copy CDs directly only from other SCSI drives, not from EIDE drives. If you have a SCSI CD recorder and an EIDE CD drive, you'll need to copy the CD to the hard disk and then burn it to CD from there.

If you don't have SCSI and want an internal drive, or if your CD player is EIDE and you want to do a lot of CD-to-CD duplicating, choose EIDE. Before you buy, make sure that you have an EIDE connector available on your computer. If it's already chock-full of drives (most modern machines can take four EIDE devices), you won't be able to add another without sacrificing an existing one.

If you're looking at an external non-SCSI drive, your current choices are a parallel-port drive, a USB drive, or a FireWire drive. Parallel-port drives perform so slowly—2X at best—that they're barely worth using. USB drives using the USB 1.0 standard are only a bit better—they're limited to 4X speeds by the limitations of USB. (USB 2.0 drives, when they arrive, will be much faster.) FireWire drives offer full speed and great convenience, but if your computer doesn't have a FireWire card, you'll need to add one. (You can get FireWire PCI cards for $100 or so and FireWire PC Cards for a few dollars more.)

Recordable CDs and Rewritable CDs

CDs on which you can record data come in two basic types:

CD-R discs   CD-R discs, usually referred to as *recordable CDs*, are CDs that you can record data to only once. Once you finish recording data, you cannot change the information on the disc. Regular CD-R discs hold 650MB, the same amount as a standard audio CD. (650MB holds 74 minutes of uncompressed audio.) Extended-capacity CD-R discs hold 700MB, a small increase that's worth having if you don't have to pay extra for it. 700MB holds 80 minutes of uncompressed audio.

CD-RW discs   CD-RW discs, usually referred to as *rewritable CDs*, are CDs that you can record data to multiple times. You can record data to the CD in multiple recording sessions until it is full. You can then erase all the data from the CD and use it again. CD-RW discs specify a theoretical safe maximum number of times that you can reuse them, but if you like your data, you'd be wise not to push them that far. CD-RW discs hold 650MB. CD-RW discs are more expensive than CD-R discs.

To simplify (or perhaps complicate) the terminology, Windows uses the term *writable CD* to refer to recordable and rewritable discs. This isn't a standard term, but it now seems destined to become one.

EXPERT KNOWLEDGE: CHOOSING CD-R AND CD-RW MEDIA

When buying CD-R and CD-RW discs, you need to balance economy with quality. Beware of cheapo discs, because they may give you skips and errors—or even lose your precious music or data. If you can, buy a few discs for testing before you buy a quantity that you'll regret if they're not up to snuff.

One way to save some money is to buy CD-R and CD-RW discs without jewel cases. This makes for a good discount, as the jewel cases are relatively expensive to manufacture and bulky to package (and easy to break, as you no doubt know from personal experience). The discs are typically sold on a spindle, which makes for handy storage until you use them—after which you'll have to find safe storage for them on your own. (One possibility is a CD wallet, which can be especially handy if you need to take your CDs with you when you travel. If you buy one, make sure it has soft pockets that won't scratch the CDs as you insert them, and sweep out travel grit frequently.)

For the faster drives, you may need to buy CD-R or CD-RW media designed for use in faster drives. For example, at this writing most 24X drives request (or perhaps require) discs rated at 24X, suggesting that regular (and less expensive) discs will have too many errors to use. Your mileage will vary depending on your discs and your drive, but it's worth testing less expensive discs to see how they perform in a fast drive. If the drive ends up burning at 20X instead of 24X, you lose all of 30 seconds. Unless you're holding your breath for the duration of the burning, you're unlikely to notice the difference.

Audio CDs and Data CDs

Broadly speaking, CDs divide into two categories:

Audio CDs   Audio CDs contain uncompressed audio in pulse code modulation (PCM) format. (PCM files are essentially WAV files with different header information at the beginning of the file.) They can be read by both audio CD players and CD-ROM drives. Audio CDs don't have names, though pressed audio CDs are identified by an ID number linked to the artist and the work.

Data CDs   Data CDs can contain any file type. They can be read by CD-ROM drives but not by audio CD players. Data CDs can have names up to 16 characters long.

WARNING   Because CD-RW discs use a different technology than regular CD-ROMs, they're not as compatible with all CD-ROM drives. If you want to share a CD with someone else, a CD-R disc is a better bet than a CD-RW disc. Likewise, only the most recent audio players can play CD-RW discs, whereas most audio players can play only pressed audio CDs and audio CD-R discs.

Configuring a Recordable CD Drive

Before you try to burn a CD, it's a good idea to check the settings that Windows has chosen for your CD recorder or CD rewriter. You may want to tweak the configuration or change the drive used for holding temporary files when burning a CD on the Desktop.

To configure a recordable CD drive, follow these steps:

1. Choose Start ➤ My Computer. Windows opens an Explorer window showing My Computer.

2. Right-click the CD drive and choose Properties from the context menu. Windows displays the Properties dialog box for the drive.

3. Click the Recording tab. Windows displays the Recording page (shown in Figure 29.1).

FIGURE 29.1

Check the configuration of your drive on the Recording page of its Properties dialog box.

4. Choose settings that meet your needs:

Enable CD Recording on This Drive check box   Select this check box to use this drive for recording. Windows lets you use only one drive at a time for recording. This check box is selected by default on the first recordable CD drive on your system and cleared by default on subsequent recordable CD drives.

Select a Drive drop-down list   In this drop-down list, select the drive on which Windows should store an *image* of the CD (temporary files containing the data to be written to the CD) when creating the CD. Windows commandeers up to 1GB of space on the drive for a high-capacity CD, so make sure the disc you choose has more than that amount available. (For a standard CD, Windows needs around 700MB of space.)

Select a Write Speed drop-down list   In this drop-down list, you can specify the speed that Windows should use when recording a CD. The default setting is Fastest—the highest speed your drive supports. If Fastest doesn't give good results, try the next lower rate. Windows automatically adjusts this speed to match the speed of the current disc, so you may not need to change it manually.

Automatically Eject the CD after Writing check box   Leave this check box selected (as it is by default) to have Windows eject the CD when it has finished writing to it. When you're burning CD-R discs, this ejection can be a useful visual signal that the disc is done, but you may want to disable this option when burning CD-RW discs or when using a laptop in a tight space.

5. Click the OK button. Windows closes the Properties dialog box and applies your choices.

EXPERT KNOWLEDGE: HOW ARE RECORDABLE CDS DIFFERENT FROM REGULAR CDS?

If you've looked at CD-R or CD-RW discs, you'll know that most of them look very different from pre-recorded audio or data CDs (*pressed* CDs). Depending on their make and type, CD-R and CD-RW discs may have a gold, green, or bluish coating on their data side. Typically, this is a polycarbonate substrate over a reflective layer of 24-carat gold or a silver-colored alloy.

Information is transferred to CD-R and CD-RW discs by a different process than for pressed CDs. While pressed CDs are pressed in a mold from a master CD, CD recorders and CD rewriters use a laser to burn the information onto the CD-R or CD-RW media. Pressed CDs use physically raised areas called *lands* and lowered areas called *pits* to store the encoded data. Recordable CDs have a dye layer in which the laser burns marks that have the same reflective properties as the lands and pits. To be pedantic, the laser doesn't actually *burn* anything, but it heats the dye layer to produce the marks. But because the term is not only evocative but also distinguishes from the CD-recording that music artists do, it has stuck: CD recorders and rewriters are widely referred to as *CD burners*, and people speak of *burning a CD*.

Not only do CD-R and CD-RW discs look different than pressed CDs, but they're also less robust. You can damage them more easily with extreme heat and moderate cold, by scratching or gouging them, or by leaving them in direct sunlight. The data is actually stored closer to the label side of the CD than to the business side, so if you're compelled to scratch one side of the CD, go for the business side over the label side.

Burning CDs from Explorer

Burning CDs from Explorer is an easy three-step process:

1. Copy the files to the storage area.

2. Check the files in the storage area to make sure that they're the right files and that there aren't too many of them.

3. Write the files to CD.

 The following sections discuss these steps. See pages 30–31 of the *Essential Skills* section for a visual guide to copying files to a CD.

Copying the Files to the Storage Area

The first step in burning files (or folders) to CD is to copy them to the storage area. You can do so in several ways, of which these three are usually the easiest:

- ◆ Select the files in an Explorer window or in a common dialog box. Then right-click in the selection and choose Send To ➤ CD Drive from the context menu. (Alternatively, choose File ➤ Send To ➤ CD Drive.) This technique is the most convenient when you're working in Explorer or in a common dialog box.

- ◆ Drag the files and drop them on the CD drive in an Explorer window or on a shortcut to the CD drive. For example, you could keep a shortcut to the CD drive on your Desktop so that you could quickly drag files and folders to it. This technique is good for copying to CD files or folders that you keep on your Desktop.

◆ Open an Explorer window to the storage area, then drag files to it and drop them there. This technique is mostly useful for adding files when you're checking the contents of the storage area. When you insert a blank CD in your CD drive, Windows displays a CD Drive dialog box offering to open a folder to the writable CD folder.

When you take one of these actions, Windows copies the files to the storage area and displays a notification-area pop-up telling you that you have files waiting to be written to the CD.

Either click the pop-up or (if it has disappeared) open a My Computer window and double-click the icon for the CD drive. Windows opens an Explorer window showing the storage area, which appears as a list called Files Ready to Be Written to the CD. (For a CD-RW that already contains files, the storage area also contains a list of Files Currently on the CD.) Figure 29.2 shows an example of the storage area. As you can see in the figure, Windows displays a downward-pointing arrow on the icon for each file or folder to indicate that it's a temporary file destined to be burned to CD and then disposed of.

FIGURE 29.2

The storage area holds the copies of files to be burned to the CD. The downward-pointing arrow on each file icon and folder icon indicates that the item is temporary and will be deleted after being burned to CD.

While Windows copies the files, the CD drive will appear to be busy, but it won't actually be writing any information to CD yet.

Checking the Files in the Storage Area

Once you've copied to the storage area all the files that you want to burn to the CD, activate the window that Explorer opened to the storage area and check that the files are all there, that you don't want to remove any of them, and that there aren't too many to fit on the CD. (If you closed the window showing the storage area, you can display the storage area again by opening an Explorer window to My Computer and double-clicking the icon for the CD drive.)

NOTE   By default, the storage area is located in the `\Local Settings\Application Data\Microsoft\CD Burning\` *folder under the folder for your account in the* `\Documents and Settings\` *folder.*

To check the size of files in the storage area, select them all (for example, by choosing Edit ➢ Select All), then right-click and choose Properties from the context menu. Windows displays the Properties dialog box for the files. Check the Size readout on the General page.

Writing the Files to CD

Once you've looked at the files in the storage area and are satisfied all is well, start the process of writing the files to CD. Take the following steps:

1. Click the Write These Files to CD link in the CD Writing Tasks list. Windows starts the CD Writing Wizard, which displays its first page (shown in Figure 29.3).

FIGURE 29.3

On the first page of the CD Writing Wizard, specify the name for the CD and choose whether the Wizard should close itself when the CD is finished.

2. Enter the name for the CD in the CD Name text box. CD names can be up to 16 characters long.

3. If you want the Wizard to close itself when the CD is finished, select the Close the Wizard after the Files Have Been Written check box. If you select this check box, you won't have the option of creating another CD containing the same files, because the Wizard automatically clears the storage area.

4. Click the Next button. The CD Writing Wizard displays the page shown in Figure 29.4 as it burns the CD. The burning goes through three stages: Adding Data to the CD Image, Writing the Data Files to the CD, and Performing Final Steps to Make the CD Ready to Use.

FIGURE 29.4

The CD Writing Wizard shows you its progress in burning the CD.

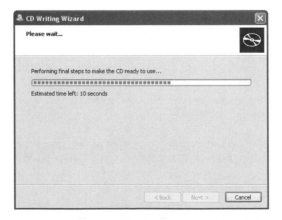

5. When the Wizard has finished burning the CD, it displays the Completing the CD Writing Wizard page (shown in Figure 29.5) and ejects the CD.

FIGURE 29.5

The CD Writing Wizard displays the Completing the CD Writing Wizard page when it has finished creating the CD.

6. If you want to create another CD containing the same files, select the Yes, Write These Files to Another CD check box.

7. Click the Finish button. The Wizard closes itself and deletes the files from the storage area unless you selected the Yes, Write These Files to Another CD check box.

When Things Go Wrong Writing the CD…

If you try to write more files to a CD than will fit on it, the CD Writing Wizard displays the Cannot Complete the CD Writing Wizard page (shown in Figure 29.6). You can remove some files from the storage area, then select the Retry Writing the Files to CD Now option button, and click the Finish button if you want to try to fix the problem while the CD is open, but in most cases you'll do best to leave the Close the Wizard without Writing the Files option button selected and click the Finish button, then return to the storage area, fix the problem, and restart the writing process.

FIGURE 29.6

The CD Writing Wizard displays its Cannot Complete the CD Writing Wizard page to warn you that the files won't fit on the CD.

The CD Writing Wizard may also warn you that there was an error in the recording process, and the disc may no longer be usable. This is the other reason why people like the term *burning* for recording CDs—when things go wrong, you get burned and the disc is toast. In this case, you'll probably want to try writing the files to another CD.

When you've finished creating the CD, test it immediately by opening an Explorer window to its contents and opening some of them. Make sure all is well with the CD before archiving it or sending it on its way.

NOTE   *If the CD you create won't read or play properly, it may have suffered recording errors. Try reducing the burning speed by using the Select a Write Speed drop-down list on the Recording page of the Properties dialog box for the drive.*

Clearing the Storage Area

If you end up deciding not to create the CD after all, clear the storage area by deleting the files in it. To do so, click the Delete Temporary Files link in the CD Writing Tasks list. Windows displays the Confirm Delete dialog box (shown in Figure 29.7) to make sure you know the files haven't yet been written to CD. Click the Yes button. Windows deletes the files and removes the Files Ready to Be Written to the CD heading from the Explorer window.

FIGURE 29.7

Windows displays the Confirm Delete dialog box to make sure you want to delete all the files from the storage area.

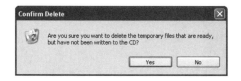

Working with Rewritable CDs

You record the first set of information to rewritable CDs (CD-RW discs) by using the same procedure as for recordable CDs (CD-R discs). But you can then add further files to them and erase all files from them. The following sections discuss how to take these actions.

ADDING FURTHER FILES TO A REWRITABLE CD

You can add further files to a rewritable CD by following the same procedure as for initially burning files to it. As mentioned earlier in the chapter, the storage area for a rewritable CD displays a Files Currently on the CD list for a CD-RW that already contains files or folders. Figure 29.8 shows an example of the storage area for a rewritable CD with a file queued for adding to the CD.

ERASING ALL FILES FROM A REWRITABLE CD

You can erase all the files off a rewritable CD so that all its space is free again. To do so, take the following steps:

1. Open an Explorer window to the CD drive.

FIGURE 29.8

The storage area for a rewritable CD displays a Files Currently on the CD list.

2. Click the Erase This CD-RW link in the CD Writing Tasks list. Windows starts the CD Writing Wizard, which displays another Welcome to the CD Writing Wizard page (shown in Figure 29.9)

FIGURE 29.9

The CD Writing Wizard walks you through the process of erasing all the files from a CD-RW.

3. If you want the Wizard to close itself after erasing the files, select the Close the Wizard when Erase Completes check box.

4. Click the Next button. The Wizard displays the Erasing the CD page (shown in Figure 29.10) while it erases the files.

5. When the Wizard has finished erasing the files on the CD-RW, it displays another Completing the CD Writing Wizard page (shown in Figure 29.11).

6. Click the Finish button. The Wizard closes itself.

FIGURE 29.10

The CD Writing Wizard displays the Erasing the CD page while it erases the files on the CD-RW.

FIGURE 29.11

The Wizard displays this Completing the CD Writing Wizard page when it has finished erasing the files on the CD-RW.

Creating an Audio CD from Explorer

To create an audio CD, you use Windows Media Player, which includes features for creating PCM files from other audio file formats. But you can start the process from Explorer by copying only audio files to the storage area. When you then start the CD Writing Wizard, it displays the Welcome to the CD Writing Wizard page as usual for you to name the CD, but after that it displays the Do You Want to Make an Audio CD? page (shown in Figure 29.12).

To create an audio CD, select the Make an Audio CD option button and click the Next button. The CD Writing Wizard launches or activates Windows Media Player, passes the information across to it, and then closes itself. Create the CD as described in the next section.

To create a data CD, select the Make a Data CD option button and click the Next button. The CD Writing Wizard then continues its usual course.

NOTE If Windows decides that the contents of the current folder displayed in an Explorer window are predominantly music, it displays the Music Tasks list. You can then select a file or folder and click the Copy to Audio CD link. Doing so opens Windows Media Player with the tracks loaded ready for copying to an audio CD.

FIGURE 29.12

When the CD Writing Wizard notices that all the files for the CD are audio files, it displays the Do You Want to Make an Audio CD? page.

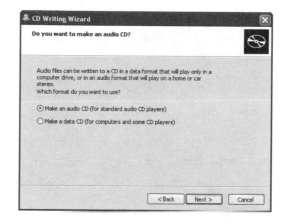

Burning CDs from Windows Media Player

Windows Media Player includes a feature for burning audio CDs directly from playlists. You can use MP3, WAV, and WMA files to create CDs up to 74 minutes long. (Windows Media Player can't create 80-minute audio CDs.)

TIP   If you want to include tracks in other formats on CDs you burn, convert them to WAV format first. Many sound programs can convert audio files. Sound Recorder (discussed in Chapter 27) can convert a wide range of formats.

Burning a CD from Windows Media Player is even easier than burning a CD from Explorer. That's because the only choice you have to make is which tracks you want to include on the CD: You don't have to name the CD (because it's an audio CD), and you don't have to specify whether it's a data CD or an audio CD (for the same reason).

The only other thing you have to worry about is this: if the tracks have digital licenses, whether the licenses allow the tracks to be copied to CD. If they don't, Windows Media Player will warn you of the problem. (If you're not clear on what you can and cannot legally do with digital-audio files, look back to Chapter 27 for a summary.)

To burn a CD from Windows Media Player, take the following steps:

1. Open the playlist you want to burn to CD, or create a new playlist containing the tracks.

2. Check the number of minutes shown: It must be 74 or fewer, otherwise the burning will grind to a halt when the disc is full. Remove tracks if necessary. (Or add more if you have space left.)

3. Choose File ➤ Copy ➤ Copy to Audio CD. Windows Media Player displays the Copy to CD or Device page and inspects the tracks to make sure that there aren't any license problems. Figure 29.13 shows the Copy to CD or Device page with a playlist queued for writing to CD.

FIGURE 29.13

Windows Media
Player ready to write
a playlist to CD

4. Click the Copy Music button. Windows begins the copying process, which consists of these three steps:

   Converting Writing out the audio files to uncompressed WAV files. While Windows Media Player converts the tracks, it displays *Converting* and a percentage readout next to the track it's working on.

   Copying to CD Copying the WAV files to the CD. Windows Media Player displays *Copying to CD* and a percentage readout next to each track in turn as it copies the track to the CD.

   Closing the disc When all of the WAV files have been written to the CD, Windows Media Player closes the disc.

5. When Windows Media Player has closed the disc, it ejects the CD. Check the CD manually to make sure that it works (for example, put it back in the drive and try playing it), then label it.

NOTE   *You can also launch Windows Media Player and get it ready to burn CDs by selecting music files, right-clicking, and choosing Copy to Audio CD from the context menu. (Alternatively, choose File ➤ Copy to Audio CD.)*

Copying a CD

You can make a copy of a CD by using the same techniques as for copying any other files: Copy the files to the storage area, and then write them to CD. Remember that copying CDs of copyrighted works involves copyright issues.

If you have a CD drive (or DVD drive) other than your CD-R or CD-RW drive, you can simply open an Explorer window to My Computer, then drag the icon for the CD and drop it on the icon for the CD-RW drive. Windows copies the files to the storage area. Click the Write to CD link to start the CD Writing Wizard.

If Windows' CD-Writing Capabilities Aren't Enough

Windows offers what might be termed strong but basic features for burning CDs, letting you burn data CDs easily from Explorer and audio CDs even more easily from Windows Media Player. But if you need more advanced CD-burning features (or more bells and whistles), you'll need to buy third-party CD software.

One package you might consider is Easy CD Creator from Roxio, Inc. (You might also consider Easy CD Creator Deluxe, which comes with not only bells and whistles but also gongs such as features for designing CD labels.) Why consider Easy CD Creator in particular? Well, for one thing, you're using Roxio technology already—the CD-burning functionality in Windows is licensed from Roxio. For another, Roxio is a company spun off in 2001 from Adaptec, Inc., a company that has long been one of the major names in CD burning.

Up Next

This chapter has discussed how to burn CDs from Explorer and from Windows Media Player. It has also provided advice on choosing recordable CD media and CD rewriter drives.

The next chapter discusses how to play games on Windows XP.

Chapter 30

Playing Games on Windows XP

GAMES AND BACKWARD COMPATIBILITY have been the eternal bane of not only Windows NT and Windows 2000 Professional but also the people who wanted to use them. Many people wanted to use NT or Windows 2000 for the extra stability they delivered for general use and business programs—but they also wanted to kick some alien butt in Duke Nukem, frag each other in Quake, or tranquilly explore a puzzle or two. To their dismay, they found that (forgive the puns) id Software games were doomed to incompatibility, Mystscapes were riven by graphics problems, and playing Rebel Assault sucked big asteroids just when they were supposed to be steering a rockless road through them.

Good news: Windows XP changes almost all that.

This chapter starts by discussing briefly the games that come with Windows XP—a handful of single-player games (including old favorites such as Solitaire and FreeCell) and about the same number of multiplayer games for the Internet. It then goes on to discuss the hardware you'll need for "serious" games, how to install and configure game controllers, how to deal with compatibility problems, and how to get the best performance from your computer when running games.

This chapter covers the following topics:

- ◆ Playing Windows XP's bundled games
- ◆ The hardware you need for serious gaming
- ◆ Adding and configuring game controllers
- ◆ Getting the best performance on games

Playing the Bundled Games

Windows XP comes with more games than previous versions of Windows. This isn't saying all that much (most distributions of Linux come with more games than Windows XP), but it does mean that you have some games to keep you entertained the next time you get stuck waiting for a connection in O'Hare—even if you're thoroughly sick of plain old Solitaire.

All the games are on the Games submenu of the Start menu (Start ➢ All Programs ➢ Games).

Playing Single-Player Games

Windows XP includes six single-player games:

FreeCell   FreeCell is a solitaire variation that involves building descending columns of cards of opposite colors until you can transfer each suit in ascending order onto the four home cells. To enable you to do so, there are four free cells (from which the game gets its name), each of which can hold one card at a time. All 1 million FreeCell games are theoretically winnable, though some are much harder than others. You can start a new random game by choosing Game ➤ New Game (or pressing the F2 key) or a new game of a specified number by choosing Game ➤ Select Game (or pressing the F3 key), entering the game number in the resulting Game Number dialog box, and clicking the OK button.

Hearts   Hearts is a computerized implementation of the classic four-person card game. In this implementation, the computer plays the other three players. The Hearts Options dialog box (Game ➤ Options, or press the F7 key) offers a choice of animation speed (Slow, Normal, or Fast) for the movement of the cards, and you can set the names of your cybernetic opponents if you wish.

Minesweeper   Minesweeper is a classic Windows game in which you attempt to clear a minefield. Click a square to detonate it. Right-click a square to mark it as a mine (one click) or a possible mine (another click). Click both left and right buttons on a square whose mines you've marked to clear the surrounding area as far as any unmarked mines. Minesweeper has three sizes of field—Beginner, Intermediate, and Expert—that you can choose from the Game menu. You can also create custom minefields up to 30 rows wide by 24 rows high by using the Custom Field dialog box (Game ➤ Custom).

Pinball   Pinball is a virtual implementation of the classic arcade and bar favorite. You can play either in a window or full screen (Options ➤ Full Screen, or press the F4 key). You can play single player (the default) or two, three, or four players (Options ➤ Select Players, then choose the number of players from the submenu). The default controls are the spacebar to launch the ball (hold the spacebar down for a moment to build up the spring), the Z key to flip the left flipper, the / (forward slash) key to flip the right flipper, the X key to bump the table left, the . (period) key to bump the table right, and the ↑ key to bump the table up. You can change the controls in the Player Controls dialog box (Options ➤ Player Controls, or press the F8 key).

Solitaire   The classic solitaire card game, Solitaire should need no introduction. The only thing worth mentioning is the Options dialog box (Game ➤ Options), in which you can choose whether to draw one card or three; whether to use standard scoring, Vegas scoring (with or without cumulative scoring), or no scoring; and whether to time the game, display the status bar, and use outline dragging (which improves display speed on older graphics cards).

Spider Solitaire   Spider Solitaire is a challenging solitaire game. You can play at three levels of difficulty (Easy, Medium, or Difficult) by choosing Game ➤ Difficulty (or pressing the F3 key). If you're new to Spider Solitaire, press the M key or choose Game ➤ Show an Available Move to see an available move. You can save one game by choosing Game ➤ Save This Game or pressing Ctrl+S, and you can open the saved game by choosing Game ➤ Open Last Saved Game or pressing Ctrl+O.

Playing Multiplayer Games

Windows XP's multiplayer games are Internet Backgammon, Internet Checkers, Internet Hearts, Internet Reversi, and Internet Spades. (More's the pity, Microsoft has chosen not to provide a chess game with Windows XP.) These games are implemented through Zone.com.

To play these games, you need to be connected to the Internet. When you start the game from the Games submenu (Start ➢ All Programs ➢ Games) on the Start menu, Windows displays an explanatory screen, of which Figure 30.1 shows an example for Hearts. If you don't want to see this screen again, clear the Show This Every Time check box.

FIGURE 30.1

Windows displays an explanatory screen when you start an Internet game.

Windows then connects to the Internet game server and searches for the appropriate number of other players. Once it has found them, it starts the game. Figure 30.2 shows a game of Internet Reversi underway.

FIGURE 30.2

Playing Internet Reversi

The Game menu offers game-appropriate options, such as Find New Opponent(s) and Skill Level. You can switch chat on or off by selecting the On option button or the Off option button in the Chat area. To use chat, select one of the canned messages from the list.

A Midsummer Gamer's Dream

Any computer that can run Windows XP at a decent pace should be able to run most games well enough for you to see what they're like. But to get the most out of more demanding games, you need heavier-duty hardware than Windows XP itself needs. At the risk of preaching to the converted, this section discusses the hardware needed for serious gaming.

Sound Card and Speakers or Headphones

Basic sound systems such as those you find in run-of-the-mill bargain PCs are fine for standard audio tasks such as Windows system sounds and listening to Internet radio, and may be good enough for a little light CD, WMA, or MP3 audio if your ears aren't too picky. But to enjoy the sonic excesses of serious gaming, you need a sound system built for it.

For most people, that means getting a sound card that delivers 3-D audio and environmental audio and a subwoofer system with surround sound or home-theater capabilities (for example, a Dolby 5.1 setup—five satellites and a subwoofer—or 7.1 setup). When buying speakers, choose ones designed for the use or uses you'll give them: Some speakers are designed for classical music, some for rock, and some for rockets and explosions. Speakers that overlap the latter two categories may be your best bet unless you have no interest in music.

Headphones come in enough styles—circumaural (over the ear), supra-aural (on the ear), and assorted buds (in the ear)—designs, and sizes that they're almost entirely a personal choice. While cheap headphones are almost guaranteed to sound bad, you don't need to spend a huge amount to get acceptable sound quality and comfort.

Generally speaking, sound quality and comfort are what you should look for in headphones. Style and looks should be secondary considerations (if you consider them at all). If headphones promise special features, evaluate them carefully rather than taking them at face value, because many aren't really worth having. For example, Evergreen Technologies (`www.evertech.com`) makes the RumbleFX Force Feedback Headphones, which claim to deliver force feedback through your ears but actually do little more than put subwoofers rather closer to your brain than any reputable doctor would recommend.

Video Card

Games are one area where an investment in a capable 3-D AGP video card with plenty of video memory pays dividends. At this writing, the amount of video memory on video cards appears to be doubling year by year: 16MB cards are now entry level, 32MB video cards are on the verge of becoming passé, and 64MB cards are in danger of being replaced by 128MB cards. (By the time you read this, 512MB video cards may well be on the way. If you use these for conventional purposes, they'll probably get bored and start arbitraging coffee futures, proving that it takes only one to contango.)

Video-card technologies change at least as fast as fashion. To find out the latest and greatest video-card technologies when you read this, consult serious gamers or visit games Web sites such as PCGaming.com (`www.pcgaming.com`) or GameSpot (`www.gamespot.com`).

Joystick, Game Pad, Steering Wheel, or Other Human Interface Device

Keyboards and mice are great for regular input to Windows computers, but to enjoy most games to the max, you'll probably want to add a game controller such as a joystick, game pad, or steering wheel with rudder pedals. These devices are commonly referred to as *game controllers* or *human interface devices*.

Which type of device you choose depends of course on the types of games that you want to play. *Force-feedback devices* (such as joysticks) provide better tactile sensation for some games (for example, flying simulations). As you'd expect, they cost more than regular devices.

Adding and Configuring Game Controllers

This section discusses how to add and configure game controllers such as those discussed in the previous section.

Adding a Game Controller

How you add a game controller usually depends on how it connects to your PC. If the controller uses a USB connection, you should be able to plug in the controller and have the Found New Hardware Wizard detect it automatically. If Windows has an appropriate driver for the controller, it loads it automatically; if not, it prompts you to supply a driver. Do so.

If the controller uses a connection that Windows is unable to detect automatically, you can install the controller either by running the Add Hardware Wizard (as described in Chapter 14) or by using the Game Controllers dialog box.

To display the Game Controllers dialog box, take the following steps:

1. Choose Start ➤ Control Panel. Windows displays Control Panel.

2. Click the Printers and Other Hardware link. Windows displays the Printers and Hardware screen.

3. Click the Game Controllers link. Windows displays the Game Controllers dialog box (shown in Figure 30.3).

FIGURE 30.3

Use the Game Controllers dialog box to add game controllers that Windows doesn't detect and install automatically.

To add a game controller, click the Add button in the Game Controllers dialog box. Windows displays the Add Game Controller dialog box (shown in Figure 30.4). Then add a listed type of game controller by using the technique described in the next section, or add an unlisted type of game controller by using the technique described in the section after that.

FIGURE 30.4

Use the Add Game Controller dialog box to add a game controller.

ADDING A GAME CONTROLLER OF A LISTED TYPE

To add a game controller of a type that Windows lists in the Add Game Controller dialog box, take the following steps:

1. Select the controller in the Game Controllers list box.

2. If the controller has rudder controls or pedals (for example, for driving games), select the Enable Rudders and Pedals check box.

3. Click the OK button. Windows closes the Add Game Controller dialog box and triggers the Found New Hardware Wizard, which searches for drivers for the new game controller. Again, if Windows has an appropriate driver for the controller, it loads it automatically; if not, it prompts you to supply a driver.

ADDING A GAME CONTROLLER THAT'S NOT LISTED

To add a game controller that's not listed, take the following steps:

1. Click the Custom button in the Add Game Controller dialog box. Windows displays the Custom Game Controller dialog box (shown in Figure 30.5).

2. In the Special Characteristics group box, select the option button that most closely describes the controller. Your choices are the Joystick option button, the Game Pad option button, the Flight Yoke or Flight Stick option button, and the Race Car Controller option button.

3. In the Axes drop-down list, specify the number of axes (plural of *axis*, not of *ax*) the controller has: 2, 3, or 4.

4. In the Buttons drop-down list, specify the number of buttons the controller has.

FIGURE 30.5

If your game controller isn't listed, use the Custom Game Controller dialog box to define a custom entry for it.

5. If the controller has a point-of-view (POV) hat, select the Includes a Point of View Control check box.

6. In the Controller Name text box, enter the name you want to use for the controller.

7. Click the OK button. Windows closes the Custom Game Controller dialog box, creates an entry for the controller you defined, and adds it to the Game Controllers list box in the Add Game Controller dialog box.

8. Click the OK button. Windows closes the Add Game Controller dialog box and triggers the Found New Hardware Wizard, which searches for drivers for the new game controller. Windows prompts you to supply a driver for the device.

Removing a Game Controller

To remove a game controller from your system, select its entry in the Installed Game Controllers list box in the Game Controllers dialog box and click the Remove button. Windows displays a Remove Controller dialog box such as that shown in Figure 30.6. Click the Yes button to remove the controller.

FIGURE 30.6

Windows displays the Remove Controller dialog box to confirm the removal of a controller.

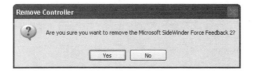

Choosing the Game Controller to Use for Legacy Programs

If you have the money and the ports, there's nothing to stop you from installing multiple game controllers on the same PC. To tell Windows which game controller to use for legacy programs that may get confused by a surfeit of game controllers, take the following steps:

1. Click the Advanced button in the Game Controllers dialog box. Windows displays the Advanced Settings dialog box (shown in Figure 30.7).

FIGURE 30.7

Use the Advanced
Settings dialog box to
tell Windows which
game controller you
want to use.

2. In the Preferred Device drop-down list, select the game controller you want to use.

3. Click the OK button. Windows closes the Advanced Settings dialog box and applies your choice.

Testing and Calibrating a Game Controller

To test and calibrate a game controller, take the following steps:

1. Select the game controller in the Installed Game Controllers list box in the Game Controllers dialog box.

2. Click the Properties button. Windows displays the Properties dialog box for the game controller with the Test page foremost. Figure 30.8 shows the Test page of the Properties dialog box for a SideWinder Force Feedback 2 Joystick.

FIGURE 30.8

Use the Test page of
the Properties dialog
box for a game con-
troller to test and
calibrate it.

3. Use the controls on the Test page to make sure that your game controller is working as it should. For example, in the Properties dialog box shown, you can check the range of movement on the axes and make sure that the buttons and the point-of-view hat control are working correctly.

4. If you decide you need to calibrate your controller, click the Settings tab. Windows displays the Settings page, of which Figure 30.9 shows an example (again for the SideWinder Force Feedback 2 Joystick).

FIGURE 30.9

The Settings page of the Properties dialog box for a game controller includes the Calibrate button for starting the Device Calibration Wizard.

5. Click the Calibrate button. Windows starts the Device Calibration Wizard.

6. Follow the prompts as the Device Calibration Wizard walks you through calibrating your game controller. When the Wizard finishes, it returns you to the Properties dialog box for the controller.

7. Click the OK button. Windows closes the Properties dialog box, applies the settings you chose, and returns you to the Game Controllers dialog box.

Troubleshooting a Game Controller

To troubleshoot a problem with a game controller, take the following steps:

1. Click the Troubleshoot button in the Game Controllers dialog box. Windows launches or activates Help and Support Center and starts the Games and Multimedia Troubleshooter (shown in Figure 30.10).

2. Select the I Am Having a Problem with a Joystick or Another Game Device option button.

3. Click the Next button. The Games and Multimedia Troubleshooter walks you through the steps for troubleshooting the game controller—for example, establishing whether the device is USB and whether the game you're trying to play is configured to use the controller.

FIGURE 30.10

Use the Games and Multimedia Troubleshooter to troubleshoot problems with a game controller.

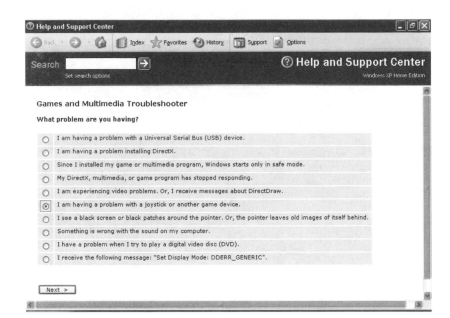

Getting the Best Performance on Games

In order to get the best performance on games, follow the recommendations in this list.

Get plenty of RAM　You've heard this before a number of times in the book—but many computers don't have enough RAM to run demanding programs effectively without frequent swapping to disk. And games are some of the most demanding programs around. For example, Unreal Tournament typically devours around 60MB of RAM and virtual memory—*each*. And if you have an AGP video card (and you should), there's another reason to have plenty of RAM. Read the next item.

Assign a big AGP aperture size　One of the reasons why AGP video cards can blow the socks off PCI video cards (apart from AGP's providing a bandwidth of 533MBps to PCI's 132MBps) is that they can offload the less exciting video-processing tasks onto system RAM so that they can devote their video RAM (VRAM) to dealing with the most exciting and demanding video-processing tasks. To get the most benefit from this, restart your computer and display the BIOS screen. (On many computers, you can do this by pressing the Delete key or the F2 key during boot-up.) Find the setting called AGP Aperture Size (or something similar, depending on your BIOS), and increase it to a value that's around half the amount of system RAM you have. (You'll be limited to the settings that the BIOS provides, but choose a setting around this amount.) Save the values and exit the BIOS screen. AGP will then be able to take as much RAM as it needs for video-processing tasks.

Assign plenty of swap-file space   Give Windows plenty of space for the paging file so that it can write to disk as much information as it needs. (See "Specifying the Size and Location of the Paging File" in Chapter 16 for details.)

Get the latest stable drivers   Get the latest stable versions of drivers for your hardware. If your hardware is from big-name manufacturers or enthusiastic manufacturers, you'll probably be able to download new drivers via Windows Update. But for the latest drivers the moment they're released, visit the hardware manufacturers' Web sites directly. Resist any temptation to test beta drivers, because they can destabilize your computer. Though System Restore (discussed in Chapter 16) can work wonders, you probably won't want to use it any more frequently than you have to.

Keep your disks defragmented   Keep your disks defragmented, as discussed in Chapter 11. This speeds up the retrieval of game data from the hard drive and optimizes the performance of virtual memory.

Choose appropriate display settings   Choose a screen resolution, color depth, and refresh rate appropriate to the game you're playing. For example, for action games, you may want to reduce the resolution, color depth, and refresh rate in order to increase the frame rate of the game and produce a smoother flow of play. For a nonaction game that uses high-quality graphics, you'll probably want a higher resolution, color depth, and refresh rate.

Stop unnecessary software   Before running a game, exit as many open programs as possible to free up memory. Check your start-up group for background services that may be running when you don't need them to. (The Microsoft Office Find Fast utility is a perennial offender.) If you're using a screen saver, disable it so that it won't try to kick in while you're playing a game.

Up Next

This chapter has discussed the games that Windows XP provides, how to install and configure game controllers, and how to get good games performance on Windows XP.

That's the end of Part IV of the book. The last part, Part V, discusses how to network your Windows XP PCs and how to share resources.

Part V

Networking Windows XP

Chapter 31

Understanding Windows Networking

THIS CHAPTER DISCUSSES WHAT a network is, why you might want to implement one in your home or home office, and what hardware you'll need to get in order to implement a network. Along the way, it tells you what you need to know about network architectures, network topologies, and network equipment. The chapter's quite short—more of an overview than seriously detailed information—so don't feel that you need to skip it. As you'll see, Windows XP includes all the software you need to create a fully functional network—and you may not even need to buy any extra hardware.

If you're already sold on the benefits of a network and you know the basics of networking, skip this chapter and go straight to the next chapter, which discusses how to start implementing a network.

This chapter covers the following topics:

◆ Why network your home?

◆ Network architectures

◆ Network topologies

◆ Planning your network

◆ Choosing between wired and wireless

◆ Choosing hardware for a wired network

◆ Choosing hardware for a wireless network

Why Network Your Home or Home Office?

A *network* is simply computers connected to each other so that they can share resources or exchange information. A network can consist of as few as two computers or as many as are connected to the Internet. In a home or a home office, you'll probably have anything from a couple of computers to a half-dozen computers networked together.

By networking your computers, you can share files and resources, so that you can perform the following actions and more:

◆ Transfer files from one computer to another. (For one-time use, such as when you're upgrading from an old computer to a new one, you might choose to use a direct connection instead of establishing a connection via network cards.)

◆ Share files. For example, if several users need to collaborate on a project from different computers, you can give them all access to a networked drive to use as a central location.

◆ Back files up easily from each of the networked computers. By centralizing backup to one computer or standard media, you can protect your files against loss and corruption.

◆ Share Internet connections, thus making better use of broadband connections (such as DSLs, cable, and satellite links) or simply reducing hardware and telephony costs.

◆ Share printers, CD-ROM and CD recorder drives, scanners, and other hardware.

Network Architectures

There are two basic network architectures: client/server networks and peer-to-peer networks. The following sections discuss the key points of each, so that you're clear on the differences. Both are worth considering for your home or home-office network, though at this writing peer-to-peer networks are far more popular for such small networks. (As you'll see, client/server networks deserve more of a look-in than they get.)

Client/Server Networks

Client/server networks are the type of networks used by most companies that have more than a dozen or so users. In a *client/server network* (also sometimes called a *server-based network*), there are two different types of computers: *server computers* that provide services such as file storage and printing, and *client computers* that use those services. The point of using servers is to centralize files, coordinate the sharing of resources, and improve security while decreasing the number of points of failure.

A client/server network can have just one server, but most corporate networks of any size have multiple servers, each with a specialized purpose. *File servers* provide networked storage for the users' files. *Print servers* manage printers, queuing the print jobs that the users send and coordinating the printers. *Applications servers* run programs so that users' desktop PCs can be 98-pound weaklings or the modern equivalent of dumb terminals. *Internet-access servers* such as proxy servers handle users' Internet requests, routing demands for URLs outward and the corresponding data inward. (Most proxy servers are set to check incoming and outgoing information for sins such as sports sites and sex sites on the way.) *E-mail servers* handle e-mail and groupware. *Fax servers*... okay, you get the idea.

The servers make it easier to manage, back up, and troubleshoot the network. Instead of having files scattered all around the building (or the campus, or offices spread right across North America) on the hard drives of individual users' computers, the administrators can have files saved on network drives that they can easily back up (and restore if necessary) from a central location. Instead of having an inexpensive and flaky printer crowding each user's cubicle, the administrators can funnel printing through centralized printers the size of refrigerators, making troubleshooting and management easy. Instead of installing programs locally (on the users' hard drives), they can install them on the applications server, where they can maintain and upgrade them with minimal effort. Security and permissions are handled centrally through the servers, so an administrator can easily prevent users from taking actions they shouldn't.

Needless to say, there's a downside to this centralization as well. If everyone in the office has been well-behaved and stored all their files on the file server (as they're usually told to do), nobody will be able to do any work on those files if the file server goes down for the count. If the Internet-access server takes an extended coffee break, all users' contact with the Internet and the Web is cut off. And if one of the cubicle-sized printers decides to eat paper rather than spit it out at 40 sheets a minute, even the network administrators won't be able to print out their resume.

That said, when client/server networks work well, they work *very* well. With proper planning, client/server networks can *scale* (grow) to have thousands of workstations on them, whereas (even with good planning) peer-to-peer networks seldom work well with more than a couple of dozen workstations.

Figure 31.1 shows part of a client/server network, omitting most of the clients so that the figure fits on the page.

FIGURE 31.1

In a client/server network, servers centralize tasks such as file storage, faxing, e-mail, and Internet access.

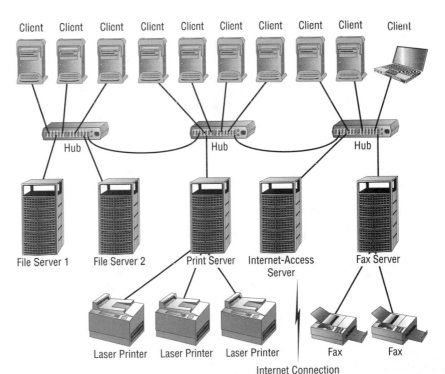

Normally, the server or servers in a client/server network run a server operating system such as Windows 2000 Server, NT Server, Novell NetWare, Linux, or Unix. But this isn't an absolute requirement. If you want, you can set up a small client/server network in which the server runs Windows XP (or even a version of Windows 9*x*). More on this in a moment.

Peer-to-Peer Networks

In a *peer-to-peer network*, the computers are all equals—*peers*—from the administration and security points of view. Instead of connecting to one or more servers, the peer computers connect to each other. Instead of getting services from servers, the peer computers get services from each other and provide each other with services. Instead of being managed centrally by administrators, each peer computer is managed by its user, making security and backup more difficult without deliberate coordination by the users.

Typically, each computer on a peer-to-peer network is both a client and a server: It's a client when it accesses a resource on another computer, and it's a server when it supplies a resource to another computer. (The word *typically* is there because quite often one or more computers in a peer network will act only as clients, in that they share no resources with their peers.) For example, when you share a folder with other users, your computer is acting as a server. And when you access the printer connected to another computer, your computer is acting as a client. But most of the time, you don't need to worry about whether your computer is acting as a client or as a server, because it all happens seamlessly behind the scenes. You set up the sharing, and after that, the resources are available, and you can use them. It's as simple as that.

Figure 31.2 shows a simple peer-to-peer network that's sharing folders, two printers, and a dial-up Internet connection. This also illustrates the main weakness of peer-to-peer networks: Each computer that's sharing a resource must be powered on and have its operating system functioning all the time that the resource is needed. If the computer that's sharing folders is switched off (or has hung or crashed), the files in those folders won't be accessible. If the computer that's sharing the printers is powered off, nobody will be able to print. And for the Internet connection to be accessible all the time, that computer must keep humming along.

Peer-to-peer networks have another disadvantage worth mentioning here—a disadvantage that you can't see in the figure. Sharing a resource occupies some of the computer's processing power and memory, making it less responsive for user-oriented duties such as running programs.

If in your mind you move around a couple of the resources shared in Figure 31.2 (and perhaps squint a bit), you can see that the line between a client/server network and a peer-to-peer network can be quite fine. If one of the computers were sharing all the resources, it'd be a server; and if the network were administered centrally, it would be a client/server network rather than a peer-to-peer network.

Network Topologies

This section discusses the two main network topologies you're likely to want to use for networking your home or home office. It also mentions two network topologies that are less used nowadays.

These topologies are physical. There are also logical topologies that describe how the data travels along the wires. We'll get to these in a few minutes' time.

FIGURE 31.2

In a peer-to-peer network, the computers share resources with each other.

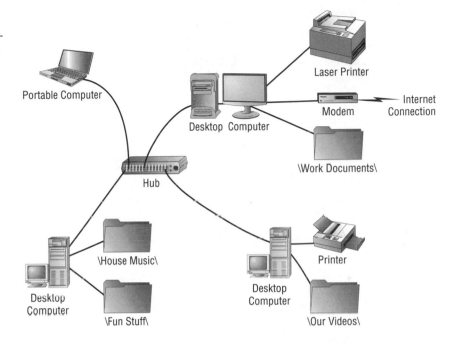

Star Topology

The *star topology* is the most used topology for networks nowadays, because it's easy to implement and fault tolerant. In a star topology, all the computers connect to a central hub or switch (or several hubs or switches connected to each other). Both the client/server network shown in Figure 31.1 and the peer-to-peer network shown in Figure 31.2 use star topologies.

A star topology uses more cable than a bus topology (discussed in the next section), because each computer is wired to the hub or switch. Extra cable costs more money, of course, but for a small network, the difference in cabling cost between a star topology and a bus topology isn't usually a significant amount. And because each computer is connected to the hub or switch, a cable failure affects only one computer.

The hub or switch in a star topology does represent a single point of failure. But because hubs and switches are typically very reliable, this isn't usually a problem.

Bus Topology

In a *bus topology*, all the computers and devices are attached to a single run of cable. As you can see in Figure 31.3, which illustrates a bus topology, the bus is a simple network design, and one that's economical on cable. The terminators at each end of the bus essentially tell the signal that it's reached the end of the cable and that it should stop rather than bouncing back along the cable.

FIGURE 31.3

In a physical bus topology, the computers and devices are attached to a single run of cable.

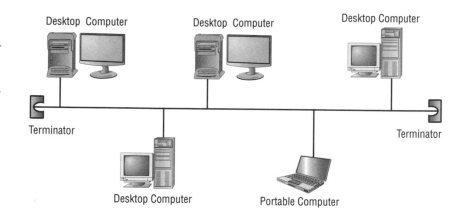

The main drawback to a bus topology is that any break in the cable takes down the entire network. Bus topologies are seldom used for Ethernet and Fast Ethernet nowadays, but they're used in other networking technologies, such as HomePNA networks.

Other Topologies: Ring and Mesh

Star and bus aren't the only topologies for networks—there are also ring topologies and mesh topologies.

In a *ring topology*, the computers are laid out in a topological ring, with each connected to its two neighbors. Ring topologies aren't fault tolerant, and because each computer on the network needs two cables, they tend to be more expensive than star or bus topologies.

Mesh topologies are fault tolerant and are used where uptime is vital. In a true mesh, each computer is directly connected to each other computer, giving a network diagram that looks like a mesh or a cat's cradle. As you can imagine, a true mesh involves a huge number of connections, and is rarely implemented for more than a handful of computers. More frequently, a partial mesh topology is implemented, with the most critical computers having multiple connections to each other so that they can maintain connectivity even if they lose a connection or two.

Logical Topologies

As mentioned a few minutes ago, the topologies discussed so far are physical topologies. A network also has a *logical topology* that describes how the data travels along the wires. A network can have the same logical topology as physical topology, or the two can be different.

There are three widely used logical topologies:

◆ In a *logical bus topology*, the signal travels to all the computers on the network, but only the computer identified by the address picks the packets of data off the wires. Ethernet uses a logical bus topology.

◆ In a *logical ring topology*, the signal travels around the network from one attached computer to the next. Each computer checks to see if the signal is intended for it; if it isn't, the computer passes the signal along to the next computer. When the signal reaches the computer identified by the address, that computer picks the packets off the wire, and they travel no further.

◆ In a *logical mesh topology*, the signal can take any of a number of paths from its source to its destination. The Internet is an example of a logical mesh topology.

Planning Your Network

This section discusses how to go about planning your network. You need to make the following decisions:

◆ Should the network be client/server or peer-to-peer?

◆ Should the network be wired or wireless?

◆ If the network will be wired, which wired networking technology will you use?

◆ Where will you keep your files?

◆ Which resources will you share on the network?

Client/Server or Peer-to-Peer?

The first question you should answer is whether you want to create a client/server network or a peer-to-peer network.

At first sight, you may be surprised by this question. Didn't the book just say that most home and many home-office networks are peer-to-peer? That's right—but just because most of these networks are peer-to-peer doesn't necessarily mean that they're better off so.

Even if your network needs are relatively modest, it's worth considering having a server, especially if you have a spare computer, or a pensioned-off old laptop or desktop, that you'd like to get a bit more use out of. A server doesn't have to have a fast processor or a ton of RAM. Nor does it need to be running the latest and greatest operating system (read: Windows XP). That Pentium-166 with 64MB RAM that you reluctantly decided couldn't handle Windows XP could still play a valuable role in your computing life. Put an old copy of Windows NT Workstation or Windows 2000 Professional on it—or Linux, if you can handle Linux—and it can provide services to the network.

TIP   Another alternative is to add to the network dedicated devices for sharing resources so that you don't need to keep as many computers running. For example, you could add a DSL modem and router or cable modem and router to share your Internet connection, or a print server to share one or more of your printers. Each of these is an independent device that connects to your network hub. Once it's connected, it can be accessed by any computer that's running.

Wired or Wireless?

After you decide between a client/server network and a peer-to-peer network, your second decision should be whether you want a wired network, a wireless network, or a combination of the two.

As with most things in life, both wired and wireless networks offer advantages and disadvantages. Wired networks have three main advantages over wireless networks: speed, cost, and reliability.

Wireless networks offer two main advantages over wired networks: flexibility and lack of cables. The following sections examine these advantages.

One point on which wired networks and wireless networks are about tied is simplicity. In theory, a wireless network should be easier to implement than a wired network, because less hardware is involved—for example, there are no cables. But because many wireless network adapters have complex setup routines, they may prove slower to set up in practice.

Wired networks are relatively simple to configure. You add a network card to each computer, attach a cable to the network card and the hub or switch, and you're in business.

ADVANTAGES OF WIRED NETWORKS OVER WIRELESS NETWORKS

This section discusses the advantages of wired networks over wireless networks: speed, cost, and reliability.

Speed

Wired networks offer higher speed than wireless networks. Fast Ethernet—as you'll see, the best choice for a wired network—provides 100Mbps. Most wireless network adapters conform to the IEEE 802.11 standard, which offers a theoretical 11Mbps. Almost all of these adapters drop down to lower speeds—5.5Mbps, 2.4Mbps, 1.1Mbps—if conditions don't allow 11Mbps. The more distance and the more walls or floors that you put between your wireless adapter and the nearest access point, the lower the transmission speed will drop.

Cost

Wired network adapters cost much less than wireless network adapters. You can get a bargain-basement wired network adapter for $10, though you'll usually be better advised to spend more like $20 to $50. Then you'll need a hub or a switch. A hub costs less than $10 per port; a switch costs $10 to $20 a port.

Most wireless network adapters cost between $100 and $200. You can create a peer-to-peer network with two or more adapters, but to improve performance, you may want to get a wireless access point instead. Most hardware wireless access points cost between $300 and $1000. Some manufacturers offer software wireless access points that are less expensive ($100 to $200). A software wireless access point usually involves putting a second, wireless network interface card in a computer that's already wired to the network. This computer then acts as a bridge between the wired portion and the wireless portion of the network. The disadvantage to software wireless access points is, needless to say, that you need to keep that computer running all the time you want to use the wireless portion of the network. However, if you decide to have a server on the network, adding a wireless software access point to it can be relatively painless.

Reliability

Wired networks tend to be more reliable than wireless networks. Unless there's a problem with one of the network cards, the cables, or the hub (or switch), a wired network should deliver its full performance all the time.

By contrast, throughput on a wireless network can be affected not only by the distance and obvious obstacles such as walls and floors but also by its immediate surroundings. For example, a PC Card wireless network adapter can be blocked by the user's hand on a laptop that has its PC Card slots toward the front, by the user's legs when the computer is being used on the user's lap, or by books or other objects placed near the adapter. It shouldn't happen, but it does.

ADVANTAGES OF WIRELESS NETWORKS OVER WIRED NETWORKS

This section discusses the advantages of wireless networks over wired networks: flexibility, and the lack of cables.

Flexibility

Because the computers in a wireless network aren't constrained by cables, a wireless network offers greater flexibility than a wired network. You can move the computers from room to room without trailing cables. Even if you're not interested in roaming with your laptop, being able to move it about freely can be a boon.

For desktop computers, of course, the mobility offered by a wireless network connection is less of a draw, though it can come in useful in shared computers. For example, if you put a desktop computer on a wheeled workstation, you can move it easily from room to room (or from schoolroom to schoolroom).

Lack of Cables

Wireless networks are great for locations where, for whatever reason, you don't want to (or cannot) install cables. For example, in a temporary office location, you can set up a wireless network without having unsightly cables strung like trip wires from room to room. Likewise, if you're renting an apartment whose landlord wouldn't appreciate your drilling holes from room to room (or floor to floor) or stapling cables along the baseboards, a wireless network will probably seem more attractive than a wired network.

COMBINING WIRED AND WIRELESS IN YOUR NETWORK

You can get the best of both worlds by combining wired and wireless in your network. For example, you might want to implement a wired network with a wireless access point that allowed your laptops to connect via wireless network interface cards from wherever in the building they happened to be. The wired portion of your network will be fast, and the wireless portion of your network will be flexible. The cost will be considerably more than that of a wired-only network, but it should be significantly less than that of a wireless-only network.

If you decide to combine wired and wireless networks, create the wired network as described in "Installing Your Network Hardware" in Chapter 32, and then add wireless to it as described in "Implementing a Wireless Network" (also in Chapter 32).

Where Will You Keep Your Files?

Your next decision is where to keep the files on the network. It's vital to make this decision when implementing the network, because it can save you a great deal of time and effort later on.

In a peer-to-peer network, each user typically saves the files they create (or download) on the hard drive of their computer. To share files, they either use the `\Shared Documents\` folder on their computer, designate another folder on their computer for sharing, or use a folder someone else is sharing on another computer.

There's nothing to stop you from keeping your files scattered about on the hard drives (or removable drives) of all the computers attached to the network. But the files will be very difficult to back up effectively from their various locations, and unless each user of the network has a good memory, it'll probably become hard to remember which file is stored in which folder on which computer.

To keep your shared files in order, designate a minimum number of shared locations. This is one of the strongest arguments for creating a client/server network rather than a peer-to-peer network. By concentrating all your shared files on the server, you'll be able to back them up easily. All the users of the network should be able to find the shared files without wasting time and effort. And because the server will be running all the time, you'll avoid the problem that arises when a user wants to access a file in a shared folder whose host computer is currently powered down or whose operating system has temporarily given up the ghost.

HOW MUCH SPACE DO YOU NEED FOR YOUR FILES?

If you decide to keep all your shared files in a central location, estimate how much space you'll need for the files. This is of course much easier said than done, because it's always difficult to know how much space you need until you find out that you have far too little. But you need to start by making an educated guess at the amount of space required so that you can provide it to start with.

How much space you need will vary wildly depending on the types of files you want to share. If you're networking your home office, you'll probably want to share documents, spreadsheets, presentations, address books, and so on. If you're networking your computers to make their entertainment resources available to each computer in the household, you may need much more space. For example, if you're planning to implement a network so that you can play your vast collection of MP3 files from any connected computer, you'll need a huge amount of storage space. If you want to share video files, the demand for storage space will be even more intense.

Which Resources Will You Share?

Next, make a list of the resources that you want to share via the network. The most obvious resources are files and folders, your Internet connection, and your printers, though not necessarily in that order.

Right out of the box, Windows XP lets you share files and folders, an Internet connection, and printers directly (as it were) from one computer to another. For example, if Computer A is sharing a printer, Computers B and C can print to it via the network. If Computer B is sharing its Internet connection, Computers A and C can use the Internet connection to access the Internet. With custom software, you can also share other resources. For example, you can network your TV or your DVD, or implement a video-communication or baby-monitoring program across the network.

You may also want to share other resources that you can't share directly like this. For example, you can't share a digital camera or scanner directly unless you unplug it and carry it from computer to computer. So the best way to share a digital camera or scanner is to set it up on a computer that any member of the household can use. If the server is in a central location, it might be the best computer for this role. (Alternatively, you could invest in enough USB or FireWire extension cords to plug the scanner or camera into each computer without moving the device itself....)

Choosing Network Hardware for a Wired Network

Once you've decided to implement a wired network, you have a further choice to make: Fast Ethernet, phone line (HomePNA), or power line. The following sections discuss how to choose hardware for each of these types of wired network.

WARNING *Network hardware is unglamorous compared to graphics cards, fast processors, and thundering subwoofer systems, but don't make the mistake of buying the cheapest hardware you can find for your network just because the network is boring. In particular, don't skimp on the hub and the cables. Sure, you can shave a few bucks off the price, but you need your network to be reliable because it will be carrying your valuable data. False economies you make here can cost you far more in troubleshooting and downtime in the future.*

Choosing Hardware for a Fast Ethernet Network

For a Fast Ethernet network, you need network interface cards, cables, and a hub or switch.

NOTE *The only reason to consider a regular Ethernet network over a Fast Ethernet network is if you already have a full set of regular Ethernet equipment ready to use. If you don't, you'll do much better to go directly to Fast Ethernet. Fast Ethernet cards, cables, and hubs used to be much more expensive than standard Ethernet ones, but now the differences are just about negligible. Even if you have regular Ethernet cards and hubs, buy Fast Ethernet cables, because you can use them for higher data rates if you upgrade your network interface cards and switches. The cables should last for many years unless you allow dogs, rodents, or small children near them.*

NETWORK INTERFACE CARDS

The main consideration when buying Fast Ethernet network interface cards is which types of slots your computers have free. In general, PCI cards are better than ISA cards, because you'll have fewer IRQ conflicts. But if your computer is stuffed to the gills with PCI cards and has only an ISA slot free, ISA will work fine.

For a portable computer that doesn't have a built-in Fast Ethernet port, your only viable choice will be a PC Card network interface card. USB network interface cards can't deliver anything like Fast Ethernet speeds, so you should use them only as a last resort for either portable computers or desktop computers.

CABLE

When choosing Fast Ethernet cable, keep these points in mind:

- For general-purpose use, go with unshielded twisted-pair (UTP) Category 5 (*Cat 5* for short) cable. This delivers excellent performance at reasonable cost.

- If you need to run cable in suspended ceilings, inside walls, or between the floors of a building, get plenum cable. Plenum cable has a Teflon coating designed to resist catching fire and to give off nontoxic smoke if it does catch fire. (A plenum is essentially an enclosed space that's full of matter.)

◆ If you need a lot of cables, or if you need custom lengths of cable, buy a reel of cable and connectors, cut lengths to match your needs, and crimp connectors to the ends. You'll need a crimping kit, which makes this approach less economical for a few cables.

◆ Cables come in a variety of colors. You may want to choose a color of cable that will blend most invisibly into your décor. But if you're creating complex wiring arrangements in the same room, you may prefer to buy different colors of cable so that it's easy to see which cable goes where.

HUB OR SWITCH

In the star network topology used for Fast Ethernet, the hub or switch forms the central point of the network, with the network cables from all the computers and other network-aware devices plugging into its ports.

When a computer sends data, the hub receives it on one port and broadcasts it on all the other connected ports so that the computer or device to which the data is addressed can receive it.

This arrangement works well enough, but it means that there's a lot of data bouncing around the network unnecessarily. Say you have eight computers, imaginatively named A through H, connected to your hub. When A is sending data to B, it sends it to the hub, and the hub broadcasts the data to all the ports but the port the data is coming in on—in other words, the ports to which computers B through H are connected. B picks the data off the wire. The data to ports C through H is unnecessary and decreases the performance of the network.

This is why you should seriously consider buying a switch rather than a hub. A *switch* (or *switching hub*) is essentially a more intelligent version of a hub. A switch builds a table of the hardware addresses of the computers and devices connected to its ports. Then, instead of taking the data passed to it on one port and blindly blasting it out on all other connected ports, it examines the address on the data and passes the data along only to the appropriate port (and thus to the appropriate computer). By doing this, a switch provides more available bandwidth on the network and improves performance.

There is, of course, a downside: A switch costs a little more than a hub. But if you're planning to use your network extensively—especially if you'll be using your network for audio and video files—you'll find the investment worthwhile.

Buy a hub or switch with enough ports for both your current needs and your future needs. If you have four computers in your home or office now, but might add either more computers or more network-aware devices in the near-ish future, it makes little sense to buy a four-port hub. Instead, buy an eight-port or twelve-port hub or switch.

Alternatively, make sure that your four-port hub or switch includes an uplink port, so that you can attach another hub or switch to it.

Choosing Hardware for a Phone-Line Network

Phone lines can be one of the easiest ways to network your home quickly, provided that you have wires and jacks where you need them. (If you don't, you *could* run extension leads—but these offer little advantage over network cable.)

Here's what you need to know about phone-line networks:

- Phone-line networks are limited in speed. The industry body, the Home Phoneline Networking Alliance (HomePNA), has so far set two standards: HomePNA 1.0 offers speeds of 1Mbps. HomePNA 2.0 offers speeds of 10Mbps—the same speed as a regular Ethernet network, a tenth of the speed of Fast Ethernet.

- Logically enough, the phone jacks you use for the network need to be on the same phone line.

- Most phone-line network adapters include a splitter, so that you can use the network and the phone at the same time.

- Most phone-line network adapters plug into a parallel port or USB port.

- Phone-line networks use a physical bus topology and a logical bus topology. This means that you don't need a hub. It also means that if you cut the phone line, the network stops working—but you'd figured that out already. Phone lines are terminated automatically, so you don't need to add termination devices to the ends of the bus.

This is about as much as you need to know. If the speed is adequate for your needs, and you have the jacks, you can buy a phone-line networking kit, plug in the adapters, and install the software, and you should be away.

EXPERT KNOWLEDGE: ETHERNET OVER PHONE WIRES

There are actually *two* ways in which you can network your home by using the existing phone lines.

One way is to use special network adapters designed for phone-line networks, as described in this section. The other is to use the spare pair of wires present in most existing phone cabling that's used for only one line to run regular Ethernet.

Regular phone cable has two pairs of wires—the telephone companies like to be able to sell you a second line without having to install more cable. Each phone line uses one pair of wires. So if you have only one telephone line, you may be able to use the second pair of wires to carry data.

Be warned that this approach to networking requires much more patience and technical skill than the other means of creating a network. Also, because phone cable has minimal shielding and isn't designed for data use, you may experience interference and slowdowns on the network... but if you have the wires free and they surface where you need the computers to be, this can be a handy solution to wiring a network.

Choosing Hardware for a Power-Line Network

Plug the network adapter into your parallel port, then plug it into the electrical socket... given the damage that a little snap of static can do to a computer's sensitive parts, this instruction seems dangerously wrong, doesn't it? But a power-line network can be one of the easiest ways to network your home, drawing ahead of phone-line networks in the simplicity stakes because most dwellings have many more electrical outlets than they do phone jacks. You shouldn't need to buy any cables for a power-line network beyond the cables for connecting the computer's parallel port or USB port to the electrical socket.

Utility companies have also been experimenting with delivering Internet connectivity via power lines, with some promising to deliver, uh, *electrifying* speeds. (Yes, at least one company has actually used that word.)

At this writing, power-line networks aren't as fast as other network types. Most offer rates of between 1Mbps and 2Mbps—enough for sharing documents among a handful of computers, but not enough for heavy-duty audio or video use. And most power-line network adapters require a power conditioner to make sure that the computer receives no untoward signal from variations in the power supply that normal electrical equipment can shrug off.

Various manufacturers make power-line network equipment. One of the leaders is Inari (formerly Intelogis; www.inari.com), which licenses power-line networking equipment to OEMs.

Given that there are various manufacturers, you'd expect there to be various types of power-line network adapters—and indeed there are. Most types plug into a parallel port or a USB port, making them easy to attach to most computers.

Power-line networks have a couple of limitations worth mentioning. One is that some power-line networks don't work well with bi-directional printer cables: You need to disable the features that let the printer give feedback to the computer, such as telling the computer that it's out of ink or that it's managed to jam again on your expensive letterhead.

A second limitation is that, because multiple apartments or even houses can be on the same ring main, power-line networking can inadvertently network you with your neighbors. (Actually, you shouldn't see this as a limitation—you should see it as a *feature*.) So it's vital that you implement security on a power-line network to protect your data and your devices.

Choosing Hardware for a Wireless Network

Choosing hardware for a wireless network is both easier and harder than choosing hardware for a wired network. It's easier in that you need less equipment—you can skip the cables for a start—but harder in that you should evaluate that equipment even more carefully than you would wired networking equipment.

For a simple wireless network involving two computers, you need nothing more than a pair of wireless network interface cards. For desktop computers, PCI card network interface cards are usually the best choice. For portable computers, PC Card network interface cards are usually the only viable choice.

NOTE   *You can get wireless network interface cards with USB connections, but even wireless' unexciting speeds can overtax USB 1.0's bandwidth. USB 1.0 can manage a maximum of 12Mbps for all the devices on the bus; 802.11 wireless devices can manage a maximum of 11Mbps, so if anything else is taking up bandwidth on the bus, you won't get the maximum wireless rate.*

For a more complex or more capable wireless network, get a wireless access point for the wireless network interface cards to connect to. The access point plugs into your Ethernet hub, forming a wireless bridge to the network and letting the wireless computers access the wired portions of the network.

Usually it's best to get all your wireless equipment from the same manufacturer or from manufacturers known to be friendly to each other. In theory, many 802.11b devices are able to interoperate with each other. In practice, many of them sulk or resort to data rates low enough to make you regret the experiment.

When evaluating wireless networking equipment, keep the following considerations in mind:

Price   With wireless networking equipment, you'll have a hard time forgetting this consideration, but don't buy anything cheap and dysfunctional.

Range   If you've used cordless phones, it'll come as no surprise that the maximum range listed for most wireless network cards turns out to be wildly optimistic or achievable only under atmospheric conditions and surroundings that can be re-created in laboratories but not real life. For example, some manufacturers claim a 300-yard range for their wireless adapters when 50 yards is in fact pushing the envelope. Try to get a demo of the range before buying rashly with plans to work wirelessly from your local coffee shop or bar.

Roaming   Usually more of a consideration in offices than in home buildings, roaming is worth thinking about if you need wireless access from an area greater than a single access point can cover. First, make sure that the network interface cards and access points you buy can handle roaming, so that you'll be able to move from one access point's coverage to the next's without dropping your network connection. (If you just need to be able to establish a connection from the garden or the garage, you won't necessarily need roaming.) And second, work out how many access points you need.

Number of access points   From the range and the need for roaming, establish the number of access points you need to provide effective coverage for your building or area.

Placement of access points   Whether you get one access point, two, or ten, you need to place them optimally in order to balance the widest possible coverage with the fastest possible connections. The nearer you are to an access point, the better your chances of getting the full 11Mbps data rate.

Up Next

This chapter has discussed why you might implement a network in your home or home office; the different network architectures, physical topologies, and logical topologies available to you; and the different types of networking equipment. It has suggested how to approach choosing the type of network you want and the types of network equipment you'll need for it.

The next chapter discusses how to set up the network.

Chapter 32

Building a Home or Home-Office Network

THIS CHAPTER DISCUSSES HOW to build an effective network for your home or your home office. It assumes that you've read the previous chapter, decided on the network type you want to use, and purchased the necessary hardware for it.

This chapter starts with arguably the simplest type of network that you can create: a direct connection from one computer to another using a parallel cable, a serial cable, or infrared rays. Direct connections are useful for infrequent networking—for example, for transferring files from one computer to another. The chapter then moves on to setting up a regular network (wired or wireless) by using the Network Setup Wizard.

This chapter covers the following topics:

◆ The different ways of setting up a network with Windows XP

◆ Setting up a direct connection via cables or infrared

◆ Installing your network hardware

◆ Setting up a network using the Network Setup Wizard

◆ Browsing the network

◆ Mapping and disconnecting network drives

◆ Changing your computer's workgroup

◆ Connecting non-XP computers to the network

The Different Ways of Setting Up a Network with Windows XP

You can set up a network with Windows XP Home in several different ways:

◆ You can connect two computers with a serial cable, a parallel cable, or infrared ports and use the New Connection Wizard to create a direct connection between them.

◆ You can run the Network Setup Wizard and perform most of your network configuration in one fell swoop. Provided that you're satisfied with a Windows-only network and a basic if effective network design, the Network Setup Wizard can get you networking very easily and efficiently.

◆ If you add additional computers to the network, you can run the Network Setup Wizard to configure their pieces of the network.

◆ If you install your network hardware piecemeal, or if you want a heterogeneous network (for example, including a Linux server), you'll need to perform some configuration manually.

The Network Setup Wizard does a creditable job of creating a peer-to-peer network with these basic parameters:

◆ It uses the nonroutable `192.168.0.x` TCP/IP subnet and implements a Dynamic Host Configuration Protocol (DHCP) server on the computer that's sharing its Internet connection. The DHCP server gets the IP address `192.168.0.1` and assigns IP addresses on-the-fly to each computer that joins the network.

◆ It creates a workgroup called MSHOME (or another name of your choosing). (As you'll see, it's a good idea to change the name of the workgroup, especially if you're using a cable modem.)

◆ It shares the Internet connection you designate with every computer on the network so that each computer can start the connection and disable it as necessary.

◆ It automatically implements Internet Connection Firewall (ICF) to protect your network from probes and attacks across your Internet connection.

◆ It automatically shares the `\Shared Documents\` folder on each computer with every computer on the network.

◆ It automatically shares any printers that it can find with every computer on the network.

You can change any of these default settings after using the Network Setup Wizard to set up your network, as described in this chapter. Alternatively, you can avoid the Network Setup Wizard almost entirely and set up your network manually, as described in the next chapter.

Setting Up a Direct Connection

If you just need to transfer files from one computer to another once or occasionally, create a direct connection using a serial port, parallel port, or infrared port. You then configure one computer as the host computer and the other computer as the guest computer, connect the two with the cables or infrared rays, and establish the connection. The guest computer can then access files on the host computer. The host computer cannot access files on the guest computer, but the guest computer can upload files to the host computer, so you can transfer files back and forth easily enough.

Infrared, Parallel, or Serial?

Which port you use depends on which ports your computer has and which of them are available. But your order of preference should be as follows:

1. Infrared port   Of these three types of port, infrared ports offer the fastest connection—up to 4Mbps for an IrDA 2.0 connection, or between a third and a half of 10BaseT speeds. This speed is fast enough for most networking purposes, including playing streaming video. (IrDA 1.0, on the other hand, offers a miserly 115Kbps—about the speed of a serial port.) Most laptop computers have IrDA ports built in; pre-1998 laptops tend to have IrDA 1.0 ports, post-1998 laptops mostly have IrDA 2.0. However, most of these ports get so little use that the manufacturers might as well not have bothered. That's because IrDA has remained firmly the province of laptop computers, and few multiple-computer people have two or more laptops—most have one laptop and one desktop. You *can* add IrDA ports to desktops, typically via USB or a serial port (USB is preferable, because a serial port isn't fast enough), but most people prefer to use parallel or serial cables or network cards for networking instead.

2. Parallel cable   Parallel cables offer as easy a way to connect two computers as serial cables, and they can be much faster. A common-or-garden parallel cable offers speeds of around 100Kbps, but you can also get enhanced parallel cables specifically designed for file transfer that offer speeds of up to 4Mbps—nothing like as fast as Fast Ethernet, but more than satisfactory for performing backups, transferring files, installing programs, and sharing anything but the fastest Internet connections.

The main disadvantage to using parallel ports is that they tend to be in use by printers, multimedia card readers, or MP3 players.

TIP   If you choose to use a parallel-cable connection, check the BIOS settings on your computers to make sure that the parallel port you're using is running in the fastest mode possible. Most modern parallel ports offer a standard setting, an Enhanced Parallel Port (EPP) setting, and an Enhanced Capabilities Port (ECP) setting. ECP mode is usually used for printers, while EPP mode is often used for scanners, digital cameras, and the like. If your BIOSes support EPP or ECP, try these, as they should give you much faster data transfer than the standard setting.

3. Serial cable   Serial cables are much slower than parallel cables, managing only 115Kbps, but they're good enough to transfer files in a pinch. If you're planning to back up a large number of files, or to install a large program over a serial connection, plan plenty of time for doing it. For example, you might want to set it running and leave it going overnight.

As with parallel ports, your serial ports (or port—many computers offer only one nowadays) may be occupied for other purposes. While you can add a couple of serial ports or parallel ports to a desktop easily enough by using an add-in card, you'd probably be better off spending the same time, money, and effort getting and installing a network card instead.

TROUBLESHOOTING: IrDA CONNECTIONS

To establish a connection via IrDA, keep the limitations of infrared firmly in mind and position the computers accordingly:

Distance Keep the distance between the computers as short as possible. In theory, IrDA works over distances of up to three feet. In practice, you'll find it much more reliable over distances of an inch to a foot.

Horizontal alignment Keep the angle of alignment between the IrDA ports as close to 90 degrees as possible. An IrDA port throws out a 15–30-degree arc of infrared light, but the signal is strongest in the middle of the arc.

Vertical alignment Position the two IrDA ports on the same level as each other. IrDA ports don't spread the beam out much vertically, so if the ports are at different levels, you may not be able to establish a satisfactory connection.

Clear path Make sure the path between the IrDA ports is clear. Even a sheet of paper can block infrared transmission quite effectively.

Avoiding direct sunlight Direct sunlight can interfere with an infrared signal because sunlight contains infrared rays. (Besides, your laptop won't thank you for being placed in direct sunlight.)

Reading this list may make you think that the IrDA ports should be just about kissing each other for maximum effect—and that's not far off true. Get the ports as close to each other as is practical, and you'll experience many fewer problems.

Direct Connection via Cable or Infrared

This section discusses how to create a direct connection via cable or infrared.

CONNECTING THE CABLE

If you're using a cable for the connection, connect it to the appropriate port on each computer.

TIP If you're buying a parallel or serial cable for the purpose, be sure to get the right type—a serial-port null-modem cable (or asynchronous modem eliminator cable) or parallel-port data-transfer cable with male connections at each end. Many serial cables have male connections at one end and female connections at the other. If you have nine-pin serial ports, get a cable with male DB9 connectors at each end. Most parallel cables are for connecting printers and have a male DB25 connection at one end and a Centronics connector at the other. You need a cable with male DB25 connectors at each end so that you can connect the two parallel ports. Make sure that the cable is specifically designed for PC-to-PC connections—you can get cables with two male DB25s that aren't designed for this purpose, and they won't work.

SETTING UP THE HOST FOR THE DIRECT CONNECTION

Next, set up the host computer for the direct connection. Before you start, be warned that because of the security features that Windows XP includes, this process is more complicated than setting up the guest computer. It's not exactly difficult, but be prepared to spend a few minutes on it.

To set up the host computer, take the following steps:

1. Choose Start ➤ Connect To ➤ Show All Connections. Windows displays the Network Connections folder.

   ◆ If you haven't created a network connection, the Connect To item doesn't appear on the Start menu. Choose Start ➤ Control Panel. Windows displays Control Panel. Click the Network and Internet Connections link. Windows displays the Network and Internet Connections screen. Click the Network Connections link. Windows displays the Network Connections folder. (You can also choose Start ➤ All Programs ➤ Accessories ➤ Communications ➤ Network Connections.)

2. Click the Create a New Connection link in the Network Tasks list. Windows starts the New Connection Wizard, which displays its Welcome to the New Connection Wizard page.

3. Click the Next button. The New Connection Wizard displays the Network Connection Type page (shown in Figure 32.1).

FIGURE 32.1

On the Network Connection Type page of the New Connection Wizard, select the Set Up an Advanced Connection option button.

4. Select the Set Up an Advanced Connection option button.

5. Click the Next button. The Wizard displays the Advanced Connection Options page (shown in Figure 32.2).

6. Select the Accept Incoming Connections option button.

7. Click the Next button. The Wizard displays the Devices for Incoming Connections page (shown in Figure 32.3).

8. Select the check box for the port or the modem that you want to use for the connection.

9. Click the Next button. The Wizard displays the Incoming Virtual Private Network (VPN) Connection page (shown in Figure 32.4).

10. Select the Do Not Allow Virtual Private Connections option button.

FIGURE 32.2

On the Advanced
Connection Options
page of the New
Connection Wizard,
select the Accept
Incoming Connec-
tions option button.

FIGURE 32.3

On the Devices for
Incoming Connec-
tions page of the
New Connection
Wizard, specify
which port or
modem you want
to use for the
connection.

FIGURE 32.4

On the Incoming
Virtual Private Net-
work (VPN) Con-
nection page of the
New Connection
Wizard, select the
Do Not Allow Vir-
tual Private Connec-
tions option button.

11. Click the Next button. The Wizard displays the User Permissions page (shown in Figure 32.5), which lists the users set up on this computer, together with a HelpAssistant user (for Remote Assistance) and a Support user (for getting help from Microsoft).

FIGURE 32.5

On the User Permissions page of the New Connection Wizard, specify which users may connect to the host computer.

12. Specify which users may connect via this connection:

◆ To enable one of the listed users to use the connection, select their check box.

● To add a user, click the Add button. The Wizard displays the New User dialog box (shown in Figure 32.6). Enter the user's details—username, full name, password, and confirmation of password—and click the OK button. The Wizard adds the user to the Users Allowed to Connect list and selects their check box.

FIGURE 32.6

You can create new users for this connection by clicking the Add button and using the resulting New User dialog box.

◆ To remove one of the listed users *from your system* (not just from the list of users allowed to use this connection), select their entry in the Users Allowed to Connect list and click the Remove button. The Wizard displays the Incoming Connections Warning dialog box (shown in Figure 32.7). If you're sure you want to remove the user, click the Yes button.

FIGURE 32.7

When you go to delete a user from the Users Allowed to Connect list, Windows displays this Incoming Connections Warning dialog box to warn you that you're about to remove the user permanently from your system.

◆ To change a user's password, select the user in the Users Allowed to Connect list and click the Properties button. The Wizard displays the Properties dialog box for the user. On the General page, change the password in the Password text box and the Confirm Password text box. Click the OK button. Windows closes the Properties dialog box.

WARNING   *Changing a user's password in the Properties dialog box changes it for logging on to Windows as well.*

◆ If you want a user to be able to use callback for a modem connection, select the user in the Users Allowed to Connect list and click the Properties button. The Wizard displays the Properties dialog box for the user. Click the Callback tab. Windows displays the Callback page. Then select the Do Not Allow Callback option button (the default setting), the Allow the Caller to Set the Callback Number option button, or the Always Use the Following Callback Number option button. Not allowing callback is the most secure option, followed by the option for specifying the number that must always be used. Allowing the caller to set the callback number is not secure but may be necessary when the caller will be calling in from the road. Click the OK button. Windows closes the Properties dialog box.

13. Click the Next button. The Wizard displays the Networking Software page (shown in Figure 32.8). If you think this dialog box looks familiar from when you set up Windows, you're right.

FIGURE 32.8

On the Networking Software page of the New Connection Wizard, specify which networking components the host computer should use for the connection.

14. Select (or leave selected) the check boxes for the networking components that you want Windows to use for the cable connection:

◆ If a component's check box is shaded, it's vital to the connection, and you can't disable the component for the connection.

◆ If you try to clear the check box for File and Printer Sharing for Microsoft Networks, Windows displays the Incoming Connections Warning dialog box shown in Figure 32.9. This dialog box warns you that in order to disable this networking component, you need to stop the Server service, and that doing so stops sharing on any currently shared folders or printers. Choose the No button in this dialog box if you don't want to take this (relatively drastic) step. If you do want to turn off sharing, click the Yes button. Windows displays the Computer Management window. Expand the Services and Applications branch of the tree, then select the Services item. In the right list box, select the Server item, then click the Stop the Service link. Windows displays the Stop Other Services dialog box, warning you that stopping Server will also stop Computer Browser (and perhaps other services, depending on your setup). Click the Yes button. Windows displays the Service Control dialog box while it stops the Server service. When the service is stopped, the Server entry in the Status column no longer displays *Started*. When you've finished using the cable connection, restart the Server service by selecting it in the Services list and clicking the Start the Service link.

FIGURE 32.9

It's best not to try to disable File and Printer Sharing for Microsoft Networks for the cable connection, because doing so also disables any shared folders or printers on your computer.

15. Click the Next button. The Wizard displays the Completing the New Connection Wizard page, which tells you that the connection is named *Incoming Connections*.

16. Click the Finish button. The New Connection Wizard closes, naming the connection *Incoming Connections* and adding it to the Incoming category in your Network Connections folder.

SETTING UP THE GUEST COMPUTER FOR THE CABLE CONNECTION

Next, follow these steps to set up the guest computer for the connection:

1. Follow steps 1 to 5 in the previous list to reach the Advanced Connection Options page of the New Connection Wizard (shown in Figure 32.2 above).

2. Select the Connect Directly to Another Computer option button.

3. Click the Next button. The Wizard displays the Host or Guest? page (shown in Figure 32.10).

4. Select the Guest option button.

5. Click the Next button. The Wizard displays the Connection Name page (shown in Figure 32.11).

6. In the Computer Name text box, enter the name you want to use for the connection. You don't need to enter the name of the other computer; this name is for your benefit.

7. Click the Next button. The Wizard displays the Select a Device page (shown in Figure 32.12).

FIGURE 32.10

On the Host or Guest? page of the New Connection Wizard, select the Guest option button.

FIGURE 32.11

On the Connection Name page of the New Connection Wizard, enter a name for the connection you're creating.

FIGURE 32.12

On the Select a Device page of the New Connection Wizard, specify which device to use.

8. In the Select a Device drop-down list, select the port to use. For example, select Direct Parallel (LPT1) to use your printer port.

9. Click the Next button. The Wizard displays the Completing the New Connection Wizard page (shown in Figure 32.13).

10. If you want the Wizard to create a shortcut on your Desktop for this connection, select the Add a Shortcut to This Connection to My Desktop check box.

11. Click the Finish button. The New Connection Wizard closes itself, creates the connection, adds it to the Network Connections window, adds a shortcut to the Desktop if appropriate, and displays the connection's Connect dialog box. Go directly to step 3 in the next section if you want to establish a connection right now.

ESTABLISHING A CABLE CONNECTION

Once you've set up the host and the guest, and connected the two via the cable (or configured infrared), you should be ready to connect.

To connect, take the following steps on the guest computer. (This example uses a parallel connection.)

1. Choose Start ➢ Connect To ➢ Show All Connections. Windows displays the Network Connections window.

2. Double-click the icon for the connection. Windows displays the Connect dialog box. Figure 32.14 shows an example.

3. Enter your username *for the other computer* in the User Name text box and your password in the Password text box. If you want Windows to save your password (a convenience, but a security threat), select the Save This User Name and Password for the Following Users check box for the connection and choose the Me Only option button or the Anyone Who Uses This Computer option button as appropriate.

4. Click the Connect button. Windows attempts to connect via the specified connection.

FIGURE 32.14

Connecting to another computer via a parallel connection

As with an Internet connection, Windows displays in the notification area on both the guest computer and the host computer an icon showing two computers to represent the direct connection. To see the status of the connection, hover the mouse pointer over this icon until Windows displays a pop-up, or click the icon to display the Status dialog box for the connection.

Once you're connected, you can work with the shared folders on the host computer by choosing Start ➤ My Computer and then clicking the My Network Places link.

HANGING UP THE DIRECT CONNECTION

To hang up the connection, right-click the icon and choose Disconnect from the context menu. You can disconnect the connection from either computer.

EXPERT KNOWLEDGE: TROUBLESHOOTING DIRECT CONNECTIONS

Direct connections can be a bit twitchy, for reasons that usually remain unexplained. If you're having trouble establishing a direct connection, here are a couple of things to try:

◆ First, check the cable (if you're using a cable): Make sure it's correctly attached at both ends, and that it's the right kind of cable. You need to do this because Windows isn't as smart with cable connections as it might be. In particular, Windows sometimes displays the Connecting *Connection Name* message box containing the *Verifying Username and Password* message when it hasn't actually contacted the other computer. If you suspect this is happening, try disconnecting the cable and seeing if Windows produces the same error when the computers are definitely not connected.

◆ Second, try switching the host and guest roles. Sometimes trying to establish a connection from Computer A to Computer B produces nothing but error messages and denials that usernames and passwords are valid when you know they're fine, but connecting from Computer B to Computer A is a snap.

Installing Your Network Hardware

To put your network together, install your network hardware by following these basic steps:

1. Install a network interface card in each computer.

2. If your network uses a hub or switch (for example, if you're creating a Fast Ethernet network using a star configuration), position the hub or switch in a convenient central location.

   ◆ If you're using multiple hubs or switches, position them so that each is located conveniently for the computers that will connect to it, and then connect the hubs or switches via the uplink port on one and a regular port on the other.

3. For a regular (wired) network interface card, connect a network cable from the card to one of the ports on the hub or switch.

4. Power on the hub or switch.

5. Power on each computer in turn. Use the Found New Hardware Wizard or Add Hardware Wizard as described in Chapter 14 to install the driver for each network card.

When the Found New Hardware Wizard or the Add Hardware Wizard has finished setting up the network card, it displays a notification-area pop-up suggesting that you run the Network Setup Wizard to configure your network settings. You can start the Network Setup Wizard by clicking this pop-up. Alternatively, you can start the Network Setup Wizard manually as described in the section after next.

Installing a Wireless Network

What you need to do when installing a wireless network depends on the type of wireless network.

For a wireless-only network—one in which all the computers communicate with each other via wireless—you won't need to install any cables. You'll need to install a wireless network card in each computer that will participate in the network and install a driver for each wireless network card. Depending on the type of wireless network card, you may need to install wireless client-management software or an additional networking service. Your wireless network cards should come with full details of all hoops you need to jump through to get the hardware working.

If you're adding a wireless section to your network by using a wireless access point that includes bridging capabilities, connect the wireless access point to the network hub with a cable. You'll then need to run some configuration software on the access point in order to set its IP address, wireless ID, and network group.

Setting Up a Network Using the Network Setup Wizard

This section discusses how to use the Network Setup Wizard to set up a network. The procedure is a little different for the computer that's sharing the Internet connection than for the other computers, so we'll deal with that first.

Setting Up the Computer That's Sharing the Internet Connection

Start with the computer that will share the Internet connection. Before running the Network Setup Wizard, set up your Internet connection as discussed in Chapter 17. Then use the Network Setup Wizard to configure the computer by taking the following steps:

1. Establish your Internet connection.

2. Choose Start ➤ All Programs ➤ Accessories ➤ Communications ➤ Network Setup Wizard. The Wizard displays the Welcome to the Network Setup Wizard screen.

3. Click the Next button. The Wizard displays the Before You Continue page (shown in Figure 32.15), which tells you to plug in your devices, turn on all the computers and devices, and connect to the Internet.

FIGURE 32.15

The Before You Continue page of the Network Setup Wizard lists the steps you need to take before running the Wizard.

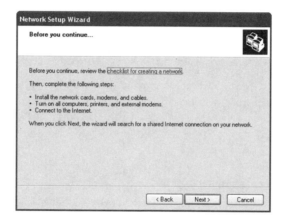

4. Click the Next button. The Wizard displays the Select a Connection Method page (shown in Figure 32.16).

FIGURE 32.16

On the Select a Connection Method page of the Network Setup Wizard, specify how this computer will connect to the Internet.

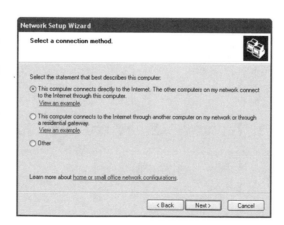

5. Make sure the This Computer Connects Directly to the Internet. The Other Computers on My Network Connect to the Internet through This Computer option button is selected.

6. Click the Next button. The Wizard displays the Select Your Internet Connection page (shown in Figure 32.17).

FIGURE 32.17

On the Select Your Internet Connection page of the Network Setup Wizard, identify your Internet connection.

7. In the Select Your Internet Connection from the Following List list box, select your Internet connection. In this example, there's no confusion, as the Wizard is listing a dial-up connection and the local area network connection. But if you have configured multiple dial-up connections or broadband connections, you may have to pay a little more attention to this choice. Windows establishes the connection you chose.

8. Click the Next button. The Wizard displays the Give This Computer a Description and Name page (shown in Figure 32.18).

FIGURE 32.18

On the Give This Computer a Description and Name page of the Network Setup Wizard, enter the name and description for the computer.

9. Enter the description for your computer in the Computer Description text box. This description is for your benefit and that of other users of the network, so make it concise and descriptive.

10. In the Computer Name text box, enter the name for your computer. Typically, for dial-up connections and DSL connections, you can choose more or less any name that suits you (within Windows' naming conventions). For cable-modem connections, you may have to use a name designated by your ISP.

11. Click the Next button. The Wizard displays the Name Your Network page (shown in Figure 32.19).

FIGURE 32.19

On the Name Your Network page of the Network Setup Wizard, specify the name for your network. For security reasons, it's best not to use the default name, MSHOME.

12. In the Workgroup Name text box, enter a name for the network. It's best to use a unique name rather than the default name, MSHOME, in case your network or Internet connection puts you on the same network loop as your neighbors. (For more details, see "Changing Your Computer's Workgroup" later in the chapter.)

13. Click the Next button. The Wizard displays the Ready to Apply Network Settings page (shown in Figure 32.20).

FIGURE 32.20

On the Ready to Apply Network Settings page of the Network Setup Wizard, double-check the information listed for mistakes before proceeding.

14. Click the Next button. The Wizard starts configuring the home network. While it works, it displays the Please Wait page (shown in Figure 32.21).

FIGURE 32.21

The Network Setup Wizard displays the Please Wait page while it configures the computer for its role in the network.

15. When the Wizard has finished configuring the computer, it displays the You're Almost Done page (shown in Figure 32.22), which offers to create a network setup disk for use on non-XP computers connecting to the same computer.

FIGURE 32.22

The You're Almost Done page of the Network Setup Wizard offers to create a network setup disk.

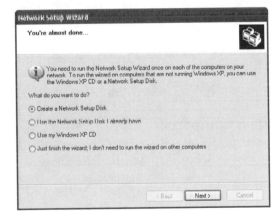

16. If you want to create a network setup disk, select the Create a Network Setup Disk option button. Otherwise, select the Just Finish the Wizard; I Don't Need to Run the Wizard on Other Computers option button. (Selecting the Use the Network Setup Disk I Already Have option button or the Use My Windows XP CD option button brings up a page of instructions for using the network setup disk or the CD.)

17. Click the Next button.

   ◆ If you chose the Create a Network Setup Disk option button, the Wizard displays the Insert the Disk You Want to Use page (shown in Figure 32.23).

FIGURE 32.23

The Insert the Disk You Want to Use page of the Network Setup Wizard lets you create a network setup disk for non-XP Windows computers.

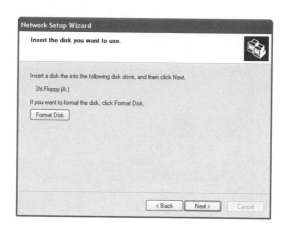

- ◆ Insert a floppy disk in the floppy drive.

- ◆ If you need to format the floppy disk, click the Format Disk button and use the resulting Format 3½ Floppy dialog box to format the disk as usual. Then click the Close button. Windows closes the dialog box.

- ◆ Click the Next button. Windows copies files to the floppy and then displays the To Run the Wizard with the Network Setup Disk page, which contains instructions for using the disk.

- ◆ Click the Next button.

18. The Wizard displays the Completing the Network Setup Wizard page, which provides links to Help and Support topics on sharing files and folders.

19. Click the Finish button. The Network Setup Wizard closes itself.

Setting Up a Client Computer

Next, set up the first of your client computers. Make sure the Internet connection is still open on the computer you set up to share it, and then take the following steps:

1. Start the Network Setup Wizard:

- ◆ On an XP computer, choose Start ➢ All Programs ➢ Accessories ➢ Communications ➢ Network Setup Wizard. The Wizard displays the Welcome to the Network Setup Wizard page.

- ◆ On a computer running an earlier version of 32-bit Windows, put the network setup disk you made earlier in the floppy drive. Open an Explorer window to the floppy drive and double-click the file named NETSETUP (or NETSETUP.EXE, if you've set Windows to show file extensions). The Wizard displays three Network Setup Wizard dialog boxes in sequence. The first dialog box tells you that the Wizard needs to install network support files on your computer. Click the Yes button. The second dialog box tells you to remove the floppy and warns you that it will prompt you to restart your computer. Remove the floppy and click the OK button. The third dialog box prompts you to restart your computer. Click the Yes button. After the restart, the Wizard displays the Welcome to the Network Setup Wizard page.

2. Click the Next button. The Wizard displays the Before You Continue page (shown in Figure 32.15 above).

3. Click the Next button. The Wizard displays the Do You Want to Use the Shared Connection? page (shown in Figure 32.24).

FIGURE 32.24

On the Do You Want to Use the Shared Connection? page of the Network Setup Wizard, consent to using the shared connection.

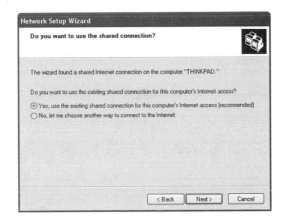

4. If the Wizard has identified the right connection, leave the Yes, Use the Existing Shared Connection for This Computer's Internet Access option button selected. If not, select the No, Let Me Choose Another Way to Connect to the Internet option button.

5. Click the Next button.

   ◆ If you chose the No, Let Me Choose Another Way to Connect to the Internet option button, Windows displays the Select a Connection Method page (shown in Figure 32.16 earlier in the chapter).

   ◆ Make sure the This Computer Connects to the Internet through Another Computer on My Network or through a Residential Gateway option button is selected.

   ◆ Click the Next button. If your computer has more than one Internet connection, the Wizard displays the Your Computer Has Multiple Connections page (shown in Figure 32.25). Otherwise, it displays the Give This Computer a Description and Name page (shown in Figure 32.18 earlier in the chapter).

   ◆ By default, the Wizard selects the Determine the Appropriate Connections for Me option button. If you leave this option button selected, the Wizard guesses which Internet connection you want to use. If you prefer to choose the connection yourself, select the Let Me Choose the Connections to My Network option button.

FIGURE 32.25

On the Your Computer Has Multiple Connections page of the Network Setup Wizard, tell the Wizard whether you want to choose the connection yourself or have it choose for you.

◆ Click the Next button. The Wizard displays the Select the Connections to Bridge page (shown in Figure 32.26), which lists the connections available for bridging.

FIGURE 32.26

On the Select the Connections to Bridge page of the Network Setup Wizard, you can specify which connections to bridge.

◆ Select the check boxes for the connections you want to bridge. Clear the check box for any direct Internet connection. Then click the Next button. The Wizard displays the Give This Computer a Description and Name page (shown in Figure 32.18 earlier in the chapter).

6. Enter the description and name for the computer. (See steps 9 and 10 in the previous list.) Because this computer isn't connecting to the Internet directly, you should be free to use any name you want for it even if your ISP requires that you use a specific name for the computer that's directly connected.

7. Click the Next button. The Wizard displays the Name Your Network page (shown in Figure 32.19 earlier in the chapter).

8. In the Workgroup Name text box, enter the name you chose earlier for the network.

9. Click the Next button. The Wizard displays the Ready to Apply Network Settings page. Figure 32.27 shows an example of this page for a client computer.

FIGURE 32.27

The Ready to Apply Network Settings page of the Network Setup Wizard for a client computer

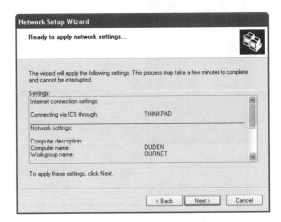

10. Click the Next button. The Wizard displays the Please Wait page while it configures the computer. It then displays the You're Almost Done page (shown in Figure 32.22 earlier in the chapter).

11. Select the Just Finish the Wizard; I Don't Need to Run the Wizard on Other Computers option button.

12. Click the Next button. The Wizard displays the Completing the Network Setup Wizard page.

13. Click the Finish button. The Wizard closes itself and displays the System Settings Change dialog box telling you that you need to restart your computer before the new settings will take effect.

14. Click the Yes button if you want to restart your computer immediately. Click the No button if you want to close some programs and then restart your computer manually.

Browsing the Network

To browse the network that the Network Setup Wizard has created, choose Start ➤ My Network Places. Windows displays the My Network Places window (shown in Figure 32.28). This window displays the resources that are directly shared. In the figure, the four SharedDocs folders represent the \Shared Documents\ folders on the four XP computers connected to the network, and the drives on Doctor are drives on a server in the workgroup.

To access one of the shared folders, double-click its icon.

FIGURE 32.28

The My Network Places window displays the resources shared on the network.

Mapping and Disconnecting Network Drives

You can access a shared folder as described in the previous section. But if you need to access the folder frequently or quickly, and especially if the folder is buried deep within the folder structure, you can save time and effort by mapping a network drive to the folder. By mapping the network drive, you essentially tell Windows that you want to refer to the folder as (say) Z: instead of (say) \\VERWIRRUNG\Andy's Documents\Reading\Recommended\Plain Text\.

You can map as many network drives as you have free letters of the alphabet on your computer. Previous versions of Windows used to start network drive mapping with the letter F, but these days, many computers need A through G (or further) for local drives—floppy, CD, CD-RW , DVD, Zip, or other removable drives, and of course one or more hard disk volumes. (B is often unused these days, because very few computers have two floppy drives.) So Windows XP automatically starts mapping drives with the letter Z, then walks backward through the alphabet with each subsequent drive. But you can override Windows' choice of drive letter with one of your own if you prefer.

Mapping a Network Drive

To map a network drive, take the following steps:

1. From an Explorer window, choose Tools ➢ Map Network Drive. Windows displays the Map Network Drive dialog box (shown in Figure 32.29).

2. In the Drive drop-down list, select the drive letter you want to use. The list shows all currently unused letters. By default, Windows selects the last available letter.

FIGURE 32.29

Use the Map Network Drive dialog box to map a drive letter to a shared network folder so that you can access the folder quickly.

3. Enter the path and folder name in the Folder text box. You can type in the path or (when you've mapped drives before) choose it from the drop-down list, but usually it's easier to click the Browse button and use the resulting Browse for Folder dialog box to select the folder, then click the OK button. As you can see in Figure 32.30, the Browse for Folder dialog box displays the My Network Places tree. You can drill down through this tree to the local network, the computers on it, and the folders they contain, or you can select one of the \SharedDocs\ folders, which appear conveniently at the first level of the My Network Places list. (You can't see them in the figure because they're too far down the list.)

FIGURE 32.30

The Browse for Folder dialog box displays the My Network Places tree so that you can easily select a networked folder.

TIP   Instead of using the procedure described in the above steps, you can browse through the network by using the Folders pane until you find the network drive or folder to which you want to connect. Then right-click the drive or folder and choose Map Network Drive from the context menu. Windows displays the Map Network Drive dialog box with the computer's name and the folder's path entered already.

4. If you want Windows to try to reconnect the network drive each time you log on to Windows, make sure the Reconnect at Logon check box is selected.

5. By default, Windows tries to log on to the network drive using the username and password (if any) under which you're currently logged on. To log on to the network drive under a different username, take the following steps:

◆ Click the Connect Using a Different User Name link. Windows displays the Connect As dialog box (shown in Figure 32.31).

FIGURE 32.31

Use the Connect As dialog box to specify a different username for connecting to the network drive.

◆ Enter the username in the User Name text box. If the network drive is in a different workgroup than the workgroup your computer is currently in, specify the network drive's workgroup and the appropriate username in it. For example, to use the username `Rikki` in the workgroup `Group2`, use `\\Group2\Rikki`.

◆ Enter the password for the username in the Password text box.

◆ Click the OK button. Windows closes the Connect As dialog box, returning you to the Map Network Drive dialog box.

6. Click the Finish button. Windows connects the network drive to the specified folder and closes the Map Network Drive dialog box.

◆ If Windows can't find the folder you specified by typing in the Folder text box, it displays a Windows message box such as that shown in Figure 32.32. Click the OK button. Windows closes the message box and returns you to the Map Network Drive dialog box so that you can try again.

FIGURE 32.32

Windows displays a message box such as this one if it can't find the folder you specified.

◆ If Windows can't connect the drive because the username is invalid or the password is wrong, it displays a Connect To dialog box such as that shown in Figure 32.33 telling you the problem. Correct the username or password and click the OK button to try again.

FIGURE 32.33

Windows displays a Connect To dialog box if the username or password isn't valid for connecting to the shared folder.

Reconnecting a Network Drive at Logon

If you selected the Reconnect at Logon check box in the Map Network Drive dialog box when mapping the drive, Windows tries to reestablish the network mapping each time you log on to Windows.

If Windows isn't able to connect a network drive, it displays a pop-up in the notification area telling you so. Click the pop-up to display a My Computer window showing all the drives. Check which drives Windows wasn't able to reconnect, and reconnect them manually if they're available. (The usual reason for not being able to reconnect a network drive is that the computer it's on is currently not sharing it.)

Disconnecting a Network Drive

To disconnect a network drive you've mapped, take the following steps from an Explorer window:

1. Choose Tools ➤ Disconnect Network Drive. Windows displays the Disconnect Network Drives dialog box (shown in Figure 32.34), which lists the network drives to which your computer is currently connected.

FIGURE 32.34

Use the Disconnect Network Drives dialog box to disconnect one or more network drives.

2. Select the drive or drives you want to disconnect.

3. Click the OK button. Windows closes the Disconnect Network Drives dialog box and disconnects the drive or drives.

◆ If you have any files or folders open on the drive or drives, Windows displays the Disconnect Network Drive dialog box (shown in Figure 32.35) to warn you that you may lose data if you disconnect the drive while files are open. Click the Yes button if you want to proceed. Click the No button if you want to close the files before you disconnect the drive.

FIGURE 32.35

Windows warns you if you have files open on the drive you're disconnecting.

You can also disconnect a single network drive by right-clicking the network drive in an Explorer window and choosing Disconnect from the context menu.

Changing Your Computer's Workgroup

As mentioned earlier, it's not a good idea to accept the default workgroup name, MSHOME, for a couple of reasons. First, MSHOME isn't the greatest name for a workgroup. It's not snappy. It's not intuitive. It's barely even pronounceable. You can come up with a much better name based on your family name, your dog's name, your knowledge of cult movies or Norse mythology, or a combination of the three.

Second, if your network is connected to the Internet via a cable modem, using a workgroup named MSHOME may be dangerous, because it can share your network with any of your neighbors who are also using a workgroup named MSHOME. You can protect your own computers and resources by using strong passwords, but even so, chances are that if you browse the network, you'll see many folders being shared without protection.

This problem is now widely recognized and, as a result, somewhat mitigated. But in the late 1990s, people in areas that had recently gotten cable Internet access reported seeing literally thousands of shared folders and printers, most of which weren't protected by a password. Apart from the security risks of having unknown people able to access drives, the amount of information about shared folders and devices bombing around the network could cause network slowdowns.

WARNING   *Should you be cruising a large MSHOME network with apparently unprotected drives and be tempted to take a peek at them, remember that this lack of security can cut both ways: An unprotected shared drive containing juicy items such as MP3 files, MPEG files, JPEGs, or (uh) sensitive information can be a great way to distribute viruses, Trojan horses, and other malware. Having people steal malware like this might also provide an interesting defense for its author, who could claim to have never intended to let it out of the lab environment in which they were testing it for security purposes. . . .*

To change your computer's workgroup, change the name in the Workgroup text box in the Computer Name Changes dialog box. For details, see the procedure described in "Changing the Computer's Name, Description, and Workgroup" in Chapter 11.

After changing the workgroup, you have to reboot your computer before the change takes effect. Do so as soon as possible.

Connecting Macs and Linux Boxes to the Network

This section gives brief details on connecting Mac and Linux clients to your Windows network.

Mac Clients

Windows XP doesn't come with any software to provide connectivity with Macs. Unless you upgrade to Windows 2000 Server (or Windows XP Server, when it arrives), your best bet is probably to buy third-party software such as DAVE (Thursby Software Systems Inc.; www.thursby.com) or Double-Talk (Connectix; www.connectix.com) that provides TCP/IP connectivity between Macs and PCs.

To give a Mac access to the Internet through Internet Connection Sharing (ICS), configure its TCP/IP Control Panel to use DHCP. Alternatively, manually assign the Mac an IP address in the 192.168.0.x subnet (192.168.0.0 to 192.168.0.255). Don't use the 192.168.0.1 address, because the computer running ICS claims that for itself.

Linux Clients

Linux clients are better equipped than the Mac for sharing files with computers running Windows XP, but this is thanks to Linux's capabilities rather than any largesse on Microsoft's part.

To enable the Linux box to access shared folders on a Windows XP computer, you have several options:

◆ Use a mount -t smbfs command to mount a shared folder on the Windows XP computer to a mount point on the Linux box.

◆ Use a smbmount command to mount a shared folder on the Windows XP computer to a mount point on the Linux box. (Using smbmount is very similar to using mount -t smbfs, but smbmount sometimes works when mount -t smbfs won't work, so it's worth keeping in mind as an alternative.)

◆ Use smbclient to attach to a shared folder. smbclient has the advantage of being much less ticklish than the previous two options, so it almost always works, even when they don't. The disadvantage is that when you make a connection via smbclient, you're stuck with using FTP-like commands to manage files. For example, you can use get and mget to copy files from the Windows XP computer and put and mput to copy files to it. You want a graphical interface? Then get one of the previous two options to work....

So far, so good—but that's only one-way traffic. If you need the Windows computers to be able to access files on the Linux box, set up Samba on the Linux box. Get it right (Samba's configuration options are good material for a GUI-lover's nightmare), and your Windows computers will be able to access the shared folders on the Linux box as if it were running Windows. (Which, incidentally, is what the Windows computers will think it's running.)

You can give a Linux box access to the Internet through ICS in the same way as you can a Mac. Either configure it to use DHCP or manually assign it an IP address in the 192.168.0.x subnet (192.168.0.0 to 192.168.0.255). Again, don't use the 192.168.0.1 address, because the computer running ICS will be using it.

Up Next

This chapter has discussed how to create a network in the two ways you're most likely to want to network your Windows XP computers: by using a direct connection for slow-and-dirty file transfer between two computers, and by using the Network Setup Wizard to configure a straightforward network sharing folders, printers, and an Internet connection. It has also discussed how to browse the network; how to map and disconnect network drives; how to change your computer's workgroup to something more appealing or obscure than MSHOME; and how to connect non-XP computers to the network.

So much for the easy way to share resources. You can also roll most of your network the hard way, as described in the next chapter. Grip those sharp-edged dice and turn the page.

Chapter 33

Sharing Resources on Your Network

IN THE PREVIOUS CHAPTER, you saw how to use the Network Setup Wizard to create a basic network configuration for sharing resources including folders, printers, and an Internet connection. This chapter discusses how to share (and unshare) resources manually. So if you set up your network with the Network Setup Wizard in the previous chapter and everything is fine, you can probably ignore this chapter for the time being.

But if you need (or want) to perform some manual configuration, here's what this chapter contains: First, it shows you how to share your Internet connection and how to use an Internet connection that another computer is sharing. It then moves on to sharing printers connected to your computer and using printers shared by other computers. After that, it shows you how to map a drive by using the `net use` command.

This chapter covers the following topics:

◆ Sharing your Internet connection with networked computers

◆ Using a shared Internet connection

◆ Sharing a printer

◆ Using a shared printer

◆ Mapping a drive by using the `net use` command

Sharing Your Internet Connection

As you know, Windows XP lets you share your Internet connection with other computers on your network. Logically enough, the feature that lets you do this is called *Internet Connection Sharing*, which gets abbreviated to *ICS*.

ICS can be a great way of saving time and money: Instead of needing a modem and phone line (or a DSL or cable modem) for each computer that needs Internet connectivity, you can get by with one modem (or equivalent) and one phone line. ICS is particularly good if you have a fast Internet connection (such as a DSL or a cable modem) that provides enough bandwidth for several computers under normal circumstances. (If someone's perpetually trying to watch streaming video, all bets are off.)

This is all good—provided your Internet connection is fast enough. It goes without saying that ICS doesn't speed up your existing Internet connection. If your connection is slow with one person using it, it'll be glacial once you've connected the whole household through it.

EXPERT KNOWLEDGE: ALTERNATIVES TO INTERNET CONNECTION SHARING

The preceding description probably makes ICS sound pretty good. And it is—up to a point. But it has two significant limitations:

♦ First, you need to keep the ICS computer running all the time so that it can handle the Internet connection and the sharing.

♦ Second, because of the way ICS is set up, you can share only one Internet connection at the same time on the same network by using ICS. To share two Internet connections, you'll need to set one up manually for sharing via another technology. (Alternatively, you can create two separate networks with an ICS connection in each, but doing so is usually much more work than setting up a second shared connection manually, because those two networks won't be able to talk to each other directly without ICS conflicts.) You can also use unshared Internet connections alongside your shared connections without any problems.

There are better alternatives—*much* better alternatives—to using ICS. Unfortunately, almost all of them require you paying for them and putting some more effort into implementing them than ICS takes. But they're worth a quick mention here in case you're interested.

Depending on your ISP, you may be able to get multiple IP addresses for your broadband connection without paying more for them. Other ISPs consider supplying multiple IP addresses to involve a different category of service than supplying a single IP address, and charge accordingly. For example, some ISPs charge around $40 a month for "residential" DSL service (which gives just one IP address) and $100–$200 for "business" DSL service (which gives multiple IP addresses—usually between five and twenty). Apart from the IP addresses and the fistful of dollars, the distinctions between the residential and business services tend to be detectable only under sustained scrutiny through an electron microscope.

If you want the residential service but need to be able to connect multiple computers through your single–IP address connection, get a cable router or DSL router designed for this purpose. All these routers have NAT built in, and most can run DHCP as well, which means that you don't need to keep one computer running the whole time to handle DHCP and NAT so that other computers can access the Internet. Some routers have firewalls built in as well, which you can use instead of or in addition to Windows XP's Internet Connection Firewall (ICF).

Some models are designed to connect to a network switch or hub and have two ports: An internal port for connecting to the switch or hub and an external port for connecting to the cable modem or DSL splitter. Others have hubs or switches built in, so if you haven't yet bought the hub or switch for your network, you can solve all your connectivity needs with a single box.

What ICS Does

In networking terms, ICS combines several elements: a proxy server, a router, and a DHCP server. As such, it's relatively simple—but it comes free with Windows, and it's easy to set up and use.

ICS uses Network Address Translation (NAT), which is also known as *IP masquerading* (particularly in the Linux world). In NAT, the host (in this case, ICS) acts as an intermediary between the client (the PC connected to the network) and the server (the Internet server that is supplying information).

In NAT, the identity of the client submitting a request is hidden: Instead, the request appears to come from the host. This can be good and bad. NAT gives you more freedom in the IP addresses you assign within the network. For example, you can use nonroutable internal IP addresses to make sure that incoming packets can reach a computer only through the router. But if someone on your network takes some illegal or offensive action (for example, posting libelous comments or downloading, uh, *unsuitable* material), the culprit will appear to be the host rather than the individual concerned. (If you had multiple IP addresses, only the specific IP address involved would appear to be guilty.)

NAT Improvements in Windows XP

The nonroutable IP addresses lead us (indirectly, sure, but that's what happens when you're routing requests) to something that's been more of a problem with NAT in the past: computers not being able to communicate with each other across *two* NAT routers.

That might sound complicated, but it really isn't. You see, what usually happens with NAT is one of the computers inside the network originates the conversation with a computer on the Internet. For example, consider Figure 33.1. This shows two simple home networks, unimaginatively named West Network (in the blue trunks) and East Network (in the red). Each network contains a computer that's connected to the Internet (West 1 and East 1) and running NAT so that it can provide Internet connectivity to the two other computers in its network (West 2, West 3, East 2, and East 3). In the middle of the figure is the Internet, represented by its traditional cloud of uncertainty. And right below the cloud (quite coincidentally) is the Sybex Web server, represented by a computer the size of a walk-in freezer.

So far, so good. Now, here's the problem that used to occur with NAT. The computers that connect through the NAT boxes have only internal IP addresses. That means they can originate a conversation with a computer on the Internet, but they can't take part in a conversation originated from beyond their NAT box. For example, West 2 can access the Sybex Web server with no problem. It sends its request to the NAT router on West 1, which says the binary equivalent of "ah, an address on the Internet" and shunts the request out through its external connection. The Sybex Web server responds to the request and sends back a response to West 1. The NAT router intercepts this response, matches it to the outgoing request, says "ah, it's for West 2" (again in binary), and passes the data on to West 2. And so it continues: West 2 (and the other internal computers) can access Internet sites provided that it starts the conversation.

But if West 3 wants to start a conversation with East 2, it can't, because it can't see East 2 through the NAT router on East 1. It can get as far as East 1, because that computer has an external IP address. But the computers beyond the NAT router are hidden from view. So you can't access them for a quick DeathMatch, for videoconferencing, for chat—well, for anything. And with NAT routers becoming widely implemented thanks to the rapid spread of broadband availability, that quickly becomes a problem. At one end of the connection, the activity has to take place on the computer running the NAT router rather than on the "inside" machine you want to use.

FIGURE 33.1

Two networks using NAT to connect internal computers to the Internet

West Network

West 1
NAT Router
External IP Address: 206.13.99.12
Internal IP Address: 192.168.0.1

East Network

East 1
NAT Router
External IP Address: 204.202.111.112
Internal IP Address: 192.168.0.1

Internet

Hub

Sybex Web Server

Hub

West 2
Internal IP Address:
192.168.0.24

West 3
Internal IP Address:
192.168.0.25

East 2
Internal IP Address:
192.168.0.69

East 3
Internal IP Address:
192.168.0.99

The good news is that Windows XP fixes this problem, letting you communicate across two NAT routers, from one inside machine to another inside machine. This is quite clever, because both the server (the NAT router) and the client (the inside machine) need to understand what's going on and work together. Some of the software has to be reworked in order to make the connection work, but you'll find that many things work.

Configuring ICS Manually

To configure ICS manually, take the following steps:

1. Choose Start ➢ Connect To ➢ Show All Connections. Windows displays the Network Connections screen.

2. Right-click the dial-up connection for which you want to implement ICS and choose Properties from the context menu. Windows displays the Properties dialog box for the connection.

3. Click the Advanced tab. Windows displays the Advanced page (shown in Figure 33.2).

4. Select the Allow Other Network Users to Connect through This Computer's Internet Connection check box.

5. If you want other computers to be able to cause ICS to start up the network connection when it's not running, make sure the Establish a Dial-up Connection whenever a Computer on My Network Attempts to Access the Internet check box is selected. Clear this check box if you want only the computer with the connection to be able to start the connection.

FIGURE 33.2

Setting up ICS on the Advanced page of the Properties dialog box for an Internet connection

6. If you want users of the other computers on the network to be able to control the Internet connection, make sure the Allow Other Network Users to Control or Disable the Shared Internet Connection check box is selected. Clear this check box if you don't want them to be able to manipulate the Internet connection directly.

7. If you want to use Internet Connection Firewall on this connection, select the Protect My Computer and Network by Limiting or Preventing Access to This Computer from the Internet check box in the Internet Connection Firewall group box.

   ◆ Unless you're using a separate firewall or you've established that ICF interferes with an Internet program that you must run, it's a good idea to use ICF on your Internet connection.

8. Click the OK button. Windows closes the Properties dialog box for the connection, changes the IP address of your network adapter to the static IP address 192.168.0.1, and starts telling the other computers to get their IP addresses from it (if there's no other DHCP server on the network).

NOTE If you have another computer on the network using the 192.168.0.1 IP address, Windows gives you an angry message telling you to change that IP address on the other computer before it will let you implement ICS on this computer. You're likely to be using this IP address only if you've previously set up ICS on another computer or the stars have decided you're due for a bad-horoscope day. If the other computer is running ICS, display the Properties dialog box for its shared connection and clear the Allow Other Network Users to Connect through This Computer's Internet Connection check box, then click the OK button. If the other computer isn't running ICS but has the 192.168.0.1 IP address set manually, either set a different address manually or switch to automatic addressing.

At this point, ICS should be up and running. The shared connection appears with a palm-upward hand on its icon to indicate that it's shared. If it's your default connection, the icon has a white check mark in a black circle. And if you're using ICF, the connection has a lock icon in its upper-right quadrant. Figure 33.3 shows one of these busy icons.

FIGURE 33.3

The icon for your Internet connection shows that it's shared (the hand), that it's the default (the check mark on the circle), and that it uses ICF (the lock icon).

ICLWay
Connected, Shared, Firewalled
U.S. Robotics 56K FAX EXT

SPECIFYING WHICH PROGRAMS AND SERVICES MAY USE THE SHARED CONNECTION

Next, if you want, you can specify which programs and services may use the shared connection. This can be useful if you need to manage the shared connection or make sure that only authorized programs are run via it. You may not want to do this, but simply let any program that wants Internet connectivity via the shared connection have it.

To specify which programs and services may use the shared connection, take the following steps:

1. Display the Advanced page of the Properties dialog box for the network connection in question.

2. Click the Settings button. Windows displays the Advanced Settings dialog box with the Services page (shown in Figure 33.4) foremost.

FIGURE 33.4

On the Services page of the Advanced Settings dialog box for a shared Internet connection, specify which network services you want Internet users to be able to access.

3. In the Services list, select the services running on your network that you want Internet users to be able to access. By default, none of these services are accessible from outside the network—you need to turn them on explicitly.

   ◆ You can add a service by clicking the Add button and working in the Service Settings dialog box (shown in Figure 33.5). Enter the description of the service, the name or IP address of the computer hosting the service, and the port number and port type (TCP or UDP) of the service, and click the OK button. Windows closes the Service Settings dialog box and adds the service to the Services list box.

FIGURE 33.5

If necessary, you can use the Service Settings dialog box to add a service for sharing.

- ◆ You can change one of the listed services by selecting it, clicking the Edit button, and working in the resulting Service Settings dialog box.

4. Click the Security Logging tab. Windows displays the Security Logging page of the Advanced Settings dialog box (shown in Figure 33.6).

FIGURE 33.6

On the Security Logging page of the Advanced Settings dialog box, choose which connection attempts to log and where to store the log file.

5. Select the Log Dropped Packets check box if you want to log dropped data packets. Select the Log Successful Connections check box if you want to log successful inbound and outbound connections (for example, to see which Internet sites the computers on your network are connecting to and which computers are connecting to your network from the Internet).

6. In the Log File Options group box, use the Name text box (and if necessary the Browse button and its resulting Browse dialog box) to specify where to store the log file. If you want, use the Size Limit text box to change the size limit for the security log file. The default setting is 4096KB—in other words, 4MB—which is enough for a large number of successful connections and a good few dropped packets.

7. Click the ICMP tab. Windows displays the ICMP page of the Advanced Settings dialog box (shown in Figure 33.7).

FIGURE 33.7

On the ICMP page of the Advanced Settings dialog box, you can set Internet Control Message Protocol options that control how the computers on the network respond to incoming requests for information.

8. Select the check boxes for the ICMP (Internet Control Message Protocol) options you want to use. When you select an item in the list box, Windows displays information about it in the Description text box. These options control how the computers on your network respond to incoming requests for information. For example, the Allow Incoming Echo Request check box controls whether the computers respond to ping packets sent to them. (Usually, it's best not to respond to ping packets, because it tells other people—including crackers—that there's a computer at that IP address. But if you're trying to establish that your network is alive from a remote location, echoing ping requests becomes very valuable.)

9. Click the OK button. Windows closes the Advanced Settings dialog box, returning you to the Properties dialog box for the connection.

10. Click the OK button. Windows closes the Properties dialog box.

   ◆ If the connection is open when you close the Properties dialog box, Windows displays the Network Connections dialog box (shown in Figure 33.8) warning you that some changes may not take effect until the next time you start the connection. Click the OK button.

FIGURE 33.8

If the connection is open, Windows displays the Network Connections dialog box to warn you that some settings you changed may not take effect immediately.

SETTING THE IP ADDRESSES OF CONNECTED COMPUTERS

If your Windows computers are set to get IP addresses via DHCP, they should automatically get IP addresses from ICS within a few minutes of your implementing ICS. If you're configuring IP addresses manually, you'll need to set each computer an IP address in the 192.168.0.2 to 192.168.0.255 range.

TURNING OFF ICS

To turn off ICS, clear the Allow Other Network Users to Connect through This Computer's Internet Connection check box on the Advanced page of the Properties dialog box for the connection, then click the OK button. Windows closes the Properties dialog box, and changes your computer's IP address from using `192.168.0.1` to obtaining an IP address automatically.

If you have a DHCP server on your network, Windows grabs an IP address from it on the next go-around of network polling. If Windows doesn't find a DHCP server (which will be the case if ICS was handling DHCP for you before you turned it off), Windows falls back on its alternate TCP/IP configuration, which uses Automatic Private IP Addressing (APIPA) to automatically assign an IP address in the range `169.254.0.1` to `169.254.255.254`.

Using a Shared Internet Connection

Depending on how a shared Internet connection is configured, you can use it in much the same way as you can use a regular Internet connection on your computer.

The shared connection appears under the Internet Gateway heading in the Network Connections window with a flashy icon. Figure 33.9 shows an example.

FIGURE 33.9

A shared connection appears in the Internet Gateway list in the Network Connections window.

To tell Windows to display an icon in the notification area when the connection is connected, take the following steps:

1. Right-click the connection and choose Properties from the context menu. Windows displays the Properties dialog box for the connection. Figure 33.10 shows an example.

FIGURE 33.10

The Properties dialog box for a shared Internet connection offers the option of displaying an icon in the notification area when the connection is connected.

2. Select the Show Icon in Notification Area when Connected check box.

3. Click the OK button. Windows closes the Properties dialog box and applies the setting.

If the connection is configured to start automatically on demand, you can start the connection by starting a program that attempts to access the Internet. For example, if you start Internet Explorer or Outlook Express, ICS automatically starts the connection.

If the connection is configured to let you control it, you can start it manually by double-clicking its entry on the Network Connections screen, and you can disconnect the connection by right-clicking its notification-area icon and choosing Disconnect from the context menu.

Sharing a Printer

Over the past few years, printer prices have dropped nearly as dramatically as printers' capabilities have risen—but even so, a printer worth having costs the best part of a year's supply of Krispy Kremes (okay, a *month's* supply if you're a heavy user), so you don't want to buy any more printers than you absolutely need for your home or office. Still, for many households and most offices that means a minimum of two or more printers to handle different printing tasks. For example, you might have a laser printer for handling home-office and school chores such as printing documents and spreadsheets, and a color printer for photographs and fun items.

In any case, the printer itself works out to be the smallest cost in the long run of printing. Ink cartridges are expensive—that's where the printer manufacturers make money, just like razor makers take losses on the razors but rake in the profits on the replacement blades. Fancy paper for high-quality color printers and photo printers runs expensive. And printers tend to break if abused or if given the evil eye more than once a week.

Bulging preamble, hidden point: To get the most out of your printers, you can share them across your network with your other networked computers. Windows XP makes it easy to share printers and to connect to shared printers. For a visual guide to the basic steps of sharing a printer and connecting to a shared printer, see pages 75–76 of the *Essential Skills* section.

To share a printer that you've already set up on your computer, take the following steps:

1. Display the Printers and Faxes screen of Control Panel. (For example, choose Start ➤ Control Panel, click the Printers and Other Hardware link in Control Panel, and click the Printers and Faxes link on the Printers and Other Hardware screen.)

2. Right-click the printer and choose Sharing from the context menu. Alternatively, select the printer and click the Share This Printer link in the Tasks list. Windows displays the Sharing page of the Properties dialog box for the printer. Figure 33.11 shows an example of the Sharing page.

3. Select the Share This Printer option button. Windows activates the Share Name text box and enters a suggested name for the shared printer. This shared name is derived from the first eight characters of the printer's existing name—an improvement on the stunningly unoriginal Printern name that the Network Setup Wizard uses for the printers it networks, but nonetheless improvable.

4. Change the name in the Share Name text box if you want. Keep the name down to eight or fewer characters if you need the printer to be accessible to computers running Windows 3.*x* or DOS. If all your computers use 32-bit versions of Windows, you can make the name longer and more descriptive. For example, you might want to include the computer's name or description so that when users print to the printer, they're clear as to where they'll find their printouts.

FIGURE 33.11

Use the Sharing page of the Properties dialog box share the printer.

5. If the computers with which you'll be sharing the printer use versions of Windows other than Windows XP, click the Additional Drivers button. Windows displays the Additional Drivers dialog box (shown in Figure 33.12).

FIGURE 33.12

If you'll be sharing this printer with computers running other versions of Windows, use the Additional Drivers dialog box to install drivers for them.

6. Select the appropriate check boxes in the Environment column. The Alpha environment is computers using the DEC Alpha processor (for which Microsoft provided versions of Windows NT). The IA64 is Intel's 64-bit chip code-named Itanium. The other environments you should recognize.

7. Click the OK button. If Windows needs you to provide drivers for any of the operating systems you chose, it displays the Printer Drivers dialog box (shown in Figure 33.13). Use the Browse button and the resulting Locate File dialog box to identify the drivers, and then click

the OK button. Windows installs the drivers and closes the Additional Drivers dialog box, returning you to the Properties dialog box for the printer.

FIGURE 33.13

In the Printer Drivers dialog box, supply the printer driver for each other operating system.

8. Click the OK button. Windows closes the Properties dialog box and displays a shared icon for the printer (a printer with an open hand in front of it).

Other computers can now connect to the shared printer as described in the next section.

Connecting to a Shared Printer

To connect to a shared printer, take the following steps:

1. Choose Start ➢ Control Panel. Windows displays Control Panel.

2. Click the Printers and Other Hardware link. Windows displays the Printers and Other Hardware screen.

3. Click the Add a Printer link in the Pick a Task list. (Alternatively, click the Add a Printer link in the Tasks list on the Printers and Faxes screen.) Windows starts the Add Printer Wizard, which displays its Welcome page.

4. Click the Next button. The Wizard displays the Local or Network Printer page (shown in Figure 33.14).

5. Select the A Network Printer, or a Printer Attached to Another Computer option button.

FIGURE 33.14

On the Local or Network Printer page of the Add Printer Wizard, select the A Network Printer, or a Printer Attached to Another Computer option button.

6. Click the Next button. The Wizard displays the Specify a Printer page (shown in Figure 33.15).

FIGURE 33.15

On the Specify a Printer page of the Add Printer Wizard, choose whether to browse for the printer or supply the printer's details.

7. Choose one of the following three ways of specifying the printer:

   ◆ Usually, it's best to leave the Browse for a Printer option button selected and use the browse procedure to locate the printer as described in the next steps.

   ◆ If you know the printer's name and location, select the Connect to This Printer option button and enter the path and printer name in the Name text box. For example, if the computer Requiem is sharing a printer named Laser1, you would enter \\Requiem\Laser1.

   ◆ Similarly, if you know the URL for the printer, select the Connect to a Printer on the Internet or on a Home or Office Network option button and enter the URL in the URL text box.

8. Click the Next button. If you chose to browse for a printer, the Wizard displays the Browse for Printer page (shown in Figure 33.16 with the network tree expanded).

FIGURE 33.16

Use the Browse for Printer page of the Add Printer Wizard to identify the shared printer you want to use.

9. In the Shared Printers list box, expand the network tree until you reach the printer you want, then select the printer. The Wizard enters the printer's full name in the Printer text box.

10. Click the Next button. The Wizard displays the Default Printer page (not shown), which asks whether you want to use the printer as your default printer.

11. Select the Yes option button or the No option button as appropriate.

12. Click the Next button. The Wizard displays the Completing the Add Printer Wizard page (shown in Figure 33.17), which details the printer you've chosen.

FIGURE 33.17

The Completing the Add Printer Wizard page summarizes your choices.

13. Click the Finish button. The Wizard closes and adds the printer to your Printers and Faxes list. The icon for the printer has a network cable underneath it, indicating that the printer is connected via the network.

You can then use the printer as you would a local printer, except that you can't set Sharing options or Advanced options for the printer.

Repairing a Network Connection

If a network connection seems not to be working or seems to be malfunctioning, you may need to repair it. To do so, choose Start ➢ Connect To ➢ Show All Connections. Windows displays the Network Connections screen. Either select the connection and click the Repair This Connection link in the Network Tasks list, or right-click the connection and choose Repair from the context menu.

EXPERT KNOWLEDGE: MAPPING DRIVES FROM THE COMMAND LINE VIA THE *NET USE* COMMAND

You can map a drive quickly from the command line by using the net use command. Choose Start ➤ All Programs ➤ Accessories ➤ Command Prompt to open a Command Prompt window, and then follow the instructions in this sidebar.

The basic syntax for the net use command is as follows:

```
net use drive path
```

Here, *drive* is the drive letter that you want to use to access the shared folder, and *path* is the path to the folder. For example, the following command connects the shared folder \\TBC\users as drive F:

```
net use f: \\TBC\users
```

If Windows is able to assign the share, it reports *The command completed successfully*. If Windows isn't able to assign the share because it can't find the network drive, it returns a system error 53 and tells you *The network path was not found*.

If you want net use to use the next available drive letter for the share, enter an asterisk in the command instead of specifying the drive letter. For example:

```
net use * \\TBC\users
```

If you need to supply an account name and a password for the drive you're connecting to, specify them in this format:

```
net use drive path password /user:domain\username
```

Here, *password* is the password, and *domain\username* is the domain or workgroup name, a backslash, and the username. For example, the following command connects drive Z to the shared folder \\TBC\users using the password 1llumin8! and the username Jaq in the workgroup MSHome:

```
net use z: \\TBC\users 1llumin8! /user:MSHome\Jaq
```

You can also use the server's IP address instead of its name. This can be especially useful if you're connecting to the server across the Internet.

If you see the message *The credentials supplied conflict with an existing set of credentials*, usually accompanied by a system error 1219, it can mean either of two things. First, that you already have a connection to this share using a different username and (valid) password, and that net use doesn't approve of your trying to connect with another username or password. Or second, that the computer to which you're trying to connect has decided, on the basis of a failed connection attempt you've made, that you're persona non grata as far as it's concerned.

In either case, use the net use *drive* /d command to disconnect from the server, then try to connect again:

```
net use Z: /d
```

If you're in doubt as to which folders are connected to which drive, type **net use** at the command prompt without any arguments and press the Enter key. Windows displays a list of the local drives, the remote folders, and their status.

Up Next

This chapter has discussed how to configure your networked devices and how to share your Internet connection, your printers, and your folders.

The next chapter—well, there isn't one. This is the end of the book, except for the "Windows Basics" appendix, which you've probably read already if it's relevant to you.

Appendix

Windows Basics

This appendix presents the basic things you need to know about the Windows graphical user interface (GUI) in order to get started with the main text of the book. If you've used Windows before and are comfortable with the GUI, you probably don't need to read this appendix, though you might want to skim through the sections about Windows controls to make sure you're clear on the terms involved.

This appendix covers the following topics:

◆ Mouse basics and terminology

◆ Selection basics

◆ Working with windows and dialog boxes

Mouse Basics and Terminology

For navigating the Windows GUI, a pointing device is almost essential. You can get a bewildering variety of pointing devices that work with Windows—everything from a conventional mouse or trackball with two, three, or more buttons to a set of foot pedals that provide mouse functionality to a head-mounted infrared reflector that reflects a beam sent from a device mounted on your monitor to track your head movements and so move the mouse pointer. But the basic principle of all these devices is the same: You move the pointer around the screen to indicate one or more objects on which you want to take an action. You then click in one of the following ways to take the action:

Click   Press the primary mouse button once (and release the button). The primary mouse button on a conventional mouse is the left button, on which your right forefinger rests.

Double-click   Press the primary mouse button twice in quick succession.

Right-click   Press the secondary mouse button once.

Drag   Press the primary mouse button to select the object, keep holding the mouse button down, and move the mouse to drag the object to where you want it to appear. Release the mouse button.

Right-drag   Drag (as described in the previous paragraph) except using the secondary mouse button.

Selection Basics

These are the basic moves for selecting objects in Windows:

- To select one object, click it with the primary mouse button. Alternatively, use the arrow keys to move the focus (the current selection) to the object, and then press the spacebar.

- To deselect a selected object, click in open space elsewhere in its window. With the keyboard, use the arrow keys to move the focus off the object.

- To select multiple objects that appear next to each other (for example, in a dialog box or in an Explorer window), click the first object to select it as usual. Then hold down the Shift key and click the last object in the range. Release the Shift key.

- To select multiple objects that don't appear next to each other, click the first object to select it as usual. Then hold down the Ctrl key while you click each of the other objects in turn. Release the Ctrl key.

- To deselect some of multiple objects you've selected, hold down the Ctrl key and click each selected object that you want to deselect in turn. Release the Ctrl key.

Working with Windows and Dialog Boxes

When you're working in Windows, most of the action takes place in windows on-screen. A *window* is essentially a rectangular area on-screen. For example, when you run a program, it typically opens one or more windows for you to work in. Figure A.1 shows two program windows—a Notepad window and a My Computer window—open on the Windows Desktop.

FIGURE A.1

Two program windows open on the Windows Desktop

Most applications also use *dialog boxes*—fixed-size windows that typically contain controls but don't let you create documents.

The distinction between a window and a dialog box is somewhat flexible. Generally speaking, a window is resizable, whereas a dialog box is not. (Some dialog boxes display an extra section when you click a button such as More or Advanced, but this is different from being able to resize a window.)

Dialog Box Modality

In addition, most dialog boxes are *modal*. This means that when they are displayed, you cannot take any further action in the program that displayed them before dismissing the dialog box. Modality is intended to focus your attention on what the dialog box is expecting you to do.

NOTE *Technically, there are two types of modality:* application modality *and* system modality. *When a dialog box is application modal, you can take no further action in its application until you dismiss the dialog box. When a dialog box is system modal, you can take no further action on your computer until you dismiss the dialog box. System modality is supposedly reserved for events of systemwide importance, such as Windows errors and crashes, but some applications display system-model dialog boxes when they should display application-modal dialog boxes.*

The opposite of a modal dialog box is a *modeless* dialog box. A modeless dialog box does not prevent you from taking actions in its program while it's displayed. At this writing, modeless dialog boxes are relatively rare, but they're used in some applications. For instance, in Word for Windows, some dialog boxes are modeless. For example, when the Find and Replace dialog box is displayed, you can click in your document and continue working around the dialog box. But most dialog boxes in Word are modal. For example, when you display the Open dialog box, the Print dialog box, or the Save As dialog box, you can't take any further action in the program until you dismiss the dialog box.

The problem with modeless dialog boxes is that, because you can continue working while a modeless dialog box is displayed on-screen, you can in theory stack up an absurd number of modeless dialog boxes on-screen while you continue to work. In practice, most people get annoyed enough by modeless dialog boxes that they close them smartly, provided that they can see them.

Maximizing, Minimizing, and Restoring Windows

Most windows have three buttons: a Minimize button, a Maximize button that swaps places with a Restore Down button, and a Close button. Figure A.2 illustrates these buttons.

FIGURE A.2

Most windows have three buttons for minimizing, maximizing or restoring, or closing the window.

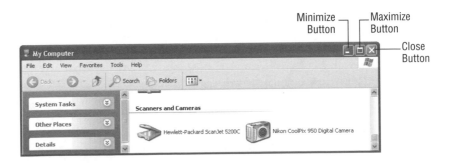

Minimize Button — Maximize Button — Close Button

These buttons are intuitive enough to use:

♦ Click the Maximize button to maximize its window. Windows expands the window to take up all the Desktop and replaces the Maximize button with a Restore Down button.

♦ Click the Restore Down button to restore the window to its former size. As you'd expect, Windows replaces the Restore Down button with the Maximize button again. The window is then said to be in a *normal* state—in other words, neither maximized nor minimized.

♦ Click the Minimize button to minimize its window down to a Taskbar button. Click the Taskbar button to restore the window to its preminimized size.

♦ Click the Close button to close its window.

You can also maximize, minimize, and restore windows by using the control menu (see the next section).

Using the Control Menu on Windows and Dialog Boxes

At the left end of its title bar, each window and dialog box has a *control menu* that contains commands for moving, resizing (windows only), and closing the window or dialog box.

When the control menu on a window is closed, it appears as a square bearing an icon representing the contents of the window. For example, the control-menu square for an Explorer window open to a hard drive displays a hard drive icon, and the control-menu square for a WordPad document bears the WordPad icon. By contrast, the control menu on a dialog box appears as part of the title bar—there's no visible indication that it's there.

To display the control menu on a window, click the square or press Alt+spacebar. To display the control menu on a dialog box, press Alt+spacebar (clicking doesn't work in a dialog box). Figure A.3 shows the control menu on a window.

FIGURE A.3

Use the control menu to move, resize, or close a window, or to move or close a dialog box.

The control menu for most dialog boxes offers just two commands: Move, and Close. The control menu for most windows offers these commands: Restore, Move, Size, Minimize, Maximize, and Close.

The Restore, Minimize, Maximize, and Close commands are self-explanatory. Only one of Restore and Maximize is available at any time: If the window is maximized, Restore is available; if the window is normal, Maximize is available.

Move is available if the window is in a normal state (because you cannot move a maximized window). To move the window by using the keyboard, select Move from the control menu, then use the arrow keys to move the window to where you want it, and press the Enter key. (You can also move the window with the mouse—but unless the window has somehow migrated to a position off your monitor, it's easier simply to drag the title bar of the window with the mouse rather than display the context menu and issue the Move command.)

Similarly, Size is available only if the window is in a normal state. Use the arrow keys to resize the window, and then press the Enter key.

TIP   Double-click the control-menu box to close a window.

Dialog Box Controls

Figure A.4 shows the main controls that you'll find in dialog boxes in Windows. The following sections discuss these controls.

FIGURE A.4

A dialog box with the most-used controls in Windows

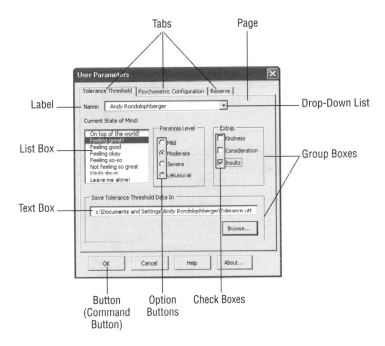

PAGE CONTROLS AND TABS

Some dialog boxes contain multiple *pages* of information. Each page typically contains a different set of controls. For example, in Figure A.4 (above), the Psychometric Configuration page and the Reserve page would contain a different set of controls than the Tolerance Threshold page.

To access one of the pages, you click its *tab*—the visible protrusion at the top of the page. Some people (including Microsoft, who should know better) refer to the pages as *tabs*, though this usage tends to be confusing.

The Windows convention is for the tab to be placed at the top of the page, though some programmers choose to place them at the bottom or at one of the sides of the pages for special effects (such as confusing the user).

LABEL CONTROLS

Labels are used to display text in dialog boxes. Typically, labels are static, though some dialog boxes use labels that you can change, either by clicking the label or by clicking a button associated with the label.

LIST BOX CONTROLS

A *list box* contains a number of items that typically are related. Most list boxes are configured so that you can choose only one of their items, but some list boxes are configured so that you can select multiple items.

DROP-DOWN LIST CONTROLS

A *drop-down list* control provides a number of preset values (presented via the list that you can access by clicking the down-arrow button) and lets you enter a new value by typing into the text box.

The formal name for drop-down list controls is *combo boxes* because they combine a text box and a list box.

GROUP BOX CONTROLS

The *group box* control is a visual aid for grouping other controls into logical sets. (The formal name for a group box control is *frame*.) For example, you'll find option buttons or check boxes arranged into group boxes to make clear that they belong together.

OPTION BUTTON CONTROLS

Option buttons (also called *radio buttons*) are groups of buttons of which only one can be chosen at any given time. (The name *radio button* comes from a physical radio with a number of preset stations. When you choose one preset button, it cancels the other buttons, because the radio can play only one station at a time.)

Selecting an option button clears all other option buttons in the set.

CHECK BOX CONTROLS

Check boxes are widely used controls for turning options on and off, or for indicating that (for multiple objects) the item specified by the check box is on for some and off for the others.

Most check boxes have two states: *selected* (with a check mark in them) and *cleared* (without a check mark in them). Clicking the check box toggles it from one state to the other. People use a variety of terms for check boxes, such as *put a check in the check box* or *click to remove the check from the check box*. For clarity, this book uses the phrases *select a check box* and *clear a check box*.

Some check boxes have a third state, in which the check box is selected but grayed out. This state, which technically is called a Null state and indicates that the check box contains no valid data, typically means that the option identified by the check box is on for part of the current selection. For example, in Microsoft Word, if you select three words, one of which has strikethrough formatting, and display the Font dialog box, the Strikethrough check box appears in a Null state, because it applies to part of the selection but not to all of it.

Some Windows applications use check boxes instead of option buttons. Their designers have wretched karma.

TEXT BOX CONTROLS

A *text box* is a control in which you can enter and edit text. Text boxes often contain a default value that you can change if necessary.

COMMAND BUTTON CONTROLS

A *command button* is a control that performs an action when you click it. For example, most dialog boxes contain a default action button (for example, a Print command button in a Print dialog box or an OK command button in many dialog boxes) to take the actions specified in the dialog box. Most dialog boxes contain a Cancel command button to cancel the actions specified in the dialog box and close the dialog box.

This book refers to command buttons as *buttons*.

CLOSING A DIALOG BOX

When you've made changes in a dialog box, you typically need to close it to apply them. To close a dialog box and apply the changes you've made, click the default command button (for example, an OK button or a Close button).

To close a dialog box without applying the changes you've made in it, click the Cancel button.

NOTE *Some dialog boxes have an Apply button that you can click to apply your changes without closing the dialog box. This lets you make further changes before closing the dialog box.*

Index

Note to reader: **Bolded** page references indicate main discussions of a topic and definitions. *Italicized* page references indicate illustrations.

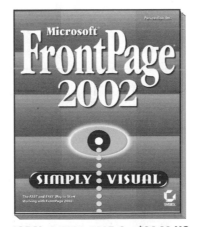

About the CD

The CD enclosed with this book contains a fully searchable electronic version of this book together with selected freeware and evaluation versions of commercial software that will help you get up to speed with Windows XP and add to Windows XP's features.

Mastering Windows XP Home Edition E-book

Use the electronic edition of the book to quickly access the full text of the book from your PC—or carry the book around on your laptop.

Utilities on the CD

The CD contains the following utilities (in alphabetical order):

Adobe Acrobat Reader   A powerful e-book reader program that allows you to view documents in the Portable Document Format (PDF). Use Acrobat Reader to read *Mastering Windows XP Home Edition Electronic Edition* from the CD and to read PDFs you create or download.

FreeAmp   A capable and extensible cross-platform audio player that you can use to play back files in the MP3 format, the WMA format, and other audio formats.

JASC Paint Shop Pro 7   An evaluation version of the powerful image-manipulation program that includes automatic photo-enhancement features.

MusicMatch Jukebox 6   A full-featured jukebox program that can rip and encode CDs to MP3, WMA, and WAV formats, organize your digital audio files into a music library, and play back audio files in many audio formats (including MP3 and WMA).

PartitionMagic   A link to the latest evaluation version of PowerQuest's disk-partitioning software.

PowerDVD   An evaluation edition of the software DVD player.

Quick View Plus   An evaluation version of the widely used preview software that lets you open more than 200 file types for viewing.

Registry Crawler   A Registry utility that lets you find, configure, and access Registry settings more quickly and easily than Windows' Registry Editor program.

RenameWiz   A powerful utility for renaming batches of files and folders.

TurboZIP and TurboZIP Express   An evaluation edition of the archive and e-mail management program, TurboZIP, together with the TurboZIP Express enhancement, which lets you access TurboZIP's functionality more easily through Windows Explorer.

VMWare   An evaluation edition of the operating system–emulation software that lets you run other operating systems in emulation on top of Windows 2000 or Windows NT 4.

Winamp   A powerful audio player for files in the MP3 format, the WMA format, and other audio formats. You can enhance Winamp with plug-ins and customize Winamp by applying skins to change its looks.

WinDVD   An evaluation edition of the software DVD player.

WinZip   An evaluation edition of the market-leading compression and archiving software for Windows.

X-Setup   A freeware utility that gives you easy access to many of Windows' hidden configuration settings.

ZoneAlarm Pro   An evaluation edition of the powerful Internet software firewall and security program.